SIXTH EDITION

AVENTURAS

PRIMER CURSO DE LENGUA ESPAÑOLA

JOSÉ A. BLANCO

PHILIP REDWINE DONLEY, LATE

VISTA®
HIGHER LEARNING

Boston, Massachusetts

On the cover: Colorful bus in Panajachel, Guatemala, with Lake Atitlán
in the background.

Creative Director: José A. Blanco
Chief Content and Innovation Officer: Rafael de Cárdenas López
Publisher: Sharla Zwirek
Editorial Director: Judith Bach
Editorial Development: Jo Hanna Kurth
Senior Video Producer: Carmen Nouel
Project Management: Faith Ryan
Rights Management: Jorgensen Fernandez, Kristine Janssens, Juan Esteban Mora
Technology Production: David Duque, Jamie Kostecki, Lauren Krolick
Design: Andrea Cubides, Paula Díaz, Daniela Hoyos, Radoslav Mateev, Gabriel Noreña, Andrés Vanegas
Production: Oscar Díez, Sebastián Díez, Andrés Escobar, Daniel Lopera, Daniela Peláez, Juliana Tobón

Student Text ISBN: 978-1-54333-191-2

Instructor's Annotated Edition ISBN: 978-1-54333-194-3

Library of Congress Control Number: 2020937034

5 6 7 8 9 10 TC 25 24 23 22 21

Printed in Canada.

Introduction

Welcome to **Aventuras, Sixth Edition!** This highly successful introductory Spanish program is designed to provide you with an active and rewarding learning experience. You are about to embark on an exciting adventure as you learn Spanish and explore the diverse cultures of the Spanish-speaking world.

NEW to the Sixth Edition

- New **Aventuras fotonovela** video
- New Video Virtual Chats
- New vocabulary tutorials
- Communicative goals and Can-Do Statements for most sections in each lesson
- New pronunciation tutorials with speech recognition
- New **Panorama cultural** videos
- New **Con ritmo hispano** music feature
- 9 new **Cultura** readings
- 8 new authentic **Videoclips** showcasing Spanish from diverse locations in the Spanish-speaking world
- Online practice tests now with diagnostics

Plus, the original hallmark features of Aventuras

- Fresh, user-friendly design and layout that support and facilitate language learning
- An abundance of illustrations, photos, and charts specifically chosen to help you learn
- Practical, high-frequency vocabulary for communicating in real-life situations
- Clear, concise grammar explanations that graphically highlight important concepts
- Guided activities that practice vocabulary and grammar so you feel confident communicating in Spanish
- Abundant opportunities to interact in communicative situations
- A process approach to reading, writing, and listening skills
- Presentation of important cultural aspects of the daily lives of Spanish speakers and coverage of the entire Spanish-speaking world
- Engaging video programs, including **Aventuras fotonovela, Flash cultura, Videoclip,** and **Panorama cultural,** that provide authentic cultural and linguistic input
- A complete set of print and technology components to make learning Spanish easier

To familiarize yourself with the program's organization, as well as its original and new features, turn to page xii and take the **Aventuras-at-a-glance** tour.

table of contents

	PREPARACIÓN	AVENTURAS

Lección 1
Hola, ¿qué tal?

Basic greetings and farewells 2
Courtesy expressions 3

Fotonovela:
Amigos de todas partes 8

Lección 2
Las clases

People and places at
the university 28
Courses of study 28

Fotonovela:
¡¿Te gustan los lunes?! 34

Lección 3
La familia

Family relationships 58
Professions. 59

Fotonovela:
Una visita inesperada 64

Lección 4
El fin de semana

Pastimes 84
Places in the city 85

Fotonovela:
¿Dónde están las entradas? 90

CULTURA	GRAMÁTICA	LECTURA
Los saludos y el espacio personal . . . . . 10 **Flash cultura:** Encuentros en la plaza 11	**1.1** Nouns and articles . . . . 12 **1.2** Numbers 0-30 . . . . 14 **1.3** Present tense of **ser** . . . . 16 **1.4** Telling time . . . . 18 **Videoclip: MasterCard** 21	**Lectura:** Teléfonos importantes y direcciones electrónicas 24
La elección de una carrera universitaria . . . . 36 **Flash cultura:** Los estudios 37	**2.1** Present tense of regular **–ar** verbs . . . . 38 **2.2** Forming questions . . . . 40 **2.3** The present tense of **estar** . . . . 42 **2.4** Numbers 31–100 . . . . 44 **Videoclip: Pruebas de selectividad** . . . 47	**Lectura:** UAE: La mejor universidad de Europa . . . . 50 **Aventuras en los países hispanos:** Estados Unidos y Canadá 53
¿Cómo te llamas? . . . . 66 **Flash cultura:** La familia 67	**3.1** Descriptive adjectives . . . . 68 **3.2** Possessive adjectives . . . . 70 **3.3** Present tense of regular **–er** and **–ir** verbs . . . . 72 **3.4** Present tense of **tener** and **venir** . . . . 74 **Videoclip: Diminutivo** 77	**Lectura:** Las familias 80
Real Madrid y Barça: rivalidad total . . . . 92 **Flash cultura:** ¡Fútbol en España! 93	**4.1** The present tense of **ir** . . . . 94 **4.2** Stem-changing verbs: **e→ie, o→ue** . . . . 96 **4.3** Stem-changing verbs: **e→i** . . . . . . 98 **4.4** Verbs with irregular **yo** forms . . . . 100 **Videoclip: Ejes** 103	**Lectura:** Guía para el fin de semana . . . . 106 **Aventuras en los países hispanos:** México 109

table of contents

	PREPARACIÓN	**AVENTURAS**

Lección 5
Las vacaciones

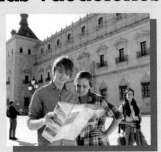

Words related to
transportation and lodging 114
Days of the week, months,
seasons, and weather
expressions. 115

Fotonovela:
De viaje en Toledo. 120

Lección 6
¡De compras!

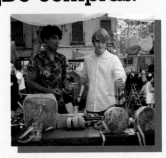

Shopping 140
Clothing and colors 141

Fotonovela:
¡Eso sí es una ganga! 146

Lección 7
La vida diaria

Daily routine and
personal hygiene. 170
Sequencing expressions. 171

Fotonovela:
¡Tengo que arreglarme!. 176

Lección 8
¡A comer!

Foods and meals 196
Adjectives that describe food 196

Fotonovela:
¡Vamos a comer tapas! 202

CULTURA	GRAMÁTICA	LECTURA

El Camino Inca 122
Flash cultura:
   ¡Vacaciones en Perú! 123

5.1 Estar with conditions
   and emotions 124
5.2 The present progressive 126
5.3 Comparing **ser** and **estar** 128
5.4 Direct object nouns and pronouns 130
Videoclip: *Xochimilco: una joya de la
herencia prehispánica de México* . . . 133

Lectura:
   Turismo ecológico
   en Puerto Rico 136

Los mercados al aire libre 148
Flash cultura:
   Comprar en los mercados 149

6.1 Numbers 101 and higher 150
6.2 The preterite tense of
   regular verbs 152
6.3 Indirect object pronouns 154
6.4 Demonstrative adjectives
   and pronouns 156
Videoclip: Juguettos 159

Lectura:
   Corona 162

Aventuras en los países hispanos:
   El Caribe 165

La siesta 178
Flash cultura:
   Tapas para todos los días 179

7.1 Reflexive verbs 180
7.2 Indefinite and
   negative words 182
7.3 Preterite of **ser** and **ir** 184
7.4 Gustar and verbs like **gustar** . . . 186
Videoclip: *Esperando el rescate* 189

Lectura:
   ¡Una mañana desastrosa! 192

Desayunos exquisitos 204
Flash cultura:
   La comida latina 205

8.1 Preterite of stem-
   changing verbs 206
8.2 Double object pronouns 208
8.3 Saber and **conocer** 210
8.4 Comparatives and
   superlatives 212
Videoclip: Receta de churros 215

Lectura:
   Cinco estrellas para
   El Palmito 218

Aventuras en los países hispanos:
   Suramérica I 221

table of contents

	PREPARACIÓN	AVENTURAS

Lección 9
Las celebraciones

Celebrations 226
Personal relationships
  and the stages of life 227

Fotonovela:
  ¡Es mi cumpleaños! 232

Lección 10
En el consultorio

Health and
  medical conditions 252
Parts of the body 252

Fotonovela:
  ¡Necesitas un médico! 258

Lección 11
El carro y la tecnología

The car and its accessories 280
Computers and technology 281

Fotonovela:
  Un carro... ¿nuevo? 286

Lección 12
Hogar, dulce hogar

The parts of a house;
  household chores 304
Table settings 304

Fotonovela:
  ¡A limpiar! 310

CULTURA

Año Nuevo 234

Flash cultura:
Las fiestas 235

GRAMÁTICA

9.1 Irregular preterites 236
9.2 Verbs that change
meaning in the preterite 238
9.3 Relative pronouns 240
9.4 ¿Qué? and ¿cuál? 242
Videoclip: Guelaguetza en Oaxaca . . . 245

LECTURA

Lectura:
Vida social 248

Servicios de salud 260

Flash cultura:
La salud 261

10.1 The imperfect tense 262
10.2 Constructions with **se** 264
10.3 Adverbs 266
**Videoclip: Asociación Parkinson
Alicante** 269

Lectura:
El consultorio 272

Aventuras en los países hispanos:
Suramérica II 275

Las redes sociales 288

Flash cultura:
Maravillas de la tecnología 289

11.1 The preterite and the
imperfect 290
11.2 **Por** and **para** 292
11.3 Stressed possessive
adjectives and pronouns 294
Videoclip: Autocine 297

Lectura:
Tira cómica: *El celular*, Tute 300

Balcones que enamoran 312

Flash cultura:
La casa de Frida 313

12.1 **Usted** and **ustedes**
commands 314
12.2 The present subjunctive 316
12.3 Subjunctive with verbs
of will and influence 318
Videoclip: Conforama 321

Lectura:
¡Bienvenidos a
la Casa Colorada! 324

Aventuras en los países hispanos:
América Central I 327

table of contents

	PREPARACIÓN	**AVENTURAS**

Lección 13
La naturaleza

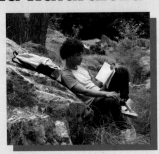

The environment 332
Conservation 332

Fotonovela:
Una excursión a la sierra 338

Lección 14
En la ciudad

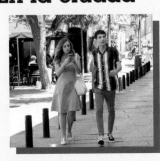

City life; giving directions 356
Banking and postal needs 356

Fotonovela:
Por las calles de Madrid 362

Lección 15
El bienestar

Personal fitness and
well-being. 384
Nutrition 385

Fotonovela:
La clase de yoga. 390

Lección 16
El mundo del trabajo

Professions and
the workplace 408
Job interviews 409

Fotonovela:
Una aspirante despistada 414

CULTURA	GRAMÁTICA	LECTURA

Jóvenes por el medio ambiente 340

Flash cultura:
Naturaleza en Costa Rica 341

13.1 The subjunctive with verbs of emotion. 342

13.2 The subjunctive with doubt, disbelief, and denial 344

13.3 The subjunctive with conjunctions 346

Videoclip: IDAE 349

Lectura:
La foto, Enrique Anderson Imbert . . . 352

Las bicicletas en la ciudad 364

Flash cultura:
El metro del D.F. 365

14.1 The subjunctive in adjective clauses. 366

14.2 Familiar (**tú**) commands 368

14.3 Nosotros/as commands 370

Videoclip: Banco Ficensa 373

Lectura:
Los bomberos, Mario Benedetti 376

Aventuras en los países hispanos:
América Central II 379

Espacios públicos saludables 392

Flash cultura:
¿Estrés? ¿Qué estrés? 393

15.1 Past participles used as adjectives. 394

15.2 The present perfect. 396

15.3 The past perfect 398

Videoclip: Azucarlito. 401

Lectura:
El viaje, Cristina Peri Rossi 404

La entrevista de trabajo 416

Flash cultura:
El mundo del trabajo. 417

16.1 The future tense 418

16.2 The conditional tense 420

16.3 The past subjunctive. 422

Videoclip: Ágatha Ruiz de la Prada . . 425

Lectura:
Imaginación y destino,
Augusto Monterroso 428

Aventuras en los países hispanos:
España 431

Lesson Openers
outline the content and goals of each lesson.

6 ¡De compras!

Communicative Goals
You will learn how to:
• talk about clothes
• negotiate and pay for items
• express preferences while shopping
• investigate markets in the Spanish-speaking world

PREPARACIÓN
pages 140–145
• Words related to clothes and shopping
• Colors and other adjectives
• Pronouncing **d** and **t**

AVENTURAS
pages 146–147
• The friends go shopping. Sara and Valentina are in a store looking for a dress. Juanjo and Manuel are at an open-air market looking for sunglasses.

CULTURA
pages 148–149
• *Los mercados al aire libre*
• Flash cultura: *Comprar en los mercados*

GRAMÁTICA
pages 150–161
• Numbers 101 and higher
• Preterite tense of regular verbs
• Indirect object pronouns
• Demonstrative adjectives and pronouns

LECTURA
pages 162–163
• Advertisement: *Corona*

PARA EMPEZAR
• ¿Dónde están los chicos, en el centro o en el campo?
• ¿Qué están haciendo: comprando o trabajando?
• ¿Hace calor o hace frío?

Photo An image from the new **Aventuras** video sets the thematic tone for the lesson.

Para empezar A series of questions on the lesson opener photo recycles the language you already know and previews the vocabulary you are about to learn.

Lesson organization Consistent, color-coded sections make navigating each lesson easy.

Communicative goals There are communicative goals on the lesson opener and throughout the lesson that let you know what you will be able to do in Spanish.

ⓢupersite

Supersite resources are available for every section of the lesson at **vhlcentral.com**. Icons show you which textbook activities are also available online. The description next to the ⓢ icon indicates what additional resources are available for each section: videos, recordings, tutorials, and more!

Preparación
introduces vocabulary central to the lesson theme.

Communicative goal There is a communicative goal for this section that lets you know what you will be able to do in Spanish.

Art Dynamic photos and illustrations present high-frequency vocabulary.

Vocabulary Theme-related vocabulary appears in easy-to-reference Spanish/English lists. For words where the visual is sufficient, the Spanish is given and the English is provided at the end of the lesson.

Así se dice This presentation of alternate words and expressions highlights the richness of the Spanish-speaking world.

Supersite

- Vocabulary tutorials: word groups with audio and images
- Vocabulary Tools: customizable word lists, flashcards with audio

Preparación
practices vocabulary in stages.

A escuchar

1 Indicar Check **invierno** or **verano** to indicate when someone would be most likely to wear each item you hear.

	Invierno	Verano
1.		
2.		
3.		
4.		
5.		
6.		
7.		
8.		

2 ¿Lógico o ilógico? Indicate whether each statement you hear is **lógico** or **ilógico**.

	Lógico	Ilógico
1.		
2.		
3.		
4.		
5.		
6.		
7.		
8.		

3 Escuchar Listen to Juanita and Vicente talk about what they're packing for their vacations. Indicate who is packing each item. If neither is packing an item, write an **X**.

	Juanita	Vicente		Juanita	Vicente
1. abrigo			7. gafas de sol		
2. zapatos de tenis			8. camisetas		
3. impermeable			9. traje de baño		
4. chaqueta			10. botas		
5. sandalias			11. pantalones cortos		
6. bluejeans			12. suéter		

A practicar

4 Escoger Indicate the item in each group that does not belong.

1. bolsa • camiseta • blusa • suéter
2. medias • calcetines • sombrero • zapatos de tenis
3. chaqueta • falda • abrigo • impermeable
4. almacén • vendedora • tienda • mercado
5. regatear • gastar • llevar • costar
6. vestido • dinero • caja • tarjeta de crédito

5 Anita la contraria Your friend Anita always contradicts you. Indicate how she would respond to each sentence.

modelo El suéter nuevo de Liliana es muy grande.
No, su suéter es muy pequeño.

1. El cinturón de Natalia es caro. _____
2. El impermeable de don José es muy feo. _____
3. La corbata del señor Ramos es larga. _____
4. Los zapatos de tenis de Noelia son viejos. _____
5. Los trajes de Mauricio son baratos. _____
6. Las botas de Marta están sucias. _____

6 Preguntas Answer these questions with a classmate.

modelo

Estudiante 1: ¿De qué color es el suéter?
Estudiante 2: El suéter es gris.

1. ¿De qué color es la corbata?
2. ¿De qué color es la planta?
3. ¿De qué color es la rosa de Texas?
4. ¿De qué color es la casa donde vive el presidente de EE.UU.?
5. ¿De qué color es la cebra?

A escuchar Practice always begins with a page of listening activities that focus on vocabulary recognition and comprehension.

A practicar Practice continues with a page of guided and transitional activities that reinforce the new vocabulary in diverse formats.

Icons Icons provide a visual cue that indicates listening, Supersite, pair, group, and chat activities.

Supersite

- Textbook activities
- Additional online-only practice activities

Preparación

wraps up vocabulary practice with communicative activities.

A conversar

7 **Marta y el señor Vega** With a classmate, answer the questions about the drawing.

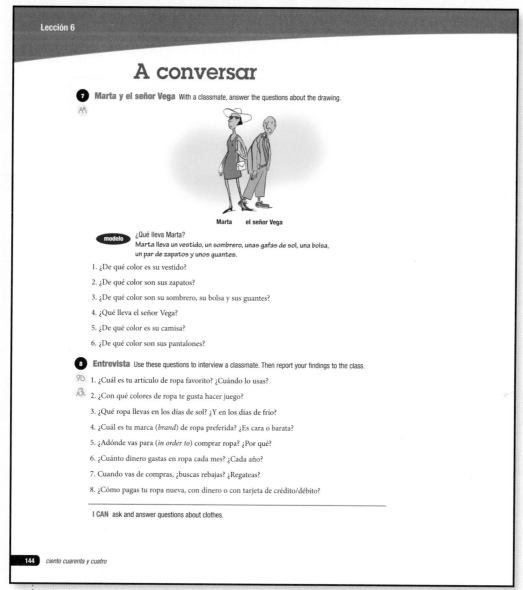

Marta   el señor Vega

modelo   ¿Qué lleva Marta?
Marta lleva un vestido, un sombrero, unas gafas de sol, una bolsa,
un par de zapatos y unos guantes.

1. ¿De qué color es su vestido?

2. ¿De qué color son sus zapatos?

3. ¿De qué color son su sombrero, su bolsa y sus guantes?

4. ¿Qué lleva el señor Vega?

5. ¿De qué color es su camisa?

6. ¿De qué color son sus pantalones?

8 **Entrevista** Use these questions to interview a classmate. Then report your findings to the class.

1. ¿Cuál es tu artículo de ropa favorito? ¿Cuándo lo usas?

2. ¿Con qué colores de ropa te gusta hacer juego?

3. ¿Qué ropa llevas en los días de sol? ¿Y en los días de frío?

4. ¿Cuál es tu marca (*brand*) de ropa preferida? ¿Es cara o barata?

5. ¿Adónde vas para (*in order to*) comprar ropa? ¿Por qué?

6. ¿Cuánto dinero gastas en ropa cada mes? ¿Cada año?

7. Cuando vas de compras, ¿buscas rebajas? ¿Regateas?

8. ¿Cómo pagas tu ropa nueva, con dinero o con tarjeta de crédito/débito?

I CAN   ask and answer questions about clothes.

A conversar This final set of activities gets you using vocabulary creatively for self-expression in interactions with a partner, a small group, or the entire class.

Can-Do Statement This section concludes with a Can-Do Statement, which shows you what you are now able to accomplish in Spanish.

Supersite

• Chat activities for conversational skill-building and oral practice
• Vocabulary activities in Activity Pack

Preparación

Pronunciación and *Ortografía* present the basics of Spanish pronunciation and spelling.

Pronunciación This section explains the sounds and pronunciation of Spanish in **Lecciones 1–9.**

Ortografía In **Lecciones 10–16,** this section focuses on topics related to Spanish spelling.

Supersite

- Pronunciation tutorials with speech recognition
- Spelling tutorials
- Record-compare textbook activities

Aventuras
tells the story of a group of students living and traveling in Spain.

Communicative goal There is a communicative goal for this section that lets you know what you will be able to do in Spanish.

Personajes The characters who appear in the episode are shown on the left.

Aventuras video The photo-based **Aventuras** conversations appear in the textbook's video program.

Expresiones útiles New words and expressions from the video are presented to help you understand and talk about the episode.

Actividades Guided exercises check your understanding and communicative activities allow you to react in a personalized way.

Nota cultural A new feature highlights some aspect of culture from the video.

Can-Do Statement This section concludes with a Can-Do Statement, which shows you what you are now able to accomplish in Spanish.

Supersite

- Streaming video of the **Aventuras** episode
- Interactive **Aventuras** videos with integrated viewing activities
- Textbook activities
- Additional online-only practice activities

Cultura

highlights engaging contemporary culture through readings and video.

Communicative goals There are two communicative goals for this section that let you know what you will be able to do in Spanish.

Feature article This focuses on a person, place, custom, event, or tradition in the Spanish-speaking world, with an emphasis on contemporary, day-to-day culture. Written in Spanish as of **Lección 7**, this feature also provides valuable reading practice.

Así se dice Additional lexical features expand cultural coverage to vocabulary from all over the Spanish-speaking world.

Flash cultura The enormously successful video offers specially shot content tied to the lesson theme. Previewing support and comprehension activities are integrated into the student text.

Can-Do Statements This section has two Can-Do Statements, which show you what you are now able to accomplish in Spanish.

Supersite

- Textbook activities
- Additional online-only practice activities
- Additional cultural reading
- **Conexión Internet** activity with questions and key words related to lesson theme
- Streaming video of **Flash cultura**

Gramática

uses innovative design to support learning Spanish.

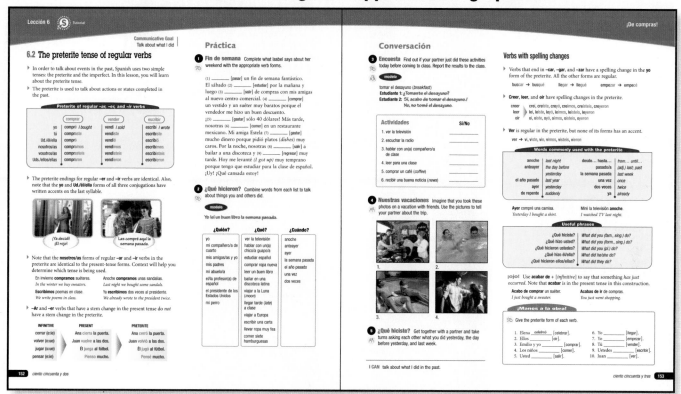

Layout For each grammar point, the explanation and practice activities appear together on two facing pages. Grammar explanations in the outside panels are the foundation for the activities in the shaded inner panels, providing you with support on the same page.

Explanations Written with the student in mind, **Aventuras'** grammar explanations are known for their clarity. Images, charts, and diagrams support the text by illustrating language and calling out key grammatical structures, patterns, and vocabulary.

Video Photos from the **Aventuras** video integrate it into the grammar explanations, providing a model and a real-life context for the structures you are studying.

(S)upersite

- Interactive grammar tutorials with quick checks
- Textbook activities
- Additional online-only practice activities
- Chat activities for conversational skill-building and oral practice
- Grammar activities in Activity Pack

Gramática
progresses from directed to communicative practice.

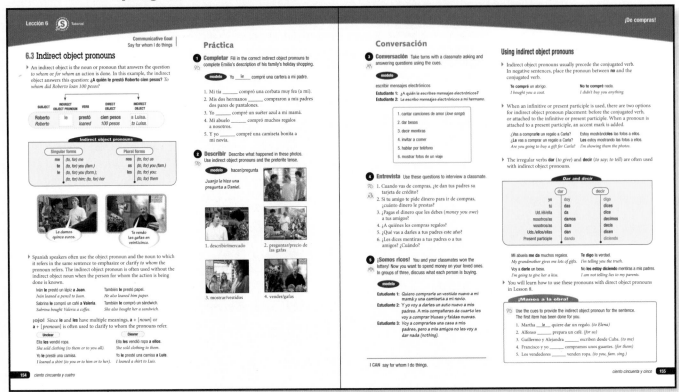

Communicative goal There is a communicative goal for each grammar point that lets you know what you will be able to do in Spanish.

¡Manos a la obra! This first practice activity gets you working with the grammar point right away in simple, easy-to-understand formats.

Práctica Activities provide a wide range of guided exercises in contexts that combine current and previously learned vocabulary with each grammar point.

Español en vivo Documents like advertisements and movie posters highlight the new grammar point in a real-life context.

Conversación Opportunities for personalized expression use the lesson's grammar and vocabulary. Activities take place with a partner, in small groups, or with the whole class.

Can-Do Statement Each grammar point concludes with a Can-Do Statement, which shows you what you are now able to accomplish in Spanish.

Supersite

- Interactive grammar tutorials with quick checks
- Textbook activities
- Additional online-only practice activities
- Chat activities for conversational skill-building and oral practice
- Grammar activities in Activity Pack

Gramática
includes additional practice and a video section.

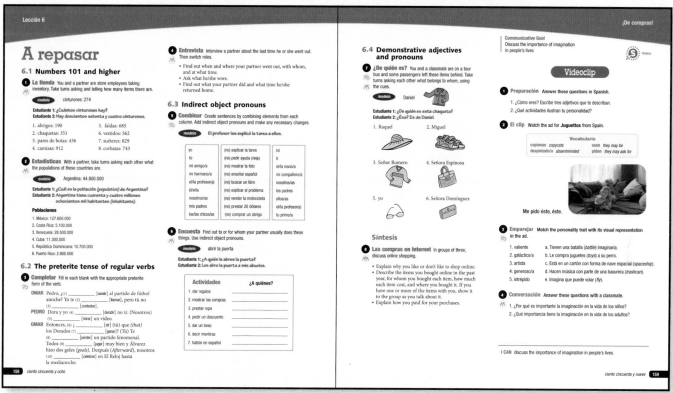

A repasar One or two directed and/or communicative exercises provide additional practice opportunities for each grammar point.

Síntesis Every **A repasar** section concludes with an open-ended, cumulative activity that allows you and your classmates to re-combine the grammar points of the lesson with the lesson's vocabulary.

Videoclip An authentic video clip synthesizes the entire lesson in a fun and engaging way. News stories, documentaries, commercials, and even a cooking show will get you excited about learning Spanish and expose you even more to the cultures of the Spanish-speaking world.

Communicative goal There is a communicative goal for the **Videoclip** section that lets you know what you will be able to do in Spanish.

Can-Do Statement The **Videoclip** section concludes with a Can-Do Statement, which shows you what you are now able to accomplish in Spanish.

Supersite

- Streaming video of **Videoclip**
- Review activities in Activity Pack

Gramática
emphasizes listening, writing, and speaking in *Ampliación*.

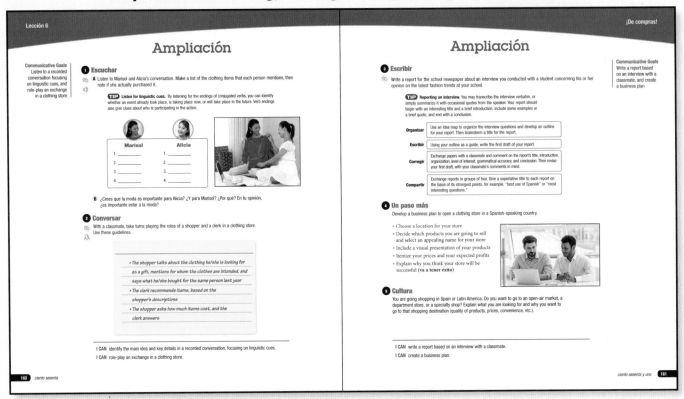

Communicative goals There are several communicative goals for this section that let you know what you will be able to do in Spanish.

Escuchar A recorded conversation or narration develops your listening skills in Spanish and checks your understanding of what you heard. Valuable on-the-spot listening tips help you carry out the activity effectively.

Conversar Your oral communication skills are developed through realistic, practical role-plays and situations.

Escribir A writing topic and plan take you step-by-step through the writing process, including planning, writing a first draft, peer review, and correcting your work. Valuable on-the-spot writing strategies (tips) help you carry out the activity effectively.

Un paso más This project guides you to research and create a tangible product such as a brochure or a web page or else give a presentation about a certain topic.

Cultura A new activity is related to the lesson theme and culture.

Can-Do Statements This section has several Can-Do Statements, which show you what you are now able to accomplish in Spanish.

Ⓢupersiteupersite

- Textbook activities
- Chat activities for conversational skill-building and oral practice
- **Conexión Internet** activity with questions and key words related to lesson theme
- Communication activities in Activity Pack

Lectura

supports the development of reading skills in the context of the lesson theme.

Communicative goal There is a communicative goal for this section that lets you know what you will be able to do in Spanish.

Antes de leer This feature presents helpful strategies (tips) and pre-reading activities to build your reading abilities in Spanish.

Readings The selections are specifically related to the lesson theme and recycle the vocabulary and grammar you have learned. **Lecciones 13–16** feature literary selections so that you can experience reading works by well-known authors in Spanish.

Después de leer Exercises check your comprehension of the reading.

Coméntalo Activities encourage you to discuss the material in the reading from your own, personal perspective.

Can-Do Statement This section concludes with a Can-Do Statement, which shows you what you are now able to accomplish in Spanish.

Supersite

- Audio-sync reading that highlights text as it is being read
- Textbook activities
- Additional reading
- Additional online-only practice

Vocabulario
summarizes the active vocabulary in each lesson.

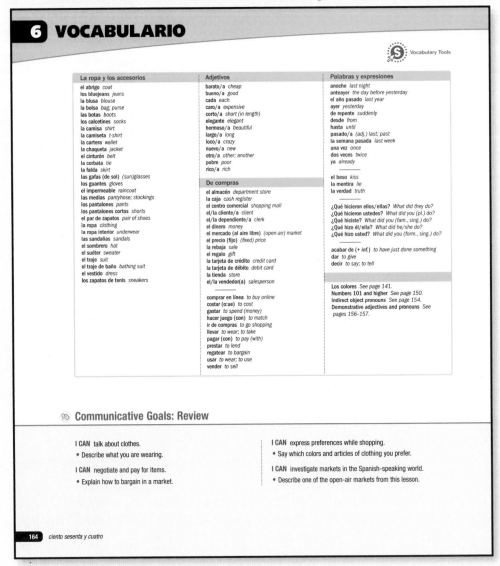

6 VOCABULARIO

Vocabulary Tools

La ropa y los accesorios

el abrigo *coat*
los bluejeans *jeans*
la blusa *blouse*
la bolsa *bag; purse*
las botas *boots*
los calcetines *socks*
la camisa *shirt*
la camiseta *t-shirt*
la cartera *wallet*
la chaqueta *jacket*
el cinturón *belt*
la corbata *tie*
la falda *skirt*
las gafas (de sol) *(sun)glasses*
los guantes *gloves*
el impermeable *raincoat*
las medias *pantyhose; stockings*
los pantalones *pants*
los pantalones cortos *shorts*
el par de zapatos *pair of shoes*
la ropa *clothing*
la ropa interior *underwear*
las sandalias *sandals*
el sombrero *hat*
el suéter *sweater*
el traje *suit*
el traje de baño *bathing suit*
el vestido *dress*
los zapatos de tenis *sneakers*

Adjetivos

barato/a *cheap*
bueno/a *good*
cada *each*
caro/a *expensive*
corto/a *short (in length)*
elegante *elegant*
hermoso/a *beautiful*
largo/a *long*
loco/a *crazy*
nuevo/a *new*
otro/a *other; another*
pobre *poor*
rico/a *rich*

De compras

el almacén *department store*
la caja *cash register*
el centro comercial *shopping mall*
el/la cliente/a *client*
el/la dependiente/a *clerk*
el dinero *money*
el mercado (al aire libre) *(open-air) market*
el precio (fijo) *(fixed) price*
la rebaja *sale*
el regalo *gift*
la tarjeta de crédito *credit card*
la tarjeta de débito *debit card*
la tienda *store*
el/la vendedor(a) *salesperson*

comprar en línea *to buy online*
costar (o:ue) *to cost*
gastar *to spend (money)*
hacer juego (con) *to match*
ir de compras *to go shopping*
llevar *to wear; to take*
pagar (con) *to pay (with)*
prestar *to lend*
regatear *to bargain*
usar *to wear; to use*
vender *to sell*

Palabras y expresiones

anoche *last night*
anteayer *the day before yesterday*
el año pasado *last year*
ayer *yesterday*
de repente *suddenly*
desde *from*
hasta *until*
pasado/a *(adj.) last; past*
la semana pasada *last week*
una vez *once*
dos veces *twice*
ya *already*

el beso *kiss*
la mentira *lie*
la verdad *truth*

¿Qué hicieron ellos/ellas? *What did they do?*
¿Qué hicieron ustedes? *What did you (pl.) do?*
¿Qué hiciste? *What did you (fam., sing.) do?*
¿Qué hizo él/ella? *What did he/she do?*
¿Qué hizo usted? *What did you (form., sing.) do?*

acabar de (+ inf.) *to have just done something*
dar *to give*
decir *to say; to tell*

Los colores *See page 141.*
Numbers 101 and higher *See page 150.*
Indirect object pronouns *See page 154.*
Demonstrative adjectives and pronouns *See pages 156-157.*

Communicative Goals: Review

I CAN talk about clothes.
• Describe what you are wearing.

I CAN negotiate and pay for items.
• Explain how to bargain in a market.

I CAN express preferences while shopping.
• Say which colors and articles of clothing you prefer.

I CAN investigate markets in the Spanish-speaking world.
• Describe one of the open-air markets from this lesson.

164 *ciento sesenta y cuatro*

Vocabulario The end-of-lesson page lists the active vocabulary from this lesson. This is the vocabulary that may appear on quizzes or tests.

Communicative Goals: Review This self-assessment gives you the opportunity to check your understanding of the lesson's communicative goals and identify any areas where you need further review and practice.

Supersite

• Audio for all vocabulary items
• Vocabulary Tools: customizable word lists, flashcards with audio
• Summative vocabulary activity with speech recognition
• Practice test with diagnostics
• Oral practice
• Task-based activity in Activity Pack

Aventuras en los países hispanos

presents the countries of the Spanish-speaking world and appears after every even-numbered lesson.

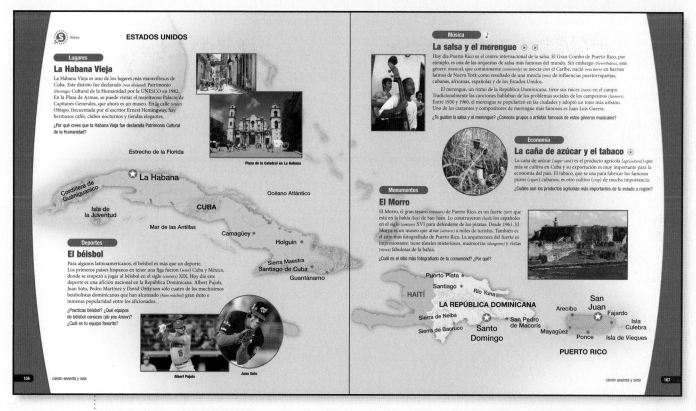

Maps These maps situate the country or region on its continent and highlight significant features.

Readings Short readings with eye-catching photos explore key facets of the location's culture, such as history, fine arts, food, celebrations, and traditions.

Panorama cultural video This video provides an exciting visual companion for one or more of the paragraphs about the featured country or region.

Con ritmo hispano This new feature highlights musicians of the Spanish-speaking world.

Opening and closing pages The opening page sets the scene for the section with a dramatic photo and statistics about the location. **¿Qué aprendiste?** activities on the closing page connect what you've learned with your own experiences. There is a communicative goal on the opening page and a Can-Do Statement on the closing page to show you what you can accomplish in Spanish.

Supersite

- Streaming video of the **Panorama cultural** program
- Textbook activities
- Additional online-only practice activities
- **Con ritmo hispano** activity
- **Conexión Internet** activity with questions and key words related to lesson theme

The Cast

Here are the main characters you will meet when you watch the **Aventuras** video.

**Olga Lucía
Pérez Soto**

**Valentina
Herrera Torres**

**Juan José
Reyes Peña**

**Manuel
Vázquez Quevedo**

**Sara
Sánchez Vázquez**

**Daniel
Acosta Campos**

Two New Video Programs

Aventuras

Fully integrated with your textbook, the **Aventuras** Video contains sixteen episodes. The episodes present the adventures of a group of friends in Madrid, Spain. Manuel, Juanjo, Valentina, and Olga Lucía are college students who live in the same apartment building. Manuel's cousin Sara also lives there with her father, Paco, the landlord. Her friend Daniel completes the group. Manuel, Valentina, Sara, don Paco, and Daniel are all from Spain. Juanjo hails from the Dominican Republic. Olga Lucía is a native of Venezuela. Their adventures take them through some of the greatest natural and cultural treasures of the Spanish-speaking world, as well as the highs and lows of everyday life.

The **Aventuras** section in each textbook lesson is actually an abbreviated version of the dramatic episode featured in the video. Therefore, each **Aventuras** section can be done before you see the corresponding video episode, after it, or as a section that stands alone.

In each dramatic segment, the characters interact using vocabulary and grammar you are studying. As the storyline unfolds, the episodes combine new vocabulary and grammar with previously taught language. The **Resumen** segment serves to recap the plot as well as to emphasize the grammar and vocabulary you are studying.

Panorama cultural

The **Panorama cultural** video provides visuals for one or more of the paragraphs in each **Aventuras en los países hispanos** section in **Aventuras**.

Flash cultura

The dynamic **Flash cultura** Video is fully integrated into the **Cultura** section of each lesson and into your Video Manual. Shot in eight countries (U.S., Puerto Rico, Mexico, Spain, Argentina, Costa Rica, Ecuador, and Peru), these contemporary and engaging episodes expand on the lesson themes. Each episode is hosted by a correspondent from the featured country; the host provides valuable information about a tradition, event, resource, or other aspect of the country's culture and talks to the locals to get their opinions about the subject at hand.

The episodes are entirely in Spanish as of **Lección 7**, but they feature authentic interviews in Spanish from the very beginning, exposing you to the diverse and authentic accents of the Spanish-speaking world. Support materials in the text, on the Supersite, and in the Video Manual make these interviews accessible so that you get the most out of them.

We hope you enjoy **Flash cultura, ¡el programa donde aprender es toda una aventura!**

Videoclip

Aventuras features an authentic video clip from the Spanish-speaking world for each lesson. Clip formats include high-interest commercials and news stories. These clips have been carefully chosen to be comprehensible for students learning Spanish. Developed by Spanish speakers for Spanish speakers, they offer another valuable window into the products, practices, and perspectives that are key to the cultures of the Spanish-speaking world. More importantly, though, these clips are a fun and motivating way to improve your Spanish!

Here are the countries represented in each lesson in **Videoclip**.

Lesson 1 U.S.	Lesson 5 Mexico	Lesson 9 Mexico	Lesson 13 Spain
Lesson 2 Spain	Lesson 6 Spain	Lesson 10 Spain	Lesson 14 Honduras
Lesson 3 Argentina	Lesson 7 Chile	Lesson 11 Argentina	Lesson 15 Uruguay
Lesson 4 Spain	Lesson 8 Spain	Lesson 12 Spain	Lesson 16 Spain

Icons

Familiarize yourself with these icons that appear throughout **Aventuras, Sixth Edition**.

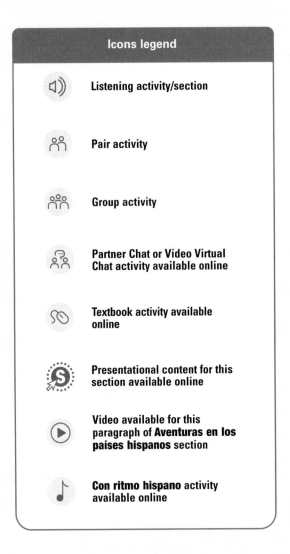

🔊	**Listening activity/section**
👥	**Pair activity**
👥👤	**Group activity**
	Partner Chat or Video Virtual Chat activity available online
	Textbook activity available online
Ⓢ	**Presentational content for this section available online**
▶	**Video available for this paragraph of Aventuras en los países hispanos section**
♪	**Con ritmo hispano activity available online**

- You will see the listening icon in **Preparación**, **Pronunciación**, and **Ampliación** sections.

- A note next to the Supersite icon will let you know exactly what type of content is available online.

New Features and Technology

Vocabulary Tutorials

Lesson vocabulary words are grouped thematically in new tutorials. Each term comes with audio, an image, and an English translation.

Interactive *Aventuras* Videos with Integrated Viewing Activities

You can check your comprehension with integrated viewing activities as you watch the new **Aventuras** video.

Refuerzo de vocabulario

There is a new summative vocabulary activity in the **Repaso** section of the Supersite in which you identify and say the terms illustrated by photos. Speech recognition lets you know if you are correct.

Video Virtual Chats

Video Virtual Chat activities provide you with opportunities to develop your listening and speaking skills and to build confidence as you practice with video recordings of native speakers. Unlike other listening activities where you can easily pause and repeat, Video Virtual Chats require you to answer questions in real time—just as you do when you engage in conversations with fluent speakers in the target language. You also benefit from nonverbal and articulatory cues that are essential for production and pronunciation.

Video Virtual Chats are available in about half of the **A conversar** sections of **Preparación** and of the **Conversación** sections of **Gramática**.

Pronunciation Tutorials with Speech Recognition

Pronunciation tutorials allow you to engage with the material via interactive quick checks throughout each tutorial.

Interactive feedback via embedded Speech Recognition gives you an opportunity to reflect on your language patterns and increases your awareness of pronunciation through low-stakes production practice.

Supersite

Each section of your textbook comes with activities on the **Aventuras** Supersite, many of which are auto-graded for immediate feedback. Plus, the Supersite can be accessed on the go! Visit **vhlcentral.com** to explore this wealth of exciting resources.

PREPARACIÓN
- Vocabulary tutorials
- Audio activities
- Textbook activities
- Additional activities for extra practice
- Chat activities for conversational skill-building and oral practice

- Pronunciation tutorials with speech recognition
- Audio files for **Pronunciación**
- Record-compare practice

AVENTURAS
- Streaming video of **Aventuras fotonovela**, with instructor-managed options for subtitles and transcripts in Spanish and English

- Textbook activities
- Additional activities for extra practice
- Record-compare practice

CULTURA
- Textbook activities
- Additional activities for extra practice
- Additional reading
- **Conexión Internet** activity

- Streaming video of **Flash cultura** series, with instructor-managed options for subtitles and transcripts in Spanish and English

GRAMÁTICA
- Interactive grammar tutorials
- Textbook activities
- Additional activities for extra practice
- Chat activities for conversational skill-building and oral practice
- **Conexión Internet** activity

- Streaming **Videoclip** with instructor-managed options for subtitles and transcripts in Spanish and English
- Audio files for listening activity in **Ampliación**
- Composition engine for **Escribir** activity

LECTURA
- Audio-sync reading in **Lectura**
- Additional reading

- Textbook activities and additional activities for extra practice

AVENTURAS EN LOS PAÍSES HISPANOS
- Textbook activities
- Additional activities for extra practice
- **Con ritmo hispano** activities
- **Conexión Internet** activity

- Streaming video of **Panorama cultural** series, with instructor-managed options for subtitles and transcripts in Spanish and English

VOCABULARIO
- Vocabulary list with audio

- Customizable study lists

*Students must use a computer for select presentations.

On behalf of its authors and editors, Vista Higher Learning expresses its sincere appreciation to the many educators nationwide who contributed their ideas and suggestions to **Aventuras, First Edition**. We are grateful to the more than eighty members of the Spanish-teaching community who reviewed the original manuscript and/or class-tested the materials. Their insights and detailed comments were invaluable to us as we created the First Edition.

Aventuras, Sixth Edition, has been informed by extensive reviews and ongoing input from instructors using the Fifth Edition. Accordingly, we gratefully acknowledge those who shared their suggestions, recommendations, and ideas as we prepared this Sixth Edition.

We acknowledge Dr. Solivia Márquez of the Massachusetts Institute of Technology for her work with us on the First Edition, and we thank her for her contributions to activities and the **Lectura** sections.

We express our appreciation to the many instructors using **Aventuras** who completed our online reviews.

Reviewers

Leyre Alegre
Michigan Technological University

Tim Altanero, PhD
College of Central Florida

Enrica J. Ardemagni, PhD
Indiana University-Purdue University Indianapolis

Mario Bahena Uriostegui, PhD
Johnson C. Smith University, NC

Stephen Barnes
College of Charleston, SC

Emily S. Beck
College of Charleston, SC

Helena S. Belío Apaolaza
Simmons University, MA

Juan Antonio Bernabeu
Laramie County Community College, WY

Amy Bomke
Indiana University-Purdue University Indianapolis

Daniel H. Briere
University of Indianapolis, IN

Orlando Bruzual
San Jacinto College, TX

Evangelina Canedo-Escarcega
University of Alaska Anchorage

Jennifer Cartan
Sierra College, CA

Marisol Castro-Calzada
College of Charleston, SC

Dr. Noel Coronel
Carroll University, WI

Adam Vincent Crofts
College of Southern Idaho

Pilar Damron
Northwest Vista College, TX

Melissa L. Fiori
Daemen College, NY

Stephanie Forgash
College of Charleston, SC

Arlene F. Fuentes
Southern Virginia University

Inés M. García
American River College, CA

Jose Garcia-Paine
Eastern Iowa Community College

Judy Haisten, PhD
College of Central Florida

Devon W. Hanahan
College of Charleston, SC

Betsy Hance
College of Charleston, SC

Ceydy B. Heiser
American River College, CA

acknowledgments

Serena M. Herter
Southwestern Community College, NC

Lauren Hetrovicz
College of Charleston, SC

Dr. Jennifer E. Irish
Ferrum College, VA

Iana Konstantinova
Southern Virginia University

William Michael Lake
Georgia State University

Gisabel Leonardo
Georgia State University

Raúl Llorente
Georgia State University

Emma B. Marquina Castillo
College of Charleston, SC

Cecilia Moix
Belmont University, TN

Vita Patrick Morales
County College of Morris, NJ

Carlos R. Naranjo
San Jacinto College, TX

Polly Nelson
Lord Fairfax Community College, VA

Noelle Parris
Trident Technical College, SC

Ana María Pinzón
Frederick Community College, MD

Thomas R. Porter
Southern Virginia University

Drew Proctor
Hill College, TX

Carola Ramirez-Castello
College of Charleston, SC

Marta Ramírez Martínez
College of Charleston, SC

Sandra L. Riveros
Eckerd College, FL

Ron Roosevelt
University of Michigan

M. Rosende
County College of Morris, NJ

Jorge Salinas
Universidad Nacional Autónoma
de México

Jean M. Scheppers
College of Central Florida

Linda M. Schumacher
William Rainey Harper College, IL

Gabriela Segal
Arcadia University, PA

Vangie Vélez-Cobb
Palo Alto College, TX

Allie Zaubi
College of Charleston, SC

1 Hola, ¿qué tal?

Communicative Goals
You will learn how to:
- greet people in Spanish
- say goodbye
- identify yourself and others
- talk about the time of day
- investigate greetings in the Spanish-speaking world

PREPARACIÓN

pages 2–7
- Words related to meeting, greeting, and saying goodbye
- Courtesy expressions
- Pronouncing the Spanish alphabet

AVENTURAS

pages 8–9
- Sara greets her friend Daniel and introduces him to her father Paco, her cousin Manuel, and other residents of her apartment building: Olga Lucía, Valentina, and Juanjo.

CULTURA

pages 10–11
- *Los saludos y el espacio personal*
- Flash cultura: *Encuentros en la plaza*

GRAMÁTICA

pages 12–23
- Nouns and articles
- Numbers 0–30
- Present tense of **ser**
- Telling time

LECTURA

pages 24–25
- Contact list: *Información importante*

🔊 PARA EMPEZAR
- Guess what the people in the photo are saying.
  - a. Por favor.
  - b. Hola.
  - c. señorita
- Most likely they would also say:
  - a. Gracias.
  - b. Adiós.
  - c. Buenas tardes.

HOLA, ¿QUÉ TAL?

SALUDOS Y DESPEDIDAS

Hola. *Hello.*

Buenos días. *Good morning.*

Buenas tardes. *Good afternoon.*

Buenas noches. *Good evening; Good night.*

Adiós. *Goodbye.*

Chau. *Bye.*

Hasta la vista. *See you later.*

Hasta luego. *See you later.*

Hasta mañana. *See you tomorrow.*

Hasta pronto. *See you soon.*

Nos vemos. *See you.*

Saludos a... *Say hello to...*

CARLA	Hola, Sofía. ¿Qué hay de nuevo?
SOFÍA	Nada. Y tú, ¿qué tal?
CARLA	Bien, gracias.
SOFÍA	Nos vemos, Carla.
CARLA	Chau, Sofía. Saludos a Roberto.

SEÑORA SALAS	Buenas tardes, señor Pérez. ¿Cómo está usted?
SEÑOR PÉREZ	Muy bien, gracias. ¿Y usted, señora Salas?
SEÑORA SALAS	Muy bien.
SEÑOR PÉREZ	Me alegro.

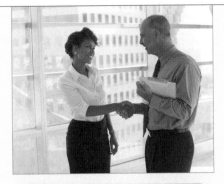

¿CÓMO ESTÁS?

¿Cómo está usted? *How are you? (formal)*

¿Cómo estás? *How are you? (familiar)*

¿Qué hay de nuevo? *What's new?*

¿Qué pasa? *What's going on?*

¿Qué tal? *How is it going?*

(Muy) bien, gracias. *(Very) well, thanks.*

Nada. *Nothing.*

No muy bien. *Not very well.*

Regular. *So-so.*

Vocabulary Tools

PRESENTACIONES

¿Cómo se llama usted? *What's your name? (form.)*

¿Cómo te llamas (tú)? *What's your name? (fam.)*

Me llamo... *My name is...*

¿Y tú? *And you? (fam.)*

¿Y usted? *And you? (form.)*

Mucho gusto. *Pleased to meet you.*

El gusto es mío. *The pleasure is mine.*

Encantado/a. *Pleased to meet you.*

Igualmente. *Likewise.*

Le presento a... *I would like to introduce you to... (form.)*

Te presento a... *I would like to introduce you to... (fam.)*

¿De dónde es usted? *Where are you from? (form.)*

¿De dónde eres? *Where are you from? (fam.)*

Soy de... *I'm from...*

LAURA	Hola. Me llamo Laura. ¿Y tú?
ESTEBAN	Hola. Me llamo Esteban. Mucho gusto.
LAURA	El gusto es mío. ¿De dónde eres?
ESTEBAN	Soy de los Estados Unidos, de Texas.

SUSANA	Leti, te presento al señor Garza.
LETICIA	Encantada.
SEÑOR GARZA	Igualmente. ¿De dónde es usted, señorita?
LETICIA	Soy de Puerto Rico. ¿Y usted?
SEÑOR GARZA	De México.

EXPRESIONES Y TÍTULOS DE CORTESÍA

De nada. *You're welcome.*

Lo siento. *I'm sorry.*

(Muchas) gracias. *Thank you (very much).*

No hay de qué. *You're welcome.*

Por favor. *Please.*

---

señor (Sr.) *Mr.; sir*

señora (Sra.) *Mrs.; ma'am*

señorita (Srta.) *Miss*

ASÍ SE DICE

Buenos días. ⟷ Buenas.
De nada. ⟷ A la orden.
Lo siento. ⟷ Perdón.
¿Qué tal? ⟷ ¿Cómo te va?,
¿Cómo vas?,
¿Qué hubo? (*Col.*)

▸ What phrases do you use when you greet friends?

A escuchar

1 Indicar Check **sí** if you might use the expression you hear to greet someone or **no** if you would not.

	Sí	No
1.	_____	_____
2.	_____	_____
3.	_____	_____
4.	_____	_____
5.	_____	_____
6.	_____	_____
7.	_____	_____
8.	_____	_____

2 Seleccionar Listen to each question or statement, and choose the correct response.

1. a. Muy bien, gracias.   b. Me llamo Graciela.
2. a. Lo siento.   b. Mucho gusto.
3. a. Soy de Puerto Rico.   b. No muy bien.
4. a. No hay de qué.   b. Regular.
5. a. Mucho gusto.   b. Hasta pronto.
6. a. Nada.   b. Igualmente.
7. a. Me llamo Guillermo Montero. b. Muy bien, gracias.
8. a. Buenas tardes. ¿Cómo está usted? b. El gusto es mío.

3 ¿Lógico o ilógico? Listen to each conversation and indicate whether the conversation is logical or illogical.

	Lógico	Ilógico
1.	_____	_____
2.	_____	_____
3.	_____	_____
4.	_____	_____
5.	_____	_____
6.	_____	_____

A practicar

4 Sinónimos For each expression, write a word or phrase that expresses a similar idea.

modelo ¿Cómo estás? _____¿Qué tal?_____

1. De nada. _____
2. Encantado. _____
3. Adiós. _____
4. Te presento a Antonio. _____
5. ¿Qué hay de nuevo? _____
6. Igualmente. _____

5 Ordenar With a classmate, put this scrambled conversation in order. Then act it out.

—Muy bien, gracias. Soy María Rosa.
—Soy de Ecuador. ¿Y tú?
—Mucho gusto, María Rosa.
—Hola. Me llamo Carlos. ¿Cómo estás?
—Soy de Cuba.
—Igualmente. ¿De dónde eres, Carlos?

CARLOS _____
MARÍA ROSA _____
CARLOS _____
MARÍA ROSA _____
CARLOS _____
MARÍA ROSA _____

6 Emparejar With a partner, match each question or statement with the correct answer.

___ 1. ¿Qué tal?
___ 2. Hasta mañana, señora Ramírez. Saludos al señor Ramírez.
___ 3. ¿Qué hay de nuevo, Alberto?
___ 4. Miguel, ésta es la señorita Perales.
___ 5. ¿De dónde eres, Antonio?
___ 6. Buenas tardes, señor. ¿Cómo está usted?

a. Muy bien, gracias.
b. Soy de México.
c. Nada. ¿Y tú?
d. Encantado. Soy Miguel Vega.
e. De nada.
f. Hasta pronto.
g. Bien. ¿Y tú?
h. Por favor.

A conversar

7 **Diálogos** With a partner, complete and act out these conversations.

DIÁLOGO 1

—Hola. Me llamo Álex. ¿Cómo te llamas tú?

_____

—Soy de Puerto Rico. ¿Y tú?

_____

DIÁLOGO 2

_____

—Muy bien, gracias. ¿Y usted, señor/señora López?

_____

—Hasta luego, señor/señora. Saludos a la señora/al señor López.

_____

8 **Conversaciones** With a partner, make up a conversation for each photo.

9 **Situaciones** Work with two classmates to act out these situations.

1. As you leave class on the first day of school, you strike up a conversation with the two students who were sitting next to you. Find out each person's name and where he or she is from before you say goodbye.

2. You meet a friend and ask how he or she is doing. As you are talking, your friend Elena walks by. Introduce Elena to your friend.

3. You say hello to your parents' friends, Mrs. Sánchez and Mr. Rodríguez, and ask how they are doing. As you say goodbye, send your regards to their spouses.

_____

I CAN greet new acquaintances, introduce myself, and say goodbye.

Pronunciación

 Tutorial

The Spanish alphabet

The Spanish and English alphabets are almost identical, with a few exceptions. For example, the Spanish letter **ñ** (**eñe**) doesn't occur in the English alphabet. Furthermore, the letters **k** (**ka**) and **w** (**doble v**) are used only in words of foreign origin. Examine the chart to find other differences.

Letra	Nombre(s)	Ejemplo(s)	Letra	Nombre(s)	Ejemplo(s)
a	a	**a**diós	n	ene	**n**acionalidad
b	be	**b**ien, pro**b**lema	ñ	eñe	ma**ñ**ana
c	ce	**c**osa, **c**ero	o	o	**o**nce
ch	che	**ch**ico	p	pe	**p**rofesor
d	de	**d**iario, na**d**a	q	cu	**q**ué
e	e	**e**studiante	r	ere	**r**egular, seño**r**a
f	efe	**f**oto			
g	ge	**g**racias, **G**erardo, re**g**ular	s	ese	**s**eñor
			t	te	**t**ú
h	hache	**h**ola	u	u	**u**sted
i	i	**i**gualmente	v	ve	**v**ista, nue**v**o
j	jota	**J**avier	w	doble ve	**w**alkman
k	ka, ca	**k**ilómetro	x	equis	e**x**istir, Mé**x**ico
l	ele	**l**ápiz			
ll	elle	**ll**ave	y	i griega, ye	**y**o
m	eme	**m**apa	z	zeta, ceta	**z**ona

Práctica Spell these words aloud in Spanish.

1. nada
2. bien
3. trece
4. muy
5. hola
6. encantado
7. Valentina
8. estudiante
9. Venezuela
10. España
11. Manuel
12. diez
13. cuatro
14. gracias
15. Juanjo

Oraciones Repeat these sentences after your instructor, then spell each word aloud.

1. Me llamo Carmen.
2. Hasta luego, señora Herrera.
3. ¿Qué tal, David?
4. Buenos días, Pedro.

Refranes Read these sayings aloud after your instructor.

Ver es creer.[1]

En boca cerrada no entran moscas.[2]

[1] Seeing is believing.
[2] Silence is golden.

Amigos de todas partes

Sara presenta un amigo a don Paco, Manuel, Valentina, Juanjo y Olga Lucía.

 Video

Antes de ver

Look at the images. Who do you think the people in the video are?

PERSONAJES

OLGA LUCÍA

DON PACO

VALENTINA

MANUEL

JUANJO

DANIEL

SARA

VALENTINA Hola. ¿Cómo estás?

OLGA LUCÍA Pues, ¡no muy bien!

VALENTINA ¿Qué te pasa?

OLGA LUCÍA ¡Ser estudiante de fotografía es agotador!

VALENTINA ¿Por qué?

OLGA LUCÍA ¡Son las seis de la tarde! ¡Todo el día tomando fotos!

MANUEL Veintidós... veintitrés...

JUANJO ¡Veintitrés no es nada! ¡¿Cómo te llamas?!

MANUEL ¡Manuel Vázquez Quevedo! Veinticuatro...

JUANJO ¡¿De dónde eres?!

MANUEL ¡Soy de Valladolid, España! ¡Veinticinco!

SARA ¡Hola, Daniel!

DANIEL Hola, Sara.

SARA Papá, te presento a Daniel. Un amigo del instituto.

PACO Paco, mucho gusto.

DANIEL El gusto es mío.

ACTIVIDADES

1 ¿Cierto o falso? Indicate if each statement is **cierto** or **falso**. Correct the false statements.

	Cierto	Falso
1. Olga Lucía es de los Estados Unidos.	○	○
2. Daniel es amigo del instituto de Olga Lucía.	○	○
3. Juanjo es de la República Dominicana.	○	○
4. El padre de Sara se llama Daniel.	○	○
5. Manuel es el primo de Sara.	○	○

2 Identificar Identify the person who made each statement.

1. ¡Soy de Valladolid, España!

2. Papá, te presento a Daniel.

3. ¡Qué bien, amigos de todas partes!

4. Foto número uno de veinticinco.

5. ¡Veintitrés no es nada!

SARA Chicos, os presento a Daniel.
VALENTINA Hola, ¿qué tal?
SARA Daniel, ella es Valentina.
DANIEL ¡Hola!
SARA Ella es Olga Lucía, de Venezuela.
DANIEL ¡De Venezuela! ¡Qué guay!

SARA Y él es mi primo, Manuel.
MANUEL ¡Hola! Manuel. ¡De Valladolid!
JUANJO Y yo soy Juanjo.
DANIEL Y tú, ¿de dónde eres?
JUANJO ¡De la República Dominicana, hermano!

DANIEL ¡Qué bien, amigos de todas partes!
VALENTINA ¡Olga Lucía, una foto!
OLGA LUCÍA ¡Foto veintiséis!
TODOS ¡Cinco, cuatro, tres, dos, uno!

Expresiones útiles

agotador(a) *exhausting*
el instituto *high school (in Spain)*
el padre *father*
el/la primo/a *cousin*
¡Qué guay! *How cool!*
(de) todas partes *everywhere*
todo/a *all*
tomando *taking*

---

la azotea *rooftop*
la brocheta *shish kebab*
las flexiones *push-ups*
la gorra *baseball cap*

Madrid

Madrid, the capital and the largest city of Spain, has beautiful squares like the **Puerta del Sol**. This is where you'll find the official symbol of Madrid, **El Oso y el Madroño**, a bronze statue of a bear nuzzling a strawberry tree. The image represents the city's coat of arms.

Is your city or town known for an iconic artwork or building? Compare it with **El Oso y el Madroño**.

3 **Conversación** With a partner, role-play a conversation between two young people who have just met in Madrid. Use these cues.

▶ Greet each other and introduce yourselves.
▶ Ask how your partner is doing.
▶ Ask where your partner is from.
▶ Say goodbye.

I CAN greet a new acquaintance, introduce myself, and say goodbye.

Communicative Goal
Identify ways in which people in
Spanish-speaking countries greet each other

Los saludos y el espacio personal

One kiss or two? A hug or a handshake? Up close or a little farther away? When you are introduced to someone, you don't always know the culturally appropriate way to greet that person. In all cultures, people have a "personal bubble" that is important to identify so that their space isn't invaded.

The acceptable amount of personal space differs according to factors such as gender, age, social status, and region. Latin American and southern European countries such as Spain are considered "high contact," that is, people come closer to each other than in other countries.

Some studies show that climate influences personal space. People in hotter regions such as the Caribbean appear to come closer to each other, while those in colder regions may keep more distance.

The tradition of kissing when greeting someone varies according to gender and region. In Spanish-speaking countries, men generally greet each other with a hug or a handshake. An exception is Argentina, where male friends and relatives lightly kiss on the cheek.

Greetings between men and women, and between women, in Spanish-speaking countries generally include a kiss (**un beso**) on the cheek or a kiss on each cheek. In Spain, it is customary to give **dos besos**, starting with the right cheek. In most Latin American countries, greetings consist of a single kiss, almost always an "air kiss," on the right cheek. In Colombia, women tend to greet each other with a pat on the right forearm or shoulder.

Tendencias

País	Beso	País	Beso
Argentina	💋	España	💋💋
Bolivia	💋	México	💋
Chile	💋	Paraguay	💋💋
Colombia	💋	Puerto Rico	💋
El Salvador	💋	Venezuela	💋/💋💋

ASÍ SE DICE

Saludos y despedidas

Chao./Ciao.	Adiós.
¿Cómo te/le va?	*How are things going?*
¿Qué hay?	*What's up?*
¿Qué hacés? (Arg.)	
¿Qué te cuentas? (Esp.)	
¿Qué onda? (Arg., Chi., Méx.)	
¿Qué más? (Col., Ven.)	

▶ How do you ask your friends what's going on?

INSTRUCTIONAL RESOURCES
Supersite: Video (Flash cultura); WebSAM
SAM: Video Manual pp. 201–202

ACTIVIDADES

1 **¿Cierto o falso?** Indicate whether each statement is true (**cierto**) or false (**falso**).

1. Social status and age influence personal space. *Cierto.*
2. In countries such as Colombia, Venezuela, and Spain, people are in closer contact than people in other countries. *Cierto.*
3. It is common for men in Spanish-speaking countries to greet each other with a kiss. *Falso.*
4. In Mexico and Chile, people greet each other with two kisses. *Falso.*
5. In Colombia, women may greet each other with a pat on the arm or shoulder. *Cierto.*

2 **Preguntas** Answer the questions.

1. What factors influence personal space? *gender, age, social status, region*
2. How do men in Spanish-speaking countries generally greet each other? *with a hug or a handshake*
3. Where do male friends and relatives lightly kiss on the cheek? *in Argentina*
4. How do women in Bolivia greet each other? *with a single kiss on the cheek*
5. How do men greet women in Spain? *with a kiss on each cheek*

3 **Comparación** Based on your experiences, compare greeting styles in the United States with those of Spanish-speaking countries.
③ Comparisons Cultural Comparisons

4 **Situaciones** With a partner, act out the following scenarios. You run into a friend at a café and want to say hello. How would you do so in Spain, Colombia, and Mexico?
④ Communication Interpersonal Communication

5 **Perspectivas** Reflect on these questions.

1. What does the acceptable amount of personal space say about countries like Spain?
2. How do you think personal space is influenced by factors such as age and social status?
3. Do you agree that climate influences personal space? Why or why not?
4. What other factors might influence personal space?

I CAN recognize variations on ways to greet someone.

Communicative Goal
Identify important social meeting places in Buenos Aires, as well as a few cultural practices

 Video

Encuentros en la plaza

1 **Preparación** Where do you usually meet your friends? Are there public places where you get together? What do you do there?

2 **El video** Watch this **Flash cultura** episode about greetings and plazas in Argentina.

Vocabulario		
abrazo *hug*	¡Cuánto tiempo!	*It's been a long time!*
encuentro *meeting*	¡Qué bueno verte!	*It's great to see you!*

Today we are at the **Plaza de Mayo.**

3 **Identificar** Identify the person or people who make(s) each of these statements.

1. ¿Cómo están ustedes? *d*   **a.** Gonzalo
2. ¡Qué bueno verte! *b*   **b.** Mariana
3. Mucho gusto, Mariana. *a*   **c.** Mark
4. Hola. *a, b, c, d*   **d.** Silvina

4 **Saludos** With a partner, role-play two Argentinians greeting each other. **④ Communication** Interpersonal Communication

I CAN identify important social meeting places in Buenos Aires.

I CAN identify the cultural practices related to formal and informal address, gestures, and behaviors when people meet.

Communicative Goal
Name familiar people and objects

1.1 Nouns and articles

▶ Nouns identify people, animals, places, things. All Spanish nouns have gender (masculine or feminine) and number (singular or plural).

▶ Most nouns that refer to males are masculine. Most nouns that refer to females are feminine.

Masculine		Feminine	
el hombre	the man	la mujer	the woman
el chico	the boy	la chica	the girl
el pasajero	the passenger	la pasajera	the passenger
el conductor	the driver	la conductora	the driver
el profesor	the professor	la profesora	the professor

el chico   **la chica**

▶ Most nouns ending in **–o**, **–ma**, and **–s** are masculine. Most nouns ending in **–a**, **–ción**, and **–dad** are feminine.

Masculine		Feminine	
el cuaderno	the notebook	la cosa	the thing
el diario	the diary	la escuela	the school
el diccionario	the dictionary	la maleta	the suitcase
el número	the number	la mochila	the backpack
el video	the video	la palabra	the word
el problema	the problem	la lección	the lesson
el programa	the program	la conversación	the conversation
el autobús	the bus	la nacionalidad	the nationality
el país	the country	la comunidad	the community

¡ojo! (*Careful!*) **El lápiz** (*pencil*), **el mapa** (*map*), and **el día** (*day*) are masculine. **La mano** (*hand*) is feminine.

▶ Some nouns have identical masculine and feminine forms. The article indicates the gender of these words.

Masculine		Feminine	
el **turista**	the tourist	la **turista**	the tourist
el **joven**	the young man	la **joven**	the young woman
el **estudiante**	the student	la **estudiante**	the student

Práctica

1 **¿Femenino o masculino?** Provide the opposite gender form for each word.

 modelo   la chica ___el chico___

1. el conductor _____   4. la mujer _____
2. el turista _____   5. el pasajero _____
3. la profesora _____

2 **Singular y plural** Make the singular words plural and the plural words singular.

modelo   el turista ___los turistas___

1. las cosas _____   6. unos números _____
2. una mujer _____   7. el conductor _____
3. la palabra _____   8. un programa _____
4. los países _____   9. una mano _____
5. el problema _____

3 **Identificar** For each photo, provide the noun and its corresponding definite and indefinite articles.

modelo

las maletas, unas maletas

1. _____   2. _____

3. _____   4. _____

Conversación

4 **Clasificar** With a partner, identify the photos and supply the definite and indefinite articles. Then indicate the plural forms of the singular nouns and vice versa.

modelo

la chica, una chica
_____
las chicas, unas chicas
_____

1. _____
_____

2. _____
_____

3. _____
_____

4. _____
_____

5. _____
_____

5 **Dibujar** In groups, play a game of *Pictionary*. Individually, think of three nouns, and taking turns, draw each noun for group members to guess. The first person to identify the singular and plural forms wins a point.

_____

I CAN name familiar objects and people.

Plural of nouns

▶ Nouns that end in a vowel form the plural by adding **–s**. Nouns that end in a consonant add **–es**. Nouns that end in **–z** change the **–z** to **–c**, then add **–es**.

SINGULAR	PLURAL	SINGULAR	PLURAL
el chico	los chicos	el país	los países
la palabra	las palabras	el lápiz	los lápices

¡ojo! In general, when a singular noun has an accent mark on the last syllable, the accent is dropped from the plural form:

la lección → las lecciones   el autobús → los autobuses

▶ The masculine plural form may refer to a mixed-gender group.

1 pasajero + 2 pasajeras = 3 pasajeros

Spanish articles

Spanish has four forms that are equivalent to the English definite article *the*. Spanish also has four forms that are equivalent to the English indefinite article, which, according to context, may mean *a, an,* or *some*.

Spanish articles

Definite articles

MASCULINE		FEMININE	
el diccionario	*the dictionary*	la computadora	*the computer*
los diccionarios	*the dictionaries*	las computadoras	*the computers*

Indefinite articles

un pasajero	*a (one) passenger*	una fotografía	*a (one) photograph*
unos pasajeros	*some passengers*	unas fotografías	*some photographs*

¡Manos a la obra!

Provide the correct articles.

¿el, la, los o las?	¿un, una, unos o unas?
1. __la__ chica	1. __un__ autobús
2. _____ chico	2. _____ lección
3. _____ nacionalidad	3. _____ computadora
4. _____ cuadernos	4. _____ hombres
5. _____ problemas	5. _____ señora
6. _____ mujeres	6. _____ lápices

Communicative Goal
Say how many people or objects there are

1.2 Numbers 0–30

Numbers 0–30				
0 cero	6 seis	12 doce	18 dieciocho	24 veinticuatro
1 uno	7 siete	13 trece	19 diecinueve	25 veinticinco
2 dos	8 ocho	14 catorce	20 veinte	26 veintiséis
3 tres	9 nueve	15 quince	21 veintiuno	27 veintisiete
4 cuatro	10 diez	16 dieciséis	22 veintidós	28 veintiocho
5 cinco	11 once	17 diecisiete	23 veintitrés	29 veintinueve
				30 treinta

▸ Before a masculine noun, **uno** shortens to **un**. Before a feminine noun, **uno** changes to **una**.

un hombre → veintiún hombres

una mujer → veintiuna mujeres

¡ojo! Uno and **veintiuno** are used when counting (**uno, dos, tres… veinte, veintiuno, veintidós…**). They are also used after a noun, even if it is feminine (**la lección uno**).

▸ To ask *how many*, use **¿Cuántos?** with a masculine noun and **¿Cuántas?** with a feminine noun. **Hay** means both *there is* and *there are*. Use **¿Hay…?** to ask *Is/Are there…?* Use **no hay** to express *there is/are not*.

—**¿Hay** chicos en la fotografía?
Are there boys in the picture?

—No, **no hay** chicos.
No, there aren't any boys.

—**¿Cuántas** chicas **hay?**
How many girls are there?

—**Hay** tres.
There are three.

¡Manos a la obra!

Provide the Spanish words for these numbers.

a. **7** _siete_
b. **16** _____
c. **29** _____
d. **1** _____
e. **0** _____

f. **15** _____
g. **21** _____
h. **9** _____
i. **23** _____
j. **11** _____

k. **30** _____
l. **4** _____
m. **12** _____
n. **28** _____
o. **14** _____

p. **10** _____
q. **2** _____
r. **5** _____
s. **22** _____
t. **13** _____

Práctica

1 **Matemáticas** Solve these math problems.

(+ más   − menos   = son)

modelo $9 + 2$ = Nueve más dos son once.

1. $3 + 10 =$ _____
2. $22 - 3 =$ _____
3. $4 + 8 =$ _____
4. $17 + 13 =$ _____
5. $22 + 1 =$ _____

6. $5 - 2 =$ _____
7. $11 + 12 =$ _____
8. $10 - 0 =$ _____
9. $3 + 14 =$ _____
10. $22 - 11 =$ _____

2 **¿Cuántos hay?** Say how many there are.

modelo

¿Cuántas maletas hay?
Hay *cuatro maletas.*

1. ¿Cuántos hombres hay?   2. ¿Cuántas fotografías hay?

_____   _____

3. ¿Cuántos chicos hay?   4. ¿Cuántos turistas hay?

_____   _____

5. ¿Cuántas conductoras hay? 6. ¿Cuántas chicas hay?

_____   _____

Conversación

3 Describir With a classmate, answer the questions about the photo.

1. ¿Cuántas personas hay en la fotografía?

_____

2. ¿Cuántos hombres hay?

_____

3. ¿Cuántas jóvenes hay?

_____

4. ¿Cuántas mochilas hay?

_____

4 En la clase With a classmate, take turns asking and answering these questions about your classroom.

1. ¿Cuántos estudiantes hay?
2. ¿Hay un profesor o (*or*) una profesora?
3. ¿Hay una computadora?
4. ¿Hay fotografías?
5. ¿Hay mapas?
6. ¿Hay diccionarios?
7. ¿Hay cuadernos?
8. ¿Cuántas mochilas hay?

Communicative Goal
Identify numbers on a poster

Español en vivo

ochenta *80*   trabaja *works*   mejor *better*   Apoye *Support*

1 Identificar Scan the poster and say the numbers out loud.

2 Preguntas Answer the questions.

1. Indicate how many of each are needed. Write the numbers as words.
   a. profesores _____
   b. estudiantes _____
2. What is the purpose of this poster: to improve existing schools, or to raise funds for new schools?
3. What would be your formula for the perfect school?

_____

I CAN ask and answer simple questions about how many there are of something.

I CAN identify numbers on a poster.

1.3 Present tense of **ser**

Communicative Goal
Tell what objects and people are and where they are from

Subject pronouns

▸ In order to use verbs, you will need to learn about subject pronouns. A subject pronoun replaces the name or title of a person and acts as the subject of a verb.

Subject pronouns

Singular		Plural	
yo	*I*	nosotros	*we (masculine)*
		nosotras	*we (feminine)*
tú	*you (familiar)*	vosotros	*you (masc., fam.)*
usted (Ud.)	*you (formal)*	vosotras	*you (fem., fam.)*
		ustedes (Uds.)	*you*
él	*he*	ellos	*they (masc.)*
ella	*she*	ellas	*they (fem.)*

Carlos **es** estudiante. → Él **es** estudiante.

▸ Spanish has four subject pronouns that mean *you*. Use **tú** when talking to a friend, a family member, or a child. Use **usted** when talking to someone with whom you have a more formal relationship, such as an employer or a professor, or to someone who is older than you. In Latin America, **ustedes** is used as the plural of both **tú** and **usted**. In Spain, **vosotros/as** is used as the plural of **tú**.

▸ **Usted** and **ustedes** are abbreviated **Ud.** and **Uds.**

▸ **Nosotros**, **vosotros**, and **ellos** refer to a group of males or to a group of males and females. **Nosotras**, **vosotras**, and **ellas** refer only to groups of females.

nosotros, vosotros, ellos   nosotros, vosotros, ellos   nosotras, vosotras, ellas

▸ There is no Spanish equivalent of the English subject pronoun *it*.

—¿Qué es?   —Es una computadora.
What is it?   *It's a computer.*

Práctica

1 **¿De quién es?** Ask your partner to name the objects and say to whom they belong.

modelo	Estudiante 1: ¿Qué es?
	Estudiante 2: Es un diccionario.
	Estudiante 1: ¿De quién es?
	Estudiante 2: Es del profesor Núñez.

1.   2.

3.   4.

2 **¿Quién es?** With a partner, take turns asking who these people are (**¿Quién es?/¿Quiénes son?**) and where they are from (**¿De dónde es?/¿De dónde son?**).

modelo	Sofía Vergara / Colombia

Estudiante 1: ¿Quién es?
Estudiante 2: Es Sofía Vergara.
Estudiante 1: ¿De dónde es?
Estudiante 2: Es de Colombia.

1. Penélope Cruz y Javier Bardem / España   2. José Altuve / Venezuela

3. René Pérez y Eduardo Cabra / Puerto Rico   4. Salma Hayek / México

5. Shakira / Colombia   6. Selena Gómez / Estados Unidos

Conversación

3 **En el dormitorio** Ask your partner questions about Susana's bedroom.

> **modelo**
> Estudiante 1: ¿Cuántos mapas hay?
> Estudiante 2: Hay un mapa.

¿Quién?	¿De dónde?	¿Cuántos?
¿Qué?	¿De quién?	¿Cuántas?

4 **Personas famosas** Pretend to be a person from **Cuba, México, España** (Spain), **Canadá** or **los Estados Unidos** (U.S.) who is famous in one of these professions. Your classmates will try to guess who you are.

actor *actor*	deportista *athlete*	cantante *singer*
actriz *actress*	escritor(a) *writer*	músico/a *musician*

> **modelo**

Estudiante 3: ¿Eres de Cuba?
Estudiante 1: Sí.
Estudiante 2: ¿Eres mujer?
Estudiante 1: Sí.
Estudiante 3: ¿Eres escritora?
Estudiante 1: No. Soy cantante.
Estudiante 2: ¿Eres Camila Cabello?
Estudiante 1: ¡Sí! ¡Sí!

Camila Cabello

I CAN ask and answer questions to describe people and objects.

The present tense of *ser*

ser (*to be*)

Singular		Plural	
yo	soy (*I am*)	nosotros/as	somos (*we are*)
tú	eres (*you are*)	vosotros/as	sois (*you are*)
Ud./él/ella	es (*you are; he/she is*)	Uds./ellos/ellas	son (*you/they are*)

▶ Use **ser** to identify people and things.

—¿Quién **es** ella?
Who is she?
—**Es** Olga Lucía.
She's Olga Lucía.

—¿Qué **es**?
What is it?
—**Es** una fotografía.
It's a photo.

▶ Use **ser** to talk about someone's occupation.[1]

Valentina **es** estudiante.
Valentina is a student.

Isabel **es** profesora.
Isabel is a professor.

▶ Use **ser** to express origin, along with **de**.

—¿**De** dónde **es** Olga Lucía?
Where is Olga Lucía from?
—**Es de** Venezuela.
She's from Venezuela.

▶ Use **ser** to express possession, with the preposition **de**. **De** combines with **el** to form the contraction **del**.[2] Note that Spanish doesn't use [*apostrophe*]+ *s* to indicate possession.

—¿**De** quién **es** la mochila?
Whose backpack is this?
—**Es** la mochila **de** Sara.
It's Sara's backpack.

—¿**De** quiénes **son** los lápices?
Whose pencils are these?
—**Son** los lápices **del** chico.
They are the boy's pencils.

---

[1] Spanish does not use **un** or **una** after **ser** when mentioning a person's occupation, unless the occupation is accompanied by an adjective.

[2] **De** does not form contractions with **la, los,** or **las.**

> **¡Manos a la obra!**

Provide the correct subject pronouns and forms of **ser.**

1. Gabriel	él	es
2. Juan y yo		
3. tú		
4. Adriana		
5. las turistas		
6. usted y el profesor Ruiz		
7. yo		
8. el señor y la señora Díaz		

1.4 Telling time

Communicative Goal
Ask and answer questions about the time of day

▶ Use numbers with the verb **ser** to tell time. To ask what time it is, use **¿Qué hora es?** To say what time it is, use **es la** with **una** and **son las** with other hours.

Es la una.   **Son las** cuatro.

▶ Express time from the hour to the half hour by adding minutes.

Son las dos **y diez**.   Son las ocho **y veinte**.

▶ Use **y cuarto** or **y quince** to say that it's fifteen minutes past the hour. Use **y media** or **y treinta** to say that it's thirty minutes past the hour.

Son las cuatro **y cuarto**.   Son las nueve **y media**.
Son las cuatro **y quince**.   Son las nueve **y treinta**.

Práctica

1   **Emparejar**   Match each watch with the correct statement.

_____   _____   _____

_____   _____   _____

1. Son las ocho menos veinticinco de la mañana.
2. Es la una menos diez de la mañana.
3. Son las tres y cinco de la mañana.
4. Son las dos menos cuarto de la tarde.
5. Son las seis y media de la mañana.
6. Son las once y veinte de la noche.

2   **¿Qué hora es?**   With a partner, take turns asking and answering the questions. Use the clocks as a guide.

modelo

Estudiante 1: Son las siete de la noche en Los Ángeles. ¿Qué hora es en San Antonio?
Estudiante 2: Son las nueve de la noche en San Antonio.

Miami   **San Antonio**   **Denver**   **Los Ángeles**

1. Son las cinco de la tarde en Los Ángeles.
   ¿Qué hora es en Miami? _____
2. Son las seis de la tarde en San Antonio.
   ¿Qué hora es en Denver? _____
3. Son las siete de la noche en Denver.
   ¿Qué hora es en Los Ángeles? _____
4. Son las dos y media de la tarde en Los Ángeles.
   ¿Qué hora es en Miami? _____
5. Son las once menos cuarto en San Antonio.
   ¿Qué hora es en Los Ángeles? _____
6. Es la una de la tarde en Los Ángeles.
   ¿Qué hora es en San Antonio? _____

Conversación

3 **En la televisión** With a partner, take turns asking and answering questions about these television listings.

modelo

Estudiante 1: ¿A qué hora es el programa *Las computadoras*?
Estudiante 2: Es a las ocho de la noche.

Programación TV ▼	
HOY	
11:00 am	Película: *El cóndor* (drama)
1:00 pm	Telenovela: *Dos mujeres y dos hombres*
3:00 pm	Programa juvenil: *Fiesta*
3:30 pm	Telenovela: *¡Sí, sí, sí!*
4:00 pm	Telenovela: *El diario de la Sra. González*
5:00 pm	Telenovela: *Tres mujeres*
5:45 pm	Clip de noticias
6:00 pm	Especial musical: *Música folclórica de México*
7:00 pm	La naturaleza: *Jardín secreto*
7:30 pm	Noticiero: *Veinticuatro horas*
8:00 pm	Documental: *Las computadoras*
9:00 pm	Telecomedia: *Don Paco y doña Tere*
10:00 pm	Película: *Pedro Páramo*

4 **Entrevista** Use these questions to interview a classmate. Compare answers with another pair.

1. ¿Qué hora es?
2. ¿A qué hora es la clase de español?
3. ¿A qué hora es el programa *60 Minutes*?
4. ¿A qué hora es el programa *Today Show*?
5. ¿Hay una fiesta (*party*) el sábado (*on Saturday*)? ¿A qué hora es?
6. ¿Hay un concierto (*concert*) el sábado? ¿A qué hora es?

I CAN ask and answer questions about the time of day.

▶ To express time from the half hour to the hour in Spanish, use **menos** to subtract minutes or a portion of an hour from the next hour.

Son las dos **menos cuarto.**

Es la una **menos cuarto**.

Son las nueve **menos diez.**

Son las ocho **menos cinco.**

Time-related expressions

▶ Here are some useful expressions related to telling time.

—**¿Qué hora es?**
What time is it?

—**Son las cuatro de la tarde.**
It's 4 o'clock in the afternoon.

—**Son las diez de la noche.**
It's 10 o'clock at night.

—**Son las nueve de la mañana.**
It's 9 o'clock in the morning.

—**Es el mediodía.**
It's noon.

—**Es la medianoche.**
It's midnight.

▶ To ask or state at what time a particular event takes place, use the constructions **¿A qué hora (...)?** and **a la(s)** + *time*.

—**¿A qué hora** es la clase?
(At) what time is the class?

—**La clase es a la una.**
The class is at one o'clock.

—**La clase es a las dos.**
The class is at two o'clock.

—**La clase es a las ocho en punto.**
The class is at 8 o'clock on the dot.

¡Manos a la obra!

Complete these sentences.

1. (1:00 a.m.) Es la ____una____ de la mañana.
2. (2:50 a.m.) Son las tres _____ diez de la mañana.
3. (4:15 p.m.) Son las cuatro y _____ de la tarde.
4. (8:30 p.m.) Son las ocho y _____ de la noche.
5. (6:00 a.m.) Son las seis de la _____.
6. (4:05 p.m.) Son las cuatro y cinco de la _____.
7. (12:00 a.m.) Es la _____.
8. (9:55 p.m.) Son las _____ menos cinco de la noche.

A repasar

1.1 Nouns and articles

1 **Combinar** Match the articles and the nouns. There are at least two correct answers for each noun.

un	chicas
una	país
unos	profesoras
unas	videos
el	mujer
la	cuaderno
los	estudiantes
las	lápiz
	conversación
	nacionalidades

2 **Completar** Make a list of at least six singular or plural nouns and their corresponding definite and indefinite articles. Then work with a partner. One person says a noun and the other responds by saying the correct article for the noun.

modelo

Estudiante 1: autobuses
Estudiante 2: los autobuses, unos autobuses

1.2 Numbers 0–30

3 **Bingo** With a partner, take turns announcing these bingo balls.

B 10   G 17   I 23
N 8   O 19   N 14   O 22
B 27   I 4   G 30

4 **¿Cuánto cuesta?** Say how much each item costs. Follow the model.

modelo
cuaderno / $3
Un cuaderno cuesta (costs) tres dólares.

1. mapa del país / $6 _____
2. diccionario / $11 _____
3. mochila / $28 _____
4. video / $20 _____
5. diario / $9 _____

1.3 Present tense of ser

5 **¿Tú, usted o ustedes?** Write which subject pronoun (**tú, usted, ustedes**) you would use when speaking directly to these people.

1	2	3	4	5	6
DON PACO	OLGA LUCÍA Y VALENTINA	FELIPE	UNA DOCTORA	JUANJO	CARMEN Y PEDRO HERRERA

1. don Paco _____
2. Olga Lucía y Valentina _____
3. Felipe _____
4. una doctora _____
5. Juanjo _____
6. Carmen y Pedro Herrera _____

6 **Presentaciones** In pairs, complete the conversation with the correct forms of the verb **ser**.

DAVID ¡Hola! Tú (1) _____ Teresa, ¿verdad?

TERESA Sí, yo (2) _____ Teresa y ella (3) _____ Elena. ¿Y quiénes (4) _____ ustedes?

DAVID (5) _____ David y él (6) _____ Roberto. ¿De dónde (7) _____ ustedes?

TERESA (8) _____ de México, de la capital. ¿Y ustedes?

DAVID Yo (9) _____ de Los Ángeles y Roberto (10) _____ de San Francisco.

TERESA Mucho gusto, David.

DAVID ¡El gusto (11) _____ mío!

1.4 Telling time

7 ¿Qué hora es? Say what time it is.

 modelo

Son las siete y diez de la mañana.

1.

2.

3.

4.

5.

6.

8 En el aeropuerto With a partner, take turns asking and answering questions about the departure times of these flights.

modelo

Estudiante 1:
¿A qué hora es el vuelo (flight) para Caracas?

Estudiante 2:
Es a las once y dos de la mañana.

Destino (Destination)	Hora
Bogotá	10:00 a.m.
Cancún	2:10 p.m.
Caracas	11:02 a.m.
La Habana	12:30 p.m.
Lima	4:40 p.m.
Montreal	1:27 p.m.
Quito	5:50 a.m.
San Juan	8:15 a.m.

Síntesis

9 En México You are in Mexico City at the start of your semester abroad. Today there is an orientation session for new students. With a classmate, act out this situation. (Use the cue in brackets to answer the last question.)

- Greet your partner, tell him/her who you are, and find out his or her name.
- Find out where your partner is from.
- Ask if he/she is a professor.
- Find out how many students are in the program. [21 students]

Communicative Goal
Watch a short TV ad and use it as a model to create my own ad

 Video

Videoclip

1 Preparación Think about three favorite activities you like to do with your family and friends. Do you have to pay for them? How much do they cost?

2 El clip Watch the ad for **MasterCard** from Argentina.

Vocabulario

aperitivo *appetizer*	no tiene precio *priceless*
plato principal *main course*	un domingo en familia
postre *dessert*	*Sunday with the family*

un domingo en familia: no tiene precio

Un domingo en familia...

3 Emparejar Match each item with its price according to the ad.

____ **1.** aperitivo

____ **2.** plato principal

____ **3.** postre

a. quince dólares

b. ocho dólares

c. treinta dólares

d. seis dólares

e. cinco dólares

f. veintiocho dólares

4 Tener un precio With a partner, brainstorm and write a TV ad about something you consider priceless. Use this MasterCard ad as a model. Then, read it to the class.

I CAN understand some information in a short TV ad using visuals and a familiar context.

I CAN create a short TV ad.

Ampliación

Communicative Goals
Listen to a short
conversation in
Spanish, and interview
a professor

1 Escuchar

A Listen to the conversation between an airline employee (Ms. Martínez) and a traveler. Then fill in the missing information on the form.

TIP **Listen for words you know.** You can get the gist of a conversation by listening for words and phrases you already know.

www.aerotur.com

aerotur

1. **Número de pasajeros**
2. **Nombre** *(first name)* **del pasajero**
3. **Apellido** *(last name)* **del pasajero**
4. **Destino**
5. **Número de maletas**

B When does this conversation take place, before or after the trip? How do you know?

2 Conversar

You are surveying professors to find out about the resources in their classrooms. With a partner, act out an interview between you and a professor. During the interview, you need to find out the following information. (Don't forget to introduce yourself and thank the professor before saying goodbye.)

- *The professor's name (Confirm the correct spelling.)*
- *The start time of the class*
- *The number of students in class*
- *The number of dictionaries in the class*
- *Whether or not there are computers in class*
- *Whether or not there are maps in class*

I CAN understand familiar words in a short recorded conversation.

I CAN interview a professor and find out basic information about his/her class.

Ampliación

3 Escribir

Write an e-mail to Mrs. Suárez, the director of a language school in Madrid where you want to take a summer course. Introduce yourself and ask her questions about the program.

TIP **Write in Spanish.** Use grammar and vocabulary that you know. Also, look at your textbook for examples of style, format, and expressions in Spanish.

Organize | Make a list of the information that you can provide about yourself in Spanish (your name, your occupation, where you are from). In addition, make a list of questions that you want to ask Mrs. Suárez, such as what time class starts, the number of students in the class, and information about the other students (where they are from, number of males/females, etc).

Write | Using the material you have compiled, write the first draft of your e-mail.

Revise | Exchange your draft with a classmate and comment on the organization, style, and grammatical accuracy of each other's work. Then, revise your first draft, taking your classmate's comments into consideration.

Share | Read your e-mail aloud in small groups. What kind of greetings and expressions of courtesy were used in the e-mails?

Communicative Goals
Write an e-mail introducing myself and asking questions about a course, and do a presentation about how Hispanic cultures have influenced a U.S. city

4 Un paso más

Prepare a presentation about how Hispanic cultures have influenced a U.S. city. Search for information about this city and include the following in your presentation.

- An introduction of yourself in Spanish
- A general description of the city
- A brief explanation of why you chose this city
- Examples of how Hispanic cultures have influenced the city
- Photos, drawings, and charts to make your presentation more interesting

5 Cultura

Choose a Spanish-speaking country and explain how to greet someone in that country. Include information about personal space, gestures, and what to say.

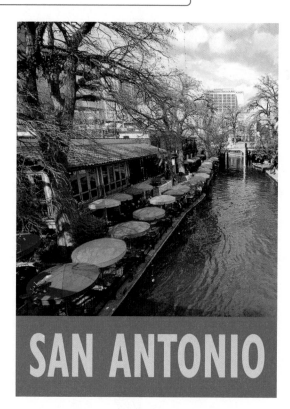

SAN ANTONIO

I CAN create an e-mail in Spanish introducing myself and asking questions about a course.

I CAN do a presentation about how Hispanic cultures have influenced a U.S. city.

Audio: Reading

Antes de leer

Cognates are words that share similar meanings and spellings in two or more languages. The Spanish words **computadora**, **problema**, and **programa** are examples of cognates.

> **TIP** **Look for cognates.** When you read in Spanish, look for cognates and use them to get the general meaning of what you're reading. Watch out for false cognates such as **librería**, which means *bookstore*, not *library*.

Laura, a university student, made a list of important names and numbers she needed to remember.

Cognados

Read the list of names and numbers and write the cognates you find. Then add their English equivalents.

Phone numbers are usually read as pairs of numbers. However, for phone numbers with an odd number of digits, the first number is read separately. For example, Mrs. Ruiz's phone number would be read as 4-24-17-11. For e-mail addresses in Spanish, the "at" symbol (@) is called **arroba** and the period is called **punto**.

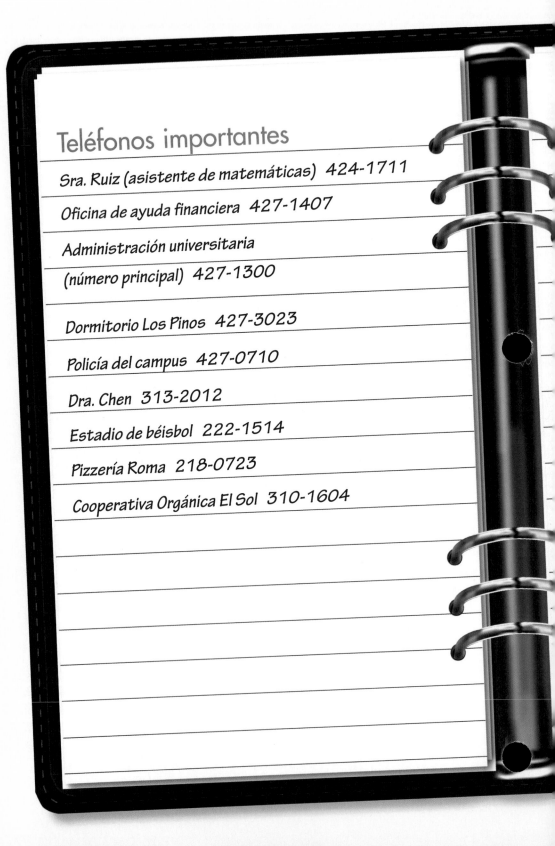

Teléfonos importantes

Sra. Ruiz (asistente de matemáticas) 424-1711

Oficina de ayuda financiera 427-1407

Administración universitaria
(número principal) 427-1300

Dormitorio Los Pinos 427-3023

Policía del campus 427-0710

Dra. Chen 313-2012

Estadio de béisbol 222-1514

Pizzería Roma 218-0723

Cooperativa Orgánica El Sol 310-1604

Direcciones electrónicas

Oficina de matemáticas

ofna@matematicas.unimetro.edu.pe

Profesora González

a.gonzalez@matematicas.unimetro.edu.pe

Farmacia

rx@farmaciagomez.com.pe

Gimnasio

informacion@gimnasio.unimetro.edu.pe

Después de leer

¿Comprendiste?

Indicate whether each statement is **cierto** (*true*) or **falso** (*false*).

Cierto	Falso	
——	——	1. Professor González works in the math department.
——	——	2. If Laura wanted to get a student loan, she would call 427-3023.
——	——	3. Laura never eats pizza.
——	——	4. If Laura needed to report a crime, she would call 427-0710.
——	——	5. To find out the price of organic apples, Laura would call 310-1604.
——	——	6. Laura would call 427-1300 to get a baseball ticket.

Coméntalo

Think about the names, phone numbers, and e-mail addresses that Laura keeps in her address book. Can you think of any others she should add?

I CAN understand a list of phone numbers and e-mail addresses.

Vocabulary Tools

Saludos y despedidas

Hola. *Hello.*
Buenos días. *Good morning.*
Buenas tardes. *Good afternoon.*
Buenas noches. *Good evening; Good night.*

———

Adiós. *Goodbye.*
Chau. *Bye.*
Hasta la vista. *See you later.*
Hasta luego. *See you later.*
Hasta mañana. *See you tomorrow.*
Hasta pronto. *See you soon.*
Nos vemos. *See you.*
Saludos a... *Say hello to...*

¿Cómo estás?

¿Cómo está usted? *How are you? (form.)*
¿Cómo estás? *How are you? (fam.)*
¿Qué hay de nuevo? *What's new?*
¿Qué pasa? *What's going on?*
¿Qué tal? *How is it going?*
(Muy) bien, gracias. *(Very) well, thanks.*
Nada. *Nothing.*
No muy bien. *Not very well.*
Regular. *So-so.*

Expresiones y títulos de cortesía

De nada. *You're welcome.*
Lo siento. *I'm sorry.*
(Muchas) gracias. *Thank you (very much).*
No hay de qué. *You're welcome.*
Por favor. *Please.*

———

señor (Sr.) *Mr.; sir*
señora (Sra.) *Mrs.; ma'am*
señorita (Srta.) *Miss*

Presentaciones

¿Cómo se llama usted? *What's your name? (form.)*
¿Cómo te llamas (tú)? *What's your name? (fam.)*
Me llamo... *My name is...*
¿Y tú? *And you? (fam.)*
¿Y usted? *And you? (form.)*
Mucho gusto. *Pleased to meet you.*
El gusto es mío. *The pleasure is mine.*
Encantado/a *Pleased to meet you.*
Igualmente. *Likewise.*
Éste/Ésta es... *This is...*
Le presento a... *I would like to introduce you to...*
(form.)
Te presento a... *I would like to introduce you to...*
(fam.)

———

¿De dónde es usted? *Where are you from? (form.)*
¿De dónde eres? *Where are you from? (fam.)*
Soy de... *I'm from...*

Verbos

ser *to be*

Expresiones adicionales

¿Cuántos/as? *How many?*
¿De quién...? *Whose...? (sing.)*
¿De quiénes...? *Whose...? (plural)*
Hay *There is; There are*
No hay *There is not; There are not*
¿Qué es? *What is it?*
¿Quién es? *Who is it?*

———

Numbers 0–30 *See page 14.*
Subject pronouns *See page 16.*
Time-related expressions *See pages 18–19.*

Sustantivos

el autobús *bus*
la chica *girl*
el chico *boy*
la computadora *computer*
la comunidad *community*
el/la conductor(a) *driver*
la conversación *conversation*
la cosa *thing*
el cuaderno *notebook*
el día *day*
el diario *diary*
el diccionario *dictionary*
la escuela *school*
el/la estudiante *student*
la foto(grafía) *photograph*
el hombre *man*
el/la joven *young person*
el lápiz *pencil*
la lección *lesson*
la maleta *suitcase*
la mano *hand*
el mapa *map*
la mochila *backpack*
la mujer *woman*
la nacionalidad *nationality*
el número *number*
el país *country*
la palabra *word*
el/la pasajero/a *passenger*
el problema *problem*
el/la profesor(a) *professor*
el programa *program*
el/la turista *tourist*
el video *video*

∞ Communicative Goals: Review

I CAN greet people in Spanish.
- Say two expressions you have learned to greet people.

I CAN say goodbye.
- Say two expressions you have learned to say goodbye.

I CAN identify myself and others.
- Say where you are from.

I CAN talk about the time of day.
- Say what time it is.

I CAN investigate greetings in the Spanish-speaking world.
- Explain how greetings in the Spanish-speaking world are different from those in the United States.

2 Las clases

Communicative Goals

You will learn how to:
- talk about classes
- discuss everyday activities
- ask questions
- describe location
- investigate universities in the Spanish-speaking world

PREPARACIÓN

pages 28–33
- Words related to people, places, and classes at the university
- Days of the week
- Pronouncing Spanish vowels

AVENTURAS

pages 34–35
- Manuel, Valentina, and Juanjo walk to their university campus, while Sara has to give a presentation at her high school.

CULTURA

pages 36–37
- *La elección de una carrera universitaria*
- Flash cultura: *Los estudios*

GRAMÁTICA

pages 38–49
- Present tense of **-ar** verbs
- Forming questions
- Present tense of **estar**
- Numbers 31–100

LECTURA

pages 50–51
- Brochure: *UAE: La mejor universidad de Europa*

∞ PARA EMPEZAR
- ¿Está la chica en la escuela?
- ¿Es estudiante o profesora?
- ¿Cuántos mapas hay en la foto?

LAS CLASES

el laboratorio

LA UNIVERSIDAD

la cafetería *cafeteria*
el estadio *stadium*
la librería *bookstore*
la residencia estudiantil *dormitory*
el salón de clases *classroom*

LOS CURSOS

la administración de empresas
  business administration
el arte *art*
la biología *biology*
la clase *class*
la contabilidad *accounting*
el curso *course*
el español *Spanish*
la física *physics*
la historia *history*
el inglés *English*
las lenguas extranjeras
  foreign languages
las matemáticas *mathematics*
el periodismo *journalism*
la psicología *psychology*
la sociología *sociology*

la biblioteca
library

la geografía

la computación
computer science

la química
chemistry

Vocabulary Tools

el reloj
clock; watch

LA CLASE

el examen *test; exam*
el horario *schedule*
el marcador *dry-erase marker*
la mesa *table*
el papel *paper*
la pluma *pen*
la prueba *test; quiz*
la puerta *door*
el semestre *semester*
la tarea *homework*
el trimestre *trimester; quarter*
la ventana *window*

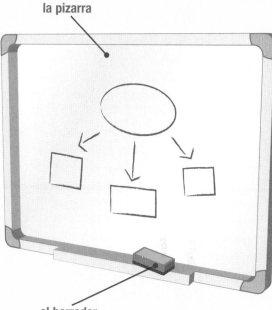

la pizarra

el borrador

LOS DÍAS DE LA SEMANA

septiembre →

lunes	3
martes	4
miércoles	5
	6
jueves	7
viernes	
sábado	1 8
domingo	2 9

OTRAS PALABRAS Y EXPRESIONES

el/la compañero/a de clase *classmate*
el/la compañero/a de cuarto *roommate*
la semana *week*
la universidad *university*

Hoy es... *Today is . . .*

el libro
book

la silla

el escritorio

ASÍ SE DICE
la pluma ←→ el bolígrafo
la pizarra ←→ el tablero (*Col.*), el pizarrón (*Amér. L.*)
la tarea ←→ la asignación (*P. Rico*); los deberes (*Esp., Arg.*)

A escuchar

1 Indicar Check **sí** if the word you hear is an academic subject or **no** if it's not.

	Sí	No
1.	_____	_____
2.	_____	_____
3.	_____	_____
4.	_____	_____
5.	_____	_____
6.	_____	_____
7.	_____	_____
8.	_____	_____

2 Mis clases Listen and fill in the calendar with María's class schedule. Then complete the sentences.

Estudiante María			**Semestre N° 1**	
lunes	**martes**	**miércoles**	**jueves**	**viernes**
AM 10:30 arte				
PM				

María

modelo Éste (*This*) es el primer (*first*) _semestre_ de María en la universidad.

1. Este semestre María toma cuatro _____.
2. La clase de _____ es el lunes a las diez y media de la mañana.
3. La clase de _____ es el martes a las dos y quince de la tarde.
4. La clase de periodismo es el _____ a las once de la mañana.
5. La clase de _____ es el jueves a las tres y media de la tarde.
6. María estudia (*studies*) en la _____ los viernes.

A practicar

3 **Clasificar** Indicate to which category each word belongs: **Persona**, **Objeto**, **Curso**, or **Lugar** (*place*).

	Persona	Objeto	Curso	Lugar
1. el periodismo	_____	_____	_____	_____
2. la residencia estudiantil	_____	_____	_____	_____
3. el compañero de cuarto	_____	_____	_____	_____
4. el estadio	_____	_____	_____	_____
5. el marcador	_____	_____	_____	_____
6. la contabilidad	_____	_____	_____	_____
7. la pluma	_____	_____	_____	_____
8. la compañera de clase	_____	_____	_____	_____

4 **Analogías** Choose the best words to complete the analogies.

modelo   dos ⟷ cuatro ⊜ martes ⟷ _jueves_

1. hoy ⟷ mañana ⊜ viernes ⟷ _____
2. país ⟷ mapa ⊜ hora ⟷ _____
3. inglés ⟷ lengua ⊜ miércoles ⟷ _____
4. mapa ⟷ geografía ⊜ computadora ⟷ _____
5. pluma ⟷ papel ⊜ marcador ⟷ _____
6. papel ⟷ cuaderno ⊜ libro ⟷ _____

biblioteca	pizarra	profesor(a)
jueves	semana	miércoles
computación	día	reloj
sábado	borrador	domingo

5 **Cursos** What is the subject matter of each class?

modelo   la cultura de España, el verbo **ser**
Es la clase de español.

1. los microbios, los animales

   _____

2. George Washington, Martin Luther King, Jr.

   _____

3. la geometría, la trigonometría

   _____

4. Frida Kahlo, Leonardo da Vinci

   _____

5. África, el río Amazonas

   _____

6. Freud, Jung

   _____

Frida Kahlo, famosa pintora (*painter*) mexicana

El río Amazonas, en Suramérica

A conversar

 6 **Horario** Create your own class schedule like this one. Then discuss it with a classmate.

modelo

Estudiante 1: ¿Cuándo tomas (*when do you take*) biología?
Estudiante 2: Los lunes, miércoles y viernes tomo (*I take*)
biología a las ocho y media de la mañana.
Estudiante 1: ¿Quién es el/la profesor(a)?
Estudiante 2: Es la profesora Morales.

Estudiante Manuel Domínguez			**Semestre N° 1**	
lunes	**martes**	**miércoles**	**jueves**	**viernes**
8:30 **biología** Profesora Morales		**8:30** **biología**		**8:30** **biología**
	9:45 **historia** Profesora Cortés		**9:45** **historia**	
10:15 **inglés** Profesor Herrera		**10:15** **inglés**		**10:15** **inglés**
	12:45 **psicología** Profesor Blanco		**12:45** **psicología**	
		1:15 **arte** Profesor Pérez		**1:15** **arte**
3:30 **laboratorio** **(biología)**				
4:30 **discusión (historia)** biblioteca				

7 **Entrevistas** Use these questions to interview classmates. See if your classmates have anything in common.

1. ¿Cómo te llamas?
2. ¿Cómo estás hoy?
3. ¿De dónde eres?
4. ¿Cuántas clases tomas?

5. ¿Cuándo tomas…?
6. ¿A qué hora es la clase de…?
7. ¿Quién es el/la profesor(a)?
8. ¿Cuál (*Which*) es tu clase favorita?

8 **Nuevos amigos** You meet a new student in the cafeteria. Have a conversation in Spanish, using these guidelines.

- Greet your new acquaintance.
- Find out how he or she is doing.
- Ask where he or she is from.
- Compare class schedules.
- Say goodbye.

I CAN meet a new student and find out basic information about him/her.

Pronunciación

  Tutorial

Spanish vowels

a　　**e**　　**i**　　**o**　　**u**

Spanish vowels are never silent; they are always pronounced in a short, crisp way without the glide sounds used in English.

. . . .

Álex　　　　**clase**　　　　**nada**　　　　**encantada**

The letter **a** is pronounced like the *a* in *father,* but shorter.

. . . .

el　　　　**ene**　　　　**mesa**　　　　**elefante**

The letter **e** is pronounced like the *e* in *they,* but shorter.

. . . .

Inés　　　　**chica**　　　　**tiza**　　　　**señorita**

The letter **i** sounds like the *ee* in *beet,* but shorter.

. . . .

hola　　　　**con**　　　　**libro**　　　　**don Francisco**

The letter **o** is pronounced like the *o* in *tone,* but shorter.

. . . .

uno　　　　**regular**　　　　**saludos**　　　　**gusto**

The letter **u** sounds like the *oo* in *room,* but shorter.

Práctica Practice the vowels by saying the names of these places in Spain.

1. Madrid　　　3. Tenerife　　　5. Barcelona　　　7. Burgos
2. Alicante　　　4. Toledo　　　6. Granada　　　8. La Coruña

Oraciones Read the sentences aloud, focusing on the vowels.

1. Hola. Me llamo Ramiro Morgado.
2. Estudio arte en la Universidad de Salamanca.
3. Tomo también (*also*) literatura y contabilidad.
4. Ay, tengo clase en cinco minutos. ¡Nos vemos!

Refranes Practice the vowels by reading these sayings aloud.

> Cada loco con su tema.[2]

> Del dicho al hecho hay un gran trecho.[1]

[1] *Easier said than done.*
[2] *To each his own.*

2 AVENTURAS

Communicative Goal
Ask and answer questions about school

¡¿Te gustan los lunes?!

Manuel, Valentina y Juanjo caminan a la universidad y Sara llega tarde a la escuela.

 Video

Antes de ver

Scan the captions and make a list of vocabulary related to school and classes.

PERSONAJES

 MANUEL

 SARA

 VALENTINA

 JUANJO

 PROFESOR

 DANIEL

 JAIME

MANUEL ¡Sara! ¿Qué pasa?
SARA La tarea... Está en la mesa... ¡Adiós!
MANUEL ¡Adiós!

MANUEL ¡Buenos días, Valentina!
VALENTINA Buenos días, Manuel.
MANUEL ¿Caminamos a la universidad?
VALENTINA Eh... sí. Busco la mochila y los libros.
MANUEL ¿Y qué clases tomas los lunes?
VALENTINA Por la mañana dibujo y por la tarde historia del arte. ¡Me gustan los lunes!

JUANJO Valentina. Buenos días.
VALENTINA Hola.
JUANJO ¿Caminan a la universidad?
MANUEL ¡No!
VALENTINA Sí. ¿Caminas con nosotros?
JUANJO ¡Por supuesto!

ACTIVIDADES

1 ¿Cierto o falso? Indicate if each statement is **cierto** or **falso**. Correct the false statements.

	Cierto	Falso
1. A Manuel le gustan los lunes.	○	○
2. El libro de Sara está en la mesa.	○	○
3. Valentina toma una clase de dibujo.	○	○
4. La Facultad de Arte está entre la biblioteca y la Facultad de Humanidades.	○	○
5. Hoy es sábado y no hay clases.	○	○

2 Ordenar Put the events in order.

_____ a. Sara llega tarde a clase.
_____ b. Valentina busca la mochila y los libros.
_____ c. Manuel mira (*looks at*) el calendario.
_____ d. Sara busca la tarea.
_____ e. Juanjo, Valentina y Manuel caminan a la universidad.

MANUEL La Facultad de Ciencias está por allá, ¿no?

JUANJO Sí.

MANUEL Gracias por caminar con nosotros. Eres un buen compañero. ¡Adiós!

VALENTINA ¡Adiós!

MANUEL A la Facultad de Bellas Artes, ¿no?

VALENTINA ¡Sí! La clase de dibujo es a las diez menos cuarto.

MANUEL ¡En diez minutos! La Facultad de Arte... está...

VALENTINA Está entre la biblioteca y la Facultad de Humanidades.

MANUEL Sí, sí, claro.

VALENTINA ¿Necesitas un mapa?

PROFESOR Gracias por la presentación, Jaime. ¡Buenos días, Sara!

SARA Buenos días, profesor.

PROFESOR ¡Llegas treinta y cinco minutos tarde! ¿Estás lista para la presentación?

SARA Sí, claro.

PROFESOR Adelante.

SARA El tema de mi presentación es ¿Cómo afecta el cambio climático a la geografía?

Expresiones útiles

adelante *go ahead*
allá *over there*
las bellas artes *fine arts*
la cama *bed*
el cambio climático *climate change*
el casco *helmet*
con *with*
el dibujo *drawing*
la energía eólica *wind energy*
la facultad *department/school of a university*
listo/a *ready*
tarde *late*
todavía *still*

Universidad Complutense

The current **Universidad Complutense de Madrid** was founded in 1499 but dates back to 1293. It has more than 70,000 students. Famous Spanish alumni include playwright Lope de Vega (1562–1635), philosopher José Ortega y Gasset (1883–1955), biochemist Severo Ochoa de Albornoz (1905–1993), and Queen of Spain Letizia Ortiz Rocasolano (1972–). Peruvian writer Mario Vargas Llosa (1936–) was also a student.

Who are some famous alumni of your school?

---

3 **Preguntas personales** Interview a classmate about school. Do you have any answers in common?

1. ¿Cuántas clases tomas este semestre?
2. ¿Qué clases tomas los lunes?
3. ¿Qué clases tomas los martes?
4. ¿Qué clases te gustan?
5. ¿Te gusta la clase de español?

I CAN ask and answer questions about school.

Communicative Goal
Identify practices related to choosing a
major in Spanish-speaking countries

La elección de una carrera universitaria

Since higher education in the Spanish-speaking world is heavily state-subsidized, tuition is almost free; as a result, public universities see large enrollments. Spanish and Latin American students generally choose their **carrera universitaria** (major) when they're eighteen, which can be during their last year of high school or their first year of college.

Estudiantes hispanos en los EE.UU.

In the 2017–18 academic year, over 15,000 Mexican students (almost 2% of all international students) studied at U.S. universities. Venezuelans were the second largest Spanish-speaking group, with over 8,000 students.

Universidad Central de Venezuela en Caracas

In order to enroll, all students must complete a high school degree, known as the **bachillerato**. In countries like Bolivia and Mexico, the last year of high school (**colegio***) tends to be specialized in an area of study, such as natural sciences or the arts. Students then choose their major according to their area of specialization. Similarly, university-bound students in Argentina focus their studies on specific fields, such as social or natural sciences, design, and business, during their five years of high school. Based on this coursework, Argentine students choose

their **carrera**. Finally, in Spain, students choose their major according to the score they receive on the **prueba de aptitud** (skills test or entrance exam).

University graduates receive a **licenciatura**, or bachelor's degree. In Argentina or Chile, a **licenciatura** takes four to six years to complete, and may be considered equivalent to a master's degree. In Peru and Venezuela, a bachelor's degree is a five-year process. Spanish and Colombian **licenciaturas** take four to five years, although some fields, such as medicine, require six or more.

*¡Ojo! **El colegio** is a false cognate. In most countries, it means *high school*, but in some regions it refers to an elementary school. All undergraduate study takes place at **la universidad**.

ASÍ SE DICE
Clases y exámenes

aprobar	to pass
la clase anual	year-long course
el examen parcial	midterm exam
la investigación	research
la materia la asignatura (Esp.)	la clase, el curso
reprobar suspender (Esp.)	to fail
sacar buenas/malas notas	to get good/bad grades
tomar apuntes	to take notes

ACTIVIDADES

1 **¿Cierto o falso?** Indicate whether each statement is **cierto** or **falso**. Correct the false statements.

1. Students in Spanish-speaking countries must pay large amounts of money toward their college tuition.
2. After studying at a **colegio**, students receive their **bachillerato**.
3. Undergraduates study at a **colegio** or an **universidad**.
4. In Latin America and Spain, students usually choose their majors in their second year at the university.
5. In Mexico, the **bachillerato** involves specialized study.
6. In Spain, majors depend on entrance exam scores.

2 **Preguntas** Answer the questions.

1. Why are there large enrollments at public universities in Spain and Latin America?
2. What is a bachelor's degree called in Spanish?
3. How long does it take to earn a bachelor's degree in Peru?
4. What is the country of origin of the largest group of Spanish-speaking students studying at U.S. universities?

3 **Comparación** Compare choosing a major in Spain or Latin America with choosing a major at your college or university.

4 **Esta universidad** In pairs, research a Spanish or Latin American university online and find five statistics about that institution (total enrollment, majors offered, number of departments/schools). Using this information, role-play a conversation between a prospective student and a university representative.

I CAN identify practices related to choosing a major in my own and other cultures.

I CAN interact at a survival level in some familiar everyday contexts.

Communicative Goal
Recognize basic details about student life in Mexico City

 Video

Los estudios

1 **Preparación** What is the name of your school or university? What degree program are you in? What classes are you taking this semester?

2 **El video** Watch this **Flash cultura** episode about a university in Mexico City.

Vocabulario
¿Qué estudias?   *What do you study?*
¿Cuál es tu materia favorita?   *What is your favorite subject?*
carrera (de medicina)   *(medical) degree program, major*
derecho   *law*

¿Conoces algún° profesor famoso que dé clases… en la UNAM?

¿Conoces algún…?   *Do you know any…?*

3 **Emparejar** Match the phrases to form sentences.

1. En la UNAM no hay
2. México, D.F. es
3. La UNAM tiene (*has*)
4. La UNAM ofrece

a. muchos profesores famosos.
b. 74 carreras de estudio.
c. residencias estudiantiles.
d. la ciudad más grande (*largest*) de Latinoamérica.

4 **Conversación** With a partner, role-play a conversation between two students at UNAM.

I CAN recognize basic details about student life in Mexico City.

Communicative Goal
Ask and answer questions about activities

2.1 The present tense of regular –ar verbs

▸ To create the forms of regular verbs, drop the infinitive endings (**–ar, –er, –ir**). Then add the endings that correspond to the different subject pronouns. This chart shows how to conjugate regular **–ar** verbs.

estudiar (*to study*)

yo	estudi**o**	*I study*
tú	estudi**as**	*you (fam.) study*
Ud./él/ella	estudi**a**	*you (form.) study; he/she studies*
nosotros/as	estudi**amos**	*we study*
vosotros/as	estudi**áis**	*you (pl.) study*
Uds./ellos/ellas	estudi**an**	*you (pl.) study; they study*

¡Llego tarde!

¡Llevas el casco, Sara!

Common *–ar* verbs

bailar	*to dance*	explicar	*to explain*
buscar	*to look for*	hablar	*to talk; to speak*
caminar	*to walk*	llegar	*to arrive*
cantar	*to sing*	llevar	*to carry*
comprar	*to buy*	mirar	*to look (at); to watch*
contestar	*to answer*	necesitar	*to need*
conversar	*to talk; to chat*	practicar	*to practice*
descansar	*to rest*	preguntar	*to ask (a question)*
desear	*to want; to wish*	preparar	*to prepare*
dibujar	*to draw*	regresar	*to return*
enseñar	*to teach*	terminar	*to end; to finish*
escuchar	*to listen (to)*	tomar	*to take; to drink*
esperar	*to wait (for); to hope*	trabajar	*to work*
estudiar	*to study*	viajar	*to travel*

▸ The Spanish present tense has several meanings in English. Note the following examples.

Ana **trabaja** en la cafetería.
Ana works in the cafeteria.
Ana is working in the cafeteria.
Ana does work in the cafeteria.

Paco **viaja** a Madrid mañana.
Paco travels to Madrid tomorrow.
Paco is traveling to Madrid tomorrow.
Paco does travel to Madrid tomorrow.

Práctica

1 **Completar** Complete the conversation with the appropriate forms of the verbs.

modelo

JUAN ¡Hola, Linda! ¿Qué clases ___tomas___ [tomar]?

LINDA Hola, Juan. (1) _____ [tomar] tres clases: química, biología y computación. Y tú, ¿cuántas clases (2) _____ [tomar]?

JUAN (3) _____ [tomar] cuatro: sociología, biología, arte y literatura. Yo (4) _____ [tomar] biología a las cuatro. ¿Y tú?

LINDA Lily, Alberto y yo (5) _____ [tomar] biología a las diez.

JUAN ¿ (6) _____ [estudiar] ustedes mucho?

LINDA Sí, porque (*because*) hay muchos exámenes. Alberto y yo (7) _____ [estudiar] dos horas juntos todos los días (*together every day*).

JUAN ¿Lily no (8) _____ [estudiar] con ustedes?

LINDA No, ella (9) _____ [estudiar] con su novio (*boyfriend*), Arturo.

2 **¿Te gusta...?** Get together with a classmate and take turns asking each other if you like these activities.

¿Te gusta...?	▷	Sí, me gusta.../No, no me gusta...

modelo

Estudiante 1: ¿Te gusta dibujar?
Estudiante 2: Sí, me gusta dibujar. /
No, no me gusta dibujar.

	Sí	No
la universidad	___	___
cantar	___	___
la historia	___	___
la computación	___	___
los exámenes	___	___
trabajar	___	___
las lenguas extranjeras	___	___

Conversación

 3 **Describir** With a partner, describe what the people in the photos are doing.

modelo

Ana María baila.

Ana María

Héctor

Ernesto

1. _____   2. _____

Gabriela

Mario y Laura

3. _____   4. _____

 4 **Entrevista** Use these questions to interview a classmate. What do you have in common?

1. ¿Qué clases tomas?
2. ¿A qué hora termina la clase de español?
3. ¿Cuántas lenguas hablas?
4. ¿Dónde estudias?
5. ¿Miras mucho la televisión? ¿Qué programas te gustan?
6. ¿Te gusta practicar el español fuera (*outside*) de clases? ¿Conversas con tus compañeros en español?

I CAN ask and answer questions about my activities and activity preferences.

Using verbs in Spanish

▶ When two verbs are used together with no change of subject, the second verb is generally in the infinitive.

Deseo hablar con Felipe.   **Necesito comprar** lápices.
I want to speak with Felipe.   *I need to buy pencils.*

▶ To make a sentence negative, use **no** before the conjugated verb.

Yo **no** miro la televisión.   Ella **no** desea bailar.
I don't watch television.   *She doesn't want to dance.*

▶ Subject pronouns are often omitted; the verb endings indicate who the subject is. They may, however, be used for clarification or for emphasis.

—¿Qué enseñan?   —**Él** enseña arte y **ella** enseña química.
What do they teach?   *He teaches art and she teaches chemistry.*

—¿Quién desea trabajar hoy?   —**Yo** no deseo trabajar.
Who wants to work today?   *I don't want to work.*

The verb *gustar*

▶ The verb **gustar,** which is used to express likes and dislikes, is different from other -**ar** verbs. The most common forms of this verb are **gusta** and **gustan**. Use a singular noun with **gusta** and a plural noun with **gustan**. Also, there is no subject pronoun (**yo, tú,...**) before **gusta(n)**.

Me gusta la historia.   **Me gustan** las lenguas extranjeras.
I like history.   *I like foreign languages.*

▶ To say what you like, use **me** before **gusta(n)**. To ask a friend what he/she likes, use **te** before **gusta(n)**. To express dislikes, insert **no** before **me** or **te**.

—¿**Te gusta** la biología?   — No, **no me gusta** la biología.
Do you like biology?   *No, I don't like biology.*

—¿**Te gustan** las clases este semestre?   — Sí, **me gustan** las clases este semestre.
Do you like your classes this semester?   *Yes, I like my classes this semester.*

▶ To talk about what you like and don't like to do, use **(no) me gusta** + [*infinitive*].

—¿**Te gusta** bailar salsa?   — Sí, **me gusta** bailar salsa.
Do you like to dance salsa?   *Yes, I like to dance salsa.*

¡Manos a la obra!

Provide the present-tense forms of the verbs.

hablar

1. Yo ___hablo___ español.
2. Ellas _____ español.
3. Tú _____ español.
4. Isabel _____ español.
5. Nosotros _____ español.

gustar

1. ___Me___ ___gusta___ la clase. *[I like]*
2. ¿_____ _____ las clases? *[Do you like?]*
3. _____ _____ _____ las pruebas. *[I don't like]*
4. _____ _____ el arte. *[You don't like]*
5. _____ _____ viajar. *[I like]*

2.2 Forming questions in Spanish

▶ One way to ask questions is simply to raise the pitch of your voice at the end of a sentence. When writing a question, use an upside-down question mark (¿) at the beginning of a question and a regular question mark (?) at the end.

¿Caminan a la universidad?

La Facultad de Ciencias está por allá, ¿no?

Statement

Ustedes trabajan los sábados.
You work on Saturdays.

Miguel regresa a las seis.
Miguel returns at six.

Question

¿Ustedes trabajan los sábados?
Do you work on Saturdays?

¿Miguel regresa a las seis?
Does Miguel return at six?

▶ You can also ask a question by placing the subject after the verb. The subject may even be placed at the end of the sentence.

Statement

SUBJECT VERB
Ustedes trabajan los sábados.
You work on Saturdays.

SUBJECT VERB
Miguel regresa a las seis.
Miguel returns at six.

Question

VERB   SUBJECT
¿Trabajan ustedes los sábados?
Do you work on Saturdays?

VERB   SUBJECT
¿Regresa a las seis **Miguel?**
Does Miguel return at six?

▶ Another way to ask questions is by adding ¿no? or ¿verdad? at the end of a statement.

Statement

Ustedes trabajan los sábados.
You work on Saturdays.

Miguel regresa a las seis.
Miguel returns at six.

Tú no tomas biología.
You don't take biology.

Question

Ustedes trabajan los sábados, **¿no?**
You work on Saturdays, don't you?

Miguel regresa a las seis, **¿verdad?**
Miguel returns at six, right?

Tú no tomas biología, **¿verdad?**
You don't take biology, right?

Práctica

1 Preguntas Change these statements into questions by inverting the word order.

modelo

Ernesto estudia español.
¿Estudia Ernesto español? /
¿Estudia español Ernesto?

1. Sandra habla con su compañera de cuarto.
   _____
   _____

2. La profesora Soto busca unos libros.
   _____
   _____

3. Tú preparas la tarea.
   _____
   _____

4. Ustedes trabajan en la cafetería.
   _____
   _____

5. Los chicos escuchan música por la radio.
   _____
   _____

2 Una conversación Complete the conversation with the appropriate questions.

modelo IRENE Hola, Manolo. *¿Cómo estás?*

MANOLO Bien, gracias. (1) _____
IRENE Muy bien. (2) _____
MANOLO Son las nueve.
IRENE (3) _____
MANOLO Estudio historia.
IRENE (4) _____
MANOLO Porque hay un examen mañana.
IRENE (5) _____
MANOLO Sí, me gusta mucho la clase.
IRENE (6) _____
MANOLO El profesor Padilla enseña la clase.
IRENE (7) _____
MANOLO No, no tomo psicología este semestre.

Conversación

3 **Encuesta** Change the phrases in the first column into questions and use them to survey two or three classmates. Then report the results of your survey to the class.

3 Communication Interpersonal Communication   *Answers will vary.*

Actividades	**Nombres**
1. estudiar contabilidad	_____
2. tomar una clase de historia	_____
3. dibujar bien	_____
4. cantar bien	_____
5. trabajar los sábados	_____
6. escuchar la radio	_____
7. necesitar comprar una computadora	_____
8. tomar el autobús a la escuela	_____
9. llevar una mochila a clase	_____
10. desear viajar a España	_____

4 **Entrevista** You are a reporter for the school newspaper. Use these questions and create three of your own to interview a classmate about student life. Write a summary of the answers. *Answers will vary.*

4 Communication Interpersonal Communication

1. ¿Dónde estudias? ¿Cuándo?
2. ¿Quién es tu profesor(a) favorito/a?
3. ¿Cuántas clases tomas?
4. ¿Necesitas estudiar más (*more*)?
5. ¿A qué hora llegas a la universidad?
6. ¿Trabajas? ¿Dónde?
7. ¿Cuál es tu día favorito de la semana? ¿Por qué?

ACTIVITY PACK For additional activities, go to the **Activity Pack** in the **Resources** section of the Supersite.

I CAN ask questions about student life.

Interrogative words

▸ These interrogative words are used to form questions in Spanish.

Interrogative words			
¿Adónde?	Where (to)?	¿De dónde?	From where?
¿Cómo?	How?	¿Dónde?	Where?
¿Cuál?, ¿Cuáles?	Which?; Which one(s)?	¿Por qué?	Why?
¿Cuándo?	When?	¿Qué?	What?; Which?
¿Cuánto/a?	How much?	¿Quién?	Who?
¿Cuántos/as?	How many?	¿Quiénes?	Who? (plural)

▸ Use interrogative words in questions that require more than a *yes* or *no* answer. Interrogative words always carry a written accent mark.

¿Cuándo descansan ustedes?
When do you rest?

¿Adónde caminamos?
Where are we walking to?

¿Qué clases tomas?
What classes are you taking?

¿De dónde son ellos?
Where are they from?

▸ In questions that contain interrogative words, the pitch of the speaker's voice falls at the end of the sentence.

¿Cómo llegas a la escuela?
How do you get to school?

¿Por qué necesitas estudiar?
Why do you need to study?

¡Manos a la obra!

Make questions out of these statements. Use intonation in column 1 and the tag **¿no?** in column 2.

Statement	Intonation	¿no?
1. Hablas inglés.	¿Hablas inglés?	Hablas inglés, ¿no?
2. Trabajamos mañana.	¿Trabajamos mañana?	Trabajamos mañana, ¿no?
3. Ustedes desean bailar.	¿Ustedes desean bailar?	Ustedes desean bailar, ¿no?
4. Usted estudia mucho.	¿Usted estudia mucho?	Usted estudia mucho, ¿no?
5. Enseño a las nueve.	¿Enseño a las nueve?	Enseño a las nueve, ¿no?
6. Luz mira la televisión.	¿Luz mira la televisión?	Luz mira la televisión, ¿no?
7. Los chicos descansan.	¿Los chicos descansan?	Los chicos descansan, ¿no?
8. Tú preparas la prueba.	¿Tú preparas la prueba?	Tú preparas la prueba, ¿no?
9. Tomamos el autobús.	¿Tomamos el autobús?	Tomamos el autobús, ¿no?
10. Necesito una pluma.	¿Necesito una pluma?	Necesito una pluma, ¿no?

2.3 The present tense of estar

Communicative Goal
Explain where people and objects are located

▶ In Lesson 1, you learned how to conjugate and use the verb **ser** (*to be*). Spanish has a second verb which means *to be*, the verb **estar**.

▶ Although **estar** ends in **–ar**, it does not follow the pattern of regular **–ar** verbs. The **yo** form (**estoy**) is irregular. Also, all forms but the **yo** and **nosotros/as** forms have an accented **á**. As you will see, **ser** and **estar** are used in different ways.

estar (to be)

yo	est**oy**	*I am*
tú	est**ás**	*you (fam.) are*
Ud./él/ella	est**á**	*you (form.) are; he/she is*
nosotros/as	est**amos**	*we are*
vosotros/as	est**áis**	*you (pl.) are*
Uds./ellos/ellas	est**án**	*you (pl.) are; they are*

¡Todavía está en la cama!

¿Estás lista para la presentación?

Uses of estar and ser

Uses of estar	Uses of ser
LOCATION	**IDENTITY**
Estoy en la biblioteca.	Hola, soy Valentina.
I am at the library.	*Hello, I'm Valentina.*
Sara está al lado de Daniel.	**OCCUPATION**
Sara is next to Daniel.	Soy estudiante.
	I'm a student.
HEALTH	
Javier está enfermo hoy.	**ORIGIN**
Javier is sick today.	¿Eres de España?
	Are you from Spain?
WELL-BEING	Sí, soy de España.
¿Cómo estás, Juanjo?	*Yes, I'm from Spain.*
How are you, Juanjo?	
Estoy muy bien, gracias.	**TELLING TIME**
I'm very well, thank you.	Son las cuatro.
	It's four o'clock.

Práctica

1 Completar Complete this phone conversation with the correct forms of **ser** or **estar**.

modelo   **MAMÁ** Hola, Daniela. ¿Cómo ___estás___?

DANIELA Hola, mamá. (1) _____ bien. ¿Dónde (2) _____ papá? ¡Ya (*already*) (3) _____ las ocho de la noche!

MAMÁ No (4) _____ aquí. (5) _____ en la oficina.

DANIELA Y Andrés y Margarita, ¿dónde (6) _____ ellos?

MAMÁ (7) _____ en el restaurante Dalí con Martín.

DANIELA ¿Quién (8) _____ Martín?

MAMÁ (9) _____ un compañero de clase. (10) _____ de México.

DANIELA Y el restaurante Dalí, ¿dónde (11) _____?

MAMÁ (12) _____ cerca de la Plaza Mayor, en San Modesto.

DANIELA Gracias, mamá. Voy (*I'm going*) al restaurante. ¡Hasta pronto!

2 En la librería You are in the school bookstore and can't find various items. Ask the clerk (your partner) where the items in the drawing are located.

modelo   **Estudiante 1:** ¿Dónde están las mochilas?
                 Estudiante 2: Las mochilas están debajo de las computadoras.

Conversación

3 **¿Dónde estás?** With a partner, take turns asking each other where you normally are at these times. Are you ever in the same place at the same time?

> **modelo**   lunes / 10:00 a.m.
>
> **Estudiante 1:** ¿Dónde estás los lunes a las diez de la mañana?
> **Estudiante 2:** Estoy en la clase de español.

1. viernes / 1:30 p.m.
2. miércoles / 9:15 a.m.
3. lunes / 11:10 a.m.
4. jueves / 12:45 p.m.
5. viernes / 2:25 p.m.
6. martes / 3:50 p.m.
7. jueves / 6:00 p.m.
8. miércoles / 8:20 p.m.

4 **La ciudad universitaria** You and your partner are at the **Facultad de Bellas Artes**. Take turns asking each other where other buildings on the campus map are located.

Facultad de Medicina

Facultad de Administración de Empresas

Facultad de Química

biblioteca

Colegio Mayor Cervantes

Facultad de Bellas Artes

1. ¿Está lejos la biblioteca de la Facultad de Bellas Artes?
2. ¿Dónde está la Facultad de Medicina?
3. ¿Está la Facultad de Administración de Empresas a la derecha de la biblioteca?
4. ¿Dónde está el Colegio Mayor Cervantes?
5. ¿Está la Facultad de Administración de Empresas detrás del Colegio Mayor Cervantes?
6. ¿Dónde está la Facultad de Química?

I CAN explain where people and objects are located.

Estar with prepositions of locations

▸ **Estar** is often used with certain prepositions to describe the location of a person or an object.

Prepositions of location

al lado de	next to	delante de	in front of
a la derecha de	to the right of	detrás de	behind
a la izquierda de	to the left of	encima de	on top of
en	in; on; at	entre	between
cerca de	near	lejos de	far from
debajo de	below	sobre	on; over

La tarea está en la mesa.

Está entre la biblioteca y la Facultad de Humanidades.

La cafetería está **al lado de** la biblioteca.
The cafeteria is next to the library.

El estadio no está **lejos de** la librería.
The stadium isn't far from the bookstore.

Los libros están **encima del** escritorio.
The books are on top of the desk.

Estamos **entre** la puerta y la ventana.
We are between the door and the window.

El laboratorio está **cerca de** la clase.
The lab is near the classroom.

Manuel está **en** la biblioteca.
Manuel is at the library.

Carla está **delante de** José.
Carla is in front of José.

El libro está **sobre** la mesa.
The book is on the table.

¡Manos a la obra!

Provide the present-tense forms of **estar**.

1. Ustedes ___están___ en la clase.
2. José _____ delante de Rosa.
3. Yo _____ muy bien, gracias.
4. Nosotras _____ en la cafetería.
5. Tú _____ en el laboratorio.
6. Elena _____ lejos de la librería.
7. Ellas _____ en la universidad.
8. Ana y yo _____ en la clase.
9. ¿Cómo _____ usted?
10. Javier y Paula _____ en el estadio.
11. Nosotros _____ enfermos.
12. Yo _____ en la biblioteca.
13. Carmen y María _____ en la residencia estudiantil.
14. Tú _____ al lado de Raúl.

2.4 Numbers 31–100

Communicative Goal
Ask for and give prices and
phone numbers

Numbers 31–100

31 treinta y uno	37 treinta y siete	50 cincuenta
32 treinta y dos	38 treinta y ocho	60 sesenta
33 treinta y tres	39 treinta y nueve	70 setenta
34 treinta y cuatro	40 cuarenta	80 ochenta
35 treinta y cinco	41 cuarenta y uno	90 noventa
36 treinta y seis	42 cuarenta y dos	100 cien

¡Llegas treinta y cinco minutos tarde!

▸ The word **y** is used in most numbers from **31** through **99**.

Hay **ochenta y cinco** exámenes.
There are eighty-five exams.

Hay **cuarenta y dos** estudiantes.
There are forty-two students.

▸ With numbers that end in **uno** (31, 41, etc.), **uno** becomes **un** before a masculine noun and **una** before a feminine noun.

Hay **treinta y un** chicos.
There are thirty-one guys.

Hay **treinta y una** chicas.
There are thirty-one girls.

▸ **Cien** is used before nouns and in counting. The words **un**, **una**, and **uno** are never used before **cien** in Spanish.

—¿Cuántos libros hay?
How many books are there?

—Hay **cien** libros.
There are one hundred books.

—¿Cuántas sillas hay?
How many chairs are there?

—Hay **cien** sillas.
There are one hundred chairs.

¡Manos a la obra!

Provide the word form of each number.

a. **56** cincuenta y seis
b. **31** _____
c. **84** _____
d. **99** _____
e. **43** _____

f. **68** _____
g. **72** _____
h. **35** _____
i. **87** _____
j. **59** _____

k. **100** _____
l. **61** _____
m. **96** _____
n. **74** _____
o. **42** _____

Práctica

1 **Baloncesto** Provide these basketball scores in Spanish.

modelo

OHIO STATE 85 MICHIGAN 74

ochenta y cinco, setenta y cuatro

DUKE 78 VIRGINIA 64

1. _____

FLORIDA 100 FLORIDA STATE 92

2. _____

KENTUCKY 63 TENNESSEE 57

3. _____

STANFORD 58 UCLA 49

4. _____

TEXAS 91 OKLAHOMA 86

5. _____

2 **Números de teléfono** Imagine that you work for directory assistance in Spain. Take turns giving the appropriate phone numbers when callers ask for them.

modelo

Estudiante 1: ¿Cuál es el número de teléfono de José Morales Ballesteros, por favor?

Estudiante 2: Es el noventa y uno, nueve, cuarenta y cuatro, sesenta y seis, sesenta y dos.

MORALES		🔍 buscar
Morales Ballesteros, José	Venerable Centenares, 2222	(91) 944-6662
Morales Benito, Francisco	Calle Flores, 16	(91) 773-1216
Morales Borrego, Flora	Mayor, 51	(91) 634-3211
Morales Calvo, Emilio	Villafuerte, 49	(91) 472-2350
Morales Campos, María	Toledo, 35	(91) 773-1382
Morales Cid, Pedro	Rosal, 98	(91) 419-7660
Morales Conde, Ángel	Alameda, 67	(91) 944-3915
Morales Crespo, Pascual	Fernando de la Peña, 13	(91) 634-7148
Morales Díaz, Luz	Buenavista, 80	(91) 834-5238
Morales Fraile, Rosa	Avenida Solares, 74	(91) 834-3371

Conversación

3 **¿Cuánto cuesta?** With a partner, take turns asking how much the items in the ad cost.

 modelo

Estudiante 1: Deseo comprar papel. ¿Cuánto cuesta (*does it cost*)?
Estudiante 2: Un paquete cuesta cuatro dólares y cuarenta y un centavos.

4 **Entrevista** Find out the phone numbers and e-mail addresses of four classmates. (They don't have to be real!)

modelo

Estudiante 1: ¿Cuál es tu (*your*) número de teléfono?
Estudiante 2: Es el (416) 635-1951.
Estudiante 1: ¿Y tu dirección de correo electrónico (*e-mail address*)?
Estudiante 2: Es jota-Smith-arroba (*at*)-pe-ele-punto-e-de-u. (*jsmith@pl.edu*).

I CAN ask for and give prices and phone numbers.

Communicative Goal
Identify numbers in a magazine table of contents

Español en vivo

This is the table of contents from a Latin American magazine.

1 **Identificar** Identify in Spanish the numbers used in the table of contents.

2 **Preguntas** Answer the questions.

1. ¿En qué página está la información sobre la familia?
2. ¿Con quién conversan en la página 74?
3. ¿En qué página buscas información sobre (*about*) opiniones de estudiantes universitarios?

I CAN identify numbers in a magazine table of contents.

A repasar

2.1 The present tense of regular –ar verbs

1 Completar Complete the sentences with the appropriate forms of these verbs. Use each verb only once.

buscar	mirar	terminar	trabajar
cantar	regresar	tomar	viajar

modelo Ella ___*trabaja*___ en la cafetería de la universidad.

1. Ustedes _____ la clase de arte, ¿no?

2. El examen _____ a las diez.

3. ¿ _____ (tú) la televisión todos los días?

4. Yo _____ un libro en la biblioteca.

5. Nosotros _____ mañana a Madrid.

6. Ellos _____ una canción (*song*) de Shakira.

2 Combinar Combine words from the columns to create sentences about yourself and these people.

modelo El *profesor no necesita explicar el examen.*

Yo	(no) desear	trabajar	hoy
Mi (*My*) compañero/a	(no) necesitar	comprar	español
El/La profesor(a)		contestar	el examen
La clase		explicar	los libros
Nosotros		hablar	la lección 2
Los/Las estudiantes		terminar	la tarea
		enseñar	en la clase
		practicar	¿?

2.2 Forming questions in Spanish

3 Preguntas Write questions for these answers using interrogative words.

modelo ¿ ___*Por qué*___ quieres estudiar geografía?

1. —¿ _____ es Patricia?
   —Patricia es de Ecuador.

2. —¿ _____ es él?
   —Él es mi compañero de cuarto.

3. —¿ _____ clases tomas?
   —Tomo cuatro clases.

4. —¿ _____ desean tomar?
   —Deseamos tomar dos cafés.

4 ¿Qué pasa? Write at least five questions about this photo using interrogative words. Then, with a partner, take turns asking and answering each other's questions.

1. _____

2. _____

3. _____

4. _____

5. _____

2.3 The present tense of estar

5 Oraciones Complete the sentences with the appropriate forms of **ser** or **estar**.

modelo ¿De dónde ___*son*___ ustedes?

1. Nosotros _____ de Barcelona.

2. ¿Por qué _____ ustedes en Madrid?

3. Nosotros _____ profesores de historia.

4. Yo _____ el doctor Ochoa y él _____ el profesor Mendoza.

5. Nosotros _____ aquí (*here*) para visitar la biblioteca.

6. La biblioteca _____ a la izquierda, ¿verdad?

6 Entrevista Use these questions to interview a classmate.

1. ¿Cómo estás hoy?

2. ¿Cómo está tu (*your*) compañero/a de cuarto?

3. ¿Dónde está tu compañero/a de cuarto ahora?

4. ¿Quién(es) no está(n) en la clase hoy?

5. ¿Dónde están tus amigos (*friends*) ahora?

6. ¿Dónde está la cafetería? ¿Y la librería?

Video

2.4 Numbers 31–100

7 Matemáticas Solve these math problems.

> + más   − menos   = son

modelo

30 + 42 = Treinta más cuarenta y dos son setenta y dos.

1. 20 + 32 = _____
2. 65 + 18 = _____
3. 46 + 51 = _____
4. 76 + 13 = _____
5. 93 − 45 = _____
6. 81 − 34 = _____
7. 77 − 66 = _____
8. 90 − 55 = _____

8 El clima With a partner, take turns asking what the high and low temperatures are in these cities today.

modelo

Estudiante 1: ¿Cuál es la temperatura máxima en Managua?
Estudiante 2: Es ochenta y siete grados (*degrees*).
Estudiante 1: ¿Y cuál es la temperatura mínima?
Estudiante 2: Es sesenta y cuatro grados.

Ciudad	Máx. / Mín.	Ciudad	Máx. / Mín.
Santiago de Chile	37/24	San Salvador	78/62
Buenos Aires	73/51	Montevideo	55/41
La Paz	48/35	Managua	87/64
Ciudad de México	58/42	Bogotá	72/46
San José	80/69	Quito	63/50

Síntesis

9 El Cuerpo de Paz (*The Peace Corps*) In pairs, imagine that one of you is a supervisor in the Peace Corps and the other is a volunteer working on starting an elementary school in a rural area in Peru. The supervisor wants some information about the project. Act out this situation, using these guidelines.

- Find out how many students there are. [31 students]
- Find out who the teacher is. [Sra. Ana Pelayo]
- Ask what furniture (*muebles*) and things she needs.
- Find out what courses she wants to teach.
- Find out if the school is located far from the town (*el pueblo*).

Communicative Goal
Watch a news report about college entrance exams in Spain

Videoclip

1 Preparación How important are college entrance exams? Did you take any? If so, how did you feel beforehand?

2 El clip Watch the news report **Pruebas de selectividad** from Spain.

Vocabulario	
empiezan *begin*	no sirve de nada *it doesn't help*
estoy temblando *I'm trembling*	se enfrentan a *they face*

Doscientos mil alumnos° se presentan a° las pruebas de selectividad° en toda España.

Doscientos mil alumnos *Two hundred thousand students*   se presentan a *are taking*
pruebas de selectividad *college entrance exams*

3 ¿Qué hay? Indicate which things appear in the video.

	Sí	No
1. mochilas	____	____
2. papel	____	____
3. biblioteca	____	____
4. plumas	____	____
5. maletas	____	____
6. cafetería	____	____
7. ventanas	____	____
8. puertas	____	____
9. mapa	____	____
10. pizarra	____	____

4 Las pruebas Discuss with a classmate how you prepare for an important test like the SAT or ACT. Use as much Spanish as you can.

I CAN watch a news report about college entrance exams in Spain.

Ampliación

1 Escuchar

A Listen to Armando and Julia's conversation. Then list the classes each person is taking.

TIP **Listen for cognates.** Cognates are words that have similar spellings and meanings in two or more languages. Listening for cognates will help you increase your comprehension.

Julia

1. _____
2. _____
3. _____
4. _____

Armando

1. _____
2. _____
3. _____
4. _____
5. _____

B ¿Cuántas clases toman Armando y Julia? ¿Cuántas clases tomas tú? ¿Qué clases te gustan y qué clases no te gustan?

2 Conversar

Greet a classmate, find out how he or she is, and get to know your classmate better by asking these questions.

- ¿Cómo te llamas?
- ¿De dónde eres?
- ¿Qué clases tomas?
- ¿Qué clases te gustan?
- ¿Cuántos estudiantes hay en tu (your) clase de...?
- ¿Cuántas horas estudias durante (during) la semana?
- ¿Dónde estudias normalmente (usually)?

I CAN use known and familiar words to understand a short conversation about classes and instructors.

I CAN greet a classmate and find out basic information about him/her.

Ampliación

on   **inicio**   perfil

Hola! Me llamo Alicia Roberts. Estudio matemáticas en la Universidad de Nueva York...

Communicative Goals
Write a short description of myself to post online, and create a poster encouraging students to study abroad

③ Escribir

Write a description of yourself to post on a website in order to meet Spanish-speaking people.

TIP **Brainstorm.** Spend ten to fifteen minutes jotting down ideas about the topic you are going to write about. The more ideas you write down, the more you'll have to choose from later when you start to organize your thoughts.

Organizar	Make a list of things you would like people to know about you, including your name, your major, where you go to school, what you're studying, where you work, and your likes and dislikes.
Escribir	Using the material you have compiled, write the first draft of your description.
Corregir	Exchange papers with a classmate and comment on the organization, style, and grammatical correctness of each other's work. Then revise your first draft, keeping your classmate's comments in mind.
Compartir	Read your descriptions aloud in small groups. Point out the three best features of each description.

④ Un paso más

Create a poster that will encourage students to study in a university in a Spanish-speaking country. The poster might include these elements:

- A title
- Photos of university locations
- A campus map
- A short summary of the university's programs
- A list of activities and sports that you can participate in at the university
- Photos of the town where the university is located
- A brief description of the town where the university is located

UNIVERSIDAD DE ANDALUCÍA

El futuro en tus manos

⑤ Cultura

Compare your school with a university in a Spanish-speaking country: the university you researched for your poster, UNAM, the **Universidad Complutense de Madrid**, or another school. Consider location, facilities, the number of students, academic departments, etc.

I CAN write a short description of myself and my preferences to post online.

I CAN create a poster encouraging students to study abroad.

Audio: Reading

Antes de leer

The format of a document can tell you a lot about it.

TIP **Predict content through formats.**
Recognizing the format of a document can help you to predict its content. For instance, invitations and classified ads follow an easily identifiable format, which usually gives you a general idea of the information they contain.

Examina el texto

Look at the format of the document on this page. What type of text is it? What information do you expect to find in this type of document?

Cognados

With a classmate, make a list of cognates in the text and guess their English meanings. What do the cognates reveal about the content of the document?

Piénsalo

If you guessed that this text is a brochure from a university, you are correct. You can now infer that the document contains information on departments, courses, and the university campus.

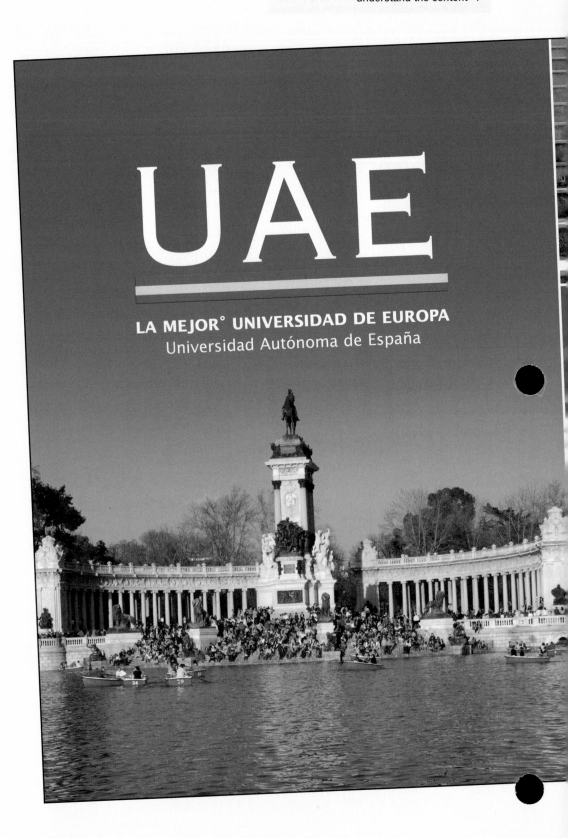

UAE

LA MEJOR° UNIVERSIDAD DE EUROPA
Universidad Autónoma de España

En el campus de la UAE hay ocho facultades:

- Ciencias
- Derecho°
- Medicina
- Psicología
- Filosofía y Letras
- Ciencias Económicas y Empresariales
- Escuela Técnica Superior de Computación
- Facultad° de Formación de Profesorado y Educación

Toma cursos de:

- Antropología Aplicada°
- Computación
- Contabilidad
- Derecho Privado
- Ecología
- Economía General
- Filosofía Antigua°
- Física General
- Geografía
- Historia Contemporánea
- Literatura Española
- Matemáticas
- Microbiología
- Psicología Social
- Química
- Sociología

UAE

INICIAMOS LAS CLASES EN SEPTIEMBRE

¡La UAE está cerca de ti!
Calle del Valle de Mena 95 ▪ 28039 Madrid, ESPAÑA
Teléfono: (34) 91.754.87.25 ▪ www.uae.edu.es

mejor *best* **derecho** *law* **facultad** *school*
aplicada *applied* **antigua** *ancient*

Después de leer

¿Comprendiste?

Indicate whether each statement is **cierto** (*true*) or **falso** (*false*).

Cierto	Falso	
_____	_____	1. La Universidad Autónoma de España está en Europa.
_____	_____	2. En la UAE hay diez facultades.
_____	_____	3. Filosofía y Letras es un curso.
_____	_____	4. Hay cursos de literatura china en la UAE.
_____	_____	5. Hay una facultad de psicología en la UAE.
_____	_____	6. La UAE está en Málaga, España.

Preguntas

Answer these questions using complete sentences.

1. ¿Hay clases de contabilidad en la UAE?

_____

2. ¿Es posible estudiar medicina en la UAE?

_____

3. ¿En qué facultad hay clases de economía general?

_____

4. ¿En qué facultad hay clases de microbiología?

_____

5. ¿En qué facultad hay clases de literatura española?

_____

Coméntalo

Look at the brochure of the **Universidad Autónoma de España** and identify the courses taught there. Does your university offer the same courses? Are you taking any of those courses? Would you be interested in studying at the UAE? Why?

I CAN read and understand key details in an ad for a university.

Vocabulary Tools

La clase y la universidad

el borrador *eraser*
el escritorio *desk*
el libro *book*
el marcador *dry-erase marker*
la mesa *table*
el papel *paper*
la pizarra *whiteboard*
la pluma *pen*
la puerta *door*
el reloj *clock; watch*
la silla *chair*
la ventana *window*

———

la biblioteca *library*
la cafetería *cafeteria*
el estadio *stadium*
el laboratorio *laboratory*
la librería *bookstore*
la residencia estudiantil *dormitory*
el salón de clases *classroom*
la universidad *university*

———

la clase *class*
el curso *course*
el examen *test; exam*
el horario *schedule*
la prueba *test; quiz*
el semestre *semester*
la tarea *homework*
el trimestre *trimester; quarter*

———

el/la compañero/a de clase *classmate*
el/la compañero/a de cuarto *roommate*

Los cursos

la administración de empresas *business administration*
el arte *art*
la biología *biology*
la computación *computer science*
la contabilidad *accounting*
el español *Spanish*
la física *physics*
la geografía *geography*
la historia *history*
el inglés *English*
las lenguas extranjeras *foreign languages*
las matemáticas *mathematics*
el periodismo *journalism*
la psicología *psychology*
la química *chemistry*
la sociología *sociology*

Los días de la semana

lunes *Monday*
martes *Tuesday*
miércoles *Wednesday*
jueves *Thursday*
viernes *Friday*
sábado *Saturday*
domingo *Sunday*

———

la semana *week*

———

Hoy es... *Today is...*

———

Interrogative words *See page 41.*
Prepositions of location *See page 43.*
Numbers 31–100 *See page 44.*

Verbos

bailar *to dance*
buscar *to look for*
caminar *to walk*
cantar *to sing*
comprar *to buy*
contestar *to answer*
conversar *to talk; to chat*
descansar *to rest*
desear *to want; to wish*
dibujar *to draw*
enseñar *to teach*
escuchar *to listen (to)*
esperar *to wait (for); to hope*
estar *to be*
estudiar *to study*
explicar *to explain*
gustar *to like; to be pleasing (lit.)*
hablar *to talk; to speak*
llegar *to arrive*
llevar *to carry*
mirar *to look (at); to watch*
necesitar *to need*
practicar *to practice*
preguntar *to ask (a question)*
preparar *to prepare*
regresar *to return*
terminar *to end; to finish*
tomar *to take; to drink*
trabajar *to work*
viajar *to travel*

Communicative Goals: Review

I CAN talk about classes.
• Make five statements about your classes.

I CAN discuss everyday activities.
• Say five things that you like or don't like to do.

I CAN ask questions.
• Ask a classmate five questions about his/her classes.

I CAN describe location.
• Say where your school supplies are.

I CAN investigate universities in the Spanish-speaking world.
• Explain how universities in the Spanish-speaking world are different from the ones in the United States.

AVENTURAS EN LOS PAÍSES HISPANOS

Todos los años *(Every year)*, en el mes de junio, Nueva York organiza un gran desfile *(parade)* en honor a los puertorriqueños.
¿Te gustan los desfiles?

ESTADOS UNIDOS Y CANADÁ

Estados Unidos

Población de los EE.UU.: 332.639.000
Población de origen hispano: 56.873.000
País de origen de hispanos en los EE.UU.:

8,3% **otros**
3,8% **Cuba**
9,2% **Puerto Rico**
15,8% **Centroamérica y Suramérica**
62,9% **México**

Estados con mayor población hispana:
California, Texas, Florida y Nueva York

SOURCE: U.S. Census Bureau

Canadá

Población de Canadá: 37.589.000
Población de origen hispano: 584.000
País de origen de hispanos en Canadá:

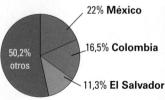

22% **México**
16,5% **Colombia**
50,2% **otros**
11,3% **El Salvador**

Ciudades con mayor población hispana:
Montreal, Toronto y Vancouver

SOURCE: Statistics Canada

Video

Lugares

La Pequeña Habana ⊙

La Pequeña Habana (*Little Havana*) es un barrio (*neighborhood*) de Miami, Florida, donde viven (*live*) muchos cubanoamericanos. Es un lugar donde se encuentran (*are found*) las costumbres (*customs*) de la cultura cubana, los aromas y sabores (*flavors*) de su comida (*food*) y la música salsa. La Pequeña Habana es una parte de Cuba en los Estados Unidos.

¿Hay barrios hispanos en tu ciudad o pueblo? Si es así (*If so*), ¿los barrios son de alguna (*any*) cultura hispana en particular?

Personalidades

Latinos famosos

Los estadounidenses de origen hispanoamericano contribuyen (*contribute*) en todos los niveles (*at all levels*) a la cultura y a la economía de los Estados Unidos.

¿Qué estadounidenses famosos de origen hispano conoces (*do you know*)?

CANADÁ

Vancouver ● ● Calgary

EE.UU.

● San Francisco

● Las Vegas

Los Ángeles ●

● San Diego

MÉXICO

Sonia Sotomayor, juez, de origen puertorriqueño

John Quiñones, periodista, de origen mexicano

Eva Mendes, actriz, de origen cubano

Ellen Ochoa, astronauta, de origen mexicano

La bachata

La bachata es un género musical de origen dominicano, derivado del bolero y con influencias del merengue y el son cubano. Combina instrumentos musicales como la guitarra, el bongó, la trompeta y las maracas. Maite Perroni (de México), Prince Royce (de los Estados Unidos) y Romeo Santos (de los Estados Unidos) son algunos de los cantantes (*singers*) de bachata más famosos.

¿Qué géneros de música latina conoces? ¿Te gusta bailar música latina?

Romeo Santos

Ottawa

Toronto

Chicago

Ciudad de Nueva York

Washington D.C.

Océano Atlántico

Golfo de México

Miami

Mar Caribe

Comida

La comida mexicana

La comida (*food*) mexicana es muy popular en los Estados Unidos. Los tacos, las enchiladas y las quesadillas son platos (*dishes*) mexicanos que frecuentemente forman parte de las comidas (*meals*) de muchos norteamericanos. También (*Also*) son populares las variaciones de la comida mexicana en los Estados Unidos... el tex-mex y el cali-mex.

¿Qué platos de comida mexicana te gustan?

Comunidad

Hispanos en Canadá ▶

La población hispana en Canadá crece (*grows*) cada año (*year*). Más (*More*) del 50% de los hispanos está en Toronto y en Montreal. La mayoría de ellos tiene (*have*) estudios universitarios y habla una de las lenguas oficiales: inglés o francés (*French*). Esto les permite (*This allows them*) participar activamente en la vida cotidiana (*daily life*) y profesional.

¿Hay una lengua oficial en tu país?

Cubanos en el festival Salsa on St. Clair, Toronto

¿Qué aprendiste?

1 **¿Cierto o falso?** Indicate whether these statements are **cierto** or **falso**, based on what you have learned about Hispanics in the U.S. and Canada.

	Cierto	Falso
1. Los mexicanos son el grupo hispano más grande (*biggest*) de los EE.UU.	_____	_____
2. En Florida no hay muchas personas de origen hispano.	_____	_____
3. En Texas hay muchos hispanos.	_____	_____
4. La Pequeña Habana está en la isla de Cuba.	_____	_____
5. John Quiñones es de origen mexicano.	_____	_____
6. Los colombianos son el grupo hispano más grande de Canadá.	_____	_____
7. Muchos hispanos en Canadá tienen estudios universitarios.	_____	_____
8. La bachata es un plato mexicano.	_____	_____

2 **Preguntas** Answer these questions.

1. ¿Cómo se llama el barrio de Miami, Florida, donde viven muchos cubanoamericanos?
2. ¿Quién es Sonia Sotomayor?
3. ¿Cuáles son las variaciones de la comida mexicana populares en los Estados Unidos?
4. ¿Dónde está más del 50% de los hispanos en Canadá?
5. ¿Quiénes son Maite Perroni, Prince Royce y Romeo Santos?

3 **¿Qué piensas?** With a partner, take turns answering the following questions with complete sentences.

1. ¿Por qué la Pequeña Habana es un lugar tan importante para los cubanos en los Estados Unidos? ¿Cuáles son las características de este lugar?
2. ¿Cómo crees que contribuyen (*contribute*) personajes como Sonia Sotomayor al progreso social en los Estados Unidos?
3. ¿Por qué la comida mexicana es tan popular en los Estados Unidos?
4. ¿Por qué es importante hablar la lengua del país en el que vives?

4 **Comparación** Compare the Hispanic populations of the United States and Canada.

I CAN identify basic facts about the Hispanic population and cultures in the United States and Canada by reading short informational texts with visuals.

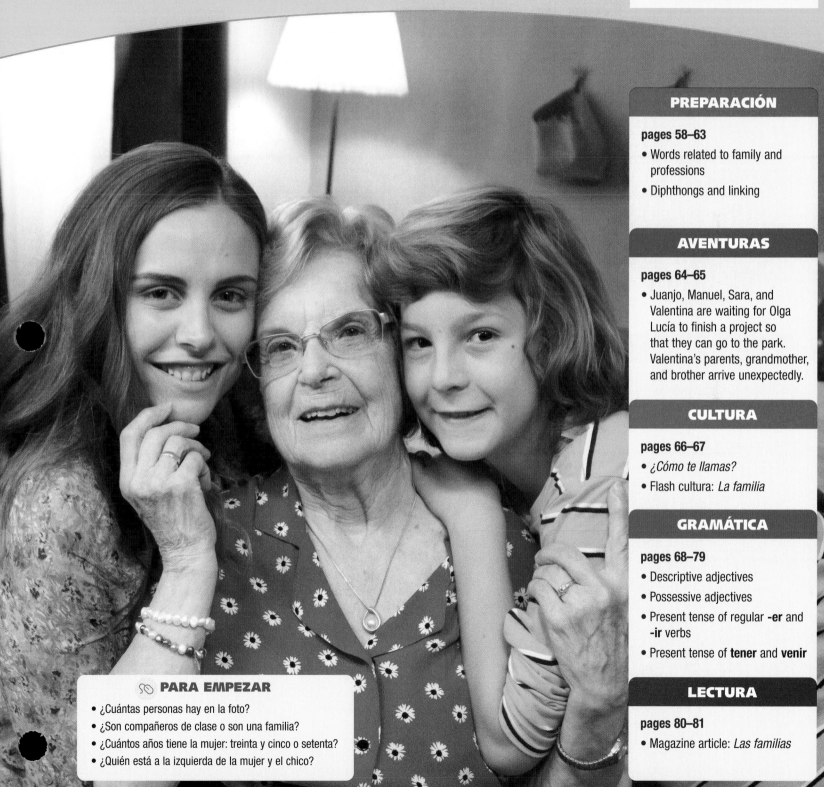

3 La familia

PREPARACIÓN

pages 58–63
- Words related to family and professions
- Diphthongs and linking

AVENTURAS

pages 64–65
- Juanjo, Manuel, Sara, and Valentina are waiting for Olga Lucía to finish a project so that they can go to the park. Valentina's parents, grandmother, and brother arrive unexpectedly.

CULTURA

pages 66–67
- *¿Cómo te llamas?*
- Flash cultura: *La familia*

GRAMÁTICA

pages 68–79
- Descriptive adjectives
- Possessive adjectives
- Present tense of regular **-er** and **-ir** verbs
- Present tense of **tener** and **venir**

LECTURA

pages 80–81
- Magazine article: *Las familias*

PARA EMPEZAR

- ¿Cuántas personas hay en la foto?
- ¿Son compañeros de clase o son una familia?
- ¿Cuántos años tiene la mujer: treinta y cinco o setenta?
- ¿Quién está a la izquierda de la mujer y el chico?

Communicative Goal
Talk about family members and their
relationship to each other

LA FAMILIA

el abuelo
grandfather

la abuela
grandmother

LA FAMILIA EXTENDIDA

el/la cuñado/a
brother-in-law/sister-in-law

el/la nieto/a *grandson/granddaughter*

la nuera *daughter-in-law*

los parientes *relatives*

el/la primo/a *cousin*

el/la sobrino/a *nephew/niece*

el/la suegro/a
father-in-law/mother-in-law

el/la tío/a *uncle/aunt*

el yerno *son-in-law*

LA FAMILIA

el/la esposo/a *husband/wife*

el/la hermanastro/a
stepbrother/stepsister

el/la hermano/a *brother/sister*

el/la hijastro/a *stepson/stepdaughter*

la madrastra *stepmother*

el/la medio/a hermano/a
half-brother/half-sister

el padrastro *stepfather*

los padres *parents*

el padre
father

la madre
mother

los hijos
sons; children

la hija
daughter

Vocabulary Tools

el artista

la niña
girl

LAS PROFESIONES

el/la ingeniero/a *engineer*

el/la médico/a *doctor*

el/la periodista *journalist*

el/la programador(a)
computer programmer

la doctora

la novia
girlfriend

el novio
boyfriend

OTRAS PALABRAS

el/la amigo/a *friend*

el/la gato/a *cat*

la gente *people*

el/la muchacho/a *boy/girl*

la persona *person*

el/la perro/a *dog*

_____

mi *my (sing.)*

mis *my (pl.)*

el niño
boy; child

ASÍ SE DICE

la madre ⟷ la mamá, mami (*colloquial*)
el padre ⟷ el papá, papi (*colloquial*)
los padres ⟷ los papás, papis (*colloquial*)

_____

▶ What do you call your parents?

A escuchar

1 Indicar Check **sí** if the word you hear indicates a family member or **no** if it does not.

	Sí	No
1.	_____	_____
2.	_____	_____
3.	_____	_____
4.	_____	_____
5.	_____	_____
6.	_____	_____
7.	_____	_____
8.	_____	_____

2 Emparejar You will hear some definitions of vocabulary words. Indicate which sentence matches each definition.

1. a. Son mis padres.   b. Son mis abuelos.   c. Son mis suegros.
2. a. Es mi yerno.   b. Es mi sobrino.   c. Es mi cuñado.
3. a. Es periodista.   b. Es programadora.   c. Es artista.
4. a. Es mi prima.   b. Es mi sobrina.   c. Es mi abuela.
5. a. Son mis perros.   b. Son mis primos.   c. Son mis abuelos.
6. a. Es mi nieto.   b. Es mi tío.   c. Es mi gato.

3 ¿Lógico o ilógico? Listen to each conversation and indicate whether it is logical or illogical.

	Lógico	Ilógico
1.	_____	_____
2.	_____	_____
3.	_____	_____
4.	_____	_____
5.	_____	_____
6.	_____	_____

A practicar

4 **Completar** Complete these sentences with the correct words.

> **modelo**
>
> El hijo de mi tío es mi ___primo___.

1. Mi madre y mi padre son mis _____.
2. El padre de mi madre es mi _____.
3. Yo soy el _____ del hijo de mi hermana.
4. La esposa de mi hijo es mi _____.
5. Yo soy el _____ de los padres de mi esposa.
6. La hija de mi hermana es mi _____.
7. El segundo (*second*) esposo de mi madre es mi _____.
8. La hija de mi padre y de mi madrastra es mi _____.

5 **Profesiones** Complete the description of each photo.

1. Rosa María Ortiz es _____.

2. Héctor Ibarra es _____.

3. Alberto Díaz es _____.

4. Elena Vargas Soto es _____.

5. Daniela López es _____.

6. Irene González es _____.

A conversar

6 ¿Y tú? With a classmate, take turns asking each other these questions. Do you have any answers in common?

tengo *I have*	**tu** *your (sing.)*
tienes *you have*	**tus** *your (pl.)*

1. ¿Cuántas personas hay en tu familia?
2. ¿Cómo se llaman tus padres? ¿De dónde son?
3. ¿Cuántos hermanos tienes? ¿Cómo se llaman?
4. ¿Cuántos primos tienes? ¿Cuántos son niños y cuántos son adultos?
5. ¿Eres tío/a? ¿Cómo se llaman tus sobrinos/as? ¿Dónde estudian o trabajan?
6. ¿Tienes novio/a? ¿Tienes esposo/a? ¿Cómo se llama?

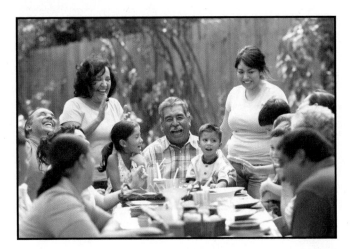

7 Una familia famosa Create a family tree for a famous family, using photos or drawings labeled with names and origins. Describe the family tree to a classmate and explain who the people are and their relationships to each other. Answer any questions your classmate may have.

8 Mi familia Draw your own family tree and then share it with a classmate. Ask your partner questions about his/her family tree.

modelo

Estudiante 1: ¿De dónde es tu cuñado David?
Estudiante 2: Es de Chicago.

I CAN ask and answer questions about family members and their relationship to each other.

Pronunciación

 Tutorial

Diphthongs and linking

. . . .

hermano   **niña**   **cuñado**

In Spanish, **a**, **e**, and **o** are considered strong vowels. The weak vowels are **i** and **u**.

. . . .

ruido   **parientes**   **periodista**

A diphthong is a combination of two weak vowels or of a strong vowel and a weak vowel.
Diphthongs are pronounced as a single syllable.

. . . .

la abuela   **mi hijo**   **una clase excelente**

Two identical vowel sounds that appear together are pronounced
like one long vowel.

. . . .

con Natalia   **sus sobrinos**   **las sillas**

Two identical consonants together sound like a single consonant.

. . . .

es ingeniera   **mis abuelos**   **sus hijos**

A consonant at the end of a word is linked with the vowel at the beginning of the next word.

. . . .

mi hermano   **su esposa**   **nuestro amigo**

A vowel at the end of a word is linked with the vowel at the beginning of the next word.

. . . .

Práctica Say these words aloud, focusing on the diphthongs.

1. historia	5. residencia	9. lenguas
2. nieto	6. prueba	10. estudiar
3. parientes	7. puerta	11. izquierda
4. novia	8. ciencias	12. ecuatoriano

Oraciones Read these sentences aloud to practice diphthongs and linking words.

1. Hola. Me llamo Anita Amaral. Soy del Ecuador.
2. Somos seis en mi familia.
3. Tengo dos hermanos y una hermana.
4. Mi papá es del Ecuador y mi mamá es de España.

Refranes Read these sayings aloud to practice
diphthongs and linking sounds.

> **Hablando del rey de Roma, por la puerta se asoma.**[2]

> **Cuando una puerta se cierra, otra se abre.**[1]

[1] *When one door closes, another opens.*
[2] *Speak of the devil and he will appear.*

Una visita inesperada

Manuel, Juanjo, Valentina y Sara esperan a Olga Lucía cuando la familia de Valentina llega.

Video

Antes de ver

Look only at the images and predict what will happen in the video.

PERSONAJES

CARMEN

OLGA LUCÍA

PEDRO

FELIPE

GLORIA

MANUEL

SARA

VALENTINA

JUANJO

CARMEN ¡Hola, guapa! ¡Tú debes ser Olga!
OLGA LUCÍA Olga Lucía. ¿Y usted quién es?
CARMEN Soy Carmen, la madre de Valentina. Él es Pedro, su padre. ¡Hijo, saluda!
FELIPE Hola, soy Felipe.
CARMEN Y ella es la abuela, Gloria.
GLORIA ¿Y mi nieta? ¡Vivimos en Zaragoza, venimos hasta Madrid y mi nieta no está!

OLGA LUCÍA Valentina está en el apartamento de al lado. Ya regreso.
JUANJO ¡Olga Lucía, por favor! ¡Es domingo! Comparte con nosotros un rato y en la tarde terminas.
OLGA LUCÍA Te presento a la familia de Valentina.
JUANJO Hola. ¡Qué simpáticos!

VALENTINA Juanjo, ¿vienes con nosotros?... Mamá... papá... Os presento a mis amigos. Él es Juanjo, vecino y compañero de universidad.
JUANJO Juan José Reyes Peña, encantado.
VALENTINA Juanjo es un chico muy inteligente. Estudia ciencias ambientales.
CARMEN ¿Y de dónde eres?
JUANJO ¡Soy dominicano!
GLORIA ¿Es mexicano?
PEDRO ¡Dominicano, mamá! ¡Dominicano!

ACTIVIDADES

1 Ordenar Put the events in order.

_____ a. Valentina, su familia y sus amigos van (*go*) al Parque del Retiro.

_____ b. La mamá de Valentina presenta a su familia.

_____ c. Juanjo busca a Olga Lucía.

_____ d. Olga Lucía abre la puerta.

_____ e. Valentina presenta a sus amigos.

2 Completar Complete the sentences about Valentina's family.

1. Felipe es el _____ de Valentina.

2. Valentina es la _____ de Gloria.

3. Carmen y Pedro son los _____ de Valentina.

4. Gloria es la _____ de Felipe.

5. Pedro es el _____ de Gloria.

6. Carmen es la _____ de Pedro.

VALENTINA Él es Manuel. También es muy inteligente.

MANUEL Manuel Vázquez Quevedo. ¡Mucho gusto!

VALENTINA La mamá de Manuel es la hermana de don Paco, nuestro casero.

MANUEL Y ella es Sara, mi prima.

SARA ¡Mucho gusto!

JUANJO Bueno, tenemos prisa.

CHICOS ¡Adiós!

FELIPE ¿Y adónde vais?

VALENTINA Al Parque del Retiro.

FELIPE ¡Pues vamos todos!

SARA ¡Olga Lucía!

OLGA LUCÍA ¡Hola!

SARA ¡Valentina!

VALENTINA ¡Hola!

SARA ¡Chicos!

FELIPE ¡Hola!

JUANJO Y MANUEL ¡Qué divertido!

Expresiones útiles

ahora *now*
el/la casero/a *landlord/landlady*
las ciencias ambientales *environmental science*
divertido/a *fun*
el proyecto *project*
también *also*
vais *you (fam. pl.) are going*
vamos *let's go*
el/la vecino/a *neighbor*

---

el bote de remos *rowboat*
el estanque *pond*
el salvavidas *life jacket*

Parque del Retiro

El Parque del Buen Retiro (*Pleasant Retreat*), also known as **el Retiro**, is a 350-acre oasis in the heart of Madrid. Once a getaway for Spanish kings, it is now a park where the public can enjoy a boat ride on a large artificial pond, take a stroll in the **Rosaleda** (*Rose Garden*), see an art exhibit at the **Palacio de Cristal** (*Glass Palace*), or have coffee at the numerous outdoor **terrazas** (*open-air cafés*).

Is there a large park or green area in your community? Compare it with **el Retiro**.

3 **Una visita inesperada** Your family has come to visit you. Introduce your roommate to your family members. Work with several classmates and switch roles.

modelo

Estudiante 1: Laura, te presento a mi familia. Ella es mi madre, Sandra.
Estudiante 2: Hola, mucho gusto.
Estudiante 3: El gusto es mío. ¿De dónde eres?

I CAN introduce my family.

Communicative Goal
Identify practices related to last names and families in Spanish-speaking countries

¿Cómo te llamas?

In the Spanish-speaking world, it is common to have two last names: one paternal and one maternal. In some cases, the words **de** or **y** are used to connect the two. For example, in the name **Juan Martínez de Velasco,** *Martínez* is the paternal surname (**el apellido paterno**), and *Velasco* is the maternal surname (**el apellido materno**); **de** simply links the two. This convention of using two last names (**doble apellido**) is a European tradition that Spaniards brought to the Americas. It continues to be practiced in many countries, including Chile, Colombia, Mexico, Peru, and Venezuela. There are exceptions, however; in Argentina, the prevailing custom is for children to inherit only the father's last name.

Gabriel García Márquez

Mercedes Barcha Pardo

Rodrigo García Barcha

Hijos en la casa

In Spanish-speaking countries, family and society place very little pressure on young adults to live on their own (**independizarse**), and children often live with their parents well into their thirties. For example, about 70% of Spaniards between the ages of 18 and 29 live at home with their parents. This delay in moving out is both cultural and economic—lack of job security or low wages coupled with a high cost of living may make it impractical for young adults to live independently before they marry.

followed by the mother's first surname, as in the name **Rodrigo García Barcha.** However, both surnames come from the grandfathers, and therefore all **apellidos** are effectively paternal.

Comparisons Language Comparisons

When a woman marries in a country where two last names are used, legally she retains her two maiden surnames. However, socially she may take her husband's paternal surname in place of her inherited maternal surname. For example, **Mercedes Barcha Pardo,** late wife of Colombian writer **Gabriel García Márquez,** might have used the names **Mercedes Barcha García** or **Mercedes Barcha de García** in social situations (although officially her name remained **Mercedes Barcha Pardo**). Adopting a husband's last name for social purposes, though widespread, is only legally recognized in Ecuador and Peru.

Most parents do not break tradition upon naming their children; regardless of the surnames the mother uses, they use the father's first surname

ASÍ SE DICE

Familia y amigos

el/la bisnieto/a	*great-grandson/ great-granddaughter*
el/la chamaco/a (Méx.) el/la chamo/a (Ven.) el/la chaval(a) (Esp.) el/la pibe/a (Arg.)	el/la muchacho/a
mi cuate (Méx.) mi parcero (Col.) mi pana (Ven., P. Rico, Rep. Dom.)	*my pal; my buddy*
la madrina; el padrino	*godmother; godfather*
el/la tatarabuelo/a	*great-great-grandfather/ great-great-grandmother*

▸ What word do you use for *friend*?

1 **¿Cierto o falso?** Indicate whether each statement is **cierto** or **falso**. Correct the false statements.

1. Hispanic last names generally consist of the paternal last name followed by the maternal last name.

2. It is common to see **de** or **y** used in a Hispanic last name.

3. Someone from Argentina would most likely have two last names.

4. Generally, married women legally retain two maiden surnames.

5. Hispanic last names are effectively a combination of the maternal surnames from the previous generation.

2 **Preguntas** Answer the questions.

1. What is the convention of using two last names called in Spanish?

2. What is the origin of this tradition?

3. Which country is an exception to the custom of using two last names?

4. When might a woman take her husband's paternal surname in place of her inherited maternal surname?

3 **Apellidos** Respond to the questions.

1. What would your two last names be if you lived in Spain?

2. What do you think of the practice of using two last names? What might be some advantages and disadvantages?

3. What do women do about their last name when they get married in the United States? How are the options similar to or different from the Spanish-speaking world?

4 **Perspectivas** What do you think are the cultural reasons for young people to live at home with their parents for so long in Spain? Discuss with a partner.

I CAN identify different practices related to family in my own and other cultures.

Communicative Goal
Identify differences in family sizes and in members that form a family unit

 Video

La familia

1 **Preparación** What is a "typical family" like where you live? Is there such a thing? What members of a family usually live together?

2 **El video** Watch this **Flash cultura** episode about families in Ecuador.

> **Vocabulario**
> **familia grande y feliz** *a big, happy family*
> **familia numerosa** *a large family*
> **hacer (algo) juntos** *to do (something) together*
> **reuniones familiares** *family gatherings, reunions*

Te presento a la familia Bolaños.

3 **Completar** Complete this paragraph with the correct options.

Los Valdivieso y los Bolaños son dos ejemplos de familias en Ecuador. Los Valdivieso son una familia (1) _____ (difícil/numerosa). Viven *(They live)* en una casa (2) _____ (grande/buena). En el patio, hacen *(they do)* muchas reuniones (3) _____ (familiares/con amigos). Los Bolaños son una familia pequeña *(small)*. Ellos comen *(eat)* (4) _____ (separados/juntos) y preparan canelazo, una bebida *(drink)* típica ecuatoriana.

4 **Entrevista** With a partner, role-play an interview with Mónica about her family.

I CAN identify different family gatherings in a Spanish-speaking country.

I CAN identify details and differences in the makeup of two families.

Communicative Goal
Describe people and places

3.1 Descriptive adjectives

▸ Descriptive adjectives describe nouns. In Spanish, adjectives agree in gender and number with the nouns or pronouns they describe.

▸ Adjectives that end in **–o** and **–or** have four forms.

Masculine	Feminine
el chico alto	la chica alta
los chicos altos	las chicas altas
el hombre trabajador	la mujer trabajadora
los hombres trabajadores	las mujeres trabajadoras

▸ Adjectives that end in **–e** or a consonant have the same masculine and feminine forms.

Masculine	Feminine
el chico inteligente	la chica inteligente
los chicos inteligentes	las chicas inteligentes
el profesor difícil	la profesora difícil
los profesores difíciles	las profesoras difíciles

▸ Adjectives describing different genders use the masculine plural form.

¿Cómo son Paco y Ana? Paco es alto. Ana es alta. → Paco y Ana son altos.

Common descriptive adjectives

alto/a	tall	gordo/a	fat	moreno/a	dark-haired
antipático/a	unpleasant	grande	big	pelirrojo/a	red-haired
bajo/a	short (in height)	guapo/a	good-looking	pequeño/a	small
bonito/a	pretty	importante	important	rubio/a	blond
bueno/a	good	inteligente	intelligent	simpático/a	nice
delgado/a	thin	interesante	interesting	tonto/a	foolish
difícil	difficult	joven	young	trabajador(a)	hard-working
fácil	easy	malo/a	bad	viejo/a	old
feo/a	ugly				

¡ojo! Note that **joven** takes an accent in the plural: **joven / jóvenes**.

Adjectives of nationality

▸ Adjectives of nationality are formed like other adjectives. Adjectives of nationality that end in a consonant add **–a** to form the feminine.

Masculine	Feminine
Toño es mexicano.	Gloria es mexicana.
Ellos son mexicanos.	Ellas son mexicanas.
Héctor es español.	Sara es española.
Ellos son españoles.	Ellas son españolas.

Práctica

1 Emparejar Read the descriptions and match them with the photos.

1. __ Mateo es moreno.
2. __ Duque es gordo.
3. __ Luisa es rubia.
4. __ Rayo es delgado.
5. __ César es muy pequeño.
6. __ Raquel es pelirroja.

2 Completar Look at the portrait of Amanda's family and imagine their personalities. Complete the sentences with appropriate adjectives.

1. Mi familia es _____.
2. Mis abuelos son _____. Mi abuelo es _____ y mi abuela es _____.
3. Mi padre se llama Julio. Él es _____.
4. Mi madre se llama Victoria. Ella es _____.
5. Mi hermana se llama Rosa. Ella es _____.
6. Y mi hermano Tomás es muy _____.

Conversación

3 Describir With a partner, take turns describing each photo. Tell your partner whether you agree (**Estoy de acuerdo**) or disagree (**No estoy de acuerdo**) with the descriptions.

modelo

Estudiante 1: Los Ángeles es una ciudad (*city*) bonita.
Estudiante 2: Estoy de acuerdo. Es muy grande también (*too*)./ No estoy de acuerdo. Es una ciudad muy fea.

Los Ángeles

1. **Rey y reina de España**

2. **La Torre (*Tower*) Sears**

3. **Taylor Swift**

4. **Enrique Iglesias**

5. **Santa Fe, Nuevo México**

6. **Bill Gates**

4 Anuncio personal Write a personal ad that describes yourself and your ideal boyfriend, girlfriend, or mate. Compare your ad with a classmate's.

★ **SOY ALTA** y bonita. Soy estadounidense, de Texas. Estudio arte en la universidad. Busco un chico similar a mí *(to me)*. Mi novio ideal es alto, inteligente y muy simpático.

I CAN describe people and places.
I CAN write a personal ad.

Some adjectives of nationality

alemán, alemana	German	estadounidense	*from the United States*
argentino/a	Argentine		
canadiense	Canadian	francés, francesa	French
chino/a	Chinese	inglés, inglesa	English
costarricense	Costa Rican	japonés, japonesa	Japanese
cubano/a	Cuban	mexicano/a	Mexican
dominicano/a	Dominican	norteamericano/a	(North) American
ecuatoriano/a	Ecuadorian	puertorriqueño/a	Puerto Rican
español(a)	Spanish	venezolano/a	Venezuelan

The position of adjectives

▶ Adjectives generally follow the nouns they modify.

La mujer **rubia** es de España. — *The blond woman is from Spain.*
¿Cómo se llama la mujer **ecuatoriana**? — *What is the Ecuadorian woman's name?*

¡ojo! Unlike descriptive adjectives, adjectives of quantity such as **mucho/a** (*much; many; a lot*) are placed before the modified noun.

Muchos ingenieros trabajan aquí. — *Many engineers work here.*
Mucha gente viaja en el verano. — *A lot of people travel in the summer.*

▶ **Bueno/a** and **malo/a** can be placed before or after a noun. Before a masculine singular noun, the forms are shortened: **bueno → buen; malo → mal.**

José es un **buen** amigo.
José es un amigo **bueno**.
José is a good friend.
Hoy es un **mal** día.
Hoy es un día **malo**.
Today is a bad day.

▶ When **grande** appears before a singular noun, it is shortened to **gran**.

¡ojo! The adjective **grande** also changes its definition depending on its position: **gran** = *great*, but **grande** = *big, large*.

Manuel es un **gran** hombre. — *Manuel is a great man.*
La familia de Inés es **grande**. — *Inés' family is large.*

¡Manos a la obra!

Give the appropriate forms of the adjectives provided.

1. Eres simpático/a.
2. Yolanda es _____.
3. Nosotros somos _____.
4. Valeria y Marta son _____.
5. Diego es _____.
6. Tomás y yo somos trabajadores.
7. Ellas son _____.
8. La médica es _____.
9. Los niños son _____.
10. Él es _____.

1. Soy español(a).
2. Ángela es _____.
3. Los turistas son _____.
4. Nosotros somos _____.
5. El periodista es _____.
6. Ellos son norteamericanos.
7. Clara y Bárbara son _____.
8. Ella es _____.
9. Rafael y yo somos _____.
10. Juan Pablo es _____.

3.2 Possessive adjectives

Communicative Goal
Indicate relationships between family members

▸ Possessive adjectives express ownership or possession.

Forms of possessive adjectives

Singular forms	Plural forms	
mi	mis	my
tu	tus	your (fam.)
su	sus	his, her, its, your (form.)
nuestro/a	nuestros/as	our
vuestro/a	vuestros/as	your (fam.)
su	sus	their, your

¡ojo! Spanish possessive adjectives show agreement in number with the nouns they modify. **Nuestro** and **vuestro** show agreement in gender and number.

mi **primo**	mis **primos**	mi **tía**	mis **tías**
nuestro **tío**	nuestros **tíos**	nuestra **tía**	nuestras **tías**

▸ Possessive adjectives are placed before the nouns they modify.

Os presento a mis amigos.

Y ella es Sara, mi prima.

▸ **Su** and **sus** have multiple meanings (*your, his, her, their, its*). To avoid confusion, use this construction instead: [*article*] + [*noun*] + **de** + [*subject pronoun*].

sus **parientes**

los parientes de él/ella	his/her relatives
los parientes de Ud./Uds.	your relatives
los parientes de ellos/ellas	their relatives

¡Manos a la obra!

Provide the appropriate form of each possessive adjective.

1. Es ___mi___ (*my*) perro.
2. _____ (*my*) familia es ecuatoriana.
3. _____ (*your, fam.*) tío Marcelo es cubano.
4. _____ (*our*) profesor es español.
5. Es _____ (*her*) reloj.
6. Es _____ (*your, fam.*) mochila.
7. Es _____ (*your, form.*) maleta.
8. _____ (*their*) sobrina es alemana.
9. _____ (*her*) primos son franceses.
10. _____ (*our*) hermanastros son canadienses.
11. Son _____ (*their*) gatos.
12. _____ (*their*) nietos son japoneses.

Práctica

1 **Completar** Complete Marta's description with the appropriate possessive adjectives.

Ésta es una foto de (1) _____ familia. Aquí están (2) _____ abuelos. Son los padres de (3) _____ papá. (4) _____ casa (*home*) está en Valparaíso, Chile. ¡Es muy bonita!

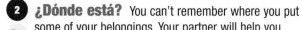

Este (*This*) hombre es (5) _____ papá. Se llama David y es doctor. (6) _____ mamá se llama Rebeca; es periodista. (7) _____ hermana, (8) _____ tía Silvia, es una gran artista. Y aquí está (9) _____ hermano Ramón. (10) _____ esposa se llama Sonia. (11) _____ hijos Javier y Laura son (12) _____ sobrinos. Son muy simpáticos.

2 **¿Dónde está?** You can't remember where you put some of your belongings. Your partner will help you by reminding you where things are. Take turns playing each role.

modelo

Estudiante 1: ¿Dónde está mi pluma?

Estudiante 2: Tu pluma está al lado de la computadora.

1.

2.

3.

4.

5.

6.

Conversación

 3 Describir With a partner, take turns describing these people and places.

 modelo La biblioteca de su universidad

La biblioteca de nuestra universidad es muy grande. Hay muchos libros en la biblioteca.

1. Tus padres
2. Tus abuelos
3. Tu mejor (*best*) amigo/a
4. Tu novio/a ideal
5. Su universidad
6. La librería de su universidad
7. Tu profesor(a) favorito/a
8. Su clase de español

4 Tres fotos Choose one of the three family photos and describe the family as if it were your own. Your partner will guess which photo you are describing. Then switch roles.

Familia 1

Familia 2

Familia 3

I CAN describe the members of a family, including the relationships between them.

Español en vivo

crecimiento *growth* **sabor** *flavor* **vaso** *glass* **huesos** *bones*

1 Identificar Scan the advertisement, and identify the instances where possessive adjectives are used.

2 Preguntas Answer the questions.
1. ¿Quiénes son las personas del anuncio (*advertisement*)?
2. ¿Cuál es su bebida (*drink*) favorita?
3. ¿Por qué bebe el niño un vaso de leche por (*per*) día?

I CAN recognize familiar words in a simple ad.

Communicative Goal
Ask and answer questions about daily activities

3.3 Present tense of regular –er and –ir verbs

▸ In Lesson 2, you learned how to form the present tense of regular **–ar** verbs. This chart contains the forms of the regular **–ar** verb **trabajar**, which is conjugated just like other **–ar** verbs you have learned. There are other regular verbs in Spanish: regular **–er** and **–ir** verbs. The chart also shows the forms of an **–er** verb and an **–ir** verb.

Present tense of –ar, –er, and –ir verbs

	trabajar	comer	escribir
	to work	*to eat*	*to write*
yo	trabajo	como	escribo
tú	trabajas	comes	escribes
Ud./él/ella	trabaja	come	escribe
nosotros/as	trabajamos	comemos	escribimos
vosotros/as	trabajáis	coméis	escribís
Uds./ellos/ellas	trabajan	comen	escriben

¡Tú debes ser Olga!

Vivimos en Zaragoza.

▸ **–Ar, –er,** and **–ir** verbs have very similar endings. Study the chart to detect the patterns that make it easier for you to use the verb endings to communicate in Spanish.

▸ Like **–ar** verbs, the **yo** forms of **–er** and **–ir** verbs end in **–o**.

    trabajo   como   escribo

▸ The endings for **–ar** verbs begin with **–a**, except for the **yo** form.

    hablo   habla   habláis
    hablas   hablamos   hablan

▸ The endings for **–er** verbs begin with **–e**, except for the **yo** form.

    como   come   coméis
    comes   comemos   comen

▸ **–Er** and **–ir** verbs have the exact same endings, except in the **nosotros/as** and **vosotros/as** forms.

    nosotros ‹ comemos   vosotros ‹ coméis
                  escribimos   escribís

Práctica

1 **Mi familia** Susana is describing her family. Complete each sentence with the correct verb form.

1. Mi familia y yo _____ [vivir] en la ciudad de Montevideo, Uruguay.

2. Mi hermano Alfredo es muy inteligente. Él _____ [asistir] a clases de lunes a viernes.

3. Los martes Alfredo y yo _____ [correr] en el parque.

4. Mis padres _____ [comer] mucho; son un poco gordos.

5. Yo _____ [creer] que (*that*) mis padres _____ [deber] comer menos (*less*).

2 **Completar** Juan is talking about what he and his friends do after school. Complete his sentences.

modelo

Yo ___*corro*___ por (*for*) una hora.

1. Nosotros _____ en el restaurante.

2. Elena _____ en su diario.

3. Juan Diego y Sofía _____ café.

4. Ana y Lía _____ el almuerzo (*lunch*).

5. Carlos _____ en la biblioteca.

Conversación

3 **Entrevista** Use these questions to interview a classmate. Then report the results of your interview to the class.

1. ¿Dónde vives?
2. ¿Con quién vives? ¿Compartes tu cuarto?
3. ¿Dónde comes al mediodía?
4. ¿Bebes leche (*milk*) todos los días?
5. ¿Qué días asistes a clases?
6. ¿Qué cursos debes tomar el próximo (*next*) semestre?
7. ¿Recibes muchos mensajes de texto (*text messages*)? ¿De quién(es)?
8. ¿Crees en extraterrestres (*aliens*)?

4 **Encuesta** Ask your classmates if they do (or should do) the things mentioned on the survey. Try to find at least two people for each item.

modelo

Estudiante 1: ¿Asistes siempre (*always*) a la clase de español?
Estudiante 2: No, no asisto siempre a la clase de español.
Estudiante 1: ¿Asistes siempre a la clase de español?
Estudiante 3: Sí, asisto siempre a la clase de español.

Actividades	Nombres
1. Asistir siempre (*always*) a la clase de español	_____
2. Correr todos los días (*every day*)	_____
3. Leer mucho (*a lot*) para los exámenes	_____
4. Compartir tus cosas con tus hermanos	_____
5. Abrir las ventanas en invierno (*winter*)	_____
6. Escribir en un blog	_____
7. Vivir en una residencia estudiantil	_____
8. Comer en la cafetería de la universidad	_____

Common –er and –ir verbs

Common –er and –ir verbs			
–er verbs		**–ir verbs**	
aprender	to learn	abrir	to open
beber	to drink	asistir (a)	to attend
comer	to eat	compartir	to share
comprender	to understand	decidir	to decide
correr	to run	describir	to describe
creer (en)	to believe (in)	escribir	to write
deber (+ *inf.*)	should	recibir	to receive
leer	to read	vivir	to live

Lucía y Marcos **corren** en el parque.

Rosa **vive** en la residencia estudiantil.

¡Manos a la obra!

Provide the correct forms of these verbs.

correr

1. Graciela __corre__ en el parque.
2. Tú _____ en el campus.
3. Mi primo y yo _____.
4. Yo _____ los domingos.
5. Mis hermanos _____.
6. Ud. _____ en la plaza.
7. Uds. _____ los lunes.
8. La familia _____.
9. Marcos y yo _____.

abrir

1. Ellos __abren__ la puerta.
2. Carolina _____ la maleta.
3. Yo _____ las ventanas.
4. Nosotras _____ los libros.
5. Ud. _____ el cuaderno.
6. Tú _____ la ventana.
7. Uds. _____ las maletas.
8. Él _____ el libro.
9. Los muchachos _____ los cuadernos.

aprender

1. Él __aprende__ español.
2. Uds. _____ español.
3. Maribel y yo _____ inglés.
4. Tú _____ japonés.
5. Uds. _____ francés.
6. Mi hijo _____ alemán.
7. Yo _____ alemán.
8. Ud. _____ inglés.
9. Nosotros _____ lenguas extranjeras.

I CAN ask and answer questions about daily activities.

3.4 Present tense of **tener** and **venir**

Communicative Goal | State basic feelings and needs

▶ The verbs **tener** (*to have*) and **venir** (*to come*) are frequently used. Since most of their forms are irregular, you will have to learn each one individually.

Present tense of *tener* and *venir*

	tener	venir
	to have	*to come*
yo	tengo	vengo
tú	tienes	vienes
Ud./él/ella	tiene	viene
nosotros/as	tenemos	venimos
vosotros/as	tenéis	venís
Uds./ellos/ellas	tienen	vienen

Juanjo, ¿vienes con nosotros?

Bueno, tenemos prisa.

▶ Note that the **yo** forms are irregular:

tengo   vengo

▶ The **nosotros** and **vosotros** forms are regular:

tenemos   venimos
tenéis   venís

▶ In the **tú, Ud./él/ella** and **Uds./ellos/ellas** forms, the **e** of the stem changes to **ie** as shown.

INFINITIVE	VERB STEM		VERB FORM
tener	ten-	tú	tienes
		Ud./él/ella	tiene
		Uds./ellos/ellas	tienen
venir	ven-	tú	vienes
		Ud./él/ella	viene
		Uds./ellos/ellas	vienen

Práctica

1 **Completar** Complete each sentence with the appropriate form of **tener** or **venir**.

modelo   Hoy nosotros __tenemos__ una reunión familiar.

1. Todos (*all*) mis parientes _____ , excepto mi tío Ricardo.
2. Él no _____ porque vive lejos, en Guayaquil.
3. Mi prima Inés y su novio no _____ hasta (*until*) las ocho porque ella _____ que trabajar.
4. En las fiestas, mis sobrinos siempre (*always*) _____ ganas de cantar y bailar.
5. Mi madre cree que mis sobrinos son muy simpáticos. Creo que ella _____ razón.

2 **Describir** Describe these people using **tener** expressions.

modelo

Tiene (*mucha*) prisa.   1. _____

2. _____   3. _____

4. _____   5. _____

Conversación

 3 **¿Sí o no?** Decide if these statements apply to you. Then interview a classmate by transforming each statement into a question. Report your results to the class.

modelo

Estudiante 1: ¿Tiene tu madre cincuenta años?
Estudiante 2: No, tiene cuarenta y dos años.

	Yo	Mi amigo/a
1. Mi madre tiene cincuenta años.	Sí	No
2. Mi padre siempre (*always*) tiene razón.	___	___
3. Mis padres vienen a la universidad con frecuencia (*frequently*).	___	___
4. Vengo a clase los jueves.	___	___
5. Tengo dos pruebas hoy.	___	___
6. Mis amigos vienen a mi casa (*house*) los sábados.	___	___
7. Hoy tengo ganas de comer en un restaurante.	___	___
8. Tengo sed.	___	___
9. Tengo miedo de vivir solo/a (*by myself*).	___	___
10. Tengo que estudiar los domingos.	___	___
11. Tengo una familia grande.	___	___
12. Siempre tengo prisa.	___	___

4 **Entrevista** Use these questions to interview a classmate.

1. ¿Cuántos años tienes? ¿Y tus hermanos/as?
2. ¿Cuándo vienes a la universidad?
3. ¿Tienes que estudiar hoy? ¿Por qué?
4. Normalmente, ¿tienes hambre a la medianoche?
5. ¿Tienes sueño ahora (*now*)?
6. ¿Qué tienes ganas de hacer (*doing*) el sábado?
7. ¿De qué tienes miedo? ¿Por qué?
8. ¿Cuándo vienen tus amigos a tu casa, apartamento o residencia estudiantil?

Expressions with **tener**

▸ In certain expressions, Spanish uses the construction **tener** + [*noun*] instead of **ser** or **estar** to express the English equivalent *to be* + [*adjective*].

Common expressions with *tener*

tener... años	to be . . . years old
tener (mucho) calor	to be (very) hot
tener (mucho) cuidado	to be (very) careful
tener (mucho) frío	to be (very) cold
tener (mucha) hambre	to be (very) hungry
tener (mucho) miedo	to be (very) afraid/scared
tener (mucha) prisa	to be in a (big) hurry
tener razón	to be right
no tener razón	to be wrong
tener (mucha) sed	to be (very) thirsty
tener (mucho) sueño	to be (very) sleepy
tener (mucha) suerte	to be (very) lucky

▸ To express an obligation, use **tener que** (*to have to*) + [*infinitive*].

—¿**Tienes que** estudiar hoy? —Sí, **tengo que** estudiar física.
Do you have to study today? *Yes, I have to study physics.*

▸ To ask people if they feel like doing something, use **tener ganas de** (*to feel like*) + [*infinitive*].

—¿**Tienes ganas de** comer? —No, **tengo ganas de** dormir.
Do you feel like eating? *No, I feel like sleeping.*

¡Manos a la obra!

Provide the appropriate forms of **tener** and **venir**.

tener

1. Ellos __tienen__ dos hermanos.
2. Yo _____ una hermana.
3. El artista _____ tres primos.
4. Nosotros _____ diez tíos.
5. Eva y Diana _____ un sobrino.
6. Ud. _____ cinco nietos.
7. Tú _____ dos hermanastras.
8. Uds. _____ cuatro hijos.
9. Ella _____ una hija.

venir

1. Mis padres __vienen__ de México.
2. Tú _____ de España.
3. Nosotras _____ de Cuba.
4. Pepe _____ de Argentina.
5. Yo _____ de Francia.
6. Uds. _____ de Canadá.
7. Alfonso y yo _____ de Puerto Rico.
8. Ellos _____ de Alemania.
9. Ud. _____ de Japón.

I CAN state basic feelings and needs.

A repasar

3.1 Descriptive adjectives

1 Corregir All of these statements are false. Change the adjectives of nationality to make them true.

1. Javier Bardem y Penélope Cruz son norteamericanos.

2. Una persona de Ecuador es estadounidense.

3. Rachel McAdams y Drake son franceses.

4. Salma Hayek es japonesa.

5. Los habitantes de Puerto Rico son cubanos.

6. David Beckham es alemán.

2 Oraciones Combine elements from each column to form complete sentences about yourself and the people you know.

modelo   Mi familia no es grande.

A		B	C	
Yo	Mis hijos/as	(no) ser	alto/a	moreno/a
Mi abuelo/a	Mi padre/		bajo/a	pelirrojo/a
Mi novio/a	madre		bonito/a	rubio/a
Mi familia	Mis padres		grande	simpático/a
Mi familia y	Mis primos		inteligente	tonto/a
yo	Mis tíos		interesante	trabajador(a)
Mi hermano/a	Mi(s) ¿?		joven	¿?

3.2 Possessive adjectives

3 Una familia Complete each sentence with the correct possessive adjective.

1. Me llamo Carmen. _____ hermano es Javier.
   a. Nuestros   b. Sus   c. Mi

2. _____ madre es médica y trabaja en un hospital.
   a. Nuestra   b. Sus   c. Mis

3. _____ padre es profesor y enseña biología.
   a. tu   b. Nuestro   c. Nuestros

4. Él admira mucho a _____ estudiantes porque trabajan mucho.
   a. tu   b. su   c. sus

5. Yo estudio en la misma (same) universidad, pero no tomo clases con _____ padre.
   a. nuestras   b. mi   c. tus

6. Y dime (tell me), ¿cómo es _____ familia?
   a. tu   b. mis   c. nuestro

4 Entrevista Get together with a classmate and take turns asking each other these questions.

1. ¿Cómo se llaman los miembros (members) de tu familia?

2. ¿Cómo es tu familia?

3. ¿Cómo son tus amigos/as?

4. ¿Cómo son tus profesores/as?

3.3 Present tense of regular –er and –ir verbs

5 Oraciones Form sentences using the cues provided.

modelo   Yo / asistir / la clase de arte
Yo asisto a la clase de arte.

1. El médico / abrir / la puerta

2. Juan Manuel y yo / comer / la cafetería

3. Tomás y Mauricio / aprender / alemán

4. Tú / leer / la biblioteca

5. Los perros / correr / el parque (park)

6 Describir Look at the drawing and describe what these people are doing using –er and –ir verbs.

Diego _____.

Marta y Susana _____.

Yo _____.

Sergio _____.

3.4 Present tense of **tener** and **venir**

7 **Completar** Complete the e-mail with the appropriate forms of **tener** or **venir**.

> ✉
>
> Juan:
> ¿Qué (1) _____ ganas de hacer (*doing*) el sábado?
> Mis hermanos César y Beatriz (2) _____ a visitarme de Madrid. César (3) _____ 15 años y Beatriz (4) _____ 17 años. Yo (5) _____ suerte porque ellos son muy simpáticos y (6) _____ a visitarme a la universidad con mucha frecuencia (*frequently*). El sábado al mediodía vamos (*we go*) a un restaurante puertorriqueño. ¿(7) _____ (tú) con nosotros?
>
> Bueno, hasta pronto. Ahora voy (*Now I go*) a la cafetería porque (8) _____ mucha hambre.
> David

8 **Tener** React to these statements logically using expressions with **tener**.

> **modelo**
> Estamos en el Polo Norte.
> **Tenemos frío.**

1. Mi hermana come dos sándwiches.
2. Estoy en una sauna.
3. ¡Mis primos ganaron (*won*) la lotería!
4. Luisa y Marta estudian a las dos de la mañana y están cansadas (*tired*).
5. Estás en *La casa del terror*.
6. Mi clase es en cinco minutos y todavía (*still*) estoy en mi apartamento.

Síntesis

9 **Describe a tu familia** In groups of three, describe your families.

- Describe your family to your classmates in several sentences. (**Mi padre es alto y moreno. Mi madre es delgada y muy inteligente. Mis hermanos son...**)
- Your classmates will work together to try to repeat your description. (**Su padre es alto y moreno. Su madre...**)
- If they forget any details, they will ask you questions. (**¿Cuántos años tiene tu abuelo?**)
- Take turns until all of you have described your families.

Communicative Goal
Watch a short TV ad and describe the characters

 Video

Videoclip

1 **Preparación** Do you like shopping or spending time in malls? What do you prefer: buying things for yourself or for others?

2 **El clip** Watch the commercial *Diminutivo* for **Banco Galicia**.

Vocabulario		
¿Te falta mucho? *Are you almost done?*	**saquito** *little coat*	**conjuntito** *little outfit*
	par de zapatitos *little pair of shoes*	**cerrar** *to close*
apurarse *to hurry*		

Tengo que buscar algo para la beba, si no, Marcos me mata°.

me mata *is going to kill me*

3 **Compras** Fill in the blanks.

comprar	esposo	hija	prisa	regresar	zapatitos

1. Marcos es el _____ de Claudia.
2. Claudia compra _____ y otras cosas.
3. Marcos y Claudia tienen una _____.
4. Claudia tiene _____ porque debe _____ pronto a casa.
5. Claudia necesita _____ algo para la beba en diez minutos.

4 **Descripción** Write a description of the characters. Then, compare your description with your partner's.

I CAN understand some information in a short TV ad.

I CAN describe characters.

Ampliación

Communicative Goals
Listen to a short
conversation in
Spanish, and describe
my family

1 Escuchar

A Listen to Cristina and Laura's conversation. Then indicate who would make each statement.

TIP **Ask for repetition.** During a conversation, you can ask someone to repeat by saying **¿Cómo?** (*What?*) or **¿Perdón?** (*Pardon me?*). In class, you can ask your teacher to repeat by saying **Repítalo, por favor** (*Repeat it, please*). If you don't understand a recorded activity, you can simply replay it.

	Cristina	Laura
1. Mi novio habla sólo (*only*) del fútbol y del béisbol.	☐	☐
2. Tengo un novio muy interesante y simpático.	☐	☐
3. Mi novio es alto y moreno.	☐	☐
4. Mi novio trabaja mucho.	☐	☐
5. Mi amiga no tiene buena suerte con los muchachos.	☐	☐
6. Mi novio es un poco (*little*) gordo, pero guapo.	☐	☐

B ¿Cómo son Laura y Cristina? ¿Cómo son sus novios? ¿Tienes novio/a? ¿Cómo es?

2 Conversar

You are taking a friend to your annual family reunion. So that there will not be any surprises for your friend, you have a conversation with him or her to talk about your relatives. During the conversation, your friend should find out about the following:

- Which family members are coming, including their names and their relationship to you
- What each family member is like
- How old each person is
- Where each person is from
- Where each person lives

I CAN recognize descriptions of a person's physical and personality traits in a short conversation.

I CAN describe my family.

Ampliación

③ Escribir

 One of your online friends wants to know about your family. Write an e-mail describing your family or an imaginary family.

TIP **Use idea maps.** Idea maps help you group your information.

Communicative Goals
Use idea maps to compose a message, and create an illustrated family tree

Idea map:

- 45 años — Simón *padre* — moreno trabajador inteligente alto
- 43 años — Rosa *madre* — trabajadora simpática bonita
- Mi familia
- José *hermano*
- moreno alto escucha música rock
- 15 años

Organizar Use an idea map to help you list and organize information about your family. See the example.

Escribir Using the material you have compiled, write the first draft of your e-mail. Use an appropriate greeting, such as **Querido/a** (*Dear*), and an appropriate closing, such as **Un abrazo** (*A hug*).

Corregir Exchange papers with a classmate and comment on the organization, style, and grammatical accuracy of each other's work. Then revise your first draft, keeping your classmate's comments in mind.

Compartir Read your e-mail aloud to a small group of classmates. Discuss how your families are similar (**semejantes**) and how they are different (**distintas**).

④ Un paso más

Create an illustrated family tree for your family and share it with the class. Your family tree might include these elements:

- A simple title
- A format that clearly shows the relationships between family members
- Photos of family members and their names, following Hispanic naming conventions
- A few adjectives that describe each family member

⑤ Cultura

Compare your family with one you learned about in this lesson: Valentina's family from the **Aventuras** video or the Valdivieso or Bolaños family from the **Flash cultura** video.

I CAN use idea maps to plan a written communication.

I CAN correspond by e-mail with a Spanish speaker using culturally appropriate greetings and closings.

I CAN create an illustrated family tree.

Communicative Goal
Infer the meaning of new words and
phrases in a familiar context

Antes de leer

Audio: Reading

As you read in Spanish, you'll often come across words you haven't learned.

TIP **Guess meaning from context.** You can guess the meaning of unfamiliar words by looking at the surrounding words and sentences.

Examina el texto

Find a few words you don't know. Using the context, guess what these words mean.

Las familias

Me llamo Armando y tengo setenta años, pero no me considero viejo. Tengo seis nietas y un nieto. Vivo con mi hija y tengo la oportunidad de pasar mucho tiempo con ella y con mi nieto. Por las tardes salgo a pasear por el parque con él y por la noche le leo cuentos°.

Armando. Tiene seis nietas y un nieto.

Diana. Vive con su prima.

◄ Mi prima Victoria y yo nos llevamos muy bien. Estudiamos juntas° en la universidad y compartimos un apartamento. Ella es muy inteligente y me ayuda° con los estudios. Además, es muy simpática y generosa. Si necesito cualquier cosa, ¡ella me la compra!

Me llamo Ramona y soy paraguaya, aunque ahora vivo en los Estados Unidos. Tengo tres hijos, uno de nueve años, uno de doce y el mayor de quince. Es difícil a veces, pero mi esposo y yo tratamos° de ayudarlos y comprenderlos siempre.

Ramona. Sus hijos son muy importantes para ella.

Tengo mucha suerte. ▶ Aunque mis padres están divorciados, tengo una familia muy unida. Tengo dos hermanos y dos hermanas. Me gusta hablar y salir a fiestas con ellos. Ahora tengo novio en la universidad y él no conoce a mis hermanos. ¡Espero que se lleven bien!

Después de leer

¿Comprendiste?

Look at the magazine article and see how the words and phrases in the first column are used in context. Then find their meanings in the second column.

1. nos llevamos muy bien _____
2. me la compra _____
3. el mayor _____
4. no conoce _____
5. películas _____
6. mejor que _____

a. *the oldest*
b. *movies*
c. *better than*
d. *buys it for me*
e. *borrows it from me*
f. *we see each other*
g. *doesn't know*
h. *we get along very well*

Preguntas

Answer these questions using complete sentences.

1. ¿Cuántas personas hay en la familia de Ramona?
   _____

2. ¿Con quién vive Diana?
   _____

3. ¿Cómo se llama el sobrino de Santiago?
   _____

4. ¿Quién no tiene hermanos ni (*nor*) primos?
   _____

5. ¿Quién tiene novio?
   _____

6. ¿Cuántos nietos tiene Armando?

Coméntalo

¿Es similar tu familia a las familias del artículo? En tu opinión, ¿son ideales las familias del artículo? ¿Cómo es la familia ideal?

_____

I CAN infer the meaning of new words and phrases in a familiar context.

Ana María. Su familia es muy unida.

◀ Antes quería° tener hermanos, pero ya no es tan importante. Ser hijo único° tiene muchas ventajas°: no tengo que compartir mis cosas con hermanos, no hay discusiones° y, como soy nieto único también, ¡mis abuelos piensan° que soy perfecto!

Fernando. Es hijo único.

◀ Como soy joven todavía, no tengo ni esposa ni hijos. Pero tengo un sobrino, el hijo de mi hermano, que es muy especial para mí. Se llama Benjamín y tiene diez años. Es un muchacho muy simpático. Siempre tiene hambre y por lo tanto vamos° frecuentemente a comer hamburguesas. Nos gusta también ir al cine° a ver películas de acción. Hablamos de todo. ¡Creo que ser tío es mejor que ser padre!

Santiago. Cree que ser tío es divertido.

cuentos *stories* juntas *together* me ayuda *she helps me* tratamos *we try* quería *I wanted* hijo único *only child* ventajas *advantages* discusiones *arguments* piensan *think* vamos *we go* ir al cine *to go to the movies*

Vocabulary Tools

WWW familia

Spanish	English
el/la abuelo/a	grandfather/grandmother
el/la cuñado/a	brother-in-law/sister-in-law
el/la esposo/a	husband/wife
la familia	family
el/la hermanastro/a	stepbrother/stepsister
el/la hermano/a	brother/sister
el/la hijastro/a	stepson/stepdaughter
el/la hijo/a	son/daughter
los hijos	children; sons
la madrastra	stepmother
la madre	mother
el/la medio/a hermano/a	half-brother/half-sister
el/la nieto/a	grandson/granddaughter
la nuera	daughter-in-law
el padrastro	stepfather
el padre	father
los padres	parents
los parientes	relatives
el/la primo/a	cousin
el/la sobrino/a	nephew/niece
el/la suegro/a	father-in-law/mother-in-law
el/la tío/a	uncle/aunt
el yerno	son-in-law

Otras palabras

Spanish	English
el/la amigo/a	friend
el/la gato/a	cat
la gente	people
el/la muchacho/a	boy/girl
el/la niño/a	child; boy/girl
el/la novio/a	boyfriend/girlfriend
la persona	person
el/la perro/a	dog

Adjetivos

alto/a	tall
antipático/a	unpleasant
bajo/a	short (in height)
bonito/a	pretty
buen, bueno/a	good
delgado/a	thin
difícil	difficult
fácil	easy
feo/a	ugly
gordo/a	fat
gran; grande	great; big
guapo/a	good-looking
importante	important
inteligente	intelligent
interesante	interesting
joven	young
mal, malo/a	bad
moreno/a	dark-haired
mucho/a	much; many; a lot
pelirrojo/a	red-haired
pequeño/a	small
rubio/a	blond
simpático/a	nice
tonto/a	foolish
trabajador(a)	hard-working
viejo/a	old

Las profesiones

el/la artista	artist
el/la doctor(a)	doctor
el/la ingeniero/a	engineer
el/la médico/a	doctor
el/la periodista	journalist
el/la programador(a)	computer programmer

Verbos

abrir	to open
aprender	to learn
asistir (a)	to attend
beber	to drink
comer	to eat
compartir	to share
comprender	to understand
correr	to run
creer (en)	to believe (in)
deber (+ inf.)	should
decidir	to decide
describir	to describe
escribir	to write
leer	to read
recibir	to receive
tener	to have
venir	to come
vivir	to live

Expresiones con tener

Spanish	English
tener... años	to be... years old
tener (mucho) calor	to be (very) hot
tener (mucho) cuidado	to be (very) careful
tener (mucho) frío	to be (very) cold
tener ganas de (+ inf.)	to feel like (doing something)
tener (mucha) hambre	to be (very) hungry
tener (mucho) miedo	to be (very) afraid/scared
tener (mucha) prisa	to be in a (big) hurry
tener que (+ inf.)	to have to (do something)
tener razón	to be right
no tener razón	to be wrong
tener (mucha) sed	to be (very) thirsty
tener (mucho) sueño	to be (very) sleepy
tener (mucha) suerte	to be (very) lucky

Nationalities *See page 69.*
Possessive adjectives *See page 70.*

᠗ Communicative Goals: Review

I CAN talk about my family and friends.
• Explain your family relationships.

I CAN describe people and things.
• Describe a friend or family member.

I CAN express possession.
• Indicate your favorite relative or pet.

I CAN investigate families in Spanish-speaking countries.
• Explain how families in Spanish-speaking countries are different from your family.

4 El fin de semana

Communicative Goals

You will learn how to:
- talk about pastimes and sports
- make plans and invitations
- say what you are going to do
- investigate the popularity of soccer in the Spanish-speaking world

PREPARACIÓN

pages 84–89
- Words related to pastimes and sports
- Places in the city
- Word stress and accent marks

AVENTURAS

pages 90–91
- Olga Lucía, Valentina, Sara, Daniel, Juanjo, and Manuel are going to a soccer game. The girls support one team, while the boys support the other.

CULTURA

pages 92–93
- *Real Madrid y Barça: rivalidad total*
- Flash cultura: *¡Fútbol en España!*

GRAMÁTICA

pages 94–105
- Present tense of **ir**
- Present tense of stem-changing verbs
- Verbs with irregular **yo** forms

LECTURA

pages 106–107
- News website article: *Guía para el fin de semana*

PARA EMPEZAR

- ¿Trabajan estas personas?
- ¿Quién está delante de Juanjo?
- ¿Cómo es el chico detrás de Olga Lucía?

Communicative Goal
Talk about pastimes

EL FIN DE SEMANA

LAS ACTIVIDADES Y LAS DISTRACCIONES

escalar montañas
to go mountain climbing

escribir una carta *to write a letter*

escribir un mensaje electrónico
to write an e-mail

escribir una (tarjeta) postal
to write a postcard

ir de excursión (a las montañas)
to go on a hike (in the mountains)

leer el correo electrónico *to read e-mail*

leer el periódico *to read the newspaper*

leer una revista *to read a magazine*

nadar en la piscina *to swim in the pool*

pasar el tiempo *to spend time*

pasear por la ciudad/el pueblo
to walk around the city/town

practicar deportes *to practice sports*

ver películas *to watch movies*

visitar un monumento
to visit a monument

pasear en bicicleta
to ride a bicycle

patinar
to skate

esquiar
to ski

bucear
to scuba dive

tomar el sol
to sunbathe

Vocabulary Tools

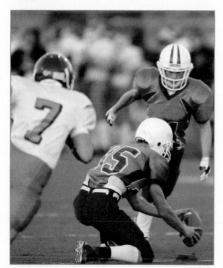

el fútbol americano
football

LOS DEPORTES

el baloncesto *basketball*
el ciclismo *cycling*
el equipo *team*
el esquí (acuático) *(water) skiing*
el/la excursionista *hiker*
el golf *golf*
el hockey *hockey*
el/la jugador(a) *player*
la natación *swimming*
el partido *game*
la pelota *ball*
el tenis *tennis*
el vóleibol *volleyball*

---

ganar *to win*
ser aficionado/a (a) *to be a fan (of)*

el fútbol
soccer

LOS LUGARES

la casa *house*
el centro *downtown*
el cine *movie theater*
el gimnasio *gym*
el museo *museum*
el restaurante *restaurant*

la iglesia
church

el café
café

el béisbol
baseball

OTRAS PALABRAS Y EXPRESIONES

la diversión *entertainment; fun activity*
el/la excursionista *hiker*
el fin de semana *weekend*
el lugar *place*
el pasatiempo *pastime, hobby*
los ratos libres *spare time*
el tiempo libre *free time*

---

deportivo/a *sports-related*
favorito/a *favorite*

ASÍ SE DICE
la piscina ⟷ la pileta (*Arg.*), la alberca (*Méx.*)
el baloncesto ⟷ el básquetbol (*Amér. L.*)
el béisbol ⟷ la pelota (*P. Rico, Rep. Dom.*)

el parque
park

A escuchar

1 **Indicar** Check **sí** if each activity you hear requires a ball or **no** if does not.

	Sí	No
1.	_____	_____
2.	_____	_____
3.	_____	_____
4.	_____	_____
5.	_____	_____
6.	_____	_____
7.	_____	_____
8.	_____	_____

2 **Escuchar** Indicate the activity that best corresponds to each statement you hear.

1. ____   a. ir de excursión

2. ____   b. tomar el sol

3. ____   c. ir a un partido de fútbol americano

4. ____   d. pasear en bicicleta

5. ____   e. practicar muchos deportes

6. ____   f. nadar

3 **Planes para el fin de semana** Berta and Julio are discussing their plans for the weekend. Listen to their conversation and mark the activities that correspond to each person.

	Berta	Julio
1. El domingo nado en la piscina.	☐	☐
2. El sábado tengo un partido de fútbol.	☐	☐
3. El domingo practico baloncesto.	☐	☐
4. El sábado trabajo en el café de mis padres.	☐	☐
5. Voy a ver una película.	☐	☐

A practicar

4 **El tiempo libre** Indicate which word or phrase doesn't belong.

1. bucear • ir de excursión • leer una revista • esquiar
2. el baloncesto • el ciclismo • el vóleibol • el fútbol
3. la natación • el cine • el café • la iglesia
4. el golf • la aficionada • el jugador • el excursionista
5. el periódico • el pasatiempo • la revista • el correo
6. ver películas • ir al museo • practicar el hockey • leer un periódico

5 **¿Cierto o falso?** Indicate whether each statement is **cierto** or **falso**.

Gustavo y Simón   **los chicos**   **José**   **don Fernando**

1. _____ Gustavo y Simón pasean en bicicleta.
2. _____ Los chicos practican fútbol.
3. _____ José escala la montaña.
4. _____ Don Fernando lee el periódico en el parque.
5. _____ Maribel patina.
6. _____ Doña Leonor pasea por la ciudad.

Maribel   **doña Leonor**

6 **Dos amigos** Complete the conversation.

LUISA ¿Cómo te gusta (1) _____ los ratos libres, Pablo?

PABLO Bueno, Luisa, no tengo mucho (2) _____ libre, pero los fines de (3) _____ me gusta ver películas. Y tú, Luisa, ¿cuáles son tus (4) _____ favoritos?

centro	pasar	semana
cine	pasatiempos	tiempo
parque	piscina	vóleibol

LUISA Nadar en la (5) _____, practicar (6) _____, correr en el (7) _____...

PABLO ¡Uf! ¿Y qué haces (*do you do*) para descansar?

LUISA Me gusta ver películas también.

PABLO ¡Excelente! Hay una buena película en un (8) _____ del (9) _____. ¿Quieres (*Do you want*) ir?

LUISA Sí, Pablo. Buena idea.

A conversar

7 **En el campus** With a partner, describe what the people in the illustration are doing. Then rank the activities from the one you like to do the most to the one you like to do the least. Compare your rankings with your partner's.

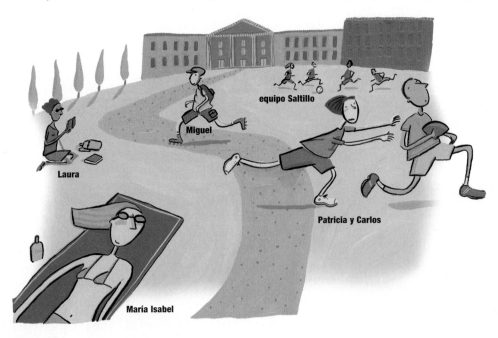

equipo Saltillo

Miguel

Laura

Patricia y Carlos

María Isabel

8 **¿Y tú?** Interview your partner. Use these questions.

1. ¿Te gustan los deportes? ¿Qué deportes practicas?

2. ¿Eres aficionado a los deportes profesionales? ¿Cuáles son tus equipos favoritos?

3. ¿Te gusta ir al cine los fines de semana? ¿Cuáles son tus películas favoritas?

4. ¿Hay lugares para esquiar o ir de excursión cerca de tu ciudad o pueblo? ¿Cuáles?

5. ¿Qué lugares del centro de tu ciudad son interesantes para visitar?

6. ¿Cuántos mensajes electrónicos escribes aproximadamente durante el día? ¿Y cuántos lees?

9 **¿Quién soy?** Using **yo** forms, describe a famous athlete to the class, mentioning the athlete's initials (**iniciales**). The class will guess the person you described.

modelo

Estudiante: Practico el tenis. Soy una jugadora profesional. Mi hermana practica el tenis también (*too*). Mis iniciales son V. W. ¿Quién soy?

Clase: ¿Eres Venus Williams?

Estudiante: ¡Sí!

I CAN talk about my favorite pastimes.

Pronunciación

 Tutorial

Word stress and accent marks

pe-lí-cu-la   **e-di-fi-cio**   **ver**   **yo**

Every Spanish syllable contains at least one vowel. When two vowels are joined in the same syllable, they form a **diphthong***. A **monosyllable** is a word formed by a single syllable.

bi-blio-te-ca   **vi-si-tar**   **par-que**   **fút-bol**

The syllable of a Spanish word that is pronounced most emphatically is the "stressed" syllable.

pe-lo-ta   **pis-ci-na**   **ra-tos**   **ha-blan**

Words that end in **n, s,** or a **vowel** are usually stressed on the next-to-last syllable.

na-ta-ción   **pa-pá**   **in-glés**   **Jo-sé**

If words that end in **n, s,** or a **vowel** are stressed on the last syllable, they must carry an accent mark on the stressed syllable.

bai-lar   **es-pa-ñol**   **u-ni-ver-si-dad**   **tra-ba-ja-dor**

Words that do **not** end in **n, s,** or a **vowel** are usually stressed on the last syllable.

béis-bol   **lá-piz**   **ár-bol**   **Gó-mez**

If words that do **not** end in **n, s,** or a **vowel** are stressed on the next-to-last syllable, they must carry an accent mark on the stressed syllable.

*The two vowels that form a diphthong are either both weak or one is weak and the other is strong.

Práctica Pronounce each word, stressing the correct syllable. Then give the word stress rule for each word.

1. profesor	4. Mazatlán	7. niños	10. México
2. Puebla	5. examen	8. Guadalajara	11. están
3. ¿Cuántos?	6. ¿Cómo?	9. programador	12. geografía

En la unión está la fuerza.²

Quien ríe de último, ríe mejor.¹

Oraciones Read the conversation aloud to practice word stress.

MARINA Hola, Carlos. ¿Qué tal?

CARLOS Bien. Oye, ¿a qué hora es el partido de fútbol?

MARINA Creo que es a las siete.

CARLOS ¿Quieres ir?

MARINA Lo siento, pero no puedo. Tengo que estudiar biología.

Refranes Read these sayings aloud to practice word stress.

¹ He who laughs last laughs loudest.
² In unity, there is strength.

¿Dónde están las entradas?

Communicative Goal
Talk about pastimes
and make plans

Olga Lucía, Valentina, Sara, Daniel, Juanjo y Manuel van a un partido de fútbol.

Video

PERSONAJES

OLGA LUCÍA

VALENTINA

DANIEL

DON PACO

MANUEL

JUANJO

SARA

CHICO

OLGA LUCÍA ¿Puedes ver mi celular?
Ahora no puedo.
VALENTINA Es un mensaje de los chicos.
OLGA LUCÍA ¡Ja! ¡Piensan que van
a ganar!

DON PACO Daniel. ¿Adónde vas?
DANIEL Voy a buscar a Sara para ir al
partido de fútbol.
DON PACO ¿Y quién crees que va a ganar?
DANIEL Pues, supongo que el mejor, ¿no?
Yo no entiendo mucho de fútbol. Mi
deporte favorito es andar en patineta.
DON PACO Yo prefiero el fútbol. El Atlético
es mi equipo favorito, el de mi hija y el de
toda mi familia. ¡Y no nos gusta perder!

MANUEL ¡Aquí están las entradas!
OLGA LUCÍA ¡Termino el videojuego
y salimos!
MANUEL ¡El metro va a estar lleno de
gente! No quiero llegar tarde al partido.
VALENTINA ¡Daniel y Sara ya están aquí!
MANUEL ¿Lista?
OLGA LUCÍA Lista.

ACTIVIDADES

1 **¿Cierto o falso?** Indicate if each statement is
cierto or **falso**. Correct the false statements.

	Cierto	Falso
1. El equipo favorito de Valentina es el Real Madrid.	○	○
2. Olga Lucía recibe un mensaje de Sara.	○	○
3. El mensaje es una foto de Manuel y Juanjo.	○	○
4. Daniel prefiere andar en patineta.	○	○
5. Los chicos ven el partido en el estadio.	○	○

2 **Ordenar** Put the events in order.

_____ a. Manuel busca las entradas.

_____ b. Valentina ve el mensaje.

_____ c. Olga Lucía termina el videojuego.

_____ d. Daniel habla con don Paco.

_____ e. Los chicos ven el partido en la televisión.

MANUEL ¡Las entradas!

VALENTINA ¿Qué dices?

MANUEL ¡No tengo las entradas!
¡¿Qué hago?!

OLGA LUCÍA ¿Dónde están?

JUANJO ¡¿Cómo pierdes las entradas?!

VALENTINA ¡No puedo creerlo!

DANIEL ¡El partido empieza en diez minutos!

SARA ¿Qué hacemos?

OLGA LUCÍA ¿Vamos a ver el partido en
un restaurante?

DANIEL Bueno...

MANUEL Lo siento, pido perdón.

OLGA LUCÍA ¡Hola!

CHICO DEL OTRO EQUIPO ¡Hala Madrid!

OLGA LUCÍA Qué bien juegan, ¿no?

VALENTINA ¿Qué haces? ¡Es del
otro equipo!

OLGA LUCÍA ¿Y?

SARA ¡Ay no! No. ¡Un contragolpe!

Expresiones útiles

andar en patineta *to skateboard*
aquí *here*
el celular *cell phone*
el contragolpe *counterattack*
la entrada *ticket (to an event)*
hala *come on (used to show support in Spain)*
lleno/a *full*
el/la mejor *the best*
el videojuego *video game*

---

el andén *platform*
la bufanda *scarf*
el güiro *percussion instrument*

El fútbol

En Madrid, hay mucha pasión por el fútbol. Los días del partido del **Derbi Madrileño**, entre el **Real Madrid** y el **Atlético de Madrid**, los bares y los restaurantes cerca del estadio están llenos de aficionados. Después, los aficionados al **Real** celebran en la **fuente** (*fountain*) **de Cibeles**; los aficionados al **Atlético** celebran en la **fuente de Neptuno**.

¿Dónde celebran los aficionados a los deportes en tu comunidad?

3 **Conversación** With a partner, talk about pastimes and plan an activity together. Use these expressions.

- ► ¿Eres aficionado/a a...?
- ► ¿Te gusta...?
- ► ¿Por qué no...?

I CAN talk about pastimes and make plans.

Communicative Goal
Identify sports rivalries in Spanish-speaking countries

Real Madrid y Barça: rivalidad total

Soccer in Spain is a force to be reckoned with, and no two teams draw more attention than **Real Madrid Club de Fútbol** and the **Fútbol Club Barcelona.** Whether the venue is Madrid's **Santiago Bernabéu** stadium or Barcelona's **Camp Nou,** both cities shut down for the game, paralyzed by **fútbol** fever. A ticket to the game is always the hottest ticket in town.

Rivalidades del fútbol

Argentina: Boca Juniors vs. River Plate

México: Águilas del América vs. Chivas del Guadalajara

Chile: Colo Colo vs. Universidad de Chile

Guatemala: Comunicaciones vs. Municipal

Uruguay: Peñarol vs. Nacional

Colombia: Millonarios vs. Independiente Santa Fe

The rivalry between **Real Madrid** and **Barça** is about more than soccer. As the two biggest, most important cities in Spain, Barcelona and Madrid are constantly compared to each other and there is a natural rivalry. There is also a political component to the dynamic. Barcelona, with its distinct language and culture, has long struggled for increased political autonomy. Under Francisco Franco's rule (1939–1975), when the repression of Catalan identity was strongest, a game between **Real Madrid** and **FC Barcelona** also symbolized the regime versus the resistance, even though both teams and both regions suffered casualties in Spain's civil war and the subsequent dictatorship.

Although the dictatorship is long over, the rivalry still sends the inhabitants of both cities into a state of anxiety in the hours leading up to the game. Once the final score is announced, one of those cities is transformed again, this time into the best party in the country.

ASÍ SE DICE
Los deportes

el/la árbitro/a	referee	empatar	to tie
el/la atleta	athlete	entrenar	to train
el campeón/la campeona	champion	el/la mejor	the best
		mundial	worldwide
la cancha (de fútbol)	soccer field	la rivalidad	rivalry
la carrera	race	el torneo	tournament
competir	to compete		

ACTIVIDADES

1 **¿Cierto o falso?** Indicate whether each statement is **cierto** or **falso**. Correct the false statements.

1. Madrid and Barcelona are the most important cities in Spain.

2. Santiago Bernabéu is a stadium in Barcelona.

3. The rivalry between Real Madrid and FC Barcelona is restricted to athletic competition.

4. Barcelona has struggled for increased political autonomy.

5. During Franco's regime, the Catalan culture thrived.

6. There are many famous rivalries between soccer teams in the Spanish-speaking world.

2 **Preguntas** Answer the questions.

1. What is the name of Barcelona's soccer stadium?

2. When did the dictatorship of Francisco Franco end?

3. Where is the **Peñarol-Nacional** soccer rivalry?

4. What is Colo Colo?

5. Which two Guatemalan soccer teams are big rivals?

3 **Comparación** What are some famous sports rivalries in the United States? Compare one of them with the **Real Madrid-Barça** rivalry.

4 **Perspectivas** Discuss with a partner why you think the **Real Madrid-Barça** rivalry continues to be so strong.

Communicative Goal
Recognize cultural practices in a video about soccer in Spain

  Video

¡Fútbol en España!

1 **Preparación** What is the most popular sport at your school? What team is your rival? How do students celebrate winning?

2 **El video** Watch this **Flash cultura** episode about soccer in Spain.

Vocabulario	
afición *fans*	**preferido** *favorite*
perder *to lose*	**se junta con** *it's tied up with*

Hay mucha afición al fútbol en España.

3 **Escoger** Select the correct answer.

1. Un partido entre el Barça y el Real Madrid es _____ (un deporte/un evento) importante en toda España.

2. Los aficionados _____ (miran/celebran) las victorias de sus equipos en las calles (*streets*).

3. La rivalidad entre el Real Madrid y el Barça está relacionada con la _____ (religión/política).

4 **Aficionados** With a partner, role-play a conversation between a **Barça** fan and a **Real Madrid** fan.

I CAN identify sports rivalries in my own and other cultures.

I CAN recognize cultural practices in a video about soccer in Spain.

Communicative Goal
Ask and answer questions about plans

4.1 The present tense of ir

▶ The verb **ir** (*to go*) is irregular in the present tense.

ir (to go)			
Singular forms		**Plural forms**	
yo	**voy**	nosotros/as	**vamos**
tú	**vas**	vosotros/as	**vais**
Ud./él/ella	**va**	Uds./ellos/ellas	**van**

▶ **Ir** is often used with the preposition **a** (*to*). When **a** is followed by the article **el,** the words form the contraction **al.** There is no contraction when **a** is followed by **la, las,** and **los.**

$$a + el = al$$

Voy al cine con María.
I'm going to the movies with María.

Ellos **van a** las montañas.
They are going to the mountains.

▶ The construction **ir a** + [*infinitive*] expresses actions that are going to happen in the future. It is equivalent to the English *to be going to* + [*infinitive*].

Voy a buscar a Sara para ir al partido de fútbol.

¿Vamos a ver el partido en un restaurante?

▶ **Vamos a** + [*infinitive*] can also express the idea of *let's (do something).*

Vamos a pasear.
Let's take a walk.

¡Vamos a ver!
Let's see!

¡ojo! Use **adónde** instead of **dónde** when asking a question with **ir.**

¿Adónde vas?
Where are you going?

¿Dónde estás?
Where are you?

¡Manos a la obra!

Provide the present tense forms of **ir.**

1. Ellos _van_.
2. Yo _____.
3. Tu novio _____.
4. Adela _____.
5. Mi prima y yo _____.
6. Tú _____.
7. Ustedes _____.
8. Nosotros _____.
9. Usted _____.
10. Nosotras _____.
11. Miguel _____.
12. Ellas _____.

Práctica

1 **Adivina** Roberto has gone to see doña Imelda, a fortune teller. Using **ir a** + [*infinitive*], say what doña Imelda predicts.

modelo

Tu hermano Gabriel __va a__ ir a Europa.

1. Tú _____ correr en el Maratón de Boston.
2. Tú y tu familia _____ escalar el monte Everest.
3. Tu primo Pablo _____ visitar las ruinas mayas.
4. Tu hermana Tina _____ recibir una carta misteriosa.
5. Tu hermana Rosario _____ patinar en los Juegos Olímpicos.
6. Tus padres _____ tomar el sol en Acapulco.
7. Tú _____ ver las pinturas (*paintings*) de tu amiga en el Museo Nacional de Arte.
8. ¡Y yo _____ ser muy, muy rica!

2 **¿Adónde vas?** You are visiting Madrid with some friends. Work with a partner and ask each other which sites you will visit today.

modelo

Estudiante 1: ¿Adónde vamos nosotros?
Estudiante 2: Nosotros vamos a la Plaza de Santo Domingo.

Conversación

3 Situaciones With a partner, say where you and your friends go in these situations.

> **modelo** Tienes ganas de tomar el sol.

Estudiante 1: Tienes ganas de tomar el sol. ¿Adónde vas?
Estudiante 2: Voy a la piscina.

1. Deseas descansar.
2. Tu novio/a tiene que estudiar.
3. Tus amigos/as necesitan practicar el español.
4. Tienes ganas de practicar deportes.
5. Tú y tus amigos/as tienen hambre.
6. Tienes tiempo libre.
7. Tus amigos/as desean esquiar.
8. Deseas leer.

4 Encuesta Ask classmates if they will do these activities today. Try to find at least two people for each item and record their names. Report your findings to the class.

Actividades	Nombres
1. comer en un restaurante	_____
2. mirar la televisión	_____
3. leer una revista	_____
4. escribir un mensaje electrónico	_____
5. correr	_____
6. ver una película	_____
7. pasear en bicicleta	_____
8. estudiar en la biblioteca	_____

5 Entrevista Talk with two classmates and find out what they are going to do this weekend. Are any of you doing the same thing?

> **modelo**

Estudiante 1: ¿Adónde vas este (this) fin de semana?
Estudiante 2: Voy a Guadalajara con mis amigos.
Estudiante 3: ¿Y qué van a hacer (to do) ustedes en Guadalajara?
Estudiante 2: Vamos a visitar unos museos. ¿Y ustedes?...

Communicative Goal
Recognize familiar words in a simple ad

Español en vivo

Esta familia siempre va a estar unida

porque el **Banco Nacional** siempre va a estar con ellos.

Luis va a trabajar lejos de su familia, pero ellos van a estar tranquilos. Luis va a depositar su sueldo en el Banco Nacional y así él va a ayudar a su familia.

Banco Nacional
Estamos siempre con usted

1 Identificar Scan the advertisement and identify where the **ir a** + [infinitive] construction is used.

2 Preguntas Answer the questions.

1. ¿Quiénes son las personas de la familia?
2. ¿Cómo va a estar la familia?
3. ¿Qué va a hacer (to do) el hijo?
4. ¿Por qué el hijo escoge (chooses) el Banco Nacional?

I CAN ask and answer questions about plans.

I CAN recognize familiar words in a simple ad.

Communicative Goal
Ask and answer questions about activity preferences and habits

4.2 Stem-changing verbs: e → ie, o → ue

▶ In stem-changing verbs, the stressed vowel of the stem has a change when the verb is conjugated.

INFINITIVE	VERB STEM	STEM CHANGE	CONJUGATED FORM
empezar	empez-	empiez-	empiezo
volver	volv-	vuelv-	vuelvo

▶ In many verbs, such as **empezar** (*to begin*), the stem vowel changes from **e** to **ie**. Note that the **nosotros/as** and **vosotros/as** forms don't have a stem change.

empezar (e:ie)

Singular forms		Plural forms	
yo	empiezo	nosotros/as	empezamos
tú	empiezas	vosotros/as	empezáis
Ud./él/ella	empieza	Uds./ellos/ellas	empiezan

¡El partido empieza en diez minutos!

¡¿Cómo pierdes las entradas?!

▶ In many other verbs, such as **volver** (*to return*), the stem vowel changes from **o** to **ue**. The **nosotros/as** and **vosotros/as** forms do not have a stem change.

volver (o:ue)

Singular forms		Plural forms	
yo	vuelvo	nosotros/as	volvemos
tú	vuelves	vosotros/as	volvéis
Ud./él/ella	vuelve	Uds./ellos/ellas	vuelven

▶ **Jugar** (*to play* a sport or a game) is the only Spanish verb that has a **u:ue** stem change. **Jugar** is followed by **a** + [*definite article*] when the name of a sport or game is mentioned.

▶ Stem-changing verbs are identified like this throughout the text:

empezar (e:ie)   volver (o:ue)

Práctica

1 **El día del partido** Complete the conversation with the appropriate verb forms.

> **modelo** PABLO Óscar, voy al centro ahora.
> ¿ _Quieres_ [querer] venir?

ÓSCAR   No, yo los fines de semana (1) _____ [preferir] descansar un poco y mirar la televisión.

PABLO   ¡Qué perezoso (*how lazy*) eres!

ÓSCAR   No, hombre. Es que yo no (2) _____ [dormir] mucho de lunes a viernes. (3) _____ [volver] a casa a la medianoche.

PABLO   Lo siento. ¿Y (4) _____ [pensar] ver el partido de fútbol hoy? (5) _____ [empezar] a las cuatro.

ÓSCAR   ¡Por supuesto! ¿Y tú?

PABLO   Yo también. ¿(6) _____ [pensar] que (*that*) que nuestro equipo (7) _____ [poder] ganar?

ÓSCAR   Claro que sí. ¡Los Pumas (8) _____ [perder] hoy! Nuestro equipo (9) _____ [jugar] mucho mejor (*much better*).

2 **Preferencias** With a partner, take turns asking and answering questions about what these people want to do.

> **modelo** Guillermo: estudiar / pasear en bicicleta
> Estudiante 1: ¿Quiere estudiar Guillermo?
> Estudiante 2: No, prefiere pasear en bicicleta.

1. **tú**: trabajar / dormir
   _____

2. **ustedes**: mirar la televisión / ir al cine
   _____

3. **tus amigos**: ir de excursión / descansar
   _____

4. **tú**: comer en la cafetería / ir a un restaurante
   _____

5. **Elisa**: ver una película / leer una revista
   _____

6. **María y su prima**: tomar el sol / esquiar
   _____

Conversación

3 **En la televisión** In pairs, read this weekend's TV listing of sporting events. Discuss what sports you want to watch on TV and try to agree on one game you will watch together each day.

 modelo

E1: ¿Qué quieres ver el sábado?
E2: Quiero ver el partido de fútbol americano.
E1: ¿A qué hora empieza?
E2: Empieza a las 4:30 de la tarde. ¿Quieres ver el partido conmigo (*with me*)?
E1: No, yo prefiero ver el partido de fútbol nacional...

🔒 www.tv.prom

TV.prom

SÁBADO

13:30 NATACIÓN
1 Copa Mundial (*World Cup*) de Natación

15:00 TENIS
8 Abierto (*Open*) Mexicano de Tenis: Cecilia Montero (México) vs. Sandra de la Paz (España). Semifinales

16:00 FÚTBOL NACIONAL
3 Chivas vs. Monterrey

16:30 FÚTBOL AMERICANO
21 Jaguares vs. Costeños

20:00 BALONCESTO PROFESIONAL
16 Knicks de Nueva York vs. Toros de Chicago

DOMINGO

13:00 GOLF
40 Campeonato (*Championship*) CME: Sei Young Kim, Nelly Korda, Brooke Henderson

14:30 VÓLEIBOL
1 Campeonato Nacional de México

16:00 BALONCESTO
3 Campeonato de Cimeba: Correcaminos de Tampico vs. Santos de San Luis. Final

17:00 ESQUÍ ALPINO
19 Eslálom

18:30 FÚTBOL INTERNACIONAL
30 Copa América: México vs. Argentina. Ronda final

20:00 PATINAJE ARTÍSTICO
16 Exhibición mundial

4 **Encuesta** Ask five classmates about each of these topics. Then, count the number of classmates who answered affirmatively to each question and report the information to the class.

1. Entender las reglas (*rules*) del fútbol americano.
2. Preferir descansar en casa en el tiempo libre.
3. Jugar al hockey.
4. Dormir más de ocho horas el fin de semana.
5. Perder las cosas frecuentemente.
6. Pensar ver una película este (*this*) fin de semana.
7. Jugar al baloncesto.
8. Volver a casa después (*after*) de las ocho de la noche.

I CAN ask and answer questions about activity preferences and habits.

Common stem-changing verbs

e:ie		o:ue	
cerrar	to close	dormir	to sleep
comenzar	to begin	encontrar	to find
empezar	to begin	jugar*	to play
entender	to understand	mostrar	to show
pensar	to think	poder	to be able to; can
perder	to lose; to miss	recordar	to remember
preferir	to prefer	volver	to return
querer	to want; to love		

*Jugar is grouped with the **o:ue** verbs because it follows a similar pattern to these verbs.

Qué bien juegan, ¿no?

▶ **Comenzar** and **empezar** require the preposition **a** when they are followed by an infinitive.

Comenzamos a jugar a las siete.
We begin playing at seven.

Ana **empieza a** trabajar hoy.
Ana starts working today.

▶ **Pensar** + [*infinitive*] means *to plan* or *to intend to do something.* **Pensar en** means *to think about someone or something.*

—¿**Piensan** ir al gimnasio?
Are you planning to go to the gym?

—Sí, **pensamos** ir al mediodía.
Yes, we are planning to go at noon.

—¿En qué **piensas**?
What are you thinking about?

—**Pienso en** el examen final.
I'm thinking about the final exam.

¡Manos a la obra!

Provide the correct forms.

cerrar (e:ie)
1. Ustedes _cierran_.
2. Tú _____.
3. Nosotras _____.
4. Mi hermano _____.
5. Yo _____.
6. Usted _____.
7. Los chicos _____.
8. Ella _____.

dormir (o:ue)
1. Mi abuela no _duerme_.
2. Yo no _____.
3. Tú no _____.
4. Mis hijos no _____.
5. Usted no _____.
6. Nosotros no _____.
7. Él no _____.
8. Ustedes no _____.

4.3 Stem-changing verbs: e → i

Communicative Goal
Talk about movies

▶ In some verbs, such as **pedir** (*to ask for; to request*), the stressed vowel in the stem changes from **e** to **i**.

INFINITIVE	VERB STEM	STEM CHANGE	CONJUGATED FORM
pedir	ped-	pid-	pido

▶ As with other stem-changing verbs, there is no stem change in the **nosotros/as** or **vosotros/as** forms in the present tense.

pedir (e:i)

Singular forms		Plural forms	
yo	pido	nosotros/as	pedimos
tú	pides	vosotros/as	pedís
Ud./él/ella	pide	Uds./ellos/ellas	piden

▶ Stem-changing verbs with the **e:i** stem change appear like this throughout the text:

pedir (e:i)

▶ Here are the most common **e:i** stem-changing verbs:

conseguir (e:i)	repetir (e:i)	seguir (e:i)
to get; to obtain	to repeat	to follow; to continue; to keep (doing something)

Pide favores todo el tiempo.
He asks for favors all the time.

Repito la pregunta.
I repeat the question.

Consiguen ver buenas películas.
They get to see good movies.

Sigue una dieta especial.
He is on a special diet.

¡ojo! The **yo** forms of **seguir** and **conseguir** have a spelling change as well as a stem change.

Sigo su plan.
I'm following their plan.

Consigo revistas en la biblioteca.
I get magazines at the library.

¡Manos a la obra!

Provide the correct forms of the verbs.

repetir (e:i)	pedir (e:i)	seguir (e:i)
1. Arturo y Eva _repiten_.	1. Yo _pido_.	1. Yo _sigo_.
2. Yo _____.	2. Él _____.	2. Nosotros _____.
3. Nosotros _____.	3. Tú _____.	3. Tú _____.
4. Julia _____.	4. Usted _____.	4. Los chicos _____.
5. Sofía y yo _____.	5. Ellas _____.	5. Usted _____.
6. Tú _____.	6. Nosotros _____.	6. Anita _____.

Práctica

1 Por la ciudad Complete the sentences with the correct form of the verb.

 modelo Mis tíos _siguen_ [seguir] el partido de fútbol por televisión.

1. Mi madre va a un café y _____ [pedir] un capuchino.
2. Mi padre va a la biblioteca y _____ [conseguir] buenas películas.
3. Mi hermano menor (*younger*) _____ [seguir] mis instrucciones.
4. Mis padres _____ [repetir] la misma pregunta: "¿Dónde está tu hermana?".
5. Mi hermana y yo _____ [pedir] permiso para volver a casa un poco más tarde (*a little later*).
6. ¿_____ [seguir] tú la misma rutina todos los fines de semana?

2 Combinar Combine words from the columns to create sentences about yourself and people you know.

modelo *Mis padres consiguen libros en Internet.*

yo	pedir muchos favores
mi compañero/a de cuarto	nunca (*never*) pedir perdón
mi mejor (*best*) amigo/a	nunca seguir las instrucciones del profesor
mi familia	siempre (*always*) seguir las instrucciones del profesor
mis amigos/as	
mis amigos/as y yo	conseguir libros en Internet
mis padres	repetir el vocabulario de la lección en voz alta (*out loud*)
mi hermano/a	
mi profesor(a) de español	conseguir viajar a lugares exóticos
	nunca repetir los cursos

Conversación

3 **¿Quién?** Talk to your classmates until you find one person who does each of these activities. Then, ask him/her a follow-up question. Use **e:ie**, **o:ue**, and **e:i** stem-changing verbs.

modelo

Tú: ¿Pides consejos con frecuencia?
Maite: No, no pido consejos con frecuencia.
Tú: ¿Pides consejos con frecuencia?
Lucas: Sí, pido consejos con frecuencia.
Tú: ¿Sigues los consejos?
Lucas: Sí, sigo los consejos. (No, no sigo los consejos).

Actividades	¿Quién?
1. Conseguir entradas gratis (*free tickets*) para conciertos o partidos de la universidad. (Preferir ir a conciertos o [*or*] a partidos de la universidad).	_____
2. Pedir consejos (*advice*) con frecuencia. (Seguir los consejos).	_____
3. Volver a casa por la noche. (¿A qué hora volver).	_____
4. Seguir las instrucciones de los manuales. (Encontrar las intrucciones fáciles de seguir).	_____
5. Perder la tarea frecuentemente. (Recordar traer [*to bring*] la tarea la clase siguiente [*next*]).	_____
6. Repetir las actividades de la clase de español en casa. (Entender mejor [*better*] la lección).	_____

4 **Las películas** Use these questions to interview a classmate. Do you have any answers in common?

1. ¿Dónde consigues información sobre (*about*) cine y televisión?

2. ¿Prefieres las películas románticas, las películas de acción o las películas de terror? ¿Por qué?

3. ¿Dónde consigues las entradas (*tickets*) para ver una película?

4. Para decidir qué películas vas a ver, ¿sigues las recomendaciones de los críticos de cine?

5. ¿Qué cines en tu comunidad muestran las mejores (*best*) películas?

6. ¿Vas a ver una película esta semana? ¿A qué hora empieza la película?

Communicative Goal
Recognize familiar words in a movie poster

Español en vivo

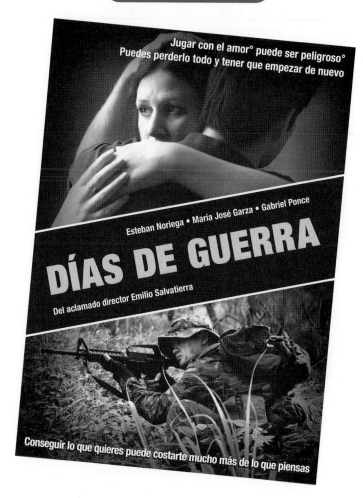

amor *love*   **peligroso** *dangerous*

1 **Identificar** Scan the movie poster and identify the stem-changing verbs.

2 **Preguntas** Answer the questions.

1. ¿Qué palabras indican que *Días de guerra* es una película dramática?

2. ¿Cuántas personas hay en el póster? ¿Cómo son? ¿Qué relación tienen?

3. ¿Cuál de los personajes (*characters*) juega con el amor? ¿Por qué lo crees?

4. ¿Te gustan las películas como ésta (*this one*)? ¿Por qué?

I CAN talk about movies.

I CAN recognize familiar words in a movie poster.

4.4 Verbs with irregular yo forms

▶ In Spanish, several verbs have irregular **yo** forms in the present tense.

▶ The verbs **hacer** (*to do, to make*), **poner** (*to put, to place*), **salir** (*to leave*), **suponer** (*to suppose*), and **traer** (*to bring*) have **yo** forms that end in **-go**. The other forms are regular.

Verbs with irregular yo forms

	hacer	poner	salir	suponer	traer
	to do; to make	to put; to place	to leave	to suppose	to bring
yo	ha**go**	pon**go**	sal**go**	supon**go**	trai**go**
tú	haces	pones	sales	supones	traes
Ud./él/ella	hace	pone	sale	supone	trae
nosotros/as	hacemos	ponemos	salimos	suponemos	traemos
vosotros/as	hacéis	ponéis	salís	suponéis	traéis
Uds./ellos/ellas	hacen	ponen	salen	suponen	traen

Pues, supongo que el mejor, ¿no?

¡¿Qué hago?!

▶ **Poner** can also mean *to turn on* a household appliance.

Carlos **pone** la radio.
Carlos turns on the radio.

María **pone** la televisión.
María turns on the television.

▶ **Salir de** is used to indicate that someone is leaving a particular place.

Salgo de casa muy temprano.
I leave home very early.

El tren **sale de** la estación a las dos.
The train leaves the station at two.

▶ **Salir para** is used to indicate someone's destination.

Mañana **salgo para** México.
Tomorrow I leave for Mexico.

Hoy **salen para** España.
Today they leave for Spain.

▶ **Salir con** means *to leave with someone or something,* or *to date someone.*

Alberto **sale con** su amigo.
Alberto is leaving with his friend.

Margarita **sale con** su mochila.
Margarita is leaving with her backpack.

Hoy voy a **salir con** mi hermana.
Today I'm going out with my sister.

Raúl **sale con** una chica muy bonita.
Raúl is going out with a very pretty girl.

Práctica

1 Completar Complete the conversation with the appropriate verb forms.

> **modelo**
>
> ERNESTO David, ¿qué <u>haces</u> [hacer] por la noche?

DAVID (1) _____ [salir] con Luisa. Vamos al cine. Queremos (2) _____ [ver] la nueva (*new*) película de Almodóvar.

ERNESTO ¿Y Diana? ¿Qué (3) _____ [hacer] ella?

DAVID (4) _____ [salir] a comer con sus padres.

ERNESTO ¿Qué (5) _____ [hacer] Andrés y Javier?

DAVID Tienen que (6) _____ [hacer] las maletas. (7) _____ [salir] para Monterrey mañana.

ERNESTO ¿Qué (8) _____ [hacer] yo entonces (*then*)?

DAVID (9) _____ [suponer] que puedes estudiar o (10) _____ [ver] la televisión.

ERNESTO No quiero estudiar. Prefiero (11) _____ [poner] la televisión.

2 Oraciones Form sentences with the cues given.

> **modelo**
>
> Tú / ? / los libros / debajo de / escritorio
> Tú *pones los libros debajo del escritorio.*

1. Nosotros / ? / mucha / tarea
2. ¿Tú / ? / la radio?
3. Yo / no / ? / el problema
4. Marta / ? / un cuaderno / clase
5. Los señores Marín / ? / su casa / siete
6. Yo / ? / que (*that*) / tú / ir / cine / ¿no?

3 Describir In pairs, say complete sentences with the cues provided.

1. Fernán/poner   2. Yo/traer

3. Nosotras/salir   4. El estudiante/hacer

Conversación

4 Preguntas Ask and answer these questions with a classmate. Are any of your habits the same? *Answers will vary.*

4 Communication Interpersonal Communication

1. ¿A qué hora sales de tu residencia o de tu casa por la mañana? ¿A qué hora llegas a la universidad?

2. ¿Traes un diccionario a la clase de español? ¿Por qué? ¿Qué más traes?

3. ¿A qué hora salimos de la clase de español?

4. Cuando vuelves a casa, ¿dónde pones tus libros? ¿Siempre (*always*) pones tus cosas en su lugar?

5. ¿Oyes la radio o prefieres ver la televisión?

6. ¿Pones la radio o la televisión en cuanto (*as soon as*) llegas a casa?

7. ¿Cuándo estudias? ¿Haces la tarea cada (*each*) noche o esperas hasta el último (*last*) día?

8. ¿Qué haces los fines de semana? ¿Adónde vas?

5 Charadas Play a game of charades. Each person should think of a phrase using **hacer, poner, salir, oír, traer,** or **ver** and act out the phrase. The first person to guess correctly acts out the next charade. *Answers will vary.*

6 Típico fin de semana Interview a classmate about what he or she does on a typical weekend. Do you have any activities in common? **6 Communication** Interpersonal Communication

modelo

Estudiante 1: ¿A qué hora sales de tu casa los fines de semana?
Estudiante 2: Salgo a la una de la tarde.
Estudiante 1: ¿Qué haces?
Estudiante 2: Voy al gimnasio...

• What time does he/she leave the house on the weekend?

• What does he/she do in the afternoon?

• What TV shows does he/she watch?

• Does he/she go out with friends?... *Answers will vary.*

ACTIVITY PACK For additional activities, go to the **Activity Pack** in the **Resources** section of the Supersite.

I CAN ask and answer questions about daily activities.

The verbs ver and oír

▶ The verb **ver** (*to see*) has an irregular **yo** form. The other forms of **ver** are regular but note that the **vosotros/as** form does not carry an accent.

ver (to see)

Singular forms		Plural forms	
yo	veo	nosotros/as	vemos
tú	ves	vosotros/as	veis
Ud./él/ella	ve	Uds./ellos/ellas	ven

Ve a su abuela todos los domingos.
He sees his grandmother every Sunday.

No **veo** el problema.
I don't see the problem.

▶ The verb **ver** also means *to watch.*

¿Cuándo **vemos** la película?
When are we watching the movie?

Veo las noticias por la mañana.
I watch the news in the morning.

Quiero **ver** el partido de béisbol.
I want to watch the baseball game.

Veo a los niños jugar en el parque.
I'm watching the kids play in the park.

▶ The verb **oír** (*to hear*) has an irregular **yo** form and a spelling change in the **tú, usted/él/ella,** and **ustedes/ellos/ellas** forms. The **nosotros/as** and **vosotros/as** forms have an accent mark.

oír (to hear)

Singular forms		Plural forms	
yo	oigo	nosotros/as	oímos
tú	oyes	vosotros/as	oís
Ud./él/ella	oye	Uds./ellos/ellas	oyen

Oigo a unas personas en la otra sala.
I hear some people in the other room.

¿**Oyes** la música?
Do you hear the music?

¡Manos a la obra!

Provide the correct forms of the verbs.

1. **salir** — Isabel _sale_. — Nosotros _salimos_. — Yo _salgo_.
2. **ver** — Yo _veo_. — Ustedes _ven_. — Tú _ves_.
3. **poner** — Rita y yo _ponemos_. — Yo _pongo_. — Los niños _ponen_.
4. **hacer** — Yo _hago_. — Tú _haces_. — Usted _hace_.
5. **oír** — Él _oye_. — Nosotros _oímos_. — Yo _oigo_.
6. **traer** — Ellas _traen_. — Yo _traigo_. — Tú _traes_.
7. **suponer** — Yo _supongo_. — Mi amigo _supone_. — Nosotras _suponemos_.

A repasar

4.1 The present tense of ir

1 **¿Qué hacemos?** You are bored today. With a partner, take turns suggesting various places to go or things to do.

modelo

Estudiante 1: Estoy aburrido/a (bored).
Estudiante 2: ¡Vamos al parque!
Estudiante 1: No, no tengo ganas de ir al parque ahora. Vamos . . .

2 **Agenda para la semana** Make a schedule listing your activities for this week. Write at least two activities for each day. Then in groups of three compare what you are going to do.

modelo

domingo: jugar al tenis, terminar la tarea
Estudiante 1: El domingo voy a jugar al tenis. ¿Van ustedes a jugar al tenis también (too)?
Estudiante 2: No, no voy a jugar al tenis el domingo. Voy a terminar la tarea.
Estudiante 3: Sí, voy a jugar al tenis también. . .

4.2 Stem-changing verbs: e → ie, o → ue

3 **Describir** It's Saturday afternoon. Describe what the Ramírez family is doing based on the cues provided.

modelo
papá / jugar / golf
Papá juega al golf.

1. los niños / preferir / nadar / piscina

_____

2. yo / pensar / jugar / béisbol

_____

3. mamá / querer / leer / revista

_____

4. las gatas Lupe y Cleo / dormir / casa

_____

5. el perro Kiko / encontrar / pelota

_____

6. la abuela / volver / casa

_____

4 **Entrevista** Use these questions to interview a classmate.

1. ¿A qué hora vuelves a casa o a la residencia hoy?
2. ¿Recuerdas la dirección de correo electrónico del/de la profesor(a)? ¿Cuál es?
3. ¿Prefieres escribir un mensaje al/a la profesor(a) o hablar con él/ella en persona?
4. ¿A qué hora empiezas a estudiar por la noche?
5. ¿Duermes mucho? ¿Cuántas horas duermes?
6. ¿Pierdes tus cosas constantemente (constantly)?

5 **Mis pasatiempos** Write a brief paragraph about one of your favorite pastimes. Use at least four of the verbs provided.

| empezar | jugar | pensar | poder | preferir | querer |

4.3 Stem-changing verbs: e → i

6 **Completar** Complete the sentences with the appropriate forms of the verbs.

modelo Tu _pides_ [pedir] dinero prestado (borrowed money) a tus padres.

1. Elena no _____ [conseguir] entradas (tickets) para el partido de mañana.
2. Los estudiantes _____ [repetir] las palabras que presenta el profesor.
3. Mis amigos y yo _____ [seguir] todos los partidos de béisbol de los Rockies.
4. Yo _____ [seguir] el camino (path) para llegar a la cima (summit) de la montaña.
5. Mi hermana siempre _____ [pedir] ayuda (help) para hacer su tarea.

7 **Los videojuegos (*video games*)** Use these questions to interview a classmate. Do you have any answers in common?

1. ¿Te gusta jugar a los videojuegos? ¿Con qué frecuencia juegas?
2. ¿Qué piensas de los videojuegos en línea (online)? En tu opinión, ¿la gente pasa mucho tiempo en línea?
3. ¿Prefieres los videojuegos de deportes o los de acción?
4. ¿Sigues las aventuras de Super Mario?
5. ¿Cómo consigues videojuegos?
6. Antes de (Before) comprar un videojuego, ¿pides recomendaciones a tus amigos?

4.4 Verbs with irregular **yo** forms

8 **Las diversiones** Complete Jorge's description with the appropriate forms of the verbs.

> **modelo**
>
> Mis amigos y yo _hacemos_ [hacer] cosas juntos todo el tiempo.

Los sábados por la noche, yo generalmente (1) _____ [salir] con ellos a la discoteca. A veces, también nos juntamos (*get together*) en una casa: (2) _____ [traer] algo para comer y (3) _____ [ver] una película, o yo (4) _____ [poner] música y bailamos. Y tú, ¿qué (5) _____ [hacer] con tus amigos?

9 **Los ratos libres** You are doing some market research on lifestyles. Interview a classmate to find out when he/she goes out with his/her friends and what they do for fun.

> **modelo**
>
> **Estudiante 1:** ¿Cuándo sales con tu familia?
> **Estudiante 2:** Salgo con mi familia los domingos por la tarde.
> **Estudiante 1:** ¿Qué hacen?
> **Estudiante 2:** Vamos a comer a un restaurante.
> **Estudiante 1:** ¿Cuándo sales con tus amigos/as (tu novio/a)?...

Síntesis

10 **Situación** With a partner, role-play a conversation between two roommates.

Estudiante 1

1. Ask your partner what he or she is doing.
2. Ask what he or she is watching.
3. Say no, because you are going out with friends.
4. Say what you are going to do, and ask your partner whether he or she wants to come along.

Estudiante 2

1. Say that you are watching TV.
2. Say what show you are watching. Ask if he or she wants to join you.
3. Ask what your partner and his/her friends are going to do.
4. Say no and tell your partner what you prefer to do instead.

 Video

Videoclip

1 **Preparación** What role do sports play in your life? Which sports do you enjoy? Why?

2 **El clip** Watch a segment of the documentary *Ejes* about extreme sports in Spain.

Vocabulario	
andar *to go*	**campeonato** *championship*
callejón *alley*	**molar** *to be cool*

Patino por pasión más que por otra cosa.

3 **Comprensión** Indicate whether each statement is **cierto** or **falso**.

1. A Diego le gusta la bici.
2. Sarini cree que patinar es un arte.
3. Pequesaurio prefiere la patineta.
4. A Pequesaurio le gusta la rampa.

4 **Conversación** With a partner, discuss these questions.

1. ¿Qué deportes se pueden practicar fácilmente en tu comunidad? ¿Qué deportes son fomentados (*encouraged*) en tu comunidad?
2. ¿Cuál es la diferencia entre un deporte y un juego? ¿Cuál es la diferencia entre un deporte y un deporte extremo?

I CAN understand the main idea and some familiar words in an authentic video.

I CAN discuss sports and recreation in my community.

Ampliación

Communicative Goals
Listen to a recorded conversation focusing on familiar words related to leisure activities, and discuss my plans

1 Escuchar

A Read the sentences and then listen as first José and then Anabela talk about themselves. Indicate who each statement describes.

TIP **Listen for gist.** When you listen for the gist, try to capture the general meaning of what you hear without focusing on individual words. You will be surprised at how much you can understand!

Descripción	José	Anabela
1. Es muy aficionado/a a los deportes.	☐	☐
2. Pasa el tiempo con sus amigos.	☐	☐
3. Va mucho al cine.	☐	☐
4. Es una persona muy activa.	☐	☐
5. Le gusta descansar por la tarde.	☐	☐
6. Es una persona estudiosa.	☐	☐
7. Su deporte favorito es el ciclismo.	☐	☐
8. A veces va a ver partidos de béisbol.	☐	☐

B ¿Tienes más cosas en común (*more in common*) con José o con Anabela? Explica tu respuesta.

2 Conversar

You and your friend, who lives in a different town, plan to meet in a nearby city. Role-play a phone conversation to discuss your plans. Include this information.

• When you are planning to arrive and go home

• What places you want to visit

• A few activities you can do together

I CAN identify the favorite activities of two people in a recorded conversation.

I CAN discuss my plans.

Ampliación

3 Escribir

Create a short article for your school's student website. Describe at least six leisure activities that students enjoy on campus. Include information about where and when these activities take place.

Communicative Goals
Create an informative text with the help of a dictionary, and prepare a radio broadcast

> **TIP** **Use bilingual dictionaries carefully.** Use a Spanish-English dictionary to look up words you don't know. Consider whether the first option given is really what you are trying to say.

Organizar	List the activities you could include in the article. Use an idea map to organize them.
Escribir	Using your idea map, write the first draft of your article.
Corregir	Exchange drafts with a classmate and comment on the organization, style, and grammatical accuracy of each other's work. Then revise your first draft, keeping your classmate's comments in mind.
Compartir	Exchange drafts with a different partner. Note any words that are new to you, so you can look them up later. Then turn your final draft in to your instructor.

4 Un paso más

You work for a radio station that caters to the Spanish-speaking community in your town. Prepare a radio spot that announces the sporting events taking place this week. Include the following information in your broadcast:

- An introduction of yourself and your program
- A list of local sports events
- The location and time of each event
- A brief sign-off

5 Cultura

Research one of the soccer teams mentioned in this lesson, and write a short report that answers these questions.

- How old is the team?
- Has it won any championships? If so, which one(s)?
- Who is its biggest rival?

I CAN create an informative text about leisure activities at my university to post online.

I CAN prepare a radio broadcast about local sporting events.

Audio: Reading

Antes de leer

This article appeared on the website of one of Mexico City's newspapers.

TIP **Predict content from visuals.**
When you are reading in Spanish, look for visual clues that will orient you to the content. Photos and illustrations, for example, will often give you a good idea of the main points.

Examina el texto

Take a quick look at the visual elements of the article. What do they tell you about the content?

Cognados

Can you guess the meaning of these cognates from the article?

baladas	_____
concierto	_____
contemporáneo/a	_____
creativo/a	_____
festival	_____
fotógrafo/a	_____
origen	_____
pasión	_____
recomendar	_____
romántico/a	_____

GUÍA
para el fin de semana

CINE
Festival de cine latinoamericano

Para los aficionados al cine, este fin de semana comienza el Festival de Cine Latinoamericano en el cine Plaza. Se muestran las últimas° producciones de Juan Pablo Reátegui, Lorena Suárez, Álvaro del Carpio y Diego Bianchi. Recomendamos especialmente *Un día sin° fútbol* del director Juan Pablo Reátegui. *Un día sin fútbol* cuenta la historia° de un grupo de aficionados al fútbol y su enorme pasión por este deporte.

Fechas: 10–14 de marzo
Hora: 8:00 p.m.
Lugar: Cine Plaza
Dirección: Calle Principal #152

CONCIERTO
Canta Maribel Puértolas

Si quiere escuchar buena música, la cantante° Maribel Puértolas va a ofrecer° un concierto en el café La Gloria. De origen puertorriqueño, esta joven cantante ha conquistado° a los románticos con *Cuando tú no estás*, su último CD de baladas. "Va a ser un concierto para recordar", dice Puértolas.

Fecha: 11 de marzo
Hora: 7:00 p.m.
Lugar: Café La Gloria
Dirección: Avenida Bolívar #345

10:00

EXPOSICIÓN

Lucía Velasco:
Cuarenta años de fotografía

Este fin de semana se va a inaugurar la exposición° de la fotógrafa uruguaya Lucía Velasco en el Museo de Arte Contemporáneo. Las cien fotografías que forman parte de la exposición muestran el desarrollo° creativo de Velasco durante sus 40 años de carrera.

Fechas: 10 de marzo – 8 de abril
Lugar: Museo de Arte Contemporáneo
Dirección: Avenida Juárez #248

Después de leer

¿Comprendiste?

Based on the reading, indicate whether each statement is **cierto** or **falso**.

Cierto	Falso	
_____	_____	1. La guía presenta noticias sobre eventos deportivos.
_____	_____	2. *Un día sin fútbol* cuenta la historia de un equipo de fútbol.
_____	_____	3. Maribel Puértolas es una cantante de baladas.
_____	_____	4. Las fotografías de Juan Pablo Reátegui se exhiben en el cine Plaza.
_____	_____	5. Lucía Velasco es una fotógrafa uruguaya.
_____	_____	6. En el café La Gloria hay una exposición de arte.

Preguntas

Answer these questions.

1. ¿De dónde es Maribel Puértolas?
   _____

2. ¿Qué clase de canciones (*songs*) canta ella?
   _____

3. ¿Cuántas fotografías de Lucía Velasco hay en la exposición?
   _____

4. ¿Dónde está la exposición de Lucía Velasco?
   _____

5. ¿Qué película recomienda la guía?
   _____

6. ¿Dónde es el festival de cine?
   _____

Coméntalo

In small groups, discuss which of the activities in the article you would each prefer to do on a weekend and why.

_____

I CAN predict and understand content in a reading supported by visuals.

últimas *latest*   **sin** *without*   **cuenta la historia** *tells the story*
cantante *singer*   **ofrecer** *offer*   **ha conquistado** *has won over*
inaugurar la exposición *to open the exhibit*   **desarrollo** *development*

Vocabulary Tools

WWLas actividades y las distracciones	Los deportes	Verbos
bucear *to scuba dive*	**el baloncesto** *basketball*	**cerrar (e:ie)** *to close*
escalar montañas *to go mountain climbing*	**el béisbol** *baseball*	**comenzar (e:ie)** *to begin*
escribir una carta *to write a letter*	**el ciclismo** *cycling*	**conseguir (e:i)** *to get; to obtain*
escribir un mensaje electrónico *to write an e-mail*	**el equipo** *team*	**dormir (o:ue)** *to sleep*
escribir una (tarjeta) postal *to write a postcard*	**el esquí (acuático)** *(water) skiing*	**empezar (e:ie)** *to begin*
esquiar *to ski*	**el fútbol** *soccer*	**encontrar (o:ue)** *to find*
ir de excursión (a las montañas) *to go for a hike (in the mountains)*	**el fútbol americano** *football*	**entender (e:ie)** *to understand*
	el golf *golf*	**hacer** *to do; to make*
leer el correo electrónico *to read e-mail*	**el hockey** *hockey*	**ir** *to go*
leer el periódico *to read the newspaper*	**el/la jugador(a)** *player*	**ir a (+ inf.)** *to be going to do something*
leer una revista *to read a magazine*	**a natación** *swimming*	**jugar (u:ue)** *to play*
nadar en la piscina *to swim in the pool*	**el partido** *game*	**mostrar (o:ue)** *to show*
pasar el tiempo *to spend time*	**la pelota** *ball*	**oír** *to hear*
pasear en bicicleta *to ride a bicycle*	**el tenis** *tennis*	**pedir (e:i)** *to ask for; to request*
pasear por la ciudad/el pueblo *to walk around the city/town*	**el vóleibol** *volleyball*	**pensar (e:ie)** *to think*
patinar *to skate*	————	**pensar (+ inf.)** *to intend; to plan*
practicar deportes *to play sports*	**ganar** *to win*	**pensar en** *to think about*
tomar el sol *to sunbathe*	**ser aficionado/a (a)** *to be a fan (of)*	**perder (e:ie)** *to lose; to miss*
ver películas *to watch movies*		**poder (o:ue)** *to be able to, can*
visitar un monumento *to visit a monument*	**Los lugares**	**poner** *to put; to place*
	el café *café*	**preferir (e:ie)** *to prefer*
Otras palabras y expresiones	**la casa** *house*	**querer (e:ie)** *to want; to love*
la diversión *entertainment; fun activity*	**el centro** *downtown*	**recordar (o:ue)** *to remember*
el/la excursionista *hiker*	**el cine** *movie theater*	**repetir (e:i)** *to repeat*
el fin de semana *weekend*	**el gimnasio** *gym*	**salir** *to leave*
el lugar *place*	**la iglesia** *church*	**seguir (e:i)** *to follow; to continue; to keep (doing something)*
el pasatiempo *pastime; hobby*	**el museo** *museum*	**suponer** *to suppose*
los ratos libres *spare time*	**el parque** *park*	**traer** *to bring*
el tiempo libre *free time*	**el restaurante** *restaurant*	**ver** *to see; to watch*
		volver (o:ue) *to return*
	Adjetivos	
	deportivo/a *sports-related*	
	favorito/a *favorite*	

∽ Communicative Goals: Review

I CAN talk about pastimes and sports.
- Describe your favorite sport or game.

I CAN make plans and invitations.
- Make plans with a classmate.

I CAN say what I am going to do.
- Say what you are going to do tomorrow.

I CAN investigate the popularity of soccer in the Spanish-speaking world.
- Explain soccer's popularity in Spanish-speaking countries.

AVENTURAS
EN LOS
PAÍSES
HISPANOS

Communicative Goal
Identify aspects of the geography
and culture of Mexico

En Acapulco, un clavadista *(diver)*
salta desde un acantilado *(cliff)* frente
al océano Pacífico. El lugar se llama
La Quebrada y miles de turistas lo
visitan cada *(each)* día.

¿Te gustaría *(would you like)* visitar
Acapulco algún *(some)* día?

MÉXICO

MÉXICO

Área: 1.972.550 km² (761.603 millas²)
Población: 127.600.000
Capital: Ciudad de México – 21.672.000
Ciudades importantes: Guadalajara,
Monterrey, Puebla
Moneda: peso mexicano

SOURCE: Population Division, UN Secretariat

Celebraciones

La independencia de México

El 16 de septiembre los mexicanos celebran la independencia de su país. En todas las ciudades se ponen decoraciones con los colores de la bandera *(flag)* mexicana y se hacen fiestas con mariachis, comida típica y bailes *(dances)* tradicionales. A estas celebraciones se les llaman las fiestas patrias.

¿Qué otras celebraciones mexicanas conoces? ¿Qué características tienen?

ESTADOS UNIDOS

Golfo de California

Baja California

Historia

El Castillo, Chichén Itzá

Los mayas

La civilización maya construyó *(built)* impresionantes ciudades con templos religiosos en forma de pirámide, que hoy en día visitan millones de turistas. Los descendientes de esta civilización siguen las tradiciones de sus antepasados *(ancestors)* y muchos aún *(still)* viven en esa misma área: el sur *(south)* de México y partes de Centroamérica.

¿Sigues alguna *(any)* tradición de tus antepasados? ¿Cuál(es)?

Océano Pacífico

Economía

La plata ▶

México es el mayor *(largest)* productor de plata *(silver)* del mundo *(world)*. Estados como Zacatecas y Durango tienen ciudades fundadas cerca de los más grandes yacimientos *(deposits)* de plata del país. Estas ciudades fueron *(were)* en la época colonial unas de las más ricas e importantes. Hoy en día, aún *(still)* conservan mucho de su encanto *(charm)* y esplendor.

¿Cuál es la actividad económica más *(more)* importante de tu ciudad o estado: la agricultura, la minería, la industria, el turismo, los servicios o el comercio *(trade)*?

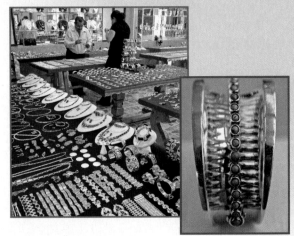

Diego Rivera y Frida Kahlo

Frida Kahlo y Diego Rivera son los pintores mexicanos más famosos. Se casaron *(They got married)* en 1929. Los dos se interesaron *(became interested)* por las condiciones sociales de los indígenas y de los campesinos *(farm workers)* de su país. Puedes ver algunas de sus obras *(works of art)* en el Museo de Arte Moderno de la Ciudad de México.

¿Por qué crees que Frida Kahlo y Diego Rivera son los pintores más famosos de México? ¿Qué características tienen sus obras?

Detalle de un mural de Diego Rivera

Ciudad Juárez

Río Bravo del Norte

Río Grande

MÉXICO

Monterrey

Golfo de México

Península de Yucatán

Puerto Vallarta

Guadalajara

Ciudad de México ★

Uxmal

Cancún

Puebla

Bahía de Campeche

Veracruz

Acapulco

Istmo de Tehuantepec

BELICE

GUATEMALA

Música ♪

La norteña

Como su nombre lo indica, la música norteña viene del norte *(north)* de México. Es popular en el suroeste *(southwest)* de los Estados Unidos y en países como Colombia y Chile. Sus instrumentos musicales tradicionales son el acordeón y el bajo *(bass)* sexto. Entre los artistas de música norteña más conocidos *(well-known)* son Ramón Ayala, Los Tucanes de Tijuana y Los Tigres del Norte.

¿Conoces la música norteña?

Los Tigres del Norte

¿Qué aprendiste?

1 **¿Cierto o falso?** Indicate whether each statement is **cierto** or **falso**.

	Cierto	Falso
1. La Quebrada está en la Ciudad de México.	_____	_____
2. Frida Kahlo es una pintora mexicana.	_____	_____
3. El 16 de septiembre en México organizan una celebración religiosa.	_____	_____
4. Los mexicanos celebran la independencia con las fiestas patrias.	_____	_____
5. En México no hay ciudades cerca de los yacimientos de plata.	_____	_____
6. Diego Rivera fue (was) el esposo de Frida Kahlo.	_____	_____
7. Puebla es la capital de México.	_____	_____
8. La moneda mexicana es el dólar mexicano.	_____	_____

2 **Preguntas** Answer the questions.

1. ¿Cuándo celebran la independencia los mexicanos?

2. ¿Dónde viven los descendientes de los mayas?

3. ¿Quién es Ramón Ayala?

4. ¿Dónde puedes ver algunas de las obras de Frida Kahlo y Diego Rivera?

5. ¿Qué estados mexicanos tienen ciudades fundadas cerca de los yacimientos más grandes de plata?

6. ¿Cuáles son tres ciudades importantes de México?

3 **¿Qué piensas?** In pairs, take turns answering the following questions. Use complete sentences.

1. ¿Por qué crees que la música norteña es popular en Colombia, Chile y el suroeste de los Estados Unidos?

2. ¿Por qué piensas que muchos descendientes de los mayas siguen las tradiciones de sus ancestros?

3. ¿Qué piensas del estilo artístico de Diego Rivera? ¿Prefieres el arte realista o el abstracto?

4. ¿Qué otras actividades económicas crees que son fundamentales en un país como México? ¿Qué productos típicos mexicanos conoces?

5. ¿Qué piensas de las fiestas patrias en México? ¿Te gustaría ver estas celebraciones?

4 **Comparación** Compare the independence celebrations of Mexico and the United States. Include food and music.

I CAN identify basic facts about Mexico by reading short informational texts with visuals.

5 Las vacaciones

Communicative Goals
You will learn how to:
- discuss and plan vacations
- talk about seasons and the weather
- talk about how you feel
- investigate travel destinations in the Spanish-speaking world

PREPARACIÓN

pages 114–119
- Words related to vacationing, travel, weather, seasons, months, ordinal numbers
- Pronouncing **b** and **v**

AVENTURAS

pages 120–121
- Manuel, Juanjo, Valentina, Olga Lucía, and Sara take the train to Toledo for the weekend. Juanjo would rather be at the beach.

CULTURA

pages 122–123
- *El Camino Inca*
- Flash cultura: *¡Vacaciones en Perú!*

GRAMÁTICA

pages 124–135
- **Estar** with conditions and emotions
- The present progressive
- Comparing **ser** and **estar**
- Direct object nouns and pronouns

LECTURA

pages 136–137
- Brochure: *Turismo ecológico en Puerto Rico*

✍ PARA EMPEZAR

- ¿Dónde están los chicos?
- ¿Qué tiene el chico en las manos?
- ¿Hacen turismo o practican deportes?

S Vocabulary Tools

Communicative Goal
Discuss and plan vacations

LAS VACACIONES

el pasaporte

el viajero

LAS VACACIONES Y LOS VIAJES

el aeropuerto *airport*
la cabaña *cabin*
el campo *countryside*
la estación de autobuses *bus station*
la estación del metro *subway station*
el/la inspector(a) de aduanas
    customs officer
la llegada *arrival*
el mar *sea*
el pasaje (de ida y vuelta)
    (round-trip) ticket
la salida *departure; exit*
la tienda de campaña *tent*

¿QUÉ TIEMPO HACE?

¿Qué tiempo hace? *How's the weather?*
Está despejado. *It's clear.*
Está (muy) nublado. *It's (very) cloudy.*
Hace buen/mal tiempo.
    The weather is nice/bad.
Hace (mucho) calor. *It's (very) hot.*
Hace fresco. *It's cool.*
Hace (mucho) frío. *It's (very) cold.*
Hace (mucho) sol. *It's (very) sunny.*
Hace (mucho) viento. *It's (very) windy.*
Hay (mucha) niebla. *It's (very) foggy.*
Llueve. *It's raining.*
Nieva. *It's snowing.*

llover (o:ue) *to rain*
nevar (e:ie) *to snow*

la estación del tren

EN EL HOTEL

el alojamiento *lodging*
el ascensor *elevator*
la cama *bed*
el/la empleado/a *employee*
el equipaje *luggage*
la habitación individual *single room*
la habitación doble *double room*
el hotel *hotel*
el/la huésped *guest*
la pensión *boarding house*
el piso *floor (of a building)*
la planta baja *ground floor*

la llave

sacar fotos (f. pl.)

LAS ACTIVIDADES

acampar *to camp*

confirmar una reservación
  to confirm a reservation

estar de vacaciones *to be on vacation*

hacer las maletas
  to pack (one's suitcase)

hacer turismo *to go sightseeing*

hacer un viaje *to take a trip*

hacer una excursión
  to go on a hike; to go on a tour

ir a la playa *to go to the beach*

ir de pesca *to go fishing*

ir de vacaciones *to go on vacation*

ir en autobús (m.) *to go by bus*

ir en auto(móvil) (m.) *to go by car*

ir en avión (m.) *to go by plane*

ir en barco *to go by boat*

ir en taxi (m.) *to go by taxi*

pasar por la aduana
  to go through customs

pescar *to fish*

montar a caballo

ir en motocicleta

LOS NÚMEROS ORDINALES

primer, primero/a *first*

segundo/a *second*

tercer, tercero/a *third*

cuarto/a *fourth*

quinto/a *fifth*

sexto/a *sixth*

séptimo/a *seventh*

octavo/a *eighth*

noveno/a *ninth*

décimo/a *tenth*

OTRAS PALABRAS Y EXPRESIONES

ahora mismo *right now*

todavía *yet; still*

¿Cuál es la fecha de hoy?
  What is today's date?

Hoy es el primero de marzo.
  Today is March first.

Hoy es el dos (tres, cuatro...)
  de marzo. *Today is March second
  (third, fourth...).*

LAS ESTACIONES Y LOS MESES

el invierno *winter*

la primavera *spring*

el verano *summer*

el otoño *autumn*

el año *year*

la estación *season*

el mes *month*

enero		
febrero		
marzo		
abril		
mayo		
junio		
julio		
agosto		
septiembre		
octubre		
noviembre		
diciembre		

ASÍ SE DICE
el automóvil ⟷ el coche (*Esp., Arg.*), el carro (*Amér. L.*)
el autobús ⟷ el camión (*Méx.*), la guagua (*P. Rico*)
la motocicleta ⟷ la moto (*colloquial*)
sacar fotos ⟷ tomar fotos

A escuchar

1 **Escuchar** Check **aeropuerto**, **hotel**, or **playa** to indicate where you would find each thing you hear.

	Aeropuerto	Hotel	Playa
1.	_____	_____	_____
2.	_____	_____	_____
3.	_____	_____	_____
4.	_____	_____	_____
5.	_____	_____	_____
6.	_____	_____	_____
7.	_____	_____	_____
8.	_____	_____	_____

2 **¿Cierto o falso?** Listen to each sentence and indicate whether it is **cierto** or **falso**. Correct the false statements.

Cierto	Falso	
_____	_____	1. _____
_____	_____	2. _____
_____	_____	3. _____
_____	_____	4. _____
_____	_____	5. _____
_____	_____	6. _____
_____	_____	7. _____
_____	_____	8. _____

A practicar

 3 **Analogías** Complete the analogies.

1. primero ⟶ segundo ⊜ enero ⟶ _____
2. aeropuerto ⟶ viajero ⊜ hotel ⟶ _____
3. invierno ⟶ nevar ⊜ primavera ⟶ _____
4. mes ⟶ año ⊜ maleta ⟶ _____
5. hotel ⟶ empleado ⊜ aduana ⟶ _____
6. pasaje ⟶ avión ⊜ llave ⟶ _____
7. acampar ⟶ campo ⊜ pescar ⟶ _____
8. agosto ⟶ verano ⊜ noviembre ⟶ _____
9. llave ⟶ abrir ⊜ pasaje ⟶ _____
10. maleta ⟶ hacer ⊜ foto ⟶ _____

equipaje	huésped	sacar
inspector	habitación	mar
febrero	llover	viajar
otoño	mayo	piso

4 **Describir** With a partner, take turns describing what these people are doing.

1. Enrique y Gustavo   **2. Yo**   **3. Tú**

4. Don Luis   **5. Marcela**   **6. Juan Martín y yo**

A conversar

5 **Contestar** With a classmate, take turns asking each other these questions. Do you have any answers in common?

modelo

¿Cuál es el primer mes de la primavera?
Estudiante 1: *¿Cuál es el primer mes de la primavera?*
Estudiante 2: Es marzo.

1. ¿Cuál es la fecha de hoy?

2. ¿Qué estación es? ¿Te gusta esta (*this*) estación?

3. ¿Prefieres el otoño o la primavera? ¿Por qué?

4. ¿Prefieres el mar o las montañas? ¿Por qué?

5. ¿Te gusta más el campo o la ciudad? ¿Por qué?

6. Cuando vas de vacaciones, ¿qué haces?

7. ¿Piensas ir de vacaciones este año?
   ¿Adónde quieres ir? ¿Por qué?

8. ¿Cómo prefieres viajar: en barco, en motocicleta…?

6 **La reservación** In pairs, role-play a conversation between a receptionist at a hotel and a tourist calling to make a reservation. Read only the information that pertains to you.

Turista	Empleado/a
Vas a viajar a la península de Yucatán con un amigo. Piensan llegar a Cancún el 23 de febrero y necesitan una habitación para cuatro noches. Ustedes quieren descansar en la playa, pero también quieren hacer una excursión a las ruinas mayas en Chichén Itzá. Llama (*Call*) al Hotel Oceanía y averigua (*find out*) toda la información que necesitas. Luego decide si (*if*) quieres hacer la reservación o no.	Trabajas en la recepción del Hotel Oceanía, en Cancún. Sólo quedan (*remain*) dos habitaciones en febrero: una habitación individual en el primer piso ($175 por noche) y una habitación doble en el quinto piso que tiene descuento (*discount*) porque no hay ascensor ($165 por noche). El hotel no ofrece excursiones a Chichén Itzá, pero hay una estación de autobuses cerca del hotel.

7 **Minidrama** With two or three classmates, act out a scene of people on vacation or planning a vacation. The scene should take place in one of these locations.

- la playa
- una casa
- un aeropuerto
- una estación del tren
- un hotel
- una cabaña

I CAN discuss and plan vacations.

Pronunciación

 Tutorial

Spanish b and v

| bueno | vóleibol | biblioteca | vivir |

There is no difference in pronunciation between the Spanish letters **b** and **v**. However, each letter can be pronounced two different ways, depending on which letters appear next to them.

| bonito | viajar | también | investigar |

B and **v** are pronounced like the English hard *b* when they appear either as the first letter of a word, at the beginning of a phrase, or after **m** or **n**.

| deber | novio | abril | cerveza |

In all other positions, **b** and **v** have a softer pronunciation, which has no equivalent in English. Unlike the hard **b**, which is produced by tightly closing the lips and stopping the flow of air, the soft **b** is produced by keeping the lips slightly open.

| bola | vela | Caribe | declive |

In both pronunciations, there is no difference between **b** and **v**. The English *v* sound, produced by friction between the upper teeth and lower lip, does not exist in Spanish. Instead, the soft **b** comes from friction between the two lips.

Verónica y su esposo cantan boleros.

When **b** or **v** begins a word, its pronunciation depends on the previous word. At the beginning of a phrase or after a word that ends in **m** or **n**, it is pronounced as a hard **b**.

Benito es de Boquerón pero vive en Victoria.

Words that begin with **b** or **v** are pronounced with a soft **b** if they appear immediately after a word that ends in a vowel or any consonant other than **m** or **n**.

Práctica Read these words aloud to practice the **b** and the **v**.

1. hablamos	4. van	7. doble	10. cabaña
2. trabajar	5. contabilidad	8. novia	11. llave
3. viajero	6. bien	9. béisbol	12. invierno

Oraciones Read these sentences aloud to practice the **b** and the **v**.

1. Vamos a Guaynabo en autobús.
2. Voy de vacaciones a la Isla Culebra.
3. Tengo una habitación individual en el octavo piso.
4. Víctor y Eva van en avión al Caribe.
5. La planta baja es bonita también.

Refranes Read these sayings aloud to practice the **b** and the **v**.

No hay mal que por bien no venga.[1]

Hombre prevenido vale por dos.[2]

[1] *Every cloud has a silver lining.*
[2] *Forewarned is forearmed.*

De viaje en Toledo

Manuel, Juanjo, Valentina, Olga Lucía y Sara pasan el fin de semana en Toledo.

 Video

Antes de ver

Predict what you will see and hear in an episode in which the characters take a trip.

PERSONAJES

SARA

JUANJO

OLGA LUCÍA

VALENTINA

MANUEL

EMPLEADA

SARA ¡Un fin de semana en Toledo!

JUANJO Pues yo prefiero la playa.

OLGA LUCÍA ¿Vas a seguir hablando de la playa todo el viaje?

VALENTINA ¡La playa está muy lejos de aquí!

MANUEL Podemos ir a la playa las próximas vacaciones.

JUANJO ¿¡Las próximas vacaciones?!

OLGA LUCÍA ¡Toledo es muy bonito!

VALENTINA Mira. Ése es el Alcázar.

MANUEL ¡Y ése, el puente de Alcántara!

SARA ¡La vista es espectacular!

JUANJO Pero no es la playa.

OLGA LUCÍA Buenos días. Tenemos una reservación.

EMPLEADA ¿A nombre de quién?

VALENTINA Valentina Herrera Torres.

EMPLEADA ¡Venís en buen tiempo! Todavía no está haciendo mucho calor.

JUANJO ¡Está perfecto para ir a la playa!

ACTIVIDADES

1 **¿Cierto o falso?** Indicate if each statement is **cierto** or **falso**. Correct the false statements.

	Cierto	Falso
1. Juanjo prefiere el campo.	○	○
2. Los chicos llegan al aeropuerto de Toledo.	○	○
3. Van a pasar un fin de semana en Toledo.	○	○
4. Juanjo tiene una habitación individual.	○	○
5. Toledo es la ciudad de las tres culturas: la cristiana, la musulmana y la judía.	○	○

2 **Identificar** Identify the person who made each statement.

1. ¡Toledo es muy bonito!
2. Yo los espero aquí.
3. Está bien. La llevo yo.
4. ¡Pues nosotros estamos bien aquí!
5. ¿Y tú estás de mal humor?
6. ¡Ya no tienes que ir a la playa!

EMPLEADA Aquí está. Habitación con tres camas en el primer piso. Ahora los chicos.

MANUEL Manuel Vázquez Quevedo.

EMPLEADA Manuel Vázquez, habitación doble en el segundo piso.

SARA ¡Llevamos las mochilas a la habitación y salimos!

JUANJO Yo los espero aquí.

MANUEL Está bien. La llevo yo.

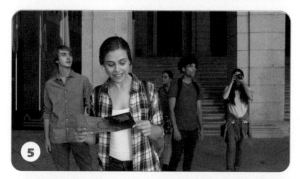

VALENTINA Estoy leyendo que en el Alcázar está el Museo del Ejército.

MANUEL ¡Este lugar es extraordinario!

JUANJO Sí, pero igual estoy aburrido.

OLGA LUCÍA ¡Juanjo! ¡Estamos de vacaciones! ¿Y tú estás de mal humor?

JUANJO ¡Soy caribeño! Quiero estar de vacaciones en el mar.

SARA Pues nosotros estamos bien aquí.

VALENTINA ¡Está sonando la Gorda!

LOS DEMÁS ¡¿La qué?!

VALENTINA ¡La campana! La llaman la Gorda porque es la más grande de España.

SARA ¡Chicos! ¡Allí está Juanjo! ¿Ya estás de buen humor?

JUANJO Sí, ya. Disculpa, es que extraño el mar.

OLGA LUCÍA Bueno, tengo que tomar una foto de Juanjo feliz en Toledo.

Expresiones útiles

la campana *bell*
caribeño/a *from the Caribbean*
cristiano/a *Christian*
el desayuno *breakfast*
Disculpa. *Forgive me.*
dulce *sweet*
estar de buen/mal humor *to be in a good/bad mood*
extrañar *to miss*
igual *just the same*
judío/a *Jewish*
musulmán, musulmana *Islamic*
el nombre *name*
próximo/a *next*
el puente *bridge*
sonar *to ring*

Toledo

Toledo es conocida como la ciudad de las tres culturas porque los cristianos, los musulmanes y los judíos vivían juntos (*lived together*) allí. Hay iglesias, mezquitas (*mosques*) y sinagogas. La ciudad es considerada Patrimonio de la Humanidad por la UNESCO.

¿Conoces (*Do you know*) una ciudad con tantas influencias como Toledo?

3 **En un hotel de Toledo** Role-play a conversation between a hotel employee and a guest checking in.

Huésped Greet the employee and ask for your reservation, say that the reservation is in your name, and ask questions about the hotel and/or Toledo.

Empleado/a Welcome the guest and ask under whose name the reservation was made, say that the reservation is for a double room and the room is on the third floor, and answer questions.

I CAN ask and respond to questions for checking in to a hotel.

I CAN interact on a survival level in some familiar everyday contexts.

El Camino Inca

Early in the morning, Larry rises, packs up his campsite, fills his water bottle in a stream, eats a quick breakfast, and begins his day. Yesterday, Larry and his group hiked seven miles to a height of 9,700 feet. By tonight, that hike will seem easy. Today the hikers will cover seven miles to a height of 14,000 feet, all the while carrying fifty-pound backpacks.

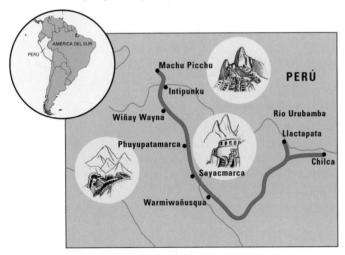

Ruta de cuatro días

While not everyone is cut out for such a rigorous trip, Larry is on the journey of a lifetime: **el Camino Inca.** Between 1438 and 1533, when the vast and powerful **Imperio Incaico** (*Incan Empire*) was at its height, the Incas built an elaborate network of **caminos** (*trails*) that traversed the Andes Mountains and converged on the empire's capital, Cuzco. Today, hundreds of thousands of tourists come to Peru

Sitios en el Camino Inca

Highlights of a four-day hike along the Inca Trail:

Warmiwañusqua (*Dead Woman's Pass*), at 13,800 feet, a hiker's first taste of the Andes' extreme sun and wind

Sayacmarca (*Inaccessible Town*), fortress ruins set on a sheer cliff

Phuyupatamarca (*Town in the Clouds*), an ancient town with stone baths, probably used for water worship

Wiñay Wayna (*Forever Young*), a town named for the pink orchid native to the area, famous for its innovative agricultural terraces which transformed the mountainside into arable land

annually to walk the surviving **caminos** and enjoy the spectacular landscapes. The most popular trail, **el Camino Inca,** leads from Cuzco to the ancient mountain city of Machu Picchu. Many trekkers opt for a guided four-day itinerary, starting at a suspension bridge over the Urubamba River, and ending at **Intipunku** (*Sun Gate*), the entrance to Machu Picchu. Guides organize campsites and meals for travelers, as well as one night in a hostel en route.

To preserve **el Camino Inca,** the National Cultural Institute of Peru limits the number of people to five hundred per day. Hikers that make the trip must book in advance and should be in good physical condition in order to endure the high altitude and difficult terrain.

Wiñay Wayna

(ASÍ SE DICE)

Viajes y turismo

el albergue (juvenil)	*(youth) hostel*
alojarse	*to stay*
el asiento del medio, del pasillo, de la ventanilla	*center, aisle, window seat*
la media pensión	*breakfast and one meal included*
el/la mochilero/a	*backpacker*
la pensión completa	*all meals included*
el puente	*long weekend (lit., bridge)*

ACTIVIDADES

1 **¿Cierto o falso?** Indicate whether each statement is **cierto** or **falso**. Correct the false statements.

1. Lima was the capital of the Incan Empire.
2. Hikers on **el Camino Inca** must camp out every night.
3. Along **el Camino Inca**, one can see village ruins, native orchids, and agricultural terraces.
4. High altitude is one of the challenges faced by hikers on **el Camino Inca**.
5. Travelers can complete **el Camino Inca** on their own at any time.

2 **Preguntas** Answer the questions.

1. When did the Incan Empire reach its height?
2. Where does **el Camino Inca** start and end?
3. What is **Intipunku**?
4. Why do hikers on **el Camino Inca** have to be in good physical condition?
5. What is **Wiñay Wayna** known for?

3 **Comparación** Compare **el Camino Inca** with a famous trail in the United States.

4 **Perspectivas** Why do you think that **el Camino Inca** is so popular? Do you agree with the National Cultural Institute of Peru's limit on the number of people allowed on the trail?

5 **De vacaciones** You want to hike **el Camino Inca** with some friends. In groups, decide how you will get there, where you prefer to stay and for how long, and what each of you will do during your free time.

I CAN identify and discuss popular travel destinations in my own and other cultures.

Communicative Goal
Identify some basic facts about a historic site and understand people's reasons for going there

 Video

¡Vacaciones en Perú!

1 **Preparación** Have you ever visited an archeological or historic site? Where? Why did you go there?

2 **El video** Watch this **Flash cultura** episode about Machu Picchu in Peru.

Vocabulario			
ciudadela	*citadel*	quechua	*Quechua (indigenous Peruvian)*
el/la guía	*guide*	sector (urbano)	*(urban) sector*

Machu Picchu se salvó° de la invasión española […] se encuentra aislada sobre° esta montaña…

se salvó *was saved* se encuentra aislada sobre *it is isolated on*

3 **Completar** Complete these sentences with the words from **Vocabulario.** Make any necessary changes.

1. Las ruinas de Machu Picchu son una antigua _____ inca.
2. La ciudadela estaba (*was*) dividida en tres sectores: _____, religioso y de cultivo (*farming*).
3. Cada año los _____ reciben a cientos (*hundreds*) de turistas de diferentes países.
4. Hoy en día, la cultura _____ está presente en las comunidades andinas (*Andean*) de Perú.

4 **Entrevista** In pairs, role-play an interview between a Peruvian journalist and a Latin American tourist at Machu Picchu.

I CAN identify some basic facts about Machu Picchu and understand people's reasons for going there.

5.1 Estar with conditions and emotions

▶ In Spanish, the verb **estar** is used to talk about how people feel and to say where people, places, and things are located. (See page 42.)

Estoy bien, gracias.
I'm fine, thanks.

Juan **está** en la biblioteca.
Juan is at the library.

▶ **Estar** is used with adjectives to describe the physical condition of things.

La puerta **está** cerrada.
The door is closed.

Todo **está** muy limpio.
Everything is very clean.

▶ Use **estar** with adjectives to describe how people feel.

Estoy aburrido.

¿Estás feliz?

Adjectives that describe emotions and conditions

abierto/a	*open*	equivocado/a	*wrong*
aburrido/a	*bored*	feliz	*happy*
alegre	*happy*	limpio/a	*clean*
avergonzado/a	*embarrassed*	listo/a	*ready*
cansado/a	*tired*	nervioso/a	*nervous*
cerrado/a	*closed*	ocupado/a	*busy*
cómodo/a	*comfortable*	ordenado/a	*orderly*
contento/a	*content*	preocupado/a (por)	*worried (about)*
desordenado/a	*disorderly*	seguro/a	*sure; safe; confident*
enamorado/a (de)	*in love (with)*	sucio/a	*dirty*
enojado/a	*angry*	triste	*sad*

¡ojo! Note that the plural of **feliz** is **felices**.

¡Manos a la obra!

Provide the correct forms of **estar**.

1. La biblioteca __está__ cerrada los domingos por la noche.
2. Nosotros _____ muy ocupados todos los lunes.
3. Ellas _____ contentas porque tienen tiempo libre.
4. Javier _____ enamorado de Maribel.
5. La habitación del hotel _____ ordenada y limpia.
6. Ustedes _____ equivocados.

Práctica

1 **Un viaje** Claudia is going on a trip. Say how she, her family, and her friends are feeling. In the first blank, fill in the correct form of **estar**. In the second blank, fill in the adjective that best fits the context. Make any necessary changes.

contento	**nervioso**	**preocupado**
enojado	**ocupado**	**triste**

modelo

¡Qué bueno! Hoy yo __estoy__ muy __contenta__ porque mañana voy a hacer un viaje a Chicago.

1. ¡Qué nervios! También _____ un poco _____ porque voy en avión y no me gusta mucho volar (*to fly*).
2. Mis papás _____ _____ porque voy sola (*alone*).
3. Mi amiga Patricia y yo _____ muy _____ porque ella no puede ir. Ella tiene que estudiar para un examen.
4. Es que Patricia _____ muy _____ porque este semestre toma muchas clases.
5. Mi novio César _____ muy _____ porque él piensa que yo voy a ir a bailar todas las noches.

2 **¿Cómo están?** Describe these people and places.

La habitación de Teresa

1. _____

La habitación de César

2. _____

Yo

3. _____

El profesor Olmos

4. _____

Conversación

3 **Situaciones** With a partner, use **estar** to talk about how you feel in these situations.

1. Durante las vacaciones...
2. En un examen...
3. Con mi familia...
4. En la clase de español...
5. En días nublados...
6. En un funeral...
7. En una cita a ciegas (*blind date*)...
8. En el invierno...

4 **Describir** With a partner, say how these people are and explain why. Use your imagination.

1. María Laura

2. Juan y Luisa

3. Sebastián

4. Olivia y Marco

5 **Preguntas** Use these questions to interview your partner.

1. ¿Estás ocupado/a este fin de semana? ¿Qué vas a hacer?
2. ¿Estás enamorado/a? ¿De quién?
3. ¿Qué haces cuando estás preocupado/a por algo (*something*)?
4. ¿Qué haces cuando estás aburrido/a?
5. ¿Cómo estás ahora? ¿Por qué?

Communicative Goal
Recognize familiar words in a simple ad

Español en vivo

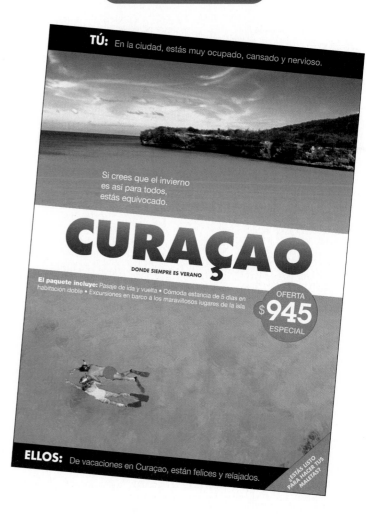

TÚ: En la ciudad, estás muy ocupado, cansado y nervioso.

Si crees que el invierno es así para todos, estás equivocado.

CURAÇAO

DONDE SIEMPRE ES VERANO

El paquete incluye: Pasaje de ida y vuelta • Cómoda estancia de 5 días en habitación doble • Excursiones en barco a los maravillosos lugares de la isla

OFERTA
$**945**
ESPECIAL

ELLOS: De vacaciones en Curaçao, están felices y relajados.

¿ESTÁS LISTO PARA HACER TUS MALETAS?

1 **Identificar** Scan the advertisement and identify the adjectives that take the verb **estar**.

2 **Preguntas** Answer the questions.

1. ¿Dónde están las personas del anuncio (*ad*)?
2. ¿Cómo están ellos?
3. ¿Te identificas (*do you identify*) con la descripción de la vida (*life*) en la ciudad? ¿Por qué?

I CAN describe how I and other people feel.

I CAN recognize familiar words in a simple ad.

5.2 The present progressive

Communicative Goal
Say what people are doing right now

▶ Both Spanish and English use the present progressive, which consists of the present tense of the verb *to be* and the present participle (the *-ing* form in English).

Los chicos **están jugando.**
The kids are playing.

Los turistas **están acampando.**
The tourists are camping.

Estoy haciendo las maletas.
I am packing.

¿**Estás mirando** la televisión?
Are you watching TV?

Todavía no está haciendo mucho calor.

Estoy leyendo que en el Alcázar está el Museo del Ejército.

▶ Form the present progressive with the present tense of **estar** and a present participle.

ESTAR + PRESENT PARTICIPLE
Están cantando.
They are singing.

Estamos esperando.
We are waiting.

ESTAR + PRESENT PARTICIPLE
Estoy comiendo.
I am eating.

Ella **está trabajando.**
She is working.

▶ The present participle of regular verbs is formed as follows:

INFINITIVE	STEM	ENDING	PRESENT PARTICIPLE
hablar	habl-	-ando	hablando
comer	com-	-iendo	comiendo
escribir	escrib-	-iendo	escribiendo

▶ When the stem of an **–er** or **–ir** verb ends in a vowel, the present participle ends in **–yendo**.

INFINITIVE	STEM	ENDING	PRESENT PARTICIPLE
leer	le-	-yendo	leyendo
oír	o-	-yendo	oyendo
traer	tra-	-yendo	trayendo

Práctica

1 De vacaciones Mauricio and his family are vacationing in Mazatlán, Mexico. Complete his description of what everyone is doing right now.

modelo

Yo _estoy tomando el sol._ 1. Mi mamá _____

2. Mi hermana Elena
_____

3. Mis hermanos _____
_____

4. Mi papá _____
_____

5. Mi prima Paula _____
_____

2 Un amigo preguntón You are on summer vacation. A nosy friend calls you at all hours to see what you are doing. Look at the clocks and tell him.

modelo

Estoy descansando.

1. _____   2. _____

3. _____   4. _____

Conversación

3 **Describir** With a partner, use the present progressive to describe what is going on in this beach scene.

María Teresa
Andrea
Nicolás
Sra. Morales
Rodrigo
José Luis
Isabel

4 **¿Qué están haciendo?** In pairs, take turns asking questions and giving answers about what these celebrities are doing right now. Be creative!

modelo

Estudiante 1: ¿Qué está haciendo Shakira?
Estudiante 2: Shakira está cantando ahora mismo.

1. LeBron James
2. Sonia Sotomayor
3. Drake
4. Zendaya
5. Stephen King
6. Venus y Serena Williams

5 **Conversar** You and a classmate are each babysitting a group of children. In pairs, role-play a phone conversation using these cues. Be creative!

Estudiante 1	Estudiante 2
1. Ask what the kids are doing.	2. Tell your partner that two of your kids are doing their homework. Then ask what the kids at his/her house are doing.
3. Tell your partner that two of your kids are running and dancing in the house.	4. Tell your partner that one of the kids is reading.
5. Tell your partner that you are tired and that two of your kids are watching TV and eating pizza.	6. Tell your partner that one of the kids is sleeping.
7. Tell your partner you have to go; the kids are playing soccer in the house.	8. Say goodbye and good luck (**¡Buena suerte!**).

I CAN say what people are doing right now.

Irregular present participles

▸ The verbs **ir, poder,** and **venir** have irregular present participles (**yendo, pudiendo, viniendo**). Several other verbs have irregular present participles.

-ir stem-changing verbs

e:ie in the present tense	PRESENT PARTICIPLE
preferir →	prefiriendo
sentir	sintiendo
e:i in the present tense	
conseguir	consiguiendo
pedir →	pidiendo
seguir	siguiendo
o:ue in the present tense	
dormir →	durmiendo

Using the present progressive

▸ The present progressive is used less in Spanish than in English. In Spanish, the present progressive emphasizes that an action is *in progress*.

Ella todavía **está escuchando** música.
She is still listening to music.

Javier **está estudiando** ahora mismo.
Javier is studying right now.

▸ In English, the present progressive is used with actions that occur over time or in the future. In Spanish, the simple present tense is used.

Tomo inglés este semestre.
I'm taking English this semester.

Salgo hoy a las tres.
I'm leaving today at three.

¡Manos a la obra!

Create complete sentences using the present progressive.

1. Mis amigos / descansar en la playa Mis amigos están descansando en la playa.
2. Nosotros / practicar deportes _____
3. Carmen / comer en casa _____
4. Nuestro equipo / ganar el partido _____
5. Yo / traer el periódico _____
6. Él / pensar en comprar una bicicleta _____
7. Ustedes / explicar la lección _____
8. José y Francisco / pedir café _____
9. Marisa / leer el correo electrónico _____
10. Yo / preparar sándwiches _____
11. Carlos / sacar fotos _____
12. ¿Tú / dormir? _____

Communicative Goal | Describe people

5.3 Comparing ser and estar

▶ **Ser** and **estar** both mean *to be,* but are used for different purposes.

Uses of ser

Nationality and place of origin	Los Gómez son peruanos. Luisa es de Cuzco.
Profession or occupation	Liliana es ingeniera. Ana y yo somos periodistas.
Characteristics of people and things	Sus padres son simpáticos. El hotel es muy grande.
Generalizations	Es necesario trabajar. ¡Es difícil estudiar en la playa!
Possession	Las maletas son de Silvia. El pasaporte es de mi amigo.
What something is made of	Las llaves son de metal. Esta botella es de plástico.
Time and date	¿Qué hora es? Son las tres. ¿Qué día es hoy? Hoy es lunes. Hoy es el dos de abril.
Where or when an event occurs	La fiesta es en mi casa. El concierto es a las ocho.

¡Estamos de vacaciones! ¿Y tú estás de mal humor?

El desayuno es de siete a nueve en la planta baja.

Uses of estar

Location or spatial relationships	El hotel no está lejos. Adrián está en el cine.
Health	¿Cómo estás? Estoy enfermo.
Physical states and conditions	El conductor está cansado. Las puertas están cerradas.
Emotional states	Ignacio está aburrido. Estoy contenta con el viaje.
Certain weather expressions	Está despejado. Está nublado.
Ongoing actions (progressive tenses)	Estamos buscando el museo. Catalina está durmiendo.

Práctica

1 **Completar** Complete this conversation with the correct forms of **ser** and **estar**.

CAMILA ¡Hola, Ricardo! ¿Cómo (1) _____ ?

RICARDO Bien, gracias. Oye... ¡Qué guapa (2) _____ hoy!

CAMILA Gracias. (3) _____ muy amable. Oye, ¿qué (4) _____ haciendo? (5) ¿ _____ ocupado?

RICARDO No, sólo (6) _____ escribiendo un mensaje electrónico a mi amigo David.

CAMILA ¿De dónde (7) _____ él?

RICARDO David (8) _____ de Ponce, pero ahora él y su familia (9) _____ de vacaciones en Miami.

CAMILA Y... ¿cómo (10) _____ David?

RICARDO (11) _____ moreno y un poco bajo. También (12) _____ muy listo. ¿Lo quieres conocer?

2 **En el aeropuerto** Use **ser** and **estar** to describe this scene at an airport in Spain. Say what these people look like, how they are feeling, and what they are doing.

modelo

Anita es una niña pequeña, delgada y morena. Ella está triste y ahora está llorando (*crying*).

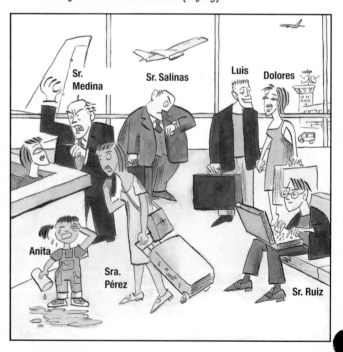

Conversación

3 **Describir** With a partner, take turns describing the people in the drawing without saying their names. Use these questions to guide your descriptions. Your partner has to guess who the person is.

- ¿Dónde está(n)?
- ¿Cómo es?/¿Cómo son?
- ¿Cómo está(n)?
- ¿Qué está(n) haciendo?

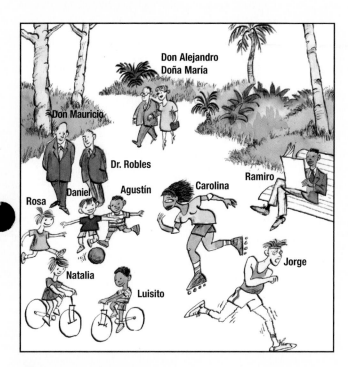

4 **Adivinar** Using these questions as a guide, describe one classmate and one celebrity to your partner. Don't mention their names. Your partner will guess whom you are describing.

- ¿Cómo es?
- ¿Cómo está?
- ¿De dónde es?
- ¿Dónde está?
- ¿Qué está haciendo?

I CAN describe people.

Ser and estar with adjectives

▶ With many adjectives, both **ser** and **estar** can be used, but the meaning changes. Statements with **ser** describe inherent qualities. **Estar** describes temporary and changeable conditions.

Juan **es** nervioso.
Juan is a nervous person.

Juan **está** nervioso hoy.
Juan is nervous today.

Ana **es** elegante.
Ana is an elegant person.

Ana **está** elegante hoy.
Ana looks elegant today.

▶ The meaning of some adjectives changes completely depending on whether they are used with **ser** or **estar**.

With *ser*	With *estar*
El chico **es listo.**	El chico **está listo.**
The boy is smart.	*The boy is ready.*
La profesora **es mala.**	La profesora **está mala.**
The professor is bad.	*The professor is sick.*
Jaime **es aburrido.**	Jaime **está aburrido.**
Jaime is boring.	*Jaime is bored.*
Las peras **son verdes.**	Las peras **están verdes.**
The pears are green.	*The pears are not ripe.*
El gato **es muy vivo.**	El gato **está vivo.**
The cat is very clever.	*The cat is alive.*
Él **es seguro.**	Él no **está seguro.**
He's a confident person.	*He's not sure.*

¡Ojo! Note that when referring to an object, **ser seguro** means *to be safe*: **El ascensor es seguro.** (*The elevator is safe.*)

¡Manos a la obra!

Form sentences with **ser** or **estar.** Make any necessary changes.

1. Alejandra / cansado
   Alejandra está cansada.
2. ellos / guapo hoy
3. Carmen / alto
4. yo / la clase de español
5. película / a las once
6. hoy / viernes
7. nosotras / enojado
8. Antonio / médico
9. Romeo y Julieta / enamorado
10. libros / de María Eugenia
11. Marisa y Juan / estudiando
12. fiesta / gimnasio

5.4 Direct object nouns and pronouns

▶ A direct object noun receives the action of the verb directly and generally follows the verb. In this example, the direct object noun answers the question *What is Valentina reading?*

SUBJECT	VERB	DIRECT OBJECT NOUN
Valentina	está leyendo	un libro.
Valentina	*is reading*	*a book.*

Yo los espero aquí.

La llevo yo.

▶ When a direct object noun is a person or a pet, it is preceded by the word **a**. This is called the "personal **a**" and it has no English equivalent.

Marta busca **a** su perro Lucas.   Escucho **al** profesor.
Marta is looking for her dog, Lucas.   *I am listening to the professor.*

▶ Direct object pronouns replace direct object nouns. Like English, Spanish sometimes uses a direct object pronoun to avoid repetition.

DIRECT OBJECT	DIRECT OBJECT PRONOUN	
Maribel hace las maletas.	Maribel las hace.	*Maribel packs them.*
Felipe compra el pasaje.	Felipe lo compra.	*Felipe buys it.*
Vicky tiene la llave.	Vicky la tiene.	*Vicky has it.*

Direct object pronouns

Singular forms		Plural forms	
me	*me*	nos	*us*
te	*you (fam.)*	os	*you (fam.)*
lo	*you (m., form.); him; it (m.)*	los	*you (m.); them (m.)*
la	*you (f., form.); her; it (f.)*	las	*you (f.); them (f.)*

Práctica

1 Sustitución Professor Vega's class is planning a trip to Costa Rica. Describe their preparations by changing the direct object nouns to direct object pronouns.

modelo

La profesora Vega tiene su pasaporte.
La profesora Vega lo tiene.

1. Gustavo y Héctor confirman las reservaciones.
2. Nosotros leemos los folletos (*brochures*).
3. Ana María estudia el mapa.
4. Yo aprendo los nombres de los monumentos de San José.
5. Alicia escucha a la profesora.
6. Miguel escribe las instrucciones para llegar al hotel.

2 Vacaciones Ramón is going to San Juan, Puerto Rico, with friends. Express his thoughts more succinctly using direct object pronouns.

modelo

Quiero hacer una excursión.
Quiero hacerla./La quiero hacer.

1. Voy a hacer mi maleta.
2. No necesitamos llevar los pasaportes.
3. Marcos está pidiendo el folleto turístico.
4. Javier debe llamar (*call*) a sus padres.
5. Ellos esperan visitar las playas.
6. No puedo llamar a Javier ahora mismo.

3 ¿Qué estás haciendo? A classmate has called to find out what you are doing to prepare for your trip to Cancún. Answer your partner's questions. Follow the model.

modelo

preparar el itinerario de viaje
Estudiante 1: ¿Estás preparando el itinerario de viaje?
Estudiante 2: No, no lo estoy preparando.
Estudiante 1: ¿Cuándo lo vas a preparar?
Estudiante 2: Voy a prepararlo mañana (el lunes, a las dos, etc.).

1. preparar los documentos de viaje
2. buscar información de hoteles en Internet
3. practicar español
4. pensar en actividades para hacer
5. hacer las maletas

Conversación

 4 **En un café** Get together with a partner and take turns asking each other questions about the drawing.

 modelo

Estudiante 1: ¿Quién está leyendo el mapa?
Estudiante 2: El Sr. Torres está leyéndolo.

Ana
Santiago
Sra. Torres
Sr. Torres
Mario

5 **Entrevista** Use these questions to interview a classmate. Your partner should respond using direct object pronouns.

modelo

Estudiante 1: ¿Quién lee el periódico en tu casa?
Estudiante 2: Mi papá lo lee.

1. ¿Quién prepara la comida (*food*) en tu casa?

2. ¿Visitas a tus parientes con frecuencia (*frequently*)?

3. ¿Cuándo ves a tus amigos/as?

4. ¿Estudias español todos los días?

5. ¿Traes tu libro a clase? ¿Y tu cuaderno?

6. ¿Cuándo vas a hacer la tarea de la clase de español?

7. ¿Ves mucho la televisión? ¿Cuándo vas a ver tu programa favorito?

8. ¿Piensas hacer un viaje pronto (*soon*)? ¿Necesitas tu pasaporte?

▶ It is common to use the direct object pronoun when the direct object noun has been mentioned before.

—¿Quieres a tu madre?
Do you love your mother?

—Sí, la quiero mucho.
Yes, I love her very much.

▶ In affirmative sentences and affirmative questions, direct object pronouns generally appear before the conjugated verb. In negative sentences and negative questions, the pronoun is placed between the word **no** and the verb.

Armando me escucha.	Armando no me escucha.
Katia las tiene.	Katia no las tiene.
¿Lo quieres?	¿No lo quieres?

▶ In the present progressive and infinitive constructions, such as **ir a** + [*infinitive*], the direct object pronoun can be placed before the conjugated form or attached to the present participle or infinitive.

Laura las está escribiendo.	Laura está escribiéndolas.
Lo vamos a hacer.	Vamos a hacerlo.
Las va a confirmar.	Va a confirmarlas.

¡ojo! When a pronoun is attached to the present participle, an accent mark is added to maintain the proper stress: **Laura está escribiéndolas. José está escuchándote.**

¡Manos a la obra!

Choose the correct response.

1. ¿Me puedes llevar al partido de fútbol?
   a. Sí, los puedo llevar.   b. Sí, te puedo llevar.

2. ¿Quién tiene los pasajes?
   a. Yo lo tengo.   b. Mónica los tiene.

3. ¿Vas a llevar a tu hermana a la playa?
   a. No, no voy a llevarla.   b. No, no voy a llevarte.

4. ¿Vas a hacer las maletas?
   a. Sí, voy a hacerla.   b. Sí, voy a hacerlas.

5. ¿Quién tiene la llave de nuestra habitación?
   a. Yo no la tengo.   b. Yo lo tengo.

6. ¿Quién revisa los documentos?
   a. El inspector te revisa.   b. El inspector los revisa.

7. ¿Vamos a confirmar los pasajes?
   a. Sí, la vamos a confirmar.   b. No, no los vamos a confirmar.

I CAN ask and answer questions about activities.

A repasar

5.1 Estar with conditions and emotions

1 **Cuando...** Describe how you feel in these situations.

1. Hace sol.
2. Tienes mucho trabajo.
3. Viajas en avión.
4. Vas al partido de tu equipo favorito.
5. Tu habitación está desordenada.
6. Pierdes las llaves de tu auto.

2 **Describir** In pairs, take turns describing these people. Say where they are from, what they are like, and how they are feeling.

1. tu mejor (*best*) amigo/a
2. tus padres
3. tu profesor(a) favorito/a
4. tu compañero/a de cuarto
5. tu primo/a favorito/a
6. tus abuelos

5.2 The present progressive

3 **De vacaciones** Gabriela and her family are on a Caribbean cruise and the ship has stopped in San Juan. Complete her e-mail with the correct forms of the present progressive.

> Nora:
> Por fin (*Finally*), tengo unos minutos libres.
> Mateo (1) _____ [comprar] tarjetas
> postales y Elenita (2) _____ [dormir]
> una siesta. Nuestros amigos César y Ángela
> (3) _____ [comer] en el café Aromas.
> Los señores Villalobos (4) _____ [pasear]
> por el centro. Nosotros (5) _____ [pensar]
> hacer una excursión con ellos mañana a El Yunque
> o al Viejo San Juan. Y tú, ¿cómo (6) _____
> [pasar] las vacaciones?
> Gabriela

4 **Situaciones** With a partner, describe what these people are doing in these situations. Write at least two activities for each item. Then get together with another pair and compare your ideas.

modelo

yo / en las montañas
Yo estoy acampando en las montañas. Yo estoy durmiendo en una tienda de campaña.

1. el inspector de aduanas / en el aeropuerto
2. mi familia / en el parque
3. los turistas / en el hotel
4. los pasajeros / en un crucero (*cruise ship*)
5. mis padres / en la estación de autobuses
6. yo / en la playa
7. mis amigos y yo / en el campo
8. mi compañero/a de cuarto / en la habitación

5.3 Comparing ser and estar

5 **Completar** Complete each sentence with the correct form of **ser** o **estar**.

1. Carolina _____ mala. Ella no me quiere ayudar con la tarea.
2. El ascensor _____ seguro.
3. Nosotros _____ listos para ir de pesca.
4. Las bananas _____ verdes. Necesitan dos días para madurar (*to ripen*).
5. Ellos _____ aburridos porque el programa _____ aburrido.
6. Ernesto _____ muy listo. Él saca buenas notas (*grades*) en los exámenes.

6 **Combinar** Combine elements from each column to form sentences about a hotel and the people there.

modelo   *Mi amiga es simpática.*

A	B	C
yo	(no) ser	bonito/a
tú	(no) estar	grande
mi amigo/a		norteamericano/a
el hotel		ocupado/a
el empleado		trabajador(a)
nosotros/as		de vacaciones
los huéspedes		en el tercer piso
las habitaciones		en la habitación
el equipaje		cómodo/a
		simpático/a

5.4 Direct object nouns and pronouns

7 Emparejar Match the video characters with the direct object pronouns in the sentences. Then form the questions that correspond to these answers.

A	B	C	D
OLGA LUCÍA Y SARA	JUANJO	MANUEL Y VALENTINA	EMPLEADA

1. Sí, la veo. _____
2. Sí, los vemos. _____
3. Sí, las vemos. _____
4. Sí, lo veo. _____

8 Entrevista Use these questions to interview a classmate. Your partner should respond using direct object pronouns.

1. ¿Te vienen a visitar tus padres este fin de semana?
2. ¿Ves a tus abuelos con frecuencia?
3. ¿Ahora mismo te están esperando tus amigos/as? ¿Dónde?
4. ¿Por qué estudias español?
5. Cuando vienes a la universidad, ¿dónde llevas los libros?
6. ¿Traes tu computadora a clase?
7. ¿Nos está mirando el/la profesor(a)?
8. ¿Me estás escuchando?

Síntesis

9 Nuestras vacaciones You are spending your vacation at one of these places: **un centro turístico** (*resort*) **en las montañas o cerca del mar, un campamento** (*campground*), or **una ciudad.** Describe your vacation to two classmates. What do your vacations have in common?

- Describe the location and who is with you.
- Describe the weather.
- Describe your accommodations.
- Describe what activities you are doing during your vacation, using the present progressive.

Communicative Goal
Watch a report and talk about tourist destinations

 Video

Videoclip

1 Preparación Have you ever visited a historic site in your country? Would you rather be in a place with a lot of history or in a brand-new city that is always changing?

2 El clip Watch the report *Xochimilco: una joya de la herencia prehispánica en México.*

Vocabulario

adornadas	decorated	joya	jewel	navegar	to sail
herencia	heritage	lagos	lakes	vestigios	remains

Antes del arribo° de los colonos españoles, los pueblos náhuatl ya vivían° en la zona de Xochimilco.

arribo *arrival* vivían *lived*

3 ¿Cierto o falso? Indicate whether these statements are **cierto** or **falso.** Correct the false statements.

1. Xochimilco está al sur de la Ciudad de México.
2. Las trajineras son barcas adornadas con muchas flores.
3. La Ciudad de México está construida sobre un sistema de lagos.
4. Xochimilco no es una zona turística actualmente.

4 Viaje a la historia With a partner, act out a dialogue at a tourist information booth. The tourist should ask for information about national parks or historic sites to visit in the area.

I CAN understand some information in a report.

I CAN talk about tourist destinations.

Ampliación

Communicative Goals
Listen to a weather report, and chat with a former classmate

1 Escuchar

A Listen to the weather report by Hernán Jiménez and indicate which of these phrases are correct.

TIP **Listen for key words.** Listening for key words and phrases will help you identify the subject and main ideas of what you hear, as well as some of the details.

Santo Domingo

___ 1. hace sol

___ 2. va a hacer frío

___ 3. una mañana de mal tiempo

___ 4. va a estar nublado

___ 5. buena tarde para tomar el sol

___ 6. buena mañana para ir a la playa

San Francisco de Macorís

___ 1. hace frío

___ 2. hace sol

___ 3. va a nevar

___ 4. va a llover

___ 5. hay niebla

___ 6. buen día para excursiones

B ¿Qué tiempo hace en tu ciudad?

2 Conversar

While you're on summer vacation, you run into a classmate from last year. With a partner, role-play a conversation that includes these topics.

• Las clases	• Las vacaciones
• La familia	• Los deportes
• Los amigos	• El tiempo
• Los pasatiempos	• Los compañeros de clase

I CAN identify the main idea and key details of a weather report in a short audio recording.

I CAN chat with a former classmate.

Ampliación

3 Escribir

Write a tourist brochure for a hotel or resort.

TIP **Make an outline.** Identify topics and subtopics in order to provide a framework for the information you want to present.

Descripción del sitio (con foto)
A. Playa Grande
1. Playas seguras y limpias
2. Ideal para tomar el sol y descansar
B. El hotel
1. Abierto los 365 días del año
2. Piscina grande

Organizar — Jot down the most attractive aspects of your hotel or resort. Then, organize your ideas into an outline.

Escribir — Using your outline, write the first draft of your brochure.

Corregir — Exchange papers with a classmate and comment on the brochure's completeness, organization, grammatical accuracy, and level of interest. Then revise your first draft, keeping your classmate's comments in mind.

Compartir — Swap brochures with a classmate. After you have read the brochure, name the three aspects of the hotel or resort that appeal to you most or least.

Communicative Goals
Use an outline to write a tourist brochure, and create a website promoting a travel package

4 Un paso más

Create a real or simulated website to promote a travel package to a resort in a Spanish-speaking country. Include images whenever possible. Your website should include these pages:

- A home page with a general description of the tour and links to the other pages, including images related to the culture of the Spanish-speaking country you chose
- A page describing the means of transportation
- A page describing hotels and accommodations
- A page describing typical food
- A page about the nearby sites to visit
- A page showing some recent history and interesting facts about the country you chose
- A page detailing activities available to travelers

5 Cultura

Pick one of the travel destinations from this lesson (Toledo, Machu Picchu, etc.) that you would like to visit and explain why you want to go there. What makes it special? Is it historic? Does it have good weather? Are there a lot of things to do?

I CAN use an outline to write a brochure with information about a hotel.

I CAN create a website promoting a travel package.

Audio: Reading

Communicative Goal
Scan, read, and understand key
details in a hotel brochure

Antes de leer

Scanning involves glancing over a document in search of specific information.

TIP **Scan.** You can scan a document to identify its format, to find cognates, to locate visual cues about its content, and to find specific facts. Scanning allows you to learn a great deal about a text without having to read it word for word.

Examinar el texto

Scan the reading selection for cognates and write a few of them down.

1. _____
2. _____
3. _____
4. _____
5. _____

Based on the cognates you found, what do you think this document is about?

_____

_____

Preguntas

Read these questions. Then scan the document again to look for answers to the questions.

1. What is the format of the reading?

_____

2. What place is the document about?

_____

3. What are some of the visual cues this document provides? What do they tell you about the content of the document?

_____

_____

4. Who produced the document, and what do you think it is for?

_____

_____

Turismo ecológico en Puerto Rico

Hotel Vistahermosa ~ Lajas, Puerto Rico

- 40 habitaciones individuales
- 15 habitaciones dobles
- Teléfono/TV por cable/Internet
- Aire acondicionado

- Restaurante (Bar)
- Piscina
- Área de juegos
- Cajero automático°

E l hotel está situado en Playa Grande, un pequeño pueblo de pescadores del mar Caribe. Es el lugar perfecto para el viajero que viene de vacaciones. Las playas son seguras y limpias, ideales para tomar el sol, descansar, tomar fotografías y nadar. Está abierto los 365 días del año. Hay una rebaja° especial para estudiantes universitarios.

DIRECCIÓN: Playa Grande 406, Lajas, PR 00667, cerca del Parque Nacional Foresta.

Atracciones cercanas

Playa Grande ¿Busca la playa perfecta? Playa Grande es el lugar que está buscando. Usted puede pescar, sacar fotos, nadar y pasear en bicicleta. Playa Grande es un paraíso para el turista que quiere practicar deportes acuáticos. El lugar es bonito e interesante y usted va a tener muchas oportunidades para descansar y disfrutar en familia.

Valle Niebla Ir de excursión, tomar café, montar a caballo, caminar, hacer picnics. Más de cien lugares para acampar.

Bahía Fosforescente Sacar fotos, salidas de noche, excursión en barco. Una maravillosa experiencia llena de luz°.

Arrecifes de Coral Sacar fotos, bucear, explorar. Es un lugar único en el Caribe.

Playa Vieja Tomar el sol, pasear en bicicleta, jugar a las cartas, escuchar música. Ideal para la familia.

Parque Nacional Foresta Sacar fotos, visitar el Museo de Arte Nativo. Reserva Mundial de la Biosfera.

Santuario de las Aves Sacar fotos, observar aves°, seguir rutas de excursión.

Después de leer

¿Comprendiste?

Indicate whether each statement is **cierto** or **falso**.

Cierto	Falso	
_____	_____	1. El hotel Vistahermosa tiene 55 habitaciones.
_____	_____	2. Playa Grande es un lugar ideal para montar a caballo.
_____	_____	3. Hay muchos lugares para acampar en Valle Niebla.
_____	_____	4. El hotel Vistahermosa está cerrado en invierno.
_____	_____	5. Es posible sacar fotos de las aves en el Santuario de las aves.
_____	_____	6. No hay museos cerca del hotel.

Preguntas

Answer these questions.

1. ¿Dónde está el hotel Vistahermosa?

_____

2. ¿Cómo son las playas cerca del hotel?

_____

3. ¿Dónde podemos hacer picnics?

_____

4. ¿Qué lugar es único en el Caribe?

_____

5. ¿Dónde podemos ir de pesca?

_____

Coméntalo

Vas de vacaciones a Lajas. ¿En qué mes del año deseas ir? ¿Por qué? ¿Cómo prefieres viajar: en avión o en barco? ¿Quieres visitar los lugares mencionados aquí? ¿Por qué?

Cajero automático *ATM* **rebaja** *discount* **llena de luz** *full of light* **aves** *birds*

I CAN scan, then read and understand key details in a hotel brochure.

Las vacaciones y los viajes

el aeropuerto *airport*
la cabaña *cabin*
el campo *countryside*
la estación de autobuses *bus station*
la estación del metro *subway station*
la estación del tren *train station*
el/la inspector(a) de aduanas *customs inspector*
la llegada *arrival*
el mar *sea*
el pasaje (de ida y vuelta) *(round-trip) ticket*
el pasaporte *passport*
la salida *departure; exit*
la tienda de campaña *tent*
el/la viajero/a *traveler*

Las actividades

acampar *to camp*
confirmar una reservación *to confirm a reservation*
estar de vacaciones *to be on vacation*
hacer las maletas *to pack (one's suitcases)*
hacer turismo *to go sightseeing*
hacer un viaje *to take a trip*
hacer una excursión *to go on a hike; to go on a tour*
ir a la playa *to go to the beach*
ir de pesca *to go fishing*
ir de vacaciones *to go on vacation*
ir en autobús (m.) *to go by bus*
ir en auto(móvil) (m.) *to go by car*
ir en avión (m.) *to go by plane*
ir en barco *to go by boat*
ir en motocicleta *to go by motorcycle*
ir en taxi (m.) *to go by taxi*
montar a caballo *to ride a horse*
pasar por la aduana *to go through customs*
pescar *to fish*
sacar fotos (f. pl.) *to take pictures*

En el hotel

el alojamiento *lodging*
el ascensor *elevator*
la cama *bed*
el/la empleado/a *employee*
el equipaje *luggage*
la habitación individual *single room*
la habitación doble *double room*
el hotel *hotel*
el/la huésped *guest*
la llave *key*
la pensión *boarding house*
el piso *floor (of a building)*
la planta baja *ground floor*

Adjetivos

abierto/a *open*
aburrido/a *bored; boring*
alegre *happy*
avergonzado/a *embarrassed*
cansado/a *tired*
cerrado/a *closed*
cómodo/a *comfortable*
contento/a *content*
desordenado/a *disorderly*
enamorado/a (de) *in love (with)*
enojado/a *angry*
equivocado/a *wrong*
feliz *happy*
limpio/a *clean*
listo/a *ready; smart*
malo/a *bad; sick*
nervioso/a *nervous*
ocupado/a *busy*
ordenado/a *orderly*
preocupado/a (por) *worried (about)*
seguro/a *sure; safe; confident*
sucio/a *dirty*
triste *sad*
verde *green; not ripe*
vivo/a *clever; alive*

¿Qué tiempo hace?

¿Qué tiempo hace? *How's the weather?*
Está despejado. *It's clear.*
Está (muy) nublado. *It's (very) cloudy.*
Hace buen/mal tiempo. *The weather is nice/bad.*
Hace (mucho) calor. *It's (very) hot.*
Hace fresco. *It's cool.*
Hace (mucho) frío. *It's (very) cold.*
Hace (mucho) sol. *It's (very) sunny.*
Hace (mucho) viento. *It's (very) windy.*
Hay (mucha) niebla. *It's (very) foggy.*
Llueve. *It's raining.*
Nieva. *It's snowing.*

llover (o:ue) *to rain*
nevar (e:ie) *to snow*

Otras palabras y expresiones

ahora mismo *right now*
todavía *yet; still*

¿Cuál es la fecha de hoy? *What is today's date?*
Hoy es el primero (dos, tres,...) de marzo. *Today is March first (second, third,...).*

Las estaciones y los meses See page 115.
Los números ordinales See page 115.
Direct object pronouns See page 130.

Communicative Goals: Review

I CAN discuss and plan vacations.
• Talk about your next vacation.

I CAN talk about seasons and the weather.
• Say what the weather is like today.

I CAN talk about how I feel.
• Say how you feel right now.

I CAN investigate travel destinations in the Spanish-speaking world.
• Explain why Machu Picchu and Toledo are important travel destinations.

6 ¡De compras!

Communicative Goals
You will learn how to:
- talk about clothes
- negotiate and pay for items
- express preferences while shopping
- investigate markets in the Spanish-speaking world

PREPARACIÓN

pages 140–145
- Words related to clothes and shopping
- Colors and other adjectives
- Pronouncing **d** and **t**

AVENTURAS

pages 146–147
- The friends go shopping. Sara and Valentina are in a store looking for a dress. Juanjo and Manuel are at an open-air market looking for sunglasses.

CULTURA

pages 148–149
- *Los mercados al aire libre*
- Flash cultura: *Comprar en los mercados*

GRAMÁTICA

pages 150–161
- Numbers 101 and higher
- Preterite tense of regular verbs
- Indirect object pronouns
- Demonstrative adjectives and pronouns

LECTURA

pages 162–163
- Advertisement: *Corona*

🔊 PARA EMPEZAR
- ¿Dónde están los chicos, en el centro o en el campo?
- ¿Qué están haciendo: comprando o trabajando?
- ¿Hace calor o hace frío?

Vocabulary Tools

Communicative Goal
Ask and answer questions about clothes

¡DE COMPRAS!

DE COMPRAS

el almacén *department store*
la caja *cash register*
el centro comercial *shopping mall*
el/la cliente/a *client*
el/la dependiente/a *clerk*
el mercado (al aire libre)
  (open-air) market
la rebaja *sale*
el regalo *gift*
la tarjeta de débito *debit card*
la tienda *store*
el/la vendedor(a) *salesperson*
_____
comprar en línea *to buy online*
costar (o:ue) *to cost*
gastar *to spend (money)*
hacer juego (con) *to match*
llevar *to wear; to take*
pagar (con) *to pay (with)*
prestar *to lend*
regatear *to bargain*
usar *to wear; to use*
vender *to sell*

el precio (fijo)
(fixed) price

el dinero

la tarjeta de crédito
credit card

las gafas (de sol)

ADJETIVOS

barato/a *cheap*

bueno/a *good*

cada *each*

caro/a *expensive*

corto/a *short (in length)*

elegante *elegant*

hermoso/a *beautiful*

largo/a *long*

loco/a *crazy*

nuevo/a *new*

otro/a *other; another*

pobre *poor*

rico/a *rich*

la corbata

el par de zapatos
pair of shoes

LA ROPA Y LOS ACCESORIOS

el abrigo *coat*

los bluejeans *jeans*

la blusa *blouse*

la bolsa *bag; purse*

las botas *boots*

los calcetines *socks*

la camisa *shirt*

la camiseta *t-shirt*

la cartera *wallet*

la chaqueta *jacket*

el cinturón *belt*

la falda *skirt*

los guantes *gloves*

el impermeable *raincoat*

las medias *pantyhose; stockings*

los pantalones *pants*

los pantalones cortos *shorts*

la ropa *clothing*

la ropa interior *underwear*

las sandalias *sandals*

el sombrero *hat*

el suéter *sweater*

el traje *suit*

el traje de baño *bathing suit*

el vestido *dress*

los zapatos de tenis *sneakers*

LOS COLORES

amarillo/a

anaranjado/a

blanco/a

rojo/a

gris

rosado/a

negro/a

morado/a

café

verde

azul

ir de compras
to go shopping

ASÍ SE DICE

los calcetines ⟷ las medias (*Amér. L.*)
el cinturón ⟷ la correa (*Col., Venez.*)
las gafas de sol ⟷ los lentes oscuros,
los lentes negros (*Amér. L.*)
los zapatos de tenis ⟷ las zapatillas de
deporte (*Esp.*), las zapatillas (*Arg., Perú*)

▶ What do you call athletic shoes?

A escuchar

1 **Indicar** Check **invierno** or **verano** to indicate when someone would be most likely to wear each item you hear.

	Invierno	Verano
1.	_____	_____
2.	_____	_____
3.	_____	_____
4.	_____	_____
5.	_____	_____
6.	_____	_____
7.	_____	_____
8.	_____	_____

2 **¿Lógico o ilógico?** Indicate whether each statement you hear is **lógico** or **ilógico**.

	Lógico	Ilógico
1.	_____	_____
2.	_____	_____
3.	_____	_____
4.	_____	_____
5.	_____	_____
6.	_____	_____
7.	_____	_____
8.	_____	_____

3 **Escuchar** Listen to Juanita and Vicente talk about what they're packing for their vacations. Indicate who is packing each item. If neither is packing an item, write an **X**.

	Juanita	Vicente		Juanita	Vicente
1. abrigo	_____	_____	7. gafas de sol	_____	_____
2. zapatos de tenis	_____	_____	8. camisetas	_____	_____
3. impermeable	_____	_____	9. traje de baño	_____	_____
4. chaqueta	_____	_____	10. botas	_____	_____
5. sandalias	_____	_____	11. pantalones cortos	_____	_____
6. bluejeans	_____	_____	12. suéter	_____	_____

A practicar

4 **Escoger** Indicate the item in each group that does not belong.

1. bolsa • camiseta • blusa • suéter
2. medias • calcetines • sombrero • zapatos de tenis
3. chaqueta • falda • abrigo • impermeable
4. almacén • vendedora • tienda • mercado
5. regatear • gastar • llevar • costar
6. vestido • dinero • caja • tarjeta de crédito

5 **Anita la contraria** Your friend Anita always contradicts you. Indicate how she would respond to each sentence.

> **modelo**
>
> El suéter nuevo de Liliana es muy grande.
>
> **No, su suéter es muy pequeño.**

1. El cinturón de Natalia es caro. _____
2. El impermeable de don José es muy feo. _____
3. La corbata del señor Ramos es larga. _____
4. Los zapatos de tenis de Noelia son viejos. _____
5. Los trajes de Mauricio son baratos. _____
6. Las botas de Marta están sucias. _____

6 **Preguntas** Answer these questions with a classmate.

> **modelo**
>
>
>
> **Estudiante 1:** ¿De qué color es el suéter?
> **Estudiante 2:** **El suéter es gris.**

1. ¿De qué color es la corbata?

2. ¿De qué color es la planta?

3. ¿De qué color es la rosa de Texas?

4. ¿De qué color es la casa donde vive el presidente de EE.UU.?

5. ¿De qué color es la cebra?

A conversar

7 **Marta y el señor Vega** With a classmate, answer the questions about the drawing.

Marta   el señor Vega

 ¿Qué lleva Marta?
Marta lleva un *vestido*, un *sombrero*, unas *gafas de sol*, una *bolsa*, un *par de zapatos* y unos *guantes*.

1. ¿De qué color es su vestido?

2. ¿De qué color son sus zapatos?

3. ¿De qué color son su sombrero, su bolsa y sus guantes?

4. ¿Qué lleva el señor Vega?

5. ¿De qué color es su camisa?

6. ¿De qué color son sus pantalones?

8   **Entrevista** Use these questions to interview a classmate. Then report your findings to the class.

1. ¿Cuál es tu artículo de ropa favorito? ¿Cuándo lo usas?

2. ¿Con qué colores de ropa te gusta hacer juego?

3. ¿Qué ropa llevas en los días de sol? ¿Y en los días de frío?

4. ¿Cuál es tu marca (*brand*) de ropa preferida? ¿Es cara o barata?

5. ¿Adónde vas para (*in order to*) comprar ropa? ¿Por qué?

6. ¿Cuánto dinero gastas en ropa cada mes? ¿Cada año?

7. Cuando vas de compras, ¿buscas rebajas? ¿Regateas?

8. ¿Cómo pagas tu ropa nueva, con dinero o con tarjeta de crédito/débito?

I CAN ask and answer questions about clothes.

Pronunciación Tutorial

The consonants **d** and **t**

| ¿**D**ón**d**e? | ven**d**er | na**d**ar | ver**d**a**d** |

Like **b** and **v**, the Spanish **d** can also have a hard sound or a soft sound, depending on which letters appear next to it.

| **D**on | **d**inero | tien**d**a | fal**d**a |

At the beginning of a phrase and after **n** or **l**, the letter **d** is pronounced with a hard sound. This sound is similar to the English *d* in *dog,* but a little softer and duller. The tongue should touch the back of the upper teeth, not the roof of the mouth.

| me**d**ias | ver**d**e | vesti**d**o | hués**p**e**d** |

In all other positions, **d** has a soft sound. It is similar to the English *th* in *there,* but a little softer.

Don **D**iego no tiene el **d**iccionario.

When **d** begins a word, its pronunciation depends on the previous word. At the beginning of a phrase or after a word that ends in **n** or **l**, it is pronounced as a hard **d**.

Doña **D**olores es **d**e la capital.

Words that begin with **d** are pronounced with a soft **d** if they appear immediately after a word that ends in a vowel or any consonant other than **n** or **l**.

| **t**raje | pan**t**alones | **t**arje**t**a | **t**ien**d**a |

When pronouncing the Spanish **t,** the tongue should touch the back of the upper teeth, not the roof of the mouth. Unlike the English *t,* no air is expelled from the mouth.

Práctica Read these phrases aloud to practice the **d** and the **t**.

1. Hasta pronto.
2. De nada.
3. Mucho gusto.
4. Lo siento.
5. No hay de qué.
6. ¿De dónde es usted?
7. ¡Todos a bordo!
8. No puedo.
9. Es estupendo.
10. No tengo computadora.
11. ¿Cuándo vienen?
12. Son las tres y media.

Oraciones Read these sentences aloud to practice the **d** and the **t**.

1. Don Teodoro tiene una tienda en un almacén en La Habana.
2. Don Teodoro vende muchos trajes, vestidos y zapatos todos los días.
3. Un día un turista, Federico Machado, entra en la tienda para comprar un par de botas.
4. Federico regatea con don Teodoro y compra las botas y también un par de sandalias.

En la variedad está el gusto. [1]

Refranes Read these sayings aloud to practice the **d** and the **t**.

Aunque la mona se vista de seda, mona se queda. [2]

[1] *Variety is the spice of life.*
[2] *You can't make a silk purse out of a sow's ear.*

¡Eso sí es una ganga!

Sara busca un vestido en una tienda y Juanjo busca gafas de sol en el mercado.

 Video

Antes de ver

Scan the captions for vocabulary related to shopping.

PERSONAJES

 SARA

 VALENTINA

 DEPENDIENTA

 JUANJO

 MANUEL

 VENDEDOR

 DANIEL

DEPENDIENTA Buenas tardes. ¿Cómo os puedo ayudar?

VALENTINA Buscamos un vestido.

DEPENDIENTA Tenemos vestidos largos y cortos. Tenemos ésos en rebaja, y también os podemos hacer un vestido a la medida.

SARA ¿Qué colores tiene?

DEPENDIENTA En su talla tenemos... rojo, verde, azul, blanco, amarillo y negro.

JUANJO ¡Ya pasamos por aquí dos veces y no está el puesto de las gafas! ¡Si no lo encontramos en cinco minutos, vamos al centro comercial!

MANUEL ¡Estamos en el mercado porque es más barato, Juanjo! Mira, esa camisa tiene muy buen precio. Y hace juego con estos pantalones.

JUANJO ¡Manuel, no busco una camisa, busco unas gafas de sol!

SARA ¡Ya decidí! ¡El rojo!

VALENTINA ¡Por fin!

SARA ¡Ahora, un par de zapatos y listo!

ACTIVIDADES

1 ¿Cierto o falso? Indicate if each statement is **cierto** or **falso**. Correct the false statements.

	Cierto	Falso
1. Manuel quiere ir al centro comercial.	○	○
2. Juanjo busca gafas de sol.	○	○
3. Sara compra el vestido amarillo.	○	○
4. Sara gasta mucho dinero en la tienda.	○	○
5. Manuel y Juanjo encuentran a Daniel en el almacén.	○	○

2 Identificar Identify which person says the equivalent of each statement.

1. ¿Cuánto cuestan estas gafas?

2. Esa camisa no es cara.

3. ¿Dónde compraste esas gafas?

4. Ese vestido es muy hermoso, ¿verdad?

5. ¡Las compré regateando!

JUANJO ¿Qué precio tienen estas gafas?
VENDEDOR Treinta euros. ¿No leíste?
JUANJO ¿Me puede hacer un descuento?
MANUEL Le damos quince euros.
VENDEDOR Te vendo las gafas en veinticinco.
MANUEL ¡Veinte!
VENDEDOR ¡Vale! Veinte.

SARA ¡Mi papá me va a matar! ¡Gasté trescientos ochenta euros!
VALENTINA El vestido que compraste es hermoso, y los zapatos son muy elegantes.
SARA Ese vestido es muy bonito, ¿no? ¡Y los zapatos!
VALENTINA ¿Vas a cambiar el vestido y los zapatos que acabas de comprar?
SARA ¡No!

MANUEL ¿Aquel chico no es Daniel? ¡Daniel!
DANIEL Hola, ¿qué tal?
JUANJO ¿Dónde conseguiste esas gafas?
DANIEL Pues, las compré aquí la semana pasada.
MANUEL ¡Seguro pagaste treinta euros!

Expresiones útiles

a la medida *custom-made*
ayudar *to help*
cambiar *to exchange*
el descuento *discount*
la estrella *star*
la ganga *bargain*
parecer *to look like*
por fin *finally*
el puesto *stall*
la talla *size (in clothes)*
vale *OK (in Spain)*

de lunares/rayas *polka-dotted/striped*
el probador *dressing room*

El Rastro

El mercado al aire libre más popular de Madrid es **El Rastro**. Es uno de los íconos de la capital. Puedes ir de compras en El Rastro los domingos y los días de fiesta entre las nueve de la mañana y las tres de la tarde. Allí venden de todo: ropa, libros, música, arte, maletas.

¿Dónde puede regatear la gente en tu comunidad?

3 **¡A regatear!** With a partner, role-play a conversation between a clothes vendor and a customer at an open-air market. Use some of these words in your conversation.

barato	costar	hermoso	precio
caro	dinero	pagar	vender

I CAN participate in a conversation at an open-air market and negotiate a price.

Communicative Goal
Identify some features of open-air markets
in Spanish-speaking countries

Los mercados al aire libre

Mercados al aire libre are an integral part of commerce and culture in the Spanish-speaking world. Whether they take place daily or weekly, these markets are an important forum where tourists, locals, and vendors interact. People come to the marketplace to shop, socialize, taste local foods, and watch street performers. Wandering from one **puesto** (*stand*) to the next, one can browse fresh fruits and vegetables, clothing, CDs and DVDs, **artesanías** (*crafts*), and more. Some markets offer a mix of products, while others specialize in food, fashion, or used merchandise, such as antiques and books.

Mercado de Otavalo

Otros mercados famosos

Mercado	Lugar	Productos
Feria Artesanal de Recoleta	Buenos Aires, Argentina	artesanías
Mercado Central	Santiago, Chile	mariscos°, pescado°, frutas, verduras°
Tianguis Cultural del Chopo	Ciudad de México, México	ropa, música, revistas, libros, arte, artesanías
El mercado de Chichicastenango	Chichicastenango, Guatemala	frutas y verduras, flores°, cerámica, textiles

every Saturday since pre-Incan times. This market is well-known for the colorful textiles woven by the **otavaleños,** the indigenous people of the area. One can also find leather goods and wood carvings from nearby towns. Another popular market is **El Rastro**, held every Sunday in Madrid, Spain. Sellers set up **puestos** along the streets to display their wares, which range from local artwork and antiques to inexpensive clothing and electronics.

mariscos *seafood* pescado *fish* verduras *vegetables* flores *flowers*

When shoppers see an item they like, they can bargain with the vendor. Friendly bargaining is an expected ritual and may result in a significantly lower price. When selling food, vendors may give the customer a little extra of what they purchase; this free addition is known as **la ñapa.**

Many open-air markets are also tourist attractions. The market in Otavalo, Ecuador, is world-famous and has taken place

El Rastro

ASÍ SE DICE

La ropa

la chamarra (Méx.)	la chaqueta
de manga corta/larga	*short/long-sleeved*
los mahones (P. Rico)	los bluejeans
el pantalón de mezclilla (Méx.)	
los tejanos (Esp.)	
los vaqueros (Arg., Cuba, Esp., Uru.)	
la marca	*brand*
la playera (Méx.) la remera (Arg.)	la camiseta
la sudadera	*sweatshirt*

ACTIVIDADES

1 ¿Cierto o falso? Indicate whether each statement is **cierto** or **falso**. Correct the false statements.

1. In the Spanish-speaking world, markets are vital centers of commerce and culture.
2. Generally, open-air markets specialize in one type of goods.
3. Bargaining is commonplace at outdoor markets.
4. Only new goods can be found at open-air markets.
5. A **ñapa** is a tax on open-air market goods.
6. The **otavaleños** weave colorful textiles to sell on Saturdays.

2 Preguntas Answer the questions.

1. What is the little extra of a purchase given by food vendors called?
2. How long has the market at Otavalo taken place?
3. Where is the market known for seafood, fish, fruits, and vegetables?
4. Which market is known for flowers, ceramics, and textiles?
5. Where does the **Feria Artesanal de Recoleta** take place?

3 Comparación Compare a market in the Spanish-speaking world with a market where you live. How popular are markets? What items can you typically find there? How do customers negotiate prices?

4 Preguntas personales Answer these questions.

1. Which of these markets would you like to visit? Why?
2. Have you ever bargained for something? If so, what happened?
3. Do you know of a U.S. tradition similar to **la ñapa**?

I CAN identify some features of open-air markets in Spanish-speaking countries.

Communicative Goal
Identify some basic facts about markets in Costa Rica

Comprar en los mercados

1 Preparación Have you ever been to an open-air market? What did you buy? Have you ever negotiated a price? What did you say?

2 El video Watch this **Flash cultura** episode about markets in Costa Rica.

Vocabulario	
colones (pl.) *currency of Costa Rica*	descuento *discount*
¿Cuánto vale? **¿Cuánto cuesta?**	el regateo *bargaining*

¿Qué compran en el Mercado Central?

3 ¿Cierto o falso? Indicate whether each statement is **cierto** or **falso**.

1. Randy lleva una camiseta.
2. El Mercado de Guadalupe está abierto cada domingo.
3. Randy regatea cuando compra papayas.
4. El Mercado Central es un mercado al aire libre.
5. Venden zapatos en el Mercado Central.

4 Conversación Role-play a conversation between Randy and a vendor at one the markets in Costa Rica.

I CAN identify some basic facts about markets in Costa Rica.

Communicative Goal
Ask and answer questions about prices and dates

6.1 Numbers 101 and higher

▶ Spanish uses a period, rather than a comma, to indicate thousands and millions.

Numbers 101 and higher			
101	ciento uno	1.000	mil
200	doscientos/as	1.100	mil cien
300	trescientos/as	2.000	dos mil
400	cuatrocientos/as	5.000	cinco mil
500	quinientos/as	100.000	cien mil
600	seiscientos/as	200.000	doscientos mil
700	setecientos/as	550.000	quinientos cincuenta mil
800	ochocientos/as	1.000.000	un millón (de)
900	novecientos/as	8.000.000	ocho millones (de)

¡Gasté trescientos ochenta euros!

▶ Use **ciento uno** for counting. Use **ciento un(a)** when describing quantity.

cien, ciento uno, ciento dos... ciento una noches

▶ The numbers **200** through **999** agree in gender with the nouns they modify.

324 tiendas	605 clientes
trescient**as** veinticuatro tiendas	seiscient**os** cinco clientes
873 habitaciones	990 euros
ochocient**as** setenta y tres habitaciones	novecient**os** noventa euros
500 mujeres	257 estudiantes
quinient**as** mujeres	doscient**os** cincuenta y siete estudiantes

▶ **Mil** can mean *a thousand* or *one thousand*. The plural form of **un millón** (*a million* or *one million*) is **millones**, which has no accent.

1.000 dólares	2.000.000 de pesos
mil dólares	**dos millones** de pesos
5.000 bicicletas	1.000.000 de aficionados
cinco mil bicicletas	**un millón** de aficionados

Práctica

1 **Completar** Complete these sequences in Spanish.

1. 100, 120, 140, ... 200
   _____
   _____

2. 5.000, 10.000, 15.000, ... 30.000
   _____
   _____

3. 50.000, 100.000, 150.000, ... 300.000
   _____
   _____

4. 100.000.000, 200.000.000, 300.000.000, ... 900.000.000
   _____
   _____

2 **Resolver** Read these math problems aloud and solve them.

modelo
$$\begin{array}{r} 300 \\ +400 \\ \hline 700 \end{array}$$

Trescientos más cuatrocientos son setecientos.

 + más − menos = es (singular)/son (plural)

1. $\begin{array}{r} 150 \\ +150 \\ \hline \end{array}$ 2. $\begin{array}{r} 3.000 \\ +753 \\ \hline \end{array}$

3. $\begin{array}{r} 43.000 \\ -10.000 \\ \hline \end{array}$ 4. $\begin{array}{r} 200.000 \\ +350.000 \\ \hline \end{array}$

5. $\begin{array}{r} 20.000 \\ +555 \\ \hline \end{array}$ 6. $\begin{array}{r} 1.000.000 \\ -75.000 \\ \hline \end{array}$

7. $\begin{array}{r} 32.000 \\ -30.000 \\ \hline \end{array}$ 8. $\begin{array}{r} 800.000 \\ +175.000 \\ \hline \end{array}$

Conversación

3 **¿Cuánto cuesta?** Ask your partner how much each item costs.

modelo

40.000 pesos

Estudiante 1: ¿Cuánto cuestan las gafas de sol?
Estudiante 2: Cuarenta mil pesos.

1.

210.000 pesos

2.

61.500 pesos

3.

160.150 pesos

4.

84.450 pesos

5.

48.200 pesos

6.

22.790 pesos

4 **¿En qué año?** Take turns with a classmate asking and answering these questions. Follow the model.

modelo

Estudiante 1: ¿En qué año terminaste (*did you finish*)
la escuela secundaria?
Estudiante 2: En el año 2017.

1. ¿En qué año llegó (*arrived*) tu familia a los Estados Unidos?

2. ¿Cuál es el año de tu nacimiento (*birth*)?

3. ¿En qué año empezaste (*started*) a estudiar en la universidad?

4. ¿En qué año vas a terminar la universidad?

▶ The plural forms **cientos** and **miles (de)** refer to *hundreds* or *thousands of* (*people or things*).

cientos de personas	**miles de** dólares
hundreds of people	*thousands of dollars*

▶ In Spanish, years are never expressed as pairs of 2-digit numbers as they sometimes are in English (*1979, nineteen seventy-nine*).

1945	**2005**
mil novecientos cuarenta y cinco	dos mil cinco
1898	**1220**
mil ochocientos noventa y ocho	mil doscientos veinte

▶ In Spanish, street numbers follow the same pattern.

¿Cuál es tu dirección? Mi dirección es Balcarce mil doscientos ochenta y tres.
What's your address? *My address is Balcarce twelve hundred eighty-three.*

▶ When **millón** or **millones** is used before a noun, place **de** between the two.

1.000.000 **de** hombres = un **millón de** hombres
12.000.000 **de** aviones = doce **millones de** aviones
15.000.000 **de** personas = quince **millones de** personas

¡ojo! Note this difference between Spanish and English:

mil millones	**un billón**
a billion (1.000.000.000)	*a trillion (1.000.000.000.000)*

Hay **mil millones** de personas en China. Hay un **billón** de planetas en el universo.
There are a billion people in China. *There are a trillion planets in the universe.*

¡Manos a la obra!

Give the Spanish equivalent of each number.

a. 102 _____ciento dos_____   i. 1999 _____

b. 935 _____   j. 113 _____

c. 5.000.000 _____   k. 204 _____

d. 2001 _____   l. 2.108 _____

e. 1776 _____   m. 17.123 _____

f. 345 _____   n. 497 _____

g. 550.300 _____   o. 30.201 _____

h. 232 _____   p. 57.507 _____

I CAN ask and answer questions about prices and dates.

6.2 The preterite tense of regular verbs

▶ In order to talk about events in the past, Spanish uses two simple tenses: the preterite and the imperfect. In this lesson, you will learn about the preterite tense.

▶ The preterite is used to talk about actions or states completed in the past.

Preterite of regular –ar, –er, and –ir verbs

	comprar	vender	escribir
yo	compré *I bought*	vendí *I sold*	escribí *I wrote*
tú	compraste	vendiste	escribiste
Ud./él/ella	compró	vendió	escribió
nosotros/as	compramos	vendimos	escribimos
vosotros/as	comprasteis	vendisteis	escribisteis
Uds./ellos/ellas	compraron	vendieron	escribieron

▶ The preterite endings for regular **–er** and **–ir** verbs are identical. Also, note that the **yo** and **Ud./él/ella** forms of all three conjugations have written accents on the last syllable.

¡Ya decidí!
¡El rojo!

Las compré aquí la semana pasada.

▶ Note that the **nosotros/as** forms of regular **–ar** and **–ir** verbs in the preterite are identical to the present-tense forms. Context will help you determine which tense is being used.

En invierno **compramos** suéteres.
In the winter we buy sweaters.

Anoche **compramos** unas sandalias.
Last night we bought some sandals.

Escribimos poemas en clase.
We write poems in class.

Ya **escribimos** dos veces al presidente.
We already wrote to the president twice.

▶ **–Ar** and **–er** verbs that have a stem change in the present tense do *not* have a stem change in the preterite.

INFINITIVE	PRESENT	PRETERITE
cerrar (e:ie)	Ana cierra la puerta.	Ana cerró la puerta.
volver (o:ue)	Juan vuelve a las dos.	Juan volvió a las dos.
jugar (u:ue)	Él juega al fútbol.	Él jugó al fútbol.
pensar (e:ie)	Pienso mucho.	Pensé mucho.

Práctica

1 **Fin de semana** Complete what Isabel says about her weekend with the appropriate verb forms.

(1) _____ [pasar] un fin de semana fantástico. El sábado (2) _____ [estudiar] por la mañana y luego (3) _____ [salir] de compras con mis amigas al nuevo centro comercial. (4) _____ [comprar] un vestido y un suéter muy baratos porque el vendedor me hizo un buen descuento. ¡(5) _____ [gastar] sólo 40 dólares! Más tarde, nosotras (6) _____ [comer] en un restaurante mexicano. Mi amiga Estela (7) _____ [gastar] mucho dinero porque pidió platos (*dishes*) muy caros. Por la noche, nosotras (8) _____ [salir] a bailar a una discoteca y (9) _____ [regresar] muy tarde. Hoy me levanté *(I got up)* muy temprano porque tengo que estudiar para la clase de español. ¡Uy! ¡Qué cansada estoy!

2 **¿Qué hicieron?** Combine words from each list to talk about things you and others did.

modelo

Yo leí un buen libro la semana pasada.

¿Quién?	¿Qué?	¿Cuándo?
yo	ver la televisión	anoche
mi compañero/a de cuarto	hablar con un(a) chico/a guapo/a	anteayer
mis amigos/as y yo	estudiar español	ayer
mis padres	comprar ropa nueva	la semana pasada
mi abuelo/a	leer un buen libro	el año pasado
el/la profesor(a) de español	bailar en una discoteca latina	una vez
el presidente de los Estados Unidos	viajar a la Luna (*moon*)	dos veces
mi perro	llegar tarde (*late*) a clase	
	viajar a Europa	
	escribir una carta	
	llevar ropa muy fea	
	comer siete hamburguesas	

Conversación

3 **Encuesta** Find out if your partner just did these activities today before coming to class. Report the results to the class.

modelo

tomar el desayuno (*breakfast*)
Estudiante 1: ¿Tomaste el desayuno?
Estudiante 2: Sí, acabo de tomar el desayuno./
No, no tomé el desayuno.

Actividades	Sí/No
1. ver la televisión	_____
2. escuchar la radio	_____
3. hablar con un(a) compañero/a de clase	_____
4. leer para una clase	_____
5. comprar un café (*coffee*)	_____
6. recibir una buena noticia (*news*)	_____

4 **Nuestras vacaciones** Imagine that you took these photos on a vacation with friends. Use the pictures to tell your partner about the trip.

1. 2. 3. 4.

5 **¿Qué hiciste?** Get together with a partner and take turns asking each other what you did yesterday, the day before yesterday, and last week.

I CAN talk about what I did in the past.

Verbs with spelling changes

▶ Verbs that end in **–car**, **–gar**, and **–zar** have a spelling change in the **yo** form of the preterite. All the other forms are regular.

buscar → busqué   llegar → llegué   empezar → empecé

▶ **Creer**, **leer**, and **oír** have spelling changes in the preterite.

creer ▸ creí, creíste, creyó, creímos, creísteis, creyeron
leer ▸ leí, leíste, leyó, leímos, leísteis, leyeron
oír ▸ oí, oíste, oyó, oímos, oísteis, oyeron

▶ **Ver** is regular in the preterite, but none of its forms has an accent.

ver → vi, viste, vio, vimos, visteis, vieron

Words commonly used with the preterite			
anoche	*last night*	desde... hasta...	*from... until...*
anteayer	*the day before yesterday*	pasado/a	*(adj.) last; past*
		la semana pasada	*last week*
el año pasado	*last year*	una vez	*once*
ayer	*yesterday*	dos veces	*twice*
de repente	*suddenly*	ya	*already*

Ayer compré una camisa.   Miré la televisión **anoche**.
Yesterday I bought a shirt.   *I watched TV last night.*

Useful phrases	
¿Qué hiciste?	*What did you (fam., sing.) do?*
¿Qué hizo usted?	*What did you (form., sing.) do?*
¿Qué hicieron ustedes?	*What did you (pl.) do?*
¿Qué hizo él/ella?	*What did he/she do?*
¿Qué hicieron ellos/ellas?	*What did they do?*

¡ojo! Use **acabar de** + [*infinitive*] to say that something *has just occurred*. Note that **acabar** is in the present tense in this construction.

Acabo de comprar un suéter.   **Acabas de ir** de compras.
I just bought a sweater.   *You just went shopping.*

¡Manos a la obra!

Give the preterite form of each verb.

1. Elena __celebró__ [celebrar].
2. Ellos _____ [oír].
3. Emilio y yo _____ [comprar].
4. Los niños _____ [comer].
5. Usted _____ [salir].
6. Yo _____ [llegar].
7. Yo _____ [empezar].
8. Tú _____ [vender].
9. Ustedes _____ [escribir].
10. Juan _____ [ver].

6.3 Indirect object pronouns

▶ An indirect object is the noun or pronoun that answers the question *to whom* or *for whom* an action is done. In this example, the indirect object answers this question: **¿A quién le prestó Roberto cien pesos?** *To whom did Roberto loan 100 pesos?*

SUBJECT	INDIRECT OBJECT PRONOUN	VERB	DIRECT OBJECT	INDIRECT OBJECT
Roberto	le	prestó	cien pesos	a Luisa.
Roberto		*loaned*	*100 pesos*	*to Luisa.*

Indirect object pronouns

Singular forms		Plural forms	
me	(to, for) me	nos	(to, for) us
te	(to, for) you (fam.)	os	(to, for) you (fam.)
le	(to, for) you (form.); (to, for) him; (to, for) her	les	(to, for) you; (to, for) them

Le damos quince euros.

Te vendo las gafas en veinticinco.

▶ Spanish speakers often use the object pronoun and the noun to which it refers in the same sentence to emphasize or clarify *to whom* the pronoun refers. The indirect object pronoun is often used without the indirect object noun when the person for whom the action is being done is known.

Iván **le** prestó un lápiz **a Juan**.
Iván loaned a pencil to Juan.

También **le** prestó papel.
He also loaned him paper.

Sabrina **le** compró un café **a Valeria**.
Sabrina bought Valeria a coffee.

También **le** compró un sándwich.
She also bought her a sandwich.

¡ojo! Since **le** and **les** have multiple meanings, **a** + [*noun*] or **a** + [*pronoun*] is often used to clarify to whom the pronouns refer.

Unclear	Clearer
Ella **les** vendió ropa.	Ella **les** vendió ropa **a ellos**.
She sold clothing (to them or to you all).	*She sold clothing to them.*
Yo **le** presté una camisa.	Yo **le** presté una camisa **a Luis**.
I loaned a shirt (to you or to him or to her).	*I loaned a shirt to Luis.*

Práctica

1 **Completar** Fill in the correct indirect object pronouns to complete Emilio's description of his family's holiday shopping.

> **modelo** Yo ___le___ compré una cartera a mi padre.

1. Mi tía _____ compró una corbata muy fea (a mí).
2. Mis dos hermanos _____ compraron a mis padres dos pares de pantalones.
3. Yo _____ compré un suéter azul a mi mamá.
4. Mi abuelo _____ compró muchos regalos a nosotros.
5. Y yo _____ compré una camiseta bonita a mi novia.

2 **Describir** Describe what happened in these photos. Use indirect object pronouns and the preterite tense.

> **modelo** hacer/pregunta
>
> **Juanjo le hizo una pregunta a Daniel.**

1. describir/mercado

2. preguntar/precio de las gafas

3. mostrar/vestidos

4. vender/gafas

Conversación

 3 Conversación Take turns with a classmate asking and answering questions using the cues.

modelo

escribir mensajes electrónicos

Estudiante 1: ¿A quién le escribes mensajes electrónicos?
Estudiante 2: Le escribo mensajes electrónicos a mi hermano.

1. cantar canciones de amor (*love songs*)
2. dar besos
3. decir mentiras
4. invitar a comer
5. hablar por teléfono
6. mostrar fotos de un viaje

4 Entrevista Use these questions to interview a classmate.

1. Cuando vas de compras, ¿te dan tus padres su tarjeta de crédito?
2. Si tu amigo te pide dinero para ir de compras, ¿cuánto dinero le prestas?
3. ¿Pagas el dinero que les debes (*money you owe*) a tus amigos?
4. ¿A quiénes les compras regalos?
5. ¿Qué vas a darles a tus padres este año?
6. ¿Les dices mentiras a tus padres o a tus amigos? ¿Cuándo?

5 ¡Somos ricos! You and your classmates won the lottery! Now you want to spend money on your loved ones. In groups of three, discuss what each person is buying.

modelo

Estudiante 1: *Quiero comprarle un vestido nuevo a mi mamá y una camiseta a mi novio.*
Estudiante 2: *Y yo voy a darles un auto nuevo a mis padres. A mis compañeras de cuarto les voy a comprar blusas y faldas nuevas.*
Estudiante 3: *Voy a comprarles una casa a mis padres, pero a mis amigos no les voy a dar nada (nothing).*

I CAN say for whom I do things.

Using indirect object pronouns

▸ Indirect object pronouns usually precede the conjugated verb. In negative sentences, place the pronoun between **no** and the conjugated verb.

Te compré un abrigo.
I bought you a coat.

No te compré nada.
I didn't buy you anything.

▸ When an infinitive or present participle is used, there are two options for indirect object pronoun placement: before the conjugated verb, or attached to the infinitive or present participle. When a pronoun is attached to a present participle, an accent mark is added.

¿Vas a comprar**le** un regalo a Carla?
¿**Le** vas a comprar un regalo a Carla?
Are you going to buy a gift for Carla?

Estoy mostrándo**les** las fotos a ellos.
Les estoy mostrando las fotos a ellos.
I'm showing them the photos.

▸ The irregular verbs **dar** (*to give*) and **decir** (*to say; to tell*) are often used with indirect object pronouns.

Dar and decir

	dar	decir
yo	doy	digo
tú	das	dices
Ud./él/ella	da	dice
nosotros/as	damos	decimos
vosotros/as	dais	decís
Uds./ellos/ellas	dan	dicen
Present participle	dando	diciendo

Mi abuela **me da** muchos regalos.
My grandmother gives me lots of gifts.

Te digo la verdad.
I'm telling you the truth.

Voy a **darle** un beso.
I'm going to give her a kiss.

No **les estoy diciendo** mentiras a mis padres.
I am not telling lies to my parents.

▸ You will learn how to use these pronouns with direct object pronouns in Lesson 8.

¡Manos a la obra!

Use the cues to provide the indirect object pronoun for the sentence. The first item has been done for you.

1. Martha ___le___ quiere dar un regalo. (*to Elena*)
2. Alfonso _____ prepara un café. (*for us*)
3. Guillermo y Alejandra _____ escriben desde Cuba. (*to me*)
4. Francisco y yo _____ compramos unos guantes. (*for them*)
5. Los vendedores _____ venden ropa. (*to you, fam. sing.*)

Communicative Goal
Talk about things located around me

6.4 Demonstrative adjectives and pronouns

Demonstrative adjectives

▶ Demonstrative adjectives demonstrate or point out nouns. They precede the nouns they modify and agree with them in gender and number.

este vestido	**esos** zapatos	**aquella** tienda
this dress	*those shoes*	*that store (over there)*

Demonstrative adjectives

Singular forms		Plural forms		
MASCULINE	FEMININE	MASCULINE	FEMININE	
este	esta	estos	estas	*this; these*
ese	esa	esos	esas	*that; those*
aquel	aquella	aquellos	aquellas	*that; those (over there)*

▶ The demonstrative adjectives **este**, **esta**, **estos**, and **estas** are used to point out things that are close to the speaker and the listener.

Me gustan estos zapatos.

▶ The demonstrative adjectives **ese**, **esa**, **esos**, and **esas** are used to point out things that are not close in space and time to the speaker. They may, however, be close to the listener.

Prefiero esos zapatos.

▶ The demonstrative adjectives **aquel**, **aquella**, **aquellos**, and **aquellas** are used to point out things that are far away from the speaker and the listener.

Aquel auto es de mi hermana.

Práctica

1 **En un almacén** Gabriel and María are shopping. Complete their conversation with the appropriate demonstrative adjectives and pronouns.

MARÍA No me gustan (1) _____ (*those*) pantalones. Voy a comprar (2) _____ (*these*).

GABRIEL Yo prefiero (3) _____ (*those over there*).

MARÍA Sí, a mí también me gustan. ¿Qué piensas de (4) _____ (*these*) cinturones?

GABRIEL (5) _____ (*these*) cuestan demasiado.

MARÍA También busco un vestido elegante. ¿Te gusta (6) _____ (*this one*)?

GABRIEL No, es muy feo. ¿Necesitas una falda nueva? (7) _____ (*this one*) es bonita.

MARÍA No, no necesito una falda. Vamos, Gabriel. Me gusta (8) _____ (*this*) almacén, pero (9) _____ (*that one over there*) es mejor (*better*).

2 **Oraciones** Form sentences using the words provided and the appropriate forms of the preterite. Make all the necessary changes.

modelo

este / clientes / gastar / mucho dinero
Estos clientes gastaron mucho dinero.

1. aquel / mujer / comprar / chaqueta
2. cliente / pagar / ese / abrigos / con tarjeta de crédito
3. tú / salir/ de compras / ese / centro comercial
4. yo / buscar / aquel / sombreros / por mucho tiempo
5. empleados / vender / este / corbatas / en rebaja

Conversación

3 **¿De qué color es?** In pairs, use demonstrative adjectives and pronouns to discuss the colors of items in your classroom.

modelo

Estudiante 1: ¿Esos zapatos son azules?
Estudiante 2: No, ésos son verdes. Aquéllos son azules.
Estudiante 1: Y esa mochila, ¿es roja?
Estudiante 2: No, ésa es blanca. Aquélla es roja.

| rojo/a | amarillo/a | azul | verde |
| anaranjado/a | blanco/a | café | negro/a |

4 **En una tienda** You and a classmate are in a small clothing store. Look at the illustration, then talk about what you see around you.

modelo

Estudiante 1: ¿Te gusta esa chaqueta de mujer que está debajo de las camisas?
Estudiante 2: No, prefiero aquélla que está al lado de los pantalones. ¿Dónde están los zapatos?
Estudiante 1: Están en el centro de la tienda.

I CAN talk about things located around me.

Demonstrative pronouns

▶ Demonstrative pronouns are identical to demonstrative adjectives, except that they traditionally carry an accent mark on the stressed vowel. They agree in number and gender with the corresponding noun.

No me gusta **este** suéter.
Prefiero **ése**.
I don't like this sweater.
I prefer that one.

Ella quiere comprar **esa** bolsa,
no **aquélla**.
She wants to buy that purse,
not that one over there.

No voy a comprar **estos** zapatos.
Quiero **aquéllos**.
I'm not going to buy these shoes.
I want those over there.

¿Qué precio tienen **esos** pantalones?
Ésos cuestan quince dólares.
How much do those pants cost?
Those cost fifteen dollars.

Demonstrative pronouns

Singular forms		Plural forms		
MASCULINE	FEMININE	MASCULINE	FEMININE	
éste	ésta	éstos	éstas	*this one; these*
ése	ésa	ésos	ésas	*that one; those*
aquél	aquélla	aquéllos	aquéllas	*that one; those (over there)*

▶ There are three neuter forms: **esto**, **eso**, and **aquello**. These forms refer to unidentified or unspecified things, situations, and ideas. They do not change in gender or number and never carry an accent mark.

¿Qué es **esto**?
What's this?

Eso es interesante.
That's interesting.

Aquello es bonito.
That's pretty.

¡Manos a la obra!

Provide the correct form of the demonstrative adjective and demonstrative pronoun for these nouns.

1. la falda / este
   esta falda; ésta/esta

2. los estudiantes / este
   _____

3. los países / aquel
   _____

4. la ventana / ese
   _____

5. los periodistas / ese
   _____

6. las empleadas / ese
   _____

7. el chico / aquel
   _____

8. las sandalias / este
   _____

9. el autobús / ese
   _____

10. las chicas / aquel
    _____

11. el abrigo / aquel
    _____

12. los pantalones / este
    _____

13. las medias / ese
    _____

14. la bolsa / aquel
    _____

A repasar

6.1 Numbers 101 and higher

1 **La tienda** You and a partner are store employees taking inventory. Take turns asking and telling how many items there are.

modelo cinturones: 274

Estudiante 1: ¿Cuántos cinturones hay?
Estudiante 2: Hay *doscientos setenta y cuatro cinturones*.

1. abrigos: 190
2. chaquetas: 351
3. pares de botas: 436
4. camisas: 912
5. faldas: 685
6. vestidos: 562
7. suéteres: 829
8. corbatas: 743

2 **Estadísticas** With a partner, take turns asking each other what the populations of these countries are.

modelo Argentina: 44.800.000

Estudiante 1: ¿Cuál es la población *(population)* de Argentina?
Estudiante 2: *Argentina tiene cuarenta y cuatro millones ochocientos mil habitantes (inhabitants).*

Poblaciones

1. México: 127.600.000
2. Costa Rica: 5.100.000
3. Venezuela: 28.500.000
4. Cuba: 11.300.000
5. República Dominicana: 10.700.000
6. Puerto Rico: 2.900.000

6.2 The preterite tense of regular verbs

3 **Completar** Fill in each blank with the appropriate preterite form of the verb.

OMAR Pedro, ¿(1) _____ [asistir] al partido de fútbol anoche? Yo te (2) _____ [llamar], pero tú no (3) _____ [contestar].

PEDRO Dora y yo (4) _____ [decidir] no ir. (Nosotros) (5) _____ [mirar] un video.

OMAR Entonces, (6) ¿ _____ [oír] (tú) que *(that)* los Dorados (7) _____ [ganar]? (Tú) Te (8) _____ [perder] un partido fenomenal. Todos (9) _____ [jugar] muy bien y Álvarez hizo dos goles *(goals)*. Después *(Afterward)*, nosotros (10) _____ [celebrar] en El Reloj hasta la medianoche.

4 **Entrevista** Interview a partner about the last time he or she went out. Then switch roles.

- Find out when and where your partner went out, with whom, and at what time.
- Ask what he/she wore.
- Find out what your partner did and what time he/she returned home.

6.3 Indirect object pronouns

5 **Combinar** Create sentences by combining elements from each column. Add indirect object pronouns and make any necessary changes.

modelo *El profesor les explicó la tarea a ellos.*

yo	(no) explicar la tarea	mí
tú	(no) pedir ayuda *(help)*	ti
mi amigo/a	(no) mostrar la foto	el/la novio/a
mi hermano/a	(no) enseñar español	mi compañero/a
el/la profesor(a)	(no) buscar un libro	nosotros/as
él/ella	(no) explicar el problema	los padres
nosotros/as	(no) vender la motocicleta	ellos/as
mis padres	(no) prestar 20 dólares	el/la profesor(a)
los/las chicos/as	(no) comprar un abrigo	tu primo/a

6 **Encuesta** Find out to or for whom your partner usually does these things. Use indirect object pronouns.

modelo abrir la puerta

Estudiante 1: ¿A quién le abres la puerta?
Estudiante 2: *Les abro la puerta a mis abuelos.*

Actividades	¿A quiénes?
1. dar regalos	_____
2. mostrar las compras	_____
3. prestar ropa	_____
4. pedir un descuento	_____
5. dar un beso	_____
6. decir mentiras	_____
7. hablar en español	_____

6.4 Demonstrative adjectives and pronouns

7 ¿De quién es? You and a classmate are on a tour bus and some passengers left these items behind. Take turns asking each other what belongs to whom, using the cues.

modelo Daniel

Estudiante 1: ¿De quién es esta chaqueta?
Estudiante 2: ¿Ésa? Es de Daniel.

1. Raquel

2. Miguel

3. Señor Romero

4. Señora Espinosa

5. yo

6. Señora Domínguez

Síntesis

8 Las compras en Internet In groups of three, discuss online shopping.

- Explain why you like or don't like to shop online.
- Describe the items you bought online in the past year, for whom you bought each item, how much each item cost, and where you bought it. If you have one or more of the items with you, show it to the group as you talk about it.
- Explain how you paid for your purchases.

Communicative Goal
Discuss the importance of imagination in people's lives

 Video

Videoclip

1 Preparación Answer these questions in Spanish.

1. ¿Cómo eres? Escribe tres adjetivos que te describan.
2. ¿Qué actividades ilustran tu personalidad?

2 El clip Watch the ad for **Juguettos** from Spain.

Vocabulario	
copionas *copycats*	sean *they may be*
despistado/a *absentminded*	pidan *they may ask for*

Me pido éste, éste.

3 Emparejar Match the personality trait with its visual representation in the ad.

1. valiente   a. Tienen una batalla (*battle*) imaginaria.
2. galáctico/a   b. Le compra juguetes (*toys*) a su perro.
3. artista   c. Está en un cartón con forma de nave espacial (*spaceship*).
4. generoso/a   d. Hacen música con parte de una basurera (*trashcan*).
5. intrépido   e. Imagina que puede volar (*fly*).

4 Conversación Answer these questions with a classmate.

1. ¿Por qué es importante la imaginación en la vida de los niños?
2. ¿Qué importancia tiene la imaginación en la vida de los adultos?

I CAN discuss the importance of imagination in people's lives.

Ampliación

Communicative Goals
Listen to a recorded conversation focusing on linguistic cues, and role-play an exchange in a clothing store

❶ Escuchar

  A Listen to Marisol and Alicia's conversation. Make a list of the clothing items that each person mentions, then note if she actually purchased it.

> **TIP** **Listen for linguistic cues.** By listening for the endings of conjugated verbs, you can identify whether an event already took place, is taking place now, or will take place in the future. Verb endings also give clues about who is participating in the action.

Marisol	Alicia
1. _____	1. _____
2. _____	2. _____
3. _____	3. _____
4. _____	4. _____

B ¿Crees que la moda es importante para Alicia? ¿Y para Marisol? ¿Por qué? En tu opinión, ¿es importante estar a la moda?

❷ Conversar

With a classmate, take turns playing the roles of a shopper and a clerk in a clothing store. Use these guidelines.

> • The shopper talks about the clothing he/she is looking for as a gift, mentions for whom the clothes are intended, and says what he/she bought for the same person last year
>
> • The clerk recommends items, based on the shopper's descriptions
>
> • The shopper asks how much items cost, and the clerk answers

I CAN identify the main idea and key details in a recorded conversation, focusing on linguistic cues.

I CAN role-play an exchange in a clothing store.

Ampliación

Communicative Goals
Write a report based on an interview with a classmate, and create a business plan

3 Escribir

Write a report for the school newspaper about an interview you conducted with a student concerning his or her opinion on the latest fashion trends at your school.

> **TIP** **Reporting an interview.** You may transcribe the interview verbatim, or simply summarize it with occasional quotes from the speaker. Your report should begin with an interesting title and a brief introduction, include some examples or a brief quote, and end with a conclusion.

Organizar | Use an idea map to organize the interview questions and develop an outline for your report. Then brainstorm a title for the report.

Escribir | Using your outline as a guide, write the first draft of your report.

Corregir | Exchange papers with a classmate and comment on the report's title, introduction, organization, level of interest, grammatical accuracy, and conclusion. Then revise your first draft, with your classmate's comments in mind.

Compartir | Exchange reports in groups of four. Give a superlative title to each report on the basis of its strongest points, for example, "best use of Spanish" or "most interesting questions."

4 Un paso más

Develop a business plan to open a clothing store in a Spanish-speaking country.

- Choose a location for your store
- Decide which products you are going to sell and select an appealing name for your store
- Include a visual presentation of your products
- Itemize your prices and your expected profits
- Explain why you think your store will be successful (**va a tener éxito**)

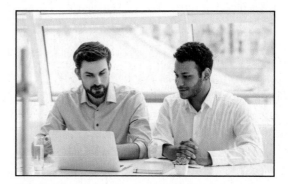

5 Cultura

You are going shopping in Spain or Latin America. Do you want to go to an open-air market, a department store, or a specialty shop? Explain what you are looking for and why you want to go to that shopping destination (quality of products, prices, convenience, etc.).

I CAN write a report based on an interview with a classmate.

I CAN create a business plan.

S Audio: Reading

Communicative Goal
Find general information by skimming a reading selection

Antes de leer

Skimming involves quickly reading through a document to absorb its general meaning.

TIP **Skim.** When you skim a text, you might want to look at its title and subtitles. You might also want to read the first sentence of each paragraph. Skimming allows you to understand the main ideas of a text without having to read word for word.

Examinar el texto

Look at the format of the reading selection. How is it organized? What does the organization of the document tell you about its content?

Buscar cognados

Scan the reading selection to locate at least five cognates. Based on the cognates, what do you think the reading selection is about?

1. _____
2. _____
3. _____
4. _____
5. _____

6. The reading selection is about _____.

Impresiones generales

Now skim the reading selection to understand its general meaning. Jot down your impressions. What new information did you learn about the document by skimming it? Based on all the information you now have, answer these questions in Spanish.

1. Who created this document?

2. What is its purpose?

3. Who is its intended audience?

 Corona

◀ ▶ ⟳ http://corona.cl

 Corona
¡Corona tiene las ofertas más locas del verano!

La tienda más elegante de la ciudad con precios increíbles

niños | **mujeres** | casa | baño | equipaje

Faldas largas
Algodón°.
De distintos colores
Talla mediana
Precio especial: 30.000 pesos

Blusas de seda°
De cuadros° y de lunares
Ahora: 31.000 pesos
40% de rebaja

Vestido de algodón
Colores blanco,
azul y verde
Ahora: 58.000 pesos
30% de rebaja

Accesorios
Cinturones, gafas de sol,
sombreros, medias
Diversos estilos
Todos con un 40% de rebaja

Carteras
Colores anaranjado,
blanco, rosado y amarillo
Ahora: 40.000 pesos
50% de rebaja

Sandalias de playa
Números° del 35 al 38
A sólo 25.000 pesos
50% de descuento

Lunes a sábado de 9 a 21 horas.
Domingo de 10 a 14 horas.

Real° Liquidación°
¡La rebaja está de moda en Corona!

¡Grandes rebajas!

y con la tarjeta de crédito más conveniente del mercado.

bebé | **hombres** | jardín | joyas | electrónica

Chaquetas
Microfibra. Colores negro,
café y gris
Tallas: P, M, G, XG
Ahora: 72.500 pesos

Traje inglés
Modelos originales
Ahora: 105.000 pesos
30% de rebaja

Pantalones
Colores negro, gris y café
Ahora: 68.000 pesos
30% de rebaja

Accesorios
Gafas de sol, corbatas,
cinturones, calcetines
Diversos estilos
Todos con un 40% de rebaja

Zapatos
Italianos y franceses
Números del 40 al 45
A sólo 60.000 pesos

Ropa interior
Tallas: P, M, G
Colores blanco, negro y gris
40% de rebaja

Real *Royal* Liquidación *Clearance sale* Algodón *Cotton*
seda *silk* De cuadros *Plaid* Números *Shoe sizes*

Por la compra de 40.000 pesos, puede llevar un regalo de nuestra tienda:

- Un cinturón de mujer
- Un par de calcetines
- Una corbata de seda
- Una bolsa para la playa
- Una mochila
- Unas medias

Después de leer

¿Comprendiste?

Indicate whether each statement is **cierto** or **falso.** Correct the false statements.

Cierto | **Falso**

_____ _____ 1. Hay sandalias de playa.

_____ _____ 2. El almacén Corona tiene un departamento de zapatos.

_____ _____ 3. Corona abre a las nueve de la mañana los domingos.

_____ _____ 4. Una elegante chaqueta café cuesta 72.500 pesos.

_____ _____ 5. Las corbatas para hombre tienen una rebaja del 25%.

_____ _____ 6. Normalmente las sandalias cuestan 25.000 pesos.

_____ _____ 7. El almacén Corona acepta tarjetas de crédito.

_____ _____ 8. Cuando gastas 30.000 pesos en la tienda, llevas un regalo.

Preguntas

Answer these questions.

1. ¿Cuánto cuestan los zapatos de hombre?
_____

2. ¿Hay rebaja de blusas de algodón?
_____

3. ¿Hay rebaja de ropa para niños?
_____

4. ¿Hay rebaja de minifaldas? _____

Coméntalo

Imagina que vas a ir a Corona. ¿Qué ropa vas a comprar? ¿Hay tiendas similares a Corona en tu comunidad? ¿Cómo se llaman? ¿Tienen muchas rebajas?

_____

I CAN skim a reading selection and find general and specific information in it.

Vocabulary Tools

La ropa y los accesorios

el abrigo *coat*
los bluejeans *jeans*
la blusa *blouse*
la bolsa *bag; purse*
las botas *boots*
los calcetines *socks*
la camisa *shirt*
la camiseta *t-shirt*
la cartera *wallet*
la chaqueta *jacket*
el cinturón *belt*
la corbata *tie*
la falda *skirt*
las gafas (de sol) *(sun)glasses*
los guantes *gloves*
el impermeable *raincoat*
las medias *pantyhose; stockings*
los pantalones *pants*
los pantalones cortos *shorts*
el par de zapatos *pair of shoes*
la ropa *clothing*
la ropa interior *underwear*
las sandalias *sandals*
el sombrero *hat*
el suéter *sweater*
el traje *suit*
el traje de baño *bathing suit*
el vestido *dress*
los zapatos de tenis *sneakers*

Adjetivos

barato/a *cheap*
bueno/a *good*
cada *each*
caro/a *expensive*
corto/a *short (in length)*
elegante *elegant*
hermoso/a *beautiful*
largo/a *long*
loco/a *crazy*
nuevo/a *new*
otro/a *other; another*
pobre *poor*
rico/a *rich*

De compras

el almacén *department store*
la caja *cash register*
el centro comercial *shopping mall*
el/la cliente/a *client*
el/la dependiente/a *clerk*
el dinero *money*
el mercado (al aire libre) *(open-air) market*
el precio (fijo) *(fixed) price*
la rebaja *sale*
el regalo *gift*
la tarjeta de crédito *credit card*
la tarjeta de débito *debit card*
la tienda *store*
el/la vendedor(a) *salesperson*

comprar en línea *to buy online*
costar (o:ue) *to cost*
gastar *to spend (money)*
hacer juego (con) *to match*
ir de compras *to go shopping*
llevar *to wear; to take*
pagar (con) *to pay (with)*
prestar *to lend*
regatear *to bargain*
usar *to wear; to use*
vender *to sell*

Palabras y expresiones

anoche *last night*
anteayer *the day before yesterday*
el año pasado *last year*
ayer *yesterday*
de repente *suddenly*
desde *from*
hasta *until*
pasado/a *(adj.) last; past*
la semana pasada *last week*
una vez *once*
dos veces *twice*
ya *already*

el beso *kiss*
la mentira *lie*
la verdad *truth*

¿Qué hicieron ellos/ellas? *What did they do?*
¿Qué hicieron ustedes? *What did you (pl.) do?*
¿Qué hiciste? *What did you (fam., sing.) do?*
¿Qué hizo él/ella? *What did he/she do?*
¿Qué hizo usted? *What did you (form., sing.) do?*

acabar de (+ *inf.*) *to have just done something*
dar *to give*
decir *to say; to tell*

Los colores *See page 141.*
Numbers 101 and higher *See page 150.*
Indirect object pronouns *See page 154.*
Demonstrative adjectives and pronouns *See pages 156–157.*

∞ Communicative Goals: Review

I CAN talk about clothes.
• Describe what you are wearing.

I CAN negotiate and pay for items.
• Explain how to bargain in a market.

I CAN express preferences while shopping.
• Say which colors and articles of clothing you prefer.

I CAN investigate markets in the Spanish-speaking world.
• Describe one of the open-air markets from this lesson.

AVENTURAS EN LOS PAÍSES HISPANOS

Communicative Goal
Identify aspects of the geography and culture of Puerto Rico, Cuba, and the Dominican Republic

Cada año miles de personas de todo el mundo *(world)* llegan al Caribe para disfrutar *(to enjoy)* de sus encantos. De aguas cálidas *(warm)* y transparentes, el mar caribeño rodea *(surrounds)* las costas *(coasts)* de Cuba, Puerto Rico y la República Dominicana. Además de sus increíbles playas, el Caribe goza de *(enjoys)* un clima tropical todo el año y posee una enorme variedad de plantas y animales exóticos.

¿Te gustaría *(Would you like)* ir al Caribe algún *(some)* día?

EL CARIBE

Puerto Rico

Área: 8.870 km² (3.425 millas²)
Población: 2.900.000
Capital: San Juan – 2.451.000
Ciudades principales: Caguas, Mayagüez, Ponce
Moneda: dólar estadounidense

SOURCE: Population Division, UN Secretariat & CIA World Factbook

Cuba

Área: 109.890 km² (42.429 millas²)
Población: 11.300.000
Capital: La Habana – 2.138.000
Ciudades principales: Santiago de Cuba, Camagüey, Holguín, Guantánamo
Moneda: peso cubano

SOURCE: Population Division, UN Secretariat & CIA World Factbook

República Dominicana

Área: 48.670 km² (18.790 millas²)
Población: 10.700.000
Capital: Santo Domingo – 3.245.000
Ciudades principales: Santiago de los Caballeros, La Vega
Moneda: peso dominicano

SOURCE: Population Division, UN Secretariat & CIA World Factbook

Video

ESTADOS UNIDOS

Lugares

La Habana Vieja

La Habana Vieja es uno de los lugares más maravillosos de Cuba. Este distrito fue declarado *(was declared)* Patrimonio *(Heritage)* Cultural de la Humanidad por la UNESCO en 1982. En la Plaza de Armas, se puede visitar el majestuoso Palacio de Capitanes Generales, que ahora es un museo. En la calle *(street)* Obispo, frecuentada por el escritor Ernest Hemingway, hay hermosos cafés, clubes nocturnos y tiendas elegantes.

¿Por qué crees que la Habana Vieja fue declarada Patrimonio Cultural de la Humanidad?

Plaza de la Catedral en La Habana

Estrecho de la Florida

★ La Habana

Cordillera de Guaniguanico

Océano Atlántico

Isla de la Juventud

CUBA

Mar de las Antillas

Camagüey •

Holguín •

Deportes

El béisbol

Para algunos latinoamericanos, el béisbol es más que un deporte. Los primeros países hispanos en tener una liga fueron *(were)* Cuba y México, donde se empezó a jugar al béisbol en el siglo *(century)* XIX. Hoy día este deporte es una afición nacional en la República Dominicana. Albert Pujols, Juan Soto, Pedro Martínez y David Ortiz son sólo cuatro de los muchísimos beisbolistas dominicanos que han alcanzado *(have reached)* gran éxito e inmensa popularidad entre los aficionados.

¿Practicas béisbol? ¿Qué equipos de béisbol conoces *(do you know)*? ¿Cuál es tu equipo favorito?

Sierra Maestra
Santiago de Cuba

Guantánamo

Albert Pujols

Juan Soto

Música

La salsa y el merengue

Hoy día Puerto Rico es el centro internacional de la salsa. El Gran Combo de Puerto Rico, por ejemplo, es una de las orquestas de salsa más famosas del mundo. Sin embargo *(Nevertheless)*, este género musical, que comúnmente *(commonly)* se asocia con el Caribe, nació *(was born)* en barrios latinos de Nueva York como resultado de una mezcla *(mix)* de influencias puertorriqueñas, cubanas, africanas, españolas y de los Estados Unidos.

El merengue, un ritmo de la República Dominicana, tiene sus raíces *(roots)* en el campo. Tradicionalmente las canciones hablaban de los problemas sociales de los campesinos *(farmers)*. Entre 1930 y 1960, el merengue se popularizó en las ciudades y adoptó un tono más urbano. Uno de los cantantes y compositores de merengue más famosos es Juan Luis Guerra.

¿Te gustan la salsa y el merengue? ¿Conoces grupos o artistas famosos de estos géneros musicales?

Economía

La caña de azúcar y el tabaco ▶

La caña de azúcar *(sugar cane)* es el producto agrícola *(agricultural)* que más se cultiva en Cuba y su exportación es muy importante para la economía del país. El tabaco, que se usa para fabricar los famosos puros *(cigars)* cubanos, es otro cultivo *(crop)* de mucha importancia.

¿Cuáles son los productos agrícolas más importantes de tu estado o región?

Monumentos

El Morro

El Morro, el gran tesoro *(treasure)* de Puerto Rico, es un fuerte *(fort)* que está en la bahía *(bay)* de San Juan. Lo construyeron *(built)* los españoles en el siglo *(century)* XVI para defenderse de los piratas. Desde 1961, El Morro es un museo que atrae *(attracts)* a miles de turistas. También es el sitio más fotografiado de Puerto Rico. La arquitectura del fuerte es impresionante: tiene túneles misteriosos, mazmorras *(dungeons)* y vistas *(views)* fabulosas de la bahía.

¿Cuál es el sitio más fotografiado de tu comunidad? ¿Por qué?

Puerto Plata •

Santiago •

Río Yuna

HAITÍ

LA REPÚBLICA DOMINICANA

Sierra de Neiba

San Pedro
de Macorís

Sierra de Baoruco

Santo
Domingo

Arecibo

San
Juan

Fajardo

Mayagüez

Isla
Culebra

Ponce

Isla de Vieques

PUERTO RICO

¿Qué aprendiste?

1 **¿Cierto o falso?** Indicate whether each statement is **cierto** or **falso**.

	Cierto	Falso
1. San Juan es la capital de Puerto Rico.	_____	_____
2. La Habana Vieja es la parte nueva de la capital de Cuba.	_____	_____
3. Los primeros países hispanos en tener una liga de béisbol fueron Cuba y Puerto Rico.	_____	_____
4. El béisbol es el deporte de afición nacional de la República Dominicana.	_____	_____
5. La salsa nació en Nueva York.	_____	_____
6. El merengue tiene sus raíces en la ciudad.	_____	_____
7. Juan Luis Guerra es un cantante de merengue.	_____	_____
8. El Morro fue construido por (*was built by*) piratas en el siglo XVI.	_____	_____

2 **Preguntas** Answer the questions.

1. ¿Cuál es el producto agícola que más se cultiva en Cuba?
2. ¿Qué género musical tiene influencias puertorriqueñas, cubanas, africanas y españolas?
3. ¿Quién es Juan Soto?
4. ¿Dónde está El Morro?
5. ¿Qué hay en la calle Obispo en la Habana Vieja?

3 **Presentación** In pairs, prepare a presentation about a Caribbean country. Your presentation should answer the following questions.

- ¿Qué atracciones hay en este país?
- ¿Cuáles son sus artistas más célebres?
- ¿Cuál es su comida más representativa?

4 **Comparaciones** Compare the flags of Puerto Rico and Cuba. Then compare them with the flag of the United States.

5 **¿Qué piensas?** Reflect on these questions.

1. ¿Por qué piensas que el béisbol es tan (*so*) popular en el Caribe?
2. ¿Por qué crees que el merengue adoptó un tono más urbano?
3. ¿Por qué piensas que la salsa tiene una mezcla de influencias?

I CAN identify basic facts about the geography and culture of Puerto Rico, Cuba, and the Dominican Republic by reading short informational texts with visuals.

7 La vida diaria

Communicative Goals
You will learn how to:
- describe daily routines
- talk about personal hygiene
- tell where you went
- investigate sleep and food customs in the Spanish-speaking world

PREPARACIÓN

pages 170–175
- Words related to personal hygiene and daily routines
- Sequencing expressions
- Pronouncing **r** and **rr**

AVENTURAS

pages 176–177
- The two sets of roommates are not getting along. There are conflicts between Olga Lucía and Valentina and between Juanjo and Manuel over sharing the bathroom and using each other's things.

CULTURA

pages 178–179
- *La siesta*
- Flash cultura: *Tapas para todos los días*

GRAMÁTICA

pages 180–191
- Reflexive verbs
- Indefinite and negative words
- Preterite of **ser** and **ir**
- **Gustar** and verbs like **gustar**

LECTURA

pages 192–193
- Magazine article: *¡Una mañana desastrosa!*

✆ PARA EMPEZAR
- ¿Cómo está el chico: contento o enojado?
- ¿Cuántas cosas tiene en las manos?
- ¿Qué ropa lleva? ¿De qué color es?

LA VIDA DIARIA

LA HIGIENE PERSONAL

afeitarse *to shave*

bañarse *to take a bath*

cepillarse el pelo *to brush one's hair*

cepillarse los dientes
to brush one's teeth

ducharse *to shower*

lavarse la cara *to wash one's face*

lavarse las manos
to wash one's hands

maquillarse *to put on makeup*

peinarse *to comb one's hair*

---

el baño *bathroom*

el champú *shampoo*

la crema de afeitar *shaving cream*

el maquillaje *makeup*

la toalla *towel*

Raúl se ducha.

Isabel se lava las manos.

el jabón

Paula se cepilla los dientes.

Daniel se afeita.

Adriana se baña.

Vocabulary Tools

Sofía se duerme.

OTRAS PALABRAS Y EXPRESIONES

la rutina diaria *daily routine*
_____

antes (de) *before*
después *afterward; then*
después de *after*
durante *during*
entonces *then*
luego *afterward; then*
más tarde *later (on)*
por la mañana *in the morning*
por la noche *at night*
por la tarde *in the afternoon; in the (early) evening*
por último *finally*
siempre *always*
también *also; too*
temprano *early*

POR LA MAÑANA Y POR LA NOCHE

acostarse (o:ue)
  to lie down; to go to bed
despertarse (e:ie) *to wake up*
dormirse (o:ue)
  to go to sleep; to fall asleep
levantarse *to get up*
vestirse (e:i) *to get dressed*

Jorge se levanta.

el espejo

el despertador

ASÍ SE DICE
afeitarse ⟷ rasurarse (*Méx., Amér. C.*)
la ducha ⟷ la regadera (*Col., Méx., Venez.*)
ducharse ⟷ bañarse (*Amér. L.*)

A escuchar

1 **Escuchar** Indica si, en general, las personas hacen las acciones que vas a escuchar por la mañana o por la noche.

	Por la mañana	Por la noche
1.	_____	_____
2.	_____	_____
3.	_____	_____
4.	_____	_____
5.	_____	_____
6.	_____	_____
7.	_____	_____
8.	_____	_____

2 **¿Lógico o ilógico?** Escucha las oraciones e indica si cada oración es **lógica** o **ilógica**.

	Lógico	Ilógico
1.	_____	_____
2.	_____	_____
3.	_____	_____
4.	_____	_____
5.	_____	_____
6.	_____	_____

A practicar

3 **Ordenar** Ordena la rutina de Francisco de manera lógica.

_____ a. Después de afeitarse, cepillarse los dientes y vestirse, sale para las clases.

_____ b. Por último, se acuesta a las once y media de la noche.

_____ c. Se ducha y luego se afeita.

_____ d. Por la noche come un poco. Luego estudia antes de acostarse.

_____ e. Asiste a todas sus clases y vuelve a casa por la tarde.

_____ f. Por la mañana, Francisco se despierta a las seis y media.

4 **Identificar** Con un(a) compañero/a, indica qué necesitan estas personas para realizar (*to perform*) estas acciones.

modelo

Miguel / vestirse
Estudiante 1: ¿Qué necesita Miguel para (*in order to*) vestirse?
Estudiante 2: Necesita una camiseta y unos pantalones.

1. **Diego / acostarse**

2. **Raúl / despertarse**

3. **Mercedes / lavarse la cara**

4. **Leonardo / afeitarse**

5. **Sofía / lavarse el pelo**

6. **Yolanda / maquillarse**

A conversar

5 **La rutina diaria** Con un(a) compañero/a, mira las fotos y describe qué hace cada persona.

modelo

Estudiante 1: ¿Qué hace Alejandro?
Estudiante 2: *Se afeita.*

Alejandro

1.

Rosa

2.

Natalia

3.

Carlos

4.

Julia

5.

María Elena

6.

Nicolás

6 **Preguntas** En parejas, túrnense para hacerse estas preguntas. ¿Qué respuestas tienen en común?

1. ¿Cómo es tu baño?

2. ¿Cuántas personas comparten tu baño?

3. ¿De qué color es tu toalla?

4. ¿Cuánto cuesta tu jabón?

5. ¿Qué champú usas?

6. ¿Cuándo estudias? ¿Por la mañana, por la tarde, por la noche?

I CAN describe daily routines and talk about personal hygiene products.

Pronunciación

  Tutorial

The consonant r

ropa	**r**utina	**r**ico	**R**amón

In Spanish, **r** has a strong trilled sound at the beginning of a word. No English words have a trill, but English speakers often produce a trill when they imitate the sound of a motor.

gusta**r**	du**r**ante	prime**r**o	c**r**ema

In any other position, **r** has a weak sound similar to the English *tt* in *better* or the English *dd* in *ladder*. In contrast to English, the tongue touches the roof of the mouth behind the teeth.

piza**rr**a	co**rr**o	ma**rr**ón	abu**rr**ido

The letter combination **rr**, which only appears between vowels, always has a strong trilled sound.

ca**r**o	ca**rr**o	pe**r**o	pe**rr**o

Between vowels, the difference between the strong trilled **rr** and the weak **r** is very important, as a mispronunciation could lead to confusion between two different words.

Práctica Lee las palabras en voz alta, prestando (*paying*) atención a la pronunciación de la **r** y la **rr**.

1. Perú
2. Rosa
3. borrador
4. madre
5. comprar
6. favor
7. rubio
8. reloj
9. Arequipa
10. tarde
11. cerrar
12. despertador

Oraciones Lee las oraciones en voz alta, prestando atención a la pronunciación de la **r** y la **rr**.

1. Ramón Robles Ruiz es programador. Su esposa Rosaura es artista.
2. A Rosaura Robles le encanta regatear en el mercado.
3. Ramón nunca regatea… le aburre regatear.
4. Rosaura siempre compra cosas baratas.
5. Ramón no es rico, pero prefiere comprar cosas muy caras.
6. ¡El martes Ramón compró un carro nuevo!

Refranes Lee en voz alta los refranes, prestando atención a la **r** y a la **rr**.

Perro que ladra no muerde.[1]

No se ganó Zamora en una hora.[2]

[1] *The dog's bark is worse than its bite.*
[2] *Rome wasn't built in a day.*

¡Tengo que arreglarme!

Hay conflictos entre los compañeros de cuarto.

 Video

Antes de ver

Mira las imágenes y haz predicciones sobre los conflictos entre los compañeros de cuarto.

PERSONAJES

OLGA LUCÍA

VALENTINA

MANUEL

JUANJO

OLGA LUCÍA ¿Dónde está mi cepillo?
VALENTINA ¡Buenos días!
OLGA LUCÍA ¡Mi cepillo rojo! ¿Lo tienes tú?
VALENTINA ¿No está en el baño?
OLGA LUCÍA ¡No! ¡No está en el baño, ni en el cuarto, ni en ninguna parte!

MANUEL ¡Juanjo!
JUANJO ¿Qué quieres?
MANUEL ¡Alguien te está llamando!

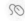

JUANJO ¡Manuel! ¡Fuiste tú! ¡Muy gracioso!... ¡Tengo clase a las nueve en punto!

ACTIVIDADES

1 **¿Cierto o falso?** Indica si lo que dicen estas oraciones es **cierto** o **falso**. Corrige las oraciones falsas.

	Cierto	Falso
1. Olga Lucía no encuentra su cepillo azul.	○	○
2. Juanjo tiene que cepillarse los dientes.	○	○
3. Manuel usa el cepillo de dientes de Juanjo.	○	○
4. Valentina tiene en su bolsa el maquillaje de Olga Lucía.	○	○
5. Manuel lleva las pantuflas de Juanjo.	○	○

2 **Preguntas** Contesta estas preguntas.

1. ¿A qué hora se levanta Olga Lucía?
2. ¿Quién hace yoga?
3. ¿De qué color es el cepillo de dientes de Juanjo?
4. ¿Quién tiene clase a las nueve en punto?
5. ¿Por qué tiene miedo Olga Lucía?
6. ¿Dónde encuentra Valentina el cepillo de Olga Lucía?

JUANJO ¡Manuel!

MANUEL Está ocupado.

JUANJO ¡Tengo que cepillarme los dientes!... ¡Ése es tu cepillo!

MANUEL ¿En serio? ¿Mi cepillo no es el rojo?

JUANJO ¡No!

MANUEL ¡Yo siempre uso éste!

VALENTINA ¿Encontraste el cepillo?

OLGA LUCÍA ¡Todavía no! ¡¿Estás usando mis calcetines?! ¿Por qué siempre te pones mis cosas?

VALENTINA ¿Son tus calcetines?

OLGA LUCÍA ¡Claro! ¡Los tienes desde hace dos meses, cuando fuimos a Toledo! ¡Por eso nunca encuentro mis cosas!

VALENTINA ¡No es por eso! ¡Pierdes todo en ese desorden!

JUANJO ¡No puedes lavarte el pelo con mi champú! ¡Me molesta! ¡Y no puedes afeitarte con mi crema de afeitar! ¡Y no puedes secarte con mi toalla! ¡Jamás! ¡Gracias!

MANUEL ¿Y tus pantuflas?

JUANJO ¡Tampoco!

MANUEL ¡Me encantan sus pantuflas!

Expresiones útiles

la araña *spider*
la ayuda *help*
el cepillo *brush*
cuando *when*
desde hace *for (a period of time)*
el desorden *mess*
¿En serio? *Really?*
gracioso/a *funny*
llamar *to call*
las pantuflas *slippers*
por eso *that's why*
secarse *to dry (oneself)*

———

la alarma *alarm*
gritar *to scream*

Los madrileños

Los habitantes de Madrid desayunan (*have breakfast*) entre las siete y las nueve de la mañana, almuerzan (*have lunch*) entre las dos y las cuatro de la tarde y cenan (*have dinner*) entre las nueve y las doce de la noche. Una teoría dice que a los madrileños se les llama gatos (*cats*) porque les gusta salir por la noche.

¿Te gustar cenar tarde y salir por la noche?

3 **Compañeros de cuarto** En parejas, representen una de estas situaciones entre dos compañeros/as de cuarto.

▸ Los/Las dos compañeros/as de cuarto quieren usar el baño al mismo tiempo.

▸ Un(a) compañero/a usa las cosas del/de la otro/a.

▸ Un(a) compañero/a no quiere prestar una cosa al/a la otro/a.

▸ Un(a) compañero/a no encuentra el champú/cepillo.

I CAN participate in a conversation between two roommates.

La **siesta**

¿Sientes cansancio° después de comer?
¿Te cuesta° volver al trabajo° o a clase después del almuerzo°? Estas sensaciones son normales. A muchas personas les gusta relajarse° después de almorzar°. Este momento de descanso es **la siesta**. La siesta es popular en los países hispanos y viene de una antigua costumbre° del área del Mediterráneo. La palabra *siesta* viene del latín y significa "sexta hora". La sexta hora del día es después del mediodía, el momento de más calor. Debido al° calor y al cansancio, los habitantes de España, Italia, Grecia y Portugal tienen la costumbre de dormir la siesta desde hace° más de° dos mil años. Los españoles y los portugueses llevaron la costumbre a los países americanos.

¿Dónde duermen la siesta?

En los lugares donde la siesta es una costumbre antigua, las personas la duermen en su casa. En los países donde la siesta es una costumbre nueva, la gente duerme en sus lugares de trabajo o en centros de siesta.

Aunque° hoy día esta costumbre está desapareciendo° en las grandes ciudades, la siesta todavía es importante en la cultura hispana. En pueblos pequeños, por ejemplo, muchas oficinas° y tiendas tienen la costumbre de cerrar por dos o tres horas después del mediodía. Los empleados van a su casa, almuerzan con sus familias, duermen la siesta o hacen actividades, como ir al gimnasio, y luego regresan al trabajo entre las 2:30 y las 4:30 de la tarde.

Algunos estudios científicos explican que una siesta corta después de almorzar ayuda° a trabajar más y mejor° durante la tarde. Pero ¡cuidado! Esta

siesta debe durar° sólo entre veinte y cuarenta minutos. Si dormimos más, entramos en la fase de sueño profundo y es difícil despertarse.

Hoy, algunas empresas° de los EE.UU., Canadá, Japón, Inglaterra y Alemania tienen salas° especiales donde los empleados pueden dormir la siesta.

Sientes cansancio *Do you feel tired* Te cuesta *Is it hard for you* trabajo *work* almuerzo *lunch* relajarse *to relax* almorzar *to have lunch* antigua costumbre *old custom* Debido al *Due to the* desde hace *for* más de *more than* Aunque *Although* está desapareciendo *is disappearing* oficinas *offices* ayuda *helps* mejor *better* durar *last* algunas empresas *some businesses* salas *rooms*

ASÍ SE DICE

El cuidado personal

el acondicionador la crema de enjuage	*conditioner*
el aseo el excusado el servicio el váter (Esp.)	*el baño*
la crema humectante	*moisturizer*
el cortaúñas	*nail clippers*
el desodorante	*deodorant*
el enjuague bucal	*mouthwash*
el hilo dental la seda dental	*dental floss*
la máquina de afeitar la máquina de rasurar (Méx.)	*electric razor*

ACTIVIDADES

1 **¿Cierto o falso?** Indica si lo que dicen las oraciones es **cierto** o **falso**. Corrige la información falsa.

1. La costumbre de la siesta empezó en Asia.
2. La palabra *siesta* está relacionada con la sexta hora del día.
3. Los españoles y los portugueses llevaron la costumbre de la siesta a Latinoamérica.
4. Los horarios de trabajo de las grandes ciudades hispanas son los mismos que los de los pueblos pequeños.
5. En los Estados Unidos, los empleados de algunas empresas pueden dormir la siesta en el trabajo.

2 **Preguntas** Contesta las preguntas.

1. ¿Cuándo es la sexta hora?
2. ¿Qué países europeos tienen la costumbre de la siesta?
3. ¿Dónde cierran muchas oficinas y tiendas por dos o tres horas después del mediodía?
4. ¿Cuántos minutos debe durar una siesta?
5. ¿Dónde duermen la siesta los españoles?

3 **Comparación** Compara la siesta en los lugares donde la siesta es una costumbre antigua con la siesta en los lugares donde es una costumbre nueva.

4 **Una nueva costumbre** Con un(a) compañero/a, imagina que las tiendas y comercios en donde vives deciden adoptar la costumbre de la hora de la siesta. ¿Es una buena idea? ¿Cómo afecta esta nueva costumbre tu vida diaria? ¿Qué debes hacer para adaptarte?

5 **Perspectivas** Responde a estas preguntas.

1. ¿Por qué piensas que la siesta es tan importante en la cultura hispana?
2. ¿Por qué crees que la costumbre de la siesta está desapareciendo en las grandes ciudades?
3. ¿Por qué piensas que la siesta es una costumbre nueva en los Estados Unidos y Canadá?

I CAN identify customs in my own and other cultures.

 Video

Tapas para todos los días

1 **Preparación** En el área donde vives, ¿qué hacen las personas normalmente después del trabajo (*work*)? ¿Van a sus casas? ¿Salen con amigos? ¿Comen?

2 **El video** Mira el episodio de **Flash cultura** sobre las tapas en España.

Vocabulario
económicas *inexpensive*
montaditos *bread slices with assorted toppings*
pagar propinas *to tip*
tapar el hambre *to take the edge off (lit. putting the lid on one's hunger)*

Éstos son los montaditos, o también llamados pinchos. ¿Te gustan?

3 **Ordenar** Ordena estos eventos.

_____ 1. El empleado cuenta los palillos (*counts the toothpicks*) de los montaditos que Mari Carmen comió.
_____ 2. Mari Carmen va al barrio de la Ribera.
_____ 3. Un hombre en un bar explica cuándo sale a tomar tapas.
_____ 4. Un hombre explica la tradición de los montaditos o pinchos.
_____ 5. Mari Carmen le pregunta a la chica si los montaditos son buenos para la salud.

4 **Las tapas** Con un(a) compañero/a, responde a estas preguntas sobre las tapas.

1. ¿Qué piensas de la costumbre de ir de tapas?
2. ¿Qué dice sobre la cultura española la costumbre?
3. ¿Quieres ir de tapas después de las clases? ¿Por qué?
4. ¿Hay restaurantes de tapas en tu comunidad?

I CAN identify a popular after-work activity in Spain.

Communicative Goal
Describe daily routines

7.1 Reflexive verbs

▶ A reflexive verb is used to indicate that the subject does something to or for himself or herself. Reflexive verbs always use reflexive pronouns.

SUBJECT   REFLEXIVE VERB

Carlos   **se afeita** todos los días.

Reflexive verbs

(lavarse)

yo	**me lavo**	*I wash (myself)*
tú	**te lavas**	*you wash (yourself)*
usted	**se lava**	*you wash (yourself)*
él/ella	**se lava**	*he/she washes (himself/herself)*
nosotros/as	**nos lavamos**	*we wash (ourselves)*
vosotros/as	**os laváis**	*you wash (yourselves)*
ustedes	**se lavan**	*you wash (yourselves)*
ellos/ellas	**se lavan**	*they wash (themselves)*

▶ When a reflexive verb is conjugated, the reflexive pronoun agrees with the subject: **Me peino**.

¿Por qué siempre te pones mis cosas?

¡No puedes lavarte el pelo con mi champú!

▶ Reflexive pronouns follow the same rules for placement as object pronouns. They are placed before the conjugated verb, or attached to the infinitive or present participle. When a pronoun is attached to the participle, an accent mark is added.

José **se** levanta temprano.
José gets up early.

José **se** va a levantar temprano.
José va a levantar**se** temprano.
José is going to get up early.

Carlos **se** afeita.
Carlos shaves.

Carlos está afeitándo**se**.
Carlos **se** está afeitando.
Carlos is shaving.

¡ojo! Unlike English, Spanish uses the definite article, not a possessive adjective, when referring to clothing or parts of the body.

La niña se quitó **los** zapatos.
*The girl took off **her** shoes.*

Me cepillé **los** dientes.
*I brushed **my** teeth.*

Práctica

1 **Conversaciones** Completa las conversaciones con la forma apropiada de los verbos.

MARIO Tú (1) _____ [lavar / lavarse] los platos ayer, ¿no?

TOMÁS Sí, los (2) _____ [lavar / lavarse] después de las clases.

• • •

BEATRIZ ¿Normalmente (tú) (3) _____ [duchar / ducharse] antes de ir a clase?

DAVID Sí, (4) _____ [duchar / ducharse] por la mañana.

• • •

MAMÁ Niños, ¿a qué hora (5) _____ [acostar / acostarse] ustedes anoche?

PABLO Daniela (6) _____ [acostar / acostarse] a las nueve, pero nosotros (7) _____ [acostar / acostarse] a las ocho.

• • •

ANA Yo (8) _____ [sentir / sentirse] nerviosa hoy.

PATRICIA Bueno... tú siempre (9) _____ [sentir / sentirse] nerviosa antes de un examen.

2 **Emparejar** Empareja cada foto con la oración correspondiente. Luego, indica qué oraciones tienen verbos reflexivos.

1.   2.

3.   4.

5.   6.

¿Reflexivo?

_____ a. Julia se enoja.   _____

_____ b. Verónica se maquilla.   _____

_____ c. Manuela baña a su hija.   _____

_____ d. Estela se pone los calcetines.   _____

_____ e. El abuelo despierta a sus nietas.   _____

_____ f. Ramón se cepilla los dientes.   _____

Conversación

 3 Preguntas En parejas, túrnense para hacerse estas preguntas. ¿Qué respuestas tienen en común?

1. ¿Cuándo te enojas?
2. ¿Cuándo te sientes feliz?
3. ¿A qué hora te despertaste ayer?
4. ¿A qué hora te levantaste hoy?
5. ¿Te cepillaste los dientes esta mañana?
6. ¿Te lavas las manos antes de comer?
7. ¿Te duermes antes o después de la medianoche?
8. ¿A qué hora te vas a acostar esta noche?

4 Charadas En grupos, jueguen a las charadas. Cada persona debe pensar en dos oraciones con verbos reflexivos. La primera persona que adivina la charada dramatiza la siguiente (*next one*).

5 Entrevista Primero, prepara una lista con las actividades que hiciste anoche. Luego, compara con un(a) compañero/a las actividades y toma apuntes (*notes*) de lo que hizo él/ella. Sigue el modelo para el primer paso (*step*).

6:00 p.m.	En el Centro Comercial. Me probé un vestido.
7:30 p.m.	Cine con Javier. Muy aburrido. Casi (*Almost*) me dormí.
9:00 p.m.	En el restaurante Cangrejo. Me enojé con Ana.
11:00 p.m.	Fiesta en casa de Antonio. Me acosté tarde.

Common reflexive verbs

Common reflexive verbs			
acordarse (de) (o:ue)	to remember	levantarse	to get up
acostarse (o:ue)	to go to bed	llamarse	to be named
afeitarse	to shave	maquillarse	to put on makeup
bañarse	to take a bath	peinarse	to comb one's hair
cepillarse	to brush	ponerse	to put on
despertarse (e:ie)	to wake up	ponerse (+ *adj.*)	to become (+ *adj.*)
dormirse (o:ue)	to go to sleep	preocuparse (por)	to worry (about)
ducharse	to shower	probarse (o:ue)	to try on
enojarse (con)	to get angry (with)	quedarse	to stay
irse	to go away; to leave	quitarse	to take off
		sentarse (e:ie)	to sit down
lavarse	to wash oneself	sentirse (e:ie)	to feel
		vestirse (e:i)	to get dressed

▶ Many Spanish verbs can be reflexive. If the verb acts upon the subject, use the reflexive form. If the verb acts upon something else, use the non-reflexive form.

Lola **lava** los platos.

Isabel **se lava** la cara.

¡ojo! Reflexive verbs and their non-reflexive counterparts sometimes have different meanings.

acordar *to agree*   **acordarse** *to remember*
levantar *to lift*   **levantarse** *to get up*

¡Manos a la obra!

Indica el presente de estos verbos reflexivos.

despertarse

1. Ellos _se despiertan_ tarde.
2. Tú _____ tarde.
3. Nosotros _____ tarde.
4. Antonio _____ tarde.
5. Yo _____ tarde.
6. Ustedes _____ tarde.

ponerse

1. Ella _se pone_ los pantalones.
2. Yo _____ los pantalones.
3. Usted _____ los pantalones.
4. Nosotros _____ los pantalones.
5. Las niñas _____ los pantalones.
6. Tú _____ los pantalones.

I CAN describe daily routines.

Communicative Goal
Talk about some places in my community

7.2 Indefinite and negative words

▸ Indefinite words, such as *someone* or *something*, refer to people and things that are not specific. Negative words, like *no one* or *nothing*, deny the existence of people and things or contradict statements.

Indefinite and negative words

Indefinite words		Negative words	
algo	something; anything	nada	nothing; not anything
alguien	someone; somebody; anyone	nadie	no one; nobody; not anyone
alguno/a(s), algún	some; any	ninguno/a, ningún	no; none; not any
o... o	either... or	ni... ni	neither... nor
		nunca, jamás	never, not ever
		tampoco	neither; not either

▸ There are two ways to form negative sentences in Spanish. You can place the negative word before the verb, or you can place **no** before the verb and the negative word after the verb.

Nadie piensa en mí.
No piensa **nadie** en mí.
Nobody thinks of me.

Ellos **nunca** se enojan.
Ellos **no** se enojan **nunca**.
They never get angry.

Ninguno me gusta.
No me gusta **ninguno**.
I don't like any.

Nada me despierta.
No me despierta **nada**.
Nothing wakes me up.

¡Alguien te está llamando!

¡No está en el baño, ni en el cuarto, ni en ninguna parte!

▸ In Spanish, sentences frequently contain two or more negative words. Once a sentence is negative, all indefinite ideas must be expressed in the negative.

Ella **no** tiene **ninguna** idea.
She doesn't have any idea.

Nunca te pido **nada**.
I never ask you for anything.

Jamás me preocupo por **nada**.
I never worry about anything.

Tampoco me acuerdo de **nadie**.
I don't remember anyone either.

Práctica

1 **La familia de Claudia** Completa las oraciones con **pero** o **sino**.

modelo

Mi abuela es aburrida, _____pero_____ amable.

1. No me ducho por la mañana, _____ por la noche.
2. A mí no me gusta nadar, _____ correr.
3. Mi hermana María Luisa es alta, _____ delgada.
4. Mi hermano Emilio no es moreno, _____ rubio.
5. Mis padres no se acuestan temprano, _____ tarde.
6. Mi primo Manuel es inteligente, _____ no es interesante.
7. Mi madre y yo siempre nos despertamos temprano, _____ nunca estamos cansadas.
8. Mi amiga Mariana es pequeña, _____ fuerte (*strong*).

2 **Completar** Completa esta conversación con oraciones que tengan (*have*) palabras negativas.

ALFONSO Ana María, ¿encontraste algún regalo para Elena?

ANA MARÍA (1) No, no encontré ningún regalo/nada para Elena.

ALFONSO ¿Viste a alguna amiga en el centro comercial?

ANA MARÍA (2) _____

ALFONSO Ana María, ¿quieres ir al teatro o al cine esta noche?

ANA MARÍA (3) _____

ALFONSO ¿Quieres salir a comer?

ANA MARÍA (4) _____

ALFONSO ¿Hay algo interesante en la televisión esta noche?

ANA MARÍA (5) _____

ALFONSO ¿Tienes algún problema?

ANA MARÍA (6) _____

ALFONSO ¿Eres siempre antipática?

ANA MARÍA (7) _____

Conversación

3 Quejas Con un(a) compañero/a, prepara una lista de cinco quejas (*complaints*) comunes que tienen los estudiantes universitarios. Usa expresiones negativas.

modelo

Nadie me entiende.
¡Jamás puedo levantarme tarde!

4 ¿Qué hay? En parejas, háganse preguntas sobre qué hay en su ciudad o pueblo: tiendas interesantes, almacenes, cines, una biblioteca, un museo, un aeropuerto, una estación del tren, etc. Sigan el modelo.

modelo

Estudiante 1: ¿Hay tiendas interesantes?
Estudiante 2: Sí, hay una/algunas. Está(n) en el centro.
Estudiante 1: ¿Hay un museo?
Estudiante 2: No, no hay ninguno.

5 Anuncios Con un(a) compañero/a, lee el anuncio (*ad*) y prepara otro similar sobre cualquier tipo de producto. Usa expresiones indefinidas y negativas.

¿Buscas algún producto especial?

¡No vas a poder resistirte jamás a las **ofertas** de las tiendas **García**!

Using indefinite words

▶ **Alguien** and **nadie** are often used with the personal **a**. The personal **a** is also used before **alguno/a**, **algunos/as**, and **ninguno/a** when these words refer to people and are the direct object of a verb.

—Carlos, ¿ves **a alguien** allí?
—No, no veo **a nadie**.

—¿Oyes **a alguno** de los chicos?
—No, no oigo **a ninguno**.

¡ojo! Before a masculine singular noun, **alguno** and **ninguno** are shortened to **algún** and **ningún**. Note that the personal **a** is not used with these words when they function as adjectives.

—¿Tienen ustedes **algún** amigo peruano?
—No, no tenemos **ningún** amigo peruano.

—¿Visitaste **algún** museo?
—No, no visité **ningún** museo.

Pero and sino

▶ Although the conjunctions **pero** and **sino** both mean *but*, they are not interchangeable. **Sino** is used when the first part of a sentence is negative and the second part contradicts it. In this context, **sino** means *but rather* or *on the contrary*. In all other cases, **pero** is used to mean *but*.

No se acuesta temprano, **sino** tarde.
*He doesn't go to bed early, **but rather** late.*

Canto, **pero** nunca en público.
*I sing, **but** never in public.*

No queremos irnos, **sino** quedarnos.
*We don't want to leave, **but rather** stay.*

Me desperté a las once, **pero** estoy cansada.
*I woke up at eleven, **but** I'm tired.*

¡Manos a la obra!

Cambia las oraciones para que sean (*they are*) negativas.

1. Siempre se viste bien. <u>Nunca</u> se viste bien.
2. Alguien se ducha. _____ se ducha _____.
3. Ellas van también. Ellas _____ van.
4. Juan también se afeita. Juan _____ se afeita.
5. Alguien se pone nervioso. _____ se pone nervioso _____.
6. Tú siempre te lavas las manos. Tú _____ te lavas las manos.
7. Voy a traer algo. _____ voy a traer _____.
8. La profesora hace algo en su escritorio. La profesora _____ hace _____ en su escritorio.
9. Mis amigos viven en una residencia o en una casa. Mis amigos _____ viven _____ en una residencia _____ en una casa.
10. Tú y yo vamos al mercado. _____ tú _____ yo vamos al mercado.
11. Tienen un espejo en su casa. _____ tienen _____ espejo en su casa.
12. Algunos niños se ponen el abrigo. _____ niño se pone el abrigo.

I CAN talk about some places in my community.

Communicative Goal
Talk about actions and states in the past

7.3 Preterite of **ser** and **ir**

▸ The preterite forms of **ser** (*to be*) and **ir** (*to go*) are irregular, so you will need to memorize them. None of these forms has an accent mark.

Preterite of *ser* and *ir*

	ser (to be)	ir (to go)
yo	fui	fui
tú	fuiste	fuiste
Ud./él/ella	fue	fue
nosotros/as	fuimos	fuimos
vosotros/as	fuisteis	fuisteis
Uds./ellos/ellas	fueron	fueron

▸ Since the preterite forms of **ser** and **ir** are identical, the context clarifies which verb is being used.

Lucía **fue** a ver una película.
Lucía went to see a film.

La película **fue** muy interesante.
The film was very interesting.

Fui a Barcelona el año pasado.
I went to Barcelona last year.

Fue un viaje maravilloso.
It was a wonderful trip.

¡Manuel!
¡Fuiste tú!

¡Los tienes desde
hace dos meses, cuando
fuimos a Toledo!

¡Manos a la obra!

Completa las oraciones usando el pretérito de **ir** y **ser**.

ir

1. Los viajeros __fueron__ a Perú.
2. Patricia _____ a Cuzco.
3. Tú _____ a Iquitos.
4. Gregorio y yo _____ a Lima.
5. Yo _____ a Trujillo.
6. Ustedes _____ a Arequipa.
7. Mi padre _____ a Lima.
8. Nosotras _____ a Cuzco.

ser

1. Usted __fue__ muy amable.
2. Yo _____ muy cordial.
3. Ellos _____ muy buenos.
4. Nosotros _____ muy impacientes.
5. Ella _____ muy antipática.
6. Tú _____ muy listo.
7. Ustedes _____ muy cordiales.
8. La gente _____ muy paciente.

Práctica

1 **Conversación** Completa esta conversación con la forma correcta del pretérito de **ser** o **ir**.

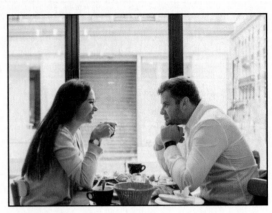

ANDRÉS Cristina y Vicente (1) _____ novios, ¿no?

LAURA Sí, pero ahora Cristina sale con Luis. Anoche ella (2) _____ a comer con él y la semana pasada ellos (3) _____ al partido de fútbol.

ANDRÉS ¿Ah, sí? Mercedes y yo (4) _____ al partido y no los vimos.

LAURA ¿(5) _____ tú con Mercedes? Y, ¿cómo (6) _____ el partido?

ANDRÉS (7) _____ muy divertido. ¡Lo pasamos genial! Pero... ¡qué extraño! Nosotros (8) _____ al café Paraíso y vimos a Vicente con la hermana de Cristina.

LAURA ¿Él (9) _____ al café Paraíso con su hermana? ¡Qué horror!

2 **Oraciones** Forma oraciones con los siguientes elementos. Usa el pretérito.

 modelo
Ustedes no fueron en autobús a Nueva York.

Sujetos	Verbos	Actividades
yo	(no) ir	a un restaurante
tú	(no) ser	en autobús a Nueva York
mis amigos/as		estudiante(s)
nosotros/as		a una discoteca en Buenos Aires
ustedes		muy amable
Lin-Manuel Miranda		a casa muy tarde
Awkwafina		a la playa con su novio/a
		dependiente/a en una tienda

Conversación

3 **Preguntas** Túrnate con un(a) compañero/a para hacerse las preguntas.

1. ¿Adónde fuiste de vacaciones el año pasado?
2. ¿Con quién fuiste?
3. ¿Cómo fueron tus vacaciones?
4. ¿Fuiste de compras esta semana? ¿Qué compraste?
5. ¿Cómo se llama la última película que viste?
6. ¿Cuándo fuiste a ver la película?
7. ¿Cómo fue la película?
8. ¿Adónde fuiste durante el fin de semana? ¿Por qué?

4 **El fin de semana pasado** Con un(a) compañero/a, habla de lo que hiciste el fin de semana pasado por la mañana, por la tarde y por la noche. Luego comparte la información con la clase.

	Yo	Mi compañero/a
Por la mañana	_____	_____
	_____	_____
	_____	_____
Por la tarde	_____	_____
	_____	_____
	_____	_____
Por la noche	_____	_____
	_____	_____
	_____	_____

5 **Veinte preguntas** En grupos pequeños, jueguen a las veinte preguntas. Una persona elige un personaje (*personality*) famoso. El resto del grupo hace preguntas hasta adivinar quién es. Los estudiantes deben hacer preguntas afirmativas o negativas con los verbos que conocen en el pretérito.

- Barack Obama
- Ariana Grande
- Alejandro González Iñárritu
- Simone Biles
- Tom Holland

Communicative Goal
Recognize familiar words in a simple ad

Español en vivo

Solario
Siempre te estamos esperando

Fue una **experiencia** increíble

"Cuando fui a Solario, me olvidé° de todo. Fui para despedirme de° todas mis preocupaciones y descubrir° los efectos calmantes del agua° de las lagunas. Después de bañarme en las aguas termales, se me fueron el cansancio° y el estrés. Fueron unas vacaciones extraordinarias."

30% de descuento sobre precios de nuestra página web

Hurtado 316 ◆ Teléfono: (506) 2327-3410 ◆ info@solario.com ◆ www.solario.com

olvidé *I forgot* **despedirme de** *to say goodbye to* **descubrir** *to discover* **agua** *water* **cansancio** *fatigue*

1 **Identificar** Lee el anuncio (*advertisement*) y busca ejemplos del pretérito de los verbos **ser** e **ir**.

2 **Preguntas** Contesta las preguntas.

1. ¿Cómo se siente el hombre del anuncio?
2. ¿Por qué fue a Solario? ¿Cómo fue su visita?
3. En tu opinión, ¿se acuerda este hombre de sus responsabilidades diarias mientras (*while*) está en Solario?
4. En tu opinión, ¿este hombre va a volver a Solario? ¿Por qué?

I CAN talk about actions and states in the past.

I CAN recognize familiar words in a simple ad.

7.4 **Gustar** and verbs like **gustar**

▸ **Me gusta(n)** and **te gusta(n)** express the concepts of *I like* and *you* (fam.) *like*. The literal meaning of **gustar** is *to be pleasing to (someone)*.

Me gusta ese champú.
That shampoo is pleasing to me.
I like that shampoo.

¿**Te gustan** los deportes?
Are sports pleasing to you?
Do you like sports?

▸ **Me gusta(n)** and similar constructions require an indirect object pronoun. In Spanish, the object or thing being liked (**el champú**) is the subject of the sentence. The person who likes the object is an indirect object that answers the question *to whom is the object pleasing?*

I.O. PRONOUN	SUBJECT	SUBJECT	DIRECT OBJECT
Me gusta	ese champú.	I like	that shampoo.

¡Me molesta!

¡Me encantan sus pantuflas!

▸ **Gustar** and similar verbs are usually used in the third-person singular and plural. When the object or person liked is singular, the form **gusta** is used. When two or more objects or persons are liked, **gustan** is used.

Me gustan el mar y la montaña.
I like the ocean and the mountains.

¿**Les gusta** la ciudad?
Do you/they like the city?

SINGULAR	me, te, le	gusta / gustó	la película / el concierto
PLURAL	nos, os, les	gustan / gustaron	las computadoras / los libros

▸ To express what someone likes or does not like to do, the singular form **gusta** is used, followed by one or more infinitives.

Me gusta levantarme tarde.
I like to get up late.

Me gusta comer y **dormir**.
I like to eat and sleep.

▸ To express the English equivalent of *would like* (*something* or *to do something*), use the construction [*i.o. pronoun*] + **gustaría(n)**.

¿**Te gustaría** ver esa película?
Would you like to see that movie?

Me gustarían unos días sin clases.
I would like a few days without class.

Práctica

1 **Completar** Completa estas oraciones con los elementos necesarios.

modelo ___A___ Ana *le encantan* [encantar] las canciones (*songs*) de Enrique Iglesias.

1. A _____ me _____ [gustar] más la música de Luis Fonsi.
2. A mis amigos _____ [molestar] la música de esa cantante.
3. _____ Juan y _____ Rafael les _____ [fascinar] la música de Shakira.
4. _____ nosotros _____ [importar] los grupos de pop latino.
5. Creo que al señor Gómez _____ [interesar] más la música clásica.
6. A _____ me _____ [aburrir] la música clásica.
7. ¿A _____ te _____ [faltar] dinero para el concierto de Jennifer López?
8. Sí. Sólo _____ [quedar] cinco dólares.
9. ¿Cuánto dinero te _____ [quedar] a _____?

2 **Describir** Describe los dibujos con uno de los siguientes verbos.

aburrir	interesar
encantar	molestar
faltar	quedar

1. A Mauricio / libros

2. A Lorena / despertador

3. A nosotros / bailar

4. A ti / camisa

Conversación

3 **Preguntas** Con un(a) compañero/a, túrnate para hacer y contestar estas preguntas.

1. ¿Te gusta levantarte temprano o tarde? ¿Por qué?

2. ¿Te molesta cuando tu compañero/a de cuarto usa tus cosas? ¿Por qué?

3. ¿Te gustaría poder dormir la siesta todos los días? ¿Por qué?

4. ¿Te gusta ducharte por la mañana o por la noche?

5. ¿Qué cosas te encantan?

6. ¿Qué cosas te aburren?

7. ¿Qué te gusta de esta universidad? ¿Qué te molesta?

8. ¿Te interesan más las ciencias o las humanidades? ¿Por qué?

4 **Conversar** Con un(a) compañero/a, representa una conversación entre un(a) cliente/a y un(a) dependiente/a en una tienda de ropa. Sigue las instrucciones.

Dependiente/a

1. Saluda al/a la cliente/a y pregúntale en qué le puedes servir.

3. Pregúntale qué estilos le interesan y empieza a mostrarle la ropa.

5. Habla de las preferencias de la temporada (*trends*).

7. Da opiniones favorables al/a la cliente/a (las botas te quedan fantásticas…).

Cliente/a

2. Saluda al/a la dependiente/a y dile (*tell him/her*) qué quieres comprar.

4. Explícale que te interesan los estilos modernos. Escoge las cosas que te interesan.

6. Habla de la ropa (me queda(n) bien/mal, me encanta(n)…).

8. Decide qué cosas te gustan y qué vas a comprar.

I CAN talk about my likes and preferences.

Using the verb *gustar*

▸ The construction **a** + [*personal pronoun*] (**a mí, a ti, a usted, a él, a ella, a nosotros/as, a vosotros/as, a ellos, a ellas, a ustedes**) clarifies or emphasizes the people who are pleased. **A** + [*noun*] can also be used.

A mí me gusta levantarme temprano. ¿Y **a ti**?
I like to get up early. How about you?

Al profesor le gustó el libro.
The teacher liked the book.

▸ Here is a list of common verbs used in the same way as **gustar.**

Verbs like *gustar*			
aburrir	to bore	importar	to be important to; to matter
encantar	to like very much; to love (objects)	interesar	to be interesting to; to interest
faltar	to lack; to need		
fascinar	to fascinate; to like very much	molestar	to bother; to annoy
		quedar	to be left over; to fit (clothing)

▸ **Faltar** expresses what is lacking or missing. **Quedar** expresses how much of something is left. Also, **quedar** is used to talk about how clothing fits or looks on someone.

Le falta dinero.
He/she is short of money.

Me faltan dos pesos.
I need two more pesos.

Nos quedan cinco libros.
We have five books left.

La falda **te queda** bien.
The skirt looks good on you.

¡Manos a la obra!

Indica el pronombre de objeto indirecto y la forma del tiempo presente adecuados en cada oración.

gustar

1. A él _le gusta_ la música pop.
2. A mí _____ bailar.
3. A nosotras _____ cantar.
4. A ustedes _____ el dibujo.
5. A ti _____ correr, ¿no?
6. A Elena _____ bucear.
7. A mis padres _____ los chocolates.
8. A usted _____ jugar al tenis.
9. A mi esposo y a mí _____ las novelas de terror.
10. A Pedro _____ estudiar.
11. A nosotros _____ la clase.
12. A Paula no _____ los exámenes.

aburrir

1. A ellos _les aburren_ los deportes.
2. A ti _____ las películas, ¿no?
3. A usted _____ los viajes.
4. A mí _____ las revistas de celebridades de Hollywood.
5. A ellas _____ los deportes.
6. A nosotros _____ las clases.
7. A ustedes _____ las fiestas.
8. A Marcela _____ leer y correr.
9. A ellos _____ los museos.
10. A ella _____ la televisión.
11. A Pedro _____ ir de compras.
12. A ti y a mí _____ bailar.

A repasar

7.1 Reflexive verbs

1 De vacaciones Estás de vacaciones con tus amigos en la playa. Forma oraciones en tiempo presente con estos elementos.

1. Martín y Mónica / sentarse / en la cafetería del hotel
   _____

2. yo / ponerse / bloqueador (sun block) / antes de tomar el sol _____

3. ustedes / quedarse / en el cuarto del hotel / durante la noche _____

4. Josefina y yo / probarse / trajes de baño / en la tienda
   _____

5. tú / ducharse / después / nadar en el mar
   _____

6. Lucía / quitarse / las sandalias / antes / entrar en la piscina _____

2 Una pareja singular Angélica y Mauricio son una pareja muy estructurada (methodical) que siempre sigue la misma rutina antes de ir al trabajo. Lee el horario de cada uno y contesta las preguntas.

modelo
¿Qué hace Mauricio a las seis de la mañana?
Mauricio se afeita a las seis de la mañana.

Hora	Angélica	Mauricio
5:50 a.m.	levantarse	levantarse
6:00 a.m.	bañarse	afeitarse
6:30 a.m.	peinarse	ducharse
7:00 a.m.	maquillarse	peinarse
7:30 a.m.	vestirse	vestirse
8:00 a.m.	irse al trabajo	irse al trabajo

1. ¿A qué hora se levantan Angélica y Mauricio?

2. ¿Qué hace Mauricio después de levantarse?

3. ¿Qué hace Angélica antes de maquillarse?

4. ¿Qué hacen Angélica y Mauricio a las siete de la mañana?

5. ¿Qué hace Mauricio después de afeitarse?

6. ¿Qué hace Angélica antes de peinarse?

7. ¿Qué hacen Mauricio y Angélica a las siete y media?

8. ¿Qué hacen Angélica y Mauricio a las ocho de la mañana?

7.2 Indefinite and negative words

3 La rutina diaria Cambia las oraciones para que sean negativas.

modelo
Algunas personas se duchan por la noche.
Ninguna persona se ducha por la noche.

1. Siempre nos acostamos a las diez en punto.
   _____

2. Mis padres se levantan a las seis o a las seis y media.
   _____

3. Alguien se baña antes de ir a la escuela.
   _____

4. Yo también trabajo por la tarde.
   _____

5. Ustedes comen algo. _____

6. Tú te lavas el pelo con algún champú caro.
   _____

4 Tu novio/a ideal Con un(a) compañero/a, describe a tu novio/a ideal. Usa expresiones indefinidas o negativas.

modelo
Es alguien que siempre dice la verdad.

7.3 Preterite of ser and ir

5 Un mensaje Completa el mensaje con el pretérito de **ser** o **ir**.

Hola, Laura:

Perdón por no escribirte antes. Ayer (1)_____ un día con muchas cosas. Mi hermano y yo nos levantamos muy temprano y (2)_____ a correr al parque. Después me duché y (3)_____ a trabajar. Por la tarde, mis primos (4)_____ a buscarme al trabajo (work) para ir a comer unas tapas. Quiero decirte que tú (5)_____ muy amable en contestar mi mensaje rápidamente y que tu familia y tú (6)_____ muy cordiales conmigo cuando los visité en Chile.

A propósito, ¿cuándo vienes a España?
Esteban

6 Ayer Con un(a) compañero/a, describe las actividades que hiciste ayer. Usa el pretérito de **ir** y **ser**.

modelo
Por la mañana, yo fui al gimnasio.

1. Por la mañana, . . .   3. Por la noche, . . .

2. Por la tarde, . . .   4. Antes de acostarme, . . .

7.4 **Gustar** and verbs like **gustar**

7 **Combinar** Combina elementos de cada columna para formar oraciones lógicas.

> **modelo** A ti te molesta ducharte con agua fría.

A	B	C
al empleado del hotel	aburrir	ducharse con agua fría
a mí	encantar	despertarse temprano
a nosotros	faltar	ponerse ropa de invierno
a Elena y a ti	fascinar	escuchar el despertador por la mañana
a ti	importar	la ropa de marca (*brand-name*)
a los estudiantes	molestar	mirarse al espejo con mucha frecuencia

8 **Encuesta** Pregúntales a dos o tres compañeros/as qué cosas o actividades les encantan, les aburren o les molestan.

Nombre	Le encanta(n)	Le aburre(n)	Le molesta(n)
____	____	____	____
____	____	____	____
____	____	____	____
____	____	____	____
____	____	____	____
____	____	____	____
____	____	____	____

Síntesis

9 **Un día típico** Con un(a) compañero/a, describe la rutina diaria de dos o tres de estas personas. Usa como mínimo tres verbos reflexivos, una expresión negativa y dos expresiones con verbos como **gustar**.

- Shakira
- Patrick Mahomes
- Brie Larson
- Dos de tus profesores
- Lionel Messi

Communicative Goal
Watch a report and talk about image consulting

 Video

Videoclip

1 **Preparación** ¿Cuidar tu apariencia personal es una prioridad para ti? ¿Cuidas tu apariencia por ti o por lo que pueden pensar los demás? Comparte tus respuestas con la clase.

2 **El clip** Mira el reportaje *Esperando el rescate* de Chile.

Vocabulario			
arreglarse	*to get ready*	mejorar	*to improve*
despreocuparse	*to stop worrying*	pareja	*partner*
embellecerse	*to make oneself beautiful*	teñir	*to dye*

Voy a estar bien vestida y alegre.

3 **¿Cierto o falso?** Indica si las oraciones son **ciertas** o **falsas**. Corrige las oraciones falsas.

1. Los mineros llevan un año sin poder salir de la mina.
2. Cristina es la pareja de Claudio, uno de los treinta y tres mineros.
3. Cristina es la única persona del campamento que se preocupa por su aspecto personal.
4. Las mujeres están nerviosas por el inminente regreso de los mineros.
5. Elizabeth Segovia descuidó (*neglected*) su aspecto durante esa larga espera.
6. A la gente de Copiapó no le importa la salida de los mineros.

4 **Ayuda** Con un(a) compañero/a, representa una conversación entre un(a) asesor(a) de moda (*image consultant*) y su cliente. El/la asesor(a) da consejos para tener un mejor aspecto en una entrevista laboral, una audición para una película, una cita romántica, etc.

I CAN understand information in a report.

I CAN talk about image consulting.

Ampliación

Communicative Goals
Use background
information to
understand an
interview, and talk
about past actions

➊ Escuchar

A Escucha la entrevista entre Carolina y Julián, teniendo en cuenta (*taking into account*) tus conocimientos sobre este tipo de situación. Elige la opción que completa correctamente cada oración.

> **TIP** **Use background information.** Use what you already know about a topic to help you guess the meaning of unknown words or linguistic structures.

1. Julián es...
   a. político.   b. deportista profesional.
   c. artista de cine.

2. El público (*audience*) de Julián quiere saber de...
   a. sus películas.   b. su vida (*life*).
   c. su novia.

3. Julián habla de...
   a. sus viajes y sus rutinas.   b. sus parientes y amigos.
   c. sus comidas (*foods*) favoritas.

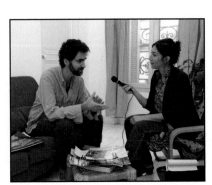

4. Julián...
   a. se levanta y se acuesta a horas diferentes todos los días.
   b. tiene una rutina diaria.   c. no quiere hablar de su vida.

B ¿Crees que Julián siempre fue rico? ¿Por qué? ¿Qué piensas de Julián como persona?

➋ Conversar

Conversa con un(a) compañero/a sobre lo que hiciste ayer. Sigue estas preguntas.

• ¿A qué hora te levantaste ayer? ¿Usaste un despertador?

• ¿Te bañaste o te duchaste? ¿Cuánto tiempo te tomó?

• ¿Qué ropa te pusiste?

• ¿Cuántas veces te cepillaste los dientes ayer?

• ¿Adónde fuiste ayer después de las clases?

• ¿A qué hora te acostaste anoche?

• ¿Te gusta mirar la televisión antes de acostarte?

I CAN understand the content of an interview, using background information.

I CAN say what I did yesterday.

Ampliación

3 Escribir

Escribe una composición en la que describes tu rutina diaria en algún lugar interesante (una isla desierta, el Polo Norte, el desierto, etc.). Considera cómo pueden cambiar los elementos básicos de tu rutina: ¿Dónde te acuestas? ¿Cómo te bañas?

TIP **Use adverbs to sequence events.** You can use adverbs and adverbial phrases as transitions between the introduction, the body, and the conclusion of a narrative.

Organizar | Utiliza estos adverbios para organizar la secuencia de tu composición: **primero, después, luego, más tarde** y **al final.** Anota ideas que respondan a estas preguntas: **¿qué?, ¿quién?, ¿cuándo?, ¿dónde?, ¿cómo?** y **¿por qué?**

Escribir | Utiliza tus notas para escribir el primer borrador (*draft*) de la composición.

Corregir | Intercambia tu composición con un(a) compañero/a. Comenta sobre la introducción, la secuencia de eventos, el nivel (*level*) de interés y los errores de gramática o de ortografía. Revisa el primer borrador según las indicaciones de tu compañero/a.

Compartir | Intercambia tu composición con otro/a compañero/a. Lee su trabajo y comparte con la clase tres ideas que te gustaron de su composición.

4 Un paso más

Planea un viaje a un lugar famoso del mundo hispano. Haz un folleto (*brochure*) con elementos visuales y esta información:

- Presenta el itinerario de cada día del viaje e indica la hora para cada actividad.
- Describe el país, una breve (*brief*) historia del lugar y también las actividades programadas para el viaje.
- Comenta sobre los restaurantes, el transporte y los hoteles.
- Describe la rutina diaria de un viajero típico.

5 Cultura

Estás en un pueblo pequeño donde muchas oficinas y tiendas cierran por dos o tres horas después del mediodía. ¿Qué vas a hacer? ¿Vas a dormir la siesta? ¿Por qué?

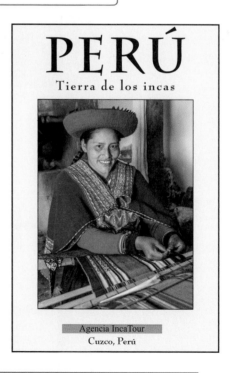

PERÚ
Tierra de los incas

Agencia IncaTour
Cuzco, Perú

Communicative Goals
Describe my daily routine in an exotic location, and create a brochure about a trip

---

I CAN write a detailed description about my daily routine in an exotic location.

I CAN create a brochure about a trip.

S Audio: Reading

Antes de leer

Prediction is an invaluable strategy in reading for comprehension.

TIP **Predict content from the title.**
You can use the title of a text to help you predict the content. For example, readers can predict the content of a news article from its headline. Predicting content from the title will help you increase your reading comprehension in Spanish.

Examinar el texto

Lee el título de la lectura y haz tres predicciones sobre el contenido. Escribe tus predicciones en una hoja de papel.

Compartir

Comparte tus ideas con un(a) compañero/a.

Cognados

Escribe una lista de cuatro cognados que encuentres en la lectura.

1. _____
2. _____
3. _____
4. _____

¿Qué te dicen los cognados sobre el tema de la lectura?

15 de octubre
¡Una mañana desastrosa!

—Me levanté de la cama a las seis y media.

Esta mañana me levanté de la cama a las seis y media y corrí a despertar a mis dos hijas. —Yolanda, Dolores, van a perder el autobús de la escuela, —les grité°. Pero ellas no se despertaron. Jamás se despiertan temprano. Siempre se sientan a ver la televisión por la noche y se acuestan muy tarde.

—Corrimos para llegar a la parada del autobús.

Yolanda y Dolores salieron de la casa sin° cepillarse los dientes, pero eso no importa. Por lo menos se acordaron de ponerse las botas y el abrigo antes de irse. Corrimos para llegar a la parada° del autobús de la escuela, que pasa a las siete de la mañana.

—Nunca llegó el autobús.

Esperamos media hora, pero nunca llegó el autobús. Regresamos a casa. Llamamos por teléfono° a la escuela, pero nadie contestó. Tomamos el automóvil y salimos de casa.

—¡Por fin se despertaron mis hijas!

¡Por fin se despertaron! Medio dormidas y medio enojadas°, ellas entraron al baño para lavarse la cara y peinarse. Luego volvieron a su habitación para vestirse. Yo fui a la cocina para prepararles el desayuno°. A mis hijas les encanta comer un buen desayuno, pero hoy les di° cereales y les preparé dos sándwiches para el almuerzo°.

—¡Hoy es sábado!

Llegamos a la escuela antes de las ocho y entonces me di cuenta de que° hoy es sábado. ¡Y los sábados no hay clases!

grité *I shouted* **medio dormidas y medio enojadas** *half asleep and half angry* **desayuno** *breakfast*
di *I gave* **almuerzo** *lunch* **sin** *without* **parada** *stop* **llamamos por teléfono** *we called on the phone*
me di cuenta de que *I realized that*

Después de leer

⚭ ¿Comprendiste?

Selecciona la respuesta correcta.

1. ¿Quién es el/la narrador(a)?
   a. el padre de las chicas   b. Yolanda
   c. Dolores

2. ¿A qué hora se despertó el papá?
   a. a las seis de la mañana   b. a las seis y media
   c. a las siete y media

3. ¿Qué comieron las chicas antes de salir de la casa?
   a. un sándwich   b. cereales
   c. dos sándwiches

4. ¿Cómo fueron las chicas a la escuela?
   a. Corrieron.   b. Fueron en autobús.
   c. Fueron en automóvil.

⚭ Preguntas

Responde estas preguntas con oraciones completas.

1. ¿Por qué nunca se despiertan temprano las chicas?
   _____

2. ¿Se bañaron las chicas esta mañana?
   _____

3. ¿A qué hora llega generalmente el autobús?
   _____

4. ¿A qué hora llegó el autobús hoy?
   _____

5. ¿Por qué no contestó nadie cuando llamaron a la escuela?
   _____

⚭ Coméntalo

¿Qué crees que le dicen Yolanda y Dolores a su papá después de volver de la escuela? Imagina que eres el papá, ¿cómo responderías (*would you respond*) a lo que te dicen las chicas?

I CAN use the title and cognates to predict the content of a text.

Vocabulary Tools

La higiene personal

el baño *bathroom*
el champú *shampoo*
la crema de afeitar *shaving cream*
el espejo *mirror*
el jabón *soap*
el maquillaje *makeup*
la toalla *towel*

Los verbos reflexivos

acordarse (de) (o:ue) *to remember*
acostarse (o:ue) *to lie down; to go to bed*
afeitarse *to shave*
bañarse *to take a bath*
cepillarse el pelo *to brush one's hair*
cepillarse los dientes *to brush one's teeth*
despertarse (e:ie) *to wake up*
dormirse (o:ue) *to go to sleep; to fall asleep*
ducharse *to shower*
enojarse (con) *to get angry (with)*
irse *to go away; to leave*
lavarse la cara *to wash one's face*
lavarse las manos *to wash one's hands*
levantarse *to get up*
llamarse *to be named*
maquillarse *to put on makeup*
peinarse *to comb one's hair*
ponerse *to put on*
ponerse (+ adj.) *to become (+ adj.)*
preocuparse (por) *to worry (about)*
probarse (o:ue) *to try on*
quedarse *to stay*
quitarse *to take off*
sentarse (e:ie) *to sit down*
sentirse (e:ie) *to feel*
vestirse (e:i) *to get dressed*

Otras palabras y expresiones

el despertador *alarm clock*
la rutina diaria *daily routine*

---

antes (de) *before*
después *afterward; then*
después de *after*
durante *during*
entonces *then*
luego *afterward; then*
más tarde *later (on)*
por la mañana *in the morning*
por la noche *at night*
por la tarde *in the afternoon; in the (early) evening*
por último *finally*
siempre *always*
también *also; too*
temprano *early*

Verbos como *gustar*

aburrir *to bore*
encantar *to like very much; to love (objects)*
faltar *to lack; to need*
fascinar *to fascinate; to like very much*
gustar *to be pleasing to; to like*
importar *to be important to; to matter*
interesar *to be interesting to; to interest*
me gustaría(n)... *I would like...*
molestar *to bother; to annoy*
quedar *to be left over; to fit (clothing)*

Pero and sino *See page 183.*

Palabras indefinidas y negativas

algo *something; anything*
alguien *someone; somebody; anyone*
alguno/a(s), algún *some; any*
jamás *never; not ever*
nada *nothing; not anything*
nadie *no one; nobody; not anyone*
ni... ni *neither... nor*
ninguno/a, ningún *no; none; not any*
nunca *never; not ever*
o... o *either... or*
tampoco *neither; not either*

∞ Communicative Goals: Review

I CAN describe daily routines.
- Describe your daily routine to a partner.

I CAN talk about personal hygiene.
- Say what personal hygiene products you use.

I CAN tell where I went.
- Say where you went yesterday.

I CAN investigate sleep and food customs in the Spanish-speaking world.
- Describe the customs of **la siesta** and **ir de tapas**.

8 ¡A comer!

Communicative Goals
You will learn how to:
- talk about food
- order at a restaurant
- discuss familiar people and places
- investigate foods in the Spanish-speaking world

PREPARACIÓN

pages 196–201
- Words related to restaurants and meals
- Adjectives that describe food
- Pronouncing **ll, ñ, c,** and **z**

AVENTURAS

pages 202–203
- Manuel, Sara, and Daniel go to a food market in Madrid. They eat a lot but still end up fighting over the last bite.

CULTURA

pages 204–205
- *Desayunos exquisitos*
- Flash cultura: *La comida latina*

GRAMÁTICA

pages 206–217
- Preterite of stem-changing verbs
- Double object pronouns
- **Saber** and **conocer**
- Comparatives and superlatives

LECTURA

pages 218–219
- Restaurant review: *Cinco estrellas para El Palmito*

∞ PARA EMPEZAR

- ¿El hombre es cliente o vendedor?
- ¿Qué está haciendo el hombre?
- ¿Tiene hambre o sueño el chico?
- ¿Qué va a hacer el chico?

¡A COMER!

el camarero

EN UN RESTAURANTE

el/la dueño/a *owner*
el plato (principal) *(main) dish*

---

el almuerzo *lunch*
la cena *dinner*
la comida *food; meal*
el desayuno *breakfast*

---

almorzar (o:ue) *to have lunch*
cenar *to have dinner*
desayunar *to have breakfast*
pedir (e:i) *to order (food)*
probar (o:ue) *to taste; to try*
recomendar (e:ie) *to recommend*
servir (e:i) *to serve*

el bistec

EL GUSTO Y LOS SABORES

agrio/a *sour*
amargo/a *bitter*
delicioso/a *delicious*
dulce *sweet*
picante *spicy*
rico/a *tasty*
sabroso/a *delicious*
salado/a *salty*

los entremeses *appetizers*

el pollo (asado) *(roast) chicken*

LAS CARNES, LOS PESCADOS Y LOS MARISCOS

el atún *tuna*
los camarones *shrimp*
la carne *meat*
la carne de res *beef*
la chuleta de cerdo *pork chop*
la hamburguesa (vegetariana)
    (veggie) hamburger
el jamón *ham*
la langosta *lobster*
el pavo *turkey*
el pescado *fish*
la salchicha *sausage*
el salmón *salmon*

los mariscos *seafood*

Vocabulary Tools

el sándwich
sandwich

LAS FRUTAS

la banana *banana*

el limón *lemon*

la manzana *apple*

la naranja *orange*

las uvas *grapes*

las frutas

LOS GRANOS Y LAS VERDURAS

el ajo *garlic*

el arroz *rice*

las arvejas *peas*

la cebolla *onion*

los cereales *cereal; grain*

los frijoles *beans*

la lechuga *lettuce*

el maíz *corn*

la papa/patata *potato*

el tomate *tomato*

las verduras *vegetables*

la zanahoria *carrot*

la pimienta

la ensalada

los champiñones

LAS BEBIDAS

la bebida *drink; beverage*

la cerveza *beer*

el jugo (de fruta) *(fruit) juice*

la leche *milk*

el refresco *soft drink*

el té (helado) *(iced) tea*

el vino (blanco/tinto) *(white/red) wine*

el menú

LOS CONDIMENTOS Y OTRAS COMIDAS

el aceite *oil*

el azúcar *sugar*

el huevo *egg*

la mantequilla *butter*

la margarina *margarine*

la mayonesa *mayonnaise*

el pan (tostado) *(toasted) bread*

las papas/patatas fritas *French fries*

el queso *cheese*

la sal *salt*

la sopa *soup*

el vinagre *vinegar*

el agua (f.) (mineral)

el café

ASÍ SE DICE

los camarones ⟷ las gambas (*Esp.*)
el refresco ⟷ la gaseosa (*Amér. L.*)
el sándwich ⟷ el bocadillo (*Esp.*), la torta (*Méx.*)
la arveja ⟷ el guisante (*Esp.*), el chícharo (*Méx.*)
la papa ⟷ la patata (*Esp.*)

▸ ¿Qué palabras hay para decir **refrescos** en inglés?

A escuchar

1 **¿Lógico o ilógico?** Escucha las oraciones e indica si son **lógicas** o **ilógicas**.

	Lógico	Ilógico
1.	_____	_____
2.	_____	_____
3.	_____	_____
4.	_____	_____
5.	_____	_____
6.	_____	_____
7.	_____	_____
8.	_____	_____

2 **¿Qué pide Nora?** Lee las opciones de comidas y después escucha la conversación entre Nora y el camarero en un restaurante. Luego, indica las comidas y las bebidas que Nora pide.

RESTAURANTE **LAS FUENTES**
• Avenida Las Lomas 22 •

ENTREMESES

___ papas fritas
___ cóctel de frutas con queso
___ sopa de verduras
___ sopa de pollo
___ pan con mantequilla

PLATOS PRINCIPALES

___ sándwich de jamón y queso
___ pollo asado
___ hamburguesa
___ hamburguesa con queso
___ enchiladas de res
___ enchiladas de queso

BEBIDAS

___ agua mineral
___ té helado
___ leche
___ café
___ jugo de naranja

A practicar

3 **La comida** Indica la palabra que no está relacionada.

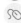

1. sabroso • manzana • banana • naranja
2. salmón • cereales • camarones • mariscos
3. frijoles • champiñón • naranja • cebolla
4. mantequilla • salchicha • carne de res • jamón
5. arvejas • lechuga • zanahoria • dulce
6. refresco • sopa • agua mineral • leche

4 **Completar** Completa las oraciones.

1. La persona que sirve la comida en un restaurante es _____.
2. Camarero, ¿puedo ver _____, por favor?
3. El bistec y el jamón son dos tipos de _____.
4. El té helado, el café y los refrescos son _____.
5. Algo de color blanco que pongo en el café es _____.
6. Las tres comidas principales del día son _____, _____ y _____.

5 **¿Qué es?** Describe cada uno de estos alimentos con alguna característica. Puedes decir de qué color es, qué sabor tiene o cuándo lo comes o lo tomas.

El limón es una fruta de color amarillo./Es una fruta agria./Le pongo limón a la ensalada.

1. _____

2. _____

3. _____

4. _____

5. _____

6. _____

7. _____

8. _____

A conversar

6 **¿Te gusta?** Lee la lista e indica si te gusta o no cada comida o bebida.

¿Te gusta(n)?	Me gusta(n)	No me gusta(n)
1. la langosta	_____	_____
2. la chuleta de cerdo	_____	_____
3. el queso	_____	_____
4. los camarones	_____	_____
5. el tomate	_____	_____
6. los champiñones	_____	_____
7. los huevos	_____	_____
8. los limones	_____	_____

Ahora compara tus opiniones con las de un(a) compañero/a.

modelo

la carne de res
Estudiante 1: A mí me gusta mucho la *carne de res.*
Estudiante 2: A mí no. Prefiero el pollo./A mí me encanta la *carne de res.*

7 **Conversación** Con un(a) compañero/a, contesta las preguntas.

1. ¿Desayunas? ¿Qué comes y bebes por la mañana?

2. ¿Qué comes generalmente a la hora del almuerzo?

3. ¿Qué comidas prefieres para la cena?

4. ¿Qué tipos de comidas te gustan más: las dulces o las saladas?

5. ¿Te gusta preparar la comida? ¿Qué comidas preparas para tus amigos? ¿Y para tu familia?

6. ¿Qué comida les recomiendas a tus amigos? ¿Por qué?

7. ¿Qué comidas quieres probar?

8. ¿Eres vegetariano/a? ¿Crees que ser vegetariano/a es una buena idea? ¿Por qué?

8 **Una cena muy especial** Trabaja con un(a) compañero/a para planear una cena sorpresa. Recuerda incluir la siguiente información.

- Qué tipo de cena es
- Dónde y cuándo va a ser
- Cuál es el motivo de la cena sorpresa
- A quiénes vas a invitar
- Qué comidas vas a preparar para el entremés, el plato principal y el postre

I CAN talk about food.

Pronunciación Tutorial

ll, ñ, c, and z

poll**o**   **ll**ave   e**ll**a   cebo**ll**a

Most Spanish speakers pronounce **ll** like the *y* in *yes*.

. . . .

ma**ñ**ana   se**ñ**or   ba**ñ**o   ni**ñ**a

The letter **ñ** is pronounced much like the *ny* in *canyon*.

. . . .

café   **c**olombiano   **c**uando   ri**c**o

Before **a, o,** or **u,** the Spanish **c** is pronounced like the *c* in *car*.

. . . .

cereales   deli**c**ioso   condu**c**ir   cono**c**er

Before **e** or **i,** the Spanish **c** is pronounced like the *s* in *sit.* (In parts of Spain, **c** before **e** or **i** is pronounced like the *th* in *think.)*

. . . .

zeta   **z**anahoria   almuer**z**o   cerve**z**a

The Spanish **z** is pronounced like the *s* in *sit.* (In parts of Spain, **z** is pronounced like the *th* in *think.)*

. . . .

Práctica Lee las palabras en voz alta.

1. mantequilla	5. español	9. quince
2. cuñado	6. cepillo	10. compañera
3. aceite	7. zapato	11. almorzar
4. manzana	8. azúcar	12. calle

Oraciones Lee las oraciones en voz alta.

1. Mi compañero de cuarto se llama Toño Núñez. Su familia es de la Ciudad de Guatemala y de Quetzaltenango.

2. Dice que la comida de su mamá es deliciosa, especialmente su pollo al champiñón y sus tortillas de maíz.

3. Creo que Toño tiene razón porque hoy cené en su casa y quiero volver mañana para cenar allí otra vez.

Refranes Lee los refranes en voz alta.

Panza llena, corazón contento.[2]

Las apariencias engañan.[1]

[1] *Looks can be deceiving.*
[2] *The way to a man's heart is through his stomach.*

Communicative Goal
Order food

¡Vamos a comer tapas!

Manuel, Sara y Daniel van al Mercado de San Miguel para comer tapas.

 Video

Antes de ver

Ojea los pies de foto (*Scan the captions*) y busca vocabulario relacionado con la comida.

PERSONAJES

SARA

DANIEL

MANUEL

VENDEDORA

VENDEDOR

GUITARRISTA

SARA Manuel, ¡vas a conocer el mejor mercado de Madrid!

DANIEL El de San Miguel. (*rapeando*) En el Mercado San Miguel de todo hay de comer. Si no te gusta el champiñón, tenemos el jamón. Si no te gusta el jamón, tenemos boquerón...

DANIEL Y SARA (*rapeando*) De merienda, pan tostado, y para almuerzo, pollo asado.

MANUEL ¡Chicos! ¡Chicos! ¡¿Podemos ir a comer ya?!

MANUEL, SARA Y DANIEL ¡Croquetas!

DANIEL ¡Quiero de... jamón! ¡Las de jamón son las mejores!

SARA Seis croquetas de jamón, por favor.

VENDEDORA ¿Qué más?

MANUEL ¡Uy! Me gustan las de pollo tanto como las de pescado.

SARA ¿Nos sirve seis de pollo y seis de pescado, por favor?

SARA ¿Cuánto es?

VENDEDORA Son dieciocho euros.

SARA Son seis euros cada uno.

VENDEDORA ¿Se las pongo con alioli?

SARA Sí, por favor.

ACTIVIDADES

1 Identificar Indica quién dice las oraciones equivalentes.

1. ¿Te gusta la comida del mercado?
2. Prefiero las croquetas de jamón.
3. Me gustan las croquetas de pollo y las croquetas de pescado.
4. Nos sirvieron unas croquetas sabrosas.
5. Me gusta la paella más que el gazpacho.
6. ¡El mercado es muy divertido!

2 Ordenar Indica el orden correcto de los eventos.

_____ a. Manuel se ahoga.
_____ b. Los chicos pagan dieciocho euros.
_____ c. Sara y Daniel rapean delante del mercado.
_____ d. Los chicos comen croquetas.
_____ e. Los chicos comen tortilla de patatas y paella.
_____ f. Manuel y Daniel juegan con la comida.

DANIEL ¡Aquí va un calamar!

MANUEL ¡Los calamares me gustan más que las croquetas!

SARA Sabéis que este juego es tontísimo, ¿no?

DANIEL ¿Qué quieres ahora?

MANUEL ¡Uno de boquerón! (*a Sara*) Te lo recomiendo.

SARA Manuel, ¿qué te parece la comida del mercado?

MANUEL Hasta ahora ¡riquísima! Nos sirvieron unas croquetas deliciosas.

DANIEL ¡Pedimos probarlas todas, y al final Manuel prefirió los calamares!

MANUEL Y ahora...

DANIEL Y MANUEL ¡Más tapas!

VENDEDOR Tortilla de patatas. Queso manchego y aceitunas.

MANUEL ¿Qué otro plato nos recomienda?

VENDEDOR La paella de marisco está muy buena y el gazpacho también.

SARA La paella está más rica que el gazpacho. Paella, por favor.

DANIEL No sé por dónde empezar.

MANUEL ¡Yo tampoco sé por dónde empezar!

VENDEDOR ¡Buen provecho!

Expresiones útiles

las aceitunas *olives*
el alioli *aioli (garlic mayonnaise)*
el boquerón *anchovy*
¡Buen provecho! *Enjoy your meal!*
el calamar *calamari (squid)*
la croqueta *croquette*
el gazpacho *cold tomato soup*
la paella *Spanish rice dish*
la tortilla *omelet (in Spain)*

---

ahogarse *to choke*
la maniobra de Heimlich *Heimlich maneuver*
tirar *to throw*
la vitrina *display case/window*

Mercado de San Miguel

Muy cerca de la Plaza Mayor de Madrid, se encuentra el Mercado de San Miguel. Abrió sus puertas en 1916 como un mercado de abastos (*wholesale food market*). Hoy en día los visitantes pueden probar en sus puestos los mejores jamones, arroces y quesos de toda España.

¿Hay lugares como este mercado en tu comunidad? ¿Qué venden?

3 **En el mercado de comida** En parejas, representen una conversación entre un(a) vendedor(a) y su cliente/a en un mercado de comida.

Vendedor(a): Saludas al/a la cliente/a, preguntas qué quiere beber, preguntas qué quiere comer, le das recomendaciones y pides su opinión sobre la comida.

Cliente/a: Saludas al/a la vendedor(a), pides una bebida, pides una de las recomendaciones y das tu opinión sobre la comida.

I CAN order food.

Communicative Goal
Identify breakfast foods and beverages in
the Spanish-speaking world

Desayunos **exquisitos**

¿Hay algo más rico que un delicioso desayuno?
Desde España hasta el Caribe, desde México a
Argentina, existe una gran oferta para elegir a la hora
de comenzar el día. Café, chocolate, mate, huevos,
frutas, queso y hasta arroz y caldo° forman parte de
la oferta gastronómica para esta comida.

el atole

Las bebidas
Como en buena parte del
mundo, el **café** es el rey° de
las bebidas para acompañar
la primera comida del día y
se consume en casi todos los
países de habla hispana, como
en España, Colombia, Costa Rica y Cuba, donde se
prepara muy dulce, con mucho azúcar. El **chocolate** es
otra bebida muy popular en estos países; está presente
en las mesas de México, Colombia y Guatemala, y
puede ser oscuro° o con leche. Muchos argentinos,
paraguayos y uruguayos optan por el **mate**, una infusión
similar al té. En México es muy popular el **atole**, una
bebida de origen prehispánico a base de una masa° de
maíz cocida° en agua a la que se le adicionan especias
como cacao, canela° o vainilla.

La harina
Si el café es el rey, la harina° es la reina° del desayuno.
De trigo° o de maíz, está siempre presente en los

las pupusas

los tamales

desayunos de los
hispanoamericanos. Además
del universal **pan**, la **arepa** es
indispensable en países como
Colombia y Venezuela, y
consiste en una torta° de maíz
con mantequilla o queso, o
bien rellena° de diversos
ingredientes. En Centroamérica
y México, las **pupusas** y
gorditas son similares a la
arepa. Hablando de México,
es la cuna° de los famosos
tamales, una masa de maíz

rellena y envuelta° en hojas° de maíz o banana. Los
tamales pueden ser dulces o salados. Son también
populares en Centroamérica, el Caribe, algunos países
de Suramérica y hasta en ciudades estadounidenses
como Miami.

el caldo de costilla

Otras opciones
Hay otras opciones muy
diversas en los diferentes
países de habla hispana.
En las zonas costeras de
Ecuador, por ejemplo, son
típicos los desayunos a base
de **pescados** y **mariscos**. En El Salvador es muy común
desayunar con **frijoles** molidos° y fritos, así como en
Nicaragua y Costa Rica no puede faltar el **gallo pinto**
(una mezcla de arroz y frijoles). Algunos colombianos
(sobre todo en las zonas frías) comienzan el día con
un **caldo de costilla**° o una **changua** (un caldo a base
de leche, huevo, queso y cilantro).

caldo *broth* rey *king* oscuro *dark* masa *dough* cocida *boiled* canela *cinnamon*
harina *flour* reina *queen* trigo *wheat* torta *cake* rellena *stuffed* cuna *cradle*
envuelta *wrapped* hojas *leaves* molidos *ground* costilla *rib*

ASÍ SE DICE
La comida

el banano (Col.) el cambur (Ven.) el guineo (Nic.) el plátano (Amér. L., Esp.)	la banana
el choclo (Amér. S.) el elote (Méx.) el jojoto (Ven.) la mazorca (Esp.)	corncob
las caraotas (Ven.) los porotos (Amér. S.) las habichuelas	los frijoles
el jitomate (Méx.)	el tomate

▸ ¿Cuáles son algunas comidas que tienen varios
nombres distintos en inglés?

ACTIVIDADES

1 **¿Cierto o falso?** Indica si las oraciones son ciertas o falsas. Corrige la información falsa.

1. Los argentinos, paraguayos y uruguayos beben mate.

2. El atole es una bebida de origen español.

3. Los colombianos y los venezolanos comen arepas.

4. Las pupusas son muy populares en Cuba.

5. El gallo pinto es una mezcla de arroz y frijoles.

2 **Preguntas** Contesta las preguntas.

1. ¿En qué país se prepara el café con mucho azúcar?

2. ¿Qué bebida es popular en México, Colombia y Guatemala?

3. ¿Cuál de los platos se come con mantequilla o queso?

4. ¿En qué países comen el gallo pinto?

5. ¿Cuáles son los ingredientes de la changua?

3 **Comparaciones** Haz una de estas comparaciones.

- las arepas con las pupusas

- el caldo de costilla con la changua

- uno de estos platos con el desayuno que tomas todos los días

4 **¿Qué piensas?** Con un(a) compañero/a, responde a estas preguntas.

1. ¿Cuál de estas comidas y bebidas te gustaría probar? ¿Por qué?

2. ¿Por qué piensas que el café es el rey de las bebidas en países como Colombia?

3. ¿Por qué crees que se toma el mate en Argentina, Uruguay y Paraguay?

4. ¿Por qué piensas que el maíz es un ingrediente tan importante?

5. ¿Por qué crees que algunos colombianos toman caldo para el desayuno?

I CAN identify breakfast foods and beverages in the Spanish-speaking world.

Communicative Goal
Identify some characteristics of Latin food

 Video

La comida latina

1 **Preparación** ¿Probaste alguna vez comida latina? ¿Qué plato? ¿La compraste en un supermercado o fuiste a un restaurante? ¿Te gustó?

2 **El video** Mira el episodio de **Flash cultura** sobre la comida latina en Los Ángeles.

Vocabulario	
cocinar *to cook*	¿Está lista para ordenar?
condimentar *to season*	*Are you ready to order?*
	pruébala *try it, taste it*

Marta nos mostrará° algunos de los platos de la comida mexicana.

mostrará *will show*

3 **¿Cierto o falso?** Indica si las oraciones son **ciertas** o **falsas**. Corrige la informacion falsa.

1. En Los Ángeles hay comida de países latinoamericanos y de España.

2. Leticia explica que la tortilla del taco americano es blanda *(soft)* y la del taco mexicano es dura *(hard)*.

3. Las ventas *(sales)* de salsa son bajas en los Estados Unidos.

4. Leticia fue a un restaurante ecuatoriano.

5. Leticia probó Inca Kola en un supermercado.

4 **¡A comer!** En parejas, representen una conversación entre un(a) cliente/a y un(a) camarero/a en la taquería o en el restaurante cubano del video.

I CAN identify characteristics of Latin food.

I CAN identify the influence of Latin food in the United States.

8.1 Preterite of stem-changing verbs

▶ As you know, **–ar** and **–er** stem-changing verbs have no stem change in the preterite. **–Ir** stem-changing verbs, however, do have a stem change.

Preterite of *–ir* stem-changing verbs

	servir	morir (*to die*)
	(e→i)	(o→u)
yo	serví *I served*	morí *I died*
tú	serviste	moriste
Ud./él/ella	sirvió	murió
nosotros/as	servimos	morimos
vosotros/as	servisteis	moristeis
Uds./ellos/ellas	sirvieron	murieron

▶ In the preterite, stem-changing **–ir** verbs have an **e** to **i** or **o** to **u** stem change in the **Ud./él/ella** and **Uds./ellos/ellas** forms.

INFINITIVE	VERB STEM	STEM CHANGE	PRETERITE
pedir	ped-	pid-	pidió, pidieron
dormir	dor-	dur-	durmió, durmieron

¡Pedimos probarlas todas, y al final Manuel prefirió los calamares!

Nos sirvieron unas croquetas deliciosas.

¡Manos a la obra!

Cambia los infinitivos al pretérito.

1. yo [servir, dormir, pedir, preferir, repetir, seguir]
   serví, dormí, pedí, preferí, repetí, seguí

2. usted [morir, conseguir, pedir, sentirse, vestirse]
   _____

3. tú [conseguir, servir, morir, pedir, dormir, repetir]
   _____

4. ellas [repetir, dormir, seguir, preferir, morir, servir]
   _____

5. nosotros [seguir, preferir, servir, vestirse, dormirse]
   _____

6. ustedes [sentirse, vestirse, conseguir, pedir, dormirse]
   _____

Práctica

1 **¡Pobre señor Suárez!** Completa las oraciones con el pretérito de los verbos.

modelo

Los señores Suárez _cenaron_ [cenar] hoy en un restaurante.

1. Los señores Suárez llegaron al restaurante a las ocho y _____ [seguir] al camarero a una mesa.

2. El señor Suárez _____ [pedir] una chuleta de cerdo. La señora Suárez decidió probar los camarones.

3. Para tomar, los dos _____ [pedir] vino.

4. El camarero _____ [repetir] el pedido (*order*) para confirmarlo.

5. La comida tardó mucho (*took a long time*) en llegar y los señores Suárez casi (*almost*) _____ [dormirse] esperándola.

6. A las nueve, el camarero les _____ [servir] la comida.

7. Después de comer la chuleta de cerdo, el señor Suárez _____ [sentirse] muy mal.

8. ¡Pobre señor Suárez! ¿Por qué no _____ [pedir] los camarones?

2 **El camarero** Indica lo que los clientes pidieron y lo que un camarero les sirvió por error.

modelo

Claudia / hamburguesa
Claudia pidió una hamburguesa, pero el camarero le sirvió zanahorias.

1. Juan y Rafael / té helado
_____

2. Laura / arroz
_____

3. Nosotros / papas fritas
_____

4. Tú / salmón
_____

Conversación

3 **¿Qué hiciste?** Averigua *(find out)* si tu compañero/a hizo estas actividades la semana pasada. Comparte los resultados con la clase.

> ¿ Pediste una pizza con salami?

> No, pedí una pizza con carne.

Actividades	Respuestas
1. pedir una pizza con salami	_____
2. dormir más de diez horas	_____
3. quedarse dormido en clase	_____
4. pedir un plato muy caro en un restaurante elegante	_____
5. preferir quedarse en casa en lugar de *(instead of)* salir con amigos	_____
6. ir a una fiesta y vestirse con ropa muy formal	_____

4 **Una cena romántica** En grupos, describan la cena de Eduardo y Rosa. Usen la foto y las preguntas como guía *(as a guide)*.

- ¿Adónde salieron a cenar?
- ¿Qué pidieron?
- ¿Les sirvieron la comida rápidamente *(quickly)*?
- ¿Les gustó la comida? ¿Qué comida prefirieron?
- ¿Cuánto costó? ¿Quién pagó?
- ¿Van a volver a ese restaurante en el futuro? ¿Van a salir juntos otra vez? ¿Por qué?

Español en vivo

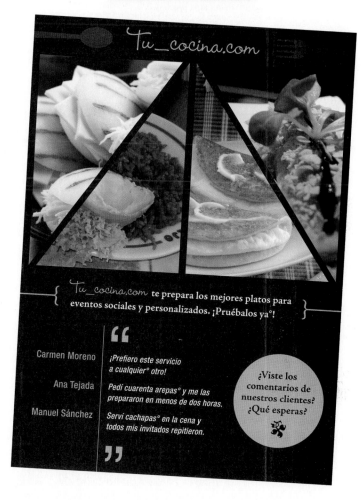

Tu_cocina.com

{ Tu_cocina.com te prepara los mejores platos para eventos sociales y personalizados. ¡Pruébalos ya°! }

Carmen Moreno — *¡Prefiero este servicio a cualquier° otro!*

Ana Tejada — *Pedí cuarenta arepas° y me las prepararon en menos de dos horas.*

Manuel Sánchez — *Serví cachapas° en la cena y todos mis invitados repitieron.*

¿Viste los comentarios de nuestros clientes? ¿Qué esperas?

ya *now* **cualquier** *any* **arepas** *a dish made of ground corn dough* **cachapas** *grilled pancakes made from fresh corn dough*

1 **Identificar** Lee el anuncio *(advertisement)* e identifica los verbos que tienen cambios en la raíz *(stem)* en el pretérito.

2 **Preguntas** Contesta las preguntas.
1. ¿Qué promociona *(promotes)* el anuncio?
2. ¿Cuáles son algunos de los platos que prepara Tu_cocina.com?
3. ¿Cómo son los comentarios de los clientes?

I CAN talk about the past.

I CAN recognize familiar words in a simple ad.

Communicative Goal
Say who does a determined action and when

8.2 Double object pronouns

▶ You have already learned that direct and indirect object pronouns replace nouns. You'll now learn how to use these pronouns together.

INDIRECT OBJECT PRONOUNS

me   te   le (se)   nos   os   les (se)

+

DIRECT OBJECT PRONOUNS

lo   la   los   las

▶ When object pronouns are used together, the indirect object pronoun precedes the direct object pronoun.

I.O.	D.O.	DOUBLE OBJECT PRONOUNS
El camarero me muestra el menú. *The waiter shows me the menu.*	▶	El camarero me lo muestra. *The waiter shows it to me.*
Nos sirven los platos. *They serve us the dishes.*	▶	Nos los sirven. *They serve them to us.*
Maribel te pidió una hamburguesa. *Maribel ordered a hamburger for you.*	▶	Maribel te la pidió. *Maribel ordered it for you.*

¿Se las pongo con alioli?

Te lo recomiendo.

▶ The indirect object pronouns **le** and **les** always change to **se** when they precede **lo, los, la,** and **las**.

I.O.	D.O.	DOUBLE OBJECT PRONOUNS
Le escribí la carta. *I wrote him/her the letter.*	▶	Se la escribí. *I wrote it to him/her.*
Les sirvió los entremeses. *He served them the appetizers.*	▶	Se los sirvió. *He served them to them.*
Le pedimos un café. *We ordered him/her a coffee.*	▶	Se lo pedimos. *We ordered it for him/her.*

Práctica

1 **¿Quién?** Cambia los sustantivos subrayados (*underlined nouns*) por pronombres de objeto directo.

modelo
¿Quién va a traerme la carne del supermercado? [Mi esposo]
Mi *esposo* va a traérmela./Mi *esposo* me la va a traer.

1. ¿Quién les mandó las invitaciones a los invitados (*guests*)? [Mi hija] _____

2. ¿Quién me puede comprar el pan? [Mi hijo]
_____

3. ¿Quién puede prestarme los platos que necesito? [Mi mamá] _____

4. Nos falta mantequilla. ¿Quién nos trae la mantequilla? [Mi cuñada] _____

5. ¡Los postres (*desserts*)! ¿Quién está preparándonos los postres? [Silvia y Renata] _____

6. ¿Quién puede pedirle la pimienta a Mónica? [Mi hijo] _____

2 **En un restaurante** Con un(a) compañero/a, representa las conversaciones entre un(a) camarero/a y unos clientes.

modelo

señora Guzmán:
Una hamburguesa, por favor.
camarero/a:
Enseguida (*right away*) se la traigo.

señora Guzmán

1. tus compañeros/as de cuarto

2. tus padres

3. tu profesor(a) de español

4. señorita Salas

5. tú

6. doctor Cifuentes

Conversación

3 Contestar Con un(a) compañero/a, haz preguntas usando las palabras interrogativas **¿Quién?** o **¿Cuándo?**

modelo

nos enseña español
Estudiante 1: ¿Quién nos enseña español?
Estudiante 2: La profesora Castro nos lo enseña.

Preguntas	Respuestas
1. te escribe mensajes electrónicos	_____
2. me vas a prestar tu computadora	_____
3. les vende los libros de texto a los estudiantes	_____
4. le enseñó español al/a la profesor(a)	_____
5. te compró esa camiseta	_____
6. me vas a mostrar tu casa o apartamento	_____

4 Preguntas Con un(a) compañero/a, haz estas preguntas e incluye pronombres de objeto directo e indirecto en cada respuesta.

modelo

Estudiante 1: ¿Quién te va a preparar el desayuno esta mañana?
Estudiante 2: Yo me lo voy a preparar.

1. ¿Quién te presta dinero cuando lo necesitas?
2. ¿Les prestas dinero a tus amigos? ¿Por qué?
3. ¿Les prestas tu casa o apartamento a tus amigos? ¿Por qué?
4. ¿Nos compras el almuerzo a mí y a los otros compañeros de clase?
5. ¿Les das regalos a tus amigos? ¿Cuándo?
6. ¿Quién te va a preparar la cena esta noche?

I CAN say who does a determined action and when.

▶ Because **se** has multiple meanings, you can clarify to whom the pronoun refers by adding **a usted, a él, a ella, a ustedes, a ellos,** or **a ellas**.

¿El sombrero? Carlos **se** lo vendió **a ella.**
The hat? Carlos sold it to her.

¿Las llaves? Yo **se** las di **a ella.**
The keys? I gave them to her.

▶ Double object pronouns are placed before a conjugated verb. With infinitives and present participles, double object pronouns may be placed before the conjugated verb or attached to the end of the infinitive or present participle.

▶ When double object pronouns are attached to an infinitive or a present participle, an accent mark is added to maintain the original stress.

DOUBLE OBJECT PRONOUNS	DOUBLE OBJECT PRONOUNS
Te lo voy a mostrar.	Voy a mostrártelo.
Nos las están sirviendo.	Están sirviéndonoslas.

Me lo estoy poniendo
Estoy poniéndo**melo.**
I am putting it on.

Se las van a traer.
Van a traér**selas.**
They are going to bring them to you.

La vendedora está sirviéndoselas.

Está haciéndosela.

¡Manos a la obra!

Escribe el pronombre que falta en cada oración.

Objeto directo

1. ¿La ensalada? El camarero nos __la__ sirvió.
2. ¿El salmón? La dueña me _____ recomienda.
3. ¿La comida? Voy a prepárarte_____.
4. ¿Las bebidas? Estamos pidiéndose_____.
5. ¿Los refrescos? Te _____ puedo traer ahora.
6. ¿Los platos de arroz? Van a servírnos_____ después.

Objeto indirecto

1. ¿Puedes traerme tu plato? No, no __te__ lo puedo traer.
2. ¿Quieres mostrarle la carta? Sí, voy a mostrár_____ la ahora.
3. ¿Les serviste la carne? No, no _____ la serví.
4. ¿Vas a leerle el menú? No, no _____ lo voy a leer.
5. ¿Me recomiendas la langosta? Sí, _____ la recomiendo.
6. ¿Cuándo vas a prepararnos la cena? _____ la voy a preparar en una hora.

8.3 Saber and conocer

Communicative Goal
Ask and answer questions about familiar people, places, and things

▸ Spanish has two verbs that mean *to know*, **saber** and **conocer**, but they are used differently. Note that only the **yo** forms of **saber** and **conocer** are irregular in the present tense.

Saber and conocer

	saber		conocer
yo	sé		conozco
tú	sabes		conoces
Ud./él/ella	sabe		conoce
nosotros/as	sabemos		conocemos
vosotros/as	sabéis		conocéis
Uds./ellos/ellas	saben		conocen

▸ **Saber** means *to know a fact or piece(s) of information* or *to know how to do something*.

No **sé** tu número de teléfono.
I don't know your phone number.

Mi hermana **sabe** hablar francés.
My sister knows how to speak French.

▸ **Conocer** means *to know* or *be familiar/acquainted with a person, place, or thing*.

¿**Conoces** la ciudad de Nueva York?
Do you know New York City?

No **conozco** a tu amigo Esteban.
I don't know your friend Esteban.

▸ As you learned in 5.4, when the direct object of **conocer** is a person or pet, the personal **a** is used. Compare these sentences.

¿**Conoces a** Rigoberta Menchú?   ¿**Conoces** ese restaurante?

¡ojo! These verbs are conjugated like **conocer** in the **yo** form in the present. You will learn how to use **saber**, **conocer**, and related verbs in the preterite in Lesson 9.

ofrecer (*to offer*)	ofrezco, ofreces, ofrece, etc.
parecer (*to seem*)	parezco, pareces, parece, etc.
conducir (*to drive*)	conduzco, conduces, conduce, conducimos, conducís, conducen
traducir (*to translate*)	traduzco, traduces, traduce, traducimos, traducís, traducen

¡ojo! **Conducir** and **traducir** are –**ir** verbs, so they differ from **conocer** in their **nosotros/as** and **vosotros/as** forms.

¡Manos a la obra!

Escribe las formas apropiadas de **saber** y **conocer**.

saber
1. José no ___sabe___ la hora.
2. Mis padres _____ hablar japonés.
3. ¿Por qué no _____ tú estos verbos?
4. Yo _____ qué hora es.

conocer
5. Usted y yo _____ bien Miami.
6. Nadie me _____ bien.
7. ¿ _____ tú a la tía de Eduardo?
8. ¿ _____ usted a Sara?

Práctica

1 Completar Completa las oraciones con la forma apropiada de **saber** o **conocer**.

modelo

Mi madre __conoce__ la ciudad maya de Tikal. Dice que es hermosa.

1. —Nosotros no _____ Guatemala.
   —Ah, ¿no? Pues yo _____ bien las ciudades de Escuintla, Quetzaltenango y Antigua.
2. —¿_____ ustedes dónde vive Pilar?
   —No, nosotras no _____.
3. Mi amiga Carla _____ conducir, pero yo no _____.
4. —¿_____ tú a Mateo, mi hermano mayor?
   —No, no lo _____.
5. —Yo todavía no _____ a tu novio.
   —Sí, ya lo _____.
6. Tú _____ esquiar, pero Tino y Luis son pequeños y no _____.
7. Roberto _____ bien el *Popol Vuh*, el libro sagrado de los mayas; también _____ leer los jeroglíficos de los templos mayas.

2 Oraciones Combina las palabras de las tres columnas para formar oraciones.

modelo

No conozco a Jennifer Lawrence. Yo conozco a Rami Malek.

Sujetos	Verbos	Objetos directos
Taylor Swift		Jennifer Lawrence
Lady Gaga		Rami Malek
Bruno Mars		cantar
Brad Pitt		la ciudad de Montreal en Canadá
Saoirse Ronan	(no) conocer	hablar dos lenguas extranjeras
Alfonso Cuarón	(no) saber	hacer reír (*laugh*) a la gente
yo		actuar (*perform*) muy bien
tú		escribir novelas de terror
tu compañero/a		programar computadoras
tu profesor(a)		muchas personas importantes

Conversación

3 Deportes Pregúntale a un(a) compañero/a qué deportes practica y por qué. Usa los verbos **saber** y **conocer**.

 modelo

Estudiante 1: ¿Sabes esquiar?
Estudiante 2: Sí, sé esquiar./
No, no sé esquiar.
Estudiante 1: ¿Por qué?
Estudiante 2: Porque me interesa el esquí./Porque no me gusta el invierno.

1.   2.   3.

4.   5.   6.

4 Contestar Con un(a) compañero/a, contesta las preguntas.

1. ¿Qué restaurantes buenos conoces? ¿Cenas en los restaurantes frecuentemente (*frequently*)?

2. En tu familia, ¿quién sabe cocinar mejor (*best*)? ¿Por qué?

3. ¿Conoces recetas de comidas latinas? ¿Cuáles?

4. ¿Conoces a algún/alguna chef famoso/a? ¿Qué tipo de comida prepara?

5. ¿Sabes preparar algún plato especial? ¿Cuál es?

6. ¿Sabes que el ajo es bueno para la salud (*health*)? ¿Qué otras comidas o condimentos saludables conoces?

Communicative Goal
Recognize familiar words in a simple ad

Español en vivo

Él sabe dónde **comer** lo que más le gusta.

Él sabe cómo **jugar** cuatro horas seguidas.

Él sabe dónde está su **regalo** de cumpleaños°.

Él sabe dónde **divertirse°**.

... y usted sabe dónde puede encontrar un poco de todo°.
¿Conoce algún otro lugar como éste?

CENTRO COMERCIAL MÁLAGA
Sabe lo que te gusta.

cumpleaños *birthday* **divertirse** *to have fun* **un poco de todo** *a little bit of everything*

1 Identificar Lee el anuncio (*advertisement*) y busca ejemplos de los verbos **saber** y **conocer**.

2 Preguntas Contesta las preguntas.

1. Después de leer el anuncio, ¿qué sabes del Centro Comercial Málaga?
2. ¿Qué puedes hacer en el Centro Comercial Málaga?
3. ¿A quién está dirigido (*directed*) el anuncio?
4. ¿Conoces un centro comercial como éste? ¿Cómo se llama? ¿En qué ciudad está?

I CAN ask and answer questions about familiar people, places, and things.

I CAN recognize familiar words in a simple ad.

8.4 Comparatives and superlatives

Communicative Goal | Compare people and things

Comparisons of inequality

▸ Comparisons of inequality are formed by placing **más** (*more*) or **menos** (*less*) before adjectives, adverbs, and nouns and **que** (*than*) after them. When the comparison involves a numerical expression, use **de** before the number.

¡Los calamares me gustan más que las croquetas!

La paella está más rica que el gazpacho.

El té es **más caro que** el jugo.
Tea is more expensive than juice.

Luis se despierta **más temprano que** yo.
Luis gets up earlier than I (do).

Susana es **menos generosa que** su prima.
Susana is less generous than her cousin.

Tomo **más clases que** Enrique.
I take more classes than Enrique.

▸ With verbs, use this construction to make comparisons of inequality:
[*verb*] + **más/menos que**.

Mis hermanos **comen más que** yo.
My brothers eat more than I (do).

Arturo **duerme menos que** su padre.
Arturo sleeps less than his father (does).

Antonio **viaja más que** tú.
Antonio travels more than you (do).

Ana **habla menos que** yo.
Ana talks less than I (do).

Comparisons of equality

▸ The constructions **tan** + [*adverb, adjective*] + **como** and **tanto/a(s)** + [*singular noun, plural noun*] + **como** are used to make comparisons of equality.

Este plato es **tan delicioso como** aquél.
This dish is as delicious as that one.

Tu amigo es **tan simpático como** tú.
Your friend is as nice as you (are).

Yo comí **tanta comida como** tú.
I ate as much food as you (did).

Ustedes probaron **tantos platos como** ellos.
You tried as many dishes as they (did).

▸ Comparisons of equality with verbs are formed by placing **tanto como** after the verb. Note that **tanto** does not change in number or gender.

No **duermo tanto como** mi tía.
I don't sleep as much as my aunt (does).

Estudiamos tanto como ustedes.
We study as much as you (do).

Práctica

1 **Lucila y Teresa** Selecciona la palabra correcta para comparar a dos hermanas muy diferentes.

Lucila   Teresa

1. Lucila es más alta y más atractiva _____ [de, más, menos, que] Teresa.

2. Teresa es más delgada porque practica _____ [de, más, menos, que] deportes que su hermana.

3. Lucila es _____ [más, menos de, más que] simpática que Teresa porque es alegre.

4. A Teresa le gusta quedarse en casa. Va a _____ [de, más, menos, que] fiestas que su hermana.

5. Teresa estudia más que Lucila. Ahora está tomando cinco clases más _____ [más, menos, que, más de] su hermana.

6. Lucila se preocupa _____ [de, más, menos, que] que Teresa por estudiar. ¡Son _____ [como, tan, tanto] diferentes!

2 **Mario y Luis** Completa las oraciones para formar comparaciones de igualdad sobre Mario y Luis, los novios de Lucila y Teresa.

| tan |
| tanto(s) |
| tanta(s) |

Mario   Luis

1. Mario es _____ interesante como Luis.

2. Mario viaja _____ como Luis.

3. Luis habla _____ lenguas extranjeras como Mario.

4. Luis cocina carnes _____ bien como Mario.

5. Mario tiene _____ amigos como Luis.

6. ¡Qué casualidad (*coincidence*)! Mario y Luis también son hermanos, pero no hay _____ diferencia entre ellos como entre Lucila y Teresa.

Conversación

3 **La familia García** En grupos, túrnense (*take turns*) para hacer comparaciones entre Rafael, Eva, Esteban y Lourdes García.

Esteban
Lourdes
Rafael
Eva

modelo

Estudiante 1: Esteban es el más activo de la familia.
Estudiante 2: Pues yo creo que Rafael es tan activo como Esteban.
Estudiante 1: Mmm, pero Esteban es mucho más delgado.

4 **Comparaciones** Con un(a) compañero/a, conversa sobre estos temas y luego comparte tres datos interesantes con la clase.

modelo artistas de moda

Estudiante 1: Creo que Adele es la mejor artista de estos tiempos.
Estudiante 2: ¡Pero qué dices! Esa artista es malísima. Rihanna y Snoop son los mejores. Además, Adele no se viste tan bien como Rihanna.
Estudiante 1: Estás loco. Adele siempre está a la moda. Además, te repito que es la mejor. Por ejemplo, ya tiene más de treinta millones de copias vendidas (*sold copies*).

cafés y restaurantes	podcasts
comidas favoritas	los profesores
los cursos que toman	música de moda
libros favoritos	ropa favorita
personas famosas	tiendas en tu comunidad

I CAN compare people and things.

Superlatives

▶ Use this construction to form the superlative. Note that the noun is preceded by a definite article. **De** is equivalent to the English *in* or *of*.

el/la/los/las + [*noun*] + más/menos + [*adjective*] + de

Es **el café más rico del** país.
It's the most delicious coffee in the country.

Son **las tiendas menos caras de** la ciudad.
They are the least expensive stores in the city.

▶ The noun in a superlative construction can be omitted if it is clear to whom or what the superlative refers.

¿El restaurante El Cráter?
Es **el más elegante de** la ciudad.
The El Cráter restaurant?
It's the most elegant (one) in the city.

Recomiendo la ensalada de papa.
Es **la más sabrosa del** menú.
I recommend the potato salad.
It's the most delicious one on the menu.

¡ojo! The absolute superlative, which ends in **–ísimo/a(s)**, is equivalent to the English *extremely/very* + [*adjective/adverb*]. For example: **muchísimo/a(s)** (*very much*), **malísimo/a(s)** (*very bad*), **facilísimo/a(s)** (*extremely easy*).

▶ Note these spelling changes.

rico ⟶ ri**qu**ísimo
joven ⟶ jove**nc**ísimo
largo ⟶ lar**gu**ísimo
trabajador ⟶ trabajador**c**ísimo
fácil ⟶ faci**l**ísimo
feliz ⟶ feli**c**ísimo

Irregular comparatives and superlatives

Irregular comparative and superlative forms					
Adjective		**Comparative form**		**Superlative form**	
bueno/a	good	mejor	better	el/la mejor	(the) best
malo/a	bad	peor	worse	el/la peor	(the) worst
grande	big; old	mayor	older	el/la mayor	(the) oldest
pequeño/a	small; young	menor	younger	el/la menor	(the) youngest
joven	young	menor	younger	el/la menor	(the) youngest
viejo/a	old	mayor	older	el/la mayor	(the) oldest

▶ When **grande** and **pequeño/a** refer to age, use the irregular comparative and superlative forms, **mayor/menor**. However, when **grande** and **pequeño/a** refer to size, use the regular forms, **más grande/más pequeño/a**.

Isabel es **la mayor**.
Isabel is the oldest.

Tu ensalada es **más grande que** ésa.
Your salad is bigger than that one.

▶ **Bien** and **mal** have the same comparative forms as **bueno/a** and **malo/a**.

Julio nada **mejor que** los otros chicos.
Julio swims better than the other boys.

Ellas cantan **peor que** las otras chicas.
They sing worse than the other girls.

A repasar

8.1 Preterite of stem-changing verbs

1 **Manuel y sus tíos** Manuel y sus tíos fueron a cenar a un restaurante. Indica las diferencias entre las acciones de Manuel y las de sus tíos. Sigue el modelo.

> **modelo**
>
> vestirse con ropa informal / ropa elegante
>
> **Manuel se vistió con ropa informal. Sus tíos se vistieron con ropa elegante.**

1. pedir dos refrescos / vino tinto

2. preferir la carne de res con papas / el pescado con ajo

3. servirse entremeses picantes / ensalada de verduras

4. repetir el plato principal / (no) repetir el plato principal.

5. sentirse mal en la noche / bien en la noche

6. dormirse tarde / temprano

2 **¿Qué desayunaron?** Con un(a) compañero/a, describe el desayuno de las personas de los dibujos. Usa el pretérito de los verbos **pedir, servir, repetir** y **sentirse.**

| 1. Elisa y Ana | 2. Marcos y Olga |

8.2 Double object pronouns

3 **En la cafetería** Cambia los sustantivos *(nouns)* por pronombres de objeto directo e indirecto. Sigue el modelo.

> **modelo**
>
> Me están sirviendo café.
> **Me lo están sirviendo. Están sirviéndomelo.**

1. Nos van a dar las patatas fritas.

2. Te van a servir los refrescos.

3. Le están preparando la ensalada.

4. Les voy a recomendar unos postres.

5. Te están pidiendo las bebidas.

6. Me voy a comer los champiñones.

4 **Camareros** Gabriel y Valeria son camareros en un restaurante. Completa la conversación que tienen con su jefe con los pronombres apropiados.

> **modelo**
>
> **JEFE** Valeria, ¿le ofreciste agua fría al cliente de la mesa 22?
>
> **VALERIA** Sí, ___se la ofrecí___ de inmediato.

JEFE Gabriel, ¿los clientes de la mesa 5 te pidieron ensaladas?

GABRIEL Sí, (1) _____.

JEFE Valeria, ¿le llevaste el pan a la señora de la mesa 10?

VALERIA Sí, (2) _____ hace cinco minutos.

VALERIA Gabriel, ¿recuerdas si ya me mostraste los vinos nuevos?

GABRIEL Sí, ya (3) _____.

JEFE Gabriel, ¿van a pagarte la cuenta *(bill)* los clientes de la mesa 5?

GABRIEL Sí, (4) _____ ahora mismo.

JEFE ¿Les dieron los clientes buenas propinas *(tips)*?

VALERIA Sí, (5) _____. ¡Estamos muy contentos!

8.3 Saber and conocer

5 **Completar** Completa las oraciones con la forma correcta de los verbos.

> **modelo**
>
> Mi amigo Juan ___traduce___ [traducir] los libros para esa editorial.

1. Mis amigos y yo vamos a ir a Perú porque no _____ [conocer] ese país.

2. En Lima, tengo un amigo que _____ [conducir] un taxi y él nos _____ [ofrecer] llevarnos a pasear por toda la ciudad.

3. Antonio y yo no _____ [saber] dónde vive nuestro amigo taxista Carlos.

4. Mis amigos _____ [parecer] preocupados porque no hablan bien español.

5. Yo no estoy preocupado porque yo sí _____ [saber] hablar español.

6 **¿Quién soy?** Imagina que eres una persona famosa. Escribe tres oraciones con los verbos **saber** y **conocer** para dar pistas *(clues)* sobre quién eres. Luego, en grupos de tres, cada persona lee sus oraciones y los demás miembros del grupo adivinan *(guess)* quién es.

> **modelo**
>
> **Estudiante 1:** *Sé cantar canciones románticas en inglés y en español. Sé bailar muy bien. Conozco a Julio Iglesias porque es mi padre.*
>
> **Estudiante 2:** ¡Enrique Iglesias!

8.4 Comparatives and superlatives

7 **En el restaurante del señor Chávez** Cambia las oraciones omitiendo *(omitting)* el sujeto y usando los superlativos.

> **modelo**
> Jorge es mal camarero. (el restaurante)
> **Es el peor camarero del restaurante.**

1. La leche es nutritiva. (las bebidas)

2. El restaurante del señor Chávez no es elegante. (la ciudad)

3. Esta taquería es muy cara. (las taquerías)

4. El arroz con pollo es un buen plato. (el menú)

5. Juliana es una camarera simpática. (las camareras)

6. El arroz con leche es sabroso. (los postres)

8 **El almuerzo familiar** La familia Solís está almorzando. Con un(a) compañero/a, escribe comparaciones usando las formas superlativas y comparativas.

> **modelo**
> El sándwich de Sandra es grandísimo. La abuela Beatriz es la mayor de la familia.

Síntesis

9 **¡Su restaurante es malísimo!** Fuiste con un(a) amigo/a a comer a un restaurante y la comida resultó no ser muy rica. Con un(a) compañero/a, escribe una carta al dueño del restaurante. Sigue la guía.

- Mencionen lo que ustedes pidieron y lo que les sirvieron.
- Expliquen que ustedes saben cocinar muy bien y que la comida fue muy mala.
- Digan que conocen otros restaurantes mejores.
- Comparen el restaurante con otros restaurantes.

Videoclip

Video

1 **Preparación** ¿Te encantan los programas de cocina? ¿Te gustaría preparar las recetas *(recipes)* de estos programas?

2 **El clip** Mira **Receta de churros** del programa de cocina *Gipsy Chef* de España.

Vocabulario	
calentar *to heat*	mezclar *to mix*
hervir *to boil*	remover *to stir*

Y ahora con el aceite muy caliente° vas apretando° la manga° y ves que te va saliendo un churro perfecto.

caliente *hot*   apretando *squeezing*   manga (pastelera) *pastry bag*

3 **Ordenar** Ordena estos pasos de la receta.

_____ a. poner los churros en el azúcar

_____ b. aromatizar *(to flavor)* el agua

_____ c. remover la masa *(dough)*

_____ d. añadir *(to add)* la sal

_____ e. calentar el agua

_____ f. añadir el queso

_____ g. poner la masa en el aceite

_____ h. añadir la harina *(flour)*

4 **Mi receta** Escribe la receta de uno de tus platos favoritos. Presenta la receta a la clase. Si es posible, prepara el plato durante tu presentación.

I CAN present a recipe.

Ampliación

Communicative Goals
Understand a conversation with the help of notes, and talk about a recent restaurant visit

1 Escuchar

A Rosa y Roberto están en un restaurante. Escucha la conversación entre ellos y la camarera y toma nota de cuáles son los especiales del día.

> **TIP** **Jot down notes as you listen.** Jotting down notes while you listen can help you keep track of the important points or details. Focus actively on comprehension rather than on remembering what you have heard.

(Los especiales del día)

_____ _____ _____

B Usa tus notas para completar las oraciones con la opción correcta.

1. La camarera les dio información sobre _____ (dos / tres / cuatro) especiales para plato principal.

2. Rosa pidió _____ (arroz con pollo / bistec a la criolla / cerdo con salsa de champiñones y papas).

3. Roberto pidió _____ (los entremeses / bistec a la criolla / cerdo con salsa de champiñones y papas).

4. Roberto va a comer _____ (más platos que / menos platos que / tantos platos como) Rosa.

2 Conversar

Con un(a) compañero/a, conversa sobre la última vez (*the last time*) que fuiste a un restaurante. Utiliza las preguntas como guía.

> • ¿Cuándo fue la última vez que fuiste a un restaurante?
>
> • ¿Con quién comiste?
>
> • ¿A qué restaurante fueron?
>
> • ¿Qué pidieron? ¿Les gustó la comida?
>
> • ¿Se la sirvieron rápidamente (quickly)?
>
> • ¿Fue mejor o peor que la comida que comes en casa? ¿Fue muy cara?
>
> • ¿Van a volver a ese restaurante en el futuro?

I CAN take notes to help me understand the details of a conversation.

I CAN talk about the last time I went to a restaurant.

Ampliación

3 Escribir

Escribe una crítica sobre un restaurante local.

TIP **Expressing and supporting opinions** Use details, facts, examples, and other forms of evidence to convince your readers to take your opinions seriously.

Organizar	Usa un mapa de ideas para organizar comentarios sobre la comida, el servicio, el ambiente (*atmosphere*) y otros datos sobre el restaurante.
Escribir	Utiliza tus notas para escribir el primer borrador de la crítica.
Corregir	Intercambia (*exchange*) tu composición con la de un(a) compañero/a. Comenta sobre el título, la organización, los detalles específicos y los errores de gramática o de ortografía.
Compartir	Revisa el primer borrador teniendo en cuenta los comentarios de tu compañero/a. Incorpora nuevas ideas o más información para reforzar (*support*) tu opinión. Luego, entrégale (*hand in*) la crítica a tu profesor(a).

4 Un paso más

Imagina que abres un nuevo restaurante en la capital de un país hispano. Sigue estos pasos para diseñar el menú.

- Decide en qué país y en qué ciudad vas a abrir el restaurante.
- Investiga cuáles son las comidas típicas y los platos más populares del país.
- Investiga cómo son los restaurantes típicos del país que elegiste y qué características tienen en común.
- Elige el nombre del restaurante.
- Diseña el menú. Piensa en el estilo y en los colores que representan la cultura del país.
- Haz una lista de los entremeses, los platos principales, las ensaladas, los postres y las bebidas que quieres incluir en el menú.
- Piensa en un plato único de tu restaurante e inclúyelo en el menú. El plato debe tener un ingrediente típico del país y representar su cultura.
- Busca información sobre los precios de los platos en la moneda del país. Indica estos precios al lado de cada plato que seleccionaste.
- Intercambia tu menú con los de tres o cuatro compañeros/as y comparen los platos que escogieron.

El Tamalito
Especialidades guatemaltecas

5.ª calle (Los Próceres)
Zona 4, Guatemala
Tel: (502) 345 89 76
Fax: (502) 243 56 34

5 Cultura

¿Adónde quieres ir para comer: el Mercado de San Miguel, el restaurante cubano, la taquería...? ¿Por qué? ¿Qué vas a pedir?

I CAN write a restaurant review.

I CAN design a menu.

Audio: Reading

Antes de leer

As you know, you can learn a great deal about a text by looking at the format and looking for cognates, titles, and subtitles. You can skim for the gist and scan for specific information. Reading for the main idea is another useful strategy.

TIP **Read for the main idea.** Reading for the main idea involves locating the topic sentence of each paragraph to determine the author's purpose for writing. Topic sentences can provide clues about the content of each paragraph, as well as the general organization of the text.

Examinar el texto

Aquí se presentan dos textos distintos. ¿Qué estrategias puedes usar para leer la crítica? ¿Cuáles son las estrategias apropiadas para familiarizarte con el menú? Utiliza las más eficaces para cada texto. Luego, identifica las estrategias similares que se aplican en los dos textos.

Identificar la idea principal

Lee la primera oración de cada párrafo de la crítica del restaurante **El Palmito**. Apunta el tema principal de cada párrafo. Luego lee el primer párrafo. ¿Crees que el restaurante le gustó a la autora? ¿Por qué? Ahora lee la crítica entera. En tu opinión, ¿cuál es la idea principal de la crítica? ¿Por qué la escribió la autora? Compara tus opiniones con las de un(a) compañero/a.

El Tiempo de Guatemala

Restaurantes
Domingo 9 de mayo, Boston, Massachusetts

37E

Cinco estrellas para El Palmito

Margarita Galán, crítica de restaurantes

El viernes pasado me sorprendí° cuando encontré un restaurante fantástico en el barrio donde vivo. Cené en el restaurante **El Palmito,** donde se mezclan° de una manera extraordinaria la comida tradicional de Centroamérica y la belleza arquitectónica de nuestra ciudad. Su propietario, Héctor Suárez, es uno de los chefs más respetados de Guatemala.

El exterior del restaurante refleja el estilo colonial de Nueva Inglaterra. Por dentro°, la decoración rústica crea un ambiente cálido°. Hay que° mencionar también el hermoso patio, lleno° de plantas y flores, donde muchas personas se reúnen para tomar un café en un ambiente° relajado° y cordial. Uno no se puede quejar° del servicio

de **El Palmito.** El personal del restaurante es muy amable y atento, desde los cocineros que preparan la comida hasta los camareros que la sirven.

La comida del restaurante es exquisita. Las tortillas, que se sirven con ajiaceite, son deliciosas. La sopa de pollo y huevo es excelente, y los frijoles enchilados, ricos. También recomiendo el tomaticán, cocinado con una gran variedad de verduras muy ricas. De postre°, don Héctor me preparó su especialidad, un rico pastel de yogur.

Les recomiendo que visiten **El Palmito** cuando tengan ocasión°.

El Palmito, Boston
de lunes a sábado 10:00a.m.-11:00p.m.
domingo 11:00a.m.-10:00p.m.

Comida *****
Servicio *****
Ambiente *****
Precio ****

M E N Ú

Entremeses
Pan tostado con
- Queso frito   • Huevos revueltos°

Tortillas con
- Ajicomino (chile, comino°)   • Ajiaceite (chile, aceite)

Sopas
- Cebolla   • Verduras   • Pollo y huevo   • Mariscos

Platos Principales
Chilaquil
(tortilla de maíz, queso y chile)

Tomaticán
(tomate, papas, maíz, chile, arvejas y zanahorias)

Tamales
(maíz, azúcar, ajo, cebolla)

Frijoles enchilados
(frijoles negros, carne de cerdo o de res, arroz, chile)

Postres
- Helado° de limón   • Plátanos° caribeños
- Uvate (uvas, azúcar y ron°)   • Pastel de yogur

Bebidas
- Té helado   • Vino tinto
- Vino blanco   • Agua mineral   • Jugos
- Chilate (maíz, chile y cacao)

sorprendí *was surprised* **mezclan** *mix* **Por dentro** *Inside* **cálido** *warm* **Hay que** *One must* **lleno** *full* **ambiente** *atmosphere* **relajado** *relaxed* **Uno no se puede quejar** *One can't complain* **postre** *dessert* **cuando tengan ocasión** *when you have the opportunity* **huevos revueltos** *scrambled eggs* **comino** *cumin* **Helado** *Ice cream* **Plátanos** *Plantains* **ron** *rum*

Después de leer

¿Comprendiste?
Completa cada oración con la opción correcta.

1. La arquitectura del restaurante es _____ [moderna, colonial, fea].
2. A muchos clientes les gusta tomar el café en _____ [las mesas, el bar, el patio].
3. El dueño del restaurante es uno de los_____ [peores, menores, mejores] chefs de Guatemala.
4. La comida en este restaurante, según la autora, es_____ [muy buena, mala, regular].
5. La crítica _____ [no da información, habla bien, se queja] del restaurante.

Preguntas
Responde estas preguntas con oraciones completas.

1. ¿Cómo se llama el dueño del restaurante?
2. ¿Qué tipo de comida se sirve en El Palmito?
3. ¿Cómo es el ambiente del restaurante?
4. ¿Quién escribió este artículo?
5. ¿Cuál es la profesión de la autora del artículo?
6. ¿Cuántos platos probó la autora del artículo?

Coméntalo
¿Te interesan las comidas y bebidas que sirven en El Palmito? ¿Cuáles te parecen más interesantes? ¿Por qué? ¿Se sirven platos y bebidas similares a éstos en donde vives?

I CAN identify the main idea of a text and of each paragraph.

Vocabulary Tools

En un restaurante

el/la camarero/a *waiter*
el/la dueño/a *owner*
el menú *menu*

el almuerzo *lunch*
la cena *dinner*
la comida *food; meal*
el desayuno *breakfast*
los entremeses *appetizers*
el plato (principal) *(main) dish*

almorzar (o:ue) *to have lunch*
cenar *to have dinner*
desayunar *to have breakfast*
pedir (e:i) *to order (food)*
probar (o:ue) *to taste; to try*
recomendar (e:ie) *to recommend*
servir (e:i) *to serve*

El gusto y los sabores

agrio/a *sour*
amargo/a *bitter*
delicioso/a *delicious*
dulce *sweet*
picante *spicy*
rico/a *tasty*
sabroso/a *delicious*
salado/a *salty*

Las bebidas

el agua (f.) (mineral) *(mineral) water*
la bebida *drink; beverage*
el café *coffee*
la cerveza *beer*
el jugo (de fruta) *(fruit) juice*
la leche *milk*
el refresco *soft drink*
el té (helado) *(iced) tea*
el vino (blanco/tinto) *(white/red) wine*

Los granos y las verduras

el ajo *garlic*
el arroz *rice*
las arvejas *peas*
la cebolla *onion*
los cereales *cereals; grains*
el champiñón *mushroom*
la ensalada *salad*
los frijoles *beans*
la lechuga *lettuce*
el maíz *corn*
la papa/patata *potato*
el tomate *tomato*
las verduras *vegetables*
la zanahoria *carrot*

Las carnes, los pescados y los mariscos

el atún *tuna*
el bistec *steak*
los camarones *shrimp*
la carne *meat*
la carne de res *beef*
la chuleta de cerdo *pork chop*
la hamburguesa (vegetariana) *(veggie) hamburger*
el jamón *ham*
la langosta *lobster*
los mariscos *seafood*
el pavo *turkey*
el pescado *fish*
el pollo (asado) *(roast) chicken*
la salchicha *sausage*
el salmón *salmon*

Las frutas

la banana *banana*
las frutas *fruit*
el limón *lemon*
la manzana *apple*
la naranja *orange*
las uvas *grapes*

Los condimentos y otras comidas

el aceite *oil*
el azúcar *sugar*
el huevo *egg*
la mantequilla *butter*
la margarina *margarine*
la mayonesa *mayonnaise*
el pan (tostado) *(toasted) bread*
las papas/patatas fritas *French fries*
la pimienta *pepper*
el queso *cheese*
la sal *salt*
el sándwich *sandwich*
la sopa *soup*
el vinagre *vinegar*

Verbos

conducir *to drive*
conocer *to know; to be acquainted with*
morir (o:ue) *to die*
ofrecer *to offer*
parecer *to seem*
saber *to know; to know how*
traducir *to translate*

Comparatives and superlatives *See pages 212–213.*

Communicative Goals: Review

I CAN talk about food.
• Describe your favorite food.

I CAN order at a restaurant.
• Say how you would order food in a restaurant.

I CAN discuss familiar people and places.
• Say the names of two people and two places you know well.

I CAN investigate foods in the Spanish-speaking world.
• Describe one of the foods you learned about in this lesson.

AVENTURAS EN LOS PAÍSES HISPANOS

El Amazonas es el río más caudaloso *(the most vast)* del mundo. Por ser muy profundo *(deep)* y ancho *(wide)*, tiene otro nombre: "río océano". Desde barcos muy grandes hasta barcos pequeños, como la canoa que vemos en la foto, navegan en él. Alrededor *(around)* del río Amazonas hay una gran selva *(jungle)* y muy poca gente vive allí.

¿Te gustaría navegar en el río Amazonas? ¿Por qué?

SURAMÉRICA I

Venezuela

Área: 912.050 km² (352.144 millas²)
Población: 28.500.000
Capital: Caracas–2.936.000
Ciudades principales: Maracaibo, Valencia, Maracay, Barquisimeto
Moneda: bolívar

SOURCE: Population Division, UN Secretariat & CIA World Factbook

Colombia

Área: 1.138.910 km² (439.734 millas²)
Población: 50.300.000
Capital: Bogotá–10.779.000
Ciudades principales: Medellín, Cali, Barranquilla, Cartagena
Moneda: peso colombiano

SOURCE: Population Division, UN Secretariat & CIA World Factbook

Ecuador

Área: 283.560 km² (109.483 millas²)
Población: 17.400.000
Capital: Quito–1.848.000
Ciudades principales: Guayaquil, Cuenca, Machala, Portoviejo
Moneda: dólar estadounidense

SOURCE: Population Division, UN Secretariat & CIA World Factbook

Perú

Área: 1.285.220 km² (496.224 millas²)
Población: 32.500.000
Capital: Lima–10.555.000
Ciudades principales: Arequipa, Trujillo, Chiclayo, Iquitos
Moneda: nuevo sol

SOURCE: Population Division, UN Secretariat & CIA World Factbook

Video

Gente

Indígenas de Ecuador

Ecuador tiene una gran población indígena *(native)*. La lengua oficial de Ecuador es el español, pero hoy día también se hablan *(are spoken)* otras lenguas. Aproximadamente unos 4.000.000 de ecuatorianos hablan lenguas indígenas; la mayoría de ellos habla quechua. Las comunidades indígenas de Ecuador son excelentes tejedoras *(weavers)*; sus tejidos son famosos en todo el mundo por sus colores vivos y sus hermosos diseños *(designs)*. En el mercado de Otavalo se venden mantas *(blankets)*, ropas tradicionales y tapices *(tapestries)* hechos por estas comunidades.

¿Qué te gustaría comprar en el mercado de Otavalo?

Lugares

El Salto Ángel

El Salto Ángel, en el sureste de Venezuela, es la catarata *(waterfall)* más alta del mundo. Tiene 979 m (3.212 pies) de altura *(height)*. Es diecisiete veces más alta que las cataratas del Niágara. James C. Angel "descubrió" esta catarata en 1937 y por eso lleva su nombre. Está en el Parque Nacional Canaima y los indígenas la llaman *Kerepakupai Merú,* que significa catarata.

¿Conoces alguna catarata similar a la de Salto Ángel? ¿Dónde está? ¿Cómo es comparada con la de Salto Ángel?

Mar Caribe

Barranquilla

Maracaibo

Medellín

★ Bogotá

Cali

R. Magdalena

Pasto

COLOMBIA

Quito
★
ECUADOR

Guayaquil

Iquitos

PERÚ

Cordillera de los Andes

Lima ★

Cuzco

Lago Titicaca

Arequipa

Océano Pacífico

Puerto España
TRINIDAD
⭐

⭐ **Caracas**
VENEZUELA

R. Orinoco

GUAYANA

BRASIL

Gabriel García Márquez

Publicó su primer cuento (*short story*) en 1947, cuando era estudiante universitario. Su libro más conocido, *Cien años de soledad*, está escrito en el estilo (*style*) literario llamado "realismo mágico", un estilo que mezcla (*mixes*) la realidad con lo irreal y lo mítico (*mythical*). García Márquez recibió el Premio Nobel de Literatura en 1982. Tras su muerte es recordado (*remembered*) como uno los escritores contemporáneos más importantes del mundo.

¿Leíste alguna obra de García Márquez? ¿Cuál? Si no, ¿crees que te gustaría leer algo de él?

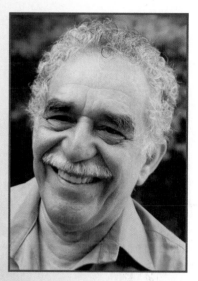

Música ♪

La música afroperuana

La música afroperuana es el resultado de la combinación de varias tradiciones musicales: la española del siglo XIX y las de las poblaciones africanas que fueron llevadas (*taken*) a Perú durante la Colonia. Entre los instrumentos tradicionales de la música afroperuana se encuentran la guitarra flamenca, el cajón y el cencerro (*cowbell*). Susana Baca, Porfirio Vásquez, la familia Ballumbrosio y Perú Negro son destacados artistas y grupos de música afroperuana.

¿Conoces la música afroperuana?

Costumbres

El Carnaval de Barranquilla ▶

Durante el Carnaval de Barranquilla, la ciudad colombiana vive para esta fiesta. Este festival es una fusión de las culturas que han llegado (*have arrived*) a las costas caribeñas de Colombia y de sus grupos autóctonos (*indigenous*). El evento más importante es la Batalla de Flores (*Battle of the Flowers*), un desfile (*parade*) de carrozas (*floats*) decoradas con flores. En 2003, la UNESCO declaró este carnaval como Patrimonio de la Humanidad.

¿Conoces una celebración como ésta en los Estados Unidos? ¿Dónde?

Susana Baca

¿Qué aprendiste?

1 **¿Cierto o falso?** Indica si las oraciones son **ciertas** o **falsas**.

	Cierto	Falso
1. El río Amazonas es el más caudaloso del mundo.	_____	_____
2. La moneda de Ecuador es el dólar estadounidense.	_____	_____
3. Arequipa es una de las ciudades principales de Venezuela.	_____	_____
4. La lengua oficial de Ecuador es el quechua.	_____	_____
5. Las cataratas del Niágara son más altas que el Salto Ángel.	_____	_____
6. García Márquez ganó el Premio Nobel en 1982.	_____	_____
7. La guitarra flamenca y el cencerro son instrumentos tradicionales de la música afroperuana.	_____	_____
8. Celebran el Carnaval de Barranquilla en las montañas de Colombia.	_____	_____

2 **Preguntas** Contesta las preguntas.

1. ¿Qué es el cajón?
2. ¿Quién es Susana Baca?
3. ¿Cuál es el evento más importante del Carnaval de Barranquilla?
4. ¿Qué catarata está en el Parque Nacional Canaima?
5. ¿Cuál es el libro más famoso de García Márquez?
6. ¿Por qué son famosos los tejidos de las comunidades indígenas de Ecuador?

3 **Comparaciones** Haz una de estas comparaciones.

1. Compara las banderas de Venezuela, Colombia y Ecuador.
2. Compara las influencias culturales en la música afroperuana y en el Carnaval de Barranquilla.

4 **¿Qué piensas?** Con un(a) compañero/a, responde a las preguntas.

1. ¿Cuáles crees que son las tradiciones españolas y africanas en la música afroperuana?
2. ¿Qué importancia crees que tiene el quechua en Ecuador?
3. ¿Por qué piensas que el Carnaval de Barranquilla es una fusión de culturas?
4. ¿Qué sabes del realismo mágico? ¿Conoces otros ejemplos?

I CAN identify basic facts about the geography and culture of Venezuela, Colombia, Ecuador, and Peru by reading short informational texts with visuals.

9 Las celebraciones

Communicative Goals

You will learn how to:
- talk about celebrations
- describe personal relationships
- talk about the past
- investigate holidays in the Spanish-speaking world

PREPARACIÓN

pages 226–231
- Words related to celebrations and desserts
- Personal relationships and stages of life
- The letters **h, j,** and **g**

AVENTURAS

pages 232–233
- It's Valentina's birthday. Friends and family are at her party, but one present has yet to arrive.

CULTURA

pages 234–235
- *Año Nuevo*
- Flash cultura: *Las fiestas*

GRAMÁTICA

pages 236–247
- Irregular preterites
- Verbs that change meaning in the preterite
- Relative pronouns
- **¿Qué?** and **¿cuál?**

LECTURA

pages 248–249
- Social news: *Vida Social: Matrimonio, Bautismo, Fiesta de quince años, Expresión de gracias*

∾ PARA EMPEZAR

- ¿Cómo se sienten estas personas, alegres o tristes?
- ¿Qué hay en la mesa?
- ¿Quién es la persona menor de la foto?

LAS CELEBRACIONES

graduarse (de)
to graduate (from)

la boda
wedding

el flan

el champán

LAS FIESTAS

el aniversario (de bodas)
(wedding) anniversary

el día de fiesta *holiday*

la fiesta *party*

el/la invitado/a *guest*

la Navidad *Christmas*

la quinceañera *young woman celebrating her fifteenth birthday*

la sorpresa *surprise*

celebrar *to celebrate*

cumplir años *to have a birthday*

dejar una propina *to leave a tip*

divertirse (e:ie) *to have fun*

invitar *to invite; to treat*

pagar la cuenta *to pay the bill*

pasarlo bien/mal
to have a good/bad time

regalar *to give (a gift)*

reírse (e:i) *to laugh*

relajarse *to relax*

sonreír (e:i) *to smile*

sorprender *to surprise*

brindar
to toast

el cumpleaños
birthday

LOS POSTRES Y OTRAS COMIDAS

la botella de vino *bottle of wine*

los dulces *sweets; candy*

el helado *ice cream*

el pastel *cake*

el pastel de cumpleaños *birthday cake*

los postres *desserts*

las galletas *cookies*

Vocabulary Tools

la niñez
childhood

la adolescencia
adolescence

la vejez
old age

la madurez
maturity; middle age

la muerte
death

LAS ETAPAS DE LA VIDA

la etapa *stage*
la juventud *youth*
el nacimiento *birth*
la vida *life*

---

jubilarse *to retire (from work)*
nacer *to be born*

LAS RELACIONES PERSONALES

la alegría *happiness*
la amistad *friendship*
el amor *love*
el divorcio *divorce*
el estado civil *marital status*
el matrimonio *marriage; married couple*
la pareja *couple; partner*
el/la recién casado/a *newlywed*

---

casado/a *married*
divorciado/a *divorced*
juntos/as *together*
separado/a *separated*
soltero/a *single*
viudo/a *widowed*

---

cambiar (de) *to change*
casarse (con) *to get married (to)*
comprometerse (con) *to get engaged (to)*
divorciarse (de) *to get divorced (from)*
enamorarse (de) *to fall in love (with)*
llevarse bien/mal (con) *to get along well/badly (with)*
odiar *to hate*
romper (con) *to break up (with)*
salir (con) *to go out (with); to date*
separarse (de) *to separate (from)*
tener una cita *to have a date; to have an appointment*

OTRAS PALABRAS

el apellido *last name*
el consejo *advice*
la respuesta *answer*

ASÍ SE DICE

comprometerse ⟷ prometerse (*Esp.*)
el pastel ⟷ la torta (*Arg., Venez.*), el queque (*C. Rica*)

A escuchar

1 Connotaciones Indica si las palabras que vas a escuchar tienen connotaciones **positivas** o **negativas**.

	Positivo	Negativo
1.	_____	_____
2.	_____	_____
3.	_____	_____
4.	_____	_____
5.	_____	_____
6.	_____	_____
7.	_____	_____
8.	_____	_____

2 ¿Lógico o ilógico? Escucha las oraciones e indica si son **lógicas** o **ilógicas**.

	Lógico	Ilógico
1.	_____	_____
2.	_____	_____
3.	_____	_____
4.	_____	_____
5.	_____	_____
6.	_____	_____

3 ¡Feliz cumpleaños! Los amigos de Silvia están preparándole una fiesta de cumpleaños. Escucha la conversación y contesta las preguntas.

1. ¿Sabe Silvia que sus amigos le van a organizar una fiesta? _____
2. ¿Qué van a comer los amigos en la fiesta? _____
3. ¿A Silvia le gusta el chocolate? _____
4. ¿Dónde compraron el helado? _____
5. ¿Por qué no quieren comer el helado de la cafetería? _____
6. ¿Qué pasa cuando llega Silvia? _____
7. ¿Cuántos años cumple Silvia? _____

A practicar

4 Completar Completa las oraciones.

dejó una propina	se jubiló
nació	se llevan bien
nos divertimos	sonrió
lo pasaron mal	tenemos una cita
se casaron	pagaron la cuenta

1. Nelson y Mónica _____ en septiembre. La boda fue maravillosa.

2. Mi tía le _____ muy grande al camarero.

3. Mi padrastro _____ el año pasado.

4. A Alejandra le gustan las galletas. Ella se puso contenta y _____ después de comérselas todas.

5. Luis y yo _____ en la fiesta. Bailamos y comimos mucho.

6. ¡Tengo una nueva sobrina! Ella _____ ayer por la mañana y se llama Sofía.

7. Irene y su esposo _____. Ellos casi nunca se pelean y disfrutan haciendo actividades juntos.

8. Isabel y yo _____ esta noche. Vamos a ir a un restaurante muy elegante.

5 La fiesta de Susana Completa las oraciones con las palabras y expresiones de la lección. Haz los cambios necesarios.

1. Susana siempre _____ su cumpleaños con su familia y sus amigos.

2. Su mamá invitó a mucha gente; todos los _____ llegaron tarde.

3. Su papá contó chistes (*told jokes*) y todos _____ porque eran (*were*) muy graciosos.

4. A Susana le _____ muchos regalos.

5. Su amiga Anabela trajo una botella de _____ para brindar después de comer el pastel.

6. El hermano de Susana comió muchos trozos (*pieces*) de _____ de chocolate.

7. Susana está un poco triste porque ayer _____ su novio y él no vino a su fiesta de cumpleaños.

8. Pero Susana _____ el próximo viernes con Jorge.

6 Cambiar Con un(a) compañero/a, túrnate para decir que las afirmaciones son falsas y corrígelas (*correct them*) cambiando las expresiones subrayadas.

modelo
Nuestros amigos <u>lo pasaron mal</u> en la playa.
Estudiante 1: Nuestros amigos lo pasaron mal en la playa.
Estudiante 2: No, te equivocas (*you're wrong*). Ellos lo pasaron bien.

1. <u>El nacimiento</u> es el fin de la vida.

2. A los sesenta y cinco años muchas personas <u>comienzan a trabajar.</u>

3. Francisco y Gloria <u>se divorcian</u> mañana.

4. Pancho <u>se comprometió</u> con Yolanda.

5. Marcela <u>lo pasa bien con</u> Ramón.

6. El abuelo murió, por eso, la abuela es <u>separada</u>.

A conversar

7 **Planes para una fiesta** Trabaja con un(a) compañero/a para planear una fiesta. Recuerda incluir la siguiente información.

1. ¿Qué tipo de fiesta es?

2. ¿Dónde va a ser? ¿Cuándo va a ser?

3. ¿A quiénes van a invitar?

4. ¿Qué van a comer? ¿Quiénes van a llevar o a preparar la comida?

5. ¿Qué van a beber? ¿Quiénes van a traer las bebidas?

6. ¿Cómo planean entretener a los invitados? ¿Van a bailar o a jugar algún juego?

7. Después de la fiesta, ¿quiénes van a limpiar (*clean*)?

8 **Encuesta** Entrevista a dos o tres compañeros/as para saber qué actitudes (*attitudes*) tienen en sus relaciones personales. Comparte los resultados con la clase.

Preguntas	Nombres	Actitudes
1. ¿Te importa la amistad? ¿Por qué?	_____	_____
2. ¿Es mejor tener un(a) buen(a) amigo/a o muchos amigos?	_____	_____
3. ¿Cuáles son las características que buscas en tus amigos/as?	_____	_____
4. ¿Tienes novio/a? ¿A qué edad (*age*) es posible enamorarse?	_____	_____
5. ¿Deben las parejas hacer todo juntos?	_____	_____
6. ¿Deben las parejas compartir las mismas opiniones? ¿Por qué?	_____	_____

9 **Una fiesta inolvidable** Cuéntale a un(a) compañero/a cómo fue la fiesta más divertida a la que fuiste. Usa estas preguntas como guía.

1. ¿Quién organizó la fiesta?

2. ¿Qué se celebró?

3. ¿Qué día se celebró? ¿Y a qué hora?

4. ¿Dónde fue?

5. ¿Quiénes fueron los invitados?

6. ¿Qué hicieron durante la fiesta?

7. ¿Por qué fue la fiesta más divertida?

I CAN plan a party.

Pronunciación Tutorial

The letters h, j, and g

. . . .

helado	**h**ombre	**h**ola	**h**ermosa

The Spanish **h** is always silent.

. . . .

José	**j**ubilarse	de**j**ar	pare**j**a

The letter **j** is pronounced much like the English *h* in *his*.

. . . .

a**g**encia	**g**eneral	**G**il	**G**isela

The letter **g** can be pronounced three different ways. Before **e** or **i**, the letter **g** is pronounced much like the English *h*.

. . . .

Gustavo, gracias por llamar el domingo.

At the beginning of a phrase or after the letter **n**, the Spanish **g** is pronounced like the English *g* in *girl*.

. . . .

Me gradué en agosto.

In any other position, the Spanish **g** has a somewhat softer sound.

. . . .

guerra	conse**g**uir	**g**uantes	a**g**ua

In the combinations **gue** and **gui**, the **g** has a hard sound and the **u** is silent. In the combination **gua**, the **g** has a hard sound and the **u** is pronounced like the English *w*.

. . . .

Práctica Lee las palabras en voz alta, prestando atención a la **h**, la **j** y la **g**.

1. hamburguesa	5. geografía	9. seguir	13. Jorge
2. jugar	6. magnífico	10. gracias	14. tengo
3. oreja	7. espejo	11. hijo	15. ahora
4. guapa	8. hago	12. galleta	16. guantes

Oraciones Lee las oraciones en voz alta, prestando atención a la **h**, la **j** y la **g**.

1. Hola. Me llamo Gustavo Hinojosa Lugones y vivo en Santiago de Chile.
2. Tengo una familia grande; somos tres hermanos y tres hermanas.
3. Voy a graduarme en mayo.
4. Para celebrar mi graduación mis padres van a regalarme un viaje a Egipto.
5. ¡Qué generosos son!

El hábito no hace al monje.[2]

Refranes Lee los refranes en voz alta, prestando atención a la **h**, la **j** y la **g**.

A la larga, lo más dulce amarga.[1]

[1] *Too much of a good thing.*
[2] *The clothes don't make the man.*

¡Es mi cumpleaños!

Todos celebran el cumpleaños de Valentina.

Video

Antes de ver

Mira las imágenes y haz predicciones sobre lo que va a pasar en el video.

PERSONAJES

FELIPE

JUANJO

VALENTINA

GLORIA

MANUEL

OLGA LUCÍA

SARA

MENSAJERO

JUANJO ¿No sabes jugar a la brisca?

VALENTINA ¡Parad de reíros, me vais a hacer perder!

GLORIA ¡Por fin!

MANUEL Y FELIPE (*a Valentina*) ¡Perdiste! ¡Perdiste!

VALENTINA ¡Chicos! Es *mi* cumpleaños.

TODOS ¡Felicidades!

MANUEL ¡La fiesta de cumpleaños ya comenzó! Quiero saber cuándo van a llegar las flores que pedí.

SARA Primo, ¿quieres un pincho de tortilla?

MANUEL ¿A qué hora? Eso no fue lo que me dijo la persona con quien hablé esta mañana. ¡No, no me importa si tuvo muchos pedidos!

SARA ¿No le trajiste un regalo a Valentina? ¡Así nunca va a enamorarse de ti!

MANUEL ¡Sí, tengo un regalo para ella!

SARA ¿Y cuál es? ¡Yo sólo veo el oso gigante que le dio Juanjo!

MANUEL Entre tú y yo... ¡es feísimo!

A C T I V I D A D E S

1 **¿Cierto o falso?** Indica si lo que dicen estas oraciones es **cierto** o **falso**. Corrige las oraciones falsas.

	Cierto	Falso
1. Valentina juega muy bien a las cartas.	○	○
2. Manuel está enojado porque no llega su regalo todavía.	○	○
3. Daniel le regala a Valentina un oso gigante.	○	○
4. Manuel dice que el regalo de Juanjo es hermoso.	○	○
5. Gloria gana en el juego de las sillas.	○	○

2 **Completar** Completa las oraciones.

1. Hoy Valentina celebra su _____.

2. Entre los _____, están Juanjo y Manuel.

3. Manuel quiere _____ a Valentina con su regalo.

4. La tarjeta para Valentina es una nota de _____.

5. Juanjo y Manuel están _____ de Valentina.

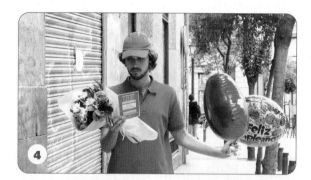

JUANJO ¿Sí?

MENSAJERO Flores para Valentina Herrera.

JUANJO ¿Quién las envía?

MENSAJERO Son de parte de Manuel.

JUANJO Aquí no es.

JUANJO Valentina no está. Puedes entregarme las flores a mí.

MENSAJERO Lo siento, tengo que dárselas a Valentina. Son para ella.

JUANJO ¿Qué dice en la tarjeta?

MENSAJERO (*leyendo la tarjeta*) Para Valentina. Con amor, de Manuel: cuando te conocí, supe que eras muy especial. ¡Feliz cumpleaños!

MANUEL ¡¿Qué pasa?!

MENSAJERO (*a los chicos en la puerta*) ¿Quién es Valentina?

OLGA LUCÍA Y SARA (*señalando a Valentina*) ¡Ella!

MENSAJERO (*a Valentina*) Las flores son para ti. Quise entregártelas pero...

VALENTINA ¿Pero?

Expresiones útiles

entregar *to hand over; to deliver*
enviar *to send*
eras *you were*
¡Felicidades! *Congratulations!*
la flor *flower*
el pedido *order*
el pincho *appetizer (in Spain)*
sólo *only*
tropezarse con *to run into*

---

el globo *balloon*
el juego de las sillas *musical chairs*
el/la mensajero/a *messenger*

La brisca

La brisca es un juego de cartas español. Se juega entre dos o más jugadores; lo más común son dos o cuatro. Cuando hay cuatro jugadores, es posible jugar en parejas. Se usa una baraja (*deck*) de cuarenta cartas.

¿Te gusta jugar a las cartas? ¿Qué juegos de cartas conoces?

3 **Preguntas personales** En parejas, túrnense para hacerse estas preguntas. ¿Tienen respuestas en común?

1. ¿Qué fiestas celebras con tu familia?
2. De las celebraciones, ¿cuál es tu favorita? ¿Por qué?
3. ¿Cómo celebras tu cumpleaños?
4. ¿Qué te gusta comer en tu cumpleaños?
5. ¿Te gusta dar y recibir regalos? ¿Por qué?

I CAN talk about celebrations.

Video

Communicative Goal
Identify holiday traditions in the
Spanish-speaking world

Año Nuevo: una sola fiesta con muchas variaciones

"Año nuevo, vida nueva, más alegres los días serán°. Año nuevo, vida nueva, con salud° y con prosperidad".

Así dice una canción° popular que se canta en varios países en los primeros minutos del primero de enero, con la esperanza° de que el nuevo año va a ser mucho mejor que el viejo. Mientras bailan y cantan esta canción, los parientes y amigos se dan abrazos° y besos, deseando lo mejor para el año que comienza.

En todo el mundo hispano se recibe el año nuevo con diversas tradiciones. Éstas son tres de las más populares:

Las doce uvas

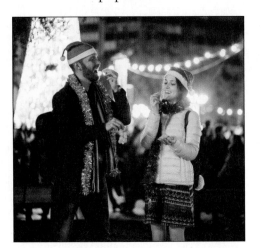

Esta tradición española está extendida por muchos países de Latinoamérica. Consiste en que exactamente a la medianoche se deben comer doce uvas para tener buena suerte en los doce meses del año nuevo. Pero ¡ojo!, se debe comer una uva con cada campanada del reloj°. Es una tradición tan extendida que se comen unos ¡500 millones de uvas cada fin de año en todo el mundo!

El muñeco de año viejo

En países como Ecuador, Colombia, Venezuela, Panamá, México, Perú y Chile, es común elaborar un muñeco de trapo°, relleno° con ropa vieja, cartón o papel, como representación del año viejo. La tradición consiste en prender fuego° al muñeco a la medianoche, para alejar° la mala suerte y las malas energías del año que termina. En algunas partes, la gente hace los muñecos como figuras políticas, como una forma de protesta, y esperando que la situación política y social mejore° en el año nuevo.

La ropa de colores

En varios países se cree que usar ropa de ciertos colores en la Nochevieja° trae suerte para el año nuevo. Los más comunes son: ropa amarilla para la prosperidad, ropa roja para el amor y ropa verde para la salud. También se llevan ropa anaranjada para la alegría y ropa azul para la serenidad.

serán *will be* salud *health* canción *song* esperanza *hope* abrazos *hugs* campanada del reloj *clock chime* muñeco de trapo *rag doll* relleno *stuffed* prender fuego *to burn* alejar *to ward off* mejore *get better* Nochevieja *New Year's Eve*

ASÍ SE DICE

Fiestas y celebraciones

la despedida de soltero/a	*bachelor(ette) party*
el día feriado/festivo	*el día de fiesta*
disfrutar	*to enjoy*
festejar	*celebrar*
los fuegos artificiales	*fireworks*
pasarlo en grande	*divertirse mucho*
salir de parranda	*to go out and have fun*
rumbear (Col., Ven.)	

▸ ¿Cuáles son algunas maneras de decir **divertirse** en inglés?

ACTIVIDADES

1 **¿Cierto o falso?** Indica si lo que dicen las oraciones es **cierto** o **falso**. Corrige las falsas.

1. Comer doce uvas para recibir el año nuevo es una tradición mexicana.

2. Las uvas representan doce días de buena suerte en el año nuevo.

3. La gente tiene que comer una uva con cada campanada del reloj.

4. En algunos países, la gente hace muñecos de trapo y les prenden fuego.

5. Se cree que llevar ropa de colores específicos trae buena suerte.

2 **Preguntas** Contesta las preguntas.

1. ¿Dónde comen doce uvas a la medianoche?

2. ¿Qué representan los muñecos de trapo?

3. ¿Qué hacen algunas personas como una forma de protesta?

4. ¿Por qué se lleva ropa roja en la Nochevieja?

5. ¿Qué color de ropa se usa para la prosperidad?

3 **Comparación** Compara una de estas tradiciones con una tradición de la Nochevieja en los Estados Unidos.

4 **Feliz Año Nuevo** Con un(a) compañero/a, representa una conversación entre dos amigos/as o parientes en una celebración de Año Nuevo en España.

5 **¿Qué piensas?** Responde a las preguntas.

1. ¿Por qué crees que la tradición de comer doce uvas es tan popular?

2. ¿Qué piensas de la costumbre de prender fuego a los muñecos?

3. ¿Por qué crees que se hacen los muñecos como figuras políticas en algunos países?

4. Estás en un país hispano en la Nochevieja. ¿Qué color vas a llevar? ¿Por qué?

I CAN identify holiday traditions in my own and other cultures.

Communicative Goal
Identify the characteristics of a celebration in Puerto Rico

 Video

Las fiestas

1 **Preparación** ¿Se celebra la Navidad en tu país? ¿Qué otras fiestas importantes se celebran? ¿Cuánto tiempo duran? ¿Cuáles son las tradiciones y actividades típicas?

2 **El video** Mira el episodio de **Flash cultura** sobre una celebración en Puerto Rico.

Vocabulario	
las artesanías	*handicrafts*
los cabezudos	*carnival figures with large heads*
los carteles	*posters*
fiesta de pueblo	*small town celebration*
máscaras	*masks*
santos de palo	*wooden sculptures of saints*

Los cabezudos son una tradición […] de España.

3 **¿Cierto o falso?** Indica si cada oración es **cierta** o **falsa**.

1. En Puerto Rico se celebra la Navidad hasta febrero.

2. San Sebastián fue un soldado romano que ayudó a los cristianos.

3. Los cabezudos son unas máscaras que vienen de las fiestas españolas.

4. Diego Palacio compra un helado de chocolate.

5. El güiro y el pandero son comidas puertorriqueñas.

4 **Conversación** Estás en Puerto Rico durante las fiestas de la Calle San Sebastián. Conversa con un(a) compañero/a sobre lo que quieren hacer.

I CAN identify the characteristics of a celebration in Puerto Rico.

Communicative Goal
Talk about the past

9.1 Irregular preterites

▶ You already know that **ir** and **ser** are irregular in the preterite. Here are some other verbs that are irregular in the preterite.

Preterite of *tener*, *venir*, and *decir*

	tener (u-stem)	venir (i-stem)	decir (j-stem)
yo	tuve	vine	dije
tú	tuviste	viniste	dijiste
Ud./él/ella	tuvo	vino	dijo
nosotros/as	tuvimos	vinimos	dijimos
vosotros/as	tuvisteis	vinisteis	dijisteis
Uds./ellos/ellas	tuvieron	vinieron	dijeron

▶ Observe the stem changes in the chart: the **e** in **tener** changes to **u**, and the **e** in **venir** and **decir** changes to **i**. Note also that the **c** in **decir** changes to **j**. None of these verbs have written accents in the **yo** or **usted/él/ella** forms.

▶ These verbs have similar stem changes to **tener**, **venir**, and **decir**.

INFINITIVE	U-STEM	PRETERITE FORMS
poder	pud-	pude, pudiste, pudo, pudimos, pudisteis, pudieron
poner	pus-	puse, pusiste, puso, pusimos, pusisteis, pusieron
saber	sup-	supe, supiste, supo, supimos, supisteis, supieron
estar	estuv-	estuve, estuviste, estuvo, estuvimos, estuvisteis, estuvieron

INFINITIVE	I-STEM	PRETERITE FORMS
querer	quis-	quise, quisiste, quiso, quisimos, quisisteis, quisieron
hacer	hic-	hice, hiciste, hizo, hicimos, hicisteis, hicieron

INFINITIVE	J-STEM	PRETERITE FORMS
traer	traj-	traje, trajiste, trajo, trajimos, trajisteis, trajeron
conducir	conduj-	conduje, condujiste, condujo, condujimos, condujisteis, condujeron
traducir	traduj-	traduje, tradujiste, tradujo, tradujimos, tradujisteis, tradujeron

¡ojo! Verbs with **j**-stems omit the letter **i** in the **ustedes/ellos/ellas** endings. For example, **tener → tuvieron**, but **decir → dijeron**.

▶ Most verbs that end in **–cir** are **j**-stem verbs in the preterite. For example, **producir → produje, produjiste**, etc.

Práctica

1 **Una fiesta sorpresa** Completa estas oraciones con el pretérito de los verbos indicados.

> **modelo**
> El sábado ___hubo___ [haber] una fiesta sorpresa para Elsa en mi casa.

1. Sofía _____ [hacer] un pastel para la fiesta y Miguel _____ [traer] un flan.
2. Los amigos y parientes de Elsa _____ [venir] y _____ [traer] regalos.
3. El hermano de Elsa no _____ [venir] porque _____ [tener] que trabajar.
4. Su tía María tampoco _____ [poder] venir.
5. Cuando Elsa abrió la puerta, todos gritaron (*shouted*): "¡Feliz cumpleaños!" y su esposo le _____ [dar] un beso.
6. Al final de la fiesta, todos _____ [decir] que se divirtieron mucho.
7. La fiesta le _____ [dar] a Elsa tanta alegría que no _____ [poder] dormir esa noche.

2 **¿Qué hicieron?** Usa los verbos para describir lo que hicieron estas personas.

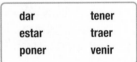
dar	tener
estar	traer
poner	venir

1. El señor López/dinero
2. Nosotros/fiesta

_____

_____

3. Norma/pavo
4. Roberto y Elena/regalo

_____

_____

Conversación

3 **Preguntas** Con un(a) compañero/a, túrnate para contestar estas preguntas.

1. ¿Qué hiciste anoche?
2. ¿Quiénes no estuvieron en clase la semana pasada?
3. ¿Hiciste la tarea esta mañana? ¿Cuándo? ¿Se la diste al/a la profesor(a)?
4. ¿Qué trajiste a clase hoy?
5. ¿Tuviste que asistir a alguna boda el año pasado? ¿De quién?
6. ¿Alguien dio una fiesta por tu cumpleaños el año pasado? ¿Quién?
7. ¿Cuándo fue la última (*last*) vez que tus parientes vinieron a visitarte?
8. ¿Les diste a tus padres un regalo para su aniversario de bodas? ¿Qué les regalaste?

4 **Encuesta** Averigua (*Find out*) quién de tus compañeros/as hizo cada una de estas actividades. Luego, comparte los resultados con la clase.

modelo

Fue a una fiesta la semana pasada.

Estudiante 1: ¿Fuiste a una fiesta la semana pasada?
Estudiante 2: No, no fui a ninguna fiesta.
Estudiante 1: ¿Fuiste a una fiesta la semana pasada?
Estudiante 3: Sí, fui a una fiesta muy buena.

Descripciones	Nombres
1. Tuvo un examen ayer.	_____
2. Trajo dulces a clase.	_____
3. Condujo su auto a clase.	_____
4. Estuvo en la biblioteca ayer.	_____
5. Le dio consejos a alguien ayer.	_____
6. Tuvo que levantarse temprano ayer.	_____
7. Hizo un viaje por más de dos semanas el verano pasado.	_____
8. Tuvo una cita anoche.	_____
9. Dijo una mentira ayer.	_____
10. Tuvo que trabajar el sábado pasado.	_____

The preterite of **dar**

The preterite of *dar*			
yo	di	nosotros/as	dimos
tú	diste	vosotros/as	disteis
Ud./él/ella	dio	Uds./ellos/ellas	dieron

▶ The endings for **dar** are the same as the regular preterite endings for **–er** and **–ir** verbs, but there are no written accent marks.

La camarera me **dio** el menú.
The waitress gave me the menu.

Los invitados le **dieron** un regalo.
The guests gave him/her a gift.

Le **di** a Juan algunos consejos.
I gave Juan some advice.

Nosotros **dimos** una gran fiesta.
We gave a great party.

▶ The preterite of **hay** (*inf.* **haber**) is **hubo** (*there was/were*).

Hubo una fiesta el sábado pasado.
There was a party last Saturday.

Hubo una sorpresa especial para mi hermana.
There was a special surprise for my sister.

Hubo muchos invitados.
There were a lot of guests.

También **hubo** muchos regalos y champán.
There were also a lot of gifts and champagne.

¡No me importa si tuvo muchos pedidos!

¿No le trajiste un regalo a Valentina?

¡Manos a la obra!

Escribe la forma correcta del pretérito de cada verbo.

1. Tú ___quisiste___ [querer].
2. Usted _____ [decir].
3. Nosotras _____ [hacer].
4. Yo _____ [traer].
5. Ellas _____ [conducir].
6. Ella _____ [estar].
7. Tú _____ [tener].
8. Ella y yo _____ [dar].
9. Yo _____ [traducir].
10. _____ [haber] muchos invitados.
11. Usted _____ [saber].
12. Ellos _____ [poner].
13. Yo _____ [venir].
14. Tú _____ [poder].
15. Ustedes _____ [querer].
16. Nosotras _____ [estar].
17. Tú _____ [decir].
18. Ellos _____ [saber].
19. Él _____ [hacer].
20. Yo _____ [poner].
21. Nosotras _____ [traer].
22. Yo _____ [tener].
23. Tú _____ [dar].
24. Usted _____ [conducir].

I CAN talk about the past.

Communicative Goal
Say what I did last weekend

9.2 Verbs that change meaning in the preterite

▶ **Conocer, saber, poder,** and **querer** change meanings in the preterite.

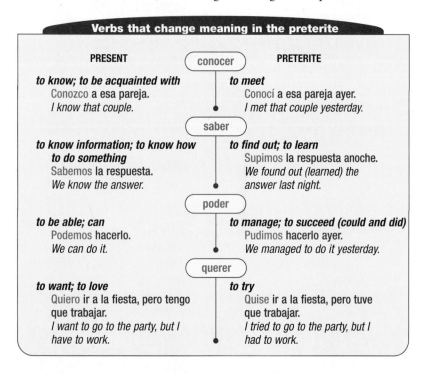

Verbs that change meaning in the preterite

conocer

PRESENT	PRETERITE
to know; to be acquainted with	**to meet**
Conozco a esa pareja.	Conocí a esa pareja ayer.
I know that couple.	*I met that couple yesterday.*

saber

to know information; to know how to do something	**to find out; to learn**
Sabemos la respuesta.	Supimos la respuesta anoche.
We know the answer.	*We found out (learned) the answer last night.*

poder

to be able; can	**to manage; to succeed (could and did)**
Podemos hacerlo.	Pudimos hacerlo ayer.
We can do it.	*We managed to do it yesterday.*

querer

to want; to love	**to try**
Quiero ir a la fiesta, pero tengo que trabajar.	Quise ir a la fiesta, pero tuve que trabajar.
I want to go to the party, but I have to work.	*I tried to go to the party, but I had to work.*

▶ In the preterite, **poder** and **querer** have different meanings, depending on whether they are used in affirmative or negative sentences.

Affirmative		Negative	
pude	*I was able (to)/succeeded*	no pude	*I failed (to)*
quise	*I tried (to)*	no quise	*I refused (to)*

¡Manos a la obra!

Cambia los verbos del presente al pretérito.

1. No quiero hacerlo. No _____quise_____ hacerlo.
2. ¿Sabes la respuesta? ¿ _____ la respuesta?
3. Las chicas pueden divertirse. Las chicas _____ divertirse.
4. ¿Conoces a los recién casados? ¿ _____ a los recién casados?
5. No puedo encontrar a Patricia. No _____ encontrar a Patricia.
6. Josefina quiere descansar. Josefina _____ descansar.
7. Conocemos a Julio. _____ a Julio el año pasado.
8. Ella no puede venir a la fiesta. Ella no _____ venir a la fiesta.
9. Queremos pasarlo bien. _____ pasarlo bien.
10. Ustedes saben del problema, ¿verdad? Ustedes _____ del problema, ¿verdad?
11. No queremos ir a la fiesta. No _____ ir a la fiesta.
12. Puedes venir conmigo. _____ venir conmigo.

Práctica

1 Oraciones Forma oraciones con estos elementos. Usa el pretérito.

modelo

Mis padres / no querer / venir / fiesta
Mis padres no quisieron venir a la fiesta.

1. Anoche / nosotros / saber / del divorcio / Carlos y Eva _____
2. Tú / conocer / Nora / clase / historia / ¿no? _____
3. ¿Poder / ustedes / visitar / la Isla de Pascua? _____
4. Pedro / querer / romper / Olivia _____
5. Irma / saber / de la fiesta sorpresa _____
6. Gustavo y Elena / conocer / mi esposo / fiesta de Ana _____
7. Yolanda / no poder / dormir / anoche _____
8. El señor Navarro / querer / jubilarse / pero / no poder _____
9. Ayer / yo / no poder / ir / partido _____
10. Nosotros / querer / pagar la cuenta _____

2 Completar Completa estas oraciones de manera lógica.

1. La semana pasada yo supe…
2. Ayer mi compañero/a de cuarto supo…
3. Esta mañana no pude…
4. El fin de semana pasado mis amigos/as y yo no pudimos…
5. Conocí a mi mejor amigo/a en…
6. Mis padres no quisieron…
7. Mi mejor amigo/a no pudo…
8. Mi novio/a y yo nos conocimos en…
9. El mes pasado quise…
10. Ayer mis amigos/as quisieron…
11. Mis abuelos pudieron…

Conversación

3 **El fin de semana** Prepara dos listas: una con las actividades que hiciste el fin de semana pasado y la otra lista con las actividades que quisiste hacer, pero no pudiste hacer. Luego, compara tu lista con la de un(a) compañero/a, y explica por qué no pudiste hacer esas cosas.

Cosas que hice	Cosas que quise hacer
1. _____	1. _____
2. _____	2. _____
3. _____	3. _____
4. _____	4. _____
5. _____	5. _____
6. _____	6. _____
7. _____	7. _____
8. _____	8. _____
9. _____	9. _____
10. _____	10. _____

4 **Telenovela** En grupos de tres, escriban el guion (*script*) de una escena amorosa entre los tres personajes de la telenovela (*soap opera*) llamada **La mujer doble**. Usen el pretérito de **conocer, poder, querer** y **saber**. ¡Sean creativos!

Daniel

Mirta

Raúl

La mujer doble
◎ Pasión ◎ Aventura ◎ Hechicería ◎ Venganza

Español en vivo

Hubo un día en el que la humanidad quiso ir más allá de sus límites.
Pudo conocer un mundo° increíble.
Supo asegurar° su futuro.

BANCO COLÓN
El banco de Puerto Rico

Ahora todos lo pueden hacer.

mundo *world*   **asegurar** *to ensure*

1 **Identificar** Lee el anuncio e identifica los verbos en el pretérito.

2 **Preguntas** Contesta las preguntas.
1. ¿Qué quiso hacer la humanidad? ¿Qué pudo conocer?
2. ¿Cuándo llegó Cristóbal Colón a América?
3. ¿Qué tipo de compañía es la del anuncio?
4. ¿Es eficaz (*effective*) la conexión entre el viaje de Colón y los servicios bancarios?

I CAN say what I did last weekend.

I CAN recognize familiar words in a simple ad.

Communicative Goal
Talk about celebrations and relationships

9.3 Relative pronouns

▶ Relative pronouns are used to combine two sentences or clauses that share a common element, such as a noun or pronoun. Study these diagrams.

> Éste es el flan.
> *This is the flan.*

> Manuela preparó el flan.
> *Manuela made the flan.*

> Éste es el flan que Manuela preparó.
> *This is the flan that Manuela made.*

> Lourdes es muy inteligente.
> *Lourdes is very intelligent.*

> Lourdes estudia español.
> *Lourdes studies Spanish.*

> Lourdes, quien estudia español, es muy inteligente.
> *Lourdes, who studies Spanish, is very intelligent.*

> El pastel que compraron fue muy rico.

> Quiero saber cuándo van a llegar las flores que pedí.

▶ Spanish has three commonly used relative pronouns. Note that relative pronouns never carry an accent, unlike interrogative words (**qué, quién,** etc.).

Common relative pronouns	
que	*that; which; who*
quien(es)	*who; whom; that*
lo que	*that which; what*

▶ **Que,** the most frequently used relative pronoun, can refer to things or to people. Unlike the English *that,* **que** is never omitted.

¿Dónde está el pastel **que** pedí?
Where is the cake (that) I ordered?

El hombre **que** sirve la comida se llama Diego.
The man who serves the food is named Diego.

Práctica

1 Una fiesta de aniversario Amparo está hablando de la fiesta de aniversario de sus abuelos. Completa las oraciones con las expresiones de la lista.

a quien conozco muy bien	que se graduó
de quienes te hablé	quien es la novia
que saqué	quien se jubiló

1. El sábado fui a la fiesta de aniversario de mis abuelos, _____ la semana pasada.
2. Éstas son las fotos _____ durante la fiesta.
3. Éste es Ramón, mi primo. Es el chico _____ de la universidad en junio.
4. Éste es mi abuelo, _____ el año pasado.
5. Esta mujer, _____, se llama Ana.
6. Y ésta es Lucía, _____ de Ramón.

2 Una fiesta de cumpleaños Describe la fiesta sorpresa que van a dar Jaime y Laura, usando los pronombres relativos **que, quien, quienes** y **lo que**.

modelo

Jaime y Laura son los amigos ___*que*___ planean la fiesta.

1. Manuela, _____ cumple veintiún años mañana, no sabe que sus amigos están planeando una fiesta.
2. Éstas son las personas _____ van a invitar.
3. Juan y Luz, _____ son los hermanos de Manuela, van a venir.
4. Marco, _____ es el novio de Manuela, va a venir también.
5. _____ Jaime y Laura van a servir de postre es un pastel.
6. Todos van a bailar salsa y rock hasta la una de la mañana, _____ va a ser muy divertido.

Conversación

3 Entrevista Con un(a) compañero/a, túrnate para contestar las preguntas. *Answers will vary.*

3 Communication Interpersonal Communication

1. ¿Qué es lo que más te gusta de las fiestas familiares? ¿Por qué?

2. ¿Qué es lo que menos te gusta de las fiestas familiares? ¿Por qué?

3. ¿Quiénes son las personas con quienes celebras tu cumpleaños?

4. ¿Quién es el/la pariente o amigo/a a quien más le gustan los cumpleaños? ¿Por qué le gustan tanto?

5. ¿Dónde compras los regalos que le regalas a tu mejor amigo/a?

6. ¿Tienes hermanos/as o amigos/as que están casados/as? ¿Dónde viven?

7. ¿Quién es la persona que más te importa?

8. ¿Quiénes son las personas con quienes te diviertes más? ¿Por qué lo pasas bien con ellos/ellas?

4 Definiciones Con un(a) compañero/a, túrnate para definir estas palabras, usando **que, quien(es)** y **lo que**. Luego, comparte las definiciones con la clase. *Answers will vary.*

4 Communication Interpersonal Communication

modelo

un pastel de cumpleaños

Estudiante 1: ¿Qué es un pastel de cumpleaños?
Estudiante 2: Es un postre que comes en tu cumpleaños./Es lo que comes en tu cumpleaños.

1. el helado
2. el champán
3. una propina
4. una boda
5. un invitado
6. la Navidad
7. una recién casada
8. los dulces
9. una viuda
10. una fiesta de quince años

ACTIVITY PACK For additional activities, go to the **Activity Pack** in the **Resources** section of the Supersite.

Uses of **quien(es)** and **lo que**

▶ **Quien** (singular) and **quienes** (plural) refer only to people and are often used after a preposition or the personal **a**.

Eva, **a quien** vi anoche, cumple veinticinco años hoy.
Eva, whom I saw last night, turns twenty-five today.

¿Son ésas las chicas **de quienes** me hablaste la semana pasada?
Are those the girls you told me about last week?

▶ **Quien(es)** is occasionally used instead of **que** in clauses set off by commas.

Lola, **quien** es cubana, es médica.
Lola, who is Cuban, is a doctor.

Su tía, **que** es alemana, ya llegó.
Her aunt, who is German, already arrived.

Mi hermana, **quien** vive en Madrid, me llamó por teléfono.
My sister, who lives in Madrid, called me on the phone.

Juan, **que** estuvo muy contento, brindó conmigo.
Juan, who was very happy, toasted with me.

▶ **Lo que** refers to an idea, a situation, or a past event and means *what* or *the thing that*.

Juana tiene todo **lo que** necesitamos.
Juana has everything we need.

Lo que me molesta es el calor.
The thing that bothers me is the heat.

Lo que quiero es verte.
What I want is to see you.

Lo que más te gusta es divertirte.
What you like most is to have fun.

¡Yo sólo veo el oso gigante que le dio Juanjo!

Eso no fue lo que me dijo la persona con quien hablé esta mañana.

¡Manos a la obra!

Completa las oraciones con pronombres relativos.

1. La chica _____que_____ me invitó a la fiesta se llama Anabel.
2. Ese mercado tiene todo _____lo que_____ necesitamos.
3. Úrsula, _____que/quien_____ es la dueña del restaurante, es de Uruguay.
4. Donaldo, a _____quien_____ viste en la fiesta, es chileno.
5. A Cecilia no le gusta el regalo _____que_____ le compré.
6. No me gusta hablar con personas a _____quienes_____ no conozco.
7. Rosana es la chica de _____quien_____ te hablé.
8. El chico _____que_____ está a la izquierda es mi primo.
9. Ana, con _____quien_____ voy a la fiesta, es muy simpática.
10. _____Lo que_____ me sorprendió fue ver a tantos invitados.

I CAN talk about celebrations and relationships.

Communicative Goal
Ask and answer questions about a wedding

9.4 ¿Qué? and ¿cuál?

▶ As you know, **¿qué?** and **¿cuál?** or **¿cuáles?** mean *what?* or *which?* However, they are not interchangeable.

▶ **¿Qué?** is used to ask for a definition or explanation.

¿Qué es el flan?
What is flan?

¿Qué estudias?
What do you study?

▶ **¿Cuál(es)?** is used when there is a choice between two or more possibilities.

¿Cuáles quieres, éstos o ésos?
Which (ones) do you want, these or those?

¿Cuál es tu apellido, Martínez o Vásquez?
What is your last name, Martínez or Vásquez?

▶ **¿Cuál(es)?** should not be used before a noun; **¿qué?** is used instead.

¿Cuál es tu color favorito?
What is your favorite color?

¿Qué colores te gustan?
What colors do you like?

▶ **¿Qué?** used before a noun has the same meaning as **¿cuál?**

Qué + noun	Cuál + verb
¿Qué regalo te gusta?	**¿Cuál** te gusta?
¿Qué dulces quieren ustedes?	**¿Cuáles** quieren ustedes?

Review of interrogative words and phrases

¿a qué hora?	at what time?	¿cuántos/as?	how many?
¿adónde?	(to) where?	¿de dónde?	from where?
¿cómo?	how?	¿dónde?	where?
¿cuál(es)?	what?; which?	¿por qué?	why?
¿cuándo?	when?	¿qué?	what?; which?
¿cuánto/a?	how much?	¿quién(es)?	who?

¡Manos a la obra!

Completa las preguntas con **¿qué?** o **¿cuál(es)?**, según el contexto.

1. ¿_Cuál_ te gusta más?
2. ¿_____ es tu teléfono?
3. ¿_____ tipo de pastel pediste?
4. ¿_____ es una boda?
5. ¿_____ haces ahora?
6. ¿_____ son tus platos favoritos?
7. ¿_____ bebidas te gustan más?
8. ¿_____ es esto?
9. ¿_____ es el mejor?
10. ¿_____ es tu opinión?
11. ¿_____ fiestas celebras tú?
12. ¿_____ jugo prefieres?
13. ¿_____ es tu clase favorita?
14. ¿_____ pones en la mesa?
15. ¿_____ restaurante prefieres?
16. ¿_____ es tu dirección?
17. ¿_____ quieres comer ahora?
18. ¿_____ es la tarea para mañana?
19. ¿_____ color prefieres?
20. ¿_____ opinas?

Práctica

1 Minidiálogos Completa los minidiálogos con las palabras interrogativas correctas.

modelo
SILVIA ¿_Cuándo_ es la fiesta de aniversario de tus padres?
ERNESTO El sábado por la noche.

• • •

MARCELA ¿ (1) _____ va a ser la fiesta de cumpleaños?
DIEGO En casa de mi primo.

• • •

CAMILA ¿ (2) _____ es tu clase favorita?
CARLOS La clase de arte es mi favorita.

• • •

TOMÁS ¿ (3) _____ dinero te van a dar tus abuelos para tu graduación de la universidad?
MERCEDES Dicen que van a darme cien dólares.

• • •

LIDIA ¿ (4) _____ compraste para tu sobrino?
MARTA Una raqueta de tenis.

• • •

IGNACIO ¿ (5) _____ vas después de la boda?
GABRIEL Mi novia y yo vamos al cine.

2 Completar Completa estas preguntas con una palabra interrogativa. En algunos casos se puede usar más de una palabra interrogativa.

modelo ¿En _qué_ país nacieron tus padres?

1. ¿_____ es la fecha de tu cumpleaños?
2. ¿_____ naciste?
3. ¿_____ es tu estado civil?
4. ¿_____ te relajas?
5. ¿_____ son tus programas de televisión favoritos?
6. ¿_____ es tu mejor amigo?
7. ¿_____ van tus amigos para divertirse?
8. ¿_____ postres te gustan? ¿_____ te gusta más?
9. ¿_____ problemas tuviste el primer día de clase?
10. ¿_____ primos tienes?

Conversación

3 **Una invitación** Con un(a) compañero/a, lee esta invitación. Luego, cada estudiante debe pensar en tres preguntas que su compañero/a debe responder sobre el texto.

modelo
Estudiante 1: ¿Quiénes se casan?
Estudiante 2: María Luisa y José Antonio

FERNANDO SANDOVAL VALERA   LORENZO VÁSQUEZ AMARAL

ISABEL ARZIPE DE SANDOVAL   ELENA SOTO DE VÁSQUEZ

TIENEN EL AGRADO DE INVITARLOS
A LA BODA DE SUS HIJOS
MARÍA LUISA Y JOSÉ ANTONIO

LA CEREMONIA RELIGIOSA TENDRÁ LUGAR
EL SÁBADO 10 DE JUNIO A LAS DOS DE LA TARDE
EN EL TEMPLO DE SANTO DOMINGO
(CALLE SANTO DOMINGO, 961).

DESPUÉS DE LA CEREMONIA, SÍRVANSE PASAR A LA RECEPCIÓN EN EL SALÓN
DE BAILE DEL HOTEL METRÓPOLI (SOTERO DEL RÍO, 465).

4 **Fotos** Con un(a) compañero/a, haz preguntas sobre estas personas.

modelo

Estudiante 1: ¿Quién es esta mujer?
Estudiante 2: Es estudiante.
Estudiante 1: ¿Dónde está?
Estudiante 2: Está en la biblioteca.
Estudiante 1: ¿Qué está haciendo?
Estudiante 2: Está estudiando para un examen.

1.   2.

3.   4.

Español en vivo

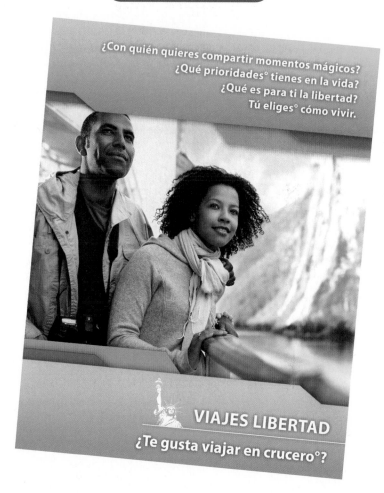

¿Con quién quieres compartir momentos mágicos?
¿Qué prioridades° tienes en la vida?
¿Qué es para ti la libertad?
Tú eliges° cómo vivir.

VIAJES LIBERTAD
¿Te gusta viajar en crucero°?

prioridades *priorities*   **eliges** *choose*   **crucero** *cruise ship*

1 **Identificar** Lee el anuncio e identifica las palabras interrogativas. ¿Cuál de las tres preguntas puede escribirse con otra palabra interrogativa sin cambiar el significado de la pregunta? ¿Con qué palabra interrogativa se puede escribir?

2 **Preguntas** Contesta las preguntas.
1. ¿Te gustaría viajar en un crucero? ¿Adónde?
2. ¿Por qué te gustaría viajar a ese lugar?
3. ¿Con quién te gustaría viajar?
4. ¿Te gusta este anuncio? ¿Por qué?

I CAN ask and answer questions about a wedding.

I CAN recognize familiar words in a simple ad.

A repasar

9.1 Irregular preterites

1 **La graduación** El fin de semana pasado fue tu fiesta de graduación y tus parientes de Colombia vinieron a la celebración. Usa estas frases para describir qué pasó en la fiesta.

conducir el automóvil	traducir del inglés
decir el discurso (*speech*)	traer un regalo
producir un video	venir desde Colombia

2 **Una fiesta importante** Con un(a) compañero/a, túrnate para describir una fiesta importante que celebraron el año pasado. Comenta qué regalos diste y qué regalos te dieron. También comenta qué hubo de cenar, de beber y de postre.

modelo

Estudiante 1: ¿Cuál fue la fiesta más importante para ti el año pasado?
Estudiante 2: Para mi, fue la Navidad. Celebré esta fiesta con toda mi familia. Mis padres me dieron una computadora. De beber, hubo vino tinto, champán y refrescos...

9.2 Verbs that change meaning in the preterite

3 **¡Qué mala suerte!** Completa el párrafo del diario de Romeo con el pretérito de los verbos **conocer, saber, poder** y **querer.**

Querido diario:
Julieta y yo nos (1) _____ en una fiesta el año pasado. Al día siguiente, yo (2) _____ invitarla a salir. La llamé por teléfono, pero no (3) _____ encontrarla. Julieta (4) _____ que yo la llamé. Ella (5) _____ escribirme un mensaje electrónico, ¡pero yo no tengo correo electrónico! Julieta y yo nunca (6) _____ tener una cita. ¡Qué mala suerte (*luck*)!
Romeo

4 **De joven...** En grupos de tres, imaginen que tienen ochenta años de edad. Escriban un párrafo diciendo las cosas que quisieron hacer de jóvenes, las cosas que no quisieron hacer, las actividades que pudieron hacer y las que no pudieron hacer.

modelo De joven, siempre quise tener una cita con una actriz de cine, pero no pude conocer a ninguna.

9.3 Relative pronouns

5 **Combinar** Combina las oraciones para formar una sola oración con los pronombres relativos **que, quien(es)** y **lo que.**

modelo Mi hermano y mi novia se llevan bien. Ellos planearon una fiesta sorpresa para mí.
Mi hermano y mi novia, quienes se llevan bien, planearon una fiesta sorpresa para mí.

1. La fiesta fue en un restaurante peruano. Mi novia lo eligió (*chose*).
2. Mi amigo Hernán es colombiano. Él vino desde Bogotá.
3. Los camareros trajeron un pastel de cumpleaños. El pastel fue de chocolate.
4. Mis tíos fueron a la fiesta. La situación fue incómoda (*uncomfortable*) porque están separados.
5. Mis hermanos son mayores que yo. Ellos le dejaron una propina al camarero.
6. Los invitados bailaron mucho. Fue bueno porque se divirtieron.

6 **Anuncio** Con un(a) compañero/a, escribe un anuncio de un salón para celebrar bodas. Usa pronombres relativos y los verbos **creer, pensar, decir** y **suponer.**

modelo ¡Creemos que este salón es perfecto para su boda! Suponemos que usted quiere una boda divertidísima.

9.4 ¿Qué? and ¿cuál?

7 Las etapas de la vida Completa las preguntas con **qué** o **cuál(es)**. Después, responde las preguntas.

> **modelo** ¿ _Qué_ etapa de la vida ocurre después de la niñez?
> La etapa de la vida que ocurre después de la niñez es la adolescencia.

1. ¿_____ es la etapa en la que nos jubilamos?

2. ¿_____ son las mejores etapas de la vida?

3. ¿_____ son las etapas que ocurren antes de la vejez?

4. ¿_____ es la etapa de la vida después de la madurez?

5. ¿_____ celebraciones son las favoritas de los niños?

8 La quinceañera Con un(a) compañero/a, escribe preguntas para entrevistar a Ana, quien celebró su fiesta de quince años. Usa todas las palabras interrogativas. Después, túrnate con tu compañero/a para hacer y responder las preguntas.

Síntesis

9 Conversar Tu amigo y tú están conversando sobre la vida de artistas famosos. Con un(a) compañero/a, comenta los últimos chismes (*gossip*) de estas celebridades.

> **modelo**
>
> **Estudiante 1:** ¿Supiste que Sofía Vergara rompió con su novio?
> **Estudiante 2:** Sí, lo supe. Creo que él se enamoró de una modelo.
> **Estudiante 1:** ¿Quién te dijo eso?
> **Estudiante 2:** Lo dijeron en el programa de entrevistas de las seis de la tarde. ¿No lo viste?
> **Estudiante 1:** No. Estuve en la biblioteca.

Communicative Goal
Watch a video about a traditional celebration in Mexico and use it to create my own video

 Video

Videoclip

1 Preparación ¿Cuál es la fiesta popular más importante de tu comunidad? ¿Cómo se celebra? ¿Cuál es la fiesta popular que más recuerdas? ¿Qué fue lo que más te llamó la atención?

2 El clip Mira el episodio **Guelaguetza en Oaxaca** del programa *Sin postal* de México.

> **Vocabulario**
>
> artesanías *crafts*   ofrenda *offering*
> diosa *goddess*   vestimentas *clothing*

Guelaguetza

La fiesta étnica y folclórica más importante de todo el continente: ¡la Guelaguetza!

3 Preguntas Contesta las preguntas.

1. ¿En qué mes se celebra la Guelaguetza?

2. ¿Cuántas regiones tiene el estado de Oaxaca?

3. ¿Cuál es el espectáculo principal de esta celebración?

4. ¿Qué significa la palabra *guelaguetza*?

5. La celebración es una mezcla de dos tradiciones. ¿Cuáles son?

4 Otra fiesta tradicional Con un(a) compañero/a, graba (*record*) un video de dos a tres minutos para presentar una fiesta tradicional de su comunidad, estado o país. Suban (*Upload*) el video y compártanlo con compañeros de su universidad y personas de otras comunidades.

I CAN understand information in a video about a traditional celebration in Mexico.

I CAN create a short video about a traditional celebration in my own culture.

Ampliación

Communicative Goals
Use context to understand unfamiliar words in a conversation, and talk about a holiday celebration

1 Escuchar

A Escucha la conversación entre Josefina y Rosa. Cuando oigas una de las palabras de la **columna A**, usa el contexto para identificar un sinónimo en la **columna B**.

> **TIP** **Guess the meaning of the words through context.** Listen to the words and phrases around an unfamiliar word to guess its meaning.

A

_____ 1. festejar

_____ 2. te divertiste

_____ 3. dicha

_____ 4. bien parecido

_____ 5. finge (fingir)

_____ 6. soporta (soportar)

B

a. conmemoración religiosa de una muerte

b. tolera

c. suerte

d. celebrar

e. lo pasaste bien

f. horror

g. pretende ser algo que no es

h. guapo

*Margarita Robles de García
y Roberto García Olmos*

*Piden su presencia en la celebración
del segundo aniversario de bodas
el día 13 de marzo de 2018
con una misa en la Iglesia Virgen del Coromoto
a las 6:30 p.m.*

❧

*Seguida por cena y baile
en el restaurante El Campanero,
Calle Principal, Las Mercedes
a las 8:30 p.m.*

B ¿Son solteras Rosa y Josefina? ¿Cómo lo sabes?

2 Conversar

Con un(a) compañero/a, conversa sobre cómo celebraron el Día de Acción de Gracias (*Thanksgiving*) el año pasado. Incluye esta información.

- ¿Dónde celebraron el día de fiesta? ¿A qué hora fue?
- ¿Cuántos invitados hubo? ¿Quiénes fueron los invitados? ¿Conocieron a alguien?
- ¿Cuál fue el menú? ¿Quiénes hicieron la comida?
- ¿Llevaron algo para comer? ¿Qué llevaron?
- ¿Qué bebida tomaron? ¿Brindaron?
- ¿Lo pasaron bien? ¿Qué fue lo que más les gustó de la celebración?

I CAN use context to understand unfamiliar words in a conversation.

I CAN talk about a holiday celebration.

Ampliación

3 Escribir

En una composición, compara dos celebraciones a las que tú asististe recientemente.

TIP **Use Venn diagrams.** Use Venn diagrams to organize your ideas visually before comparing and contrasting people, places, objects, events, or issues. Differences are listed in the outer rings of the two circles; similarities appear where the circles overlap.

Boda de Silvia Reyes y Carlos Espinoza

Diferencias:
1. Primero hay una celebración religiosa.
2. Se celebra el matrimonio de dos personas.

Similitudes:
1. Las dos fiestas se celebran por la noche.
2. Hay música y baile.

Fiesta de quince años de Ana Ester Larenas Vera

Diferencias:
1. Se celebra en un club.
2. Vienen invitados especiales.

Organizar	Utiliza un diagrama de Venn para anotar las similitudes y las diferencias entre las dos celebraciones.
Escribir	Utiliza tus notas para escribir el primer borrador de la composición.
Corregir	Intercambia tu composición con la de un(a) compañero/a. Dale sugerencias para mejorar su borrador y si ves errores gramaticales u ortográficos, coméntaselos.
Compartir	Revisa el primer borrador según las indicaciones de tu compañero/a. Incorpora nuevas ideas o más información para ampliar la comparación. Luego, comparte tu composición con otro/a compañero/a.

4 Un paso más

Imagina que eres periodista en un país hispano. Escribe un artículo sobre un día de fiesta o una celebración que viste.

• Investiga las fiestas, las celebraciones y los festivales de ese país.

• Explica el nombre de la celebración que escogiste, cuándo fue y cómo la celebraron.

• Incluye información sobre la ropa especial que llevaron, la comida, la música y el baile.

• Indica qué hiciste tú durante la celebración.

• Presenta el artículo a la clase. Explica los detalles y muestra fotos.

5 Cultura

Puedes asistir a una de las celebraciones mencionadas en esta lección. ¿A cuál quieres ir? ¿Por qué?

I CAN write a composition in which I compare two celebrations.

I CAN write an article about a holiday or celebration in a Spanish-speaking country.

Audio: Reading

Antes de leer

Analyzing words will help you understand a text.

TIP **Recognize word families.** Recognizing root words and word families can help you guess the meaning of words in context, ensuring better comprehension of a reading selection. Using this strategy will enrich your Spanish vocabulary as well.

∞ Examinar el texto

Familiarízate con el texto usando las estrategias de lectura más efectivas para ti. ¿Qué tipo de documento es? ¿De qué tratan las cuatro secciones del documento? Explica tus respuestas.

∞ Raíces

Completa el cuadro para ampliar tu vocabulario. Usa palabras de la lectura de esta lección y vocabulario de las lecciones anteriores. ¿Qué significan las palabras que escribiste?

Verbs	Nouns	Other forms
1. agradecer *to thank, to be grateful for*	agradecimiento/ gracias *gratitude/thanks*	agradecido *grateful, thankful*
2. estudiar	_____	_____
3. _____	_____	celebrado
4. _____	baile	_____
5. bautizar	_____	_____

EL INFORMANTE

| Actualidad | Opinión | Vida social | Entretenimiento |

Matrimonio

Espinoza Álvarez- Reyes Salazar

El día sábado 17 de junio a las 19 horas, se celebró el matrimonio de Silvia Reyes y Carlos Espinoza en la catedral de Santiago. La ceremonia fue oficiada por el pastor Federico Salas y participaron los padres de los novios, el señor Jorge Espinoza y señora y el señor José Alfredo Reyes y señora. Después de la ceremonia, los padres de los recién casados ofrecieron una fiesta bailable en el restaurante La Misión.

Bautismo

José María recibió el bautismo el 26 de junio.

Sus padres, don Roberto Lagos Moreno y doña María Angélica Sánchez, compartieron la alegría de la fiesta con todos sus parientes y amigos. La ceremonia religiosa tuvo lugarº en la catedral de Aguas Blancas. Después de la ceremonia, padres, parientes y amigos celebraron una fiesta en la residencia de la familia Lagos.

10:00 ▶ ⅞▭

Lunes, 30 de junio de 2018

| Tecnología | Deportes | Economía |

Fiesta de quince años *Señorita Ana Ester*

El doctor don Amador Larenas Fernández y la señora Felisa Vera de Larenas celebraron los quince años de su hija Ana Ester junto a sus parientes y amigos. La quinceañera reside en la ciudad de Valparaíso y es estudiante del Colegio Francés. La fiesta de presentación en sociedad de la señorita Ana Ester fue el día viernes 2 de junio a las 19 horas en el Club Español. Entre los invitados especiales asistieron el alcalde° de la ciudad, don Pedro Castedo, y su esposa. La música estuvo a cargo de la Orquesta Americana. ¡Feliz cumpleaños, le deseamos a la señorita Ana Ester en su fiesta bailable!

Expresión de gracias *Carmen Godoy Tapia*

Agradecemos° sinceramente a todas las personas que nos acompañaron en el último adiós a nuestra apreciada esposa, madre, abuela y tía, la señora Carmen Godoy Tapia. El funeral tuvo lugar el día 28 de junio en la ciudad de Viña del Mar. La vida de Carmen Godoy fue un ejemplo de trabajo, amistad, alegría y amor para todos nosotros. Su esposo, hijos y familia agradecen de todo corazón° su asistencia° al funeral a todos los parientes y amigos.

Después de leer

∞ ¿Comprendiste?

Indica si lo que dice cada oración es **cierto** o **falso**. Corrige las oraciones falsas.

Cierto	Falso	
_____	_____	1. El alcalde y su esposa asistieron a la boda de Silvia y Carlos.
_____	_____	2. Todos los anuncios (*announcements*) describen eventos felices.
_____	_____	3. Ana Ester Larenas cumple quince años.
_____	_____	4. Roberto Lagos y María Angélica Sánchez son hermanos.
_____	_____	5. La familia de Carmen Godoy Tapia les dio las gracias a las personas que asistieron al funeral.

∞ Preguntas

Responde estas preguntas con oraciones completas.

1. ¿Quién murió en junio?

_____

2. ¿Dónde tuvo lugar el funeral?

_____

3. ¿Dónde fue la fiesta de bautismo de José María?

_____

4. ¿Qué hicieron los recién casados y sus invitados después de la ceremonia?

_____

5. ¿Quién estuvo a cargo de la música en la fiesta de quince años de Ana Ester?

_____

∞ Coméntalo

¿Hay una sección de notas sociales en el periódico de tu universidad, comunidad o región? ¿Qué tipo de información encuentras en la sección de notas sociales? ¿La lees normalmente? ¿Por qué?

I CAN use word families to understand a text.

tuvo lugar *took place* **alcalde** *mayor* **Agradecemos** *We thank* **de todo corazón** *sincerely*
asistencia *attendance*

Las fiestas

el aniversario (de bodas) *(wedding) anniversary*
la boda *wedding*
el cumpleaños *birthday*
el día de fiesta *holiday*
la fiesta *party*
el/la invitado/a *guest*
la Navidad *Christmas*
la quinceañera *young woman celebrating her fifteenth birthday*
la sorpresa *surprise*

———

brindar *to toast (drink)*
celebrar *to celebrate*
cumplir años *to have a birthday*
dejar una propina *to leave a tip*
divertirse (e:ie) *to have fun*
graduarse (de) *to graduate (from)*
invitar *to invite; to treat*
pagar la cuenta *to pay the bill*
pasarlo bien/mal *to have a good/bad time*
regalar *to give (a gift)*
reírse (e:i) *to laugh*
relajarse *to relax*
sonreír (e:i) *to smile*
sorprender *to surprise*

Los postres y otras comidas

la botella de vino *bottle of wine*
el champán *champagne*
los dulces *sweets; candy*
el flan *baked custard*
las galletas *cookies*
el helado *ice cream*
el pastel *cake*
el pastel de cumpleaños *birthday cake*
los postres *desserts*

Las relaciones personales

la alegría *happiness*
la amistad *friendship*
el amor *love*
el divorcio *divorce*
el estado civil *marital status*
el matrimonio *marriage; married couple*
la pareja *couple; partner*
el/la recién casado/a *newlywed*

———

casado/a *married*
divorciado/a *divorced*
juntos/as *together*
separado/a *separated*
soltero/a *single*
viudo/a *widowed*

———

cambiar (de) *to change*
casarse (con) *to get married (to)*
comprometerse (con) *to get engaged (to)*
divorciarse (de) *to get divorced (from)*
enamorarse (de) *to fall in love (with)*
llevarse bien/mal (con) *to get along well/badly (with)*
odiar *to hate*
romper (con) *to break up (with)*
salir (con) *to go out (with); to date*
separarse (de) *to separate (from)*
tener una cita *to have a date; to have an appointment*

Otras palabras

el apellido *last name*
el consejo *advice*
la respuesta *answer*

Las etapas de la vida

la adolescencia *adolescence*
la etapa *stage*
la juventud *youth*
la madurez *maturity; middle age*
la muerte *death*
el nacimiento *birth*
la niñez *childhood*
la vejez *old age*
la vida *life*

———

jubilarse *to retire (from work)*
nacer *to be born*

Relative pronouns *See page 240.*
Interrogative words and phrases *See page 242.*

Communicative Goals: Review

I CAN talk about celebrations.

- Describe an annual celebration you attend.

I CAN describe personal relationships.

- Talk about the marital status of three people you know.

I CAN talk about the past.

- Say what you did yesterday. Did you meet anyone? Did you learn anything? Did you drive somewhere?

I CAN investigate holidays in the Spanish-speaking world.

- Describe one of the holidays you learned about in this lesson.

10 En el consultorio

Communicative Goals
You will learn how to:
- talk about health
- discuss medical conditions and symptoms
- describe the past
- investigate health systems in the Spanish-speaking world

PREPARACIÓN

pages 252–257
- Words related to sickness, symptoms, medicine, and the doctor's office
- Parts of the body
- Written accent marks and word stress

AVENTURAS

pages 258–259
- Juanjo falls while posing for a picture and hurts his ankle. His friends want to take him to the hospital, but he's reluctant.

CULTURA

pages 260–261
- *Servicios de salud*
- Flash cultura: *La salud*

GRAMÁTICA

pages 262–271
- The imperfect tense
- Constructions with **se**
- Adverbs

LECTURA

pages 272–273
- Online health column: *El consultorio: Dra. Fernanda Jiménez Ocaña*

PARA EMPEZAR
- ¿Se divierte el chico?
- ¿La mujer es doctora o periodista?
- ¿Están en un almacén o en un hospital?
- ¿Cómo es la mujer?

EN EL CONSULTORIO

la oreja

el ojo

la nariz

la boca

EL CUERPO

el corazón *heart*
el cuerpo *body*
el estómago *stomach*
el hueso *bone*
la rodilla *knee*
el tobillo *ankle*

la pierna
leg

el pie
foot

la cabeza
head

la garganta
throat

el cuello
neck

el brazo
arm

el dedo
finger

LA SALUD

el accidente *accident*
la clínica *clinic*
el consultorio *doctor's office*
el/la doctor(a) *doctor*
el/la enfermero/a *nurse*
el examen médico *physical exam*
el hospital *hospital*
la operación *operation*
el/la paciente *patient*
la radiografía *X-ray*
la sala de emergencia(s)
    emergency room
la salud *health*

la farmacia

el dentista

Vocabulary Tools

tomar(le) la temperatura (a alguien)
to take (someone's) temperature

LOS MEDICAMENTOS

el antibiótico *antibiotic*
el medicamento *medication*
la medicina *medicine*
las pastillas *pills*
la receta *prescription*

ADJETIVOS

embarazada *pregnant*
grave *grave; serious*
médico/a *medical*
saludable *healthy*
sano/a *healthy*

LAS ENFERMEDADES Y LOS SÍNTOMAS

el dolor (de cabeza) *(head)ache; pain*
la enfermedad *illness*
la gripe *flu*
la infección *infection*
el resfriado *cold*
el síntoma *symptom*
la tos *cough*
_____
congestionado/a *congested*
mareado/a *dizzy; nauseated*

VERBOS

caerse *to fall*
doler (o:ue) *to hurt*
enfermarse *to get sick*
estar enfermo/a *to be sick*
lastimarse (el pie) *to injure (one's foot)*
poner una inyección
   to give an injection
recetar *to prescribe*
romperse (la pierna)
   to break (one's leg)
sacar(se) una muela
   to have a tooth pulled
ser alérgico/a (a) *to be allergic (to)*
tener fiebre (f.) *to have a fever*
torcerse (o:ue) (el tobillo)
   to sprain (one's ankle)
toser *to cough*

la aspirina

estornudar
to sneeze

ASÍ SE DICE

el resfriado ⟷ el resfrío (*Cono Sur*), el catarro (*Méx.*)
la sala de emergencia(s) ⟷ la sala de urgencias
romperse ⟷ quebrarse (*Amér. L.*)

A escuchar

1 Escuchar Escucha las preguntas y selecciona la respuesta más adecuada.

1. _____
2. _____
3. _____
4. _____
5. _____
6. _____
7. _____
8. _____

a. Tengo dolor de cabeza y fiebre.
b. No fui a la clase porque estaba (*I was*) enfermo.
c. Me caí ayer jugando al tenis.
d. Debes ir a la farmacia.
e. Porque tengo gripe.
f. Sí, tengo mucha tos por las noches.
g. Lo llevaron directamente a la sala de emergencia.
h. No sé. Todavía tienen que tomarme la temperatura.

2 Me duele Escucha la conversación entre Virginia Castillo y el doctor Dávila. Luego, indica si (*if*) las oraciones que resumen (*sum up*) la conversación son correctas.

_____ 1. Virginia le dice a la enfermera que le duelen las rodillas.
_____ 2. Virginia dice que tomó una aspirina anoche.
_____ 3. El médico le pregunta a Virginia si se cayó o tuvo un accidente.
_____ 4. Virginia dice que ayer corrió cinco kilómetros con un amigo.
_____ 5. El doctor Dávila le receta un antibiótico a Virginia.
_____ 6. El médico le dice a Virginia que puede correr mañana si se toma las pastillas.
_____ 7. El médico le recomienda tomar dos pastillas al día.
_____ 8. El doctor Dávila le dice a Virginia que no debe correr por siete días.

A practicar

3 **Actividades** Con un(a) compañero/a, identifica las partes del cuerpo asociadas con estas actividades.

modelo

nadar
Estudiante 1: *Usamos los brazos para nadar.*
Estudiante 2: *También usamos las piernas.*

1. conducir	5. comprar un perfume	9. jugar al fútbol
2. caminar	6. ver una película	10. escuchar música
3. toser	7. hablar por teléfono	11. levantar pesas (*weights*)
4. comer arroz con pollo	8. correr en el parque	12. tomar unas pastillas

4 **Cuestionario** Selecciona las respuestas que mejor reflejen tu estado de salud. Suma (*add*) los puntos de cada respuesta y anota el resultado. Después, compara los resultados con el resto de la clase.

¿Tienes buena salud?

27-30 puntos   Salud y hábitos excelentes
23-26 puntos   Salud y hábitos buenos
22 puntos o menos Salud y hábitos problemáticos

1. ¿Con qué frecuencia te enfermas (resfriados, gripe, etc.)?
   • Cuatro veces por año o más. (1 punto)
   • Dos o tres veces por año. (2 puntos)
   • Casi nunca. (3 puntos)

2. ¿Con qué frecuencia tienes dolor de estómago o problemas digestivos?
   • Con mucha frecuencia. (1 punto)
   • A veces. (2 puntos)
   • Casi nunca. (3 puntos)

3. ¿Con qué frecuencia tienes dolor de cabeza?
   • Frecuentemente. (1 punto)
   • A veces. (2 puntos)
   • Casi nunca. (3 puntos)

4. ¿Comes verduras y frutas?
   • No, casi nunca. (1 punto)
   • Sí, a veces. (2 puntos)
   • Sí, todos los días. (3 puntos)

5. ¿Eres alérgico/a a algo?
   • Sí, a muchas cosas. (1 punto)
   • Sí, a algunas cosas. (2 puntos)
   • No. (3 puntos)

6. ¿Haces ejercicios aeróbicos?
   • No, casi nunca hago ejercicios aeróbicos. (1 punto)
   • Sí, a veces. (2 puntos)
   • Sí, con frecuencia. (3 puntos)

7. ¿Con qué frecuencia te haces un examen médico?
   • Nunca o casi nunca. (1 punto)
   • Cada dos años. (2 puntos)
   • Cada año o antes de practicar un deporte. (3 puntos)

8. ¿Con qué frecuencia vas al dentista?
   • Nunca voy al dentista. (1 punto)
   • Sólo cuando me duele una muela. (2 puntos)
   • Por lo menos una vez por año. (3 puntos)

9. ¿Qué desayunas normalmente por la mañana?
   • No como nada. (1 punto)
   • Tomo una bebida dietética. (2 puntos)
   • Como cereales y fruta. (3 puntos)

10. ¿Con qué frecuencia te sientes mareado/a?
   • Frecuentemente. (1 punto)
   • A veces. (2 puntos)
   • Casi nunca. (3 puntos)

A conversar

5 **¿Qué le pasó?** En un grupo de tres, hablen de lo que les pasó y de cómo se sienten estas personas.

1. Víctor

2. La señora Núñez

3. Gabriela

4. El señor Álvarez

6 **¿Cuáles son sus síntomas?** Con un(a) compañero/a, túrnate para representar los papeles (*roles*) de un(a) médico/a y su paciente.

> **modelo**
>
> **Estudiante 1:** ¿Cuáles son sus síntomas?
> **Estudiante 2:** Me duele la garganta y toso.
> **Estudiante 1:** Creo que usted tiene una infección en la garganta.
> Voy a recetarle un antibiótico.

7 **Un accidente** Con un(a) compañero/a, conversa sobre un accidente que ustedes, un(a) amigo/a o un miembro de la familia tuvo. Usa estas preguntas como guía.

- ¿Qué ocurrió?
- ¿Cómo ocurrió?
- ¿Dónde y cuándo ocurrió?
- ¿Quién te ayudó y cómo?
- ¿Te lastimaste?
- ¿Tomaste medicamentos para sentirte mejor?
- ¿Fuiste al médico?
- ¿Fuiste a trabajar?

I CAN discuss medical conditions and symptoms.

Ortografía

 Tutorial

El acento y las sílabas fuertes

In Spanish, written accent marks are used on many words. Here is a review of some of the principles governing word stress and the use of written accents.

. . . .

as-pi-ri-na   **gri-pe**   **to-man**   **an-tes**

In Spanish, when a word ends in a vowel, **-n**, or **-s**, the spoken stress usually falls on the next-to-last syllable. Words of this type are very common and do not need a written accent.

a-sí   **in-glés**   **in-fec-ción**   **hé-ro-e**

When a word ends in a vowel, **-n**, or **-s**, and the spoken stress does *not* fall on the next-to-last syllable, then a written accent is needed.

. . . .

hos-pi-tal   **na-riz**   **re-ce-tar**   **to-ser**

When a word ends in any consonant *other* than **-n** or **-s**, the spoken stress usually falls on the last syllable. Words of this type are very common and do not need a written accent.

. . . .

lá-piz   **fút-bol**   **hués-ped**   **sué-ter**

When a word ends in any consonant *other* than **-n** or **-s,** and the spoken stress does *not* fall on the last syllable, then a written accent is needed.

. . . .

far-ma-cia   **bio-lo-gí-a**   **su-cio**   **frí-o**

Diphthongs (two weak vowels or a strong and weak vowel together) are normally pronounced as a single syllable. A written accent is needed when a diphthong is broken into two syllables.

. . . .

sol   **pan**   **mar**   **tos**

Spanish words of only one syllable do not usually carry a written accent.

. . . .

 Práctica Busca las palabras que necesitan acento y escribe su forma correcta.

1. sal-mon	6. a-bri-go	11. o-pe-ra-cion	16. far-ma-cia
2. ins-pec-tor	7. ra-pi-do	12. im-per-me-a-ble	17. es-qui
3. nu-me-ro	8. sa-ba-do	13. a-de-mas	18. pen-sion
4. fa-cil	9. vez	14. re-ga-te-ar	19. pa-is
5. ju-go	10. me-nu	15. an-ti-pa-ti-co	20. per-don

El ahorcado Juega al ahorcado (*hangman*) para adivinar las palabras.

1. __ l __ __ __ __ a   Vas allí cuando estás enfermo.
2. __ __ __ e __ c __ __ n   Se usa para poner una vacuna (*vaccination*).
3. __ __ d __ o __ __ __ __ a   Se usa para ver los huesos.
4. __ __ __ i __ o   Trabaja en un hospital.
5. a __ __ __ b __ __ __ __ __ __   Es una medicina.

¡Necesitas un médico!

Juanjo se lastima el tobillo y no quiere ir al hospital.

 Video

PERSONAJES

 VALENTINA

 MANUEL

 OLGA LUCÍA

 JUANJO

 DANIEL

 SARA

 CARICATURISTA

 DOCTORA

Antes de ver

Mira el título del episodio. Con base en el título y las imágenes que ves, describe lo que piensas que va a pasar en el video.

VALENTINA (a Olga Lucía) ¿Puedes tomar la foto rápido?
MANUEL ¡Ya me duele la boca!
OLGA LUCÍA ¡Tres, dos, uno!
JUANJO ¡Ay! ¡Mi tobillo!
DANIEL ¿Te duele?
JUANJO No, no es nada...

MANUEL A lo mejor se te rompió el tobillo.
OLGA LUCÍA ¡Tenemos que llevarte a la sala de emergencias!
DANIEL Seguramente te tienen que hacer una radiografía.
JUANJO ¡Ya, por favor! ¡Sólo me lastimé un poco!
VALENTINA ¿Te puedo ayudar?
JUANJO ¡Por favor!

JUANJO La verdad es que me duele bastante.
VALENTINA ¡Pobrecito!
OLGA LUCÍA ¡Chicos! ¡Valentina, Juanjo! ¡Estamos aquí!
VALENTINA ¿Vamos?
JUANJO No, mejor espero aquí. Me duele.
VALENTINA Ya vuelvo.

ACTIVIDADES

1 ¿Cierto o falso? Indica si lo que dicen estas oraciones es **cierto** o **falso**. Corrige las oraciones falsas.

	Cierto	Falso
1. Manuel dice que le duele la garganta.	○	○
2. Juanjo se cae y se tuerce el tobillo.	○	○
3. Los chicos van a la farmacia.	○	○
4. La doctora mira una radiografía.	○	○
5. Al final, Juanjo se siente muy bien.	○	○

2 Identificar Identifica quién dice las oraciones equivalentes.

1. ¡Necesitamos ir a la sala de emergencias!
2. ¿Tienes dolor?
3. Tengo que ir a una farmacia.
4. ¡Necesitas un doctor!
5. ¿Va a darme una receta?

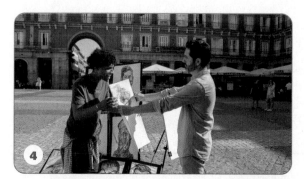

VALENTINA ¿Te estás haciendo un dibujo?

JUANJO ¿Qué?

VALENTINA ¡Él te está dibujando!

JUANJO ¿Quién?

VALENTINA (apuntando al caricaturista) ¡Él!

JUANJO (al caricaturista) ¡No, no, no, no, no! Lo siento, señor, estaba distraído, no sabía que...

CARICATURISTA Son diez euros.

JUANJO Necesito ir a una farmacia.

SARA ¡Necesitas un médico!

JUANJO ¡Me torcí el tobillo, eso es todo! Con una aspirina el dolor se me pasa rápidamente... ¡Ay! Bueno, mejor vamos al hospital, ¿no?

DOCTORA Aquí no veo nada roto. ¿Cómo te caíste?

JUANJO Me caí en la Plaza Mayor y apenas me levanté me empezó el dolor.

DOCTORA ¿Y todavía te duele?

JUANJO Sí, un poco. ¿Me va a recetar algún medicamento?

DOCTORA No, no hace falta.

JUANJO ¡Sabía que no tenía que venir al hospital! ¡Gracias, doctora!

Expresiones útiles

a lo mejor *maybe*
distraído/a *distracted*
menos mal *it's a good thing*
no hace falta *there's no need*
pobrecito/a *poor thing*
roto/a *broken*

---

el brinco *leap*
cojear *to limp*
la cojera *limp*

Plaza Mayor de Madrid

La Playa Mayor de Madrid es la plaza principal de la ciudad. Esta plaza, que tiene ya 400 años, es de forma rectangular y tiene diez accesos (*entrances*). Uno de ellos es el Arco de Cuchilleros, donde Juanjo se cae. En la plaza, se pueden encontrar artistas callejeros (*street performers*), probar platos deliciosos en sus restaurantes y, cada diciembre, se puede visitar el mercado de Navidad.

¿Qué lugares históricos hay en tu ciudad o pueblo?

---

3 **En el consultorio** En parejas, representen una conversación entre un(a) médico/a y su paciente.

▶ El/La médico/a le pregunta al/a la paciente qué le pasó.

▶ El/La paciente se cayó en la casa y se lastimó.

▶ El/La médico/a le pregunta al/a la paciente si le duele.

▶ El/La paciente describe el dolor.

▶ El/La médico/a le recomienda un tratamiento (*treatment*).

I CAN participate in a medical consultation.

Servicios de salud

¿Sabías que en algunos países hispanos no necesitas pagar por los servicios de salud?
Ésta es una de las diferencias que hay entre países como los Estados Unidos y los países hispanos.

En la mayor parte de estos países, el gobierno ofrece servicios médicos muy baratos o gratuitos° a sus ciudadanos°. Los turistas y extranjeros también pueden tener acceso a los servicios médicos a bajo° costo. La Seguridad Social y organizaciones similares son las responsables de gestionar° estos servicios.

Cruz verde de farmacia en Madrid, España

Las farmacias

Farmacia de guardia: Las farmacias generalmente tienen un horario comercial. Sin embargo°, en cada barrio° hay una farmacia de guardia que abre las veinticuatro horas del día.

Productos farmacéuticos: Hay muchas farmacias especializadas en medicinas y productos farmacéuticos. No venden productos de otro tipo.

Recetas: Muchos medicamentos se venden sin receta. Los farmacéuticos aconsejan° a las personas sobre problemas de salud y les dan las medicinas.

Cruz° verde: En muchos países, las farmacias tienen el signo de una cruz verde. Cuando la cruz verde está encendida°, la farmacia está abierta.

acceso a ellos y en muchos casos son completamente gratuitos. Según un informe de la Organización Mundial de la Salud, el sistema de salud español ocupa uno de los primeros diez lugares del mundo. Esto se debe no sólo al buen funcionamiento° del sistema, sino también al nivel de salud general de la población. Impresionante, ¿no?

gratuitos *free (of charge)* ciudadanos *citizens* bajo *low* gestionar *to manage* igual *in the same way* cuentan con *have* desarrollados *developed* funcionamiento *operation* Sin embargo *However* barrio *neighborhood* aconsejan *advise* Cruz *Cross* encendida *lit (up)*

Consulta médica en la República Dominicana

Naturalmente, esto no funciona igual° en todos los países. En Ecuador, México y Perú, la situación varía según las regiones. Los habitantes de las ciudades y pueblos grandes tienen acceso a más servicios médicos, mientras que quienes viven en pueblos remotos sólo cuentan con° pequeñas clínicas.

Por su parte, Costa Rica, Colombia, Cuba y España tienen sistemas de salud muy desarrollados°. En España, por ejemplo, la mayoría de la gente tiene

ASÍ SE DICE

La salud

la ambulancia	*ambulance*
el chequeo (Esp., Méx.)	el examen médico
la cirugía	*surgery*
la droguería (Col.)	la farmacia
la herida	*injury; wound*
el jarabe para la tos	*cough syrup*
los primeros auxilios	*first aid*
la sala de espera	*waiting room*
la sangre	*blood*

ACTIVIDADES

1 ¿Cierto o falso? Indica si lo que dicen las oraciones es **cierto** o **falso**. Corrige la información falsa.

1. En los países hispanos los gobiernos ofrecen servicios de salud accesibles a sus ciudadanos.

2. En los países hispanos los extranjeros tienen que pagar mucho dinero por los servicios médicos.

3. El sistema de salud español es uno de los mejores del mundo.

4. Los farmacéuticos de los países hispanos venden algunas medicinas sin necesidad de receta.

5. En México y otros países, los pueblos remotos cuentan con grandes centros médicos.

6. Muchas farmacias usan una cruz verde como símbolo.

2 Preguntas Contesta las preguntas.

1. ¿Qué países hispanos tienen sistemas de salud muy desarrollados?

2. ¿Cuándo están abiertas las farmacias de guardia?

3. ¿Cómo sabes que una farmacia está abierta?

4. ¿Por qué no venden jabón y champú las farmacias?

3 Comparación Con un(a) compañero/a, compara el sistema de salud de los países hispanos con el de tu país. ¿En qué se parecen? ¿En qué se diferencian? ¿Cuál prefieres? ¿Por qué?

4 ¿Qué piensas? Responde a estas preguntas.

1. ¿Por qué crees que los servicios médicos son muy baratos o gratuitos en algunos países hispanos?

2. ¿Piensas que los medicamentos deben venderse sin receta? ¿Por qué?

I CAN identify characteristics of the health systems in my own country and in Spanish-speaking countries.

Communicative Goal
Identify characteristics of the health system in Argentina

La salud

1 Preparación ¿Qué haces si tienes un pequeño accidente o quieres hacer una consulta? ¿Visitas a tu médico general o vas al hospital? ¿Debes pedir un turno (*appointment*)?

2 El video Mira el episodio de **Flash cultura** sobre el sistema de salud en Argentina.

Vocabulario	
la cita previa *previous appointment*	Me di un golpe. *I hurt myself.*
la guardia *emergency room*	la práctica *rotation (hands-on medical experience)*

¿Le podría° pedir que me explique qué es la guardia?

podría *could*

3 ¿Cierto o falso? Indica si las oraciones son **ciertas** o **falsas**.

1. Silvina tuvo un accidente en su automóvil.
2. Silvina fue a la guardia del hospital.
3. La guardia del hospital está abierta sólo durante el día y es necesario tener cita previa.
4. Los entrevistados (*interviewees*) tienen enfermedades graves.
5. En Argentina, los médicos reciben la certificación cuando terminan la práctica.

4 Los sistemas de salud Escribe una comparación entre el sistema de salud en Argentina y el sistema de salud en los Estados Unidos.

I CAN identify characteristics of the health system in Argentina.

10.1 The imperfect tense

▶ In Lessons 6–9, you learned the preterite tense. Now you will learn the imperfect tense, which describes past activities in a different way.

The imperfect of regular verbs

	cantar	beber	escribir
yo	cantaba	bebía	escribía
tú	cantabas	bebías	escribías
Ud./él/ella	cantaba	bebía	escribía
nosotros/as	cantábamos	bebíamos	escribíamos
vosotros/as	cantabais	bebíais	escribíais
Uds./ellos/ellas	cantaban	bebían	escribían

¡ojo! The imperfect endings of **–er** and **–ir** verbs are the same. The **nosotros** form of **–ar** verbs has an accent on the first **a** of the ending. **–Er** and **–ir** verb forms carry an accent on the first **i** of the ending.

Lo siento, señor, estaba distraído, no sabía que...

¡Sabía que no tenía que venir al hospital!

▶ There are no stem changes in the imperfect tense.

Me **duelen** los pies.
My feet hurt.

Me **dolían** los pies.
My feet were hurting.

▶ The imperfect form of **hay** is **había** (*there was/were/used to be*).

Había sólo un médico.
There was only one doctor.

Había dos pacientes allí.
There were two patients there.

¡ojo! **Ir, ser,** and **ver** are the only irregular verbs in the imperfect.

Irregular verbs in the imperfect

	ir	ser	ver
yo	iba	era	veía
tú	ibas	eras	veías
Ud./él/ella	iba	era	veía
nosotros/as	íbamos	éramos	veíamos
vosotros/as	ibais	erais	veíais
Uds./ellos/ellas	iban	eran	veían

Práctica

1 La salud Completa las oraciones con el imperfecto de los verbos de la lista. Algunos verbos se repiten.

caerse	esperar	mirar	sentirse
doler	estar	poder	tener
enfermarse	estornudar	querer	toser

modelo Después de correr, a Dora le ___dolían___ los pies.

1. Ana _____ el termómetro; con tanta fiebre no _____ leerlo.
2. El paciente _____, mientras la enfermera _____ muy ocupada atendiendo a otros pacientes.
3. Lorenzo _____ dolor de muelas, pero no _____ ir al dentista porque tenía miedo.
4. Paco y Luis _____ dolor de estómago y _____ unas pastillas para el dolor.
5. Le _____ la cabeza y _____ mareado.
6. Luisa _____ siempre porque era alérgica al polen.
7. Antes de la operación, le _____ todo el cuerpo y se sentía muy débil (*weak*).
8. Juan Carlos siempre _____ de la bicicleta cuando era pequeño.
9. De niño, Julio _____ todos los inviernos. Siempre _____ resfriados y fiebre. _____ muchas veces por la noche. ¡Pobre su garganta!

2 ¡Pobre Miguelito! Completa las oraciones con el imperfecto de los verbos. Luego, ponlas en orden lógico.

_____ a. Finalmente, Miguelito no tenía ganas de jugar más. Ahora _____ [querer] ir a casa a descansar.
_____ b. El doctor dijo que la inflamación no _____ [ser] nada grave.
_____ c. El niño le dijo a la enfermera que _____ [dolerle] la nariz.
_____ d. _____ [ser] las dos de la tarde y los niños _____ [jugar] en el patio.
_____ e. Su mamá _____ [estar] dibujando cuando Miguelito entró llorando.
_____ f. Miguelito _____ [tener] mucho dolor. Fueron a la sala de emergencias.
_____ g. El doctor examinó la nariz del niño y le dijo que _____ [ver] una pequeña inflamación (*swelling*).

Conversación

3 Entrevista Sigue las preguntas como guía y entrevista a un(a) compañero/a. Luego, comparte los resultados con la clase.

1. ¿Cuántos años tenías en 2010?
2. ¿Veías mucha televisión cuando eras niño/a?
3. Cuando eras niño/a, ¿qué hacía tu familia durante las vacaciones?
4. Cuando eras estudiante de primaria, ¿te gustaban tus profesores/as?
5. Cuando tenías diez años, ¿cuál era tu programa de televisión favorito?
6. Cuando tenías once años, ¿cuál era tu grupo musical favorito?
7. Cuando estabas en el quinto año escolar, ¿qué hacías con tus amigos/as?
8. Antes de tomar esta clase, ¿sabías hablar español?

4 Describir Con un(a) compañero/a, túrnate para describir lo que hacías de niño/a. Elige una de estas preguntas guía y comparte la anécdota con tu compañero/a.

modelo

De niña, mi familia y yo siempre íbamos a Tortuguero. Tomábamos un barco desde Limón, y por las noches mirábamos las tortugas (*turtles*) en la playa. Algunas veces teníamos suerte, porque las tortugas venían a poner (*lay*) huevos. Otras veces, volvíamos al hotel sin ver ninguna tortuga.

- ¿Qué hacías durante las vacaciones cuando eras niño/a?
- ¿Qué hacían en ocasiones especiales?
- ¿Cómo eran las celebraciones con tus amigos/as o familia?
- ¿Cómo era tu escuela? ¿Te gustaban tus profesores/as y compañeros/as?
- ¿Cómo eran tus amigos/as? ¿A qué jugabas con ellos/as?
- ¿Cuáles eran sus comidas favoritas?
- ¿Qué deportes practicaban? ¿Con qué frecuencia?

Uses of the imperfect

▶ The imperfect is used to describe past events in a different way than the preterite. Generally, the imperfect describes actions that are seen by the speaker as incomplete or continuing, while the preterite describes actions that have been completed. The imperfect expresses what was happening at a certain time or how things used to be.

—¿Qué te **pasó**?
What happened to you?

—Me **torcí** el tobillo.
I sprained my ankle.

—¿Dónde **vivías** de niño?
Where did you live as a child?

—**Vivía** en San José.
I lived in San José.

▶ Use these expressions with the imperfect to express habitual or repeated actions: **de niño/a** (*as a child*), **todos los días** (*every day*), **mientras** (*while*).

Uses of the imperfect

Habitual or repeated actions	Íbamos al parque los domingos. *We used to go to the park on Sundays.*
Events or actions that were in progress	Yo leía mientras él estudiaba. *I was reading while he was studying.*
Telling time	Eran las tres y media. *It was 3:30.*
Age	Los niños tenían seis años. *The children were six years old.*
Physical characteristics	Era alto y guapo. *He was tall and handsome.*
Mental or emotional states	Quería mucho a su familia. *He loved his family very much.*

¡Manos a la obra!

Escribe la forma correcta de cada verbo en el imperfecto.

1. Yo [hablar, bailar, descansar, correr, comer, decidir, vivir]
   hablaba, bailaba, descansaba, corría, comía, decidía, vivía

2. Tú [nadar, encontrar, comprender, venir, ir, ser, ver]

3. Usted [hacer, regatear, asistir, ser, pasear, poder, ir]

4. Nosotras [ser, tomar, ir, poner, seguir, ver, pensar]

5. Ellos [salir, viajar, ir, querer, ser, pedir, empezar]

6. Yo [ver, estornudar, sufrir, ir, dar, ser, toser] .

I CAN describe the past.

10.2 Constructions with se

Impersonal constructions with se

▶ As you know, **se** can be used as a reflexive pronoun (**Él se despierta.**). **Se** is also used in other ways.

▶ Non-reflexive verbs can be used with **se** to form impersonal constructions. In impersonal constructions, the person performing the action is not defined. In English, the passive voice or indefinite subjects (*you, they, one*) are used.

Se habla español en Costa Rica.
Spanish is spoken in Costa Rica.

Se puede leer en la sala de espera.
You can read in the waiting room.

¡ojo! The third person singular verb form is used with singular nouns and the third person plural form is used with plural nouns.

Se vende ropa.   **Se venden camisas.**

▶ You often see the impersonal **se** in signs and advertisements.

**SE PROHÍBE
NADAR**

Se necesitan programadores
GRUPO TECNO
Tel. 778-34-34

ENTRADA

Se entra por la izquierda

Se for unplanned events

▶ **Se** can also be used to de-emphasize the person who performs an action, implying that the accident or event is not his or her direct responsibility. Use this construction:

se	+	INDIRECT OBJECT PRONOUN	+	VERB	+	SUBJECT
Se		me		cayó		la pluma.

I dropped the pen.

▶ In this construction, what would normally be the direct object of the sentence becomes the subject and agrees with the verb.

I.O. PRONOUN	VERB	SUBJECT
me	perdieron	las llaves.
te	cayó	la pelota.
Se le	dañó	el radio.
nos	rompieron	las botellas.
os	olvidaron	las pastillas.
les		

Práctica

1 **¿Cierto o falso?** Lee estas oraciones sobre la vida en 1901. Indica si lo que dice cada oración es **cierto** o **falso**. Luego, corrige las oraciones falsas.

Cierto   Falso

_____ _____ 1. Se veía mucha televisión.

_____ _____ 2. Se escribían muchos libros.

_____ _____ 3. Se viajaba mucho en tren.

_____ _____ 4. Se montaba a caballo.

_____ _____ 5. Se mandaban mensajes electrónicos.

_____ _____ 6. Se preparaban comidas en casa.

_____ _____ 7. Se llevaban minifaldas.

_____ _____ 8. Se pasaba mucho tiempo con la familia.

2 **Letreros** Reescribe los letreros (*signs*) con el **se** impersonal.

 modelo
Buscamos vendedores con experiencia
Se buscan vendedores con experiencia

1. Necesitamos profesores de matemáticas

2. Hablamos español

3. Aceptamos tarjetas de crédito

4. Está prohibido hablar por teléfono

5. Vendemos libros

6. Buscamos dentista con experiencia

3 **¿Qué pasó?** Forma oraciones con estos elementos para indicar qué pasó. Sigue el modelo.

modelo
Luis / caer / pastel
A Luis se le cayó el pastel.

1. Gabriel / dañar / computadora

2. Carla y Lupe / romper / botellas

3. Julia / quedar / bolsa

4. Antonio / olvidar / huevos

5. Rosa / perder / llaves

Conversación

4 Preguntas Usa estas preguntas para entrevistar a un(a) compañero/a.

1. ¿Qué comidas se sirven en tu restaurante favorito?
2. ¿Se te olvidó invitar a alguien a tu última fiesta o cena? ¿A quién?
3. ¿A qué hora se abre la cafetería de tu universidad?
4. ¿Alguna vez se te perdió algo importante durante un viaje? ¿Qué?
5. ¿Qué se vende en la librería de la universidad?
6. ¿Alguna vez se te rompió algo caro? ¿Qué?

5 Minidiálogos Con un(a) compañero/a, representa uno de estos minidiálogos.

1. Un(a) profesor(a) de español le pide a un(a) estudiante su cuaderno de práctica (*workbook*). El/La estudiante le explica por qué él/ella no lo tiene.
2. Un(a) turista le pregunta al/a la empleado/a dónde se sirve la mejor comida en la ciudad. El/La empleado/a hace varias sugerencias.
3. Un(a) paciente le dice al/a la doctor(a) que él/ella no puede caminar. El/La doctor(a) examina al/a la paciente y le explica el problema.
4. Un padre/una madre le pregunta a su hijo/a qué le pasó al plato que está roto (*broken*) en el piso. El/La hijo/a le explica lo que sucedió.

6 Anuncios En grupos, preparen dos anuncios (*ads*) de televisión para presentar a la clase. Deben usar el imperfecto y dos construcciones con **se**.

modelo

Se me cayeron unos libros sobre el pie. Me dolía mucho. Pero ahora no, gracias a Superaspirina 500. ¡Tomé dos pastillas y se me fue el dolor! Se puede comprar Superaspirina 500 en todas las farmacias Recetamax.

These verbs are often used with **se** to describe unplanned events.

caer	to fall; to drop	perder (e:ie)	to lose
dañar	to damage; to break down	quedar	to be left behind
olvidar	to forget	romper	to break

¡ojo! **Dejar caer** (*to let fall*) is often used to mean *to drop*.

Elena **dejó caer** el libro.
Elena dropped the book.

El médico **dejó caer** la aspirina.
The doctor dropped the aspirin.

A lo mejor se te rompió el tobillo.

Con una aspirina el dolor se me pasa rápidamente.

A + [*noun*] or **a** + [*prepositional pronoun*] is frequently used to clarify or emphasize who is involved in the action.

Al estudiante se le perdió la tarea.
The student lost his homework.

A mí se me olvidó ir a clase ayer.
I forgot to go to class yesterday.

¡Manos a la obra!

Completa las oraciones de la primera columna con **se** impersonal y verbos en presente. Completa las oraciones de la segunda columna con **se** para sucesos imprevistos (*unplanned events*) y verbos en pretérito.

Presente

1. *Se enseñan* [enseñar] cinco lenguas en esta universidad.
2. _____ [comer] muy bien en El Cráter.
3. _____ [vender] muchas camisetas allí.
4. _____ [servir] platos exquisitos cada noche.
5. _____ [necesitar] mucho dinero.
6. _____ [buscar] secretaria.

Pretérito

1. *Se me rompieron* [I broke] las gafas.
2. _____ [you (fam.) dropped] las pastillas.
3. _____ [they lost] la receta.
4. _____ [you (form.) left] aquí la radiografía.
5. _____ [we forgot] pagar la medicina.
6. _____ [they left] los cuadernos en casa.

I CAN explain what happened.

10.3 Adverbs

▸ Adverbs describe how, when, and where actions take place. They modify verbs, adjectives, and even other adverbs. This list contains some adverbs you have already learned.

bien	nunca	temprano
mal	hoy	ayer
muy	siempre	ya

▸ Most adverbs end in **–mente**. These are equivalent to the English adverbs that end in *-ly*.

lentamente	*slowly*	**generalmente**	*generally*
verdaderamente	*truly, really*	**simplemente**	*simply*

▸ To form adverbs that end in **–mente**, add **–mente** to the feminine form of the adjective. If the adjective does not have a feminine form, just add **–mente** to the standard form.

ADJECTIVE	FEMININE FORM	SUFFIX	ADVERB
lento	lenta	-mente	lentamente
fabuloso	fabulosa	-mente	fabulosamente
enorme		-mente	enormemente
feliz		-mente	felizmente

▸ Adverbs that end in **–mente** generally follow the verb, while adverbs that modify an adjective or another adverb precede the word they modify.

Javier dibuja **maravillosamente**.	Inés está **casi siempre** ocupada.
Javier draws wonderfully.	*Inés is almost always busy.*

Common adverbs and adverbial expressions

a menudo	*often*	así	*like this; so*	menos	*less*
a tiempo	*on time*	bastante	*enough; quite*	muchas veces	*a lot; many times*
a veces	*sometimes*	casi	*almost*	poco	*little*
además (de)	*furthermore; besides*	con frecuencia	*frequently*	por lo menos	*at least*
apenas	*hardly; scarcely*	de vez en cuando	*from time to time*	pronto	*soon*

¡Manos a la obra!

Transforma los adjetivos en adverbios.

1. alegre _alegremente_
2. constante _____
3. gradual _____
4. perfecto _____
5. real _____
6. frecuente _____
7. tranquilo _____
8. regular _____
9. maravilloso _____
10. normal _____
11. básico _____
12. afortunado _____

Práctica

1 **En la clínica** Completa las oraciones con los adverbios adecuados.

1. La cita era a las nueve, pero llegamos _____ [de vez en cuando, nunca, tarde].

2. El problema fue que _____ [alegremente, ayer, así] se nos rompió el despertador.

3. La recepcionista no se enojó porque sabía que normalmente llegamos _____ [a veces, a tiempo, poco].

4. _____ [Por lo menos, Muchas veces, Poco] el doctor estaba listo.

5. _____ [Lentamente, Además, Apenas] tuvimos que esperar cinco minutos.

6. El doctor dijo que nuestra hija Irene necesitaba una operación _____ [casi, a veces, inmediatamente].

7. Cuando Irene salió de la operación, le preguntamos _____ [con frecuencia, nerviosamente, muchas veces] al doctor cómo estaba nuestra hija.

8. _____ [Bastante, Afortunadamente, A menudo], el médico nos contestó que Irene estaba bien.

2 **Oraciones** Combina palabras de las tres columnas para formar oraciones completas.

> **modelo**
>
> Mi mejor amigo se enferma frecuentemente.

Sujetos	Verbos	Adverbios
mi mejor amigo/a	caerse	bien
mi(s) padre(s)	casarse	fabulosamente
el/la profesor(a) de español	conducir	felizmente
yo	divertirse	mal
los jóvenes	enfermarse	frecuentemente
Donald Glover	estornudar	muchas veces
Jennifer López	ir	poco
las celebridades	levantarse	rápidamente
todos nosotros	llevarse	pronto
	vestirse	tarde
		temprano
		ya

Conversación

Communicative Goal
Identify adverbs in an ad

3 Preguntas Usa estas preguntas para entrevistar a un(a) compañero/a. ¿Tienen respuestas en común?

1. ¿Qué sabes hacer muy bien?
2. ¿Qué estudias además de español?
3. ¿Hay compañeros/as de clase a quienes apenas conoces?
4. ¿Qué gustos (*treats*) te das de vez en cuando?
5. ¿Cenas bastante en restaurantes?
6. ¿Te enfermas a menudo?
7. ¿Con qué frecuencia vas al doctor?
8. ¿Qué haces si te sientes congestionado/a y estornudas muchas veces?

4 ¿Con qué frecuencia? Averigua (*Find out*) con qué frecuencia tus compañeros/as hacen estas actividades. Comparte los resultados con la clase.

> **modelo** pasear en bicicleta

Estudiante 1: ¿Paseas en bicicleta con mucha frecuencia?
Estudiante 2: Sí, paseo en bicicleta con mucha frecuencia./No, casi nunca paseo en bicicleta.

Actividades	con mucha frecuencia	de vez en cuando	casi nunca	nunca
1. Nadar				
2. Jugar al tenis				
3. Hacer la tarea				
4. Salir a bailar				
5. Mirar la televisión				
6. Dormir en clase				
7. Perder las gafas				
8. Tomar medicina				
9. Ir al dentista				
10. Comer ensalada				

Español en vivo

No hay tiempo para el dolor de cabeza.

Si tienes prisa, o simplemente quieres que tu dolor de cabeza se vaya muy pronto, piensa en Aspirina. Se asimila mejor y actúa rápidamente. Ya no se puede perder tiempo por un dolor de cabeza.

1 Identificar Lee el anuncio e identifica los adverbios.

2 Preguntas Contesta las preguntas.

1. ¿Cuáles son las ventajas (*advantages*) de este medicamento?
2. ¿Qué tan a menudo te duele la cabeza? ¿Qué tomas cuando te duele la cabeza?
3. ¿Necesitas una receta del médico para comprar ese medicamento?

I CAN say how often I do things.

I CAN identify adverbs in an ad.

A repasar

10.1 The imperfect tense

1 **Cuando éramos niños...** Usa estas oraciones para contar los sucesos que le ocurrían a ti y a tus amigos cuando eran niños. Sigue el modelo.

> **modelo**
> Rosalinda (estar enferma) / su mamá (llevarla al doctor)
> *Cuando Rosalinda estaba enferma, su mamá la llevaba al doctor.*

1. Rosalinda (ir a la clínica) / ella (llorar (*cry*) mucho)
2. Gustavito (tener dolor de cabeza) / su abuela (no darle una aspirina)
3. Gustavito (tener temperatura alta) / él (sentirse mareado)
4. la enfermera (ponerle una inyección a Rosalinda) / ella (sentir mucho dolor)
5. Rosalinda y Gustavito (no tomarse las medicinas) / sus padres (enojarse)
6. nosotros (no hacer la tarea) / nuestros padres (no dejarnos ver la televisión)

2 **El doctor Rodríguez** Completa el párrafo con el imperfecto de los verbos **ir**, **ver** y **ser**.

Cuando nosotros (1) _____ niños, mi hermano y yo (2) _____ al doctor Rodríguez. Nosotros (3) _____ a su consultorio después de las clases. Mi madre (4) _____ con nosotros. El doctor Rodríguez (5) _____ muy simpático. El doctor y la enfermera (6) _____ muy amables con nosotros. ¿Ustedes (7) _____ al consultorio del doctor Rodríguez?

3 **El dentista** Describe a un(a) compañero/a cómo eran tus visitas al dentista cuando eras niño/a. Usa el imperfecto.

> **modelo**
> *Iba al dentista cuando me dolía alguna muela. Siempre había muchos pacientes en el consultorio del dentista.*

10.2 Constructions with se

4 **Oraciones** Forma oraciones con estos elementos. Usa **se** para sucesos imprevistos (*unplanned events*) y los verbos en pretérito.

> **modelo**
> A Cecilia / olvidar / la medicina en la farmacia.
> *A Cecilia se le olvidó la medicina en la farmacia.*

1. A ti / romper / el brazo y la pierna
2. A los enfermeros / dañar / las radiografías
3. Al paciente / perder / los antibióticos
4. A mí / quedar / la receta en el consultorio
5. A Hugo y a ti / caer / la bicicleta en los pies
6. A nosotros / olvidar / el teléfono del doctor Gómez

5 **El enfermero** La doctora Suárez tiene un enfermero nuevo. Escribe las preguntas que el enfermero le hace. Usa **se** y **cómo**, **dónde**, **cuándo**.

> **modelo**
> Vamos a tomar la temperatura del paciente.
> *¿Cómo se toma la temperatura del paciente?*

1. Vamos a poner una inyección.
   _____
2. Vamos a llevar a un enfermo a la sala de emergencia.
   _____
3. Vamos a sacar las radiografías.
   _____
4. Vamos a recetar dos medicamentos.
   _____
5. Vamos a hacer un examen médico.
   _____
6. Vamos a buscar un antibiótico nuevo.
   _____

6 **¿Qué se debe hacer?** Con un(a) compañero/a, escribe qué se debe hacer en estas situaciones. Después, comparte tus respuestas con la clase.

> **modelo**
> Para estar sanos
> *Se debe hacer ejercicio. No se debe fumar.*

1. Para curarse de un resfriado
2. Para relajarse
3. Para curarse de la gripe
4. Para tener dientes sanos
5. Para ser saludable
6. Para ser médico/a

10.3 Adverbs

7 **¡Tristemente!** Escribe seis oraciones para describir lo que le pasó a Héctor. Usa los adverbios necesarios.

> **modelo**
> Héctor paseaba felizmente
> en su bicicleta.

1.

2.

3.

8 **Consejos** Tu amiga Elsa está embarazada. En grupos de tres, escriban consejos para Elsa usando los adverbios adecuados.

además (de)	a veces	poco
a menudo	con frecuencia	por lo menos
así	muchas veces	pronto

> **modelo**
> Debes caminar por lo menos durante
> media hora cada día.
> Si te sientes mal, debes ir pronto
> al doctor.

Síntesis

9 **La primera vez** Cuéntale a un(a) compañero/a cómo fue la primera vez que te pusieron una inyección, te rompiste un hueso, pasaste la noche en un hospital, estuviste mareado/a, etc. Incluye estos puntos en la conversación.

- una descripción del tiempo que hacía
- cuántos años tenías
- qué pasó
- cómo te sentías

Communicative Goal
Create an ad campaign for an organization

Video

Videoclip

1 **Preparación** ¿Conoces alguna ONG (organización no gubernamental)? ¿Cuál? ¿Qué cosas se hacen en esa organización para ayudar a los demás?

2 **El clip** Mira el anuncio de la **Asociación Parkinson Alicante** de España.

Vocabulario	
aullar *to howl*	manada *pack (of wolves)*
hombre lobo *werewolf*	subvenciones *subsidies*

Queremos que la gente conozca la asociación y nos ayude en esta lucha°.

lucha *fight*

3 **Escoger** Elige la opción correcta.

1. Las _____ a la asociación estaban fallando.
   a. subvenciones   b. peticiones

2. La asociación decidió inventar una _____ para el Parkinson.
   a. pastilla   b. causa

3. Michael J. Fox hizo el papel de un _____ y tiene Parkinson.
   a. hombre lobo   b. hombre araña

4. La forma para llegar a todo el mundo es _____ lo más fuerte (*loud*) posible.
   a. cantar   b. aullar

4 **Una campaña** Con un(a) compañero/a, crea una campaña para transformar una organización, real o ficticia. Luego, compartan su campaña con el resto de la clase.

I CAN create an ad campaign for an organization.

Ampliación

Communicative Goals
Understand a
conversation by
listening for specific
information, and
discuss medical
conditions and
symptoms

1 Escuchar

A Escucha la conversación de la señorita Méndez y Carlos Peña. Marca las oraciones donde se mencionan los síntomas de Carlos.

> **TIP** **Listen for specific information.** Identify the subject of a conversation and use your background knowledge to predict what kinds of information you might hear. For example, what would you expect to hear in a conversation between a sick person and a doctor's receptionist?

_____ 1. Tiene infección en los ojos.

_____ 2. Se lastimó el dedo.

_____ 3. Tiene tos.

_____ 4. Está congestionado.

_____ 5. Está mareado.

_____ 6. Le duele la cabeza.

_____ 7. Le duele el estómago.

_____ 8. No puede dormir.

_____ 9. Es alérgico a la aspirina.

_____ 10. Le duele la garganta.

_____ 11. Tiene frío.

_____ 12. Se rompió la pierna.

_____ 13. Le duele la rodilla.

_____ 14. Siente dolor en los huesos.

B En tu opinión, ¿qué tiene Carlos? ¿Gripe? ¿Un resfriado? ¿Alergia? Explica tu opinión.

2 Conversar

Con un(a) compañero/a, representa una conversación entre un(a) estudiante hipocondríaco/a y un(a) enfermero/a.

> • Decidan qué síntomas tiene el/la estudiante y con qué frecuencia los tiene.
>
> • Decidan qué preguntas le va a hacer el/la enfermero/a. Por ejemplo: ¿Cuánto tiempo hace que comenzaron los síntomas? ¿Tenía el mismo problema cuando era niño/a? ¿Lo tenía la semana pasada?
>
> • Decidan qué consejos le va a dar el/la enfermero/a.

I CAN understand a conversation by listening for specific information.

I CAN discuss medical conditions and symptoms.

Ampliación

3 Escribir

Imagina que eres enfermero/a en la sala de emergencias de un hospital. Tienes que escribir cada día un parte (*report*) médico para tu supervisor(a).

> **TIP** **Avoid redundancies.** To avoid repetition of verbs and nouns, consult a Spanish-language thesaurus. You can also use direct object pronouns, possessive adjectives, demonstrative adjectives and pronouns, and prepositional pronouns to streamline your writing.

Susana se lastimó la rodilla ayer. ~~Susana~~ Ella estaba corriendo por el parque cuando se cayó y se lastimó la ~~la~~ rodilla.

Communicative Goals
Write a medical report, and create a presentation about the health system of a Spanish-speaking country

Organizar	Utiliza un mapa de ideas para organizar tu parte médico. Incluye información sobre los pacientes, sus síntomas y el resultado de los tratamientos.
Escribir	Utiliza tus apuntes para escribir el primer borrador del parte médico.
Corregir	Intercambia tu composición con un(a) compañero/a. Lee su borrador y anota los aspectos mejor escritos (*written*). Ofrécele sugerencias para evitar (*avoid*) redundancias, y si ves algunos errores gramaticales u ortográficos, coméntaselos.
Compartir	Revisa el primer borrador según las indicaciones de tu compañero/a. Incorpora nuevas ideas o más información si es necesario antes de escribir la versión final del parte médico.

4 Un paso más

Prepara una presentación sobre el sistema de servicios médicos de un país hispano. Tu presentación debe contestar estas preguntas.

- ¿Qué servicios médicos públicos hay en el país?
- ¿Cuál es el papel (*role*) de las clínicas y los hospitales privados?
- ¿Cómo son los servicios médicos en las ciudades y en las áreas rurales?
- ¿Son populares los tratamientos alternativos?
- ¿Hay personas reconocidas por sus contribuciones a la medicina?

5 Cultura

Estás en un país hispano y te lastimas o te enfermas. ¿Qué haces? ¿Adónde vas? ¿A la farmacia? ¿A la sala de emergencias?

I CAN write a medical report.

I CAN create a presentation about the health system of a Spanish-speaking country.

Audio: Reading

Antes de leer

Using what you already know about a particular subject will often help you better understand a reading selection.

TIP **Activate background knowledge.** Think about what you already know. For example, if you read an article about a recent medical discovery, you might think about what you already know about health in order to understand unfamiliar words or concepts.

Examinar el texto

1. A primera vista, ¿cuál es el tema de esta lectura?

_____

_____

2. ¿Qué tipo de documento es? ¿Cómo lo sabes?

_____

_____

3. Basándote en documentos similares que conoces, ¿qué tipo de información esperas encontrar en esta lectura?

_____

_____

El consultorio

Usuario [_____]   Contraseña [_____]

Soy una madre española y le escribo para hacerle una consulta sobre mi hijo. Tiene ocho años y hace una semana que ni come ni duerme bien. Además, desde hace cuatro días° tose constantemente. Al no consumir la cantidad de alimentos° necesarios ni dormir lo suficiente, mi hijo no tiene energía para realizar sus actividades diarias. Estoy un poco preocupada porque es la primera vez que el niño presenta este tipo de síntomas. Todavía no hemos ido° al médico porque me interesa conocer primero su punto de vista°. Muchísimas gracias por su ayuda.

Querida° madre española: Gracias por escribir en mi columna. Cuando un niño de la edad de su hijo presenta este tipo de síntomas, puede ser señal° de que tiene una pequeña infección en las vías° respiratorias, producida por una bacteria o por un virus. Creo que debe llevar pronto a su hijo al consultorio de su médico para evitar° la aparición de una enfermedad crónica como la bronquitis. Si tiene alguna pregunta más o si desea contarme cómo evoluciona su hijo, ya sabe que puede escribirme otra vez.

Hola, doctora. Soy un ciclista profesional de Colombia. Hace dos semanas° tuve un accidente con mi bicicleta y me lastimé la rodilla. Fui a la sala de emergencias y el médico me hizo una radiografía para ver si tenía un hueso roto°. Afortunadamente, los resultados de la radiografía fueron muy buenos y sólo me recetaron unas pastillas y mucho reposo. Le escribo porque, después de este tiempo, sigo sintiendo dolor en la zona de la rodilla. ¿Qué puedo hacer?

www.elconsultorio.com

10:00 ▶ ⚡🔋

Dra. Fernanda Jiménez Ocaña

Querido amigo ciclista: Creo que, en su caso, necesita tener más paciencia. Hay que° comprender que algunas veces el cuerpo requiere más tiempo para recuperarse. Pienso que tiene que esperar dos semanas más para ver si el dolor va desapareciendo o no. Si sigue las indicaciones de su médico y no nota ningún cambio, debe volver al hospital. En mi opinión, no debe hacer ningún movimiento con la pierna y debe seguir tomándose las pastillas que le recetaron.

Le escribo desde Puerto Rico para pedirle su opinión. Desde hace un mes tengo los síntomas de un resfriado que no desaparece nunca. Toso, estoy congestionado y tengo la garganta y los ojos irritados. Mi novia opina que puedo ser alérgico a algo. ¿Cree usted que eso es posible?

Estimado° amigo puertorriqueño: Debe empezar por observar dónde y cuándo aparecen sus síntomas. El otoño y la primavera son las épocas del año en que suele haber° más reacciones alérgicas del tipo que usted presenta. Creo que debe ir al médico y esperar los resultados de las pruebas. Si le diagnostican un tipo de alergia, no debe preocuparse. En la actualidad, existen tratamientos excelentes, incluyendo antihistamínicos e inyecciones que calman los efectos de las reacciones alérgicas y lo ayudan a llevar una vida normal.

¡Salud! *Dra. Fernanda Jiménez Ocaña*

Después de leer

¿Comprendiste?

Indica si cada oración es **cierta** o **falsa**. Corrige las oraciones falsas.

Cierto	Falso	
_____	_____	1. La madre española no come bien.
_____	_____	2. La doctora piensa que el hijo de la española puede tener una infección.
_____	_____	3. La doctora piensa que el ciclista debe practicar más el ciclismo.
_____	_____	4. La radiografía indica que el ciclista colombiano tiene algunos huesos rotos.
_____	_____	5. La doctora cree que el chico puertorriqueño puede tener alergias.
_____	_____	6. Hace un mes que el puertorriqueño tiene los síntomas de un resfriado.

Preguntas

Responde estas preguntas con oraciones completas.

1. ¿Con qué frecuencia tose el hijo de la madre española?
2. ¿Por qué fue a la sala de emergencias el colombiano?
3. ¿Qué debe hacer la madre española?
4. ¿Qué hizo el médico cuando el ciclista fue a la sala de emergencias?
5. ¿Por qué debe ser paciente el ciclista?
6. Según (*According to*) la doctora, ¿cuándo ocurren más frecuentemente las reacciones alérgicas?

Coméntalo

¿Conoces alguna columna de consejos médicos en Internet? ¿La lees frecuentemente? ¿Por qué sí o por qué no? Imagina que tú escribes las respuestas de esta columna, ¿qué deben hacer las tres personas que pidieron consejos?

I CAN use my background knowledge to understand a text.

desde hace cuatro días *for four days* **alimentos** *foods* **hemos ido** *have been* **punto de vista** *point of view* **Querido/a** *Dear* **señal** *sign* **vías** *passages* **evitar** *avoid* **Hace dos semanas** *Two weeks ago* **roto** *broken* **Hay que** *It is necessary to* **Estimado/a** *Dear* **suele haber** *there tend to be*

Vocabulary Tools

El cuerpo

la boca *mouth*
el brazo *arm*
la cabeza *head*
el corazón *heart*
el cuello *neck*
el cuerpo *body*
el dedo *finger*
el estómago *stomach*
la garganta *throat*
el hueso *bone*
la nariz *nose*
el ojo *eye*
la oreja *(outer) ear*
el pie *foot*
la pierna *leg*
la rodilla *knee*
el tobillo *ankle*

Las enfermedades y los síntomas

el dolor (de cabeza) *(head)ache; pain*
la enfermedad *illness*
la gripe *flu*
la infección *infection*
el resfriado *cold*
el síntoma *symptom*
la tos *cough*

———

congestionado/a *congested*
mareado/a *dizzy; nauseated*

Verbos

caer *to fall, to drop*
caerse *to fall*
dañar *to damage; to break down*
doler (o:ue) *to hurt*
enfermarse *to get sick*
estar enfermo/a *to be sick*
estornudar *to sneeze*
lastimarse (el pie) *to injure (one's foot)*
olvidar *to forget*
perder (e:ie) *to lose*
poner una inyección *to give an injection*
prohibir *to prohibit*
quedar *to be left behind*
recetar *to prescribe*
romper *to break*
romperse (la pierna) *to break (one's leg)*
sacar(se) una muela *to have a tooth pulled*
ser alérgico/a (a) *to be allergic (to)*
tener fiebre (f.) *to have a fever*
tomar(le) la temperatura (a alguien) *to take (someone's) temperature*
torcerse (o:ue) (el tobillo) *to sprain (one's ankle)*
toser *to cough*

La salud

el accidente *accident*
la clínica *clinic*
el consultorio *doctor's office*
el/la dentista *dentist*
el/la doctor(a) *doctor*
el/la enfermero/a *nurse*
el examen médico *physical exam*
la farmacia *pharmacy*
el hospital *hospital*
la operación *operation*
el/la paciente *patient*
la radiografía *X-ray*
la sala de emergencia(s) *emergency room*
la salud *health*

Los medicamentos

el antibiótico *antibiotic*
la aspirina *aspirin*
el medicamento *medication*
la medicina *medicine*
las pastillas *pills*
la receta *prescription*

Adjetivos

embarazada *pregnant*
grave *grave; serious*
médico/a *medical*
saludable *healthy*
sano/a *healthy*

Otras palabras y expresiones

de niño/a *as a child*
mientras *while*
todos los días *every day*

Adverbs *See page 266.*

∞ Communicative Goals: Review

I CAN talk about health.
• Say how you feel today.

I CAN discuss medical conditions and symptoms.
• Describe your last injury or illness to a partner.

I CAN describe the past.
• Talk about something you used to do as a child.

I CAN investigate health systems in the Spanish-speaking world.
• Describe the health system of a Spanish-speaking country.

AVENTURAS
EN LOS
PAÍSES
HISPANOS

Un *snowboarder* salta *(jumps)* en el centro de esquí Portillo, uno de los más famosos y antiguos *(old)* de Chile. El esquí y el *snowboard* se pueden practicar en las montañas nevadas *(snow-capped)* de la cordillera de los Andes, que se extiende por todo el país. Gente de todo el mundo va a Chile a practicar los deportes de invierno.

¿Te gustaría esquiar en Chile?

SURAMÉRICA II

Argentina

Área: 2.780.400 km^2
(1.074.000 millas^2)
Población: 44.800.000
Capital: Buenos Aires –
15.057.000
Ciudades principales: Córdoba, Rosario, Mendoza
Moneda: peso argentino

Chile

Área: 756.100 km^2
(292.000 millas^2)
Población: 19.000.000
Capital: Santiago de Chile –
6.724.000
Ciudades principales: Valparaíso, Concepción, Viña del Mar, Temuco
Moneda: peso chileno

Uruguay

Área: 176.220 km^2
(68.039 millas^2)
Población: 3.500.000
Capital: Montevideo – 1.745.000
Ciudades principales: Salto, Paysandú, Las Piedras, Rivera
Moneda: peso uruguayo

Paraguay

Área: 406.750 km^2
(157.046 millas^2)
Población: 7.000.000
Capital: Asunción – 3.279.000
Ciudades principales: Ciudad del Este, San Lorenzo, Lambaré, Fernando de la Mora
Moneda: guaraní

Bolivia

Área: 1.098.580 km^2
(424.171 millas^2)
Población: 11.500.000
Capital: La Paz, sede del gobierno *(seat of government)*, capital administrativa – 1.835.000;
Sucre, capital constitucional y judicial
Ciudades principales: Santa Cruz de la Sierra, Cochabamba, Oruro, Potosí
Moneda: peso boliviano

Artes

El tango argentino ▶

El tango es un símbolo cultural muy importante de Argentina. Este género *(genre)* musical es una mezcla de ritmos de origen africano, italiano y español, y surgió a finales del siglo XIX entre los porteños *(people of Buenos Aires)*. Poco después se hizo popular entre el resto de los argentinos y su fama llegó hasta París. Como baile, el tango en un principio *(at first)* era provocativo y violento, pero se hizo más romántico durante los años treinta. Hoy en día, este estilo musical es popular en muchas partes del mundo *(world)*.

¿Sabes bailar tango? ¿Te gusta ese tipo de baile? ¿Por qué?

Lugares

El lago Titicaca ▶

Situado en los Andes de Bolivia y Perú, éste es el lago navegable más alto del mundo, a una altitud de 3.812 metros (12.506 pies). Con un área de más de 8.000 kilómetros² (3.000 millas²), también es el segundo lago más grande de Suramérica, después del lago de Maracaibo en Venezuela. La mitología inca cuenta que los hijos del dios *(god)* Sol emergieron de las profundas aguas del lago Titicaca para fundar su imperio *(empire)*.

¿Qué otros lagos navegables conoces? ¿Cuál te gustaría visitar?

PERÚ

Océano Pacífico

BOLIVIA

⭐ La Paz

Arica

⭐ Sucre

Iquique

Antofagasta

Salta

CHILE

Córdoba

Valparaíso ⭐ Mendoza

Santiago

ARGENTINA

Concepción

Cordillera de los Andes

Puerto Montt

Estrecho de Magallanes

Punta Arenas · Tierra del Fuego

BRASIL

Costumbres

La carne y el mate ▷

En Chile, Uruguay y Argentina, la carne de res es un elemento esencial de la dieta diaria. Los platos más representativos de estas naciones son el asado *(barbecue)* y la parrillada *(grilled meat)*.

El mate, una infusión similar al té, también es típico de la región. Esta bebida de origen indígena se bebe a diario y reemplaza al café. Tradicionalmente se toma en una calabaza *(gourd)* con una bombilla *(straw)* de metal.

¿Probaste alguna vez el mate? ¿Te gustaría probarlo? ¿Qué otras comidas y bebidas típicas de estos países conoces?

PARAGUAY

⭐ Asunción

Río Paraná

Naturaleza

Los ríos Paraguay y Paraná

Los ríos Paraguay y Paraná sirven de frontera *(border)* natural entre Argentina y Paraguay, y son las principales rutas de transporte de este último *(last)* país. El río Paraguay divide el Gran Chaco de la meseta *(plateau)* Paraná, donde vive la mayoría de los paraguayos. El Paraná tiene unos 3.200 kilómetros navegables, y por esta ruta pasan barcos de más de 5.000 toneladas, los cuales viajan desde el estuario *(estuary)* del Río de la Plata hasta la ciudad de Asunción. El río Paraná confluye *(meets)* con el río Iguazú en la frontera entre Brasil, Argentina y Paraguay. Allí forman las cataratas *(waterfalls)* del Iguazú, uno de los sitios turísticos más visitados en Suramérica. Estas extensas cataratas miden unos 70 metros (230 pies) de altura *(height)*.

¿Qué otras cataratas conoces? ¿Qué río(s) afecta(n)?

URUGUAY

• Rosario   ⭐ Montevideo
⭐
Buenos
Aires

Música ♪

La música andina

La música andina incluye numerosos estilos musicales típicos de las culturas indígenas de los Andes. Los ritmos actuales de la música andina tienen influencias españolas y africanas. Varios tipos de flauta *(flute)*, entre ellos la quena y la zampoña, caracterizan esta música. Algunos de los grupos de música andina más importantes son Los Kjarkas (Bolivia), Illapu (Chile), Los Chaskis (Argentina), Inti-Illimani (Chile) y Chila Jatun (Bolivia).

¿Conoces la música andina? ¿Te gusta?

Islas
Malvinas

¿Qué aprendiste?

1 **¿Cierto o falso?** Decide si lo que dicen las oraciones es **cierto** o **falso**.

	Cierto	Falso
1. Viña del Mar y Concepción son dos de las ciudades principales de Chile.	_____	_____
2. Asunción es la capital de Uruguay.	_____	_____
3. El tango es uno de los símbolos culturales más importantes de Argentina.	_____	_____
4. El lago Titicaca es el más bajo del mundo.	_____	_____
5. La carne de res forma parte de la dieta diaria de Argentina y de Uruguay.	_____	_____
6. El mate es una bebida similar al té.	_____	_____
7. En la meseta Paraná vive muy poca gente.	_____	_____
8. Las cataratas del Iguazú están en la frontera entre Brasil, Paraguay y Argentina.	_____	_____

2 **Preguntas** Contesta las preguntas.

1. ¿Qué es Portillo?
2. ¿Cómo era el tango en un principio?
3. ¿Dónde está el lago Titicaca?
4. ¿Qué país tiene dos capitales?
5. ¿Cuál es la moneda de Paraguay?
6. ¿Qué es Inti-Illimani?

3 **¿Qué piensas?** Responde a estas preguntas.

1. ¿Por qué crees que hay una mezcla de influencias culturales en el tango y en la música andina?
2. ¿Por qué piensas que el tango y la música andina son tan populares?
3. ¿Qué piensas que dice el tango sobre la cultura de Argentina?
4. ¿Por qué crees que el lago Titicaca era importante en la mitología inca?

4 **Comparación** Haz una de estas comparaciones.

- el mate y otra bebida
- el tango y la música andina
- el tango y otro baile

I CAN identify basic facts about the geography and culture of Argentina, Chile, Uruguay, Paraguay, and Bolivia by reading short informational texts with visuals.

11 El carro y la tecnología

Communicative Goals
You will learn how to:
- talk about cars
- describe your use of technology
- talk about the past
- investigate technology use in the Spanish-speaking world

PREPARACIÓN

pages 280–285
- Cars and driving
- Technology and the Internet
- Written accents with homophones

AVENTURAS

pages 286–287
- Manuel has just bought a car. He and Valentina, Juanjo, and Sara take it for a spin.

CULTURA

pages 288–289
- *Las redes sociales*
- Flash cultura: *Maravillas de la tecnología*

GRAMÁTICA

pages 290–299
- The preterite and the imperfect
- **Por** and **para**
- Stressed possessive adjectives and pronouns

LECTURA

pages 300–301
- Comic strip: *El celular*

PARA EMPEZAR

- ¿Está feliz o triste la persona de la foto?
- ¿Qué está mostrando?
- ¿De qué color es?
- ¿Qué tiempo hace?

Communicative Goal
Talk about cars and technology

EL CARRO Y LA TECNOLOGÍA

LAS PARTES DEL CARRO

el carro *car*
el coche *car*
los frenos *brakes*

el semáforo

el parabrisas
el baúl
el volante
el capó
el motor
la llanta

la licencia de conducir

EN LA CALLE

la calle *street*
el camino *route*
el garaje
    garage; (mechanic's) repair shop
la gasolina *gasoline*
la gasolinera *gas station*
el kilómetro *kilometer*
el/la mecánico/a *mechanic*
la milla *mile*
la multa *fine; ticket*
el policía/la mujer policía *police officer*
la policía *police (force)*
el taller (mecánico)
    (mechanic's) repair shop
el tráfico *traffic*
la velocidad máxima *speed limit*

arrancar *to start*
arreglar *to fix; to arrange*
bajar *to go down*
bajar(se) de *to get out of (a vehicle)*
chocar (con) *to run into; to crash into*
conducir *to drive*
estacionar *to park*
llenar (el tanque) *to fill (the tank)*
manejar *to drive*
parar *to stop*
revisar (el aceite) *to check (the oil)*
subir *to go up*
subir(se) a *to get into (a vehicle)*

Vocabulary Tools

INTERNET Y LA COMPUTADORA

el archivo *file*

la computadora portátil *laptop*

la conexión inalámbrica *wireless (connection)*

Internet *Internet*

la página principal *home page*

el programa de computación *software*

la red *network; Web*

el sitio web *website*

la tableta *tablet (computer)*

---

cargar *to charge; to upload*

chatear *to chat*

conectarse a Internet *to get connected to the Internet*

descargar *to download*

escanear *to scan*

guardar *to save*

imprimir *to print*

la calculadora

el televisor

la computadora

la pantalla

la impresora

el teclado

el ratón

LA TECNOLOGÍA

la aplicación *app*

el buzón de voz *voicemail*

el cargador *charger*

el control remoto *remote control*

el mensaje de texto *text message*

el navegador GPS *GPS*

el puerto USB *USB port*

el radio *radio (set)*

el teléfono celular *cell phone*

---

apagar *to turn off*

funcionar *to work*

grabar *to record*

llamar *to call*

poner *to turn on*

prender *to turn on*

sonar (o:ue) *to ring*

textear *to text*

ADJETIVOS

descompuesto/a *not working; out of order*

lento/a *slow*

lleno/a *full*

la cámara digital

ASÍ SE DICE

el baúl ⟷ la cajuela (*Méx.*), la maletera (*Perú*)
la computadora ⟷ el ordenador (*Esp.*)
la gasolinera ⟷ la bencinera (*Chile*)
el radio ⟷ la radio (*Esp., Cono Sur*)
el teléfono celular ⟷ el móvil (*Esp.*)

A escuchar

1 **¿Lógico o ilógico?** Indica si las situaciones que vas a escuchar son **lógicas** o **ilógicas**.

	Lógico	Ilógico
1.	_____	_____
2.	_____	_____
3.	_____	_____
4.	_____	_____
5.	_____	_____
6.	_____	_____
7.	_____	_____
8.	_____	_____

2 **En una gasolinera** Escucha la conversación entre un joven y el empleado de una gasolinera. Después, completa las oraciones.

1. El empleado de la gasolinera llena el tanque, revisa el aceite y
   a. estaciona el carro.　　b. limpia el parabrisas.　　c. usa el navegador.

2. La próxima semana el joven tiene que
   a. manejar hasta Córdoba.　　b. llenar el tanque.　　c. revisar las llantas.

3. El joven va a volver mañana porque el empleado
   a. va a llenar el tanque.　　b. va a revisar los frenos.　　c. va a darle una multa.

4. Para revisar los frenos, el empleado necesita
   a. un par de minutos.　　b. un par de días.　　c. un par de horas.

5. Hoy el joven va
   a. a Córdoba.　　b. a las montañas.　　c. a la playa.

6. La gasolina cuesta
   a. 22 pesos.　　b. 32 pesos.　　c. 24 pesos.

A practicar

3 **Problemas con la computadora** Completa la conversación.

el archivo	la impresora	la pantalla
arreglar	imprimir	prendiste
descompuesto	llamar	el ratón
funciona	llenar	el teléfono celular

JUAN CARLOS Mariana, la computadora no (1) _____. No veo nada en (2) _____.

MARIANA Pues, ¿la (3) _____?

JUAN CARLOS Ah sí, tienes razón; no estaba prendida. Mariana, ahora no puedo conectarme a Internet. Parece que el sistema de conexión inalámbrica está (4) _____. ¿Sabes cómo lo puedo (5) _____?

MARIANA ¡Ay, mi amor! Si (*If*) quieres, puedo (6) _____ a la compañía de Internet para ver qué pasa. Mientras tanto, creo que es mejor que uses (7) _____ para conectarte.

JUAN CARLOS Sí, gracias… Bueno, ahora sí estoy conectado. Voy a (8) _____ el trabajo para mi clase de historia… Pero... ¡Mariana! ¿dónde está (9) _____?

MARIANA Lo siento, ésa sí que está descompuesta. Pablo la está arreglando. No sé cómo vas a imprimir tu trabajo ahora.

JUAN CARLOS No te preocupes. Voy a guardar (10) _____ para imprimirlo en la universidad.

MARIANA ¡Qué buena idea!

4 **Oraciones** Escribe oraciones usando los siguientes elementos. Usa el pretérito y añade (*add*) las palabras necesarias.

> **modelo** Juan Diego / guardar / archivo / su / computadora
> *Juan Diego guardó el archivo en su computadora.*

1. Jaime / comprar / televisor / nuevo

   _____

2. Yo / apagar / radio / diez / noche

   _____

3. teléfono / sonar / pero / yo / no contestar

   _____

4. Luis y yo / ir / gasolinera / para / llenar / tanque

   _____

5. Sandra / perder / tableta

   _____

6. Marisa / poner / su / maletas / baúl

   _____

A conversar

5 **Preguntas** Con un(a) compañero/a, contesta las preguntas. Después, comparte las respuestas con la clase.

1. ¿Tienes carro? ¿Cómo es? ¿Para qué lo usas?

2. ¿Siempre paras cuando ves la luz amarilla del semáforo? ¿Manejas rápidamente? ¿A veces excedes la velocidad máxima?

3. ¿Cuáles de estas actividades haces tú normalmente: llenar el tanque, limpiar el parabrisas, lavar el coche, revisar el aceite, cambiar el aceite, revisar las llantas?

4. ¿Cómo miras tus programas favoritos?

5. ¿Cómo escuchas música: por radio, por teléfono celular o en Internet?

6. ¿Cómo te comunicas más: llamas por teléfono, escribes mensajes electrónicos, texteas o chateas? ¿Cuáles son las ventajas (*advantages*) y desventajas de los diferentes modos de comunicación?

7. ¿Cómo usas la tecnología para divertirte? ¿Y para comunicarte? ¿Y para trabajar?

6 **En el taller** Con un(a) compañero/a, representa una conversación entre un(a) mecánico/a y un(a) cliente/a cuyo (*whose*) coche se dañó en un accidente. El/La cliente/a le dice al/a la mecánico/a qué ocurrió en el accidente y los dos hablan de las partes dañadas.

7 **Situación** Con un(a) compañero/a de clase, elige un(a) cliente/a de la lista y representa una conversación entre el/la director(a) de ventas (*sales*) de una tienda de computadoras y esta persona. El/La director(a) de ventas pregunta lo que el/la cliente/a desea hacer con la computadora y le muestra la computadora que éste/a necesita.

- El padre o la madre de un niño de seis años
- Una jubilada (retired woman) que quiere aprender a conectarse a Internet
- Una mujer que va a crear una nueva empresa (business) en su casa
- Un estudiante que no sabe nada de computadoras
- Un hombre de negocios (businessman) que viaja mucho
- Un programador que necesita comprar una computadora buena y rápida

I CAN talk about cars and technology.

I CAN interact at a survival level in some familiar everyday contexts.

Ortografía

 Tutorial

La acentuación de palabras similares

Although accent marks usually indicate which syllable in a word is stressed, they are also used to distinguish between words that have the same or similar spellings.

· ·

Él maneja el coche.   **Sí, voy si quieres.**

Although one-syllable words do not usually carry written accents, some *do* have accent marks to distinguish them from words that have the same spelling but different meanings.

· ·

Sé cocinar.   **Se baña.**   **¿Tomas té?**   **Te duermes.**

Sé (*I know*) and **té** (*tea*) have accent marks to distinguish them from the pronouns **se** and **te**.

· ·

para mí   **mi cámara**   **Tú lees.**   **tu estéreo**

Mí (*me*) and **tú** (*you*) have accent marks to distinguish them from the possessive pronouns **mi** and **tu**.

· ·

¿Por qué vas?   **Voy porque quiero.**

Several words of more than one syllable also have accent marks to distinguish them from words that have the same or similar spellings.

· ·

Éste es rápido.   **Este tren es rápido.**

Demonstrative pronouns may have accent marks to distinguish them from demonstrative adjectives.

· ·

¿Cuándo fuiste?   **Fui cuando me llamó.**

¿Dónde trabajas?   **Voy al taller donde trabajo.**

Adverbs have accent marks when they are used to convey a question.

· ·

Práctica Marca los acentos en las palabras que los necesitan.

ANA Hola, soy Ana. ¿Que tal?
JUAN Hola, pero… ¿por que me llamas tan tarde?
ANA Porque mañana tienes que llevarme a la universidad. Mi auto esta dañado.
JUAN ¿Como se daño?
ANA Se daño el sabado. Un vecino (*neighbor*) choco con el.

Crucigrama Utiliza las siguientes pistas (*clues*) para completar el crucigrama. ¡Ojo con los acentos!

Horizontales
1. Él _____ levanta.
4. No voy _____ no puedo.
7. Tú _____ acuestas.
9. ¿ _____ es el examen?
10. Quiero este video y _____.

Verticales
2. ¿Cómo _____ usted?
3. Eres _____ mi hermano.
5. ¿ _____ tal?
6. Me gusta _____ suéter.
8. Pongo las maletas _____ el baúl.

Un carro... ¿nuevo?

Manuel acaba de comprar un coche.

 Video

Antes de ver

Mira los pies de foto (*captions*) y haz una lista de los cognados.

PERSONAJES

SARA

JUANJO

MANUEL

VALENTINA

POLICÍA

SARA ¡Chicos! ¡Ahí viene!

JUANJO ¡¿Ése es el carro que se compró Manuel?!

MANUEL ¿Qué te parece?

SARA ¡Éste es!

VALENTINA Manuel, ¿no tiene puerto USB para cargar el móvil?

JUANJO Es un carro viejo, Valentina. No tiene puerto USB, ni navegador GPS.

VALENTINA Por lo menos tiene radio, ¿no?

MANUEL No funciona.

SARA ¿Qué te parece el coche de Manuel?

VALENTINA Aunque no es muy moderno, y no tiene nada de tecnología, es bonito.

JUANJO ¿Damos un paseo para probarlo?

SARA Ten cuidado. ¡Vas muy rápido!

VALENTINA ¡No estamos en la autopista, Manuel!

MANUEL ¡Sé conducir!

VALENTINA ¡Vamos a chocar!

JUANJO ¡Nos va a parar la policía!

A C T I V I D A D E S

1 **¿Cierto o falso?** Indica si lo que dicen estas oraciones es **cierto** o **falso**. Corrige las oraciones falsas.

	Cierto	Falso
1. Manuel se compró un coche moderno.	○	○
2. El radio del carro no funciona.	○	○
3. Manuel tiene problemas con la policía porque olvidó su licencia de conducir.	○	○
4. Manuel tiene que pagar una multa.	○	○
5. Al final, el coche arranca sin problemas.	○	○

2 **Preguntas** Answer the questions.

1. ¿Cómo es el coche que se compró Manuel?
2. ¿Qué cosas no tiene el coche?
3. ¿Es posible escuchar música en el coche? ¿Por qué?
4. ¿Cómo se sienten los pasajeros mientras Manuel conduce?
5. ¿Cómo se puede pagar la multa?

POLICÍA Buenas tardes.

MANUEL ¿Cómo le va?

POLICÍA Su licencia de conducir, por favor.

MANUEL ¿Por qué nos paró, señor policía?

POLICÍA Por sobrepasar la velocidad máxima. Iba a cincuenta y cinco kilómetros por hora y la velocidad permitida es cincuenta.

MANUEL ¡¿En serio?! (*a los chicos*) ¡La culpa es vuestra! ¡Os lo dije! ¡Nos van a parar por ir tan rápido!

POLICÍA ¿De quién es el coche?

MANUEL Mío, acabo de comprarlo. Lo estábamos probando y ellos pidieron ir más rápido.

POLICÍA Tiene veinte días para pagar la multa. Puede pasar por la oficina de tráfico o hacerlo por teléfono o Internet. Buenas tardes.

MANUEL Gracias.

MANUEL Pagamos la multa entre todos, ¿no? Son cien euros. Los amigos se ayudan.

VALENTINA Nos ayudamos, Manuel, ¡pero la multa es tuya!

MANUEL ¡La próxima vez os vais a pasear en taxi!

Expresiones útiles

aunque *although*
la autopista *highway*
ayudarse *to help each other*
la culpa *blame; fault*
dar un paseo *to go for a ride*
empujar *to push*
sobrepasar *to exceed*

———

el asiento delantero *front seat*
el asiento trasero *back seat*
el cinturón de seguridad *seat belt*
la sirena *siren*

Puerta de Alcalá

La Puerta de Alcalá está en la Plaza de la Independencia en Madrid. Este monumento neoclásico se inauguró en 1778. Se inspiró en los arcos triunfales romanos. Cada lado del monumento tiene un diseño distinto.

¿Hay un monumento famoso en tu ciudad o pueblo? ¿Cómo es?

---

3 Preguntas personales En parejas, túrnense para hacerse estas preguntas. ¿Tienen respuestas en común?

1. ¿Qué piensas del coche de Manuel?
2. ¿Te gustan los coches con toda la tecnología? ¿Por qué?
3. ¿Qué marca (*brand*) de coche es tu favorita? ¿Por qué?
4. ¿Prefieres conducir o ser pasajero/a? ¿Por qué?
5. ¿Con qué frecuencia usas tu teléfono celular?
6. ¿Te gusta grabar videos y ponerlos en Internet? ¿Por qué?

I CAN ask and answer questions about cars and technology.

Communicative Goal
Compare the use of social networks in my community
with their use in the Spanish-speaking world

Las **redes sociales**

¿Cómo te comunicas con tu familia y con tus amigos? Al igual que° en los Estados Unidos, en los países hispanohablantes las redes sociales han tenido° un gran impacto en los últimos años. Los usos básicos de los teléfonos celulares ya no son las llamadas°, sino el contacto entre amigos y parientes por medio de° redes sociales y de aplicaciones como Facebook, Twitter, WhatsApp, Instagram o Snapchat.

Mensajes de texto en español

Al igual que otros idiomas, el chateo está cambiando la forma en que la gente escribe el español. Ésta es una lista de expresiones comunes al chatear.

¿K TL?	¿Qué tal?	CONT, XFA	Contesta, por favor.
Toy cansada	Estoy cansada.	TB	también
TQ MXO	Te quiero mucho.	1 BSO	Un beso.
A2	Adiós.	¿Q T PARECE?	¿Qué te parece?
¿XQ?	¿Por qué?	T MANDO 1	Te mando un
GNL	genial	MSG DSPS	mensaje después.

La mayoría de hispanos tiene un perfil° en Facebook o en Twitter, pero el método de comunicación más popular en los países hispanohablantes es WhatsApp. Por medio de esta aplicación de mensajería los usuarios° pueden crear grupos y enviarse° un número ilimitado de imágenes, videos y mensajes de texto y de audio. Su popularidad se debe a que es una forma rápida y prácticamente gratuita° de comunicarse.

Hoy en día, los teléfonos inteligentes y los contratos telefónicos son más asequibles°, por lo que la mayoría de los hispanos disfruta de estos celulares y de sus ventajas tecnológicas. Gracias a las redes sociales y a las aplicaciones, las personas pueden estar en constante comunicación con sus seres queridos° más lejanos°. La inevitable pregunta es: ¿qué ocurre con los seres queridos que están cerca? La influencia que tienen las redes sociales en las relaciones humanas es un tema cada vez más polémico.

Al igual que *Like* han tenido *have had* llamadas *calls* por medio de *through* perfil *profile* usuarios *users* enviarse *send each other* gratuita *free* asequibles *affordable* seres queridos *loved ones* lejanos *distant*

ACTIVIDADES

1 **¿Cierto o falso?** Indica si lo que dicen estas oraciones es **cierto** o **falso**. Corrige la información falsa. Communication
Interpretive Communication

1. Los hispanos prefieren las llamadas para comunicarse con sus parientes y con sus amigos.

2. Twitter no se usa en Latinoamérica.

3. WhatsApp es un método de comunicación muy común en los países hispanos.

4. WhatsApp permite enviar fotos a los contactos del celular.

5. TB significa "también".

2 **Preguntas** Contesta las preguntas.

1. ¿Dónde tiene un perfil la mayoría de los hispanos?

2. ¿Cuál es el método de comunicación más popular en los países hispanos?

3. ¿Qué se puede hace por medio de WhatsApp?

4. ¿Por qué es tan popular WhatsApp?

5. ¿Qué significa A2?

3 **¿Cómo te comunicas?** Escribe un párrafo breve para explicar qué utilizas para comunicarte con tus amigos/as (correo electrónico, teléfono, chat, etc.). Luego, haz comparaciones con la forma como los hispanos se comunican.

4 **¿Qué piensas?** Con un(a) compañero/a, responde a estas preguntas.

1. ¿Cuáles son los aspectos positivos y negativos de las redes sociales?

2. ¿Qué influencia piensas que tienen las redes sociales en las relaciones personales en los países hispanos?

Communicative Goal
Recognize the use and importance of technology in Peru

 Video

Maravillas de la tecnología

1 **Preparación** ¿Con qué frecuencia te conectas a Internet? ¿Dónde lo haces: en tu casa o en un lugar público?

2 **El video** Mira el episodio de **Flash cultura** sobre la tecnología en Perú.

Vocabulario	
comunidad indígena *indigenous community*	romper con la barrera de la distancia *to break the distance barrier*
localizados *located*	usuarios *users*

… el primer *hotspot* de Cuzco, que permite a los usuarios navegar de manera inalámbrica…

3 **¿Cierto o falso?** Indica si lo que dice cada oración es **cierto** o **falso**.

1. A Omar lo llama su tía.

2. Omar entrevista a varios habitantes de Cuzco.

3. No hay cibercafés en la ciudad de Cuzco.

4. Los peruanos no van a los cibercafés.

5. Algunos peruanos utilizan Internet para vender sus productos.

4 **Entrevista** En parejas, dramaticen una entrevista con Omar sobre su uso de la tecnología.

I CAN compare the use of social networks in my community with their use in the Spanish-speaking world.

I CAN recognize the use and importance of technology in Peru.

Communicative Goal
Talk about the past

11.1 The preterite and the imperfect

▸ The preterite and the imperfect are not interchangeable. The choice between these two tenses depends on the context and on the point of view of the speaker.

¡¿Ése es el carro que se compró Manuel?!

Lo estábamos probando y ellos pidieron ir más rápido.

Uses of the preterite

To express actions that are viewed by the speaker as completed	Manuel estacionó el coche. *Manuel parked the car.*
	Fueron a Valparaíso ayer. *They went to Valparaíso yesterday.*
To express the beginning or end of a past action	La película empezó a las nueve. *The movie began at nine o'clock.*
	Ayer terminé el proyecto. *Yesterday I finished the project.*
To narrate a series of past actions or events	Manuel paró el coche, abrió la ventanilla y saludó a Sara. *Manuel stopped the car, opened the window, and greeted Sara.*

Uses of the imperfect

To describe an ongoing past action with no reference to its beginning or end	Manuel conducía muy rápido en Madrid. *Manuel was driving very fast in Madrid.*
	Sara esperaba en el apartamento. *Sara was waiting in the apartment.*
To express habitual past actions and events	Cuando era joven, jugaba al tenis. *When I was young, I used to play tennis.*
	Juanjo siempre revisaba su correo electrónico a las tres. *Juanjo always checked his e-mail messages at three o'clock.*
To describe physical and emotional states or characteristics	La chica quería descansar. Se sentía mal y tenía dolor de cabeza. *The girl wanted to rest. She felt ill and had a headache.*
	Ellos eran altos y tenían ojos verdes. *They were tall and had green eyes.*
	Estábamos felices de ver a la familia. *We were happy to see the family.*

Práctica

1 Un accidente Completa este artículo de periódico con las formas correctas del pretérito o del imperfecto.

Un trágico accidente

Ayer en la mañana (1) _____ [haber] un trágico accidente en el centro de Lima, cuando un autobús (2) _____ [chocar] con un carro. La mujer que (3) _____ [manejar] el carro (4) _____ [morir] al instante. Los paramédicos llevaron al conductor del autobús al hospital porque (5) _____ [tener] varias fracturas. Su estado de salud es todavía muy grave. El conductor del autobús (6) _____ [decir] que no (7) _____ [ver] el carro hasta el último momento porque (8) _____ [haber] mucha niebla y (9) _____ [llover]. Él (10) _____ [intentar] (*to attempt*) dar un viraje brusco (*to swerve*), pero (11) _____ [perder] el control del autobús y no (12) _____ [poder] evitar (*to avoid*) el accidente. Según nos informaron, no (13) _____ [lastimarse] ninguno de los pasajeros que (14) _____ [viajar] en el autobús.

2 Combinar Combina elementos de las tres columnas para hablar de lo que hicieron y lo que hacían las personas de la primera columna. Usa el imperfecto o el pretérito para formar las oraciones.

Sujetos	Verbos	Adverbios
el mecánico	arreglar	ayer
Rafael Nadal	caerse	bien
la mujer policía	chocar	con frecuencia
Timothée Chalamet	conducir	de vez en cuando
mis padres	decir	fácilmente
mis amigos y yo	enamorarse	lentamente
Rihanna	lastimarse	mal
yo	llamar	siempre
	mirar	todos los días
	olvidar	la semana pasada

Conversación

3 Oraciones Con un(a) compañero/a, completa las oraciones usando el pretérito o el imperfecto. Luego, compara tus respuestas.

modelo De niño/a, yo...

Estudiante 1: De niña, yo vivía con mis abuelos en un apartamento cerca de la escuela.
Estudiante 2: Pues mi mamá, mis hermanos y yo vivíamos en una casita con un jardín.
Estudiante 1: De niña, me lastimé una vez la rodilla. Mientras corría, me caí.
Estudiante 2: En cambio, yo nunca me lastimé la rodilla, pero me torcía constantemente el tobillo.

1. El verano pasado…
2. Yo manejaba el coche mientras…
3. Anoche mi novio/a…
4. Ayer el/la profesor(a)…
5. La semana pasada un(a) amigo/a…
6. A menudo mi madre…
7. Esta mañana en la cafetería…
8. Chateábamos cuando…

4 Tu primer(a) novio/a Entrevista a un(a) compañero/a acerca de su primer(a) novio/a. Si quieres, puedes añadir (*add*) otras preguntas.

1. ¿Quién fue tu primer(a) novio/a?
2. ¿Cuántos años tenías cuando lo/la conociste?
3. ¿Cómo era él/ella?
4. ¿Qué le gustaba hacer? ¿Tenían ustedes los mismos pasatiempos?
5. ¿Por cuánto tiempo salieron ustedes?
6. ¿Adónde iban ustedes cuando salían?
7. ¿Pensaban casarse?
8. ¿Cuándo y por qué rompieron ustedes?

5 Un robo misterioso Anoche alguien robó (*stole*) el examen de la Lección 11 de la oficina de tu profesor(a) y tú tienes que averiguar (*to find out*) quién lo hizo. Pregúntales a varios compañeros dónde estaban, con quién estaban y qué hicieron entre las ocho y las doce de la noche. Luego, decide quién robó el examen.

▸ When the preterite and the imperfect appear in the same sentence, the imperfect describes what was happening, while the preterite describes the action that "interrupted" the ongoing activity.

Escuchaba música cuando **sonó** el teléfono.
I was listening to music when the phone rang.

Sara **leía** una revista cuando **llegó** Daniel.
Sara was reading a magazine when Daniel arrived.

▸ You will see the preterite and the imperfect together in narratives such as fiction, news, and retelling of events. The imperfect provides background information, such as time, weather, and location. The preterite indicates the specific events that occurred.

Eran las dos de la mañana y el detective ya no **podía** mantenerse despierto. **Se bajó** lentamente del coche, **estiró** las piernas y **levantó** los brazos hacia el cielo oscuro.

It was two in the morning, and the detective could no longer stay awake. He slowly stepped out of the car, stretched his legs, and raised his arms toward the dark sky.

La luna **estaba** llena y no **había** en el cielo ni una sola nube. De repente, el detective **escuchó** un grito espeluznante proveniente del parque.

The moon was full and there wasn't a single cloud in the sky. Suddenly, the detective heard a terrifying scream coming from the park.

NASA·La sonda se estrelló° antes de orbitar

Mars cayó en Marte

La agencia espacial estadounidense perdió la comunicación con la sonda *Mars Climate Orbiter*, justo en el momento en que se ponía en órbita alrededor° de Marte. La nave se estrelló por un error de navegación importante. Se habían invertido° 25 millones de dólares e iba a ser la primera estación meteorológica interplanetaria.

se estrelló *crashed* **alrededor** *around* **Se habían invertido** *had been invested*

¡Manos a la obra!

Escribe la forma correcta de los verbos.

Pretérito

1. Tomás y yo ___fuimos___ [ir] al parque ayer.
2. _____ [nadar] por la tarde.
3. Después _____ [tomar] el sol.
4. _____ [regresar] a casa a las cinco.
5. Tomás preparó la cena. Yo _____ [leer] una revista.
6. Mientras Tomás veía una película, yo _____ [dormirse].

Imperfecto

1. ___Eran___ [ser] las doce.
2. _____ [haber] mucha gente en la calle.
3. Los novios _____ [estar] en el café.
4. Todos los días ellos _____ [almorzar] juntos.
5. El camarero siempre les _____ [servir] ensaladas.
6. Cuando los novios salieron del café, _____ [llover].

I CAN talk about the past.

11.2 Por and para

▶ Both **por** and **para** mean *for*, but they are not interchangeable. Study their uses in the charts.

> Manuel, ¿no tiene puerto USB para cargar el móvil?

> Iba a cincuenta y cinco kilómetros por hora.

Uses of *por*

Motion or a general location *(around, through, along, by)*	La excursión nos llevó por el centro. *The tour took us through downtown.*
	Pasamos por el parque y por el río. *We passed by the park and along the river.*
Duration of an action *(for, during, in)*	Estuve en Montevideo por un mes. *I was in Montevideo for a month.*
	Juanjo estudió por la noche. *Juanjo studied during the night.*
Object of a search *(for, in search of)*	Vengo por ti a las ocho. *I'm coming for you at eight.*
	Olga Lucía fue por su cámara. *Olga Lucía went in search of her camera.*
Means by which something is done *(by, by way of, by means of)*	Ellos viajan por la autopista. *They travel by (by way of) the highway.*
	¿Hablaste con la policía por teléfono? *Did you talk to the police by (on the) phone?*
Exchange or substitution *(for, in exchange for)*	Le di dinero por el cargador. *I gave him money for the charger.*
	Cambiamos este carro por uno nuevo. *We exchanged this car for a new one.*
Unit of measure *(per, by)*	Manuel manejaba a 55 kilómetros por hora. *Manuel was driving 55 kilometers per hour.*

▶ **Por** is used in several idiomatic expressions.

por aquí	*around here*		**por eso**	*that's why; therefore*
por ejemplo	*for example*		**por fin**	*finally*

¡ojo! When giving an exact time, **de** is used instead of **por** before **la mañana, la tarde,** and **la noche.**

Llegué a las diez **de la noche.**
I arrived at ten p.m.

Me gusta estudiar **por la noche.**
I like to study at night.

Práctica

1 **Un viaje a Buenos Aires** Completa este párrafo con las preposiciones **por** o **para**.

El mes pasado, mi esposo y yo hicimos un viaje a Buenos Aires y sólo pagamos dos mil dólares (1) _____ los pasajes. Estuvimos en Buenos Aires (2) _____ una semana y exploramos toda la ciudad. Durante el día caminamos (3) _____ la Plaza San Martín, el microcentro y el barrio de La Boca, donde viven muchos artistas. (4) _____ la noche fuimos a una tanguería, que es un tipo de teatro, (5) _____ ver a la gente bailar tango. Dos días después decidimos hacer una excursión (6) _____ las Pampas (7) _____ ver el paisaje y un rodeo con gauchos. (8) _____ eso, alquilamos (*we rented*) un carro y pasamos unos días muy agradables. El último día fuimos a Galerías Pacífico (9) _____ comprar recuerdos (*souvenirs*) (10) _____ nuestros hijos y nietos. Compramos tantos regalos que, al regresar, tuvimos que pagar impuestos (*duties*) cuando pasamos (11) _____ la aduana.

2 **¿Qué pasa aquí?** Usa **por** o **para** y el tiempo presente para describir estos dibujos.

modelo
Él trabaja para el Taller Juárez. / Él abre el taller por la mañana.

1. _____

2. _____

3. _____

4. _____

5. _____

Conversación

3 **Encuesta** Averigua (*Find out*) a cuáles de tus compañeros/as corresponde cada descripción. Luego, presenta los resultados a la clase.

> **modelo**
>
> Usa el celular para ver películas.

Estudiante 1: ¿Usas el celular para ver películas?
Estudiante 2: No, no uso el celular para ver películas.

	Nombres
1. Trabaja para la universidad.	_____
2. Ayer no durmió por la noche.	_____
3. Viajó por Europa.	_____
4. Hoy pasó por la gasolinera.	_____
5. Se preocupa por sus amigos.	_____
6. Habla por teléfono celular.	_____
7. Quiere estudiar para médico/a.	_____
8. Las clases son fáciles para él/ella.	_____

4 **Completar** Habla con un(a) compañero/a para completar estas oraciones sobre él/ella. Usa **por** y **para** en las respuestas.

1. El año pasado compró un regalo…
2. Ayer fue al taller…
3. Necesita hacer la tarea…
4. En casa, habla con sus amigos/as…
5. Los miércoles tiene clases…
6. A veces va a la biblioteca…
7. Necesita… dólares…
8. Su mejor amigo/a estudia…

5 **Una subasta** En grupos, dramaticen una subasta (*auction*). Cada estudiante debe traer a la clase un objeto o una foto del objeto para vender. Luego, un(a) estudiante es el/la vendedor(a) y los otros son los postores (*bidders*).

> **modelo**
>
> **Vendedor(a):** Aquí tengo una cámara digital. ¿Quién ofrece $400 por ella?
> **Postor(a) 1:** Te doy $175.

I CAN participate in an auction.

Uses of *para*

Destination *(toward, in the direction of)*	Salimos para Mérida el sábado. *We are leaving for Mérida on Saturday.* Voy para el banco. *I'm going to the bank.*
Deadline or a specific time in the future *(by, for)*	Él va a arreglar el carro para el viernes. *He will fix the car by Friday.*
Purpose or goal + [*infinitive*] *(in order to)*	Roberto estudia para (ser) mecánico. *Roberto is studying to be a mechanic.*
Purpose + [*noun/verb*] *(for, used for)*	Es una llanta para el carro. *It's a tire for the car.* Uso mi celular para ver mi correo electrónico. *I use my cell phone to read my e-mail.*
The recipient of something *(for)*	Compré una calculadora para mi hijo. *I bought a calculator for my son.*
Comparisons or opinions *(for, considering)*	Para ser joven, es demasiado serio. *For a young person, he is too serious.* Para mí, esta lección no es difícil. *For me, this lesson isn't difficult.*
Employment *(for)*	Ana trabaja para Telecom. *Ana works for Telecom.*

▶ Often, either **por** or **para** can be used in a sentence. The meaning of the sentence changes, depending on which one is used.

Caminé **por** el parque.
I walked through (around) the park.

Caminé **para** el parque.
I walked to (toward) the park.

Trabajó **por** su padre.
He worked for (in place of) his father.

Trabajó **para** su padre.
He worked for his father('s business).

Se exhibió **por** todo el pueblo.
It was shown throughout (around) the whole town.

Se exhibió **para** todo el pueblo.
It was shown for the whole town.

¡Manos a la obra!

Completa las oraciones con **por** o **para**.

1. Dormimos __por__ la mañana.
2. Necesitas conexión inalámbrica _____ conectarte a Internet.
3. Entraron _____ la puerta.
4. Es un pasaje _____ Buenos Aires.
5. _____ arrancar el carro, necesito la llave.
6. Arreglé el televisor _____ ti.
7. Estuvieron nerviosos _____ el examen.
8. ¿Hay una gasolinera _____ aquí?
9. Esta computadora es _____ usted.
10. Juan está enfermo. Tengo que trabajar _____ él.
11. Estuvimos en Cancún _____ dos meses.
12. _____ mí, el español es difícil.
13. Tengo que estudiar la lección _____ el lunes.
14. Voy a ir _____ ese camino.
15. Compré un radio _____ mi novia.
16. Lo compró _____ un buen precio.

Communicative Goal |
Talk about my belongings

11.3 Stressed possessive adjectives and pronouns

▶ Spanish has two types of possessive adjectives: the unstressed (short) forms you learned in Lesson 3 and the stressed (long) forms. The stressed possessive adjectives are used for emphasis or to express *(of) mine, (of) yours, (of) his,* and so on.

Stressed possessive adjectives

Singular forms		Plural forms		
MASCULINE	FEMININE	MASCULINE	FEMININE	
mío	mía	míos	mías	*my; (of) mine*
tuyo	tuya	tuyos	tuyas	*your; (of) yours (fam.)*
suyo	suya	suyos	suyas	*your; (of) yours (form.); his; (of) his; her; (of) hers; its*
nuestro	nuestra	nuestros	nuestras	*our; (of) ours*
vuestro	vuestra	vuestros	vuestras	*your; (of) yours (fam.)*
suyo	suya	suyos	suyas	*your; (of) yours; their; (of) theirs*

▶ Stressed possessive adjectives must agree in gender and number with the nouns they modify.

mi **impresora**	la **impresora** mía
my printer	*my printer*
nuestros **televisores**	los **televisores** nuestros
our television sets	*our television sets*

▶ Stressed possessive adjectives are placed after the nouns they modify. Unstressed possessive adjectives are placed before the noun.

Son **mis** llaves.   Son las llaves **mías.**
They are my keys.   *They are my keys.*

▶ A definite article, an indefinite article, or a demonstrative adjective usually precedes a noun modified by a stressed possessive adjective.

Alberto tenía
- **unos** discos **tuyos.**   *Alberto had some disks of yours.*
- **los** discos **tuyos.**   *Alberto had your disks.*
- **estos** discos **tuyos.**   *Alberto had these disks of yours.*

▶ Since **suyo, suya, suyos,** and **suyas** have more than one meaning, you can avoid confusion by using the construction: [*article*] + [*noun*] + **de** + [*subject pronoun or noun*].

el teclado **suyo**
- el teclado **de él/ella**   *his/her keyboard*
- el teclado **de Ud./Uds.**   *your keyboard*
- el teclado **de ellos/ellas**   *their keyboard*
- el teclado **de Ramón**   *Ramón's keyboard*

▶ **El** and **la** are usually omitted when a stressed possessive adjective follows the verb **ser.**

¿**Es suya** esta cámara?   No, no **es mía.**

Práctica

1 **Oraciones** Forma oraciones con estos elementos. Usa el presente y haz todos los cambios necesarios.

1. yo / necesitar / usar / impresora / de Miguel / porque / mío / no / funcionar
2. pero / él / no poder / ayudarme / porque / suyo / tampoco / funcionar
3. me gustaría / pedirle / a Juana / su ratón, / pero / suyo / estar / descompuesto
4. yo / no poder / usar / teclado / de Valeria / porque / suyo / también / estar descompuesto
5. si / yo / pedirte / computadora, / estar / seguro/a / de que / ir / decirme / que / no poder / usar / tuyo

2 **¿Es suyo?** Un policía ha capturado (*has captured*) al hombre que robó (*robbed*) en tu casa. Ahora quiere saber qué cosas son tuyas. Túrnate con un(a) compañero/a para hacer el papel del policía y usa las pistas (*clues*) para contestar las preguntas.

 modelo   No / pequeño

Policía: Esta computadora, ¿es suya?
Estudiante: No, no es mía. La mía es más pequeña.

1. Sí

2. No / viejo

3. Sí

4. Sí

5. No / nuevo

6. No / caro

Conversación

3 **Identificar** Trabajen en grupos. Cada estudiante trae tres objetos. Pongan todos los objetos juntos. Luego, un(a) estudiante escoge uno o dos objetos y le pregunta a otro/a si esos objetos son suyos. Usen adjetivos posesivos.

modelo

Estudiante 1: *José Luis, ¿son tuyos estos ratones?*
Estudiante 2: *Sí, son míos. / No, no son míos. Son los ratones de Felipe.*

4 **Anuncios** Lee este anuncio con un(a) compañero/a. Luego, preparen su propio (*own*) anuncio usando adjetivos o pronombres posesivos. Después, conviértanlo en un anuncio de televisión y preséntenlo a la clase.

Esta **computadora**
y esta **impresora**
pueden ser suyas **por sólo**

$699

Características de la computadora

- Procesador: Intel Dual Core a 3000 MHz
- 4GB DDR3 de memoria
- Disco duro de 250 GB
- Sistema operativo: Linux

Impresora

- Impresora, fotocopiadora y escáner
- Velocidad: 40 páginas por minuto a color

El precio incluye un año de servicio de Internet gratis. Para más información, llame al 3 62 19 90 o visite nuestro sitio web www.tecnolibre.com

I CAN talk about my belongings.

Possessive pronouns

▶ Possessive pronouns are used to replace [*noun*] + [*possessive adjective*]. In Spanish, possessive pronouns have the same forms as stressed possessive adjectives, and they are preceded by a definite article.

la **calculadora** nuestra	la nuestra
el **radio** tuyo	el tuyo
los **archivos** suyos	los suyos

¿De quién es el coche?

Mío, acabo de comprarlo.

Nos ayudamos, Manuel, ¡pero la multa es tuya!

▶ Possessive pronouns agree in number and gender with the nouns they replace.

—Aquí está **mi coche.** ¿Dónde está **el tuyo**?
Here's my car. Where is yours?

—¿Tienes **los archivos** de Carlos?
Do you have Carlos's files?

—**El mío** está en el taller de mi hermano Armando.
Mine is at my brother Armando's garage.

—No, pero tengo **los nuestros**.
No, but I have ours.

¡Manos a la obra!

Indica las formas tónicas *(stressed)* de estos adjetivos posesivos y los pronombres posesivos correspondientes.

	adjetivos	pronombres
1. su navegador GPS	el navegador GPS suyo	el suyo
2. mi televisor		
3. nuestras tabletas		
4. tus teléfonos		
5. su pantalla		
6. mis videos		
7. nuestra impresora		
8. tu calculadora		
9. nuestro carro		
10. mi computadora		

A repasar

11.1 The preterite and the imperfect

1 Seleccionar Utiliza el tiempo verbal adecuado, según el contexto.

1. La semana pasada, Manuel y Andrea _____ [querer] dar una fiesta. _____ [decidir] invitar a seis amigos y servirles mucha comida.

2. Manuel y Andrea _____ [estar] preparando la comida cuando Elena _____ [llamar]. Como siempre, _____ [tener] que estudiar para un examen.

3. A las seis, _____ [volver] a sonar el teléfono. Su amigo Francisco tampoco _____ [poder] ir a la fiesta, porque _____ [tener] fiebre. Manuel y Andrea _____ [ponerse] muy tristes.

4. Después de otros quince minutos _____ [sonar] el teléfono. Sus amigos, los señores Vega, _____ [estar] en camino al hospital: a su hijo le _____ [doler] mucho el estómago. Sólo dos de los amigos _____ [poder] ir a la cena.

5. Por supuesto, _____ [ir] a tener demasiada comida. Finalmente, cinco minutos antes de las ocho, _____ [llamar] Ramón y Javier. Ellos _____ [pensar] que la fiesta _____ [ser] la próxima semana.

6. Tristes, Manuel y Andrea _____ [sentarse] a comer solos. Mientras _____ [comer], pronto _____ [llegar] a la conclusión de que _____ [ser] mejor estar solos. ¡La comida _____ [estar] feísima!

2 La sala de emergencia Con un(a) compañero/a, mira la lista e inventa qué les pasó a estas personas que están en la sala de emergencia.

modelo
Eran las tres de la tarde. Como todos los días, Pablo jugaba al fútbol con sus amigos. Estaba muy contento. De repente, se cayó y se rompió el brazo. Después fue a la sala de emergencia.

Paciente	Edad	Hora	Condición
1. Pablo	9 años	15:20	hueso roto (el brazo)
2. Estela	45 años	15:25	tobillo torcido
3. Lucía	29 años	15:37	embarazada, dolores
4. Marta	3 años	16:00	temperatura muy alta
5. Roberto	32 años	16:06	dolor de muelas
6. Ana	66 años	16:29	reacción alérgica

3 La multa Sergio Reyes tuvo un accidente y le dieron esta multa. Con un(a) compañero/a, escribe un párrafo que explique cómo sucedió el accidente, usando el pretérito y el imperfecto.

Multa

Fecha: 05/01/13 **Conductor:** Sergio Reyes
Hora: 8:25 p.m. **N° de licencia:** 483 699
Lugar: Calle Paz #12
Infracciones
- Pasar el semáforo en rojo
- Exceder la velocidad máxima
- Chocar con un carro estacionado

Multa: 120 pesos

11.2 Por and para

4 Para arreglar computadoras Gerardo está hablando de su trabajo. Completa las oraciones.

de la mañana	para mañana	por aquí	por eso
de la noche	para mi padre	por ejemplo	por la tarde

Yo trabajo (1) _____. Él tiene un taller para arreglar computadoras. ¡Trabajamos mucho! (2) _____, entro a las siete (3) _____ y salgo a las ocho (4) _____. (5) _____, tomo un descanso (*break*) de una hora. (6) _____ no hay muchos talleres para arreglar computadoras. ¡(7) _____ tenemos tanto trabajo! (8) _____ debemos tener listas once computadoras.

5 Oraciones Crea oraciones originales con los elementos de las columnas. Une los elementos usando **por** y **para**.

modelo
Fuimos a Mar del Plata por razones de salud, para visitar a una especialista en alergias.

(No) fuimos a la tienda	por/para	comprar tabletas	por/para	¿?
(No) fuimos a las montañas	por/para	tres días	por/para	¿?
(No) fuiste a Medellín	por/para	razones de trabajo	por/para	¿?
(No) fueron a Buenos Aires	por/para	tomar el sol	por/para	¿?

6 Lista de regalos Imagina que es Navidad y quieres regalarles a tus amigos aparatos electrónicos. En parejas, escriban los nombres de cinco amigos y decidan qué regalo es el mejor para cada uno. Expliquen sus razones usando **por** y **para**.

modelo
El mejor regalo para Olga es una cámara digital. Puede usarla en todas las celebraciones para sacar fotos.

11.3 Stressed possessive adjectives and pronouns

7 Computación Completa estas conversaciones con las formas adecuadas de los pronombres posesivos.

1.—Éste es mi sitio web. ¿Cómo es el de ustedes?
— _____ tiene música y fotografías.

2.—Tu radio no funciona. ¿Necesitas uno nuevo?
—Sí, mi papá me va a prestar _____.

3.—Mi tableta está descompuesta. ¿Cómo funciona _____?
— _____ funciona bien.

4.—¿Cómo es la pantalla de tu computadora?
— _____ es pequeña y plana (*flat*).

5.—Las computadoras de nuestra escuela son lentísimas. ¿Y las de tu escuela?
— _____ son muy rápidas.

8 No es así Contesta cada oración diciendo que las cosas no son como te dicen. Sigue el modelo.

> **modelo**
> Mi impresora es lenta. (yo, rápida)
> La impresora mía no es así.
> La mía es rápida.

1. El carro de Julio es viejo. (tú, nuevo)
2. Nuestras cámaras son caras. (ellas, baratas)
3. Su buzón de voz está descompuesto. (yo, no descompuesto)
4. Tu control remoto es grande. (ustedes, pequeño)
5. El navegador GPS de Antonio es fácil de usar. (nosotros, difícil de usar)

Síntesis

9 ¡No puedo imprimir! Tu impresora está descompuesta. Vas a hablarle por teléfono a tu hermano/a para pedirle ayuda. Con un(a) compañero/a, representa la conversación.

- Expliquen qué pasaba con su impresora.
- Expliquen cuántas veces rompió alguna hoja (*sheet*) o cuántas veces no funcionó.
- Expliquen para qué clase es el trabajo que tienen que imprimir.
- Indiquen adónde pueden llevar la impresora a arreglar, dónde pueden imprimir el trabajo y cómo pueden llegar a esos lugares.

Communicative Goal
Watch a short TV ad and talk about annoying actions

 Video

Videoclip

1 Preparación ¿Cuáles son las cosas que más te molestan de los demás (por ejemplo, cuando te interrumpen o te cuentan el final de una película)? Haz una lista y compárala con la de un(a) compañero/a.

2 El clip Mira el anuncio **Autocine** para Banco Galicia de Argentina.

Vocabulario	
está bueno *it's cool*	**¡Cuidado el tapizado!** *Be careful with the upholstery!*
el tipo *dude*	**¡Basta!** *Enough!*

Está bueno venir al autocine.

3 ¿Cierto o falso? Indica si las oraciones son **ciertas** o **falsas**. Corrige las oraciones falsas.

1. Los pasajeros prefieren no comer en el taxi.
2. Van al autocine en taxi porque no tienen auto.
3. El taxista interrumpe y comenta la película.
4. La pareja se ríe de la situación.
5. El cielo está despejado y es una noche perfecta para estar en el autocine.
6. La mujer quiere tener un auto.

4 ¡Basta! En parejas, dramaticen una situación en la que uno/a de ustedes hace algo que molesta al otro, por ejemplo, colarse en la fila (*skipping the line*). Uno/a trata de explicarle al/a la otro/a qué le molestó. El/La otro/a no entiende, y la discusión continúa.

I CAN understand some information in a short TV ad.

I CAN talk about annoying actions.

Ampliación

Communicative Goals
Identify the genre of a spoken discourse, and talk about driving

1 Escuchar

A Escucha a Ricardo Moreno y luego contesta las preguntas.

> **TIP** **Recognize the genre of spoken discourse.** Identifying the genre (for example: political speech, radio interview, news broadcast) of what you hear can help you figure out what kinds of things you are likely to hear. It will also help you identify the speaker's motives and intentions.

1. ¿Qué tipo de género es?
   a. noticias (*news*) por radio o televisión   b. un anuncio comercial
   c. una reseña (*review*) de una película
2. ¿De qué habla?
   a. de su vida   b. de un producto o servicio   c. de algo que oyó o vio
3. ¿Cuál es el propósito (*purpose*)?
   a. relacionarse con alguien   b. informar   c. vender

B ¿Qué pistas (*clues*) te ayudaron a identificar el género de la grabación (*recording*)?

2 Conversar

Con un(a) compañero/a, representa una conversación sobre la primera vez que manejaste un carro o el día en que fuiste al Departamento de Tráfico para conseguir tu licencia de conducir. Incluye la siguiente información:

- ¿Cuántos años tenías?
- ¿A qué hora fue?
- ¿Cómo estaba el tiempo?
- ¿Quién fue contigo (*with you*)?
- ¿Cómo te sentías antes de hacerlo? ¿Y cómo te sentiste después?
- ¿Fue una experiencia agradable? ¿Te gustaría repetirla? ¿Por qué?

I CAN listen to a short message and identify the genre, theme, and purpose.

I CAN talk about driving.

Ampliación

3 Escribir

Escribe una historia acerca de una experiencia tuya con una máquina electrónica o con un carro.

TIP **Master the simple past tenses.** To write about events that occurred in the past, you will need to know when to use the preterite and the imperfect. The box on this page contains a summary of their uses.

Preterite
- Past actions viewed as completed
- Beginning or end of past actions
- Series of past actions

Imperfect
- Ongoing past actions
- Habitual past actions
- Physical and emotional states in the past

Communicative Goals
Write about an experience with electronics or a car, and create an ad for a technology product or a car

Organizar	Prepara una lista de todos los detalles que quieres narrar (*narrate*). Identifica qué acciones fueron completadas (pretérito) y cuáles están incompletas (imperfecto).
Escribir	Utiliza tu lista para escribir el primer borrador de tu historia.
Corregir	Intercambia tu historia con un(a) compañero/a. Lee su borrador y reflexiona sobre las partes mejor escritas. Da sugerencias sobre los detalles, la lógica de la secuencia de eventos y el uso del pretérito y del imperfecto.
Compartir	Revisa el primer borrador según las indicaciones de tu compañero/a. Incorpora las nuevas ideas y prepara la versión final. Luego, comparte la historia con la clase.

4 Un paso más

Crea un anuncio para promocionar un producto electrónico o un carro. El anuncio debe incluir estos elementos:

- Nombre del producto o carro
- Una descripción del producto o carro
- Una descripción de la tecnología y de los servicios que se ofrecen a los clientes
- Fotos o dibujos
- Por qué este producto o carro es mejor que otros
- El precio

5 Cultura

Describe el uso de las redes sociales en los países hispanos.

I CAN write about an experience with electronics or a car.

I CAN create an ad for a technology product or a car.

Audio: Reading

Antes de leer

One way languages grow is by borrowing words from each other.

TIP **Recognize borrowed words.** English words that relate to technology are often borrowed by Spanish and other languages throughout the world. Sometimes the words are modified slightly to fit the sounds of the languages that borrow them. When reading in Spanish, you can often increase your understanding by looking for words borrowed from English or other languages you know.

Examinar el texto

Observa la tira cómica (*comic strip*). ¿De qué trata (*is it about*)? ¿Cómo lo sabes?

Buscar

Esta lectura contiene una palabra tomada (*taken*) del inglés. Trabaja con un(a) compañero/a para encontrarla.

_____

Repasa (*Review*) las nuevas palabras relacionadas con la tecnología que aprendiste en **Preparación** y expande la lista de palabras tomadas del inglés.

_____ _____

_____ _____

_____ _____

Juan Matías Loiseau (1974–). Más conocido como *Tute*, este artista nació en Buenos Aires, Argentina. Estudió diseño gráfico, humorismo y cine. Sus tiras cómicas se publican en los Estados Unidos, Francia y toda Latinoamérica.

te viene *comes with* **tipo** *guy, dude* **te avisa** *alerts you* **escuchás** *hear (Arg.)* **distraídos** *careless* **piso** *floor* **bolsa de dormir** *sleeping bag* **darle de baja** *to cancel* **harto** *fed up* **revolear** *throw away forcefully (S. America)* **bien hecho** *well done* **llamada perdida** *missed call*

Después de leer

¿Comprendiste?

Indica si las oraciones son **ciertas** o **falsas**. Corrige las falsas.

Cierto   **Falso**

_____   _____   1. Hay tres personajes en la tira cómica: un usuario de teléfono, un amigo y un empleado de la empresa (*company*) telefónica.

_____   _____   2. El nuevo servicio de teléfono incluye las llamadas telefónicas únicamente.

_____   _____   3. El empleado duerme en su casa.

_____   _____   4. El contrato de teléfono dura (*lasts*) un año.

_____   _____   5. El usuario y el amigo están trabajando (*working*).

Preguntas

Responde estas preguntas con oraciones completas. Usa el pretérito y el imperfecto.

1. ¿Al usuario le gustaba usar el teléfono celular todo el tiempo?

_____

2. ¿Por qué el usuario decidió tirar el teléfono al mar?

_____

3. Según el amigo, ¿para qué tenía el usuario que tirar el teléfono celular al mar?

_____

4. ¿Qué ocurrió cuando el usuario tiró el teléfono?

_____

5. ¿Qué le dijo el empleado al usuario cuando salió del mar?

_____

Coméntalo

¿Cuáles son los aspectos positivos y los negativos de tener teléfono celular? ¿Te sientes identificado/a con el usuario del teléfono? ¿Por qué?

_____

I CAN read and understand a comic strip in Spanish.

I CAN express my opinions about the use of technology.

Vocabulary Tools

En la calle

la calle *street*
el camino *route*
el garaje *garage; (mechanic's) repair shop*
la gasolina *gasoline*
la gasolinera *gas station*
el kilómetro *kilometer*
la licencia de conducir *driver's license*
el/la mecánico/a *mechanic*
la milla *mile*
la multa *fine; ticket*
el policía/la mujer policía *police officer*
la policía *police (force)*
el semáforo *traffic light*
el taller (mecánico) *(mechanic's) repair shop*
el tráfico *traffic*
la velocidad máxima *speed limit*

———

arrancar *to start*
arreglar *to fix; to arrange*
bajar *to go down*
bajar(se) de *to get out of (a vehicle)*
chocar (con) *to run into; to crash*
conducir *to drive*
estacionar *to park*
llenar (el tanque) *to fill (the tank)*
manejar *to drive*
parar *to stop*
revisar (el aceite) *to check (the oil)*
subir *to go up*
subir(se) a *to get into (a vehicle)*

Las partes del carro

el baúl *trunk*
el capó *(car) hood*
el carro *car*
el coche *car*
los frenos *brakes*
la llanta *tire*
el motor *motor*
el parabrisas *windshield*
el volante *steering wheel*

La tecnología

la aplicación *app*
el buzón de voz *voicemail*
la calculadora *calculator*
la cámara digital *digital camera*
el cargador *charger*
el control remoto *remote control*
el mensaje de texto *text message*
el navegador GPS *GPS*
el puerto USB *USB port*
el radio *radio (set)*
el teléfono celular *cell phone*
el televisor *television set*

———

apagar *to turn off*
funcionar *to work*
grabar *to record*
llamar *to call*
poner *to turn on*
prender *to turn on*
sonar (o:ue) *to ring*
textear *to text*

———

descompuesto/a *not working; out of order*
lento/a *slow*
lleno/a *full*

Internet y la computadora

el archivo *file*
la computadora *computer*
la computadora portátil *laptop*
la conexión inalámbrica *wireless (connection)*
la impresora *printer*
Internet *Internet*
la página principal *home page*
la pantalla *screen*
el programa de computación *software*
el ratón *mouse*
la red *network, Web*
el sitio web *website*
la tableta *tablet (computer)*
el teclado *keyboard*

———

cargar *to charge; to upload*
chatear *to chat*
conectarse a Internet *to get connected to the Internet*
descargar *to download*
escanear *to scan*
guardar *to save*
imprimir *to print*

Otras palabras y expresiones

para *toward; in the direction of; by; for; in order to; used for; considering*
por *around; through; along; by; for; during; in; in search of; by way of; by means of; in exchange for; per*
por aquí *around here*
por ejemplo *for example*
por eso *that's why; therefore*
por fin *finally*

Stressed possessive adjectives and pronouns *See pages 294–295.*

Communicative Goals: Review

I CAN talk about cars.
• Describe your car or the car of someone you know.

I CAN describe my use of technology.
• Tell how you use your cell phone or computer.

I CAN talk about the past.
• Describe a car trip you took or an experience with technology you had.

I CAN investigate technology use in the Spanish-speaking world.
• Describe an aspect of technology use in Spanish-speaking countries.

12 Hogar, dulce hogar

Communicative Goals

You will learn how to:
- describe homes
- talk about household chores
- give advice
- investigate architectural features in the Spanish-speaking world

PREPARACIÓN

pages 304–309
- Words related to the home
- Household chores
- Capital and lowercase letters

AVENTURAS

pages 310–311
- Juanjo and Valentina are busy cleaning their apartments. Will Manuel and Olga Lucía do their share of the work?

CULTURA

pages 312–313
- *Balcones que enamoran*
- Flash cultura: *La casa de Frida*

GRAMÁTICA

pages 314–323
- **Usted** and **ustedes** commands
- The present subjunctive
- Subjunctive with verbs of will and influence

LECTURA

pages 324–325
- Brochure: *¡Bienvenidos a la Casa Colorada!*

∞ PARA EMPEZAR

- ¿Dónde están las chicas: en el apartamento o en la universidad?
- ¿Están contentas?
- ¿Está ordenado o desordenado el cuarto?
- ¿Qué lleva Valentina en las manos?

HOGAR, DULCE HOGAR

LA CASA Y SUS CUARTOS

la alcoba *bedroom*
el altillo *attic*
el balcón *balcony*
la cocina *kitchen*
el comedor *dining room*
la entrada *entrance*
el garaje *garage*
la oficina *office*
el pasillo *hallway*
el patio *patio; yard*
la sala *living room*
el sótano *basement*

la escalera
stairs

LA MESA

la copa *wineglass*
la taza *cup; mug*
el vaso *glass*

la servilleta

el cuchillo

el tenedor

la cuchara

el plato

el jardín
garden; yard

LOS ELECTRODOMÉSTICOS

la estufa *stove*
el horno *oven*
la lavadora *washing machine*
el lavaplatos *dishwasher*
el microondas *microwave*
el refrigerador *refrigerator*
la secadora *clothes dryer*

los electrodomésticos
electrical appliances

barrer el suelo
to sweep the floor

Vocabulary Tools

LOS MUEBLES Y OTRAS COSAS

la alfombra *carpet; rug*

la almohada *pillow*

el armario *closet*

la cómoda *chest of drawers*

las cortinas *curtains*

el cuadro *picture*

el estante *bookcase; bookshelf*

la lámpara *lamp*

la luz *light; electricity*

la manta *blanket*

la mesita *end table*

la mesita de noche *nightstand*

la pared *wall*

la pintura *painting*

el sillón *armchair*

el sofá *sofa*

los muebles
furniture

LOS QUEHACERES DOMÉSTICOS

arreglar *to straighten up*

cocinar *to cook*

hacer los quehaceres domésticos
  to do household chores

lavar (el suelo, los platos)
  to wash (the floor, the dishes)

limpiar la casa *to clean the house*

pasar la aspiradora *to vacuum*

poner la mesa *to set the table*

quitar la mesa *to clear the table*

sacar la basura *to take out the trash*

sacudir los muebles
  to dust the furniture

OTRAS PALABRAS

las afueras *suburbs; outskirts*

la agencia de bienes raíces
  real estate agency

el alquiler *rent (payment)*

el amo/a (m., f.) de casa *homemaker*

el barrio *neighborhood*

el edificio de apartamentos
  apartment building

el hogar *home*

el/la vecino/a *neighbor*

la vivienda *housing*

---

alquilar *to rent*

ensuciar *to get (something) dirty*

mudarse *to move (residences)*

hacer la cama
to make the bed

planchar la ropa
to iron clothes

ASÍ SE DICE

la alcoba ⟷ el aposento (*Rep. Dom.*), la recámara (*Méx.*),
la habitación, el dormitorio (*Esp.*), el cuarto (*Amér. L.*), la pieza (*Col., Arg.*)
el apartamento ⟷ el departamento (*Amér. L.*), el piso (*Esp.*)
lavar los platos ⟷ fregar los trastes (*Amér. C.*)

A escuchar

1 **Escoger** Escucha las preguntas e indica la respuesta correcta.

1. _____ Al pasillo.

_____ Al balcón.

2. _____ En el lavaplatos.

_____ En la mesita de noche.

3. _____ Al edificio.

_____ A las afueras.

4. _____ En la secadora.

_____ En la basura.

5. _____ El balcón.

_____ La escalera.

6. _____ En las paredes.

_____ En el horno.

7. _____ La estufa.

_____ La aspiradora.

8. _____ En la alfombra.

_____ En la alcoba.

2 **Escuchar** Escucha la conversación y completa las oraciones con las palabras o expresiones adecuadas.

1. Paula va a comenzar por _____.

2. Pedro va a limpiar _____ primero.

3. Pedro también va a limpiar _____.

4. Pedro le dice a Paula que debe _____ en la alcoba de huéspedes.

5. Pedro va a _____ en el sótano.

6. Ellos están limpiando la casa porque _____ va a visitarlos.

A practicar

3 Emparejar Empareja cada dibujo con su descripción. Luego, nombra los dibujos.

_____ 1. Lo usas para tomar agua.

_____ 2. Lo necesitas para comer un bistec.

_____ 3. Necesitas este objeto para la sopa.

_____ 4. La necesitas para tomar café.

_____ 5. La necesitas para tomar vino.

_____ 6. Necesitas este objeto para limpiarte la boca después de comer.

a._____ b._____ c._____

d._____ e._____ f._____

4 Definiciones Con un(a) compañero/a, túrnate para identificar cada elemento que se describe. Luego, cada uno/a debe agregar dos descripciones propias de palabras y expresiones de **Preparación**.

modelo

Es lo que pagan cada mes las personas que viven en un apartamento.
Estudiante 1: Es lo que pagan cada mes las personas que viven en un apartamento.
Estudiante 2: el alquiler
Estudiante 1: Estacionas el carro en este lugar. Pones...

1. Pones la cabeza en este objeto cuando duermes.

2. Es el quehacer doméstico que haces después de comer.

3. Cubren (they cover) las ventanas y decoran la sala a la vez (at the same time).

4. Algunos ejemplos son las cómodas, las mesitas y los sillones.

5. Son las personas que viven en tu barrio.

5 Los quehaceres domésticos Trabajen en grupos para indicar quién hace los siguientes quehaceres domésticos en sus casas. Luego contesten las preguntas.

barrer el suelo	lavar la ropa	planchar la ropa
cocinar	lavar los platos	sacar la basura
hacer las camas	pasar la aspiradora	sacudir los muebles

• ¿Quién es la persona de mi grupo que hace más quehaceres?

• ¿Cúales son los quehaceres que más te molestan y los que más te gustan? ¿Por qué?

• ¿Piensas que debes hacer más quehaceres? ¿Por qué?

A conversar

6 **Dos habitaciones** Con un(a) compañero/a, describe las habitaciones que se ven en las fotos. Identifica cuatro muebles o adornos (*adornments*) de cada foto e indica tres quehaceres que se pueden hacer en cada habitación.

1.

2.

7 **¿Una casa o un apartamento?** Con un(a) compañero/a, compara las ventajas y desventajas de vivir en una casa o en un apartamento. Considera el espacio, la comodidad, el precio del alquiler, las reglas para las visitas, la organización de fiestas, etc.

8 **Un(a) agente de bienes raíces** Trabajen en grupos para representar a un(a) agente de bienes raíces y a sus clientes. El/La agente tiene varias casas para vender; debe mostrarlas y hablar de los muebles y del barrio que más les convienen (*suit*) a estos clientes.

> • Una pareja que está esperando su segundo hijo
>
> • Un grupo de estudiantes universitarios que quiere vivir fuera del campus (off-campus)
>
> • Una familia con cinco niños
>
> • Una pareja con tres mascotas (pets)
>
> • Un joven profesional dedicado (devoted) a la agricultura y a los deportes acuáticos

I CAN describe homes.

Ortografía

 Tutorial

Las mayúsculas y las minúsculas

Here are some of the rules that govern the use of capital letters (**mayúsculas**) and lowercase letters (**minúsculas**) in Spanish.

....

Los estudiantes llegaron al aeropuerto a las dos. Luego fueron al hotel.

In both Spanish and English, the first letter of every sentence is capitalized.

....

Rubén Blades   **Panamá**   **Colón**   **los Andes**

The first letter of all proper nouns (names of people, countries, cities, geographical features, etc.) is capitalized.

....

Cien años de soledad   ***Don Quijote de la Mancha***   ***El País***   ***Muy Interesante***

The first letter of the first word in titles of books, films, and works of art is generally capitalized, as well as the first letter of any proper names. In newspaper and magazine titles, as well as other short titles, the initial letter of each word is often capitalized.

....

la señora Ramos   **don Francisco**   **el presidente**   **Sra. Vives**

Titles associated with people are *not* capitalized unless they appear as the first word in a sentence. Note, however, that the first letter of an abbreviated title is capitalized.

....

Último   **Álex**   **MENÚ**   **PERDÓN**

Accent marks should be retained on capital letters. In practice, however, this rule is often ignored.

....

lunes   **viernes**   **marzo**   **primavera**

The first letter of days, months, and seasons is *not* capitalized.

....

español   **estadounidense**   **japonés**   **panameños**

The first letter of nationalities and languages is *not* capitalized.

....

Práctica Corrige las mayúsculas y minúsculas incorrectas.

1. soy lourdes romero. Soy Colombiana.
2. éste Es mi Hermano álex.
3. somos De panamá.
4. ¿es ud. La sra. benavides?
5. ud. Llegó el Lunes, ¿no?

Oraciones Lee el diálogo de las serpientes. Ordena las letras para saber de qué palabras se trata. Después, escribe las letras indicadas para descubrir por qué llora Pepito.

Profesor Herrera, ¿es cierto que somos venenosas°?

Sí, Pepito. ¿Por qué lloras?

m n a a P á   ⬤_ _ _ _ _   y a U r u g u   _ _ _ ⬤ _ _

s t e m r a   ⬤_ _ _ _ _   r o ñ e s a   _ _ _ _ _ ⬤

i g s l é n   _ _ _ ⬤ _ _

¡ _orque _e acabo de morder° la _ en _u _|!

venenosas *venomous*
morder *to bite*

¹ *Respuestas: Panamá, martes, inglés, Uruguay, señora. ¡Porque me acabo de morder la lengua!*

INSTRUCTIONAL RESOURCES
Supersite: WebSAM
SAM: Video Manual
pp. 191–192

Communicative Goal
Say how often I do chores

¡A limpiar!

Juanjo y Valentina están limpiando.

 Video

Antes de ver

Mira la primera imagen y describe lo que piensas que está pasando.

VIDEO RECAP Before showing this **Aventuras** episode, review the previous episode with these questions: 1. ¿Quién se compró un coche? (Manuel) 2. ¿Por qué paró el coche el policía? (por sobrepasar la velocidad máxima) 3. ¿A qué velocidad iba Manuel? (iba a 55 kilómetros por hora) 4. ¿Cómo puede pagar la multa Manuel? (pasar por la oficina de tráfico o pagarla por teléfono o Internet)

VIDEO SYNOPSIS Juanjo is cleaning the living room when Manuel enters their apartment with groceries. Juanjo doesn't want Manuel to move because the floor has just been washed. Valentina is vacuuming the living room in her apartment; Olga Lucía is upset that everything is such a mess. Juanjo wants Manuel to clean the kitchen. Daniel runs into Don Paco on the stairs. Don Paco gives Daniel and Sara the trash to take out. Olga Lucía sees that the living room is now very clean and says that she owes an apology to Valentina, who is sleeping on the couch. Manuel knocks at the door in an attempt to get away from Juanjo.

PERSONAJES

JUANJO

MANUEL

VALENTINA

OLGA LUCÍA

DON PACO

DANIEL

SARA

JUANJO ¡Detente! ¡Es mejor que no des ni un paso más!
MANUEL ¿Qué pasa?
JUANJO ¡¿No ves?!
MANUEL ¿Qué?
JUANJO ¡Estoy limpiando!
MANUEL ¡Está limpiando!

VALENTINA ¡La aspiradora que te compraste funciona muy bien!
OLGA LUCÍA ¿Qué haces?
VALENTINA ¡Estoy limpiando!
OLGA LUCÍA ¡Cuando yo limpio, no hago tanto desorden! Me voy a estudiar a mi cuarto. ¡En un rato espero que esté todo ordenado!
VALENTINA ¡No me puede prohibir que limpie!

MANUEL Juanjo, ¿es necesario que me quede aquí?
JUANJO ¡No, ven a la cocina! A ti te gusta mucho cocinar, ¿no?
MANUEL ¿Quieres que cocine?
JUANJO No. ¡Lo que quiero es que limpies!
MANUEL Que limpie ¿qué?
JUANJO ¡El microondas donde explotó tu pizza! La estufa, el horno, la cafetera, ¡y todo lo que ensucias!

ACTIVIDADES

1 **¿Cierto o falso?** Indica si lo que dicen las oraciones es **cierto** o **falso**. Corrige las oraciones falsas.
1 Communication Interpretive Communication

	Cierto	Falso
1. Manuel pasa la aspiradora.	○	✓
Valentina pasa la aspiradora.		
2. Valentina está en la sala de su apartamento.	✓	○
3. A Olga Lucía no le gusta el desorden que hace Valentina.	✓	○
4. Juanjo hace la cama.	○	✓
Juanjo limpia el apartamento.		
5. Daniel y Sara sacan la basura.	✓	○

2 **Ordenar** Indica el orden de los eventos.
2 Communication Interpretive Communication

a. Valentina duerme en el sofá. *4*

b. Manuel vuelve de comprar comida. *1*

c. Juanjo empieza a lavar los platos. *3*

d. Valentina pasa la aspiradora. *2*

e. Manuel va al apartamento de las chicas. *5*

PACO ¡Tened cuidado!
DANIEL Disculpe, no estábamos mirando...
PACO Hacedme un favor.
DANIEL Claro, diga.
PACO ¡Sacad la basura!
DANIEL Eh... cómo no.
SARA (*a Paco*) ¡De nada!

OLGA LUCÍA ¿Qué pasa?
MANUEL ¡Me estoy escapando de Juanjo!
OLGA LUCÍA ¿Por qué?
MANUEL ¡Quiere que limpie la cocina!

JUANJO ¡Déjenme entrar! ¡Abran la puerta!

Expresiones útiles

la cafetera *coffee maker*
cómo no *of course*
dejar *to let*
detenerse *to stop (moving)*
la disculpa *apology*
explotar *to explode*
¡Guau! *Wow!*
la limpieza *cleaning*

---

la escoba *broom*
esconderse *to hide*

Malasaña

Este barrio tiene calles angostas (*narrow*) y edificios con balcones. Los cafés, restaurantes, museos, librerías y tiendas de segunda mano le dan vida a Malasaña tanto de día como de noche, exactamente lo que buscan los jóvenes.

¿Hay en tu comunidad un barrio que les guste mucho a los jóvenes? Descríbelo.

3 **Los quehaceres** En parejas, túrnense para preguntarse con qué frecuencia hacen estos quehaceres domésticos. ¿Tienen respuestas en común?

1. sacar la basura
2. cocinar
3. lavar los platos
4. hacer la cama
5. pasar la aspiradora
6. poner y quitar la mesa
7. sacudir los muebles
8. lavar y planchar la ropa

I CAN say how often I do chores.

Communicative Goal
Identify architectural features in the
Spanish-speaking world

Balcones que enamoran

Cartagena, Colombia

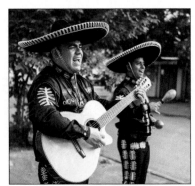

la serenata

Grandes o pequeños, curvos o rectos°, de hierro° o de madera°, los balcones siempre han sido° parte importante de las viviendas de los países hispanos, sobre todo en las regiones más cálidas°, como el sur de España (en especial Andalucía) o el Caribe, pero también en las ciudades andinas, como Lima, Perú. El centro histórico de esta ciudad fue declarado patrimonio histórico de la humanidad, en especial por sus balcones.

Desde la época° colonial, los balcones fueron siempre fundamentales en las construcciones de estos países, tanto que en algunas partes se consideraba que una casa sin° balcón estaba "inacabada°". Esta parte de la casa tuvo durante mucho tiempo una función social, pues las mujeres jóvenes salían a "balconear", con el objetivo no sólo de refrescarse° sino también de coquetear° con el chico que les gustaba. ¡Cuántas relaciones amorosas nacieron y se desarrollaron° en los balcones de las ciudades hispanoamericanas! Decorados con plantas y muchas flores, son también escenario de las famosas serenatas, una tradición que todavía se conserva en muchas partes y que consiste en que el novio le lleva en la noche un grupo musical a su amada°, quien lo escucha desde el balcón de su casa.

Hoy en día, aunque los balcones han desaparecido° de muchas construcciones modernas, siguen siendo parte esencial de casas o apartamentos en pueblos y ciudades, donde son utilizados no sólo para balconear, sino también para otras actividades como tomar el desayuno o recibir a las visitas°.

rectos *straight* **hierro** *iron* **madera** *wood* **han sido** *have been* **cálidas** *hot* **época** *era* **sin** *without* **inacabada** *unfinished* **refrescarse** *to cool off* **coquetear** *to flirt* **se desarrollaron** *developed* **amada** *loved one* **han desaparecido** *have disappeared* **visitas** *visitors*

Lima, Perú

ASÍ SE DICE
La vivienda

el ático el desván	el altillo
la cobija (Méx.) la frazada (Arg., Cuba, Ven.)	la manta
el escaparate (Cuba, Ven.) el ropero (Méx.)	el armario
el fregadero	*kitchen sink*
el frigidaire (Perú) el frigorífico (Esp.) la heladera (Arg.) la nevera	el refrigerador
el lavavajillas (Arg., Esp., Méx.)	el lavaplatos

ACTIVIDADES

1 **¿Cierto o falso?** Indica si lo que dicen las oraciones es **cierto** o **falso**. Corrige la información falsa.

1. Los balcones son una parte importante de las viviendas en las regiones más cálidas de los países hispanos.

2. Las mujeres jóvenes salían a balconear para refrescarse y coquetear.

3. En algunas partes se consideraba que una casa sin balcón estaba "inacabada".

4. Durante la serenata el grupo musical canta en el balcón.

5. Hay balcones en casi todas las construcciones modernas.

2 **Preguntas** Contesta las preguntas.

1. Además del sur de España y el Caribe, ¿dónde son una parte importante de las viviendas los balcones?

2. ¿Cómo se llama la tradición de llevar un grupo musical al balcón de la amada?

3. ¿Qué ciudad tiene un centro histórico que ha sido declarado patrimonio histórico de la humanidad, especialmente por sus balcones?

4. ¿Cómo son utilizados los balcones hoy en día?

3 **La serenata** Con un(a) compañero/a, representa una conversación entre un novio y su amada cuando él le lleva una serenata a ella.

4 **¿Qué piensas?** Responde a las preguntas.

1. ¿Por qué crees que los balcones son una parte tan importante de las viviendas en las regiones más cálidas de los países hispanos?

2. ¿Qué piensas de la tradición de las serenatas?

3. ¿Por qué crees que la tradición de las serenatas todavía se conserva?

4. ¿Qué balcones famosos (reales o ficticios) conoces? ¿Para qué se usan o se usaban?

I CAN identify architectural features in the Spanish-speaking world.

Communicative Goal
Identify characteristics of the house of Frida Kahlo

  Video

La casa de Frida

1 **Preparación** Imagina que eres un(a) artista, ¿cómo sería (*would be*) tu casa? ¿Sería muy diferente de la casa en donde vives ahora?

2 **El video** Mira el episodio de **Flash cultura** sobre la casa de la artista mexicana Frida Kahlo.

Vocabulario	
jardinero *gardener*	la silla de ruedas *wheelchair*
muros *walls*	las valiosas obras *valuable works*

El hogar en que nació la pintora Frida Kahlo en 1907 se caracteriza por su arquitectura típicamente mexicana…

3 **¿Cierto o falso?** Indica si lo que dicen estas oraciones es **cierto** o **falso**.

1. La casa de Frida Kahlo está en el centro de la Ciudad de México.

2. La casa de Frida se transformó en un museo en los años cincuenta.

3. Frida Kahlo vivió sola (*alone*) en su casa.

4. Entre las obras que se exhiben está el cuadro de *Las dos Fridas*.

5. El jardinero actual (*current*) jamás conoció ni a Frida ni a Diego.

6. En el museo se exhiben la silla de ruedas y los aparatos ortopédicos de Frida.

4 **Comparación** Compara la casa de Frida Kahlo con otra casa famosa que conoces.

I CAN identify characteristics of the house of Frida Kahlo.

12.1 Usted and ustedes commands

▸ Command forms are used to give orders or advice. **Usted** and **ustedes** can be used to refer to a group of people or in formal situations.

Hable con ellos, don Paco.
Talk to them, Don Paco.

Laven los platos ahora mismo.
Wash the dishes right now.

Coma frutas y verduras.
Eat fruits and vegetables.

Beban menos té y café.
Drink less tea and coffee.

▸ The **usted** and **ustedes** commands (**mandatos**) are formed by dropping the final **–o** of the **yo** form of the present tense. For **–ar** verbs, add **–e** or **–en**. For **–er** and **–ir** verbs, add **–a** or **–an**.

Formal commands (*Ud.* and *Uds.*)

Infinitive	Present tense *yo* form	*Ud.* command	*Uds.* command
limpiar	limpio	limpie	limpien
barrer	barro	barra	barran
sacudir	sacudo	sacuda	sacudan
decir (e:i)	digo	diga	digan
pensar (e:ie)	pienso	piense	piensen
volver (o:ue)	vuelvo	vuelva	vuelvan
servir (e:i)	sirvo	sirva	sirvan

Claro, diga.

¡Déjenme entrar!
¡Abran la puerta!

▸ Verbs with irregular **yo** forms have the same irregularity in their formal commands. These verbs include **conducir, conocer, decir, hacer, ofrecer, oír, poner, salir, tener, traducir, traer, venir,** and **ver**.

Oiga, don Paco…
Listen, Don Paco…

Pongan la mesa, por favor.
Set the table, please.

¡Salga inmediatamente!
Leave immediately!

Hagan la cama antes de salir.
Make the bed before leaving.

▸ Stem-changing verbs maintain their stem changes in **usted** and **ustedes** commands.

e:ie
No **pierda** la llave.
Cierren la puerta.

o:ue
Vuelva temprano, joven.
Duerman bien, chicos.

e:i
Sirva la sopa, por favor.
Repitan las oraciones.

Communicative Goal
Give advice

Práctica

1 ¡A mudarse! La señora González quiere mudarse. Ayúdala a organizarse, indicando el mandato formal de cada verbo.

modelo
_____ *Lea* [leer] los anuncios (*ads*) del periódico y *guárdelos* [guardarlos].

1. _____ [ir] personalmente y _____ [ver] las casas usted misma.

2. Decida qué casa quiere y _____ [llamar] al agente. _____ [pedirle] un contrato de alquiler.

3. _____ [alquilar] un camión (*truck*) para el día de la mudanza (*moving day*) y _____ [preguntarles] a los empleados la hora exacta de llegada.

4. _____ [decirles] a todos en casa que tienen que ayudar. No _____ [decirles] que usted va a hacerlo todo.

5. _____ [tomarse] su tiempo para hacer las maletas tranquilamente. _____ [sacar] toda la ropa que no use y _____ [dar] a alguien que la necesite.

6. El día de la mudanza no _____ [estar] nerviosa.

7. No _____ [preocuparse]. _____ [saber] que todo va a salir bien.

2 ¿Qué dicen? Mira los dibujos y escribe un mandato lógico para cada uno.

modelo

Arreglen estas cosas, por favor.

1. _____   2. _____

3. _____   4. _____

Conversación

3 **Consejos** Con un(a) compañero/a, representa a un(a) estudiante y a un(a) profesor(a). El/La estudiante cuenta sus problemas y el/la profesor(a) le da órdenes.

modelo

Me torcí el tobillo jugando al tenis.
Es la tercera vez.

Estudiante 1: Me torcí el tobillo jugando al tenis. Es la tercera vez.

Estudiante 2: No juegue más al tenis. / Vaya a ver a un médico.

1. Me enfermé después de volver de las vacaciones.
2. Mi compañero/a de cuarto y yo siempre llegamos tarde a la clase.
3. Nuestro cuarto es demasiado ruidoso (*too noisy*) para estudiar.
4. Me duele la cabeza y no puedo hacer la presentación para la clase hoy.
5. ¡Se me olvidó estudiar para el examen!

4 **Un programa de consejos** Con un(a) compañero/a, representa los papeles de una persona que da consejos en la radio y de los radioyentes (*radio listeners*) que la llaman con estos problemas.

- problemas sentimentales o familiares
- problemas académicos
- problemas con los amigos
- problemas financieros
- problemas médicos
- problemas con la casa o el apartamento
- problemas con el coche
- problemas con los vecinos
- problemas para dormir

5 **Un anuncio de televisión** En grupos, presenten un anuncio de televisión a la clase. Debe tratar de (*be about*) un detergente, un electrodoméstico o una agencia de bienes raíces. Usen mandatos, los pronombres relativos y el **se** impersonal.

modelo

Compre el lavaplatos Cristal. Tiene todo lo que usted desea. Es el lavaplatos que mejor funciona. Venga a verlo ahora mismo… No pierda ni un minuto más.

I CAN give advice.

Irregular commands

▶ Verbs ending in **-car, -gar,** and **-zar** have a spelling change in the command forms.

sacar	c	qu	saque, saquen
jugar	g	gu	juegue, jueguen
almorzar	z	c	almuerce, almuercen

▶ These verbs have irregular formal commands.

INFINITIVE	Ud. COMMAND	Uds. COMMAND
dar	dé	den
estar	esté	estén
ir	vaya	vayan
saber	sepa	sepan
ser	sea	sean

▶ To make a command negative, place **no** before the verb.

No ponga las maletas en la cama.
Don't put the suitcases on the bed.

No ensucien los sillones.
Don't get the armchairs dirty.

▶ In affirmative commands, reflexive and object pronouns are always attached to the end of the verb. Note that when a pronoun is attached to a verb that has two or more syllables, an accent mark is added.

Siénten**se**, por favor.
Díga**melo**.

Acuésten**se** ahora.
Póngan**las** en el suelo, por favor.

▶ In negative commands, the pronouns precede the verb.

No **se** preocupe.
No **me lo** dé.

No **los** ensucien.
No **nos las** traigan.

▶ **Usted** and **ustedes** can be used after command forms for a more formal, polite tone.

Muéstrele usted la casa a su amigo.
Show the house to your friend.

Tomen ustedes esta alcoba.
Take this bedroom.

¡Manos a la obra!

Indica los mandatos afirmativos y negativos.

	Afirmativo	Negativo
1. escucharlo (Ud.)	Escúchelo	No lo escuche
2. decírmelo (Uds.)	_____	_____
3. salir (Ud.)	_____	_____
4. servírnoslo (Uds.)	_____	_____
5. barrerla (Ud.)	_____	_____
6. hacerlo (Ud.)	_____	_____
7. ir (Uds.)	_____	_____
8. sentarse (Uds.)	_____	_____

Communicative Goal
Talk about things that are necessary or important

12.2 The present subjunctive

▶ The subjunctive mood expresses the speaker's attitude toward events, actions, or states that the speaker views as uncertain or hypothetical.

Es bueno **que estudies** más.	Es necesario **que** no **lleguemos** tarde.
It is good that you study more.	*It is necessary that we don't arrive late.*

▶ The subjunctive is mainly used to express 1) will and influence; 2) emotion; 3) doubt, disbelief, and denial; and 4) indefiniteness and nonexistence.

▶ The subjunctive is most often used in sentences that consist of a main clause and a subordinate clause. The main clause contains a verb or expression that triggers the use of the subjunctive in the subordinate clause. The word **que** connects the subordinate clause to the main clause.

▶ Some expressions are always followed by clauses in the subjunctive. These include:

Es bueno (malo, mejor) que...
It's good (bad, better) that...

Es importante (necesario, urgente) que...
It's important (necessary, urgent) that...

Es mejor que vayas con él.
It's better that you go with him.

Es urgente que sepa la verdad.
It's urgent that she know the truth.

▶ Note the following endings for the subjunctive.

Present subjunctive of regular verbs

	hablar	comer	escribir
yo	hable	coma	escriba
tú	hables	comas	escribas
Ud./él/ella	hable	coma	escriba
nosotros/as	hablemos	comamos	escribamos
vosotros/as	habléis	comáis	escribáis
Uds./ellos/ellas	hablen	coman	escriban

▶ To form the present subjunctive of regular verbs, drop the **–o** ending from the **yo** form of the indicative, and replace it with the subjunctive endings.

INFINITIVE	PRESENT INDICATIVE	PRESENT SUBJUNCTIVE
hablar	hablo	hable
comer	como	coma
escribir	escribo	escriba

▶ Verbs ending in **-car, -gar,** and **-zar** have a spelling change in all forms.

sacar	saque, saques, saque, saquemos, saquéis, saquen
jugar	juegue, juegues, juegue, juguemos, juguéis, jueguen
almorzar	almuerce, almuerces, almuerce, almorcemos, almorcéis, almuercen

Práctica

1 **Emparejar** Completa las oraciones con el subjuntivo de los verbos. Luego, empareja las oraciones del grupo **A** con las del grupo **B**.

A

1. Es mejor que _____ [nosotros, cenar] en casa.
2. Es importante que _____ [yo, tomar] algo para el dolor de cabeza.
3. Señora, es urgente que le _____ [yo, sacar] la muela. Parece que tiene una infección.
4. Es malo que Ana les _____ [dar] tantos dulces a los niños.
5. Es necesario que _____ [Uds., llegar] a la una de la tarde.
6. Es importante que _____ [nosotros, acostarse] temprano.

B

a. Es importante que _____ [ellos, comer] más verduras.
b. No, es mejor que _____ [nosotros, salir] a comer a un restaurante.
c. Y yo creo que es urgente que _____ [tú, llamar] al médico.
d. En mi opinión, no es necesario que _____ [nosotros, dormir] tanto.
e. ¿Ah, sí? ¿Es necesario que me _____ [yo, tomar] un antibiótico también?
f. Para llegar a tiempo, es necesario que _____ [nosotros, almorzar] temprano.

2 **Oraciones** Combina los elementos de las tres columnas para formar oraciones. Usa el subjuntivo.

Expresiones	Sujetos	Actividades
Es bueno que	yo	hacer la cama
Es mejor que	mi hermano	levantarse
Es malo que	los padres	sacar la basura
Es importante que	Sofía Vergara	mudarse
Es necesario que	mis amigos/as	lavar los platos
Es urgente que	Kevin Durant	cocinar
	el/la profesor(a)	barrer el suelo
		despertarse
		ensuciar la casa
		comer

Conversación

3 Minidiálogos Con un(a) compañero/a, completa los minidiálogos de una manera lógica, usando el subjuntivo.

> **modelo**
>
> **Miguelito:** Mamá, no quiero arreglar mi cuarto.
> **Sra. Torres:** *Es necesario que lo arregles.*
> *Y es importante que sacudas los*
> *muebles también.*

MIGUELITO Mamá, no quiero estudiar. Quiero salir a
jugar con mis amigos.
SRA. TORRES (1) _____.

. . .

MIGUELITO Mamá, es que no me gustan las
verduras. Prefiero comer pasteles.
SRA. TORRES (2) _____.

. . .

MIGUELITO ¿Tengo que poner la mesa, mamá?
SRA. TORRES (3) _____.

. . .

MIGUELITO No me siento bien, mamá. Me duele
todo el cuerpo y tengo fiebre.
SRA. TORRES (4) _____.

4 Entrevista Usa estas preguntas para entrevistar a un(a) compañero/a. Explica tus respuestas.

1. ¿Es importante que los niños ayuden con los quehaceres domésticos?

2. ¿Es urgente que los norteamericanos aprendan otras lenguas?

3. Si un(a) norteamericano/a quiere aprender francés, ¿es mejor que lo aprenda en Francia?

4. En tu universidad, ¿es necesario que los estudiantes vivan en residencias estudiantiles?

5. ¿Es bueno que todos los estudiantes practiquen algún deporte?

6. ¿Es importante que los estudiantes asistan a las clases?

▶ **-Ar** and **-er** stem-changing verbs have the same stem changes in the subjunctive as they do in the present indicative.

pensar (e:ie)	piense, pienses, piense, pensemos, penséis, piensen
mostrar (o:ue)	muestre, muestres, muestre, mostremos, mostréis, muestren
entender (e:ie)	entienda, entiendas, entienda, entendamos, entendáis, entiendan
volver (o:ue)	vuelva, vuelvas, vuelva, volvamos, volváis, vuelvan

▶ **–Ir** stem-changing verbs have the same stem changes in the subjunctive as in the present indicative. In addition, the **nosotros/as** and **vosotros/as** forms also undergo a stem change. The unstressed **e** changes to **i** and the unstressed **o** changes to **u**.

pedir (e:i)	pida, pidas, pida, pidamos, pidáis, pidan
sentir (e:ie)	sienta, sientas, sienta, sintamos, sintáis, sientan
dormir (o:ue)	duerma, duermas, duerma, durmamos, durmáis, duerman

▶ Verbs with irregular **yo** forms in the present indicative tense have the same irregularity in the present subjunctive.

INFINITIVE	PRESENT INDICATIVE	PRESENT SUBJUNCTIVE
conducir	conduzco	conduzca
conocer	conozco	conozca
decir	digo	diga
hacer	hago	haga
ofrecer	ofrezco	ofrezca
oír	oigo	oiga
parecer	parezco	parezca
poner	pongo	ponga
tener	tengo	tenga
traducir	traduzco	traduzca
traer	traigo	traiga
venir	vengo	venga
ver	veo	vea

▶ These five verbs are irregular in the present subjunctive.

Irregular verbs in the present subjunctive					
	dar	estar	ir	saber	ser
yo	dé	esté	vaya	sepa	sea
tú	des	estés	vayas	sepas	seas
Ud./él/ella	dé	esté	vaya	sepa	sea
nosotros/as	demos	estemos	vayamos	sepamos	seamos
vosotros/as	deis	estéis	vayáis	sepáis	seáis
Uds./ellos/ellas	den	estén	vayan	sepan	sean

¡ojo! The subjunctive form of **hay** (*there is, there are*) is **haya**.

I CAN talk about things that are necessary or important.

12.3 Subjunctive with verbs of will and influence

Communicative Goal | Give advice and recommendations

▸ The subjunctive is used with verbs and expressions of will and influence.

QUIERO QUE TENGAS
DIENTES MÁS BLANCOS
DENTABRIT BLANQUEADOR
Nueva fórmula

▸ Verbs of will and influence are often used when someone wants to affect the actions or behavior of other people.

Enrique **quiere** que **salgamos** a cenar.
Enrique wants us to go out for dinner.

Paola **prefiere** que **cenemos** en casa.
Paola prefers that we have dinner at home.

Ana **insiste** en que la **llamemos.**
Ana insists that we call her.

Mi madre nos **ruega** que **vayamos** a verla.
My mother begs us to come see her.

▸ Here are some verbs of will and influence.

Verbs of will and influence			
aconsejar	to advise	pedir (e:i)	to ask (for)
desear	to wish; to desire	preferir (e:ie)	to prefer
importar	to be important; to matter	prohibir	to prohibit
		querer (e:ie)	to want
insistir (en)	to insist (on)	recomendar (e:ie)	to recommend
mandar	to order	rogar (o:ue)	to beg
necesitar	to need	sugerir (e:ie)	to suggest

▸ Some impersonal expressions convey will or influence, such as **es necesario que, es importante que, es mejor que,** and **es urgente que.**

Es importante que duermas bien.
It's important that you sleep well.

Es urgente que él lo **haga** hoy.
It's urgent that he do it today.

▸ When the main clause contains an expression of will or influence and the subordinate clause has a different subject, the subjunctive is required.

Main clause	Connector	Subordinate clause
VERB OF WILL		SUBJUNCTIVE
Mi mamá prefiere	**que**	**yo saque la basura.**

Práctica

1 **Entre amigas** Completa el diálogo.

cocina	mires	quiere	sea
diga	ponga	saber	ser
haga	prohíbe	sé	vaya

IRENE Tengo problemas con Vilma. ¿Qué me recomiendas que le (1) _____?

JULIA Necesito (2) _____ más para aconsejarte.

IRENE Me (3) _____ que mire televisión cuando llego de la escuela.

JULIA Tiene razón. Es mejor que tú no (4) _____ tanta televisión.

IRENE Quiero que (5) _____ más flexible, pero insiste en que yo (6) _____ todo en la casa.

JULIA No es verdad. Yo (7) _____ que Vilma (8) _____ y hace los quehaceres todos los días.

IRENE Sí, pero siempre me pide que (9) _____ los cubiertos en la mesa y que (10) _____ al sótano por las servilletas.

JULIA ¡Vilma sólo (11) _____ que ayudes en la casa!

2 **Unos consejos** Lee lo que dice cada persona. Luego, da consejos lógicos usando verbos como **aconsejar, recomendar** y **prohibir.** Sigue el modelo.

 modelo

El presidente: Quiero comprar la Casa Blanca.
Le aconsejo que compre otra casa.

1. **Tu mamá:** Pienso poner la secadora en la entrada de la casa.

2. **Martha Stewart:** Voy a ir a la gasolinera para comprar unas elegantes copas de cristal.

3. **Tu profesor(a):** No voy a corregir los exámenes.

4. **Enrique Iglesias:** Pienso llevar todos mis muebles nuevos al altillo.

5. **Katy Perry:** Hay una fiesta en mi casa esta noche, pero no quiero arreglar la casa.

6. **Tu papá:** Hoy no tengo ganas de hacer las camas.

Conversación

3 Preguntas Con un(a) compañero/a, túrnate para contestar las preguntas. Usa el subjuntivo.

1. ¿Te dan consejos tus amigos/as? ¿Qué te aconsejan? ¿Aceptas sus consejos? ¿Por qué?

2. ¿Qué te sugieren tus profesores que hagas antes de terminar los cursos que tomas?

3. ¿Insisten tus amigos/as en que salgas mucho con ellos/as?

4. ¿Qué quieres que te regalen tu familia y tus amigos/as para tu cumpleaños?

5. ¿Qué le recomiendas tú a un(a) amigo/a que no quiere salir los sábados con su novio/a?

6. ¿Qué les aconsejas a los nuevos estudiantes de tu universidad?

4 Recomendaciones Con un(a) compañero/a, prepara una lista de seis personas famosas. Un(a) estudiante da el nombre de una persona famosa y el/la otro/a le da un consejo.

modelo

Estudiante 1: Tom Holland.
Estudiante 2: Le aconsejo que haga más películas.

5 El apartamento de Luisa Con un(a) compañero/a, mira la ilustración. Da consejos a Luisa sobre cómo arreglar su apartamento. Usa expresiones impersonales y verbos como **aconsejar**, **sugerir** y **recomendar**.

modelo

Es mejor que arregles el apartamento más a menudo. Te aconsejo que guardes (*put away*) la tabla de planchar (*ironing board*).

I CAN give advice and recommendations.

¡Es mejor que no des ni un paso más!

¡No me puede prohibir que limpie!

▸ Indirect object pronouns are often used with the verbs **aconsejar, mandar, pedir, recomendar, rogar,** and **sugerir**.

Te aconsejo que estudies.
I advise you to study.

Le sugiero que vaya a casa.
I suggest that he go home.

Les recomiendo que barran el suelo.
I recommend that you sweep the floor.

Les ruego que no vengan.
I beg you not to come.

▸ Note that all the forms of **prohibir** in the present tense carry a written accent, except for the **nosotros/as** form: **prohíbo, prohíbes, prohíbe, prohibimos, prohibís, prohíben.**

Ella les **prohíbe** que miren la televisión.
She prohibits them from watching television.

Nos **prohíben** que nademos en la piscina.
They prohibit us from swimming in the pool.

▸ The infinitive is used with expressions of will and influence if there is no change of subject.

No quiero **sacudir** los muebles.
I don't want to dust the furniture.

Don Paco prefiere **descansar**.
Don Paco prefers to rest.

Es importante **sacar** la basura.
It's important to take out the trash.

No es necesario **quitar** la mesa.
It's not necessary to clear the table.

¡Manos a la obra!

Completa cada oración con la forma correcta del verbo indicado.

1. Te sugiero que __vayas__ [ir] con ella al supermercado.
2. Él necesita que yo le _____ [prestar] dinero.
3. No queremos que tú _____ [hacer] nada especial para nosotros.
4. Mis papás quieren que yo _____ [limpiar] mi cuarto.
5. Nos piden que la _____ [ayudar] a preparar la comida.
6. Quieren que tú _____ [sacar] la basura todos los días.
7. Quiero _____ [descansar] esta noche.
8. Es importante que ustedes _____ [limpiar] la casa.
9. Su tía les manda que _____ [poner] la mesa.
10. Te aconsejo que no _____ [salir] con él.
11. Mi tío insiste en que mi prima _____ [hacer] la cama.
12. Prefiero _____ [ir] al cine.
13. Es necesario _____ [estudiar].
14. Recomiendo que ustedes _____ [pasar] la aspiradora.

A repasar

12.1 Used and ustedes commands

1 Los consejos de la abuela La abuela les da muchos consejos a sus nietos. Completa los consejos con los mandatos de los verbos.

> **modelo** <u>Planchen</u> su ropa. (planchar)

1. No _____ el volumen de la música muy alto. (poner)
2. _____ sus camas después de levantarse. (hacer)
3. _____ los dientes después de comer. (cepillarse)
4. _____ sus platos después de cenar. (lavar)
5. _____ la tarea antes de salir a la calle. (terminar)
6. No _____ la televisión hasta la medianoche. (ver)

2 Órdenes Don José se va de viaje y deja su casa al cuidado de su vecina, doña Lucía. Lee lo que dice doña Lucía y contesta dándole órdenes como si fueras (*as if you were*) don José. Usa la información entre paréntesis.

> **modelo** DOÑA LUCÍA Voy a descansar.
> DON JOSÉ (comenzar a preparar la cena)
> No descanse. Comience a preparar la cena.

DOÑA LUCÍA Voy a apagar la luz del garaje.
DON JOSÉ (dejarla así) (1) _____

DOÑA LUCÍA Voy a barrer el suelo de toda la casa.
DON JOSÉ (barrer sólo el suelo de la cocina)
(2) _____

DOÑA LUCÍA Voy a lavar y secar los platos.
DON JOSÉ (ponerlos en el lavaplatos) (3) _____

DOÑA LUCÍA Voy a pasear el perro por la calle.
DON JOSÉ (dejarlo adentro de la casa) (4) _____

DOÑA LUCÍA Voy a sacar la basura por la noche.
DON JOSÉ (sacarla por la mañana) (5) _____

DOÑA LUCÍA Voy a quitar los libros del estante.
DON JOSÉ (no ser desordenada) (6) _____

3 Josefina Josefina se va de viaje y les deja una lista a sus hijos de lo que (no) tienen que hacer. Con un(a) compañero/a, escribe cinco mandatos formales con los verbos **dar, estar, ir, saber** y **ser**.

> **modelo** Miren solamente una hora de televisión por día.

12.2 The present subjunctive

4 Es importante que... Forma oraciones con **es importante que...** y estos elementos.

> **modelo** tú / ir / pagar / el alquiler
> Es importante que tú vayas a pagar el alquiler.

1. nosotros / dormir / siesta / por la tarde
2. los adolescentes / saber / hacer / los quehaceres domésticos
3. ustedes / conocer / sus vecinos
4. yo / ser / ordenado / la cocina
5. siempre / haber / comida / refrigerador
6. el vecino / estar / su apartamento / por la noche

5 El apartamento ideal Con un(a) compañero/a, describe el apartamento ideal. Explica el número de habitaciones y los muebles que deseas tener en cada habitación. Usa el subjuntivo con expresiones impersonales.

> **modelo** Es necesario que mi apartamento tenga tres alcobas y una oficina. Es importante que... También es necesario que...

12.3 Subjunctive with verbs of will and influence

6 Los quehaceres domésticos Di lo que estas personas quieren que se haga.

> **modelo** Los vecinos (pedir) / tú (barrer el patio)
> Los vecinos piden que tú barras el patio. /
> Los vecinos te piden que barras el patio.

1. El ama de casa (mandar) / los chicos (sacudir los estantes)
2. Yo (recomendar) / nosotros (usar el lavaplatos)
3. Raúl (insistir) / yo (apagar la luz del pasillo)
4. Tú (sugerir) / Sandra (cocinar la cena)
5. Nosotros (necesitar) / José y tú (poner las copas en la mesa)
6. Ustedes (rogar) / Esteban (planchar la ropa)

7 ¿Dónde quieres que lo ponga? Te estás mudando de casa y tus amigos deciden ayudarte. Con un(a) compañero/a, túrnate para preguntar dónde deben poner las cosas en la nueva casa. Usa el subjuntivo y los verbos **desear, preferir** y **querer** con los verbos **poner, colocar** (*to put*) y **llevar.**

modelo

Estudiante 1: *¿Dónde deseas que pongamos estas pinturas?*
Estudiante 2: *Deseo que pongan las pinturas en el sótano. / Deseo que las pongan en el sótano.*

- alfombras
- platos
- vasos
- almohadas
- cortinas
- mesa
- cuadro
- lámparas
- mantas
- sillón
- cómoda
- mesita

8 ¡Por favor! Tus padres van a visitar tu apartamento, por lo que necesitas ayuda para limpiarlo. Con un(a) compañero/a, escribe qué les vas a pedir a tus compañeros/as de apartamento. Usa el subjuntivo y los verbos **necesitar, pedir** y **rogar.**

modelo

Por favor, necesito que hagan sus camas y arreglen sus cuartos.

Síntesis

9 Una fiesta en la cuadra Imagina que tú y tu compañero/a son vecinos/as y están organizando una fiesta en su cuadra (*street block*). Prepara una conversación sobre los preparativos que tienen que hacer. Usa los mandatos formales y el subjuntivo.

modelo

Estudiante 1: *Para la fiesta del domingo, necesito que usted arregle las mesas en la calle.*
Estudiante 2: *Así lo voy a hacer. Compre usted la comida y vaya por el pastel.*

Communicative Goal
Talk about furniture and home decor

 Video

Videoclip

1 Preparación ¿Qué muebles tienes en tu casa? ¿Qué muebles te faltan o te gustaría comprar para decorar más tu casa?

2 El clip Mira el anuncio de **Conforama** de España.

Vocabulario	
caber *to fit*	duro *hard*
colchón *mattress*	madera *wood*

Tenemos la cama de rayas, la colcha° de rayas, el sofá de rayas, las cortinas de rayas.

colcha *bedspread*

3 ¿Qué buscan? Indica lo que buscan estas personas en la tienda.

_____ 1. chico   a. un sofá
_____ 2. familia de cinco   b. una cama
_____ 3. niña   c. una cocina de madera
_____ 4. Juan y su esposa   d. un televisor
_____ 5. hombre   e. un colchón

4 De compras En parejas, representen una conversación entre dos compañeros de cuarto o dos esposos que van a Conforama para comprar algo. Utilicen el subjuntivo.

modelo

Esposo: *Es importante que compremos un sofá cómodo.*
Esposa: *Quiero que el sofá sea grande...*

I CAN talk about furniture and home decor.

Ampliación

Communicative Goals
Use visual cues to help me understand a conversation, and give professional advice

1 Escuchar

A Mira los anuncios y escucha la conversación entre el señor Núñez, Adriana y Felipe. Luego, indica si cada descripción se refiere a la casa del anuncio o al apartamento del anuncio.

TIP **Use visual cues.** Visual cues, like illustrations and headings, provide useful clues about what you will hear.

18G

Bienes raíces

 Se vende.
4 alcobas, 3 baños, cocina moderna, jardín con árboles frutales.
B/. 225.000

 Se alquila.
2 alcobas, 1 baño.
Balcón. Urbanización Las Brisas. 525

Descripciones	La casa del anuncio	El apartamento del anuncio
1. Es barato.	☐	☐
2. Tiene cuatro alcobas.	☐	☐
3. Tiene oficina.	☐	☐
4. Tiene balcón.	☐	☐
5. Tiene una cocina moderna.	☐	☐
6. Tiene un jardín muy grande.	☐	☐
7. Tiene patio.	☐	☐

B Vuelve a escuchar la conversación e indica cómo es la casa ideal de Adriana y Felipe.

2 Conversar

Con un(a) compañero/a, representa una conversación entre un(a) psicólogo/a y un(a) paciente que le consulta sobre un problema personal (la familia, el/la novio/a, etc.). Incluye la siguiente información:

- *¿Cómo se siente el/la paciente?*
- *¿Cuál es el problema que tiene el/la paciente?*
- *¿Por qué tiene este problema?*
- *¿Desde cuándo lo tiene?*
- *¿Qué soluciones le da el/la psicólogo/a?*

I CAN understand a conversation by using visual cues.

I CAN give professional advice.

Ampliación

③ Escribir

Eres el/la administrador(a) de un edificio de apartamentos. Prepara un contrato de arrendamiento (*lease*) para los nuevos inquilinos (*tenants*).

> **TIP** **Use linking words.** To make your writing more cohesive, use linking words to connect simple sentences or ideas. Some common linking words are **cuando, mientras, o, pero, porque, pues, que, quien(es), sino,** and **y.**

Organizar	Utiliza un mapa de ideas para organizar la información sobre las fechas del contrato, el precio del alquiler y otros aspectos importantes.
Escribir	Escribe el primer borrador de tu contrato de arrendamiento.
Corregir	Intercambia el contrato con un(a) compañero/a. Anota los mejores aspectos, especialmente el uso de las palabras de enlace (*linking words*). Dale sugerencias y, si ves algunos errores, coméntaselos.
Compartir	Revisa el primer borrador según las indicaciones de tu compañero/a. Incorpora nuevas ideas o más información si es necesario, antes de escribir la versión final.

> Here are some technical terms that might help you in writing your contract:
> **el/la arrendatario/a** *tenant*
> **el/la arrendador(a)** *landlord*
> **el/la propietario/a** *owner*
> **las estipulaciones** *stipulations*
> **la parte** *party*
> **de anticipación, de antelación** *in advance*

Communicative Goals
Write a lease agreement, and do a presentation about a vacation house

④ Un paso más

Imagina que quieres construir (*to build*) una casa de vacaciones en un país hispano. Prepara una presentación sobre la casa. Considera estas preguntas.

- ¿Dónde quieres construir la casa? ¿Prefieres que esté en la selva (*jungle*), en una isla, en una montaña o en un lugar con vista al mar?

- ¿Cómo va a ser la casa? ¿Quieres que sea grande? ¿Cuántos pisos y cuántos cuartos va a tener?

- ¿Qué muebles quieres poner en cada cuarto?

- ¿Qué efectos visuales puedes usar para hacer más interesante la presentación? ¿Tienes mapas, fotos o planos (*blueprints*) de la casa?

⑤ Cultura

Describe uno de los barrios mencionados en esta lección: Malasaña en Madrid o Coyoacán en la Ciudad de México. Compáralo con el barrio donde vives, trabajas o pasas el tiempo libre.

I CAN write a lease agreement.

I CAN do a presentation about a vacation house.

Audio: Reading

Antes de leer

Did you know that a text written in Spanish is often longer than the same text written in English? Because the Spanish language often uses more words to express ideas, you will often encounter long sentences when reading in Spanish. Of course, sentence length varies with genre and with authors' individual styles.

TIP **Locate the main parts of a sentence.** To help you understand long sentences, identify the main parts of the sentence before trying to read it in its entirety. First, locate the main verb of the sentence, along with its subject, ignoring any words or phrases set off by commas. Then re-read the sentence, adding details like direct and indirect objects, transitional words, and prepositional phrases.

Examinar el texto

Locate the main subject and verb in the first sentence of this reading: _____

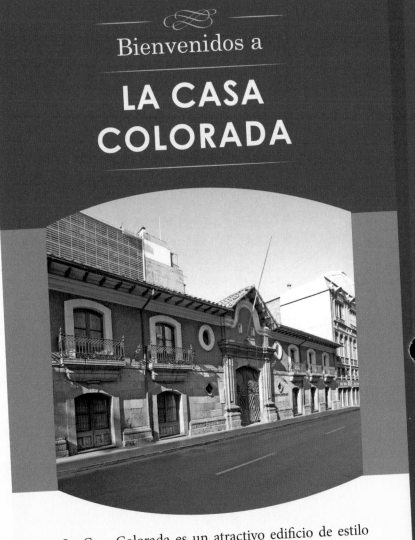

Bienvenidos a

LA CASA COLORADA

La Casa Colorada es un atractivo edificio de estilo colonial, construido° en 1769. Está situado en el centro de Santiago de Chile, en la calle Merced. En sus orígenes fue la vivienda de Mateo de Toro y Zambrano, un aristócrata chileno conocido por sus actividades en el ejército°, los negocios° y la administración de la ciudad. En la actualidad°, la Casa Colorada no está habitada por nadie.

El edificio se convirtió en un espacio público en el siglo° XX y en su interior están el Museo de Santiago, la Oficina de Turismo y la Fundación Vicente Huidobro, donde se encuentra abundante información sobre la vida y la obra° de este escritor chileno. El Museo de Santiago ofrece una exhibición permanente sobre la historia de la ciudad, desde la época precolombina hasta nuestros días.

La Casa Colorada es una obra del arquitecto portugués Joseph de la Vega. Los materiales fundamentales que se utilizaron en su construcción fueron el adobe, la madera° y la cal°. Desde el primer momento, esta casa se convirtió en el centro de atención de la sociedad santiaguina° por la elegancia de su diseño°. Además, una característica que la diferenciaba de otras viviendas del mismo estilo arquitectónico es que su fachada° estaba recubierta de piedra° hasta el primer piso. El edificio empezó a llamarse Casa Colorada en 1888, año en que pintaron su fachada de color rojo.

La composición exterior del edificio es simétrica. En el centro de la fachada hay una gran puerta que sirve de acceso principal a la vivienda; a los lados se ven unos arcos que forman puertas adicionales en el primer piso y ventanas con balcones de hierro forjado° en el segundo. Otra característica interesante del exterior de la casa es la elevación triangular del tejado° sobre la puerta principal.

construido *built* ejército *army* negocios *business* En la actualidad *At the present time*
siglo *century* obra *work* madera *wood* cal *lime* santiaguina *of Santiago* diseño *design*
fachada *façade* recubierta de piedra *covered with stone* hierro forjado *wrought iron* tejado *roof*

Después de leer

¿Comprendiste?

Completa las oraciones con las palabras adecuadas.

1. En el siglo XVIII, Mateo de Toro y Zambrano, un aristócrata de _____, vivió en la Casa Colorada.
2. Ahora _____ vive en la Casa Colorada.
3. El exterior de la casa es de color _____.
4. La _____ principal está en el centro de la fachada.
5. Los materiales que se utilizaron en su construcción fueron _____, la madera y la cal.
6. En el Museo de Santiago hay una exhibición sobre la _____ de la ciudad.

Preguntas

Responde estas preguntas con oraciones completas.

1. ¿Cuándo se construyó la Casa Colorada?
   _____
2. ¿Cuándo se convirtió en lugar público?
   _____
3. ¿Dónde están el Museo de Santiago, la Oficina de Turismo y la Fundación Vicente Huidobro?
   _____
4. ¿Cómo se llamaba el arquitecto de la Casa Colorada?
   _____
5. ¿En qué se diferenciaba la Casa Colorada de otras viviendas del mismo estilo arquitectónico?
   _____
6. ¿Por qué este edificio se llama la Casa Colorada?
   _____

Coméntalo

¿Te gustaría visitar la Casa Colorada? ¿Por qué? ¿Te gustaría vivir en una casa similar a ésta? Explica tu respuesta. ¿Hay edificios históricos en tu ciudad o comunidad? Descríbelos.

I CAN understand a text by identifying the main parts of its sentences.

Vocabulary Tools

La casa y sus cuartos

la alcoba *bedroom*
el altillo *attic*
el balcón *balcony*
la cocina *kitchen*
el comedor *dining room*
la entrada *entrance*
la escalera *stairs*
el garaje *garage*
el jardín *garden; yard*
la oficina *office*
el pasillo *hallway*
el patio *patio; yard*
la sala *living room*
el sótano *basement*

Los electrodomésticos

el electrodoméstico *electrical appliance*
la estufa *stove*
el horno *oven*
la lavadora *washing machine*
el lavaplatos *dishwasher*
el microondas *microwave*
el refrigerador *refrigerator*
la secadora *clothes dryer*

La mesa

la copa *wineglass*
la cuchara *spoon*
el cuchillo *knife*
el plato *plate*
la servilleta *napkin*
la taza *cup; mug*
el tenedor *fork*
el vaso *glass*

Los quehaceres domésticos

arreglar *to straighten up*
barrer el suelo *to sweep the floor*
cocinar *to cook*
hacer la cama *to make the bed*
hacer los quehaceres domésticos *to do household chores*
lavar (el suelo, los platos) *to wash (the floor, the dishes)*
limpiar la casa *to clean the house*
pasar la aspiradora *to vacuum*
planchar la ropa *to iron clothes*
poner la mesa *to set the table*
quitar la mesa *to clear the table*
sacar la basura *to take out the trash*
sacudir los muebles *to dust the furniture*

Los muebles y otras cosas

la alfombra *carpet; rug*
la almohada *pillow*
el armario *closet*
la cómoda *chest of drawers*
las cortinas *curtains*
el cuadro *picture*
el estante *bookcase; bookshelf*
la lámpara *lamp*
la luz *light; electricity*
la manta *blanket*
la mesita *end table*
la mesita de noche *nightstand*
los muebles *furniture*
la pared *wall*
la pintura *painting*
el sillón *armchair*
el sofá *sofa*

Otras palabras

las afueras *suburbs; outskirts*
la agencia de bienes raíces *real estate agency*
el alquiler *rent (payment)*
el amo/a (m., f.) de casa *homemaker*
el barrio *neighborhood*
el edificio de apartamentos *apartment building*
el hogar *home*
el/la vecino/a *neighbor*
la vivienda *housing*

———

alquilar *to rent*
ensuciar *to get (something) dirty*
mudarse *to move (residences)*

Verbs of will and influence *See page 318.*

∞ Communicative Goals: Review

I CAN describe homes.

• Describe your dorm room, apartment, or house. Mention the furniture and what is on the walls.

I CAN talk about household chores.

• Rank household chores, ending with your least favorite.

I CAN give advice.

• Write five pieces of advice for one of your professors. Use **usted** commands and the subjunctive with verbs of will and influence.

I CAN investigate architectural features in the Spanish-speaking world.

• Describe the role of balconies in Spanish-speaking countries.

AVENTURAS EN LOS PAÍSES HISPANOS

La ropa tradicional de los guatemaltecos se llama *huipil* y en ella se puede observar el amor de la cultura maya por la naturaleza *(nature)*. El diseño *(design)* y los colores de cada *huipil* indican el pueblo de origen y, a veces, también el sexo y la edad *(age)* de la persona que lo lleva.

¿Conoces la ropa tradicional de algún lugar en el mundo? ¿De dónde? ¿Tiene muchos colores como la ropa tradicional de Guatemala?

AMÉRICA CENTRAL I

Guatemala

Área: 108.890 km^2 (42.042 millas^2)
Población: 17.600.000
Capital: Ciudad de Guatemala – 2.891.000
Ciudades principales: Quetzaltenango, Escuintla, Mazatenango, Puerto Barrios
Moneda: quetzal

SOURCE: Population Division, UN Secretariat & CIA World Factbook

Honduras

Área: 112.492 km^2 (43.870 millas^2)
Población: 9.800.000
Capital: Tegucigalpa – 1.403.000
Ciudades principales: San Pedro Sula, El Progreso
Moneda: lempira

SOURCE: Population Division, UN Secretariat & CIA World Factbook

El Salvador

Área: 21.040 km^2 (8.124 millas^2)
Población: 6.500.000
Capital: San Salvador – 1.106.000
Ciudades principales: Soyapango, Santa Ana, San Miguel
Moneda: dólar estadounidense

SOURCE: Population Division, UN Secretariat & CIA World Factbook

Video

Deportes

El surfing

El Salvador es uno de los destinos favoritos en Latinoamérica para la práctica del *surfing*. Cuenta con 300 kilómetros de costa a lo largo del océano Pacífico y sus olas *(waves)* altas son ideales para quienes practican este deporte. De sus playas, La Libertad es la más visitada por surfistas de todo el mundo, gracias a que está muy cerca de la capital salvadoreña.

¿En qué lugares de los Estados Unidos se puede practicar el surfing? ¿Te gustaría practicarlo en las playas de América Central?

Ciudades

Antigua Guatemala ▶

Antigua Guatemala fue fundada en 1543. Fue una capital de gran importancia hasta 1773, cuando un terremoto *(earthquake)* la destruyó. Hoy día, conserva el carácter original de su arquitectura y es un gran centro turístico. Su celebración de la Semana Santa es, para muchas personas, la más importante del hemisferio.

¿Conoces algún país donde se celebra la Semana Santa? ¿Cómo se celebra?

MÉXICO

Lago Petén Itza

BELICE

Río de la Pasión

Golfo de Honduras

Lago de Izabal

Puerto Barrios

La Ceiba

GUATEMALA

Río Motagua

Sierra Espíritu Santo

San Pedro Sula

El Progreso

Lago de Atitlán

Sierra Grita

Sierra Rijol

Quetzaltenango

Ciudad de Guatemala

Lago de Guija

Lago de Yojoa

Antigua Guatemala

Río Lempa

Mazatenango

Tegucigalpa

Escuintla

Río de la Paz

Santa Ana

San Salvador

La Libertad

Río Lempa

San Miguel

EL SALVADOR

La Unión

Río Choluteca

Océano Pacífico

Mar Caribe

Islas de la Bahía

HONDURAS

Sierra de Payas

Río Patuca

Montañas de Colón

Río Coco

Laguna de Caratasca

NICARAGUA

Lugares

Copán

Copán es una zona arqueológica muy importante de Honduras. Fue construida por los mayas y se calcula que en el año 400 d. C. era una ciudad con más de 150 edificios y una gran cantidad de plazas, patios, templos y canchas *(courts)* para el juego de pelota *(ceremonial ball game)*. Las ruinas más famosas del lugar son los edificios adornados con esculturas pintadas a mano, los cetros *(scepters)* ceremoniales de piedra y el templo Rosalila. Una de las actividades más importantes de Copán era la astronomía. ¡Hasta se hacían congresos *(conventions)* de astrónomos!

Además de Honduras, ¿qué otros países en el mundo son famosos por sus ruinas arqueológicas?

Naturaleza

El Parque Nacional Montecristo

El Parque Nacional Montecristo se encuentra en la región norte de El Salvador. Se le conoce también como El Trifinio porque se ubica *(it is located)* en el punto donde se unen las fronteras de Guatemala, Honduras y El Salvador. Este bosque reúne muchas especies vegetales y animales, como orquídeas, monos araña *(spider monkeys)*, pumas, quetzales y tucanes. En este hermoso bosque, las copas de sus enormes árboles forman una bóveda que impide *(blocks)* el paso de la luz solar.

¿Cuáles son algunos de los parques nacionales más famosos en los Estados Unidos?

Música

La música garífuna

La música es una parte fundamental de la cultura de los garífunas, un grupo étnico que se extiende por la costa atlántica de Nicaragua, Honduras, Belice y Guatemala, y que es el producto del mestizaje *(mixing)* de los indígenas y los africanos. Festiva y vibrante, la música garífuna se interpreta en lengua arahuaca, con guitarra, bajo, tambores *(drums)*, clave y maracas. Aurelio Martínez y Andy Palacio son dos importantes artistas garífunas. En 2001, la música garífuna fue proclamada por la UNESCO Patrimonio Cultural Inmaterial de la Humanidad.

¿Conoces la música garífuna? ¿Te gusta?

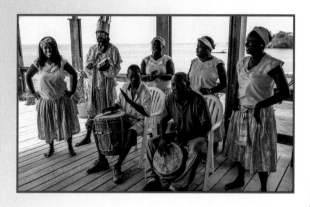

¿Qué aprendiste?

1 **¿Cierto o falso?** Indica si lo que dicen estas oraciones es **cierto** o **falso**.

	Cierto	Falso
1. La Libertad es una ciudad principal de El Salvador.	_____	_____
2. Los diseños del *huipil* indican el origen de la persona que lo lleva.	_____	_____
3. Tegucigalpa es la capital de Honduras.	_____	_____
4. Los garífunas viven en Guatemala, Honduras, Nicaragua y El Salvador.	_____	_____
5. En Copán se hacían congresos de geografía.	_____	_____
6. Antigua Guatemala es muy famosa por su celebración de la Semana Santa.	_____	_____
7. El Parque Nacional Montecristo está en El Salvador, en el límite con Honduras y Guatemala.	_____	_____
8. La vegetación del bosque del Parque Nacional Montecristo permite el paso de la luz del sol.	_____	_____

2 **Preguntas** Contesta estas preguntas.

1. ¿Cuál es la moneda de Guatemala?
2. ¿Qué país tiene 300 kilómetros de costa a lo largo del océano Pacífico?
3. ¿Quién es Andy Palacio?
4. ¿Qué ciudad fue la capital de Guatemala hasta 1773?
5. ¿Dónde está el templo Rosalila?
6. ¿Cómo se llama la ropa tradicional de los guatemaltecos?

3 **Por América Central** Con un(a) compañero/a, prepara un folleto (*brochure*) turístico en el que se hable de las características principales de Antigua Guatemala, Copán o el Parque Nacional Montecristo. Después, intercambia los folletos con otras parejas y elige el que más te guste.

4 **¿Qué piensas?** Responde a estas preguntas.

1. ¿Por qué piensas que la celebración de la Semana Santa es tan importante en Antigua Guatemala?
2. ¿Cuáles crees que son las influencias indígenas y africanas en la música garífuna?
3. ¿Por qué piensas que el dólar estadounidense es la moneda de El Salvador?

I CAN identify basic facts about the geography and culture of Guatemala, Honduras, and El Salvador by reading short informational texts with visuals.

13 La naturaleza

PREPARACIÓN

pages 332–337
- Words related to nature and the environment
- Animals
- Spanish punctuation

AVENTURAS

pages 338–339
- Juanjo, Valentina, Olga Lucía, Sara, and Daniel go hiking in the **Sierra de Madrid**. Why didn't Manuel go with them?

CULTURA

pages 340–341
- *Jóvenes por el medio ambiente*
- Flash cultura: *Naturaleza en Costa Rica*

GRAMÁTICA

pages 342–351
- The subjunctive with verbs of emotion
- The subjunctive with doubt, disbelief, and denial
- The subjunctive with conjunctions

LECTURA

pages 352–353
- Short story: *La foto*

PARA EMPEZAR

- ¿Dónde está Juanjo? ¿Qué hace?
- ¿Qué lleva? ¿Por qué?
- ¿Le interesa la naturaleza?

LA NATURALEZA

LA NATURALEZA

el árbol *tree*

el bosque (tropical)
   (tropical; rain) forest

el césped *grass*

el cielo *sky*

el cráter *crater*

el desierto *desert*

la estrella *star*

la hierba *grass*

el lago *lake*

la luna *moon*

el mundo *world*

la naturaleza *nature*

la nube *cloud*

el océano *ocean*

el paisaje *landscape*

la piedra *stone*

la planta *plant*

la región *region; area*

el río *river*

la selva *jungle*

el sendero *trail*

el sol *sun*

la tierra *land; soil*

el valle *valley*

el mono

la flor
flower

el pájaro
bird

VERBOS

conservar *to conserve*

contaminar *to pollute*

controlar *to control*

cuidar *to take care of*

dejar de (+ inf.)
   to stop (doing something)

desarrollar *to develop*

descubrir *to discover*

destruir *to destroy*

estar afectado/a (por)
   to be affected (by)

evitar *to avoid*

mejorar *to improve*

proteger *to protect*

reciclar *to recycle*

recoger *to pick up*

reducir *to reduce*

resolver (o:ue)
   to resolve; to solve

respirar *to breathe*

LOS ANIMALES

el animal *animal*

la ballena *whale*

el pez *fish*

Vocabulary Tools

el volcán

EL MEDIO AMBIENTE

el calentamiento global
  global warming

la caza *hunting*

la conservación *conservation*

la contaminación (del aire; del
  agua) *(air; water) pollution*

la deforestación *deforestation*

la ecología *ecology*

el/la ecologista *ecologist*

el ecoturismo *ecotourism*

la energía (nuclear; solar)
  (nuclear; solar) energy

la extinción *extinction*

la fábrica *factory*

el gobierno *government*

la ley *law*

el medio ambiente *environment*

el peligro *danger*

la población *population*

el reciclaje *recycling*

el recurso natural *natural resource*

la solución *solution*

───────────────────

ecológico/a *ecological*

renovable *renewable*

OTRAS PALABRAS Y EXPRESIONES

el envase de plástico
  plastic container

puro/a *pure*

la botella de vidrio
  glass bottle

la tortuga marina
sea turtle

la lata de aluminio
aluminum can

la energía nuclear
nuclear energy

estar contaminado/a
to be polluted

ASÍ SE DICE

césped/hierba ⟷ la grama (*Ec., Hond., Pan.,
Perú, P. Rico*), el pasto (*Arg., Col., Méx., Urug.*),
el zacate (*Amér. C., Méx.*)

A escuchar

1 **Escuchar** Escucha estas oraciones y anota los sustantivos (*nouns*) que se refieren a **las plantas**, **los animales**, **la tierra** y **el cielo**.

Plantas	Animales	Tierra	Cielo
_____	_____	_____	_____
_____	_____	_____	_____

2 **Seleccionar** Escucha las descripciones y escribe el número que corresponda a cada foto.

a. _____

b. _____

c. _____

d. _____

A practicar

3 **La naturaleza** Selecciona la palabra que no pertenece al grupo.

1. sol • desierto • luna • estrella
2. océano • lago • sendero • río
3. naturaleza • paisaje • ecoturismo • mono
4. piedra • pájaro • pez • perro
5. volcán • ballena • cráter • piedra
6. recurso natural • caza • contaminación • deforestación
7. nube • aire • cielo • lago
8. solución • selva • bosque • desierto
9. botella • envase • peligro • lata
10. tortuga • árbol • hierba • flor

4 **Completar** Completa las oraciones.

1. Si vemos basura en las calles, la debemos _____.
2. Los científicos trabajan para _____ nuevas soluciones.
3. Es necesario que todos trabajemos juntos para _____ los problemas del medio ambiente.
4. Debemos _____ el medio ambiente porque está en peligro.
5. Muchas leyes nuevas _____ el número de árboles que se pueden cortar (*cut down*).
6. Las primeras civilizaciones _____ cerca de los ríos, los lagos y los océanos.
7. Todas las personas del mundo _____ por la contaminación.
8. Los turistas deben tener cuidado y no _____ las regiones que visitan.
9. Podemos conservar los recursos si _____ el aluminio, el vidrio y el plástico.
10. La contaminación y la deforestación _____ el medio ambiente.

contaminar	destruyen	reciclamos
controlan	están afectadas	recoger
cuidan	mejoramos	resolver
descubrir	proteger	se desarrollaron

5 **Definiciones** Indica la palabra adecuada para cada definición.

modelo
lugar que está lleno de árboles
el bosque

1. estrella más grande de nuestro sistema planetario _____
2. lugar donde llueve poco _____
3. cuando la temperatura del planeta sube _____
4. cuando una especie animal ya no existe más _____
5. parte de un volcán _____
6. animal grande que vive en el océano _____

A conversar

6 **Preguntas** En parejas, túrnense para hacerse estas preguntas. ¿Tienen respuestas en común?

1. ¿Te preocupas por el medio ambiente? ¿Por qué?
2. ¿Qué forma de energía prefieres? ¿Por qué?
3. ¿Cómo podemos reducir la cantidad de basura que producimos?
4. ¿Crees que es importante reciclar? ¿Lo haces? ¿Por qué?
5. ¿Cómo podemos proteger los animales en peligro de extinción?
6. ¿Qué lugares están contaminados en tu estado o región?
7. ¿Qué podemos hacer para mejorar la calidad del aire?
8. ¿Quiénes deben resolver los problemas del medio ambiente? ¿Los gobiernos, los ecologistas…?

7 **Alternativas** En parejas, hablen sobre las alternativas y el efecto que tienen en el medio ambiente.

- manejar en coche o pasear en bicicleta
- ser vegetariano/a o comer carne
- ducharse o bañarse
- lavar los platos a mano o usar el lavaplatos
- leer libros en papel o electrónicos
- hacer ecoturismo o turismo tradicional

8 **Situaciones** En grupos pequeños, representen estas situaciones.

- Un(a) ecologista habla con un grupo de familias sobre qué se puede hacer en la casa para proteger el medio ambiente.
- Un(a) representante de una universidad habla con un grupo de estudiantes nuevos sobre la campaña (*campaign*) ambiental de la universidad.
- Un(a) candidato/a presidencial da un discurso (*speech*) sobre el problema de la deforestación.

I CAN talk about nature and the environment.

Ortografía

 Tutorial

Los signos de puntuación

In Spanish, as in English, punctuation marks are important because they help you express your ideas in a clear, organized way.

. . . .

No podía ver las llaves. Las buscó por los estantes, las mesas, las sillas, el suelo; minutos después, decidió mirar por la ventana. Allí estaban…

The **punto y coma (;)**, the **tres puntos (…)**, and the **punto (.)** are used in very similar ways in Spanish and English.

. . . .

Argentina, Brasil, Paraguay y Uruguay son miembros de Mercosur.

In Spanish, the **coma (,)** is not used before **y** or **o** in a series.

. . . .

3,5%   **29,2%**   **3.000.000**   **$2.999,99**

In numbers, Spanish uses a **coma** where English uses a decimal point and a **punto** where English uses a comma.

. . . .

¿Cómo te llamas?   **¿Dónde está?**   **¡Ven aquí!**   **¡Hola!**

Questions in Spanish are preceded and followed by **signos de interrogación (¿ ?)**, and exclamations are preceded and followed by **signos de exclamación (¡ !)**.

. . . .

Práctica Lee el párrafo e indica los signos de puntuación necesarios. Recuerda que la primera letra de una oración siempre debe estar en mayúscula.

Ayer recibí la invitación de boda de Marta mi amiga colombiana inmediatamente empecé a pensar en un posible regalo fui al almacén donde Marta y su novio tenían una lista de regalos había un montón de cosas para regalar finalmente decidí regalarles un perro ya sé que es un regalo extraño pero espero que les guste a los dos

¿Palabras de amor? El siguiente diálogo tiene diferentes significados (*meanings*), dependiendo de los signos de puntuación que utilizas y el lugar donde los pones. Intenta encontrar los diferentes significados.

JULIÁN   me quieres

MARISOL   no puedo vivir sin ti

JULIÁN   me quieres dejar

MARISOL   no me parece mala idea

JULIÁN   no eres feliz conmigo

MARISOL   no soy feliz

Una excursión a la sierra

Juanjo, Valentina, Olga Lucía, Sara y Daniel hacen una excursión a la Sierra de Madrid.

 Video

Antes de ver

Haz predicciones sobre lo que vas a ver y oír en un episodio en el cual los personajes hacen una excursión.

PERSONAJES

JUANJO

VALENTINA

SARA

DANIEL

OLGA LUCÍA

JUANJO ¡Estamos en la naturaleza! ¡Respiren el aire puro!

VALENTINA Es una lástima que Manuel no esté aquí.

SARA Dijo que se sentía... mal.

OLGA LUCÍA Dudo mucho que esté enfermo.

DANIEL Seguro que no quiso levantarse temprano.

JUANJO ¡Ojalá podamos ver un oso pardo!

VALENTINA Daniel, no creo que debas darles comida a los peces.

DANIEL ¡Tienen hambre!

JUANJO ¡No seas tonto, Daniel, eso afecta el ecosistema!

SARA Juanjo, ¡deja de dibujar plantitas y come!

JUANJO En cuanto termine.

OLGA LUCÍA No olviden recogerlo todo, para que no contaminemos.

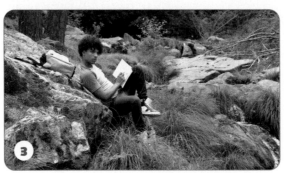

JUANJO ¡Me encanta el sonido del río! Es tan relajante. Aunque dudo que veamos un oso pardo, están en peligro de extinción.

VALENTINA Pero es probable que veamos una cabra, ¿no?

JUANJO Pues sí, aquí en la sierra hay una sobrepoblación de cabras.

ACTIVIDADES

1 **¿Cierto o falso?** Indica si lo que dicen las oraciones es **cierto** o **falso**. Corrige las oraciones falsas.

	Cierto	Falso
1. Daniel quiere ver un oso pardo.	○	○
2. En la Sierra de Madrid hay muchísimas cabras.	○	○
3. Juanjo dibuja plantas.	○	○
4. La playa del lago está llena de basura.	○	○
5. Manuel se quedó en casa.	○	○

2 **Ordenar** Indica el orden de los eventos.

a. Juanjo piensa que ve un oso. _____

b. Daniel les da comida a los peces. _____

c. Los chicos ven botellas. _____

d. El agua daña los dibujos de Juanjo. _____

e. Juanjo quiere recoger la basura. _____

DANIEL ¡Guau! ¡Es hermoso!

JUANJO ¡Es terrible!

VALENTINA Mirad todo ese plástico.

OLGA LUCÍA ¡Hay botellas en todas partes!

SARA Me molesta que la gente no sepa cuidar la naturaleza.

JUANJO ¡Tranquilos! ¡Cuando veo basura, la recojo! El reciclaje en una bolsa y la basura en otra. (*a Valentina y Olga Lucía*) ¿Qué?

VALENTINA Y OLGA LUCÍA ¡¿Tenemos que recoger la basura de otros?!

SARA Chicos, ¡¿visteis eso?!

VALENTINA ¡Tal vez sea una cabra!

JUANJO ¡Toma una foto antes de que se vaya!

Expresiones útiles

atrapar *to catch*
la cabra *goat*
de verdad *real*
el oso pardo *brown bear*
relajante *relaxing*
la sobrepoblación *overpopulation*
el sonido *sound*
Tranquilo(s)/a(s). *Relax.*

---

el disfraz *costume; disguise*
disfrazarse de *to dress up as*
mojado/a *wet*
la señal *signal*

Sierra de Madrid

A una hora de la ciudad en coche, se encuentra la Sierra de Madrid. Incluye el Parque Nacional de la Sierra de Guadarrama. Allí se pueden visitar altas montañas, pastizales (*pastures*) y valles, pero también lagunas, embalses (*reservoirs*) y ríos, con bosques de pinos y robles (*pine and oak trees*). Este parque es el hogar del 40% de las especies animales de España y más de mil especies de plantas.

¿Hay un parque nacional cerca de tu ciudad o pueblo? ¿Cómo es?

3 **El medio ambiente** En parejas, discutan los problemas ambientales mencionados en el video y sus posibles soluciones.

- ▶ la basura
- ▶ los animales en peligro de extinción
- ▶ la sobrepoblación de una especie de animales

I CAN discuss environmental issues.

Communicative Goal |
Talk about environmental activism in
Spanish-speaking countries

Jóvenes por el medio ambiente

No hay duda de que la crisis climática afecta a todo el mundo, pero Latinoamérica en particular ha sufrido° los estragos° de esta crisis. La continua reducción de lagos en Bolivia, el retroceso de los glaciares en los Andes, la destrucción de Puerto Rico por el huracán María en 2017 y los incendios° recientes en la Amazonia y otras regiones en varios países son algunos ejemplos de los retos° que enfrentan° los gobiernos y las comunidades de la región.

Ante esta situación, los jóvenes han cumplido° un rol fundamental y no están esperando a que las personas adultas o los países más ricos propongan las soluciones. Muchos adolescentes y jóvenes de toda la región se están movilizando para exigir° que se lleven a cabo° acciones que mitiguen los efectos de la crisis.

Por ejemplo, Xiye Bastida, original de San Pedro Tultepec, Estado de México, y miembro de la nación indígena otomí-tolteca, ha estado° al frente del movimiento de la juventud para salvar° el clima del planeta. Después de que su pueblo sufrió sequías° e inundaciones°, y tras presenciar los daños del huracán Sandy en Long Island, la joven, quien ahora vive en la ciudad de Nueva York, se convirtió en líder de las protestas del movimiento Fridays for Future (FFF), que pide a los gobiernos tomar acciones frente al cambio climático. Su activismo es tan intenso que ahora es conocida como "la Greta Thunberg de América".

Como Xiye, son muchos los jóvenes de Latinoamérica y España que están levantando la voz° por la defensa de un ambiente saludable y sostenible. El argentino Bruno Rodríguez, por ejemplo, en el otro extremo del continente, lidera la asociación

Xiye Bastida

Jóvenes por el Clima, que lucha° por la justicia climática, los derechos° humanos y la justicia social.

A Xiye y a Bruno los acompañan miles de jóvenes de España y Latinoamérica, agrupados en organizaciones como Jóvenes Verdes (España), Guateambiente (Guatemala) o Pacto X El Clima (Colombia), todas ellas conformadas por jóvenes entre catorce y treinta años.

ha sufrido *has suffered* **estragos** *ravages* **incendios** *fires* **retos** *challenges* **enfrentan** *face* **han cumplido** *have played* **exigir** *to demand* **lleven a cabo** *carry out* **ha estado** *has been* **salvar** *to save* **sequías** *droughts* **inundaciones** *floods* **levantando la voz** *raising their voices* **lucha** *fights* **derechos** *rights*

ASÍ SE DICE

La naturaleza

el arco iris	*rainbow*
la cascada la catarata	*waterfall*
el cerro la colina la loma	*hill, hillock*
la cima la cumbre el tope (Col.)	*summit; mountaintop*
la maleza los rastrojos (Col.) la yerba mala (Cuba) los hierbajos (Méx.) los yuyos (Arg.)	*weeds*

ACTIVIDADES

1 **¿Cierto o falso?** Indica si lo que dicen las oraciones es **cierto** o **falso**. Corrige la información falsa.

1. Hay una continua reducción de lagos en Puerto Rico.
2. San Pedro Tultepec sufrió sequías e indundaciones.
3. Xiye Bastida es conocida como "la Greta Thunberg de América".
4. Bruno Rodríguez lidera la organización Jóvenes Verdes.
5. Pacto X El Clima es una organización española.

2 **Preguntas** Contesta las preguntas.

1. ¿Dónde hay un retroceso de los glaciares?
2. ¿De dónde es Xiye Bastida?
3. ¿Quién lidera la asociación Jóvenes por el Clima?
4. ¿Cómo se llama la organización guatemalteca?
5. ¿De qué país es la organización Jóvenes Verdes?
6. ¿Cuántos años tienen los miembros de estas organizaciones?

3 **Activistas** En parejas, representen una conversación entre un miembro de una de estas organizaciones y otro/a joven, quien piensa en participar.

4 **¿Qué piensas?** Responde a las preguntas sobre los activistas medioambientales.

1. ¿Por qué crees que tantos jóvenes de Latinoamérica como de España se están movilizando por el medio ambiente?
2. ¿Qué piensas de Xiye Bastida y Bruno Rodríguez? ¿Por qué?
3. ¿Por qué crees que la asociación Jóvenes por el Clima conecta la justicia climática, los derechos humanos y la justicia social?
4. ¿Te inspiran estos activistas? ¿Por qué?

Communicative Goal
Identify different aspects of nature in Costa Rica

 Video

Naturaleza en Costa Rica

1 **Preparación** ¿Qué sabes de los volcanes de Costa Rica? ¿Y de sus aguas termales? Si no sabes nada, escribe tres predicciones sobre cada tema.

2 **El video** Mira el episodio de **Flash cultura** sobre un volcán en Costa Rica.

Vocabulario		
aguas termales *hot springs*	los poderes curativos *healing powers*	
hace erupción *erupts*	rocas incandescentes *incandescent rocks*	

Aquí existen más de cien volcanes. Hoy visitaremos el Parque Nacional Volcán Arenal.

3 **¿Cierto o falso?** Indica si estas oraciones son **ciertas** o **falsas**.

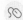

1. Centroamérica es una zona de pocos volcanes.
2. El volcán Arenal está en un parque nacional.
3. El volcán Arenal hace erupción pocas veces.
4. Las aguas termales cerca del volcán vienen del mar.
5. Cuando Alberto sale del agua, tiene calor.
6. Se pueden ver las rocas incandescentes desde algunos hoteles.

4 **Comparación** Compara el Parque Nacional Volcán Arenal con un parque nacional que conoces.

I CAN talk about environmental activism in Spanish-speaking countries.

I CAN identify different aspects of nature in Costa Rica.

Communicative Goal
Express my feelings about environmental problems

13.1 The subjunctive with verbs of emotion

Main clause	Connector	Subordinate clause
Marta espera	que	yo vaya al lago este fin de semana.

▸ When the main clause of a sentence expresses an emotion or feeling, use the subjunctive in the subordinate clause.

Nos alegramos de que te **gusten** las flores.
We are happy that you like the flowers.

Temo que Ana no **pueda** ir mañana con nosotros.
I'm afraid Ana won't be able to go with us tomorrow.

Siento que tú no **vengas** mañana.
I'm sorry that you're not coming tomorrow.

Le **sorprende** que Juan **sea** tan joven.
It surprises him that Juan is so young.

Es una lástima que Manuel no esté aquí.

Me molesta que la gente no sepa cuidar la naturaleza.

Common verbs and expressions of emotion

alegrarse (de)	to be happy	tener miedo (de)	to be afraid (of)
esperar	to hope; to wish	es extraño	it's strange
gustar	to be pleasing;	es una lástima	it's a shame
	to like	es ridículo	it's ridiculous
molestar	to bother	es terrible	it's terrible
sentir (e:ie)	to be sorry; to regret	es triste	it's sad
sorprender	to surprise	ojalá (que)	I hope (that);
temer	to be afraid		I wish (that)

Me molesta que la gente no **recicle** el plástico.
It bothers me that people don't recycle plastic.

Es una lástima que no **controlemos** la deforestación.
It's a shame that we don't control deforestation.

Es terrible que no **respiremos** aire puro.
It's terrible that we don't breathe clean air.

Espera que el gobierno **proteja** el medio ambiente.
He hopes that the government protects the environment.

Práctica

1 **Julia y Rosa** Completa la conversación. Hay dos palabras que no vas a usar.

alegro	molesta	temer
conozcan	ojalá	tengo miedo de
estén	puedan	vayan
lleguen	sorprender	visitar

JULIA Me alegro de que Adriana y Raquel (1) _____ a Colombia.

ROSA Sí... Es una lástima que (2) _____ cuando ya comenzaron las clases. Ojalá que la universidad las ayude a buscar casa. (3) _____ que no consigan dónde vivir.

JULIA Me (4) _____ que seas tan pesimista. Yo espero que (5) _____ gente simpática.

ROSA ¿Sabías que ellas van a estudiar la deforestación en las costas? Es triste que en tantos países los recursos naturales (6) _____ en peligro.

JULIA Me (7) _____ de que no se queden en la capital por la contaminación, pero (8) _____ tengan tiempo de viajar por el país.

ROSA Sí, espero que (9) _____ ir al Museo del Oro. Sé que también esperan (10) _____ la Catedral de Sal de Zipaquirá.

2 **Oraciones** Combina elementos de las tres columnas para formar oraciones.

 modelo Es triste que algunas personas no cuiden la naturaleza.

Expresiones	Sujetos	Actividades
Me alegro de que	yo	desarrollar programas de reciclaje
Espero que	tú	proteger las ballenas
Es extraño que	el gobierno	destruir los bosques
Me gusta que	el/la profesor(a)	contaminar el aire
Tengo miedo de que	la universidad	poner en peligro las tortugas marinas
Es triste que	las fábricas	cuidar la naturaleza
Ojalá que	algunas personas	utilizar el transporte público para usar menos gasolina
	los centros comerciales	
	mis amigos y yo	

Conversación

3 Diálogo Usa los elementos para crear una conversación entre Juan y la madre de su novia. Añade palabras si es necesario. Luego, con un(a) compañero/a, preséntala a la clase.

modelo

Juan, / esperar / (tú) llamar / Raquel. / Ser / tu / novia. / Ojalá / no / sentirse / sola

Juan, espero que llames a Raquel. Es tu novia. Ojalá no se sienta sola.

1. molestarme / (usted) decirme / lo que / tener / hacer. / Ahora / mismo / estarla / llamando
2. alegrarme / oírte / decir / eso. / Ser / terrible / estar / lejos / cuando / nadie / recordarte
3. señora, / ¡yo / tener / miedo / (ella) no recordarme / mí! / Ser / triste / estar / sin / novia
4. ser / ridículo / (tú) sentirte / así. / Mi hija / esperar / (tú) casarte / con ella
5. ridículo / o / no, / sorprenderme / todos preocuparse / ella / y / nadie acordarse / mí

4 Comentar Con un(a) compañero/a, comparte tus opiniones sobre las clases que más te gustan y las que menos te gustan. Usa expresiones como **me alegro de que, temo que** y **es extraño que**.

modelo

Estudiante 1: Mi clase favorita es español. Me alegro de que mi profesor nos ayude con la tarea.
Estudiante 2: Yo, en cambio, odio las matemáticas. Temo que mi profesor piense darnos más tarea.

5 Problemas Prepara una lista de tres o cuatro problemas ambientales en tu universidad. Luego, utilizando el subjuntivo, escribe una oración en la que expreses tu reacción. Comparte la información con la clase.

modelo

la basura de la cafetería
Temo que la basura de la cafetería no se pueda reducir.

6 Ecologistas En grupos, preparen un anuncio de una campaña ecológica. Usen expresiones como **esperar, sentir** y **temer**. Recuerden incluir:

- el nombre de la campaña ecológica
- un eslogan
- un mensaje para la comunidad
- una imagen que los identifique

I CAN express my feelings about environmental problems.

Using the subjunctive

▶ Use the infinitive after an expression of emotion when there is no change of subject.

Temo **llegar** tarde.
I'm afraid I'll arrive late.

Temo que mi novio **llegue** tarde.
I'm afraid my boyfriend will arrive late.

Me molesta **ver** el bosque tropical en peligro.
It bothers me to see the rain forest in danger.

Me alegro de que algunas fábricas **se preocupen** por el medio ambiente.
I'm happy that some factories worry about the environment.

▶ The expression **ojalá (que)** is always followed by the subjunctive. The use of **que** is optional.

Ojalá (que) se conserven nuestros recursos naturales.
I hope (that) our natural resources will be conserved.

Ojalá (que) recojan la basura muy pronto.
I hope (that) they collect the garbage soon.

Esperamos que nuestros hijos vean el cielo azul y que naden en aguas limpias... Tenemos que enseñarles a conservar y a reciclar.

¡Manos a la obra!

Completa las oraciones con el subjuntivo o el infinitivo.

1. Ojalá que ellos ___descubran___ [descubrir] nuevas formas de energía.
2. Temo que la energía nuclear _____ [ser] uno de los grandes peligros del futuro.
3. Es una lástima que la gente no _____ [reciclar] la basura orgánica.
4. Esperamos _____ [proteger] el aire de nuestra comunidad.
5. Me alegro de que mis amigos _____ [querer] hacer ecoturismo en el Amazonas.
6. A mis padres les gusta que nosotros _____ [participar] en programas de conservación.
7. Es terrible que _____ [haber] tantos animales en peligro de extinción.
8. El gobierno siente no _____ [poder] hacer nada para encontrar una solución.
9. Es triste que nuestras ciudades _____ [estar] afectadas por la contaminación.
10. Ojalá yo _____ [poder] hacer algo para reducir la contaminación.

Communicative Goal
Express my doubts about the future

13.2 The subjunctive with doubt, disbelief, and denial

▸ The subjunctive is used with expressions of doubt, disbelief, and denial.

Main clause	Connector	Subordinate clause
Dudan	que	su hijo les diga la verdad.

▸ The subjunctive is used in a subordinate clause when there is a change of subject and the main clause implies negation or uncertainty.

Dudo mucho que esté enfermo.

Daniel, no creo que debas darles comida a los peces.

Expressions of doubt, disbelief, or denial

dudar	to doubt	no es seguro	it's not certain
negar (e:ie)	to deny	no es verdad	it's not true
no creer	not to believe	es imposible	it's impossible
no estar seguro/a (de)	not to be sure (of)	es improbable	it's improbable
no es cierto	it's not true; it's not certain	(no) es posible	it's (not) possible
		(no) es probable	it's (not) probable

El gobierno **niega** que el agua **esté** contaminada.
The government denies that the water is polluted.

Dudo que el gobierno **resuelva** el problema.
I doubt that the government will solve the problem.

▸ In English, the expression *it is probable/possible* indicates a fairly high degree of certainty. In Spanish, however, **es probable/posible** implies inherent uncertainty and therefore triggers the subjunctive in the subordinate clause.

Es posible que **haya** menos bosques y selvas en el futuro.
It's possible that there will be fewer forests and jungles in the future.

Es muy probable que **contaminemos** el medio ambiente.
It's very probable that we're polluting the environment.

▸ Use the infinitive after an expression of uncertainty, doubt, disbelief, or denial when there is no change of subject.

Dudo **llegar** temprano.
I doubt I will arrive early.

Él duda **llegar** temprano.
He doubts he will arrive early.

Práctica

1 Conversación Completa el diálogo con la opción adecuada.

RAÚL Ustedes dudan que yo (1) _____ [estudio/estudie]. No niego que a veces me (2) _____ [divierto/divierta], pero no cabe duda de que (3) _____ [tomo/tome] mis estudios en serio. Creo que no (4) _____ [tienen/tengan] razón.

PAPÁ Es posible que tu mamá y yo no (5) _____ [tenemos/tengamos] razón. Es cierto que a veces (6) _____ [dudamos/dudemos] de ti. Pero no hay duda de que te (7) _____ [pasas/pases] toda la noche en Internet y escuchando música. No es seguro que (8) _____ [estás/estés] estudiando.

RAÚL Es verdad que (9) _____ [uso/use] Internet por las noches, pero ¿no es posible que (10) _____ [es/sea] para buscar información para mis clases? ¡No hay duda de que Internet (11) _____ [es/sea] el mejor recurso del mundo! Es obvio que ustedes (12) _____ [piensan/piensen] que no hago nada.

PAPÁ Dudo que esta conversación nos (13) _____ [va/vaya] a ayudar. Pero tal vez (14) _____ [puedes/puedas] estudiar sin música.

2 Dudas Carolina siempre miente. Exprésale a Carolina tus dudas sobre sus afirmaciones. Sigue el modelo.

modelo
El próximo año mi familia y yo vamos a ir de vacaciones por diez meses. [dudar]
Dudo que vayan a ir de vacaciones por diez meses.

1. Estoy escribiendo una novela en español. [no creer]

2. Mi tía es la directora del Sierra Club. [no ser verdad]

3. Dos profesores míos juegan para los Osos (*Bears*) de Chicago. [ser imposible]

4. Mi mejor amiga conoce al chef Emeril. [no ser cierto]

5. Mi padre es dueño del Rockefeller Center. [no ser posible]

6. Yo ya tengo un doctorado en lenguas. [ser improbable]

Conversación

3 **Hablando con un(a) burócrata** Con un(a) compañero/a, dramatiza una conversación entre un(a) activista ambiental y un(a) funcionario/a público/a (*government official*). Usa el subjuntivo.

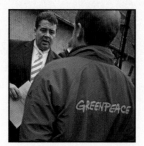

modelo

Activista: Queremos reducir la contaminación del aire, pero dudo que el gobierno nos ayude.

Funcionario: No es cierto. ¡Lea el periódico! Es obvio que el gobierno está haciendo muchas cosas para reducir la contaminación del aire.

4 **Adivinar** Escribe cinco oraciones sobre tu vida presente y futura. Cuatro deben ser falsas y sólo una debe ser cierta. Preséntalas al grupo. El grupo adivina (*guesses*) cuál es la oración cierta y expresa sus dudas sobre las falsas.

modelo

Estudiante 1: Quiero irme un año a trabajar en la selva.
Estudiante 2: Dudo que te guste vivir en la selva.
Estudiante 3: En cinco años voy a ser presidente de los Estados Unidos.
Estudiante 2: No creo que vayas a ser presidente de los Estados Unidos en cinco años. ¡Tal vez en treinta! Algún día pienso enseñar arte a los niños.
Estudiante 1: No dudo que vas a ser profesor. Te gustan mucho los niños.

5 **Debate** Con un(a) compañero/a, conversa sobre tus dudas y miedos para cuando te gradúes de la universidad.

modelo

Estudiante 1: Es improbable que me case inmediatamente.
Estudiante 2: Dudo que podamos comprarnos una casa después de terminar la universidad.

I CAN express my doubts about the future.

▶ **Quizás** and **tal vez** imply an uncertain possibility and are usually followed by the subjunctive.

> **Quizás haga** sol mañana.
> *Perhaps it will be sunny tomorrow.*

> **Tal vez veamos** la luna esta noche.
> *Perhaps we will see the moon tonight.*

▶ Use the indicative in a subordinate clause when the main clause expresses certainty.

Expressions of certainty			
no dudar	*not to doubt*	estar seguro/a (de)	*to be sure (of)*
no cabe duda de	*there is no doubt*	es cierto	*it's true; it's certain*
no hay duda de	*there is no doubt*	es seguro	*it's certain*
no negar (e:ie)	*not to deny*	es verdad	*it's true*
		es obvio	*it's obvious*

No negamos que **hay** demasiados carros en las carreteras.
We don't deny that there are too many cars on the highways.

No hay duda de que el Amazonas **es** uno de los ríos más largos del mundo.
There is no doubt that the Amazon is one of the longest rivers in the world.

Es verdad que Colombia **es** un país bonito.
It's true that Colombia is a beautiful country.

Es cierto que los tigres **están** en peligro de extinción.
It's certain that tigers are in danger of extinction.

▶ The verb **creer** expresses belief or certainty, so it is followed by the indicative. **No creer** implies doubt and is followed by the subjunctive.

No creo que **haya** vida en el planeta Marte.
I don't believe that there is life on the planet Mars.

Creo que **debemos** usar exclusivamente la energía solar.
I believe we should exclusively use solar energy.

¡Manos a la obra!

Completa estas oraciones con la forma correcta de los verbos.

1. Dudo que ellos __trabajen__ [trabajar].
2. Es cierto que él _____ [comer] mucho.
3. Es imposible que ellos _____ [salir].
4. Es probable que ustedes _____ [ganar].
5. No creo que ella _____ [volver].
6. Es posible que nosotros _____ [ir].
7. Dudamos que tú _____ [reciclar].
8. Creo que ellos _____ [jugar] al fútbol.
9. No niego que ustedes _____ [estudiar].
10. Es probable que ellos _____ [dormir].
11. Es posible que Marta te _____ [llamar].
12. Tal vez Juan no nos _____ [oír].

13.3 The subjunctive with conjunctions

No olviden recogerlo todo, para que no contaminemos.

¡Toma una foto antes de que se vaya!

▶ Conjunctions are words or phrases that connect clauses in sentences. Certain conjunctions introduce adverbial clauses, which describe *how, why, when,* and *where* an action takes place. These conjunctions always require the subjunctive.

Conjunctions that require the subjunctive

a menos que	*unless*	en caso (de) que	*in case (that)*
antes (de) que	*before*	para que	*so that*
con tal (de) que	*provided that*	sin que	*without*

Voy a dejar un recado **en caso de que** Gustavo me **llame**.
I'm going to leave a message in case Gustavo calls me.

Algunos animales van a morir **a menos que haya** leyes para protegerlos.
Some animals are going to die unless there are laws to protect them.

Voy al supermercado **para que tengas** algo de comer.
I'm going to the supermarket so that you'll have something to eat.

Voy a tomar esa clase **con tal de que** tú la **tomes** también.
I'm going to take that class provided that you take it too.

¡ojo! Use the infinitive after the prepositions **antes de, para,** and **sin** when there is no change of subject. Compare these sentences.

Te llamamos el viernes **antes de salir** de la casa.
We will call you on Friday before leaving the house.

Tus padres trabajan muchísimo **para vivir** bien.
Your parents work very hard in order to live well.

Te llamamos mañana **antes de que salgas.**
We will call you tomorrow before you leave.

Tus padres trabajan mucho **para que tú puedas** vivir bien.
Your parents work a lot so that you are able to live well.

Práctica

1 **Una excursión** Completa las oraciones.

modelo Voy a llevar a mis hijos al parque para que ___hagan___ [hacer] actividades al aire libre.

1. Vamos a pasar todo el día allí con tal de que ellos no _____ [aburrirse] en casa.

2. Vamos a alquilar bicicletas en cuanto _____ [llegar] al parque.

3. En bicicleta, podemos explorar el parque sin _____ [caminar] demasiado.

4. Siempre llevamos al perro cuando _____ [ir] al parque.

5. En caso de que _____ [llover], vamos a regresar temprano a la casa.

6. Queremos almorzar a la orilla (*shore*) del río cuando _____ [tener] hambre.

7. Mis hijos van a ver muchas cosas interesantes antes de _____ [salir] del parque.

2 **Oraciones** Completa las oraciones.

1. No podemos controlar la contaminación del aire a menos que…

2. Voy a reciclar los productos de papel en cuanto…

3. Protegemos los animales en peligro de extinción para que…

4. Mis amigos y yo vamos a recoger la basura de la universidad después de que…

5. Todos podemos conservar energía cuando…

6. No podemos desarrollar nuevas fuentes (*sources*) de energía sin…

7. Debemos comprar coches eléctricos tan pronto como…

8. Los gobiernos deben alertar a la población de que las tortugas marinas están en peligro de extinción, antes de que…

Conversación

3 **¿Yo, ambientalista?** Con un(a) compañero/a, túrnate para preguntar sobre sus conductas (*behavior*) ambientales. Usa el subjuntivo para las acciones que todavía no has hecho y el indicativo para las acciones que haces habitualmente.

modelo reciclar la basura

Estudiante 1: ¿Reciclas la basura?
Estudiante 2: Sí, siempre reciclo la basura después de comer. / No, no voy a reciclar la basura a menos que tenga recipientes para reciclar.

1. Venir en bicicleta a la universidad
2. Comer alimentos orgánicos
3. Usar excesiva calefacción (*heating*) en invierno
4. Comprar productos ecológicos
5. Interesarse por los animales en peligro de extinción
6. Pensar en las consecuencias del calentamiento global

4 **Instrucciones** Vas de viaje. Escribe una lista de instrucciones para tu compañero/a de cuarto. Usa el subjuntivo y las conjunciones de la lista.

modelo Apaga las luces cuando salgas de la casa.

> a menos que
> cuando
> en caso de que
> en cuanto
> tan pronto como

5 **Preguntas** En parejas, túrnense para hacerse estas preguntas.

1. ¿Qué haces cada noche antes de acostarte?
2. ¿Qué haces después de salir de la universidad?
3. ¿Qué hace tu familia para que puedas asistir a la universidad?
4. ¿Qué piensas hacer tan pronto como te gradúes?
5. ¿Qué quieres hacer mañana, a menos que haga mal tiempo?
6. ¿Qué haces en tus clases sin que los profesores lo sepan?

Conjunctions with subjunctive or indicative

En cuanto termine.

¡Cuando veo basura, la recojo!

Conjunctions used with subjunctive or indicative

cuando	*when*	hasta que	*until*
después (de) que	*after*	tan pronto como	*as soon as*
en cuanto	*as soon as*		

▶ With these conjunctions, use the subjunctive in the subordinate clause if the main clause expresses a future action or command.

Vamos a resolver el problema **cuando desarrollemos** nuevas tecnologías.
We are going to solve the problem when we develop new technology.

Después de que ustedes **tomen** sus refrescos, reciclen las botellas.
After you drink your soft drinks, recycle the bottles.

▶ Use the indicative if the verb in the main clause expresses an action that habitually happens or that happened in the past.

Contaminan los ríos **cuando construyen** nuevos edificios.
They pollute the rivers when they build new buildings.

Contaminaron el río **cuando construyeron** ese edificio.
They polluted the river when they built that building.

Siempre vamos de excursión **tan pronto como llega** Rafael.
We always go hiking as soon as Rafael arrives.

Salimos **tan pronto como llegó** Rafael.
We left as soon as Rafael arrived.

¡Manos a la obra!

Completa las oraciones con las formas correctas de los verbos.

1. Voy a estudiar ecología cuando ___vuelva___ [volver] a la universidad.
2. No podemos evitar el calentamiento global a menos que todos nosotros _____ [trabajar] juntos.
3. No podemos conducir sin _____ [contaminar] el aire.
4. Siempre recogemos mucha basura cuando _____ [ir] al parque.
5. Elisa habló con el presidente del club de ecología después de que _____ [terminar] la reunión.
6. Vamos de excursión para _____ [observar] los animales y las plantas.
7. La contaminación va a ser un problema muy grave hasta que _____ [cambiar] nuestros sistemas de producción y transporte.
8. El gobierno debe crear más parques nacionales antes de que los bosques y ríos _____ [estar] completamente contaminados.
9. Los ecologistas luchan para que se _____ [proteger] la naturaleza.

A repasar

13.1 The subjunctive with verbs of emotion

1 Agua contaminada Completa estos comentarios sobre la contaminación del agua con el infinitivo o el subjuntivo.

1. Siento mucho que mi ciudad _____ [tener] un problema de contaminación del agua.

2. Me molesta _____ [ver] fábricas que contaminan ríos.

3. Es triste que muchísimos peces _____ [morir] cada día.

4. Temo _____ [enfermarse] por beber agua contaminada.

5. Ojalá que el gobierno _____ [resolver] esto pronto.

2 ¿Qué piensas? Con un(a) compañero/a, túrnate para expresar sus reacciones a estos problemas. Escriban tres oraciones y compártanlas con la clase.

> **modelo**
> En mi ciudad nadie recicla envases.
> Es terrible que nadie recicle envases.
> Es necesario que aprendamos a reciclar.
> Es importante que yo dé el ejemplo.

1. Nadie protege a los animales en los bosques tropicales.
2. Millones de personas respiran aire contaminado.
3. Pocas leyes controlan la deforestación en las selvas.
4. Hay un aumento de la caza ilegal de ballenas.

3 ¡Es terrible! Con un(a) compañero/a, mira el dibujo y di qué piensas sobre el comportamiento (*behavior*) de esta familia. Usa el subjuntivo y expresiones como **es una lástima que, es ridículo que** y **es terrible que**.

> **modelo**
> Es terrible que la hija no recicle la botella.

13.2 The subjunctive with doubt, disbelief, and denial

4 Opuestos Escribe lo opuesto (*the opposite*) de cada oración. Sigue el modelo.

> **modelo**
> No es seguro que esta familia recicle las latas de aluminio.
> Es seguro que esta familia recicla las latas de aluminio.

1. Luisa y tú dudan que la deforestación dañe a los animales.
_____

2. Algunos científicos están seguros de que el calentamiento global existe.
_____

3. Es verdad que esas plantas están en peligro de extinción.
_____

4. Negamos que nuestros océanos estén contaminados.
_____

5. Es cierto que las leyes protegen a los animales.
_____

6. Creo que la población cuida los recursos naturales.
_____

5 Carta Con un(a) compañero/a, escribe una carta al/a la presidente/a de una compañía de tu comunidad, pidiéndole su apoyo (*support*) para resolver un problema ambiental. Usa el subjuntivo o el indicativo y las expresiones de la lista. Después, comparte la carta con la clase.

Creemos	Es probable
Es obvio	No creemos
Estar seguros/as (de)	Quizás
No hay duda de	Tal vez

6 Entrevista Con un(a) compañero/a, túrnate para hacer estas preguntas. Usa las pistas para responder.

1. ¿Es mejor la energía nuclear que la energía solar? (dudar)
2. ¿Es posible reducir la contaminación de los ríos? (ser improbable)
3. ¿Se deben reciclar todos los envases de plástico? (ser obvio)
4. ¿Están los monos en peligro de extinción? (no ser cierto)
5. ¿Están los pájaros afectados por la contaminación del agua? (creer)
6. ¿Son las piedras un recurso natural? (ser verdad)

13.3 The subjunctive with conjunctions

7 **Planes para el futuro** ¿Cuáles son tus planes para el futuro? Escríbelos usando las conjunciones **a menos que, antes (de) que, con tal (de) que, en caso (de) que, para que** y **sin que**. Incluye a tu familia y amigos en tus planes.

modelo

Voy a aprender a nadar en caso de que vaya de vacaciones a la playa.

8 **Oraciones** Con un(a) compañero/a, escribe una oración con el subjuntivo y una oración con el indicativo, con cada una de las siguientes conjunciones: **cuando, después (de) que, en cuanto, hasta que** y **tan pronto como**. Después, intercambien sus oraciones con otra pareja para que identifiquen el tiempo verbal usado en cada caso.

modelo

Vamos a respirar aire contaminado hasta que el gobierno controle el número de automóviles en la ciudad. (*subjuntivo*)
Los camiones pasaban por la ciudad hasta que construyeron la nueva carretera. (*indicativo*)

Síntesis

9 **¡Participa!** En parejas, imaginen que son dos celebridades que deciden organizar una campaña (*campaign*) para proteger una especie animal en peligro de extinción. Preparen un anuncio publicitario de 30 segundos y preséntenlo a la clase.

modelo

Soy Bono y para mí es muy importante cuidar el medio ambiente. Hoy te quiero invitar a que participes en esta campaña para salvar el puma en Chile. ¡Ayúdalo antes de que sea demasiado tarde!

Communicative Goal
Discuss geothermal energy

 Video

Videoclip

1 **Preparación** ¿Qué tipos de energía conoces? ¿Cuáles son más limpios? ¿Cuáles son renovables? Si no sabes la respuesta, busca en Internet o en tu libro de ciencias.

2 **El clip** Mira el anuncio de **IDAE** de España.

Vocabulario	
calefacción *heating*	geotérmica *geothermal*
dañino *harmful*	madalena *cupcake*

¿Qué es la energía geotérmica?

3 **Elegir** Selecciona las expresiones que, según el anuncio, se relacionan con la energía geotérmica.

a. recurso natural
b. contamina
c. peligrosa
d. en el interior de la tierra
e. dulce
f. ecológica
g. afuera de la tierra
h. limpia

4 **Ventajas y desventajas** En grupos de tres, describan con sus propias palabras cuáles son las características de la energía geotérmica. ¿De qué se trata? ¿Cuáles son sus ventajas o sus posibles desventajas?

I CAN discuss geothermal energy.

Ampliación

Communicative Goals
Use background knowledge and context to help me understand a speech, and talk about endangered animals

1 Escuchar

A Soledad Morales es una activista preocupada por el medio ambiente. Observa el dibujo y escribe tres predicciones sobre lo que piensas que va a decir.

> **TIP** **Use your background knowledge. / Guess meaning from context.** Your background knowledge helps you anticipate the content. If you hear words or expressions you do not understand, you can often guess their meanings based on the surrounding words.

B Escucha lo que Soledad dice e indica si estas oraciones son **ciertas** o **falsas**.

	Cierto	Falso
1. Soledad conversa con unos compañeros de trabajo.	_____	_____
2. Soledad teme que el futuro del medio ambiente no sea bueno.	_____	_____
3. Soledad cree que las distintas formas de vida —la naturaleza y los humanos— están relacionadas.	_____	_____
4. Soledad dice que la caza ilegal de animales es un problema grave.	_____	_____
5. La contaminación del río afecta la ecología de las playas de Barranquilla.	_____	_____
6. Soledad dice que la comunidad debe dejar de cazar animales en peligro de extinción.	_____	_____

¡Protejamos la Tierra!

NUESTRO

PATRIMONIO

C Compara tus predicciones con las respuestas correctas. ¿Fueron tus predicciones correctas? ¿Qué elementos te ayudaron a anticipar el discurso de Soledad?

2 Conversar

Conversa con un(a) compañero/a sobre los animales en peligro de extinción. Usa las preguntas como guía:

En América, el puma del este o de montaña está en peligro de extinción debido a la caza excesiva y a la falta de hábitat.

- ¿Cuáles son las causas de la extinción de los animales?
- ¿Cuáles son sus consecuencias?
- ¿Cómo se puede controlar este problema?
- ¿Que medidas (measures) debería (should) tomar el gobierno?
- ¿Qué medidas debería tomar cada persona para que los animales no estén en peligro de extinción?

I CAN understand a speech by using background knowledge and context.

I CAN talk about endangered animals.

Ampliación

3 Escribir

Escribe una carta al editor en la que hables sobre una situación importante que afecta el medio ambiente en tu comunidad.

TIP **Consider your audience and purpose.** Once you have defined both your audience and your purpose, you will be able to decide which tone, vocabulary, and grammatical structures will best serve your needs.

• Are you going to comment on one topic or several?

• Do you intend to register a complaint or to inform others?

• Are you hoping to persuade others to adopt your point of view or to take specific action?

Communicative Goals
Write a letter to the editor and a letter to the president of a Spanish-speaking country about the environment

Organizar	Decide cuál es el propósito de tu carta y planéala.
Escribir	Utiliza tus apuntes para escribir el primer borrador de la carta.
Corregir	Intercambia tu carta con un(a) compañero/a. Lee su carta y anota los mejores aspectos. Dale sugerencias para mejorarla. Si ves algunos errores, coméntaselos.
Compartir	Revisa el primer borrador y ten en cuenta las indicaciones de tu compañero/a. Si es necesario, incorpora nuevas ideas y/o más información.

4 Un paso más

Escribe una carta al/a la presidente/a de un país hispano para hablarle de tus dudas, deseos y preocupaciones sobre el futuro de una de las atracciones naturales del país.

• Investiga algunas de las atracciones naturales del mundo hispano.

• Escoge una con base en las características y el peligro en que se encuentra esta atracción natural.

• Piensa en lo que se puede hacer para protegerla. Presenta diferentes ideas que ayuden a mejorar las condiciones de esta atracción natural en la actualidad.

• Explica lo que temes de los problemas ambientales, lo que esperas y tus dudas sobre el futuro.

• Presenta recomendaciones para proteger este lugar en el futuro. Menciona qué se debe y no se debe hacer para que esta atracción se conserve.

Las tortugas marinas están en grave peligro de extinción.

5 Cultura

Imagina que vives en un país hispano. ¿Qué puedes hacer para proteger el medio ambiente de ese país? Piensa en los jóvenes activistas de esta lección.

I CAN write a letter about an environmental issue in my community.

I CAN write a letter about the future of a natural attraction in a Spanish-speaking country.

Audio: Reading

Antes de leer

Use any strategies you can to read a short story in Spanish.

TIP **Examine the title and visual elements.** Examining the title and visual elements can help you predict a story's content and understand it better. The title and visual elements may tell you what a story is about and what details are important.

Examinar el texto

Look at the title and the illustration. What do you think the story is about?

_____

_____

_____

Sobre el autor

Enrique Anderson Imbert (1910–2000) fue un escritor y crítico literario argentino. Escribió ensayos (*essays*) y novelas, pero sus obras (*works*) más famosas son sus microcuentos, o cuentos (*short stories*) muy breves, que se sitúan (*are situated*) entre lo fantástico y el realismo mágico. En este estilo literario se presentan elementos fantásticos e irreales como ordinarios o comunes.

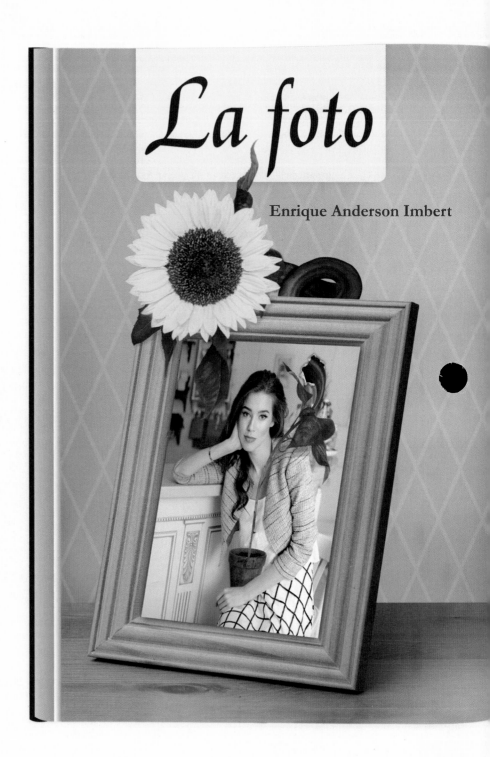

La foto

Enrique Anderson Imbert

Jaime y Paula se casaron. Ya durante la luna de miel° fue evidente que Paula se moría. Apenas unos pocos meses de vida le pronosticó el médico. Jaime, para conservar° ese bello rostro°, le pidió que se dejara fotografiar. Paula, que estaba plantando una semilla de girasol° en una maceta°, lo complació°: sentada con la maceta en el regazo° sonreía y...

¡Clic!

Poco después, la muerte. Entonces Jaime hizo ampliar° la foto —la cara de Paula era bella como una flor—, le puso vidrio, marco° y la colocó° en la mesita de noche.

Una mañana, al despertarse, vio que en la fotografía había aparecido una manchita°. ¿Acaso° de humedad? No prestó° más atención. Tres días más tarde: ¿qué era eso? No una mancha que se superpusiese° a la foto sino un brote° que dentro de la foto surgía° de la maceta. El sentimiento de rareza se convirtió en miedo cuando en los días siguientes comprobó que la fotografía vivía como si, en vez de reproducir la naturaleza, se reprodujera en la naturaleza. Cada mañana, al despertarse, observaba un cambio°. Era que la planta fotografiada crecía°. Creció, creció hasta que al final un gran girasol cubrió° la cara de Paula.

3

Después de leer

¿Comprendiste?

Ordena los eventos del cuento del 1 al 7.

_____ 1. Paula muere.

_____ 2. Paula va al médico.

_____ 3. Jaime le saca una foto a Paula.

_____ 4. La cara de Paula se cubre totalmente por el girasol.

_____ 5. Paula y Jaime se casan.

_____ 6. El girasol empieza a crecer.

_____ 7. Jaime pone la foto de Paula en su mesita de noche.

Preguntas

Responde estas preguntas con oraciones completas.

1. ¿Por qué quiere Jaime una foto de Paula?
2. ¿Con qué se compara la cara de Paula?
3. ¿Cómo reacciona Jaime cuando ve una manchita en la foto?
4. ¿Qué observa Jaime en los días siguientes? ¿Cómo se siente?
5. ¿Qué ocurre al final? ¿Cómo crees que va a reaccionar Jaime?

Coméntalo

¿Crees que las fotos pueden representar fielmente la realidad? ¿Existe alguna forma de distorsión o manipulación de la realidad en las fotos? Explica.

luna de miel *honeymoon*   conservar *to preserve*   rostro *face*   semilla de girasol *sunflower seed*
maceta *flowerpot*   complació *obliged*   regazo *lap*   ampliar *to enlarge*   marco *frame*   colocó *he put*
manchita *stain, mark*   Acaso *Maybe*   No prestó *He didn't pay*   se superpusiese *was covering*
brote *sprout*   surgía *was emerging*   cambio *change*   crecía *was growing*   cubrió *covered*

I CAN read and understand a short story in Spanish.

Vocabulary Tools

La naturaleza

el árbol *tree*
el bosque (tropical) *(tropical; rain) forest*
el césped *grass*
el cielo *sky*
el cráter *crater*
el desierto *desert*
la estrella *star*
la flor *flower*
la hierba *grass*
el lago *lake*
la luna *moon*
el mundo *world*
la naturaleza *nature*
la nube *cloud*
el océano *ocean*
el paisaje *landscape*
la piedra *stone*
la planta *plant*
la región *region; area*
el río *river*
la selva *jungle*
el sendero *trail*
el sol *sun*
la tierra *land; soil*
el valle *valley*
el volcán *volcano*

Conjunciones

a menos que *unless*
antes (de) que *before*
con tal (de) que *provided that*
cuando *when*
después (de) que *after*
en caso (de) que *in case (that)*
en cuanto *as soon as*
hasta que *until*
para que *so that*
sin que *without*
tan pronto como *as soon as*

El medio ambiente

el calentamiento global *global warming*
la caza *hunting*
la conservación *conservation*
la contaminación (del aire; del agua) *(air; water) pollution*
la deforestación *deforestation*
la ecología *ecology*
el/la ecologista *ecologist*
el ecoturismo *ecotourism*
la energía (nuclear; solar) *(nuclear; solar) energy*
la extinción *extinction*
la fábrica *factory*
el gobierno *government*
la ley *law*
el medio ambiente *environment*
el peligro *danger*
la población *population*
el reciclaje *recycling*
el recurso natural *natural resource*
la solución *solution*

conservar *to conserve*
contaminar *to pollute*
controlar *to control*
cuidar *to take care of*
dejar de (+ inf.) *to stop (doing something)*
desarrollar *to develop*
descubrir *to discover*
destruir *to destroy*
estar afectado/a (por) *to be affected (by)*
estar contaminado/a *to be polluted*
evitar *to avoid*
mejorar *to improve*
proteger *to protect*
reciclar *to recycle*
recoger *to pick up*
reducir *to reduce*
resolver (o:ue) *to resolve; to solve*
respirar *to breathe*

la botella de vidrio *glass bottle*
el envase de plástico *plastic container*
la lata de aluminio *aluminum can*

ecológico/a *ecological*
puro/a *pure*
renovable *renewable*

Las emociones

alegrarse (de) *to be happy*
esperar *to hope; to wish*
sentir (e:ie) *to be sorry; to regret*
temer *to be afraid*

es extraño *it's strange*
es una lástima *it's a shame*
es ridículo *it's ridiculous*
es terrible *it's terrible*
es triste *it's sad*
ojalá (que) *I hope (that); I wish (that)*

Las dudas y las certezas

(no) creer *(not) to believe*
(no) dudar *(not) to doubt*
(no) estar seguro/a (de) *(not) to be sure (of)*
(no) negar (e:ie) *(not) to deny*

es imposible *it's impossible*
es improbable *it's improbable*
es obvio *it's obvious*
no cabe duda de *there is no doubt*
no hay duda de *there is no doubt*
(no) es posible *it's (not) possible*
(no) es probable *it's (not) probable*
(no) es cierto *it's (not) true; it's (not) certain*
(no) es verdad *it's (not) true*
(no) es seguro *it's (not) certain*

Los animales

el animal *animal*
la ballena *whale*
el mono *monkey*
el pájaro *bird*
el pez *fish*
la tortuga marina *sea turtle*

Communicative Goals: Review

I CAN talk about nature.
- Describe a natural attraction in or near your community.

I CAN discuss environmental issues.
- Describe an environmental issue in your community.

I CAN express emotions and doubts.
- List five doubts you have about the future. Use the subjunctive.

I CAN investigate environmentalism in the Spanish-speaking world.
- Describe efforts to protect the environment in a Spanish-speaking country.

Communicative Goals
You will learn how to:
- talk about errands
- ask for and give directions
- tell someone what to do
- make suggestions
- investigate city transportation in Spanish-speaking countries

PREPARACIÓN

pages 356–361
- City life
- At the bank and post office
- Abbreviations

AVENTURAS

pages 362–363
- Sara is dancing in a flamenco presentation. Daniel, Valentina, Manuel, Olga Lucía, and Juanjo need to pick up their tickets and buy flowers and chocolates for Sara.

CULTURA

pages 364–365
- *Las bicicletas en la ciudad*
- Flash cultura: *El metro del D.F.*

GRAMÁTICA

pages 366–375
- The subjunctive in adjective clauses
- Familiar (**tú**) commands
- **Nosotros/as** commands

LECTURA

pages 376–377
- Short story: *Los bomberos*

⌔ PARA EMPEZAR

- ¿Dónde están Valentina y Daniel: en una ciudad o en un pueblo?
- ¿Qué están haciendo?
- ¿Qué plantas hay?

Vocabulary Tools

EN LA CIUDAD

EN LA CIUDAD

el banco *bank*
la carnicería *butcher shop*
el correo *post office*
la heladería *ice cream shop*
la joyería *jewelry store*
la lavandería *laundromat*
la panadería *bakery*
la pastelería *pastry shop*
la peluquería *hair salon*
la pescadería *fish market*
el salón de belleza *beauty salon*
el supermercado *supermarket*
la zapatería *shoe store*

hacer cola *to stand in line*
hacer diligencias *to run errands*

la cartera

la frutería
fruit shop

las estampillas

EN EL CORREO

el correo *mail; post office*
el paquete *package*
los sellos *stamps*
el sobre *envelope*

echar (una carta) al buzón *to put (a letter) in the mailbox; to mail (a letter)*
enviar *to send*
mandar *to send*

EN EL BANCO

la cuenta corriente *checking account*

la cuenta de ahorros *savings account*

---

ahorrar *to save (money)*

cobrar *to cash (a check); to charge (for a product or service)*

depositar *to deposit*

llenar (un formulario) *to fill out (a form)*

pagar al contado *to pay in cash*

pagar a plazos *to pay in installments*

pedir prestado/a *to borrow*

pedir un préstamo *to apply for a loan*

ser gratis *to be free of charge*

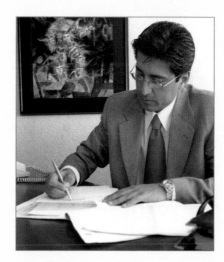

firmar
to sign

CÓMO LLEGAR

la cuadra *(city) block*

la dirección *address*

la esquina *corner*

---

cruzar *to cross*

doblar *to turn*

estar perdido/a *to be lost*

quedar *to be located*

(al) este *(to the) east*

(al) norte *(to the) north*

(al) oeste *(to the) west*

(al) sur *(to the) south*

---

derecho *straight (ahead)*

enfrente de *opposite; facing*

hacia *toward*

SERIE KY 5296221
Diamante 787
Valparaíso

0-744679-00-5
JUAN FLORES GARCÍA

044-0365
011

$ 2387.00

8 de noviembre de 2021

Páguese a la orden de *María Eugenia Castaño*

o, al portador

la suma de *dos mil trescientos ochenta y siete con* 00/100

pesos m/l

Juan Flores García
Firma autorizada

Este cheque tiene papel de seguridad con marca de agua, verifíquela antes de aceptarlo.

|||| BANCO NACIONAL

:54892332·A 0440900657008- 01

el cheque

el cajero automático
ATM

PARE

el letrero ←
sign

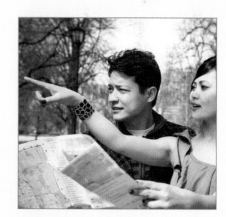

indicar cómo llegar
to give directions

ASÍ SE DICE
la cuadra ⟷ la manzana (*Esp.*)
doblar ⟷ girar (*Esp.*), virar, voltear (*Amér. L.*)
hacer diligencias ⟷ hacer mandados (*Amér. L.*)

A escuchar

1 **¿Lógico o ilógico?** Escucha las oraciones e indica si cada oración es **lógica** o **ilógica.**

	Lógico	Ilógico
1.	_____	_____
2.	_____	_____
3.	_____	_____
4.	_____	_____
5.	_____	_____
6.	_____	_____
7.	_____	_____
8.	_____	_____

2 **Cita** Indica si cada afirmación es **cierta** o **falsa.**

Cierto	Falso	
_____	_____	1. Jorge fue al banco.
_____	_____	2. Sandra fue a la peluquería.
_____	_____	3. El supermercado está al lado del banco.
_____	_____	4. Jorge fue a la zapatería.
_____	_____	5. Sandra fue a la lavandería.
_____	_____	6. Jorge va a encontrarse con Sandra en la pastelería.
_____	_____	7. Sandra también quiere ir a una heladería.
_____	_____	8. La panadería queda en la esquina.

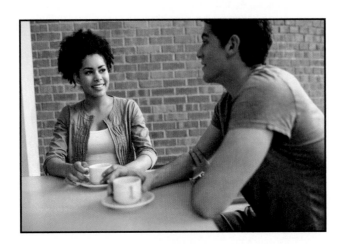

A practicar

3 **Emparejar** Indica la actividad que se puede hacer en cada lugar.

Lugares	Actividades
1. carnicería _____	a. comprar galletas
2. pastelería _____	b. conseguir manzanas
3. frutería _____	c. comprar un collar (*necklace*)
4. joyería _____	d. cortarse (*to cut*) el pelo
5. lavandería _____	e. lavar la ropa
6. pescadería _____	f. comprar pescado
7. salón de belleza _____	g. comprar pollo
8. zapatería _____	h. probarse unas sandalias

4 **Completar** Completa las oraciones.

1. El banco me regaló un reloj. Lo conseguí _____ .
2. Me gusta _____ dinero, pero no me molesta gastarlo.
3. Tengo que _____ el cheque en el dorso (*on the back*) para cobrarlo.
4. Para pagar con un cheque, necesito tener dinero en mi _____ .
5. Mi madre va a un _____ para obtener dinero.
6. Ana _____ un cheque en su cuenta de ahorros.
7. Anoche en el restaurante, Marcos _____ en vez de usar una tarjeta de crédito.
8. Para pedir un préstamo, Miguel y Susana tuvieron que _____ cuatro formularios.

ahorrar	firmar
cajero automático	gratis
cuenta corriente	llenar
deposita	pagó al contado

5 **Conversación** Completa esta conversación con el vocabulario de la lección.

CARTERO Buenas tardes, ¿es usted la señorita Ramírez? Le traigo un (1) _____ .

JUANITA Sí, soy yo. ¿Quién lo envía?

CARTERO La señora Ortega. Y también tiene usted dos (2) _____ .

JUANITA Ay, pero ¡ninguna es de mi novio! ¿No llegó nada de Manuel Fuentes?

CARTERO Sí, pero él echó la carta al (3) _____ sin poner un (4) _____ en el sobre.

JUANITA Entonces, ¿qué me recomienda usted que haga?

CARTERO Le sugiero que vaya al (5) _____ . Si usted paga el costo del sello, se le puede dar la carta.

A conversar

6 **Situaciones** Con un(a) compañero/a, escoge una de estas situaciones y represéntala.

- un(a) cliente/a habla con un(a) empleado/a de banco sobre abrir una cuenta corriente
- una pareja de recién casados quiere pedir un préstamo para comprar una casa
- una persona habla con un(a) empleado/a de correo sobre mandar un paquete

7 **El Hatillo** Con un(a) compañero/a, representa una conversación entre un(a) turista que está perdido/a en El Hatillo, Venezuela, y un(a) residente de la ciudad que quiere ayudarlo/la.

🏰	Plaza Bolívar
🏛️	Plaza Sucre
$	Banco
🏛️	Casa de la Cultura
➕	Farmacia
⛪	Iglesia
🚉	Terminal
🏫	Escuela
E	Estacionamiento
💍	Joyería
👠	Zapatería
🍽️	Café Primavera

modelo

Plaza Sucre, Café Primavera
Estudiante 1: Perdón, ¿por dónde queda la Plaza Sucre?
Estudiante 2: Del Café Primavera, camine derecho por la calle Sucre hasta llegar a la calle Comercio. Doble a la izquierda y camine una cuadra. Allí está la plaza.

1. Plaza Bolívar, farmacia
2. Casa de la Cultura, Plaza Sucre
3. banco, terminal
4. estacionamiento (este), escuela
5. Plaza Sucre, estacionamiento (oeste)

6. joyería, banco
7. farmacia, joyería
8. zapatería, iglesia
9. terminal, Plaza Bolívar
10. escuela, zapatería

8 **¿Dónde está?** En grupos, representen un minidrama en el que unos/as turistas piden ayuda para llegar a tres sitios diferentes de la comunidad en la que ustedes viven.

I CAN ask for and give directions.

I CAN interact at a survival level in some familiar everyday contexts.

Ortografía

 Tutorial

Las abreviaturas

In Spanish, as in English, abbreviations are often used in order to save space and time while writing. Here are some of the most commonly used abbreviations in Spanish.

· ·

usted ⟶ Ud.   **ustedes** ⟶ Uds.

As you have already learned, the subject pronouns **usted** and **ustedes** are often abbreviated.

· ·

don ⟶ D.   **doña** ⟶ Dña.   **doctor(a)** ⟶ Dr(a).

señor ⟶ Sr.   **señora** ⟶ Sra.   **señorita** ⟶ Srta.

These titles are frequently abbreviated.

· ·

centímetro ⟶ cm   **metro** ⟶ m   **kilómetro** ⟶ km

litro ⟶ l   **gramo** ⟶ g   **kilogramo** ⟶ kg

The abbreviations for these units of measurement are often used, but without periods.

· ·

por ejemplo ⟶ p. ej.   **página(s)** ⟶ pág(s).

These abbreviations are often seen in books.

· ·

derecha ⟶ dcha.   **izquierda** ⟶ izq. (izqda.)

código postal ⟶ C.P.   **número** ⟶ n.º

These abbreviations are often used in mailing addresses.

Sra. Emilia F. Bazán
Cía. Romero, S.A.
3336
Calle Lozano, n.º 37
Caracas, Venezuela

· ·

Banco ⟶ Bco.   **Compañía** ⟶ Cía.

cuenta corriente ⟶ c/c.   **Sociedad Anónima (*Inc.*)** ⟶ S.A.

These abbreviations are frequently used in the business world.

· ·

Práctica Escribe otra vez la siguiente información usando las abreviaturas adecuadas.

1. doña María
2. señora Pérez
3. Compañía Mexicana de Inversiones
4. usted

5. Banco de Santander
6. doctor Medina
7. Código Postal 03697
8. cuenta corriente número 20-453

Emparejar En la tabla hay nueve abreviaturas. Empareja los cuadros necesarios para formarlas.

S.	c.	C.	c	co.	U
B	c/	Sr	A.	D	dc
ta.	P.	ña.	ha.	m	d.

Por las calles de Madrid

Los chicos tienen que hacer diligencias antes de ir a la presentación de flamenco de Sara.

Video

Antes de ver

Lee la primera oración de cada pie de foto (*caption*) y adivina lo que pasa en el video.

PERSONAJES

OLGA LUCÍA

VALENTINA

DANIEL

MANUEL

JUANJO

ANCIANA

EMPLEADA

SEÑORA

DANIEL (*a Manuel*) ¡Por fin llegaste! ¡Sara es la primera que baila!

MANUEL ¡Lo siento!

OLGA LUCÍA ¡Es tarde!

JUANJO ¡Calma, calma! Olga Lucía, tú y yo compremos las flores.

DANIEL (*a Valentina*) Tú y yo vamos a recoger las entradas.

JUANJO (*a Manuel*) Tú, ve por los chocolates.

JUANJO ¡Hay demasiada gente! Vamos a otra floristería.

OLGA LUCÍA ¡Sólo necesitamos a alguien que nos deje pasar!

OLGA LUCÍA Disculpe, señora.

JUANJO ¿Nos permite pasar?

ANCIANA Y eso, ¿por qué?

JUANJO Es que hoy una amiga nuestra...

OLGA LUCÍA ...murió.

ANCIANA Ay, lo siento mucho. Pasen, pasen.

OLGA LUCÍA Con permiso...

ACTIVIDADES

1 **Identificar** Identifica quién(es) hace(n) las diligencias y otras acciones.

1. comprar los chocolates
2. ir a recoger las entradas
3. bailar
4. comprar las flores
5. ir al cajero automático
6. estacionar el coche

2 **Preguntas** Contesta las preguntas. Usa oraciones completas.

1. ¿Por qué llegó tarde Manuel?
2. ¿Cuál es el problema con las entradas?
3. ¿Por qué es un problema que Daniel y Valentina no tienen suficiente dinero?
4. ¿Qué problema tienen Juanjo y Olga Lucía en la floristería?
5. ¿Qué hace Sara al final?

DANIEL Sara Sánchez nos reservó cinco entradas para la presentación.

EMPLEADA Aquí están. Son cincuenta euros.

DANIEL ¡¿Qué?!

EMPLEADA Están reservadas, pero tenéis que pagarlas. Y no aceptamos tarjeta de crédito. Sólo efectivo.

VALENTINA ¡No tenemos suficiente dinero!

DANIEL (*a la empleada*) ¿Hay algún cajero automático que esté cerca?

DANIEL ¡Estamos perdidos!

VALENTINA Espera. ¡Encontré uno, vamos, crucemos la calle!

DANIEL ¡Ahí está!

VALENTINA ¡Está dañado!

DANIEL ¡Rápido! ¡Necesitamos uno que funcione! ¡Busca en el móvil!

OLGA LUCÍA ¿Dónde estaban?

JUANJO La presentación ya comenzó.

DANIEL Las entradas no eran gratis. Fuimos al cajero a buscar dinero. Casi nos arrestan...

OLGA LUCÍA Y JUANJO ¿Qué?

JUANJO Seguramente Sara ya bailó.

---

3 **Conversación** En parejas, dramaticen una conversación entre dos personas que hacen una diligencia en uno de estos lugares o entre una persona que hace una diligencia y un(a) empleado/a de uno de estos lugares.

- ▶ el banco
- ▶ el correo
- ▶ la frutería
- ▶ la lavandería
- ▶ la pastelería
- ▶ el supermercado

I CAN talk about errands.

Expresiones útiles

¡Auxilio! *Help!*
la caja *box*
Con permiso. *Excuse me. (to request permission)*
el efectivo *cash*
el estacionamiento *parking lot*
la floristería *florist's shop*
Perdón. *Excuse me. (to get someone's attention or excuse oneself)*
respetar *to respect*
tardar *to be late*
el teatro *theater*
tener vergüenza *to be ashamed*

———

la ventanilla *ticket window*

Las tiendas especializadas

En Madrid, como en muchas ciudades del mundo hispano, muchas personas hacen las diligencias en tiendas especializadas. Van a la carnicería, la frutería, la panadería, la pastelería, la pescadería y la floristería en lugar de comprar todo en el supermercado.

¿Vas a tiendas especializadas o siempre vas al supermercado?

Communicative Goal
Compare bicycle use in Latin American
cities with its use in my community

Las bicicletas en la ciudad

La bicicleta es un medio de transporte que tiene múltiples beneficios. Es ideal a la hora de recorrer la ciudad si se quieren evitar los atascos° y, además, su uso no sólo evita la contaminación ambiental, también es una forma de cuidar la salud.

En este sentido°, las ciudades de Latinoamérica están desarrollando políticas para la promoción del uso de las bicicletas en la vida urbana. El objetivo es lograr° que las calles se conviertan en un espacio seguro y respetuoso° para todos.

Desde hace años, Bogotá está a la cabeza de la iniciativa que propone el uso de la bicicleta como medio de transporte alternativo y amigable° con el medio ambiente. De esta manera, todos los domingos y días festivos, desde las siete de la mañana hasta las dos de la tarde, se prohíbe la circulación de carros por las principales calles de esta ciudad de casi once millones de habitantes: sólo pueden pasear por estas calles los peatones° y las bicicletas. Se calcula que cerca de un millón y medio de bicicletas llenan la ciudad en esos días. Hay también ciclovías° nocturnas, es decir, vías vehiculares que, por unas horas en las noches, permiten el uso exclusivo de bicicletas, y ciclopaseos, que son visitas programadas a lugares históricos de la ciudad.

Otras ciudades tienen sistemas de bicicletas compartidas. En Buenos Aires, el programa Ecobici

nació en 2010 y funciona todos los días del año durante las 24 horas. Cualquier persona (incluso los turistas) puede buscar una bicicleta en una estación automática cercana, pasear en ella

por la ciudad y devolverla° en otra estación. ¡Y es totalmente gratis! La ciudad tiene 230 kilómetros de ciclovías y 400 estaciones con 4.000 bicicletas públicas. Y el programa sigue aumentando.

Otros sistemas de bicicletas compartidas

Caracas, Venezuela: Caracas Rueda Libre (2015)
Ciudad de México, México: ECOBICI (2010)
Medellín, Colombia: EnCicla (2011)
Montevideo, Uruguay: Movete (2014)
Quito, Ecuador: BiciQuito (2012)

atascos *traffic jams* sentido *regard* lograr *to achieve* respetuoso *respectful* amigable *friendly* peatones *pedestrians* ciclovías *bikeways* devolverla *return it*

ASÍ SE DICE

En la ciudad

el aparcamiento (Esp.)	el estacionamiento
el parqueadero (Bol., Col.)	
el parqueo (Bol., Col., Cuba, El Salv., Nic.)	
dar un aventón (Amér. C.)	*to give (someone) a ride*
dar botella (Cuba)	
el subterráneo, el subte (Arg.)	el metro

▶ ¿Qué palabras hay para decir **metro** en inglés?

Communicative Goal
Identify some characteristics of
Mexico City's subway

ACTIVIDADES

 ¿Cierto o falso? Indica si lo que dice cada oración es **cierto** o **falso**. Corrige la información falsa.

1. Todos los domingos y días festivos, sólo los peatones y las bicicletas pueden pasear por las principales calles de Bogotá.

2. Los ciclopaseos son calles para el uso exclusivo de bicicletas.

3. Ecobici es un sistema de bicicletas compartidas en Buenos Aires.

4. Los ciclistas pagan para usar Ecobici.

5. El sistema de bicicletas compartidas de Medellín se llama EnCicla.

 Preguntas Contesta las preguntas.

1. ¿A qué horas se prohíbe la circulación de carros en Bogotá?

2. ¿Cómo se llaman las vías vehiculares que permiten el uso exclusivo de bicicletas?

3. ¿Cuántas bicicletas públicas tiene Ecobici?

4. ¿Cómo se llama el sistema de bicicletas compartidas de Quito?

 Ecobici En parejas, representen una conversación entre dos amigos/as que quieren usar Ecobici en Buenos Aires.

 ¿Qué piensas? Responde a las preguntas.

1. ¿Por qué crees que las ciudades de Latinoamérica están desarrollando políticas para la promoción del uso de las bicicletas?

2. ¿Qué piensas de la prohibición de la circulación de carros por las calles principales los domingos y días festivos en Bogotá? ¿Por qué?

3. ¿Por qué crees que tantas personas pasean en bicicleta los domingos y días festivos en las calles de Bogotá?

 Comparación Compara el uso de bicicletas en las ciudades latinoamericanas con su uso en tu comunidad.

I CAN compare bicycle use in Latin American cities with its use in my community.

 Video

El metro del D.F.

 Preparación Imagina que estás en la Ciudad de México, una de las ciudades más grandes del mundo. ¿Qué transporte usas para ir de un lugar a otro? ¿Por qué?

El video Mira el episodio de **Flash cultura** sobre el metro de la Ciudad de México.

Vocabulario	
concurrido *busy, crowded*	transbordo *transfer, change*
se esconde *is hidden*	el rincón *corner*

Para la gente mayor de 60 años, el transporte es totalmente gratuito.

Seleccionar Selecciona la respuesta correcta.

1. El Parque de _____ (Chapultepec/Los Leones) es uno de los lugares más concurridos de la ciudad.

2. En las estaciones _____ (de transbordo/de una sola línea) los pasajeros pueden cambiar de trenes para llegar fácilmente a su destino.

3. Algunas líneas de metro son _____ (subterráneas/superficiales), es decir, circulan al nivel de la calle.

4. Dentro de algunas estaciones hay _____ (danzas indígenas/ exposiciones de arte).

El transporte público Compara el metro de la Ciudad de México con el metro o con otro tipo de transporte público de una ciudad que conoces.

I CAN identify some characteristics of Mexico City's subway.

Communicative Goal
Talk about people that might or might not exist

14.1 The subjunctive in adjective clauses

▸ Adjective clauses modify nouns or pronouns. The subjunctive can be used in adjective clauses to indicate that the existence of someone or something is uncertain or indefinite.

¡Sólo necesitamos a alguien que nos deje pasar!

¿Hay algún cajero automático que esté cerca?

▸ The subjunctive is used in an adjective clause that refers to a person, place, thing, or idea that either does not exist or whose existence is uncertain or indefinite.

Busco **un profesor** que **enseñe japonés**.
I'm looking for a professor who teaches Japanese.

¿Conoces **un buen restaurante** que **esté** cerca de mi casa?
Do you know a good restaurant that is near my house?

▸ The indicative is used when the adjective clause refers to a person, place, thing, or idea that is clearly known, certain, or definite.

Quiero ir **al restaurante** que **está** enfrente de la biblioteca.
I want to go to the restaurant that's in front of the library.

Conozco a **alguien** que **va** a esa peluquería.
I know someone who goes to that hair salon.

Adjective clauses

Indicative	Subjunctive
Necesito el libro que tiene **información sobre Venezuela.** *I need the book that has information about Venezuela.*	**Necesito** un libro que tenga **información sobre Venezuela.** *I need a book that has information about Venezuela.*
Quiero vivir en esta casa **que** tiene **jardín.** *I want to live in this house that has a garden.*	**Quiero vivir en** una casa **que** tenga **jardín.** *I want to live in a house that has a garden.*
En mi barrio, hay una heladería **que** vende **helado de mango.** *In my neighborhood, there's an ice cream shop that sells mango ice cream.*	**En mi barrio, no hay** ninguna heladería **que** venda **helado de mango.** *In my neighborhood, there is no ice cream shop that sells mango ice cream.*

Práctica

1 **Minidiálogos** Completa los minidiálogos con la forma correcta de los verbos indicados.

MARCELA Buscamos un hotel que (1) _____ [tener] piscina.

MARTÍN Hay tres o cuatro hoteles por aquí que (2) _____ [tener] piscina.

• • •

EDUARDO ¿Hay algún buzón por aquí donde yo (3) _____ [poder] echar una carta?

SUSANA Sí, hay uno en la esquina donde (4) _____ [poder] echar una carta.

• • •

ANA Queremos encontrar un restaurante que (5) _____ [servir] comida venezolana.

ROBERTO Creo que el restaurante en esta cuadra (6) _____ [servir] comida venezolana.

• • •

VICENTE Necesitas hablar con José, el empleado que (7) _____ [entender] este nuevo programa de computación.

MARISOL No hay nadie que (8) _____ [entender] este programa.

2 **Completar** Completa estas oraciones de manera lógica. Luego, compara tus respuestas con las de un(a) compañero/a.

1. Tengo un(a) amigo/a que...
2. Algún día espero tener un apartamento o una casa que...
3. Quiero visitar un país que...
4. No tengo ningún/ninguna profesor(a) que...
5. Es importante conocer a alguien que...
6. Mi compañero/a de cuarto busca una lavandería que...
7. Un(a) consejero/a (*advisor*) debe ser una persona que...
8. Mi novio/a desea un perro que...
9. En esta clase no hay nadie que...
10. Mis padres buscan un carro que...

Conversación

3 Encuesta Averigua (*Find out*) cuál de tus compañeros/as conoce a alguien que haga estas actividades. Si responden que sí, pregunta quién es y anota sus respuestas. Comparte los resultados con la clase.

¿Conoces una joyería que esté cerca?	Nombres	Respuestas
1. Conocer muy bien su ciudad	_____	_____
2. Hablar japonés	_____	_____
3. Comprender el subjuntivo	_____	_____
4. Odiar ir de compras	_____	_____
5. Estudiar música	_____	_____
6. Trabajar en una zapatería	_____	_____
7. No tener tarjeta de crédito	_____	_____
8. Graduarse este año	_____	_____
9. Ser periodista	_____	_____
10. Jugar al béisbol	_____	_____

4 Anuncios clasificados En parejas, lean estos anuncios y describan el tipo de persona u objeto que se busca. Usen el subjuntivo.

CLASIFICADOS

CLASES DE INGLÉS Profesor de Inglaterra con diez años de experiencia ofrece clases para grupos o instrucción privada para individuos. Llamar al 0416-933-4110 de 16:30 a 18:30.

SE BUSCA CONDOMINIO Se busca condominio en Sabana Grande con 3 alcobas, 2 baños, sala, comedor y aire acondicionado. Tel: 0412-977-2018.

PELUQUERÍA UNISEX Se busca persona con experiencia en peluquería y maquillaje para trabajar tiempo completo. Llamar de 9 a 13h. Tel: 0212-261-3548.

EJECUTIVO DE CUENTAS Se requiere joven profesional con al menos dos años de experiencia en el sector financiero. Se ofrecen beneficios excelentes. Enviar *currículum vitae* al Banco Mercantil, Avda. Urdaneta 263, Caracas.

COMPARTIR APARTAMENTO Se necesita compañera para compartir apartamento de 2 alcobas en Chacao. Alquiler 3.000 bolívares por mes. No fumar. Llamar al 0212-951-3642 entre 19 y 22h.

▶ The personal **a** is not used with direct objects that are hypothetical people. However, **alguien** and **nadie** are always preceded by the personal **a** when they function as direct objects.

Necesitamos **un empleado** que **sepa** usar computadoras.
We need an employee who knows how to use computers.

Necesitamos **al empleado** que **sabe** usar computadoras.
We need the employee who knows how to use computers.

Busco **a alguien** que **pueda** cocinar hoy.
I'm looking for someone who can cook today.

No conozco **a nadie** que **pueda** cocinar hoy.
I don't know anyone who can cook today.

▶ The subjunctive is commonly used in questions when the speaker is uncertain. However, if the person who responds to the question knows the information, the indicative is used.

—¿Hay un parque que **esté** cerca de nuestro hotel?
Is there a park that's close to our hotel?

—Sí, hay un parque que **está** muy cerca del hotel.
Yes, there's a park that's very close to the hotel.

http://paginasamarillas.com

paginas amarillas.com

Busque cualquier información que necesite.

¡Manos a la obra!

Completa cada oración con el subjuntivo o el indicativo.

1. Necesito una persona que _____*pueda*_____ [puede/pueda] cantar bien.
2. Buscamos a alguien que _____ [tiene/tenga] paciencia.
3. ¿Hay restaurantes aquí que _____ [sirven/sirvan] comida japonesa?
4. Tengo una amiga que _____ [saca/saque] fotografías muy bonitas.
5. Hay una carnicería que _____ [está/esté] cerca de aquí.
6. No vemos ningún apartamento que nos _____ [interesa/interese].
7. Conozco a un estudiante que _____ [come/coma] hamburguesas todos los días.
8. ¿Hay alguien que _____ [dice/diga] la verdad?

I CAN talk about people that might or might not exist.

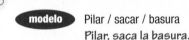

14.2 Familiar (tú) commands

▶ Use familiar (**tú**) commands when you want to give an order or advice to someone you normally address with **tú**.

Tú, ve por los chocolates.

¡Busca en el móvil!

▶ Affirmative **tú** commands usually have the same form as the **usted/él/ella** of the present indicative. The pronoun **tú** is used only for emphasis.

Paga al contado.
Pay in cash.

Pide un préstamo.
Ask for a loan.

Affirmative *tú* commands

Infinitive	Present indicative	Affirmative *tú* command
cuidar	Ud./él/ella cuida	cuida (tú)
tocar	Ud./él/ella toca	toca (tú)
temer	Ud./él/ella teme	teme (tú)
volver	Ud./él/ella vuelve	vuelve (tú)
insistir	Ud./él/ella insiste	insiste (tú)
pedir	Ud./él/ella pide	pide (tú)

▶ Negative **tú** commands have the same form as the **tú** form of the present subjunctive.

Carlos, **no eches** eso al buzón.
Carlos, don't put that in the mailbox.

Julia, **no cruces** la calle.
Julia, don't cross the street.

Negative *tú* commands

Infinitive	Present subjunctive	Negative *tú* command
cuidar	que tú cuides	no cuides (tú)
tocar	que tú toques	no toques (tú)
temer	que tú temas	no temas (tú)
volver	que tú vuelvas	no vuelvas (tú)
insistir	que tú insistas	no insistas (tú)
pedir	que tú pidas	no pidas (tú)

▶ The negative familiar commands keep the same stem changes as the indicative.

No pierdas el mapa.
Don't lose the map.

No vuelvas a esa gasolinera.
Don't go back to that gas station.

Práctica

1 **Unas diligencias** Completa los pedidos que la señora Ramos le hace a su esposo. Usa las formas correctas de los mandatos informales.

> **modelo** Enrique, ___ve___ [ir] al banco, por favor.

1. Cuando llegues al banco, _____ [depositar] este cheque en nuestra cuenta corriente.

2. No _____ [depositarlo] en la cuenta de ahorros y, por favor, no _____ [pedir] un préstamo.

3. Luego, _____ [pasar] por la zapatería y _____ [recoger] mis zapatos.

4. No _____ [pagar] al contado, sino con un cheque.

5. Luego, _____ [comprar] un pastel en la pastelería. Por favor, no _____ [comprar] un pastel de chocolate. Mi tío Felipe viene a cenar y es alérgico al chocolate.

2 **Quehaceres** Lee los quehaceres que Pedro le da a Miguel. Después, usa la información entre paréntesis para formar las contraórdenes que, a su vez, le da Marina. Sigue el modelo.

> **modelo** Recoge los libros. (poner la mesa)
> *No los recojas, Miguel. Pon la mesa.*

1. Barre el suelo. (pasar la aspiradora)

2. Plancha la ropa. (hacer las camas)

3. Saca la basura. (quitar la mesa)

4. Ve a la joyería. (ir a la frutería)

5. Dale los libros a Isabel. (dárselos a Juan)

6. Prepara la cena. (limpiar el carro)

7. Echa las cartas al buzón. (dárselas al cartero)

8. Corta el césped. (bañar al gato)

3 **Oraciones** Forma los mandatos que la señora Morales les da a su esposo y a sus hijos.

> **modelo** Pilar / sacar / basura
> *Pilar, saca la basura.*

1. Gloria / poner / sello / este / sobre

2. Manolo / ir / banco / cobrar / este / cheques

3. Lidia / no poner / televisión

4. Esteban / hacer / camas

5. Gloria / no lavar / platos

6. Manolo / firmar / este / formularios

Conversación

4 **Estoy perdido/a** Con un(a) compañero/a, representen una conversación breve entre un(a) estudiante nuevo/a en la universidad y otro/a estudiante que le indica cómo llegar a varios lugares.

modelo

Estudiante 1: Quiero ir al laboratorio de Ciencias, pero estoy perdido. ¿Me puedes ayudar?

Estudiante 2: Sí. Sigue derecho hasta llegar a la Facultad de Negocios. Dobla a la izquierda...

5 **¡Te lo ordeno!** En parejas, representen una conversación entre dos compañeros/as de cuarto que tenían que estar en una fiesta y todavía se están arreglando. Usen mandatos afirmativos y negativos.

modelo

Luisa: ¡Te lo ordeno! ¡Sal del baño ya!

Ramón: ¡No me des órdenes!

Luisa: Pero tengo que maquillarme.

Ramón: Y yo tengo que ducharme. Oye, ¿qué hora es?

Luisa: Son las siete menos veinte.

Ramón: ¡Ay! ¡Tráeme una toalla!

6 **Órdenes** En grupos, intercambien tres órdenes con cada uno. Luego, cada uno debe seguir las órdenes que el resto del grupo le da o reaccionar apropiadamente.

modelo

Estudiante 1: Dame todo tu dinero.
Estudiante 2: No, no quiero dártelo. Muéstrame tu cuaderno.
Estudiante 1: Aquí está.
Estudiante 3: Ve a la pizarra y escribe tu nombre.
Estudiante 4: No quiero. Hazlo tú.

I CAN tell someone what to do.

Irregular tú commands

▸ There are eight irregular affirmative **tú** commands.

decir	di	salir	sal
hacer	haz	ser	sé
ir	ve	tener	ten
poner	pon	venir	ven

¡Ten cuidado con el perro!
Be careful with the dog!

¡Sal de aquí ahora mismo!
Leave here at once!

Pon la estampilla en el sobre.
Put the stamp on the envelope.

Haz los ejercicios.
Do the exercises.

▸ **Ir** and **ver** have the same **tú** command. Context will determine the meaning.

Ve al supermercado con José.
Go to the supermarket with José.

Ve ese programa… es muy interesante.
Watch that program… it's very interesting.

Ve al banco esta tarde.
Go to the bank this afternoon.

Ve esa película con tu hermano.
See that movie with your brother.

▸ The placement of reflexive and object pronouns in **tú** commands follows the same rules as in formal commands. When a pronoun is attached to a command of more than two syllables, a written accent is used.

Informal	Formal
¡Alégrate!	**¡Alégrese!**
Be happy!	*Be happy!*
No **te** sientas triste.	No **se** sienta triste.
Don't feel sad.	*Don't feel sad.*
Dime.	**Dígame.**
Tell me.	*Tell me.*
No **me lo** digas.	No **me lo** diga.
Don't tell me (it).	*Don't tell me (it).*

¡Manos a la obra!

Indica los mandatos familiares de estos verbos.

	Mandato afirmativo	Mandato negativo
1. cambiar	<u>Cambia</u> el aceite.	No <u>cambies</u> el aceite.
2. correr	_____ más rápido.	No _____ más rápido.
3. salir	_____ ahora.	No _____ ahora.
4. tocar	_____ las flores.	No _____ las flores.
5. venir	_____ aquí.	No _____ aquí.
6. levantarse	_____ temprano.	No _____ temprano.
7. volver	_____ pronto.	No _____ pronto.
8. hacerlo	_____ ya.	No _____ ahora.

14.3 Nosotros/as commands

▸ **Nosotros/as** commands, which correspond to the English *let's* + [*verb*], are used to give orders or suggestions that include yourself and other people.

Crucemos la calle.
Let's cross the street.

No crucemos la calle.
Let's not cross the street.

▸ Both affirmative and negative **nosotros/as** commands are generally formed by using the first-person plural form of the present subjunctive.

▸ The affirmative *let's* + [*verb*] may also be expressed with **vamos a** + [*infinitive*]. Remember, however, that **vamos a** + [*infinitive*] can also mean *we are going to (do something)*. Context and tone will determine which meaning is being expressed.

Vamos a caminar por la ciudad.
Let's walk around the city.

Vamos a ir a Chile este verano.
We're going to Chile this summer.

Olga Lucía, tú y yo compremos las flores.

¡Encontré uno, vamos, crucemos la calle!

▸ To express *let's go*, the present indicative form of **ir** (**vamos**) is used, not the subjunctive. For the negative command, however, the subjunctive is used.

Affirmative	Negative
Vamos a la pescadería.	**No vayamos** a la pescadería.
Let's go to the fish market.	*Let's not go to the fish market.*
Vamos a tomar un café.	**No vayamos** a tomar un café.
Let's go have a coffee.	*Let's not go have a coffee.*

¡Pidamos un préstamo!

¡Hagamos un viaje!

¡Compremos un caballo!

BANCOSUR. LLÁMANOS.

Práctica

1 **Conversación** Completa esta conversación con mandatos de **nosotros/as.**

MARÍA Sergio, ¿quieres hacer diligencias ahora o por la tarde?

SERGIO No (1) _____ [dejarlas] para más tarde. (2) _____ [hacerlas] ahora.

MARÍA Necesito mandar un paquete.

SERGIO Yo también. (3) _____ [ir] al correo.

MARÍA Pues, antes de ir al correo, necesito sacar dinero de mi cuenta corriente.

SERGIO Bueno, (4) _____ [buscar] un cajero automático.

MARÍA ¿Tienes hambre?

SERGIO Sí. (5) _____ [cruzar] la calle y (6) _____ [comer] algo en ese café.

MARÍA Buena idea.

SERGIO ¿Nos sentamos aquí?

MARÍA No, no (7) _____ [sentarse] aquí; (8) _____ [sentarse] enfrente de la ventana.

SERGIO ¿Qué pedimos?

MARÍA (9) _____ [pedir] café y pan dulce.

2 **Hagámoslo** Responde a cada oración; sigue el modelo.

> **modelo**
> Vamos a vender el carro. (Sí)
> Sí, vendámoslo.

1. Vamos a levantarnos a las seis. (Sí)

2. Vamos a enviar los paquetes. (No)

3. Vamos al supermercado. (No)

4. Vamos a mandar esta tarjeta postal a nuestros amigos. (No)

5. Vamos a limpiar la habitación. (Sí)

6. Vamos a mirar la televisión. (No)

7. Vamos a bailar. (Sí)

8. Vamos a arreglar la sala. (No)

9. Vamos a comprar estampillas. (Sí)

Conversación

3 Decisiones Imagina que estás con un(a) amigo/a. Túrnense para hacerse estas preguntas. Usen mandatos de **nosotros/as** en sus respuestas.

1. ¿Cruzamos la calle aquí o caminamos una cuadra más?
2. ¿Vamos a casa o comemos en un restaurante?
3. ¿Salimos para el cine a las seis o a las seis y media?
4. ¿Pagamos la cuenta al contado o con tarjeta de crédito?

4 Preguntar Tú y tu compañero/a están de vacaciones y se hacen sugerencias para resolver las situaciones. Usen mandatos de **nosotros/as**.

Se nos olvidaron las tarjetas de crédito.
Paguemos al contado. /No compremos más regalos.

A

1. El museo está a sólo una cuadra de aquí.
2. Tenemos hambre.
3. Hay una cola larga en el cine.

B

1. Perdimos una maleta en el aeropuerto.
2. Tenemos prisa para llegar al cine.
3. Estamos cansados y queremos dormir.

5 Turistas Imaginen que están en Caracas. En grupos pequeños, lean esta guía turística y decidan qué van a hacer hoy. Usen mandatos de **nosotros/as**.

Visitemos el Museo de Arte Contemporáneo de Caracas esta mañana. Quiero ver las esculturas de Jesús Rafael Soto.

Guía de Caracas

MUSEOS

- **Museo de Arte Colonial**
  Avenida Panteón
- **Museo de Arte Contemporáneo de Caracas**
  Parque Central. Esculturas de Jesús Rafael Soto y pinturas de Miró, Chagall y Picasso.
- **Galería de Arte Nacional**
  Parque Central. Colección de más de 4.000 obras de arte venezolano.

SITIOS DE INTERÉS

- **Plaza Bolívar**
- **Jardín Botánico**
  Avenida Interna UCV. De 8:00 a 5:00.
- **Parque del Este**
  Avenida Francisco de Miranda. Parque más grande de la ciudad con serpentario.
- **Casa Natal de Simón Bolívar**
  Esquinas San Jacinto y Traposos. Casa colonial donde nació Simón Bolívar.

RESTAURANTES

- **El Barquero**
  Avenida Luis Roche
- **Restaurante El Coyuco**
  Avenida Urdaneta
- **Restaurante Sorrento**
  Avenida Francisco Solano
- **Café Tonino**
  Avenida Andrés Bello

I CAN make suggestions.

Nosotros commands and object pronouns

▶ Object pronouns are attached to affirmative **nosotros/as** commands. A written accent is added to maintain the original stress.

Firmemos el cheque.	**Firmémoslo.**
Let's sign the check.	*Let's sign it.*
Escribamos a Ana y a Raúl.	**Escribámosles.**
Let's write to Ana and Raúl.	*Let's write to them.*

▶ When **nos** or **se** is attached to an affirmative **nosotros/as** command, the final **–s** of the command verb is dropped.

Démoselo a ella.	**Mandémoselo** a ellos.
Let's give it to her.	*Let's send it to them.*
Sentémonos allí.	**Levantémonos** temprano.
Let's sit down there.	*Let's get up early.*

▶ Object pronouns are placed in front of negative **nosotros/as** commands.

No **les paguemos** el préstamo.	No **se lo digamos** a ellos.
Let's not pay them the loan.	*Let's not tell them.*
No **lo compremos.**	No **se la presentemos.**
Let's not buy it.	*Let's not introduce her (to him).*

▶ The **nosotros/as** command form of **irse** (*to go away*) is **vámonos.** Its negative form is **no nos vayamos.**

¡Vámonos de vacaciones!	**No nos vayamos** de aquí.
Let's go away on vacation!	*Let's not go away from here.*

¡Manos a la obra!

Indica los mandatos afirmativos y negativos de **nosotros/as** de estos verbos.

	Afirmativo	Negativo
1. estudiar	estudiemos	no estudiemos
2. cenar	_____	_____
3. leer	_____	_____
4. decidir	_____	_____
5. perder	_____	_____
6. seguir	_____	_____
7. practicar	_____	_____
8. conocer	_____	_____
9. decir	_____	_____
10. cerrar	_____	_____
11. levantarse	_____	_____
12. irse	_____	_____
13. dormir	_____	_____
14. escribirle	_____	_____
15. comprarlo	_____	_____
16. pedírselo	_____	_____

A repasar

14.1 The subjunctive in adjective clauses

1 **Un nuevo barrio** Acabas de mudarte y quieres saber qué puedes encontrar en tu nuevo barrio. Con un(a) compañero/a, túrnate para formular las preguntas y contestarlas.

modelo   algún / banco / estar / abierto / domingos / (no)

Estudiante 1: ¿Hay algún banco que esté abierto los domingos?
Estudiante 2: No, no hay ningún banco que esté abierto los domingos.

1. alguna / frutería / vender / frutas frescas / (sí)

2. alguna / peluquería / no / ser / cara / (sí)

3. alguna / joyería / vender / a plazos / (no)

4. alguna / zapatería / aceptar / cheques / (no)

5. alguna / lavandería / cerrar / diez de la noche / (sí)

6. alguien / poder / llevar / este paquete / correo / (no)

2 **¡Queremos vivir ahí!** En grupos de tres, describan qué características buscan en una ciudad para vivir. Después, compartan sus respuestas con la clase.

modelo   Queremos vivir en un lugar que tenga restaurantes de todo tipo.

14.2 Familiar (tú) commands

3 **En la ciudad** Tu amigo/a y tú tienen que hacer muchas diligencias, pero ninguno de los dos quiere hacer nada. Túrnense para dar mandatos familiares. Sigan el modelo.

modelo   enviar los paquetes
Estudiante 1: Envía los paquetes.
Estudiante 2: ¡Envíalos tú!

1. pagar la cuenta

2. comprar los sellos

3. hacer la comida

4. firmar el cheque

5. pedir un préstamo

6. llenar estos formularios

4 **Consejos** Tienes un sobrino que es un desastre. Dale por lo menos ocho consejos usando mandatos familiares de los verbos **decir, hacer, ir, poner, salir, ser, tener** y **venir**.

modelo   No digas mentiras. Di la verdad.

_____

_____

_____

_____

_____

_____

_____

5 **¡Un día muy ocupado!** Teresa hizo una lista de sus diligencias y de cuánto tiempo tarda en (*it takes her*) hacerlas. Con un(a) compañero/a, escribe el horario ideal para Teresa. Usa mandatos familiares.

modelo   Teresa, ve al banco a las nueve de la mañana y cobra tus cheques. A las nueve y media...

Diligencias	Tiempo	Lugares	Horarios
Cortarme el pelo	1 hr.	salón de belleza	12:00 p.m.–1:00 p.m.
Comprar un pastel para Eva	30 min.	pastelería	10:00 a.m.–2:00 p.m.
Visitar a Eva en el hospital	1 hr.	hospital	4:00 p.m.–5:00 p.m.
Cobrar cheques	30 min.	banco	9:00 a.m.–12:00 p.m.
Lavar ropa	2 hrs.	lavandería	12:00 p.m.–2:00 p.m.
Enviar cartas	30 min.	correo	9:00 a.m.–1:00 p.m.

14.3 Nosotros/as commands

6 **Planes** Con un(a) compañero/a, escribe las cosas que ustedes pueden hacer para realizar estos planes. Usa mandatos de **nosotros/as**.

modelo   Divertirnos este fin de semana
Vamos al cine con nuestros amigos.
No nos quedemos en casa.

1. Graduarse con honores

2. Vivir hasta los cien años

3. Comprar una casa

4. Estar en forma (*in shape*)

5. Conseguir una licencia de conducir

6. Pedir un préstamo en el banco

7 **Aniversario** Es el aniversario de bodas de tus abuelos. Escribe lo que les dices a tus familiares, usando mandatos de **nosotros/as**.

modelo

hacerles una fiesta sorpresa /
no decirles nuestros planes
Hagámosles una fiesta sorpresa.
No les digamos nuestros planes.

1. sorprenderlos / preparar sus platos favoritos
2. no alquilar un salón de fiestas / celebrar en casa
3. invitar a sus amigos / llamarles por teléfono
4. comprarles flores / no darles chocolates
5. bailar toda la noche / no quedarse sentados
6. llevar la cámara / tomarles muchas fotografías

8 **¿Cómo llegamos?** Con un(a) compañero/a, dibuja un mapa de una ciudad imaginaria. Escribe los nombres de las calles y marca los lugares de la lista. No olvides marcar el norte, el sur, el este y el oeste. Después, túrnense para preguntarse cómo llegar de un lugar a otro.

| banco | correo | lavandería | salón de belleza |
| carnicería | heladería | pescadería | supermercado |

modelo

Estudiante 1: ¿Cómo llegamos del banco a la heladería?
Estudiante 2: Caminemos hacia el este y lleguemos a la esquina de Colón y Morelos. Sigamos derecho por Morelos. Crucemos la calle...

Síntesis

9 **Una tienda** Conversa con un(a) compañero/a sobre abrir una tienda en tu ciudad. Decidan dónde va a estar ubicada (*located*), qué cosas harán juntos/as y qué cosas hará cada uno/a por separado. Usen mandatos de **tú** y de **nosotros/as**.

modelo

Estudiante 1: En nuestra ciudad no hay un supermercado que venda productos latinos. ¡Vamos a abrir uno!
Estudiante 2: ¡Excelente! Busquemos un lugar que esté cerca del centro de la ciudad. Hagamos una lista de los productos que vamos a vender. ¿Qué más necesitamos?
Estudiante 1: Tú piensa en un nombre para el supermercado. Yo voy a averiguar cuánto dinero necesitamos. Y vamos a pedir un préstamo en el banco.

Communicative Goal
Describe the steps for opening a joint savings account

 Video

Videoclip

1 **Preparación** ¿Quién eligió tu nombre? ¿Te gusta tu nombre o prefieres otro? ¿Cuál? ¿Por qué?

2 **El clip** Mira el anuncio de **Banco Ficensa** de Honduras.

Vocabulario	
cargar *to carry*	peluquero *hairdresser*
parecerse a *to look like*	segundo nombre *middle name*

Bueno, yo le puse° José.

le puse *named him*

3 **Escoger** Elige la opción correcta.

1. El peluquero de la mamá del bebé se llama _____.
   a. José   b. Tomás

2. Al papá del bebé le gustan las películas de _____.
   a. Harry Potter   b. Sylvester Stallone

3. Tomás es el nombre del _____ de la mamá del bebé.
   a. abuelo   b. hermano

4. El regalo para el bebé está _____.
   a. en el banco   b. personalizado

4 **En el banco** En parejas, describan cinco pasos para abrir una cuenta de ahorros conjunta (*joint*). Usen mandatos de **nosotros/as**.

I CAN describe the steps for opening a joint savings account.

Ampliación

Communicative Goals
Understand a
conversation by
listening for specific
details, and talk
about solutions to
economic problems

1 Escuchar

 A Lee estas oraciones y luego escucha la conversación entre Alberto y Eduardo. Indica si cada verbo se refiere a algo en el pasado, en el presente o en el futuro.

> **TIP** **Listen for specific information and linguistic cues.** You can often get the facts you need by listening for specific pieces of information. You should also be aware of the linguistic structures you hear. By listening for verb endings, you can figure out whether the verbs describe past, present, or future actions. Verb endings also indicate who is performing the action.

1. Demetrio / comprar en Macro _____
2. Alberto / comprar en Macro _____
3. Alberto / estudiar psicología _____
4. carro / tener frenos malos _____
5. Eduardo / comprar un anillo (*ring*) para Rebeca _____
6. Eduardo / estudiar _____

B ¿Crees que Alberto y Eduardo viven en una ciudad grande o en un pueblo? ¿Cómo lo sabes?

2 Conversar

 Tú y tu compañero/a de cuarto tienen problemas económicos. Representen una conversación en la que hablen de cuatro problemas y propongan soluciones para cada uno. Usen mandatos de **nosotros/as**.

modelo

Estudiante 1: No sé qué hacer. Casi no tengo el dinero para el alquiler.

Estudiante 2: Debes ahorrar más dinero... y yo también. No comamos en restaurantes. Preparemos comida en casa.

Estudiante 1: Tal vez necesitemos mudarnos. Necesitamos un apartamento que sea más barato.

Estudiante 2: ¡Uy! No quiero mudarme. Pídele un préstamo a tu papá, mejor.

Estudiante 1: No lo puedo hacer cada mes. Pero tienes razón, podemos ahorrar dinero comiendo en casa.

Estudiante 2: Y no usemos más los cajeros automáticos. Paguemos todo al contado para saber mejor adónde va el dinero.

I CAN understand a conversation by listening for specific details.

I CAN talk about solutions to economic problems.

Ampliación

Communicative Goals
Write a letter giving directions, and create a promotional brochure

3 Escribir

Escribe una carta a un(a) amigo/a en la cual le explicas claramente cómo llegar a tu casa desde el aeropuerto. Incluye también un mapa detallado para que no se confunda.

> **TIP** **List key words.** When you give directions, you use prepositions that describe location, such as **enfrente de, al lado de**, and **detrás de**. Making a list of these expressions will help you write your directions more efficiently.

Organizar	Planea la mejor ruta para llegar a tu casa. Apunta las expresiones útiles para indicar cómo llegar, como los nombres de las calles y de los monumentos.
Escribir	Dibuja un mapa y utilízalo para escribir el primer borrador de tu carta.
Corregir	Intercambia tu carta con un(a) compañero/a. Anota los aspectos mejor escritos. Ofrécele sugerencias. ¿Hay suficientes detalles? ¿Está claro el mapa? Si ves algunos errores, coméntaselos.
Compartir	Revisa el primer borrador de la carta y el mapa, según las indicaciones de tu compañero/a. Incorpora nuevas ideas y prepara la versión final.

4 Un paso más

Imagina que eres miembro de un grupo que está promocionando una comunidad modelo en un país hispano. Diseña un folleto (*brochure*) informativo para dar a conocer la comunidad.

- Escoge el lugar ideal para el proyecto. Considera el acceso a las ciudades grandes, los eventos culturales y los recursos naturales.
- Incluye un mapa del país elegido que indique dónde está localizada la comunidad modelo.
- Crea un mapa de la zona que muestre las atracciones principales del centro de la comunidad.
- Explica las características de la comunidad.

5 Cultura

Estás en una ciudad grande de Latinoamérica como Buenos Aires, la Ciudad de México o Bogotá. ¿Cómo vas a transitar por la ciudad? ¿Vas a pasear en bicicleta o ir en metro/autobús/taxi? ¿Por qué? ¿Vas a ir a las tiendas especializadas como las panaderías y las pastelerías?

I CAN write a letter giving directions.

I CAN create a promotional brochure.

Audio: Reading

Antes de leer

Readers often visualize a text as they read.

TIP Visualize. Visualizing a text as you read can help you comprehend it. Before you begin, read the title and create a picture in your mind. Then skim each paragraph and visualize what you read. As you create these mental pictures, think about not only the sights, but also the sounds, smells, tastes, and feelings that are conveyed in the text. These visualizations will help you create an image of what the story will be about.

 Visualizar

The reading selection for this lesson consists of a **microcuento**, or very short story, by Mario Benedetti. Why do you think that visualizing might be important in the *Los bomberos* short story?

_____

_____

Sobre el autor

Mario Benedetti (1920–2009) fue un escritor uruguayo. Aunque es conocido principalmente por sus poemas, escribió también ensayos, novelas y cuentos. Gran parte de la obra de Benedetti se centra en la temática urbana y se caracteriza por su compromiso político y social.

Los bomberos
Mario Benedetti

Olegario no sólo fue un as° del presentimiento, sino que además siempre estuvo muy orgulloso° de su poder. A veces se quedaba absorto° por un instante, y luego decía: "Mañana va a llover". Y llovía. Otras veces se rascaba la nuca° y anunciaba: "El martes saldrá° el 57 a la cabeza". Y el martes salía el 57 a la cabeza. Entre sus amigos gozaba de° una admiración sin límites.

Algunos de ellos recuerdan el más famoso de sus aciertos°. Caminaban con él frente a la Universidad, cuando de pronto el aire matutino° fue atravesado° por el sonido y la furia de los bomberos°. Olegario sonrió de modo casi imperceptible, y dijo: "Es posible que mi casa se esté quemando°".

Llamaron un taxi y encargaron° al chofer que siguiera de cerca a los bomberos. Éstos tomaron por Rivera, y Olegario dijo: "Es casi seguro que mi casa se esté quemando". Los amigos guardaron un respetuoso y afable silencio; tanto lo admiraban.

Los bomberos siguieron por Pereyra y la nerviosidad llegó a su colmo°. Cuando doblaron por la calle en que vivía Olegario, los amigos se pusieron tiesos° de expectativa. Por fin, frente mismo a la llameante° casa de Olegario, el carro de bomberos se detuvo° y los hombres comenzaron rápida y serenamente los preparativos de rigor. De vez en cuando, desde las ventanas de la planta alta, alguna astilla° volaba por los aires.

Con toda parsimonia°, Olegario bajó del taxi. Se acomodó el nudo° de la corbata, y luego, con un aire de humilde vencedor°, se aprestó° a recibir las felicitaciones y los abrazos de sus buenos amigos.

as *ace* **orgulloso** *proud* **absorto** *absorbed* **se rascaba la nuca** *he scratched the back of his neck* **saldrá** *will leave* **gozaba de** *he enjoyed* **aciertos** *correct predictions* **matutino** *morning* **atravesado** *pierced* **bomberos** *firefighters* **quemando** *burning* **encargaron** *asked* **colmo** *peak* **tiesos** *tense, stiff* **llameante** *flaming* **se detuvo** *stopped* **astilla** *splinter* **parsimonia** *lack of urgency* **nudo** *knot* **vencedor** *victor* **se aprestó** *he prepared*

Después de leer

¿Comprendiste?

Indica si las oraciones son **ciertas** o **falsas**. Corrige las falsas.

Cierto	Falso	
_____	_____	1. Las predicciones de Olegario a veces son correctas.
_____	_____	2. Los amigos de Olegario dudan de sus predicciones.
_____	_____	3. Un día, Olegario y sus amigos caminaban por la calle cuando escucharon el carro de los bomberos.
_____	_____	4. Olegario y sus amigos siguieron a los bomberos en un taxi.
_____	_____	5. Los amigos de Olegario tuvieron miedo al ver que su casa se quemaba.

Preguntas

Responde estas preguntas con oraciones completas.

1. Busca las dos predicciones de Olegario en el primer párrafo del cuento. ¿Expresan un grado de certeza (*certainty*) alto o bajo?

_____

2. Ahora, busca las dos predicciones que hace sobre la casa. ¿Expresan certeza o dejan lugar a dudas?

_____

3. Al final, ¿crees que a Olegario le importa que se queme la casa? Explica.

_____

4. ¿Tiene Olegario una actitud arrogante con respecto a su talento? ¿Por qué?

_____

5. ¿Cómo crees que ocurrió el incendio (*fire*)?

_____

Coméntalo

¿Te gustaría predecir el futuro? ¿Conoces a alguien que diga tener este poder? ¿Cómo usarías tú el poder de predecir el futuro? Explica.

I CAN read a story and visualize the text.

Vocabulary Tools

En la ciudad

el banco *bank*
la carnicería *butcher shop*
el correo *post office*
la frutería *fruit shop*
la heladería *ice cream shop*
la joyería *jewelry store*
la lavandería *laundromat*
la panadería *bakery*
la pastelería *pastry shop*
la peluquería *hair salon*
la pescadería *fish market*
el salón de belleza *beauty salon*
el supermercado *supermarket*
la zapatería *shoe store*

———

hacer cola *to stand in line*
hacer diligencias *to run errands*

En el correo

el/la cartero/a *mail carrier*
el correo *mail; post office*
las estampillas *stamps*
el paquete *package*
los sellos *stamps*
el sobre *envelope*

———

echar (una carta) al buzón *to put (a letter) in the mailbox; to mail (a letter)*
enviar *to send*
mandar *to send*

En el banco

el cajero automático *ATM*
el cheque *check*
la cuenta corriente *checking account*
la cuenta de ahorros *savings account*

———

ahorrar *to save (money)*
cobrar *to cash (a check); to charge (for a product or service)*
depositar *to deposit*
firmar *to sign*
llenar (un formulario) *to fill out (a form)*
pagar al contado *to pay in cash*
pagar a plazos *to pay in installments*
pedir prestado/a *to borrow*
pedir un préstamo *to apply for a loan*
ser gratis *to be free of charge*

Cómo llegar

la cuadra *(city) block*
la dirección *address*
la esquina *corner*
el letrero *sign*

———

cruzar *to cross*
doblar *to turn*
estar perdido/a *to be lost*
indicar cómo llegar *to give directions*
quedar *to be located*

———

(al) este *(to the) east*
(al) norte *(to the) north*
(al) oeste *(to the) west*
(al) sur *(to the) south*

———

derecho *straight (ahead)*
enfrente de *opposite; facing*
hacia *toward*

℘ Communicative Goals: Review

I CAN talk about errands.
• Name two errands that you need to do.

I CAN ask for and give directions.
• Say how to get to your dorm, apartment, or house from Spanish class.

I CAN tell someone what to do.
• Give three pieces of advice to a classmate. Use familiar commands.

I CAN make suggestions.
• You and your friends are bored. Use **nosotros/as** commands to make two suggestions of things to do.

I CAN investigate city transportation in Spanish-speaking countries.
• Describe a mode of transportation in a Latin American city.

AVENTURAS
EN LOS
PAÍSES
HISPANOS

Communicative Goal
Identify aspects of the geography
and culture of Nicaragua,
Costa Rica, and Panama

▶ El Canal de Panamá conecta el
océano Pacífico con el océano Atlántico.
La construcción de este cauce *(channel)*
artificial empezó en 1903 y concluyó
diez años después. Es la fuente *(source)*
principal de ingresos *(income)* del país,
gracias al dinero que aportan los más
de 14.000 buques *(ships)* que transitan
anualmente por esta ruta.

¿Te gustaría visitar el Canal de Panamá?

AMÉRICA CENTRAL II

Nicaragua

Área: 130.370 km^2 (50.336 millas^2)
Población: 6.600.000
Capital: Managua – 1.055.000
Ciudades principales: León,
Masaya, Granada
Moneda: córdoba
SOURCE: Population Division,
UN Secretariat & CIA World Factbook

Costa Rica

Área: 51.100 km^2 (19.730 millas^2)
Población: 5.100.000
Capital: San José – 1.379.000
Ciudades principales: Alajuela, Cartago,
Puntarenas, Heredia
Moneda: colón costarricense
SOURCE: Population Division,
UN Secretariat & CIA World Factbook

Panamá

Área: 75.420 km^2 (29.119 millas^2)
Población: 4.300.000
Capital: Ciudad de Panamá – 1.822.000
Ciudades principales: Colón, David
Moneda: balboa (es equivalente al
dólar estadounidense)
SOURCE: Population Division,
UN Secretariat & CIA World Factbook

Video

Sociedad

Costa Rica: una nación progresista

Costa Rica es un país progresista. Tiene un nivel de alfabetización del 96%, uno de los más altos de Latinoamérica. Además, en 1871, Costa Rica abolió la pena de muerte *(death penalty)* y, en 1948, disolvió el ejército *(army)* e hizo la educación gratis y obligatoria para todos los costarricenses.

¿Fuiste a Costa Rica o conoces a alguien que visitó alguna vez Costa Rica? ¿Qué sabes sobre ese país?

Museo Nacional de Costa Rica, antiguo cuartel *(barracks)* del ejército *(army)*.

Indígenas

La mola

La mola es una forma de arte textil de los kunas, una tribu indígena que vive en las islas San Blas de Panamá. Las molas se hacen con fragmentos de tela *(material)* de colores vivos. Las molas tradicionales tienen diseños *(patterns)* geométricos. Antes se usaban como ropa, pero hoy día también sirven para decorar casas.

¿Te gustan las molas y su variedad de colores?

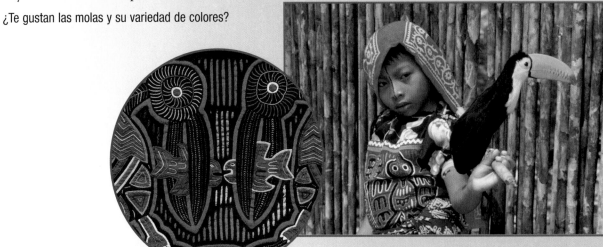

NICARAGUA

Río Coco

Cordillera Isabella

Río Tuma

Sierra Madre

Cordillera de Yolaina

León
Lago de Managua

⭐ Managua

Masaya
Granada

Lago de Nicaragua
Isla Zapatera
Isla Ometepe

Océano Pacífico

Río San Juan

Cordillera de Guanacaste

Puntarenas

San José

COSTA RICA

Cartago

Río Reventazón

Cordillera de Talamarca

Música 🎵

El tamborito

El tamborito es el género musical más representativo del folclor panameño. Su origen se remonta *(dates back)* al siglo XVII; es el resultado de la fusión de ritmos indígenas, africanos y españoles. Tiene la forma de un diálogo entre un coro *(chorus)* y una **cantalante**, voz principal que marca la melodía y el compás *(beat)*. Esta conversación musical se complementa con tambores *(drums)*, cajas y palmadas *(claps)*. Tradicionalmente, las mujeres cantan el tamborito. La **cantalante** y folclorista Lucila Aura Jaén Córdoba, mejor conocida como Lucy Jaén, es considerada la mayor exponente de este género musical.

¿Qué géneros de música folclórica conoces?

Política

Óscar Arias

Óscar Arias es expresidente de Costa Rica. Fue elegido presidente dos veces. Su primer período presidencial fue de 1986 a 1990 y su segundo período fue de 2006 a 2010. Arias tiene una amplia formación académica: estudió en Costa Rica, los Estados Unidos e Inglaterra y fue profesor de Ciencias Políticas en la Universidad de Costa Rica. Durante su primer período como presidente, trabajó incansablemente *(tirelessly)* para establecer la paz *(peace)* en Centroamérica. Finalmente, logró *(he achieved)* un acuerdo *(agreement)* de paz con los presidentes de El Salvador, Nicaragua, Honduras y Guatemala. Por sus esfuerzos *(efforts)*, ganó el Premio Nobel de la Paz en 1987.

¿Conoces a alguna persona importante en el área de la política en Latinoamérica?

Escritores

Ernesto Cardenal

El nicaragüense Ernesto Cardenal (1925–2020) fue poeta, escultor y sacerdote *(priest)* católico. Es uno de los escritores más famosos de Latinoamérica. Escribió más de treinta y cinco obras. Desde joven creyó en el poder *(power)* de la poesía para mejorar la sociedad, y trabajó por establecer la igualdad y la justicia en su país.

¿Conoces a artistas o escritores de Latinoamérica? ¿A quién conoces?

Mar Caribe

Canal de Panamá

Islas San Blas

Cordillera de San Blas

Río Chepo

Bocas del Toro

Colón

Serranía de Tabasará

Ciudad de Panamá

PANAMÁ

David

Isla del Rey

Isla de Coiba

Golfo de Panamá

Colombia

¿Qué aprendiste?

1 **¿Cierto o falso?** Indica si estas oraciones son **ciertas** o **falsas**.

	Cierto	Falso
1. El Canal de Panamá conecta los océanos Pacífico y Atlántico.	_____	_____
2. San José es la capital de Panamá.	_____	_____
3. Costa Rica disolvió el ejército en 1948.	_____	_____
4. La mola es una tribu indígena que vive en Panamá.	_____	_____
5. Las molas se usan hoy para decorar casas.	_____	_____
6. Ernesto Cardenal es uno de los escritores más famosos de Latinoamérica.	_____	_____
7. El tamborito es un género musical de Nicaragua.	_____	_____
8. Óscar Arias fue presidente de Panamá.	_____	_____

2 **Preguntas** Contesta estas preguntas.

1. ¿Cuál es la capital de Nicaragua?
2. ¿Qué país tiene un nivel de alfabetización del 96%?
3. ¿Quién ganó el Premio Nobel de la Paz en 1987?
4. ¿Dónde viven los kunas?
5. ¿Quiénes cantan el tamborito tradicionalmente?

3 **¿Qué piensas?** Responde a las preguntas.

1. ¿Por qué crees que el Canal de Panamá es tan importante para el comercio de los países del continente americano?
2. ¿Qué dice sobre Costa Rica que la educación es gratis y obligatoria para todos los costarricenses?
3. ¿Crees que la poesía puede mejorar la sociedad? ¿Por qué?
4. ¿Qué piensas que representan las molas para los kunas?

4 **Comparación** Haz una de estas comparaciones.

- la mola y un arte textil que conoces
- el progresismo en Costa Rica y en los Estados Unidos
- el tamborito y otro género musical

I CAN identify basic facts about the geography and culture of Nicaragua, Costa Rica, and Panama by reading short informational texts with visuals.

15 El bienestar

PREPARACIÓN

pages 384–389
- Words related to being healthy
- The gym and nutrition
- The letters **b** and **v**

AVENTURAS

pages 390–391
- Juanjo and Manuel join Valentina, Olga Lucía, and Sara for an outdoor yoga class. Will they enjoy it?

CULTURA

pages 392–393
- *Espacios públicos saludables*
- Flash cultura: *¿Estrés? ¿Qué estrés?*

GRAMÁTICA

pages 394–403
- Past participles used as adjectives
- The present perfect
- The past perfect

LECTURA

pages 404–405
- Short story: *El viaje*

PARA EMPEZAR

- ¿Qué están haciendo los chicos?
- ¿Dónde están?
- ¿Tienen estrés?
- ¿Qué lleva la chica en la mano?

EL BIENESTAR

EN EL GIMNASIO

el músculo *muscle*

calentarse (e:ie) *to warm up*

entrenarse *to train*

estar en buena forma
to be in good shape

hacer ejercicio *to exercise*

hacer ejercicios aeróbicos
to do aerobics

hacer gimnasia *to work out*

levantar pesas *to lift weights*

mantenerse en forma *to stay in shape*

sudar *to sweat*

hacer ejercicios de estiramiento
to do stretching exercises

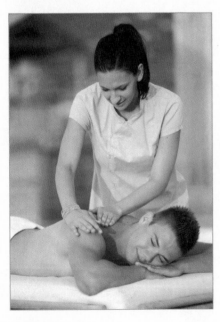

el masaje
massage

EL BIENESTAR

el bienestar *well-being*

aliviar el estrés/la tensión
to relieve stress/tension

disfrutar (de)
to enjoy; to reap the benefits (of)

llevar una vida sana
to lead a healthy lifestyle

(no) fumar *(not) to smoke*

la clase de ejercicios aeróbicos
aerobics class

Vocabulary Tools

LA NUTRICIÓN

la bebida alcohólica
alcoholic beverage

la caloría *calorie*

el colesterol *cholesterol*

la grasa *fat*

la merienda *(afternoon) snack*

los minerales *minerals*

la nutrición *nutrition*

la proteína *protein*

---

adelgazar *to lose weight; to slim down*

aumentar de peso *to gain weight*

consumir alcohol *to consume alcohol*

engordar *to gain weight*

estar a dieta *to be on a diet*

seguir una dieta equilibrada
to eat a balanced diet

---

descafeinado/a *decaffeinated*

merendar (e:ie)
to have a(n) (afternoon) snack

ADJETIVOS

activo/a *active*

débil *weak*

flexible *flexible*

sedentario/a *sedentary*

tranquilo/a *calm; quiet*

OTRAS PALABRAS Y EXPRESIONES

la droga *drug*

el/la drogadicto/a *drug addict*

el/la teleadicto/a *couch potato*

---

apurarse *to hurry; to rush*

darse prisa *to hurry; to rush*

sufrir muchas presiones
to be under a lot of pressure

tratar de (+ inf.)
to try (to do something)

---

en exceso *in excess; too much*

sin *without*

fuerte
strong

las vitaminas

ASÍ SE DICE

hacer ejercicios aeróbicos ⟷ hacer aeróbic (*Esp., Arg.*)

A escuchar

1 **¿Lógico o ilógico?** Escucha las oraciones e indica si son **lógicas** o **ilógicas**.

	Lógico	Ilógico
1.	_____	_____
2.	_____	_____
3.	_____	_____
4.	_____	_____
5.	_____	_____
6.	_____	_____
7.	_____	_____
8.	_____	_____

2 **Seleccionar** Escucha el anuncio del gimnasio Sucre. Marca los servicios que se ofrecen.

_____ 1. dietas para adelgazar

_____ 2. programa para aumentar de peso

_____ 3. clases de gimnasia

_____ 4. entrenador personal

_____ 5. programas privados de pesas

_____ 6. clases de estiramiento

_____ 7. masajes

_____ 8. programa para dejar de fumar

_____ 9. programas para teleadictos

_____ 10. clases de ejercicios aeróbicos

A practicar

3 **Identificar** Identifica la palabra o expresión opuesta de la lista.

1. activo
2. adelgazar
3. débil
4. rígido

5. no tener prisa
6. estar sano
7. engordar
8. nervioso

apurarse	**mantenerse en forma**
aumentar de peso	**sedentario**
en exceso	**sin**
estar enfermo	**sudar**
flexible	**sufrir muchas presiones**
fuerte	**tranquilo**

4 **Combinar** Combina las frases de las dos columnas para formar ocho oraciones lógicas.

_____ 1. David levanta pesas…

_____ 2. Estás en buena forma…

_____ 3. Felipe se lastimó…

_____ 4. Mi hermano…

_____ 5. Sara hace ejercicios de…

_____ 6. Mis primos se entrenan…

_____ 7. Para llevar una vida sana,

_____ 8. Los médicos sufren muchas…

a. aumentó de peso por sufrir estrés.

b. estiramiento.

c. presiones de sus pacientes.

d. para correr en un maratón.

e. porque haces ejercicio.

f. un músculo de la pierna.

g. no se debe fumar.

h. y corre mucho.

5 **Describir** Describe lo que ocurre en los dibujos.

1.

2.

3.

4.

A conversar

6 **La nutrición** Con un(a) compañero/a, conversa sobre tus hábitos alimenticios (*eating habits*).

1. ¿Cuántas comidas con mucha grasa consumes regularmente? ¿Piensas que debes comer menos comidas de este tipo? ¿Por qué?

2. ¿Compras comidas con muchos minerales y vitaminas? ¿Necesitas consumir más comidas que los contienen? ¿Por qué?

3. ¿Tiene algún miembro de tu familia problemas con el colesterol? ¿Qué hace para cuidarse?

4. ¿Qué piensas de la idea de no comer carne u otros productos animales? ¿Es posible seguir una dieta equilibrada sin comer carne?

5. ¿Consumes cafeína en exceso? ¿Cuáles son los productos que contienen cafeína? ¿Qué ventajas (*advantages*) y desventajas tiene la cafeína?

6. ¿Crees que llevas una vida sana? ¿Y tus amigos/as? ¿Crees que, en general, los estudiantes llevan una vida sana? ¿Por qué?

7 **Comparaciones** Con un(a) compañero/a, conversa sobre estos temas y luego comparte tres datos interesantes con la clase.

el yoga

modelo
Estudiante 1: *Creo que el yoga es muy bueno para la salud.*
Estudiante 2: *Sí, pero las clases de yoga son muy caras. Además, son muy aburridas.*
Estudiante 1: *Yo prefiero pagar y estar en buena forma física y mental.*

la meditación	la comida orgánica	pilates	correr al aire libre
las pesas	los ejercicios aeróbicos	la natación	el baile

8 **Un anuncio** En grupos de cuatro, imaginen que son dueños/as de un gimnasio con un equipo (*equipment*) moderno, entrenadores cualificados y un(a) nutricionista. Preparen un anuncio para la televisión que atraiga (*attracts*) a nuevos clientes. Incluyan esta información.

- Las ventajas de estar en buena forma

- El equipo que tienen y las características únicas del gimnasio

- Los servicios y las clases que ofrecen

- La dirección y el teléfono del gimnasio

- El precio para los socios (*members*) del gimnasio

9 **Recomendaciones** Imagina que tú y tu compañero/a están preocupados por los malos hábitos de un(a) amigo/a suyo/a que no está bien últimamente (*lately*). Representen un diálogo en el cual hablan de lo que está pasando en la vida de su amigo/a y los cambios que necesita hacer para llevar una vida sana.

10 **El teleadicto** Con un(a) compañero/a, representa una conversación entre un(a) nutricionista y un(a) teleadicto/a. La persona sedentaria habla de sus malos hábitos de salud. El/La nutricionista debe sugerir una dieta equilibrada y una rutina para mantenerse en forma.

I CAN discuss well-being.

Ortografía

 Tutorial

Las letras b y v

Since there is no difference in pronunciation between the Spanish letters **b** and **v**, spelling words that contain these letters can be tricky. Here are some tips.

....

nomb**re**   **b**lusa**   **a**b**soluto**   **descu**b**rir**

The letter **b** is always used before consonants.

....

bon**ita**   **bo**t**ella**   **bu**s**car**   **bie**n**estar**

At the beginning of words, the letter **b** is usually used when it is followed by the letter combinations **-on, -or, -ot, -u, -ur, -us, -ien,** and **-ene.**

....

adelgazab**a**   **disfruta**b**an**   **i**b**as**   **í**b**amos**

The letter **b** is used in the verb endings of the imperfect tense for **–ar** verbs and **ir**.

....

voy   **v**amos   **estu**v**o**   **tu**v**ieron**

The letter **v** is used in the present tense forms of **ir** and in the preterite forms of **estar** and **tener**.

....

octa**v**o   **hu**e**v**o   **act**i**v**a   **gra**v**e**

The letter **v** is used in these noun and adjective endings: **-avo/a, -evo/a, -ivo/a, -ave, -eve**.

....

Práctica Completa las palabras con las letras **b** o **v**.

1. Una __ez me lastimé el __razo cuando esta__a __uceando.
2. Manuela ol__idó sus li__ros en el auto__ús.
3. Ernesto tomó el __orrador y se puso todo __lanco de tiza.
4. Para tener una __ida sana y saluda__le, necesitas tomar __itaminas.
5. En mi pue__lo hay un __ule__ar que tiene muchos ár__oles.

El ahorcado Juega al ahorcado (*hangman*) para adivinar las palabras.

1. __ _u_ __ __ _s_   Están en el cielo.
2. __ _u_ __ _n_   Relacionado con el correo.
3. __ _o_ __ _e_ __ __ _a_   Está llena de líquido.
4. __ _i_ __ _e_   Fenómeno meteorológico.
5. __ _e_ __ __ __ __ __ _s_   Los "ojos" de la casa.

La clase de yoga

Los chicos asisten a una clase de yoga en Madrid Río.

Video

Antes de ver

Ojea los pies de foto (*Scan the captions*) y busca vocabulario relacionado con el ejercicio, la nutrición y el bienestar.

PERSONAJES

JUANJO

MANUEL

SARA

OLGA LUCÍA

VALENTINA

INSTRUCTORA

SARA ¿Has ido a clase de yoga alguna vez?

MANUEL No, pero Valentina dijo que para hacer yoga es mejor ser flexible.

JUANJO Nunca he sido flexible. Yo prefiero levantar pesas.

SARA (*a Olga Lucía y Valentina*) ¡Hola!

OLGA LUCÍA ¿Qué hacen aquí tan temprano?

MANUEL ¿No nos habíais invitado a ir a la clase de yoga por la mañana?

VALENTINA ¡¿Y os lo tomasteis en serio?!

VALENTINA Siempre vamos corriendo para calentar.

SARA ¡Así también hacemos ejercicios aeróbicos y nos mantenemos en forma!

OLGA LUCÍA (*a Juanjo y Manuel*) Desayunaron ligero, ¿verdad?

JUANJO ¡¿Ligero?! Desayunamos huevos, jamón, salchichas...

MANUEL ...tostadas y zumo de naranja. Eso. Ah, y café.

SARA ¿Y los chicos?

OLGA LUCÍA Allá los veo, vienen lentísimo.

VALENTINA Cuando llegaron, ni siquiera nos habíamos vestido, y ahora los tenemos que esperar.

OLGA LUCÍA ¡Pude haber dormido más!

SARA (*a Manuel y Juanjo*) ¡Daos prisa, que va a empezar la clase!

ACTIVIDADES

1 **¿Cierto o falso?** Indica si lo que dicen las oraciones es **cierto** o **falso**. Corrige las oraciones falsas.

	Cierto	Falso
1. Manuel y Juanjo se despiertan temprano.	○	○
2. Juanjo quiere ir en autobús a la clase de yoga.	○	○
3. Las chicas siempre hacen ejercicios aeróbicos antes de la clase de yoga.	○	○
4. Juanjo y Manuel desayunan algo ligero antes de la clase.	○	○

2 **Asociar** Identifica a quién(es) asocias con estas comidas y bebidas.

1. huevos
2. gazpacho
3. jamón
4. ensalada de atún
5. café

INSTRUCTORA Repitamos el saludo al sol: inhalamos, brazos al cielo, exhalamos. Pie derecho atrás.

JUANJO (*a Valentina*) ¡¿No decías que el yoga servía para relajarse?!

VALENTINA (*a Juanjo*) Sí, el yoga te ayuda a aliviar la tensión y el estrés.

JUANJO ¡Pues yo no me siento nada aliviado!

SARA Tienes que respirar, Juanjo.

OLGA LUCÍA ¡Shh! ¡No se puede hablar!

INSTRUCTORA Y ahora levantamos la pierna. No importa que se caigan, lo importante es que traten de hacerlo.

INSTRUCTORA (*a Manuel*) ¿Quieres que te ayude a hacer la pose una vez más?

INSTRUCTORA Estiramos. Levantamos la pierna.

INSTRUCTORA (*a Manuel*) Lo has hecho muy bien.

MANUEL ¡Namaste!

OLGA LUCÍA ¿Les gustó la clase?

JUANJO ¡Nunca he sudado tanto en mi vida!

MANUEL Yo estoy muy relajado.

SARA ¿Queréis ir a comer algo?

MANUEL ¡Claro!

Expresiones útiles

la chistorra *type of cured pork sausage*
estirar *to stretch*
exhalar *to exhale*
inhalar *to inhale*
ligero/a *light*
ni siquiera *not even*
la sobrasada *spicy pork sausage*
el zumo *juice (in Spain)*

──────────

la estera *mat*

Madrid Río

Desde 2011 los madrileños disfrutan de un nuevo pulmón verde (*green area*): Madrid Río. Situado al lado de la ribera (*riverbank*) del río Manzanares, el parque ofrece casi veinte áreas de juegos infantiles (*playgrounds*), espacios para jugar al fútbol, baloncesto, tenis y pasear en bicicleta, ¡y hasta una playa! Gracias a Madrid Río, los madrileños ya no tienen excusas para no mantenerse en forma.

¿Haces ejercicio al aire libre? ¿Qué pulmones verdes ofrece el lugar donde vives?

---

3 **Preguntas personales** En parejas, háganse estas preguntas. ¿Tienen respuestas en común?

1. ¿Qué ejercicios haces?
2. ¿Te gusta correr? ¿Por qué?
3. ¿Qué haces para aliviar la tensión y el estrés?
4. ¿Asistes a clases de yoga? ¿Por qué?
5. ¿Qué desayunaste hoy?
6. ¿Qué te gusta comer después de hacer ejercicio?

I CAN talk about well-being.

Communicative Goal
Discuss outdoor exercise spaces in Spanish-speaking
countries and in the United States

Espacios públicos **saludables**

Los médicos de todo el mundo insisten en la importancia de la actividad física y el deporte para el bienestar físico y mental de todos. Aun así, los niveles° de actividad física siguen siendo bajos. Según la Organización Mundial de la Salud (OMS), el 39% de la población latinoamericana no practica ningún tipo de actividad física. Y en España el valor es del 46%.

Con el objetivo de aumentar° la actividad física entre la población, varias ciudades del mundo hispano promueven la creación de espacios públicos para que los residentes hagan ejercicio. En Madrid, España, por ejemplo, se han instalado los llamados "parques calistenia" en diferentes partes de la ciudad, donde las personas pueden hacer ejercicio al aire libre a cualquier hora del día y sin tener que pagar un gimnasio caro. Estos parques también se están volviendo° muy populares en Latinoamérica, no sólo porque son gratuitos y permiten hacer ejercicio al aire libre, sino también porque favorecen la conformación de grupos de amigos que comparten el interés por el ejercicio y se motivan mutuamente.

En Lima, Perú, se encuentra uno de los espacios públicos más amplios y agradables para la práctica de la actividad física: el Malecón° de Miraflores. Por su gran extensión, su hermosa vista y el fresco aire marino que se respira, el malecón es el lugar preferido por los limeños° para hacer ejercicio. Todos los días, desde muy temprano en la mañana hasta las horas de la noche, y durante todo el año, es posible ver personas practicando todo tipo de actividades físicas, como caminar, correr, patinar o pasear en bicicleta, pero también hay quienes levantan pesas y practican yoga.

Para los más aventureros y que prefieren más adrenalina, la ciudad de Buenos Aires, Argentina, ofrece muchos espacios públicos para la práctica de actividades como el skate y el parkour, maneras diferentes y divertidas de hacer ejercicio que se han extendido por muchos países hispanos. En 2015, Buenos Aires inauguró el primer espacio público de Latinoamérica para practicar parkour: el Parque Alberdi de Mataderos. Es un amplio espacio con una variedad de volúmenes y estructuras tubulares donde se pueden practicar estas disciplinas. Con éste, ya son cinco los parques públicos que promueven los deportes extremos en la ciudad.

Área X en Buenos Aires, Argentina

niveles *levels* aumentar *increase* se están volviendo *are becoming* Malecón *coastal walkway* limeños *residents of Lima*

Malecón de Miraflores en Lima, Perú

ACTIVIDADES

 1 **¿Cierto o falso?** Indica si lo que dicen las oraciones es **cierto** o **falso**. Corrige la información falsa.

1. Los niveles de actividad física entre la población todavía son bajos.

2. Los "parques calistenia" de Madrid son caros.

3. En el Malecón de Miraflores se puede correr y practicar yoga.

4. El primer parque público de Latinoamérica para la práctica de parkour se encuentra en Lima, Perú.

5. Los jóvenes de Buenos Aires no tienen espacios para practicar deportes extremos.

 2 **Preguntas** Contesta las preguntas.

1. ¿Qué porcentaje (*percentage*) de españoles no practica ningún tipo de actividad física?

2. ¿Dónde está el Malecón de Miraflores?

3. ¿Qué es el Parque Alberdi de Mataderos?

4. ¿Cuántos parques públicos para deportes extremos hay en Buenos Aires?

5. ¿Por qué son populares los "parques calistenia"?

 3 **Conversación** Conversa con un(a) compañero/a sobre estas preguntas.

1. ¿Por qué crees que los espacios públicos para la práctica de la actividad física son importantes para las ciudades?

2. ¿En qué lugares de tu comunidad se puede realizar actividad física al aire libre?

3. ¿Estos espacios son similares a los que hay en algunos países hispanos?

 4 **Carta al editor** Escribe una carta al editor para proponer la creación de más espacios públicos para practicar actividades físicas en tu comunidad. Menciona la importancia que tienen estas actividades y presenta soluciones.

I CAN discuss outdoor exercise spaces in Spanish-speaking countries and in my community.

Communicative Goal
Identify the ways people deal with stress in Madrid

  Video

¿Estrés? ¿Qué estrés?

1 **Preparación** ¿Sufres de estrés? ¿Qué situaciones te producen estrés? ¿Qué haces para combatirlo?

2 **El video** Mira el episodio de **Flash cultura** sobre la manera como las personas combaten el estrés in Madrid.

Vocabulario	
árabe *Moorish, Arab*	**combatir el estrés** *to fight against stress*
el bullicio *hustle and bustle*	**el ruido** *noise*

... es un lugar donde la gente viene a "retirarse", a escapar del estrés y el bullicio de la ciudad.

3 **¿Cierto o falso?** Indica si las oraciones son **ciertas** o **falsas**. Corrige la información falsa.

1. Madrid es la segunda ciudad más grande de España, después de Barcelona.

2. Madrid es una ciudad muy poco congestionada (*congested*) gracias a los policías de tráfico.

3. Un turista estadounidense intenta saltearse la cola (*cut the line*) para conseguir unos boletos para un espectáculo.

4. En el Parque del Retiro, puedes descansar, hacer gimnasia, etc.

5. Los baños termales Medina Mayrit son de influencia cristiana.

6. En Medina Mayrit es posible bañarse en aguas termales, tomar el té y hasta comer.

4 **Comparación** Compara las maneras como las personas combaten el estrés en Madrid y en tu comunidad.

I CAN identify the ways people deal with stress in Madrid.

Communicative Goal
Describe situations

15.1 Past participles used as adjectives

Forming past participles

▸ The past participles of English verbs often end in **–ed** (*to turn* ➔ *turned*), but many are irregular (*to buy* ➔ *bought; to drive* ➔ *driven*).

▸ In Spanish, regular **–ar** verbs form the past participle with **–ado**. Regular **–er** and **–ir** verbs form the past participle with **–ido**.

INFINITIVE	STEM	PAST PARTICIPLE
bailar	bail-	bailado
comer	com-	comido
vivir	viv-	vivido

▸ You already know several past participles used as adjectives: **aburrido, cansado, enamorado, nublado, perdido,** etc.

Sólo tomo café descafeinado.

Estoy cansada.

▸ Note that all irregular past participles, except for those of **decir (dicho)** and **hacer (hecho)**, end in **–to**.

Irregular past participles

abrir	abierto		morir	muerto
decir	dicho		poner	puesto
describir	descrito		resolver	resuelto
descubrir	descubierto		romper	roto
escribir	escrito		ver	visto
hacer	hecho		volver	vuelto

¡ojo! The past participles of **–er** and **–ir** verbs whose stems end in **–a**, **–e**, or **–o** carry a written accent mark on the **i** of the **–ido** ending.

caer	caído	oír	oído	sonreír	sonreído
creer	creído	reír	reído	traer	traído
leer	leído				

Práctica

1 Completar Completa estas oraciones con la forma adecuada del participio pasado.

> **modelo**
> El hombre *descrito* [describir] en ese panfleto es un entrenador personal de gimnasia.

1. Megan Rapinoe es una atleta muy _____ [conocer].

2. ¿Está _____ [hacer] la cena?

3. Los libros _____ [usar] son más baratos que los nuevos.

4. Los documentos están _____ [firmar].

5. Creo que el gimnasio está _____ [abrir] veinticuatro horas al día.

2 Describir Completa las oraciones con las palabras de la lista. Haz los cambios necesarios.

estar cerrado	estar aburrido
estar muerto	estar descrito
estar roto	estar firmado
estar abierto	no estar hecho

> **modelo**

Los estudiantes *están aburridos*.

1. Los cheques _____.

2. La ventana _____.

3. La cama _____.

4. La puerta _____.

5. El señor Vargas _____.

Conversación

3 **Preguntas** Túrnate con un(a) compañero/a para responder estas preguntas.

1. ¿Qué haces cuando no estás preparado/a para una clase?

2. ¿Qué haces cuando estás perdido/a en una ciudad?

3. ¿Está ordenado tu cuarto?

4. ¿Dejas la luz prendida en tu cuarto?

5. ¿Prefieres comprar libros usados o nuevos? ¿Por qué?

6. ¿Tienes mucho dinero ahorrado?

7. ¿Necesitas pedirles dinero prestado a tus padres?

8. ¿Quiénes están aburridos en la clase?

4 **Encuesta** Averigua quién de tus compañeros/as se identifica con estas descripciones. Anota sus respuestas y comparte los resultados con la clase.

Descripciones	Nombres	Respuesta
1. Tiene un electrodoméstico roto en casa. (¿Qué es?)	_____	_____
2. Lleva algo hecho en Europa o en un país hispano. (¿Qué es?)	_____	_____
3. Deja la puerta de su cuarto abierta por la noche. (¿Por qué?)	_____	_____
4. Toma café descafeinado. (¿Cuándo?)	_____	_____
5. Está interesado/a en trabajar en un banco. (¿Por qué?)	_____	_____
6. Le gusta comprar ropa usada. (¿Dónde y por qué?)	_____	_____
7. Tiene un pariente o un(a) amigo/a muy conocido/a. (¿Quién?)	_____	_____
8. Es teleadicto/a. (¿Cuáles son sus programas favoritos?)	_____	_____

I CAN describe situations.

Past participles used as adjectives

La ventana está rota.   **La puerta está abierta.**

▶ In Spanish, as in English, past participles can be used as adjectives. They are often used with the verb **estar** to describe a condition or state that results from an action. Like other Spanish adjectives, past participles must agree in gender and number with the nouns they modify.

El gimnasio **está cerrado**.
The gym is closed.

El cheque ya **está firmado**.
The check is already signed.

En la entrada, hay algunos letreros **escritos** en español.
At the entrance, there are some signs written in Spanish.

Tenemos la mesa **puesta** y la cena **hecha**.
We have the table set and dinner made.

> ### Revista Capital
> Consejos financieros escritos
> por gente que sabe.
>
> Incluso si su negocio va mal, su compañía no está acabada. ¡Tenemos la solución y montones de ideas listas para poner en práctica!

¡Manos a la obra!

Indica la forma correcta del participio pasado de estos verbos.

1. hablar	*hablado*	11. ver	_____
2. beber	_____	12. hacer	_____
3. decidir	_____	13. morir	_____
4. romper	_____	14. reír	_____
5. escribir	_____	15. mirar	_____
6. cantar	_____	16. abrir	_____
7. oír	_____	17. decir	_____
8. traer	_____	18. volver	_____
9. correr	_____	19. poner	_____
10. leer	_____	20. descubrir	_____

Communicative Goal
Describe recent actions and events

15.2 The present perfect

▸ The present perfect indicative tense (**el pretérito perfecto de indicativo**) is used to talk about what someone *has done*. It is formed with the present tense of **haber** and a past participle.

Nunca he sido flexible.

Lo has hecho muy bien.

Present indicative of *haber*

Singular forms		Plural forms	
yo	he	nosotros/as	hemos
tú	has	vosotros/as	habéis
Ud./él/ella	ha	Uds./ellos/ellas	han

Tú no **has cerrado** la puerta.
You haven't closed the door.

¿**Ha asistido** Juan a la clase?
Has Juan attended class?

Yo ya **he leído** esos libros.
I've already read those books.

Hemos presentado el proyecto.
We have presented the project.

▸ The past participle agrees with the noun when it functions as an adjective, but not when it is part of the present perfect tense.

Clara **ha abierto** las ventanas.
Clara has opened the windows.

Las ventanas están **abiertas**.
The windows are open.

Yo **he cerrado** la puerta.
I've closed the door.

La puerta está **cerrada**.
The door is closed.

▸ The present perfect is generally used just as in English: to talk about what *has occurred*. It usually refers to the recent past.

He trabajado cuarenta horas.
I have worked forty hours.

¿Cuál es el último libro que **has leído**?
What is the last book that you have read?

¡ojo! To say that someone has *just done something*, **acabar de** + [*infinitive*] is used.

Juan **acaba de llegar**.
Juan has just arrived.

Ellos **acaban de salir**.
They have just left.

Acabo de terminar mi tarea.
I have just finished my homework.

Acabamos de cenar.
We have just eaten dinner.

Práctica

1 Completar Completa estas oraciones sobre el estado de salud y bienestar de algunos estudiantes con el pretérito perfecto de indicativo de estos verbos.

adelgazar	llevar
aumentar	seguir
hacer	sufrir

modelo Luisa ___ha sufrido___ muchas presiones.

1. Juan y Raúl _____ de peso porque no hacen ejercicio.
2. Pero María _____ porque trabaja demasiado y siempre se olvida de comer.
3. Hasta ahora, yo _____ una vida muy sana.
4. Pero tú y yo no _____ gimnasia este semestre.
5. Tú tampoco _____ una dieta equilibrada recientemente.

2 Estilos de vida Indica si has hecho estas actividades. Sigue el modelo.

modelo

Encontrar un buen gimnasio
He encontrado un buen gimnasio. / Yo no he encontrado un buen gimnasio.

1. Tratar de estar en forma
2. Estar a dieta los últimos dos meses
3. Dejar de tomar refrescos
4. Hacerse una prueba de colesterol
5. Entrenarse cinco días a la semana
6. Cambiar de una vida sedentaria a una vida activa
7. Tomar vitaminas por las noches y por las mañanas
8. Practicar yoga para relajarse
9. Consumir mucha proteína
10. Quedarse despierto/a toda una noche
11. Levantar pesas tres días a la semana
12. Aliviar el estrés

Conversación

3 ¿Qué han hecho? Con un(a) compañero/a, describe lo que han hecho y lo que no han hecho estas personas. Usen la imaginación.

1. Jorge y Raúl

2. Natalia y Diego

3. Luisa

4. Ricardo

5. Jorge

6. Carmen

4 Describir Con un(a) compañero/a, piensa en una persona que conozcas bien o en una celebridad que lleva una vida muy sana. Luego, describe en un párrafo lo que la persona ha hecho para llevar una vida sana.

modelo

Coco Gauff ha llevado una vida muy sana. Ha hecho todo lo posible para mantenerse en forma. Para ganar las competencias de tenis, ella ha…

5 Cosas en común Con un(a) compañero/a, encuentra una película, un libro y un lugar que han visto, leído y visitado los/las dos. Luego, coméntenlo al resto de la clase.

modelo

Estudiante 1: *¿Has visto la película Relatos salvajes?*
Estudiante 2: *¿Relatos salvajes?*
Estudiante 1: *Sí, la película de Damián Szifron. Los actores principales son Ricardo Darín y Óscar Martínez.*
Estudiante 2: *Ah. Sí, la he visto. Me gustó mucho.*

I CAN describe recent actions and events.

Using the present perfect

▸ **Haber** and the past participle cannot be separated by any word.

Siempre **hemos vivido** en Bolivia.
We have always lived in Bolivia.

Usted nunca **ha venido** a mi oficina.
You have never come to my office.

¿Has ido a clase de yoga alguna vez?

¡Nunca he sudado tanto en mi vida!

▸ The word **no** and any object or reflexive pronouns are placed immediately before **haber**.

Yo **no he cobrado** el cheque.
I have not cashed the check.

¿Por qué **no lo has cobrado**?
Why haven't you cashed it?

Susana ya **lo ha hecho**.
Susana has already done it.

Ellos **no lo han arreglado**.
They haven't fixed it.

▸ In English, *to have* can be either a main verb or an auxiliary verb. As a main verb, it corresponds to **tener**; as an auxiliary, it corresponds to **haber**.

Tengo muchos amigos.
I have a lot of friends.

No **he** visto el programa.
I have not seen the program.

Tengo un problema.
I have a problem.

He resuelto mi problema.
I have resolved my problem.

▸ The present perfect of **hay** is **ha habido**.

Ha habido muchos problemas con el nuevo profesor.
There have been a lot of problems with the new professor.

Ha habido un accidente en la calle Central.
There has been an accident on Central Street.

¡Manos a la obra!

Indica el pretérito perfecto de indicativo de los verbos.

1. yo <u>he disfrutado, he comido, he vivido</u> [disfrutar, comer, vivir]
2. tú _____ [traer, adelgazar, compartir]
3. usted _____ [venir, estar, correr]
4. ella _____ [leer, resolver, poner]
5. ellos _____ [decir, romper, hacer]
6. nosotros _____ [mantenerse, dormirse]
7. yo _____ [estar, escribir, ver]
8. él _____ [vivir, correr, morir]

15.3 The past perfect

▶ The past perfect indicative (**el pretérito pluscuamperfecto de indicativo**) is used to talk about what someone *had done* or what *had occurred* before another past action, event, or state. The past perfect uses the imperfect of **haber** plus the past participle.

Las chicas habían invitado a los chicos a ir a la clase de yoga.

Cuando llegaron, ni siquiera nos habíamos vestido, y ahora los tenemos que esperar.

Past perfect indicative

	cerrar	perder	asistir
yo	había cerrado	había perdido	había asistido
tú	habías cerrado	habías perdido	habías asistido
Ud./él/ella	había cerrado	había perdido	había asistido
nosotros/as	habíamos cerrado	habíamos perdido	habíamos asistido
vosotros/as	habíais cerrado	habíais perdido	habíais asistido
Uds./ellos/ellas	habían cerrado	habían perdido	habían asistido

Pensé que ya se **habían ido.**
I thought you had already left.

Cuando llegamos, Luis ya **había salido.**
When we arrived, Luis had already left.

▶ The past perfect is often used with the word **ya** (*already*). Note that **ya** cannot be placed between **haber** and the past participle.

Ella **ya había empezado** cuando llamaron.

She had already begun when they called.

Cuando llegué a casa, Raúl **ya se había acostado.**

When I arrived home, Raúl had already gone to bed.

¡Manos a la obra!

Indica el pretérito pluscuamperfecto de indicativo de cada verbo.

1. Nosotros ya __habíamos cenado__ [cenar] cuando nos llamaron.
2. Antes de tomar esta clase, yo no _____ [estudiar] nunca español.
3. Antes de ir a México, ellos nunca _____ [ir] a otro país.
4. Eduardo nunca _____ [entrenarse] antes de este año.
5. Pensé que Ana y Raúl ya _____ [casarse].
6. Yo ya te _____ [ver] muchas veces antes de conocerte.

Práctica

1 Completar Completa los minidiálogos con las formas correctas del pretérito pluscuamperfecto de indicativo.

SARA Antes de cumplir los 15 años, ¿(1)_____ [estudiar] tú otra lengua?

JOSÉ Sí, (2) _____ [tomar] clases de inglés y de italiano.
• • •

DIANA Antes del 2017, ¿(3)_____ [viajar] tú y tu familia a Europa?

TOMÁS Sí, (4) _____ [visitar] Europa tres veces.
• • •

ANTONIO Antes de este año, ¿(5)_____ [correr] usted en un maratón?

SRA. VERA No, nunca lo (6) _____ [hacer].
• • •

SOFÍA Antes de su enfermedad, ¿(7)_____ [sufrir] muchas presiones tu tío?

IRENE Sí... y mi tío nunca antes (8)_____ [mantenerse] en forma.

2 Quehaceres Indica lo que ya había hecho cada miembro de la familia antes de la llegada de la madre, la señora Ferrer.

3 Tu vida Indica si ya habías hecho las siguientes cosas cuando cumpliste los dieciséis años.

1. Hacer un viaje en avión
2. Escalar una montaña
3. Escribir un poema
4. Leer una novela
5. Enamorarte
6. Tomar una clase de ejercicios aeróbicos
7. Montar a caballo
8. Ir de pesca
9. Manejar un carro
10. Acampar

Conversación

4 Oraciones Túrnate con un(a) compañero/a para completar estas oraciones, usando el pretérito pluscuamperfecto de indicativo.

1. Cuando yo llamé a mi mejor amigo/a la semana pasada, él/ella ya…
2. Antes de este año, mis amigos/as y yo nunca…
3. Hasta el año pasado, yo siempre…
4. Antes de cumplir los veinte años, mi mejor amigo/a…
5. Antes de cumplir los treinta años, mis padres ya…
6. Hasta que cumplí los dieciocho años, yo nunca…
7. Antes de este semestre, el/la profesor(a) de español nunca…
8. Antes de tomar esta clase, yo nunca…

5 Lo dudo Escribe cinco oraciones, algunas ciertas y otras falsas, sobre cosas que habías hecho antes de venir a la universidad. Luego, en grupos, túrnense para leer sus oraciones. Cada miembro del grupo debe decir "es cierto" o "lo dudo" después de cada oración. Cada uno escribe la reacción de cada compañero/a para ver quién obtiene más respuestas ciertas.

modelo

Estudiante 1: *Cuando tenía diez años, ya había manejado el carro de mi papá.*

Estudiante 2: *Lo dudo.*

Estudiante 3: *Es cierto.*

6 Entrevista Con un(a) compañero/a, dramatiza una conversación en la que un(a) periodista de televisión está entrevistando (*interviewing*) a un(a) actor/actriz famoso/a que está haciendo un video de ejercicios aeróbicos. El/La periodista le hace preguntas para descubrir esta información:

- Si siempre se había mantenido en forma antes de hacer este video
- Si había seguido alguna dieta especial antes de hacer este video
- Qué le recomienda a la gente que quiere mantenerse en forma
- Qué le recomienda a la gente que quiere adelgazar
- Qué va a hacer cuando termine este video

Communicative Goal
Recognize the past perfect in an ad

Español en vivo

¡Acabo de descubrir UNA NUEVA VIDA!

Hasta el año pasado, siempre había mirado la tele sentado en el sofá durante mis ratos libres. ¡Era un sedentario y un teleadicto! Había aumentado mucho de peso porque jamás había practicado ningún deporte.

Este año, he empezado a tener una dieta más sana y voy al gimnasio todos los días. He comenzado a ser una persona muy activa y he adelgazado. Disfruto de una vida sana y… ¡me siento muy feliz!

MANTÉNGASE EN FORMA

GIMNASIO OLÍMPICO

1 Identificar Identifica los ejemplos del pretérito pluscuamperfecto del indicativo en el anuncio.

2 Preguntas Contesta las preguntas.

1. ¿Cómo era la vida de este joven hasta el año pasado? ¿Cómo es ahora?
2. ¿Te identificas con algunos de los hábitos, presentes o pasados, de este joven? ¿Con cuáles?
3. ¿Qué les recomienda el joven del anuncio a los lectores (*readers*)?

I CAN describe events that occurred before other past events.

I CAN recognize the past perfect in an ad.

A repasar

15.1 Past participles used as adjectives

1 ¡Ya está hecho! Tus padres te piden ayuda con los quehaceres de la casa. Como eres un(a) hijo/a muy responsable, ya hiciste todo. Responde a sus preguntas.

> **modelo** ¿Puedes planchar la ropa?
> La ropa ya está planchada.

1. ¿Puedes arreglar la computadora?
2. ¿Puedes estacionar el carro en el garaje?
3. ¿Puedes apagar la luz del pasillo?
4. ¿Puedes preparar el almuerzo?
5. ¿Puedes sacudir los estantes?
6. ¿Puedes poner los platos en la mesa?

2 ¡Qué miedo! En parejas, imaginen que son compañeros/as de apartamento. Ayer, mientras ustedes estaban en clase, alguien rompió una ventana y entró a su apartamento. Describan a la policía lo que vieron cuando llegaron. Usen el participio pasado.

> **modelo** Cuando llegamos al apartamento, nuestra
> puerta estaba cerrada, pero la ventana
> estaba rota...

15.2 The present perfect

3 ¡En forma! Son las 8:45 de la mañana. Describe las actividades que Carla ha hecho en el gimnasio y las que no ha hecho todavía.

Hora	Actividades
6:30 a.m.	hacer ejercicios de estiramiento
7:00 a.m.	tomar clase de ejercicios aeróbicos
8:00 a.m.	levantar pesas
8:30 a.m.	recibir un masaje
9:00 a.m.	ducharse
9:30 a.m.	desayunar en la cafetería
10:00 a.m.	irse a su oficina

> **modelo** Carla ya ha hecho ejercicios de estiramiento.

4 ¡A dieta! Emilio ha seguido una dieta especial durante tres meses. Lee su dieta y contesta las preguntas.

Desayuno	Almuerzo	Cena
una taza de café	ensalada de atún con verduras	pollo o pescado asado
cereal con leche	un pan	ensalada de tomate y
una manzana	una naranja	queso
	té helado sin azúcar	una copa de vino tinto

1. ¿Qué alimentos con proteínas ha consumido Emilio?
2. ¿Qué frutas ha comido?
3. ¿Te gustan los alimentos que ha comido Emilio?
4. ¿Crees que Emilio ha seguido una dieta equilibrada? ¿Por qué?
5. ¿Crees que Emilio ha engordado o adelgazado con esta dieta?
6. ¿Piensas que esta dieta ha mejorado la salud de Emilio? ¿Por qué?

5 ¿Alguna vez...? Túrnate con un(a) compañero/a para hacer y responder estas preguntas. Usen el pretérito perfecto de indicativo en sus respuestas.

> **modelo** tomar una clase de yoga (tú)
> **Estudiante 1:** ¿Alguna vez has tomado una clase
> de yoga?
> **Estudiante 2:** No, nunca he tomado una clase de yoga,
> pero he hecho ejercicios para aliviar
> el estrés.

1. levantar pesas (tu hermano/a)
2. tener problemas con el colesterol (tus papás)
3. entrenarse para un maratón (tu amigo/a)
4. llevar una vida sedentaria (tu hermano/a)
5. consumir alcohol en exceso (alguien que conoces)
6. seguir una dieta baja en grasas (tus amigos/as y tú)
7. ver televisión más de cinco horas en un día (tú)

15.3 The past perfect

6 Oraciones Forma oraciones con estos elementos. Usa el pretérito pluscuamperfecto de indicativo y haz los cambios necesarios.

> **modelo** Mi abuela / nunca / tener / problemas / de colesterol
> Mi abuela nunca había tenido problemas de colesterol.

1. Nosotros / jamás / cuidar / nuestro / nutrición
2. Todos (nosotros) / llevar / vida / sedentario
3. En agosto / mis hermanos y yo / resolver / estar a dieta
4. Yo / no / ver / mis hermanos / en dos meses
5. En octubre / ellos / adelgazar / diez libras

Video

7 **¡Ya lo había hecho!** Imagina que tú y tu compañero/a tienen setenta años de edad. Un(a) estudiante dice algo que ya había hecho a los diez años de edad. El/La otro/a responde con algo que ya había hecho a los quince años. Terminen a los setenta años. ¡Usen su imaginación!

modelo

Estudiante 1: A los diez años de edad, ya había aprendido a hablar tres idiomas.
Estudiante 2: Antes de cumplir quince años, yo ya había conocido Nueva York.
Estudiante 1: Pues a los veinte años, yo…

8 **Anuncio de radio** Con un(a) compañero/a, prepara un anuncio de radio para vender las vitaminas Energía 2000. Describan qué productos habían tomado ustedes antes de probar estas vitaminas y cómo se habían sentido. Usen el pretérito pluscuamperfecto de indicativo y **antes de, cuando** y **nunca**. Presenten el anuncio a la clase.

modelo ¡Nunca nos habíamos sentido mejor!

Síntesis

9 **El maratón** Con un(a) compañero/a, dramatiza una conversación entre dos deportistas que se están entrenando para su cuarto maratón en Nueva York. Compara los entrenamientos que han tenido y los planes de nutrición que han seguido. Incluye esta información.

• ¿Cuántas horas a la semana se han entrenado? ¿Qué ejercicios han hecho?
• ¿Cómo ha sido su dieta? ¿Qué alimentos o bebidas no han consumido?
• ¿Cómo había sido su entrenamiento en años anteriores (previous)? ¿Qué cosas habían hecho diferente en otros años?
• ¿Se sienten preparados/as para ganar el maratón este año? ¿Por qué?

Communicative Goal
Talk about solutions to personal challenges

Videoclip

1 **Preparación** ¿Es fácil o difícil para ti comunicar tus emociones y sentimientos (feelings)? ¿Los prefieres comunicar oralmente o por escrito?

2 **El clip** Mira el anuncio de **Azucarlito** de Uruguay.

Vocabulario	
abrazo *hug*	gesto *gesture*
dulzura *sweetness*	mensajero *messenger*

Mañana a primera hora° se lo digo… ¿A quién?

mañana a primera hora *first thing tomorrow morning*

3 **Seleccionar** Selecciona la opción correcta para cada oración.

1. En el pueblo las personas necesitaban un mensajero de sentimientos porque (eran tímidos / estaban ocupados).
2. Pedro dejó de ser mensajero porque (se enfermó / se enamoró).
3. Los mejores regalos (no se compran / son los que dan los padres).
4. La dulzura (puede cambiar el mundo / ni se compra ni se vende).

4 **Soluciones** Con un(a) compañero/a, conversa sobre soluciones que han aplicado en sus vidas ante estos retos (challenges): aliviar el estrés durante los exámenes, resolver un conflicto con un amigo, correr más rápidamente en competencias, dormir mejor en período de clases. Luego, compartan sus ideas con la clase.

modelo Para aliviar el estrés durante los exámenes, yo he tomado clases de yoga.

I CAN talk about solutions to personal challenges.

Ampliación

Communicative Goals
Use cognates to understand a radio show, and talk about recent health problems

❶ Escuchar

A Escucha lo que dice Ofelia Cortez de Bauer. Anota algunos de los cognados que escuchas y también la idea general del discurso.

> **TIP** **Listen for the gist and cognates.** By listening for the gist, you can get the general idea of what you're hearing. Listening for cognates will help you to fill in the details.

Cognados

_____
_____
_____

Idea general

_____
_____
_____

Ahora indica si estas oraciones son **ciertas** o **falsas**.

Cierto **Falso**

____ ____ 1. La señora Bauer habla de la importancia de estar en buena forma.

____ ____ 2. Según la señora Bauer, es importante que todos sigan el mismo programa.

____ ____ 3. La señora Bauer participa en actividades individuales y de grupo.

____ ____ 4. Según la señora Bauer, el objetivo más importante de cada persona debe ser adelgazar.

B ¿Qué piensas de los consejos que ella da? ¿Hay otra información que ella debía haber incluido (_included_)?

❷ Conversar

Con un(a) compañero/a, dramatiza una conversación entre el/la enfermero/a de la clínica de la universidad y un(a) estudiante que no se siente bien. Usa estas preguntas guía.

> • _¿Qué problema tiene y de dónde viene?_
>
> • _¿Tiene buenos hábitos el/la estudiante?_
>
> • _¿Qué ha hecho el/la estudiante en los últimos meses? ¿Cómo se ha sentido?_
>
> • _¿Qué recomendaciones tiene el/la enfermero/a para el/la estudiante?_
>
> • _¿Qué va a hacer el/la estudiante para llevar una vida más sana?_

I CAN understand a radio show by using cognates.

I CAN talk about recent health problems.

Ampliación

3 Escribir

Desarrolla un plan personal para mejorar tu bienestar físico y emocional. Considera la nutrición, el ejercicio y el descanso.

> **TIP** **Organize your information logically.** To make your writing and message clearer to your readers, organize information chronologically, sequentially, or in order of importance.

Organizar	Escribe tus objetivos. Anota lo que has hecho hasta ahora, lo que no has hecho y lo que todavía tienes que hacer para conseguir tus objetivos.
Escribir	Organiza tus apuntes y escribe el primer borrador de tu plan personal.
Corregir	Intercambia tu plan personal con un(a) compañero/a. Dale sugerencias para mejorar la organización. ¿Incluye toda la información pertinente? ¿Es lógica la organización? Si ves algunos errores, coméntaselos.
Compartir	Prepara la versión final, tomando en cuenta los comentarios de tu compañero/a. Luego, con otro/a compañero/a, compara lo que han escrito. ¿Son similares sus planes? ¿Son diferentes?

Communicative Goals
Develop a personal wellness plan, and create an adventure travel brochure

4 Un paso más

Imagina que estás a cargo de (*in charge of*) promocionar una excursión de aventuras con actividades deportivas en algún país hispano. Crea un atractivo folleto (*brochure*) para vender la idea de la excursión. Luego, compara tu folleto con los de tus compañeros/as.

- Escoge el país y los lugares que van a visitar.
- Describe las actividades deportivas y de aventura que van a hacer en cada lugar.
- Explica los aspectos de la excursión que son importantes para la salud.
- Incluye el costo del viaje.

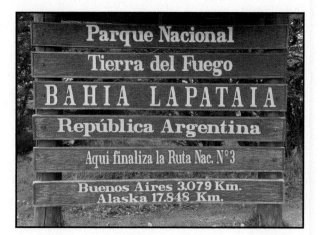

5 Cultura

Estás en Madrid, Lima o Buenos Aires. ¿Vas a utilizar uno de los espacios públicos para la práctica de la actividad física? Explica tu respuesta.

I CAN develop a personal wellness plan.

I CAN create an adventure travel brochure.

Audio: Reading

Antes de leer

For dramatic effect and to achieve a smoother writing style, authors often do not explicitly supply the reader with all the details of a story.

> **TIP** **Make inferences.** Clues in the text can help you infer those things the writer chooses not to state in a direct manner. You simply "read between the lines" to fill in the missing information and draw conclusions about the story.

Inferencias

To practice making inferences, read these statements.

> A Liliana le encanta ir al gimnasio. Empezó a levantar pesas en el año 2010.

Based on these statements alone, what inferences can you make about Liliana?

Sobre la autora

Cristina Peri Rossi (1941–) nació en Uruguay, pero actualmente vive en España. En sus cuentos, novelas y poemas explora las pasiones, el aislamiento (*isolation*) y las incertidumbres (*uncertainties*) que sentimos como seres humanos (*human beings*).

El viaje

Cristina Peri Rossi

Ella me ha entregado la felicidad dentro de una caja° bien cerrada, y me la ha dado, diciéndome:

—Ten cuidado, no vayas a perderla, no seas distraída, me ha costado un gran esfuerzo° conseguirla: los mercados estaban cerrados, en las tiendas ya no había y los pocos vendedores ambulantes que existían se han jubilado, porque tenían los pies cansados. Ésta es la única que pude hallar° en la plaza, pero es de las legítimas. Tiene un poco menos brillo° que aquella que consumíamos mientras éramos jóvenes y está un poco arrugada°, pero si caminas bien, no notarás° la diferencia. Si la apoyas en alguna parte°, por favor, recógela antes de irte, y si decides tomar un ómnibus, apriétala° bien entre las manos: la ciudad está llena de ladrones° y fácilmente te la podrían arrebatar°.

Después de todas estas recomendaciones soltó° la caja y me la puso entre las manos. Mientras caminaba, noté que no pesaba° mucho pero que era un poco incómoda de usar: mientras la sostenía no podía tocar otra cosa, ni me animaba a dejarla depositada, para hacer las compras. De manera que no podía entretenerme, y menos aún, detenerme a explorar, como era mi costumbre. A la mitad de la tarde tuve frío. Quería abrirla, para saber si era de las legítimas, pero ella me dijo que se podía evaporar. Cuando desprendí° el papel, noté que en la etiqueta° venía una leyenda°:

"Consérvese sin usar."

Desde ese momento tengo la felicidad guardada en una caja. Los domingos de mañana la llevo a pasear, por la plaza, para que los demás me envidien° y lamenten su situación; de noche la guardo en el fondo del ropero°. Pero se aproxima el verano y tengo un temor: ¿cómo la defenderé° de las polillas°?

me... caja *handed me happiness in a box*   esfuerzo *effort*   la única... hallar *the only one I could find*   brillo *shine*   arrugada *wrinkled*   no notarás *you won't notice*   Si... parte *If you set it down somewhere*   apriétala *hold it tight*   ladrones *thieves*   podrían arrebatar *could snatch*   soltó *she let go of*   no pesaba *it didn't weigh*   desprendí *I took off*   etiqueta *label*   leyenda *inscription*   envidien *envy*   en... ropero *in the back of the closet*   defenderé *will I defend*   polillas *moths*

Después de leer

¿Comprendiste?

Responde las preguntas de acuerdo con la lectura.

1. La persona que narra el cuento, ¿es hombre o es mujer?
2. El regalo, la felicidad, ¿fue fácil o difícil de conseguir?
3. ¿Dónde compró la persona la felicidad: en la calle o en una tienda?
4. Según la persona que la dio, ¿esta felicidad es de mejor o de peor calidad que la que tenía de joven?
5. Según ella, ¿hay mucho o poco riesgo (*risk*) de perder la felicidad?
6. ¿Por qué no puede abrir la caja la narradora?
7. Al final, ¿qué hace la narradora con la felicidad?

Preguntas

Responde estas preguntas con oraciones completas.

1. ¿Qué debe hacer la narradora para cuidar la felicidad?
2. ¿Qué límites le impone la felicidad a la narradora?
3. ¿Cómo quiere la narradora que su felicidad afecte a otras personas?
4. ¿Por qué la narradora tiene miedo de las polillas?

Coméntalo

Con un(a) compañero/a, conversa sobre estas preguntas:

- ¿Por qué a la persona le resulta (*results*) difícil conseguir la felicidad?
- ¿Por qué está encerrada en una caja?
- ¿Vale la pena (*Is it worth it*) tener la "felicidad" guardada en una caja sin usar?
- ¿Qué simboliza la felicidad en este cuento?

I CAN read a literary text and make inferences about it.

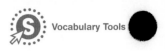 Vocabulary Tools

El bienestar

el bienestar *well-being*
el masaje *massage*

---

aliviar el estrés/la tensión *to relieve stress/tension*
disfrutar (de) *to enjoy; to reap the benefits (of)*
(no) fumar *(not) to smoke*
llevar una vida sana *to lead a healthy lifestyle*

activo/a *active*
débil *weak*
flexible *flexible*
fuerte *strong*
sedentario/a *sedentary*
tranquilo/a *calm; quiet*

En el gimnasio

la clase de ejercicios aeróbicos *aerobics class*
el músculo *muscle*
calentarse (e:ie) *to warm up*
entrenarse *to train*
estar en buena forma *to be in good shape*
hacer ejercicio *to exercise*
hacer ejercicios aeróbicos *to do aerobics*
hacer ejercicios de estiramiento *to do stretching exercises*
hacer gimnasia *to work out*
levantar pesas *to lift weights*
mantenerse en forma *to stay in shape*
sudar *to sweat*

La nutrición

la bebida alcohólica *alcoholic beverage*
la caloría *calorie*
el colesterol *cholesterol*
la grasa *fat*
la merienda *(afternoon) snack*
los minerales *minerals*
la nutrición *nutrition*
la proteína *protein*
las vitaminas *vitamins*

---

adelgazar *to lose weight; to slim down*
aumentar de peso *to gain weight*
consumir alcohol *to consume alcohol*
engordar *to gain weight*
estar a dieta *to be on a diet*
merendar (e:ie) *to have a(n) (afternoon) snack*
seguir una dieta equilibrada *to eat a balanced diet*

---

descafeinado/a *decaffeinated*

Otras palabras y expresiones

la droga *drug*
el/la drogadicto/a *drug addict*
el/la teleadicto/a *couch potato*

---

apurarse *to hurry; to rush*
darse prisa *to hurry; to rush*
sufrir muchas presiones *to be under a lot of pressure*
tratar de (+ inf.) *to try (to do something)*

en exceso *in excess; too much*
sin *without*

Irregular past participles *See page 394.*

⟡ Communicative Goals: Review

I CAN discuss well-being.

• Describe three things you do to lead a healthy lifestyle.

I CAN describe an action or event in the immediate past.

• Tell a partner five things you have done recently. Use the present perfect.

I CAN describe an event that occurred before another.

• Describe three things that you had done before the age of ten. Use the past perfect.

I CAN investigate exercise spaces.

• Describe one of the exercise spaces you learned about in this lesson.

16 El mundo del trabajo

Communicative Goals
You will learn how to:
- discuss the world of work
- participate in a job interview
- talk about future plans
- investigate job interviews in Spanish-speaking countries

PREPARACIÓN

pages 408–413
- Words related to working
- Occupations
- **y**, **ll**, and **h**

AVENTURAS

pages 414–415
- Olga Lucía has a job interview. With Valentina and Manuel's help, will she make it to the interview on time and get a job offer?

CULTURA

pages 416–417
- *La entrevista de trabajo*
- Flash cultura: *El mundo del trabajo*

GRAMÁTICA

pages 418–427
- The future tense
- The conditional tense
- The past subjunctive

LECTURA

pages 428–429
- Short story: *Imaginación y destino*

PARA EMPEZAR
- ¿Está sonriendo la joven?
- ¿Qué clase de ropa lleva?
- ¿Dónde está?
- ¿Va bien la entrevista?

Communicative Goal
Participate in a job interview

EL MUNDO DEL TRABAJO

el actor

LAS OCUPACIONES

el/la abogado/a *lawyer*

la actriz *actress*

el/la arqueólogo/a *archeologist*

el/la arquitecto/a *architect*

el bailarín *dancer*

la bailarina *dancer*

el/la cantante *singer*

el/la carpintero/a *carpenter*

el/la científico/a *scientist*

el/la consejero/a *counselor; advisor*

el/la contador(a) *accountant*

el/la corredor(a) de bolsa *stockbroker*

el/la diseñador(a) *designer*

el/la electricista *electrician*

el/la escritor(a) *writer*

el/la escultor(a) *sculptor*

el/la gerente *manager*

el hombre/la mujer de negocios
   businessperson

el/la jefe/a *boss*

el/la maestro/a *teacher*

el/la pintor(a) *painter*

el/la poeta *poet*

el/la político/a *politician*

el/la reportero/a *reporter*

el/la secretario/a *secretary*

el/la técnico/a *technician*

la peluquera

el psicólogo

el cocinero

la reunión
meeting

Vocabulary Tools

EL MUNDO DEL TRABAJO

el ascenso *promotion*
el aumento de sueldo *raise*
la carrera *career*
la compañía *company; firm*
el empleo *job; employment*
la empresa *company; firm*
la especialización *field of study*
los negocios *business; commerce*
la ocupación *occupation*
el oficio *trade*
la profesión *profession*
el teletrabajo *telecommuting*
el trabajo *job; work*
la videoconferencia *videoconference*

dejar *to quit; to leave behind*
despedir (e:i) *to fire*
invertir (e:ie) *to invest*
renunciar (a) *to resign (from)*
tener éxito *to be succesful*

comercial *commercial; business-related*

el anuncio
advertisement

la entrevista
interview

el bombero

el currículum
résumé

LAS ENTREVISTAS

el/la aspirante *candidate; applicant*
los beneficios *benefits; profit*
el/la entrevistador(a) *interviewer*
el puesto *position; job*
el salario *salary*
la solicitud (de trabajo)
    (job) application
el sueldo *salary*

contratar *to hire*
entrevistar *to interview*
ganar *to earn*
obtener *to obtain; to get*
solicitar *to apply (for a job)*

ASÍ SE DICE
el/la abogado/a ⟷ el/la licenciado/a (*Amér. C.*)
el/la contador(a) ⟷ el/la contable (*Esp.*)

A escuchar

1 **¿Lógico o ilógico?** Escucha las oraciones e indica si son **lógicas** o **ilógicas**.

	Lógico	Ilógico
1.	_____	_____
2.	_____	_____
3.	_____	_____
4.	_____	_____
5.	_____	_____
6.	_____	_____
7.	_____	_____
8.	_____	_____

2 **Escuchar** Escucha la descripción que hace Alejandro Dávila de su profesión y luego completa las oraciones con las palabras o expresiones adecuadas.

1. Alejandro Dávila es un

    a. poeta.   b. hombre de negocios.   c. escultor.

2. El señor Dávila trabaja como _____ en una compañía multinacional.

    a. secretario   b. técnico   c. gerente

3. Al señor Dávila le interesaba _____ en la cual pudiera (*he could*) trabajar en otros países.

    a. una carrera   b. un ascenso   c. un aumento de sueldo

4. En sus negocios con empresas extranjeras, el señor Dávila prefiere

    a. usar las videoconferencias.   b. conocer a la gente personalmente.

    c. mandar mensajes electrónicos.

A practicar

3 **Completar** Escoge la respuesta que completa cada oración.

1. Quiero conseguir un puesto con _____.

   a. oficios   b. beneficios   c. ocupación

2. Luisa tiene la oportunidad de _____ la empresa donde trabaja.

   a. despedir   b. entrevistar   c. invertir en

3. Mi vecino dejó su _____ porque no le gustaba su jefe.

   a. puesto   b. anuncio   c. sueldo

4. Raúl va a _____ su empleo antes de empezar su propia empresa.

   a. solicitar   b. tener éxito   c. renunciar a

5. Mi madre _____ su carrera como escultora.

   a. tuvo éxito en   b. contrató   c. entrevistó

6. ¿Cuándo obtuviste _____ más reciente?

   a. los negocios   b. la videoconferencia   c. el aumento de sueldo

7. Jorge llegó tarde a la _____ esta mañana.

   a. reunión   b. especialización   c. carrera

4 **Ocupaciones** Escoge la ocupación que corresponde a cada definición.

1. Arregla las computadoras.

2. Enseña a los niños.

3. Diseña ropa.

4. Canta para el público.

5. Nos ayuda a iluminar nuestras casas.

6. Desarrolla teorías de biología, química, física, etc.

7. Construye (*Builds*) sillas, mesas, casas y otras cosas de madera (*wood*).

8. Ayuda a la gente a invertir su dinero.

9. Trabaja con números y arregla las cuentas de diferentes negocios.

10. Combate los incendios (*fires*) que destruyen edificios y bosques.

el bombero	**el corredor de bolsa**
la cantante	**el diseñador**
la carpintera	**la electricista**
el científico	**el maestro**
la contadora	**la técnica**

5 **Asociaciones** Escribe las profesiones que asocias con estas palabras.

1. pelo _____
2. novelas _____
3. emociones _____
4. teatro _____
5. periódico _____
6. pinturas _____
7. elecciones _____
8. baile _____
9. leyes _____
10. luz artificial _____

A conversar

6 **Conversación** Contesta las preguntas con un(a) compañero/a.

1. ¿Te gusta tu especialización?

2. ¿Lees los anuncios de empleos con regularidad?

3. ¿Obtienes siempre los puestos que quieres?

4. ¿Qué características tiene un(a) buen(a) jefe/a?

5. ¿Te gustaría más un teletrabajo o un trabajo en una oficina? ¿Por qué?

6. ¿Quieres tener tu propia empresa?

7. ¿Cuál es tu carrera ideal? ¿Por qué?

8. ¿Cómo son tus compañeros de trabajo ideales?

7 **Entrevista** Trabaja con un(a) compañero/a para representar los papeles de un(a) aspirante a un puesto de trabajo y el de un(a) entrevistador(a).

El/La entrevistador(a) debe describir…
- el empleo
- las responsabilidades
- el salario
- los beneficios

El/La aspirante debe…
- presentar su experiencia
- obtener más información sobre el puesto

Entonces…
- el/la entrevistador(a) debe decidir si va a contratar al/a la aspirante
- el/la aspirante debe decidir si va a aceptar el puesto

8 **Una feria de trabajo** La clase va a organizar una feria (*fair*) de trabajo. Unos estudiantes son representantes de compañías y otros están buscando empleo.

Representantes	**Aspirantes**
• Preparan carteles con el nombre de su compañía. • Escriben los puestos de trabajo que ofrecen. • Contestan las preguntas de los aspirantes y describen los puestos disponibles. • Consiguen los nombres y referencias de los aspirantes.	• Circulan por la feria de trabajo. • Hablan con tres representantes y formulan preguntas sobre los puestos que tienen. • Muestran sus referencias y sus currículums. • Escogen el puesto que les gustó más.

I CAN participate in a job interview.

Ortografía

 Tutorial

y, ll y h

The digraph **ll** and the letter **y** were not pronounced alike in Old Spanish. Nowadays, however, **ll** and **y** have the same or similar pronunciations in many parts of the Spanish-speaking world. This similarity results in frequent misspellings. The letter **h**, as you already know, is silent in Spanish, and it is often difficult to know whether words should be written with or without it. Here are some of the word groups that are spelled with each letter.

| ta**lla** | se**llo** | bote**lla** | amari**llo** |

The digraph **ll** is used in these endings: **–allo/a**, **–ello/a**, **–illo/a**.

| **lla**ve | **lle**ga | **llo**rar | **llu**via |

The digraph **ll** is used at the beginning of words in these combinations: **lla-**, **lle-**, **llo-**, **llu-**.

| ca**y**endo | le**y**eron | o**y**e | inclu**y**e |

The letter **y** is used in some forms of the verbs **caer**, **leer**, and **oír**, and in verbs ending in **–uir**.

| **hiper**activo | **hosp**ital | **hipo**pótamo | **hum**or |

The letter **h** is used at the beginning of words in these combinations: **hiper-**, **hosp-**, **hidr-**, **hipo-**, **hum-**.

| **hia**to | **hie**rba | **hue**so | **hui**r |

The letter **h** is also used in words that begin with these combinations: **hia-**, **hie-**, **hue-**, **hui-**.

Práctica Llena los espacios con **h**, **ll** o **y**. Después escribe una frase con cada una de las palabras.

1. cuchi___o
2. ___ielo
3. cue___o
4. estampi___a
5. estre___a
6. ___uésped
7. destru___ó
8. pla___a

Adivinanza Aquí tienes una adivinanza (*riddle*). Intenta descubrir de qué se trata.

> Una cajita chiquita, blanca como la nieve: todos la saben abrir, nadie la sabe cerrar.[1]

> Pista: Es una comida.

[1] El huevo

Communicative Goal
Talk about job interviews
and the future

Una aspirante despistada

Olga Lucía se prepara para una entrevista de trabajo, con la ayuda de Valentina y Manuel.

Video

Antes de ver

Haz predicciones sobre lo que vas a ver y oír en un episodio en el cual un personaje tiene una entrevista de trabajo.

PERSONAJES

VALENTINA

OLGA LUCÍA

MANUEL

PORTERO

RECEPCIONISTA

EJECUTIVA

OLGA LUCÍA Gracias por darme la oportunidad de esta entrevista.

VALENTINA Dígame, ¿por qué le interesa trabajar en esta empresa?

OLGA LUCÍA En poco tiempo terminaré mi segundo año de universidad y me gustaría hacer...

VALENTINA ¿Cómo piensa que podrá aplicar sus conocimientos en el puesto de asistente del departamento creativo?

MANUEL A ver. Por última vez. ¿Por qué estás interesada en este puesto?

OLGA LUCÍA Porque quiero especializarme en fotografía publicitaria y trabajar en una agencia me ayudará a obtener experiencia en el campo.

MANUEL ¡Bien!

OLGA LUCÍA ¿Podrías ir rápido? No quiero llegar tarde.

OLGA LUCÍA Buenos días. Vengo a la agencia de publicidad Martín y Llobet. ¿Me puede decir dónde es?

PORTERO Martín y Llobet... oficina tres cero seis, señorita.

OLGA LUCÍA ¡Gracias!

PORTERO De nada.

1 Ordenar Indica el orden de los eventos.

a. La entrevistadora felicita a Olga Lucía por su portafolio.

b. Manuel lleva en carro a Olga Lucía a la entrevista.

c. Olga Lucía le da su currículum a la recepcionista.

d. Valentina entrevista a Olga Lucía.

e. Olga Lucía dice que puede estudiar y trabajar al mismo tiempo.

2 Completar Completa las oraciones.

1. Olga Lucía está nerviosa porque hoy tiene _____.

2. Olga Lucía le da su currículum a la recepcionista de _____.

3. Olga Lucía presenta _____ con sus trabajos de fotografía.

4. En el futuro, Olga Lucía quiere ser _____.

5. Olga Lucía va a saber el resultado de la entrevista _____.

OLGA LUCÍA Buenos días. ¡Vengo para la entrevista!

RECEPCIONISTA Perfecto, tome asiento que usted es la próxima.

OLGA LUCÍA Aquí está mi currículum y me pidieron que trajera mi portafolio con mis trabajos de fotografía...

RECEPCIONISTA ¿Fotografías? El puesto es para un asistente legal. ¡Esto es un despacho de abogados!

OLGA LUCÍA ¡Ay...! ¡Perdón!

OLGA LUCÍA Señor. ¡Me dijo que Martín y Llobet estaba en la trece cero seis, pero ésa es una oficina de abogados!

PORTERO Señorita, le dije oficina tres cero seis.

OLGA LUCÍA ¡Ay! ¡Qué despiste! ¡Tres cero seis!

OLGA LUCÍA Desde niña me interesé por la fotografía, aunque mis padres querían que estudiara una carrera científica. Sin duda, en el futuro me veo como fotógrafa publicitaria.

EJECUTIVA Ya veo. ¿Y crees que podrás organizarte bien para trabajar y estudiar al mismo tiempo?

OLGA LUCÍA Claro, el horario de media jornada me permitirá seguir con mis estudios de forma exitosa.

EJECUTIVA La semana que viene tomaremos la decisión final.

Expresiones útiles

la agencia de publicidad *ad agency*
contar (o:ue) *to tell*
de media jornada *part-time*
el despacho *office*
el despiste *mistake*
especializarse *to specialize*
felicitar *to congratulate*
el/la fotógrafo/a *photographer*
mismo/a *same*
la oportunidad *opportunity*
la torre *tower*

---

el/la ejecutivo/a *executive*
interrumpir *to interrupt*
el/la portero/a *concierge*

Cuatro Torres

El Área de Negocios de Cuatro Torres en Madrid es un gran parque empresarial (*business park*) formado por cuatro rascacielos (*skyscrapers*). La Torre de Cristal, el rascacielos más alto de España, tiene cincuenta y dos pisos. En estas torres, no sólo hay muchísimas oficinas, sino también un hotel y un jardín en una de sus azoteas.

¿Hay algún parque empresarial en tu comunidad? ¿Te gustaría trabajar allí?

3 **Entrevista** En parejas, háganse estas preguntas. ¿Tienen respuestas en común?

1. ¿Cómo te preparas para una entrevista?
2. ¿Puedes organizarte bien para trabajar y estudiar al mismo tiempo? Explica tu respuesta.
3. ¿Tienes las cualidades de puntualidad, responsabilidad y atención a los detalles? Explica tu respuesta.
4. ¿Qué piensas hacer después de graduarte?
5. ¿Dónde vas a trabajar en diez años?
6. ¿Cómo te ves en veinte años?

I CAN talk about job interviews and the future.

Communicative Goal
Identify practices related to interviewing for a job
in Spanish-speaking countries

La entrevista de trabajo

En casi todos los países del mundo hay recomendaciones generales para la presentación de una entrevista de trabajo, como llegar a tiempo, ir bien vestido/a, mirar al/a la entrevistador(a) a los ojos o dar respuestas claras y concisas, pero hay algunas diferencias culturales que se deben tener en cuenta al presentar una entrevista de trabajo en otro país. Uno de los errores que cometen muchos aspirantes extranjeros a la hora de realizar una entrevista de trabajo en un país nuevo es que no toman en cuenta las diferencias culturales del país.

Una entrevista de trabajo no se realiza de igual manera en México, España o los Estados Unidos. El dominio° del idioma del país no es la única cosa de la que debes preocuparte.

El *currículum vitae*

- El *currículum vitae* contiene información personal y es fundamental que sea muy detallado. En general, mientras más páginas tenga, mejor.
- Normalmente, incluye la educación completa del aspirante, todos los trabajos que ha tenido e, incluso, sus gustos personales y pasatiempos.
- Puede también incluir detalles que no se suele incluir en los Estados Unidos: una foto del aspirante, su estado civil e, incluso, si tiene auto y de qué tipo.

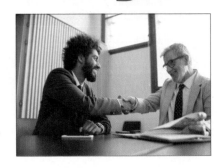

En el contexto europeo, los entrevistadores son más analíticos. Revisan minuciosamente° los hechos° de tu vida laboral, así como las motivaciones, los cambios de trabajo, etc. Los vacíos° o errores en la cronología o en la narración de tu historia laboral son muy mal vistos y pueden generar sospechas° sobre tus capacidades para desempeñar° el puesto que solicitaste.

En España, al igual que en algunos países latinoamericanos, las entrevistas de trabajo se caracterizan por ser un poco más relajadas. En primer lugar, en general se hace una sola entrevista, mientras que en países como los Estados Unidos o Canadá es común hacer hasta tres entrevistas. Obviamente, todo depende de la personalidad del/de la entrevistador(a) y del tipo de empresa, pero en general, los entrevistadores en países hispanos dejan un espacio durante la entrevista para hablar de temas más personales (como el fútbol, la situación familiar, etc.), con el fin de establecer una relación cordial con el/la aspirante.

Es por eso que, tanto en los currículums españoles como en los latinoamericanos, se indican al final los pasatiempos o intereses de las personas, con el fin de tener un tema de conversación con el/la entrevistador(a).

Otra diferencia es la inclusión de una foto en el currículum. Si bien en Norteamérica y Europa no es común incluir una foto, hay muchos latinoamericanos que incluyen su foto, lo cual es mal visto en otros países, pues puede dar lugar a sesgos° por la apariencia física del/de la aspirante.

dominio *command* minuciosamente *thoroughly* hechos *facts* vacíos *gaps* sospechas *suspicions* desempeñar *to carry out* sesgos *biases*

ASÍ SE DICE

El trabajo

la chamba (Amér. C., Ec., Méx.)	el trabajo
el curro (Esp.)	
el laburo (Arg., Urug.)	
la pega (Bol., Chile, Cuba, Ec., Perú)	
el/la cirujano/a	*surgeon*
la huelga, el paro	*strike*
el/la niñero/a	*babysitter*
el impuesto	*tax*

ACTIVIDADES

1 **¿Cierto o falso?** Indica si lo que dicen las oraciones es **cierto** o **falso**. Corrige la información falsa.

1. El dominio del idioma del país extranjero es suficiente para tener éxito en una entrevista de trabajo.

2. En ciertos países hispanos, las entrevistas son más relajadas que en otros países.

3. En los países hispanos, los entrevistadores evitan hablar de temas personales.

4. En Latinoamérica nadie pone una foto en su currículum.

2 **Preguntas** Contesta las preguntas.

1. En general, ¿cuántas entrevistas para un puesto hay en los países hispanos?

2. ¿Por qué hablan de temas personales los entrevistadores en los países hispanos?

3. ¿Por qué se incluyen los pasatiempos o intereses en el currículum en los países hispanos?

4. ¿Cuál es el aspecto negativo de incluir una foto en el currículum?

3 **Conversar** Habla con un(a) compañero/a sobre estas preguntas.

1. ¿Crees que una entrevista de trabajo debe ser muy estricta o puede ser un poco más relajada? ¿Por qué?

2. ¿Por qué crees que las entrevistas de trabajo son más relajadas en los países hispanos?

3. ¿Crees que está bien hablar de los pasatiempos o los intereses personales en una entrevista de trabajo? ¿Por qué?

4 **Una entrevista** Tienes una entrevista de trabajo en un país hispano. Describe cómo vas a prepararte. ¿Qué vas a incluir en tu currículum? ¿Cómo se diferencia de tu preparación para una entrevista de trabajo en tu comunidad?

I CAN identify practices related to interviewing for a job in Spanish-speaking countries.

Communicative Goal
Identify aspects of the world of work in Ecuador

 Video

El mundo del trabajo

1 **Preparación** ¿Trabajas? ¿Cuáles son tus metas (*goals*) profesionales?

2 **El video** Mira el episodio de **Flash cultura** sobre el mundo del trabajo en Ecuador.

Vocabulario	
el desarrollo *development*	promover *to promote*
el horario *schedule*	las ventas *sales*

Gabriela, ¿qué es lo más difícil de ser una mujer policía?

3 **Escoger** Escoge la opción correcta de cada par de afirmaciones.

1. A. Todos los ecuatorianos que trabajan en Ecuador son muy felices en su trabajo.

B. En Ecuador, como en todos los países del mundo, hay personas que aman su trabajo y hay otras que lo odian.

2. A. El objetivo principal de la agencia Klein Tours es mostrar al mundo las maravillas de Ecuador.

B. La agencia de viajes Klein Tours quiere mostrar al mundo que tiene los empleados más fieles y profesionales de toda Latinoamérica.

4 **Entrevista** En parejas, dramaticen una entrevista con otro/a trabajador(a) ecuatoriano/a.

I CAN identify aspects of the world of work in Ecuador.

16.1 The future tense

▶ You have already learned how to use **ir a** + [*infinitive*] to express the near future. You will now learn the future tense. Compare these different ways of expressing the future in Spanish.

Present indicative

Voy al cine mañana.
I'm going to the movies tomorrow.

Present subjunctive

Ojalá **vaya al cine** mañana.
I hope I will go to the movies tomorrow.

ir a + infinitive

Voy a ir al cine.
I'm going to go to the movies.

Future

Iré al cine.
I will go to the movies.

Future tense of regular verbs

	estudiar	aprender	recibir
yo	estudiaré	aprenderé	recibiré
tú	estudiarás	aprenderás	recibirás
Ud./él/ella	estudiará	aprenderá	recibirá
nosotros/as	estudiaremos	aprenderemos	recibiremos
vosotros/as	estudiaréis	aprenderéis	recibiréis
Uds./ellos/ellas	estudiarán	aprenderán	recibirán

¡ojo! All the forms of the future tense have written accents, except the **nosotros/as** form.

▶ In Spanish, the future tense consists of one word, whereas in English it is made up of the auxiliary verb *will* or *shall* and the main verb.

¿Cuándo **recibirás** el ascenso?
When will you receive the promotion?

Mañana **aprenderemos** más.
Tomorrow we will learn more.

▶ The future endings are the same for all verbs. For regular verbs, add the endings to the infinitive. For irregular verbs, add the endings to the irregular stem.

Irregular verbs in the future

INFINITIVE	STEM	FUTURE FORMS
decir	dir-	diré
hacer	har-	haré
poder	podr-	podré
poner	pondr-	pondré
querer	querr-	querré
saber	sabr-	sabré
salir	saldr-	saldré
tener	tendr-	tendré
venir	vendr-	vendré

Práctica

1 Planes Celia está hablando de sus planes. Repite lo que dice, usando el tiempo futuro.

modelo
Voy a consultar un diccionario en la biblioteca.
Consultaré un diccionario en la biblioteca.

1. Julián me va a decir dónde puedo buscar trabajo.
2. Voy a buscar un puesto que ofrezca ascensos.
3. Álvaro y yo nos vamos a casar pronto.
4. Voy a obtener un puesto en mi especialización.
5. Mis amigos van a intentar (*try*) obtener un teletrabajo.

2 En el futuro Forma oraciones con los elementos dados, usando el tiempo futuro.

modelo
Yo / estudiar / para / exámenes finales / mañana
Estudiaré para mis exámenes finales mañana.

1. Yo / tener / entrevista de trabajo / en una semana
2. La próxima semana / mis tíos / poner / anuncio para buscar un empleado
3. Pronto / mi hermana / dejar / puesto de cocinera
4. Mis padres / tener mucho éxito / como políticos
5. Mis amigos y yo / tener / puestos interesantes

3 Preguntas Túrnate con un(a) compañero/a para hablar del puesto que prefieren y por qué, basándose en los anuncios. Usen las preguntas como guía y hagan también sus propias preguntas.

SE BUSCA DIRECTOR
de mercadeo para empresa privada. Mínimo de 5 años de experiencia en turismo y conexiones con INTUR (Instituto Nicaragüense de Turismo) y ANTUR (Asociación Nicaragüense de Turismo Receptivo). Debe hablar inglés, español y alemán. Salario anual: 306.000 córdobas. Horario flexible. Buenos beneficios. Envíe currículum por fax al 492-38-67.

MUEBLERÍA MANAGUA
busca carpintero/a. Experiencia en fabricación de muebles finos. Horario: lunes a viernes de 7:30 a 11:30 y de 1:30 a 5:30. Sueldo semanal: 462 córdobas (y beneficios). Comenzará inmediatamente. Solicite en persona: Calle El Lago, Managua.

1. ¿Cuál será tu trabajo?
2. ¿Qué harás?
3. ¿Cuánto te pagarán?
4. ¿Te ofrecerán beneficios?
5. ¿Qué horario tendrás?
6. ¿Crees que te gustará? ¿Por qué?
7. ¿Cuándo comenzarás a trabajar?
8. ¿Qué crees que aprenderás?

Conversación

4 Conversar Tú y tu compañero/a viajarán a la República Dominicana por siete días. Indiquen lo que harán y no harán. Digan dónde, cómo, con quién o cuándo lo harán, usando el anuncio como guía. Pueden usar sus propias ideas también.

modelo

Estudiante 1: ¿Qué haremos el martes?
Estudiante 2: Visitaremos el Jardín Botánico.
Estudiante 1: Pues, tú visitarás el Jardín Botánico y
yo caminaré por el Mercado Modelo.

www.republicadominicana.com

¡BIENVENIDO a la República Dominicana!

Se divertirá desde el momento en que llegue al **Aeropuerto Internacional de las Américas**.

• Visite la ciudad colonial de **Santo Domingo** con su interesante arquitectura.
• Vaya al **Jardín Botánico** y disfrute de nuestra abundante naturaleza.
• En el **Mercado Modelo** no va a poder resistir la tentación de comprar artesanías.
• No deje de escalar el **Pico Duarte** (se recomiendan 3 días).
• ¿Le gusta bucear? **Cabarete** tiene todo el equipo que usted necesita.
• ¿Desea nadar? **Punta Cana** le ofrece hermosas playas.

5 Una empresa privada En grupos pequeños, hagan planes para formar una empresa privada. Usen las preguntas como guía. Después, presenten su plan a la clase.

1. ¿Cómo se llamará y qué tipo de empresa será?
2. ¿Cuántos empleados tendrá y cuáles serán sus oficios?
3. ¿Qué tipo de beneficios se ofrecerán?
4. ¿Quién será el/la gerente y quién será el/la jefe/a?
5. ¿Permitirá su empresa el teletrabajo? ¿Por qué?
6. ¿Qué se hará para que los empleados no dejen el trabajo?
7. ¿Dónde pondrán anuncios para buscar empleados?
8. ¿Qué harán los gerentes para que la empresa tenga éxito?

6 Predicciones En grupos pequeños, especulen sobre lo que ocurrirá en estos años: 2040, 2060 y 2090. Usen su imaginación. Luego, compartan sus predicciones con la clase.

I CAN talk about future plans.

¡ojo! The future of **hay** (*inf.* **haber**) is **habrá** (*there will be*).

La próxima semana **habrá** dos reuniones.
Next week there will be two meetings.

Habrá muchos gerentes en la conferencia.
There will be many managers at the conference.

▸ Although the English verb *will* can refer to future time, it also refers to someone's willingness to do something. In this case, Spanish uses **querer** + [*infinitive*].

¿**Quieres llamarme**, por favor?
Will you please call me?

¿**Quieren ustedes escucharnos**, por favor?
Will you please listen to us?

▸ English sentences involving expressions such as *I wonder, I bet, must be, may, might,* and *probably* are often conveyed in Spanish using the future of probability. This use of the future tense expresses conjecture about *present* conditions, events, or actions.

—¿Dónde **estarán** mis llaves?
I wonder where my keys are.

—**Estarán** en la cocina.
They're probably in the kitchen.

—¿Qué hora **será**?
What time can it be? (I wonder what time it is.)

—**Serán** las once o las doce.
It must be (It's probably) eleven or twelve.

▸ The future may be used in the main clause of sentences in which the present subjunctive follows a conjunction of time such as **cuando, después (de) que, en cuanto, hasta que,** and **tan pronto como**.

Cuando llegues a la oficina, **hablaremos**.
When you arrive at the office, we will talk.

Saldremos tan pronto como termine su trabajo.
We will leave as soon as you finish your work.

Después de que obtengas el ascenso, te **invitaré** a cenar.
After you get the promotion, I'll invite you to dinner.

Hasta que contrate otro empleado, el jefe **tendrá** que hacer el trabajo.
Until he hires another employee, the boss will have to do the work.

¡Manos a la obra!

Conjuga los verbos indicados en futuro.

1. yo [dejar, correr, invertir] _____ dejaré, correré, invertiré
2. tú [renunciar, beber, vivir] _____
3. Lola [hacer, poner, venir] _____
4. nosotros [tener, decir, querer] _____
5. ustedes [ir, ser, estar] _____
6. usted [solicitar, comer, repetir] _____
7. yo [saber, salir, poder] _____
8. tú [encontrar, jugar, servir] _____

Communicative Goal
Say what I would do

16.2 The conditional tense

▸ The conditional tense in Spanish expresses what you *would do* or what *would happen* under certain circumstances. In Lesson 7, you learned the polite expression **me gustaría...** (*I would like...*), which uses a conditional form of **gustar**.

	visitar	comer	aplaudir
yo	visitaría	comería	aplaudiría
tú	visitarías	comerías	aplaudirías
Ud./él/ella	visitaría	comería	aplaudiría
nosotros/as	visitaríamos	comeríamos	aplaudiríamos
vosotros/as	visitaríais	comeríais	aplaudiríais
Uds./ellos/ellas	visitarían	comerían	aplaudirían

▸ The conditional endings are the same for all verbs, and all forms carry a written accent. For regular verbs, add the endings to the infinitive. For irregular verbs, add the endings to the irregular stem.

INFINITIVE	STEM	CONDITIONAL
decir	dir-	diría
haber	habr-	habría
hacer	har-	haría
poder	podr-	podría
poner	pondr-	pondría
querer	querr-	querría
saber	sabr-	sabría
salir	saldr-	saldría
tener	tendr-	tendría
venir	vendr-	vendría

¡ojo! The conditional form of **hay** is **habría** (*there would be*).

▸ While in English the conditional is made up of the auxiliary verb *would* and a main verb, in Spanish it consists of one word.

Este aspirante **sería** perfecto para el puesto.
This candidate would be perfect for the job.

Querría un puesto con un buen salario.
I would like a job with a good salary.

¿**Vivirían** ustedes en otro país por un trabajo?
Would you live in another country for a job?

Ganarían más en otra compañía.
They would earn more at another company.

Práctica

1 **Un viaje** Completa las oraciones con el condicional del verbo indicado.

> **modelo**
> Diana ___querría___ [querer] conocer otros lugares en el viaje.

1. Me _____ [gustar] llegar unos días antes de la conferencia para viajar.
2. Ana y Rubén _____ [salir] primero a la playa para descansar.
3. Yo _____ [decir] que fuéramos a San Juan porque es una ciudad muy divertida.
4. Nosotras _____ [preferir] tener las reuniones por la mañana. Así, por la tarde _____ [poder] visitar la ciudad.
5. Y nosotros _____ [visitar] la zona comercial de la ciudad. Y tú, Luisa, ¿qué _____ [hacer]?
6. Estamos seguros de que el jefe _____ [tener] interés en hacer una videoconferencia. El fin de semana él _____ [visitar] los museos.

2 **Preguntas** Forma preguntas con estos elementos. Luego, inventa las respuestas. Usa el condicional.

> **modelo**
>
> hacer (ustedes) / videoconferencia / con / empresa de Chile
> —¿Harían ustedes una videoconferencia con una empresa de Chile?
> —Sí, haríamos una videoconferencia con una empresa de Chile.

1. contratar (tú) / un miembro de tu familia / para / puesto nuevo
2. invertir (ellos) / dinero / en / compañía nueva
3. solicitar (ella) / trabajo / de abogado
4. renunciar (tú) / puesto / por otro trabajo con mejores beneficios
5. tener (nosotros) / dinero / para empezar / empresa privada

3 **Sugerencias** Beatriz busca trabajo. Dile ocho cosas que tú harías si fueras (*if you were*) ella. Usa el condicional. Luego, compara tus sugerencias con un(a) compañero/a.

> **modelo**
>
> Buscaría trabajo en la red.

Conversación

4 En tu lugar… Lee las situaciones. Responde con lo que harías en esta situación usando la frase **Yo en tu lugar…** (*If I were you…*). Después, compara tus ideas con las de un(a) compañero/a.

 modelo

Me encanta mi puesto, pero mi jefe nunca me deja hablar.

Estudiante 1: *Me encanta mi puesto, pero mi jefe nunca me deja hablar.*

Estudiante 2: *Pues, yo en tu lugar, hablaría con mi jefe sobre este problema.*

1. El año pasado escogí contabilidad como mi especialización, pero ahora he descubierto que no me gusta trabajar con números todo el día. Si cambio, mis padres quizás se enojen.

2. Me ofrecen un puesto interesantísimo, con un buen sueldo y excelentes beneficios, pero tiene un horario horrible. No volveré a ver a mis amigos jamás.

3. Mi peluquero es maravilloso, pero se va de viaje por dos meses a San Juan. Los otros peluqueros que trabajan en su salón no me gustan. Y tengo que hacer varias presentaciones públicas para mi empresa durante esos dos meses.

5 ¿Qué harías? Quieres saber qué harían tus compañeros/as por un millón de dólares. Escribe siete preguntas usando el tiempo condicional. Circula por la clase y hazles las preguntas a tus compañeros/as. Anota las respuestas e informa a la clase de los resultados de la encuesta.

modelo

Estudiante 1: *¿Trabajarías como cantante en Las Vegas?*
Estudiante 2: *Sí, lo haría. Sería un puesto muy interesante.*

Actividades	Nombre de compañero/a
_____	_____
_____	_____
_____	_____
_____	_____
_____	_____
_____	_____
_____	_____

I CAN say what I would do.

Uses of the conditional

▸ The conditional is commonly used to make polite requests.

¿Podrías llamar al gerente, por favor?
Would you call the manager, please?

¿Sería tan amable de venir ahora?
Would you be so kind as to come now?

▸ In both Spanish and English, the conditional expresses the future in relation to a past action or state of being. The future indicates what *will happen*, whereas the conditional indicates what *would happen*. The future tense is often used if the main verb is in the present tense. The conditional is often used if the main verb is in one of the past tenses.

Creo que mañana **hará** sol.
I think it will be sunny tomorrow.

Creía que hoy **haría** sol.
I thought it would be sunny today.

▸ The English *would* can also mean *used to*, in the sense of past habitual action. To express past habitual actions, Spanish uses the imperfect.

Íbamos al parque los sábados.
We would go to the park on Saturdays.

De adolescentes, **comíamos** mucho.
As teenagers, we used to eat a lot.

▸ English sentences involving expressions such as *I wondered if, probably,* and *must have been* are often conveyed in Spanish using the conditional of probability. This use of the conditional expresses conjecture or probability about *past* conditions, events, or actions.

Serían las nueve cuando el jefe me llamó.
It must have been (It was probably) 9 o'clock when the boss called me.

Sonó el teléfono. **¿Llamaría** Tina para cancelar nuestra cita?
The phone rang. I wondered if it was Tina calling to cancel our date.

Sin ti, no sé qué haría.

Sólo tú sabes ordenar mi vida.

¡Manos a la obra!

Indica la forma apropiada del condicional de estos verbos.

1. yo [escuchar, leer, escribir] _____ escucharía, leería, escribiría
2. tú [invertir, comprender, compartir] _____
3. Marcos [poner, venir, querer] _____
4. nosotras [ser, saber, ir] _____
5. ustedes [presentar, deber, despedir] _____
6. ella [salir, poder, hacer] _____
7. yo [tener, tocar, acostarse] _____
8. tú [decir, ver, renunciar] _____

Communicative Goal
Express past hopes and requests

16.3 The past subjunctive

▶ The past subjunctive (**el pretérito imperfecto de subjuntivo**) is also called the imperfect subjunctive. Like the present subjunctive, it is used mainly in multiple-clause sentences that express will, influence, emotion, commands, indefiniteness, and non-existence.

The past subjunctive

	estudiar	aprender	recibir
yo	estudiara	aprendiera	recibiera
tú	estudiaras	aprendieras	recibieras
Ud./él/ella	estudiara	aprendiera	recibiera
nosotros/as	estudiáramos	aprendiéramos	recibiéramos
vosotros/as	estudiarais	aprendierais	recibierais
Uds./ellos/ellas	estudiaran	aprendieran	recibieran

¡ojo! The past subjunctive endings are the same for all verbs. Also, note that the **nosotros/as** form always has a written accent.

▶ For *all* verbs, the past subjunctive is formed with the **Uds./ellos/ellas** form of the preterite. By dropping the **–ron** ending, you establish the stem for all the past subjunctive forms. You then add the past subjunctive endings.

INFINITIVE	PRETERITE FORM	STEM	PAST SUBJUNCTIVE
hablar	ellos hablaron	habla-	hablara, hablaras, habláramos
beber	ellos bebieron	bebie-	bebiera, bebieras, bebiéramos
escribir	ellos escribieron	escribie-	escribiera, escribieras, escribiéramos

▶ For verbs with irregular preterites, add the past subjunctive endings to the irregular stem.

INFINITIVE	PRETERITE FORM	STEM	PAST SUBJUNCTIVE
dar	dieron	die-	diera, dieras, diéramos
decir	dijeron	dije-	dijera, dijeras, dijéramos
estar	estuvieron	estuvie-	estuviera, estuvieras, estuviéramos
hacer	hicieron	hicie-	hiciera, hicieras, hiciéramos
ir/ser	fueron	fue-	fuera, fueras, fuéramos
poder	pudieron	pudie-	pudiera, pudieras, pudiéramos
poner	pusieron	pusie-	pusiera, pusieras, pusiéramos
querer	quisieron	quisie-	quisiera, quisieras, quisiéramos
saber	supieron	supie-	supiera, supieras, supiéramos
tener	tuvieron	tuvie-	tuviera, tuvieras, tuviéramos
venir	vinieron	vinie-	viniera, vinieras, viniéramos

Práctica

1 **Conversaciones** Completa los minidiálogos con el pretérito imperfecto de subjuntivo de los verbos.

PACO ¿Qué le dijo el consejero a Andrés? Quisiera saberlo.

JULIA Le aconsejó que (1) _____ [dejar] los estudios de arte y que (2) _____ [estudiar] una carrera que (3) _____ [pagar] mejor.

PACO Siempre el dinero. ¿No se enojó Andrés de que le (4) _____ [aconsejar] eso?

JULIA Sí, y le dijo que no creía que ninguna carrera le (5) _____ [ir] a gustar más.

• • •

EVA Qué lástima que ellos no te (6) _____ [ofrecer] el puesto de gerente.

LUIS Querían a alguien que (7) _____ [tener] más experiencia.

EVA Pero, ¿cómo? ¿No te molestó que te (8) _____ [decir] eso?

LUIS No, porque les gustó mucho mi currículum. Me pidieron que (9) _____ [volver] en un año y (10) _____ [solicitar] el puesto otra vez.

• • •

CARLA Cuánto me alegré de que tus hijas (11) _____ [venir] ayer a visitarte. ¿Cuándo se van?

ANA Bueno, yo esperaba que (12) _____ [quedarse] dos semanas, pero no pueden. Ojalá (13) _____ [poder]. Hace muchísimo tiempo que no las veo.

2 **Transformar** Cambia las oraciones al pasado. Sigue el modelo.

modelo

Temo que Juanita no consiga el trabajo.
Temía que Juanita no consiguiera el trabajo.

1. Esperamos que Miguel no renuncie.

2. No hay nadie que responda al anuncio.

3. Me sorprende que ellos no inviertan su dinero.

4. Te piden que no llegues tarde a la oficina.

5. Juan quiere que Marta tome el puesto de contadora.

6. Siento mucho que no tengas éxito en el trabajo.

7. Quiero que te entrevistes con esta compañía.

8. Temen que usted no firme el contrato esta mañana.

Conversación

3 Preguntas Con un(a) compañero/a, contesta las preguntas.

1. De pequeño/a, ¿qué querías que hicieran tus padres?
2. Cuando eras niño/a, ¿esperaban tus padres que trabajaras en una profesión específica?
3. ¿Dudaban tus profesores que tú pudieras llegar a ser lo que querías?
4. ¿Insistían tus padres en que fueras a la universidad? ¿Insistían en otras cosas?
5. ¿Qué te aconsejaron tus amigos que hicieras para tener éxito?
6. ¿Cuál esperabas que fuera tu profesión?

4 Minidiálogos Trabaja con un(a) compañero/a. Uno/a de ustedes ha comprado una casa; la otra persona es el/la gerente de la empresa responsable de las reformas (*improvements*) de la casa. El/La cliente/a llama al/a la gerente para quejarse (*to complain*). Usen estas palabras y el modelo como guía.

modelo el/la técnico/a / conectar / módem

Estudiante 1: Le pedí al técnico que conectara el módem, pero todavía no ha venido.
Estudiante 2: No se preocupe. Yo también le pedí al técnico que fuera a su casa.

1. el/la electricista / poner / electricidad
2. el/la carpintero/a / construir / balcón
3. el/la diseñador(a) / escoger / muebles
4. el/la pintor(a) / pintar / paredes

5 Situación Claudia dejó su puesto por la forma en que le hablaba el gerente, por el aumento que les dieron a otros empleados (¡pero no a ella!) y por el horario que no le permitía seguir con sus clases. Con un(a) compañero/a, dramatiza una conversación entre Claudia y el gerente.

modelo

Estudiante 1: No estoy contenta. No me dieron un aumento de sueldo.
Estudiante 2: ¿Quería usted que le diéramos un aumento? ¡No lo sabía!

I CAN express past hopes and requests.

Past subjunctive of stem-changing verbs

▶ **–Ir** stem-changing verbs and other verbs with spelling changes follow a similar process to form the past subjunctive.

INFINITIVE	PRETERITE FORM	STEM	PAST SUBJUNCTIVE
preferir	prefirie~~ron~~	prefirie-	prefiriera, prefirieras, prefiriéramos
repetir	repitie~~ron~~	repitie-	repitiera, repitieras, repitiéramos
dormir	durmie~~ron~~	durmie-	durmiera, durmieras, durmiéramos
conducir	conduje~~ron~~	conduje-	condujera, condujeras, condujéramos
creer	creye~~ron~~	creye-	creyera, creyeras, creyéramos
destruir	destruye~~ron~~	destruye-	destruyera, destruyeras, destruyéramos
oír	oye~~ron~~	oye-	oyera, oyeras, oyéramos

Aquí está mi currículum y me pidieron que trajera mi portafolio con mis trabajos de fotografía...

Desde niña me interesé por la fotografía, aunque mis padres querían que estudiara una carrera científica.

▶ The past subjunctive is used in the same contexts and situations as the present subjunctive, except that it generally describes actions, events, or conditions that have already happened. The verb in the main clause is usually in the preterite or the imperfect.

Me pidieron que no **llegara** tarde.
They asked me not to arrive late.

Ellos querían que yo les **escribiera**.
They wanted me to write to them.

¡ojo! **Quisiera** is often used to make polite requests.

Quisiera hablar con Marco.
I would like to speak to Marco.

¿**Quisiera** usted algo más?
Would you like anything else?

¡Manos a la obra!

Completa estas oraciones con el pretérito imperfecto de subjuntivo.

1. Quería que tú __vinieras__ [venir] más temprano.
2. Esperábamos que ustedes _____ [hablar] mucho más en la reunión.
3. No creían que yo _____ [poder] hacerlo.
4. Se opuso a que nosotros _____ [invertir] el dinero ayer.
5. Sentí mucho que usted no _____ [estar] con nosotros anoche.
6. No era necesario que ellas _____ [hacer] todo.
7. Me pareció increíble que tú _____ [saber] dónde encontrarlo.
8. No hubo nadie que _____ [creer] tu historia.
9. Mis padres insistieron en que yo _____ [ir] a la universidad.
10. Queríamos salir antes de que ustedes _____ [llegar].

A repasar

16.1 The future tense

1 Los detalles del trabajo ¡Felicidades! Obtuviste el empleo que querías. Completa el diálogo con tu nuevo jefe sobre los detalles de tu próximo trabajo. Usa el tiempo futuro.

TÚ Gracias por ofrecerme el puesto de contador. ¿Cuándo _____ (empezar) a trabajar?

JEFE _____

TÚ ¿Cuántos días de vacaciones _____ (tener) al año?

JEFE _____

TÚ ¿Cuándo _____ (obtener) un aumento de sueldo?

JEFE _____

TÚ ¿Cuáles _____ (ser) mis beneficios?

JEFE _____

TÚ ¿_____ (poder) tener una computadora?

JEFE _____

TÚ ¿Dónde _____ (estar) mi oficina?

JEFE _____

2 ¿Qué ocurrirá...? Completa estas frases de una manera lógica, usando el tiempo futuro.

modelo En cuanto Javier termine su especialización, él...
obtendrá un ascenso.

1. Tan pronto como nos graduemos, nosotros...
2. Después de que el gerente me entreviste, yo...
3. En cuanto Eva llene la solicitud de trabajo, ella...
4. Hasta que obtengan un aumento de sueldo, ellos...
5. Cuando contratemos a una secretaria, ustedes...
6. Después de que te expliquen los beneficios del puesto, tú...

3 ¿Cuál será su profesión? Con un(a) compañero/a, utiliza el futuro de probabilidad para preguntar y responder sobre las profesiones que tienen las personas.

modelo **Estudiante 1:** *¿Trabajará este hombre en un banco?*
Estudiante 2: *Creo que sí. ¿Cuántas horas trabajará?*

16.2 The conditional tense

4 El gerente dijo que... Tu empresa contrató a un gerente nuevo. Lee el discurso que dio en su primer día de trabajo. Después, cuéntale a tu novio/a lo que dijo el gerente, usando el condicional.

"Habrá muchos cambios en la empresa. Mejoraré los beneficios de los trabajadores, pero no aumentaré los sueldos. Despediré a los empleados perezosos *(lazy)*. Tendremos una reunión todos los lunes a las siete de la mañana. Y juntos, solucionaremos los problemas de la compañía. ¡Será un buen año!"

modelo El *gerente nuevo dijo que habría muchos cambios en la empresa...*

5 Peticiones Túrnate con un(a) compañero/a para hacer preguntas y responder con la información indicada. Usen **¿Podrías...?, ¿Serías tan amable de...?** y **por favor** en sus preguntas. Contesten en forma negativa a cada petición *(request)*.

modelo darme información acerca del puesto

Estudiante 1: *¿Podrías darme información acerca del puesto, por favor?*
Estudiante 2: *Te la daría, pero no puedo. El gerente hablará contigo.*

1. explicarme mis beneficios
2. ayudarme a escribir mi currículum
3. enviarme una solicitud de trabajo
4. decirme el sueldo que ofrecen
5. hablarnos de tu experiencia profesional
6. venir a una entrevista
7. decirme qué hora es
8. contratarme lo antes posible
9. organizar una videoconferencia
10. entrevistar al aspirante a contador

6 Situaciones Túrnate con un(a) compañero/a para decir qué harían en estas situaciones.

- Estás perdido/a en un país donde no hablan tu lengua. Es de noche y tu automóvil está descompuesto.
- Tu computadora no funciona y tienes que imprimir un trabajo final. Son las once de la noche y tienes que dárselo a tu profesor a las ocho de la mañana.
- Hoy es el cumpleaños de tu novio/a, pero se te olvidó. No le compraste ningún regalo.
- Estás en un restaurante y llega Javier Bardem a cenar. Se sienta en una mesa cerca de ti.

16.3 The past subjunctive

7 Reacciones Tu hermano y tú son cantantes famosos. Pero en el pasado, su familia y sus amigos les decían que siguieran otra profesión. Escribe las reacciones que tenían.

A mis padres les molestaba mucho que	(no) escoger la profesión de cantantes
Mis mejores amigos nos insistían en que	(no) ser arquitectos
A mi abuelo le sorprendía siempre que	(no) tener éxito
Mi novia nos sugería que	(no) aprender a cantar
Los maestros nos recomendaban que	(no) ganar mucho dinero
Ustedes se alegraban de que	(no) hacer el ridículo
Tú nos decías que era muy difícil que	(no) estudiar otra especialización

8 Películas En grupos de tres, escriban sobre una película, usando el pretérito imperfecto de subjuntivo. Después, lean sus composiciones a la clase para que ellos adivinen el nombre de la película.

modelo

Willy no quería que nadie entrara a su empresa. Le daba miedo que alguien robara su receta para hacer chocolates. Por eso, contrataba a gente pequeña para que manejaran las máquinas. Un día, decidió invitar a cinco niños a que visitaran su fábrica... (*Charlie and the Chocolate Factory*)

Síntesis

9 Cambio de profesión Con un(a) compañero/a, dramatiza una conversación entre un(a) psicólogo/a y un(a) cocinero/a que no está contento/a con su profesión. El/La psicólogo/a escucha a la persona hablar sobre su vida y después recomienda futuras acciones. Incluye esta información en la conversación. Luego, preséntala a la clase.

- ¿Que profesión querían tus padres que tú siguieras?
- ¿Qué especialización querías estudiar?
- ¿Cambiarías de profesión en este momento?
- ¿Cómo te sentirías si cambiaras de empleo?
- ¿Qué acciones recomienda el/la psicólogo/a para que esta persona sea más feliz?
- ¿Qué va a hacer el/la cocinero/a para encontrar una nueva ocupación?

Communicative Goal
Write a commentary

Video

Videoclip

1 Preparación ¿Dónde se realizan los grandes eventos de moda en el mundo? ¿Crees que la moda es una industria importante en los países latinoamericanos?

2 El clip Mira el reportaje sobre Ágatha Ruiz de la Prada.

Vocabulario	
apretadito *tight*	desfile *fashion show*
atrevido *audacious*	destacar *to highlight*

Hay mucho color en la forma de vestir en América Latina.

3 ¿Cierto o falso? Indica si estas oraciones son **ciertas** o **falsas**. Corrige las falsas.

1. En América Latina, la moda no es tan importante como en Europa.
2. Los países latinoamericanos están atrasados en relación con las nuevas tendencias de la moda.
3. Según la diseñadora, la ropa apretada no está de moda.
4. La principal característica de países como México y Brasil son sus grandes desfiles de moda.
5. Para Ruiz de la Prada, la moda se representa con una gran variedad de colores y con diseños atrevidos.

4 Un comentario Imagina que en tu ciudad se celebrará próximamente un importante evento de moda. Prepara con un(a) compañero/a un comentario sobre el evento, utilizando el tiempo futuro. Usa el modelo como guía.

modelo Esta semana habrá un importante evento de moda... El evento se realizará en... Vendrá la diseñadora...

I CAN write a commentary.

Ampliación

Communicative Goals
Use background
knowledge to
understand a
conversation, and talk
about future plans

1 Escuchar

A Escucha la entrevista de la señora Sánchez y Rafael Ventura Romero. Antes de escucharla, prepara una lista de la información que esperas oír, según tu conocimiento previo (*prior knowledge*) del tema.

> **TIP** **Use background knowledge. / Listen for specific information.** Knowing the subject of what you are going to hear will help you use your background knowledge to anticipate words and phrases that you are likely to hear, and to determine important information that you should listen for.

Llena el formulario con la información necesaria. Si no oyes un dato (*piece of information*) que necesitas, escribe *Buscar en el currículum.* ¿Oíste toda la información de tu lista?

Puesto solicitado _____

Nombre y apellidos del solicitante _____

Dirección _____ **Tel.** _____

Educación _____

Experiencia profesional: Puesto _____

Empresa _____

¿Cuánto tiempo? _____

Referencias:

Nombre _____

Dirección _____ Tel. _____

Nombre _____

Dirección _____ Tel. _____

B ¿Cómo sabes si los resultados de la entrevista han sido positivos para Rafael Ventura?

_____

2 Conversar

Conversa con un(a) compañero/a sobre sus planes para el futuro. Incluye esta información en su conversación.

- ¿Qué profesión u oficio seguirás en el futuro?
- ¿Por qué te interesa esta carrera?
- ¿En qué compañía te gustaría trabajar?
- ¿Te gustaría tener un teletrabajo?
- ¿Qué se necesita hacer para tener éxito?
- ¿Te mudarías de país por un puesto excelente?

I CAN use background knowledge to understand a conversation.

I CAN talk about future plans.

Ampliación

③ Escribir

Escribe una composición sobre tus planes para el futuro. Formula planes para tu vida personal, profesional y financiera. Termina tu composición con una lista de metas (*goals*).

> **TIP** **Use note cards.** Note cards (**fichas**) can help you organize and sequence your information. Label the top of each card with a general subject, such as **lugar** or **empleo**. Number the cards so you can easily flip through them to find information.

Organizar | Utiliza fichas para apuntar cada plan o meta para el futuro. Asigna un año a cada meta.

Escribir | Organiza tus fichas y escribe el primer borrador de tu composición.

Corregir | Intercambia tu composición con un(a) compañero/a. Léela y anota sus mejores aspectos. ¿Habla de las metas específicas para su futuro? Ofrécele sugerencias para mejorar la organización. Si ves algunos errores, coméntaselos.

Compartir | Revisa el primer borrador de tu composición, según las indicaciones de tu compañero/a. Incorpora nuevas ideas y/o más información si es necesario, antes de escribir la versión final.

Communicative Goals
Write a composition about my future plans, and create a time line

④ Un paso más

Imagina que en el futuro trabajarás para una empresa multinacional que tiene sus oficinas más importantes en algún país hispano. Crea una cronología con texto y fotos de tu futura carrera profesional y compártela con la clase.

- Escoge el país y busca información sobre las industrias y las compañías que operen allá.
- Describe la empresa y sus productos.
- Incluye fotos relacionadas con la empresa y con sus productos.
- Describe tu carrera, desde el comienzo hasta tu jubilación.
- Incluye los puestos que vas a tener en la empresa, y también fotos relacionadas con tu carrera.

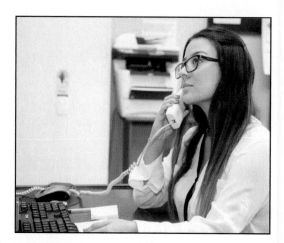

⑤ Cultura

Te gustaría solicitar un puesto en un país hispano. ¿Qué tipo de puesto te interesaría? ¿Cómo solicitarías el puesto? ¿Cómo adaptarías tu currículum?

I CAN write a composition about my future personal and professional plans.

I CAN create a time line with text and photos.

Audio: Reading

Antes de leer

Summarizing a text in your own words can help you understand it better.

TIP **Summarize.** Before you begin, you may find it helpful to skim the text and jot down a few notes about its general meaning. You can then read it again, writing down important details or noting special characteristics that occur in the text. Your notes will help you summarize what you have read.

Examinar el texto

The reading selection for this lesson consists of a short story by Augusto Monterroso. What special characteristics in this text could help you summarize it? Skim the story and jot down your ideas.

_____

_____

_____

_____

Sobre el autor

Augusto Monterroso (1921–2003) fue un escritor guatemalteco. Sus textos son concisos, sencillos (*simple*) y accesibles. Su trabajo incluye la parodia, el humor negro, la fábula y el ensayo.

Imaginación y destino
Augusto Monterroso

En la calurosa° tarde de verano un hombre descansa acostado°, viendo° al cielo, bajo un árbol; una manzana cae sobre su cabeza; tiene imaginación, se va a su casa y escribe la Oda a Eva.

En la calurosa tarde de verano un hombre descansa acostado, viendo al cielo, bajo un árbol; una manzana cae sobre su cabeza; tiene imaginación, se va a su casa y establece la Ley de la Gravitación Universal.

En la calurosa tarde de verano un hombre descansa acostado, viendo al cielo, bajo un árbol; una manzana cae sobre su cabeza; tiene imaginación, observa que el árbol no es un manzano sino una encina° y descubre, oculto° entre las ramas°, al muchacho travieso° del pueblo que se entretiene° arrojando° manzanas a los señores que descansan bajo los árboles, viendo al cielo, en las calurosas tardes del verano.

El primero era, o se convierte entonces para siempre en el poeta sir James Calisher; el segundo era, o se convierte entonces para siempre en el físico sir Isaac Newton[1]; el tercero pudo ser o convertirse entonces para siempre en el novelista sir Arthur Conan Doyle[2]; pero se convierte, o era ya irremediablemente desde niño, en el Jefe de Policía de San Blas, S.B.[3]

[1] Sir Isaac Newton (1642–1727), matemático y físico británico. Es considerado uno de los científicos más importantes de la historia. Formuló la Ley de la Gravitación Universal.

[2] Sir Arthur Conan Doyle (1859–1930), escritor británico. Sus más famosos protagonistas son Sherlock Holmes y su ayudante, el doctor Watson.

[3] S.B. Abreviatura de San Blas, unas islas en Panamá. Una de las novelas de Monterroso tiene lugar en San Blas.

calurosa *hot*   **acostado** *lying down*   **viendo** *looking*   **encina** *oak tree*   **oculto** *hidden*
ramas *branches*   **travieso** *mischievous*   **se entretiene** *entertains himself*
arrojando *throwing*

Después de leer

∞ ¿Comprendiste?

Responde las preguntas de acuerdo con la lectura.

1. ¿Qué estación del año es y qué tiempo hace?

2. ¿Qué hace el primer hombre después de descansar?

3. ¿Qué hace el segundo hombre después de descansar?

4. ¿Qué encuentra el tercer hombre en el árbol?

5. ¿Cuáles son las profesiones de estos tres hombres?

∞ Preguntas

Responde estas preguntas con oraciones completas.

1. ¿Por qué lleva el cuento el título "Imaginación y destino"?

2. ¿Por qué utiliza el autor la repetición?

3. La misma situación les ocurre a los tres hombres, pero tienen reacciones distintas. ¿Por qué?

4. El autor escribe "o era ya irremediablemente desde niño". ¿Qué significa esta frase en relación con el resto del cuento?

5. Imagina que hay una cuarta persona en la historia. Escribe un párrafo con el estilo del autor sobre qué le pasa a esta persona "cuando una manzana cae sobre su cabeza".

∞ Coméntalo

En el cuento, tres personajes tienen la misma experiencia con distintos resultados. ¿Has tenido una experiencia así? Un ejemplo es la graduación: un grupo de personas se gradúa el mismo día, pero ¿qué pasa después? ¿Podemos controlar nuestros destinos? ¿Afectarán tus experiencias actuales tu futuro? ¿Cómo sabes qué profesión quieres ejercer (*carry out*) en el futuro?

I CAN read a short story and summarize it.

Vocabulary Tools

Las ocupaciones

el/la **abogado/a** *lawyer*
el **actor** *actor*
la **actriz** *actress*
el/la **arqueólogo/a** *archeologist*
el/la **arquitecto/a** *architect*
el **bailarín** *dancer*
la **bailarina** *dancer*
el/la **bombero/a** *firefighter*
el/la **cantante** *singer*
el/la **carpintero/a** *carpenter*
el/la **científico/a** *scientist*
el/la **cocinero/a** *cook; chef*
el/la **consejero/a** *counselor; advisor*
el/la **contador(a)** *accountant*
el/la **corredor(a) de bolsa** *stockbroker*
el/la **diseñador(a)** *designer*
el/la **electricista** *electrician*
el/la **escritor(a)** *writer*
el/la **escultor(a)** *sculptor*
el/la **gerente** *manager*
el **hombre/la mujer de negocios** *businessperson*
el/la **jefe/a** *boss*
el/la **maestro/a** *teacher*
el/la **peluquero/a** *hairdresser*
el/la **pintor(a)** *painter*
el/la **poeta** *poet*
el/la **político/a** *politician*
el/la **psicólogo/a** *psychologist*
el/la **reportero/a** *reporter*
el/la **secretario/a** *secretary*
el/la **técnico/a** *technician*

Las entrevistas

el **anuncio** *advertisement*
el/la **aspirante** *candidate; applicant*
los **beneficios** *benefits; profits*
el **currículum** *résumé*
la **entrevista** *interview*
el/la **entrevistador(a)** *interviewer*
el **puesto** *position; job*
el **salario** *salary*
la **solicitud (de trabajo)** *(job) application*
el **sueldo** *salary*

———

contratar *to hire*
entrevistar *to interview*
ganar *to earn*
obtener *to obtain; to get*
solicitar *to apply (for a job)*

El mundo del trabajo

el **ascenso** *promotion*
el **aumento de sueldo** *raise*
la **carrera** *career*
la **compañía** *company; firm*
el **empleo** *job; employment*
la **empresa** *company; firm*
la **especialización** *field of study*
los **negocios** *business; commerce*
la **ocupación** *occupation*
el **oficio** *trade*
la **profesión** *profession*
la **reunión** *meeting*
el **teletrabajo** *telecommuting*
el **trabajo** *job; work*
la **videoconferencia** *videoconference*

———

dejar *to quit; to leave behind*
despedir (e:i) *to fire*
invertir (e:ie) *to invest*
renunciar (a) *to resign (from)*
tener éxito *to be successful*

———

comercial *commercial; business-related*

Communicative Goals: Review

I CAN discuss the world of work.
• Describe three professions that interest you.

I CAN participate in a job interview.
• List three questions you would ask at a job interview.

I CAN talk about future plans.
• Tell a partner five things you will do in the next six months. Use the future tense.

I CAN investigate job interviews in Spanish-speaking countries.
• Describe how job interviews are different in the Spanish-speaking world.

AVENTURAS
EN LOS
PAÍSES
HISPANOS

Communicative Goal
Identify aspects of the geography
and culture of Spain

 Una mujer baila flamenco en Sevilla.
El flamenco, el baile y su música, expresa
las pasiones de la gente de España.
Tiene raíces *(roots)* judías *(Jewish)*, árabes
y africanas. Hoy es popular en todo el
mundo, en parte gracias a la influencia
de cantantes como Rosario Flores,
Diego el Cigala o Rosalía.

¿Te gusta la música flamenca?

ESPAÑA

España

Área: 505.370 km^2 (195.124 millas^2),
incluyendo las islas Baleares y las
islas Canarias
Población: 46.700.000
Capital: Madrid – 6.559.000
Ciudades principales: Barcelona,
Valencia, Sevilla, Zaragoza
Moneda: euro

SOURCE: Population Division, UN Secretariat & CIA
World Factbook

Lugares

Madrid: La Plaza Mayor

La Plaza Mayor de Madrid es uno de los lugares turísticos más importantes de la capital. Fue construida *(built)* en 1617 y está totalmente rodeada *(surrounded)* por edificios de tres pisos con balcones y pórticos antiguos. En la Plaza Mayor hay muchas cafeterías, donde la gente pasa el tiempo bebiendo café y hablando con amigos.

¿Dónde pasas tiempo con tus amigos?

Celebraciones

La Tomatina

En Buñol, un pequeño pueblo de Valencia, la producción de tomates es un recurso económico muy importante. Cada año en agosto se celebra el festival de La Tomatina. Durante todo un día, miles de personas se tiran *(throw)* tomates. Llegan turistas de todo el mundo, y se usan varias toneladas *(tons)* de tomates.

¿Te gustaría ir al festival de La Tomatina? ¿Conoces algún otro festival o celebración fuera de lo común *(out of the ordinary)*? ¿Cuál es y dónde se celebra?

Mar Cantábrico

La Coruña

Salamanca

Madrid ☆

ESPAÑA

PORTUGAL

Sevilla

Sierra Nevada

Estrecho de Gibraltar

Ceuta

Melilla

Islas Canarias

La Palma

Tenerife

Gran Canaria

Lanzarote

Fuerteventura

Gomera

Hierro

MARRUECOS

FRANCIA

San Sebastián

ANDORRA

Pirineos

Zaragoza

Barcelona

Islas Baleares

Valencia

Menorca

Mallorca

Ibiza

Mar
Mediterráneo

Artes

Velázquez y el Prado ▶

El Prado, en Madrid, es uno de los museos más famosos del mundo. En el Prado hay miles de pinturas importantes, incluyendo obras *(works)* de Botticelli, de El Greco, y de los españoles Goya y Velázquez. Diego Velázquez pintó *(painted) Las meninas* en 1656 y es su obra más famosa. Actualmente, *Las meninas* está en el Museo del Prado.

¿Cuál es tu museo favorito? ¿Recuerdas alguna obra de arte que se encuentra en ese museo? ¿Cuál?

Lugares

La Universidad de Salamanca

La Universidad de Salamanca, fundada en 1218, es la más antigua *(oldest)* de España. Alrededor de 32.000 estudiantes toman clases en esta institución. La universidad está en la ciudad de Salamanca, famosa por sus edificios históricos, tales como *(such as)* los puentes *(bridges)* romanos y las catedrales góticas.

¿Cuál es la universidad más antigua que conoces? ¿Sabes en qué año fue fundada?

Comida

La paella ▶

La paella es uno de los platos más típicos de España. Siempre se prepara con arroz y azafrán *(saffron)*, pero hay diferentes recetas *(recipes)*. La paella valenciana, por ejemplo, es de pollo y conejo *(rabbit)*, y la paella marinera es de mariscos.

¿Has probado la paella alguna vez? ¿Te gustó?

¿Qué aprendiste?

1 **¿Cierto o falso?** Indica si estas oraciones son **ciertas** o **falsas**.

	Cierto	Falso
1. La moneda de España es la peseta.	⎯⎯	⎯⎯
2. Hay mariscos en la paella valenciana.	⎯⎯	⎯⎯
3. El flamenco es hoy popular en todo el mundo.	⎯⎯	⎯⎯
4. En Buñol, los tomates son un recurso importante.	⎯⎯	⎯⎯
5. Durante La Tomatina, se tiran pelotas.	⎯⎯	⎯⎯
6. En el Museo del Prado hay miles de pinturas importantes.	⎯⎯	⎯⎯
7. *Las meninas* es la obra más famosa de Botticelli.	⎯⎯	⎯⎯
8. En la ciudad de Salamanca se ve la influencia del Imperio romano en la arquitectura.	⎯⎯	⎯⎯

2 **Preguntas** Contesta estas preguntas.

1. ¿Quién es Rosalía?
2. ¿Qué lugar de Madrid está rodeado por edificios de tres pisos con balcones y pórticos antiguos?
3. ¿Dónde puedes ver *Las meninas*?
4. ¿Cuándo se celebra La Tomatina?
5. ¿Cuáles son los dos ingredientes básicos de la paella?

3 **¿Qué piensas?** Piensa en estas preguntas.

1. ¿Por qué crees que el flamenco es tan popular en todo el mundo?
2. ¿Qué piensas de La Tomatina?
3. ¿Cómo crees que empezó La Tomatina?
4. ¿Qué te dice la Plaza Mayor sobre los residentes de Madrid?
5. ¿Por qué crees que hay diferentes recetas para la paella?
6. ¿Cuál es tu opinión de *Las meninas*?

4 **Comparaciones** Escribe un párrafo haciendo una de estas comparaciones.

- el flamenco con otro género musical
- La Tomatina con otro festival
- El Prado con otro museo
- la Universidad de Salamanca con otra universidad
- la paella con otro plato

I CAN identify basic facts about the geography and culture of Spain by reading short informational texts with visuals.

Apéndice A

Maps   436–439

Apéndice B

Glossary of
Grammatical Terms   440–443

Apéndice C

Verb Conjugation Tables   444–453

Vocabulario

Spanish–English   454–467
English–Spanish   469–483

Índice

485–488

Credits

489–492

About the Authors

493

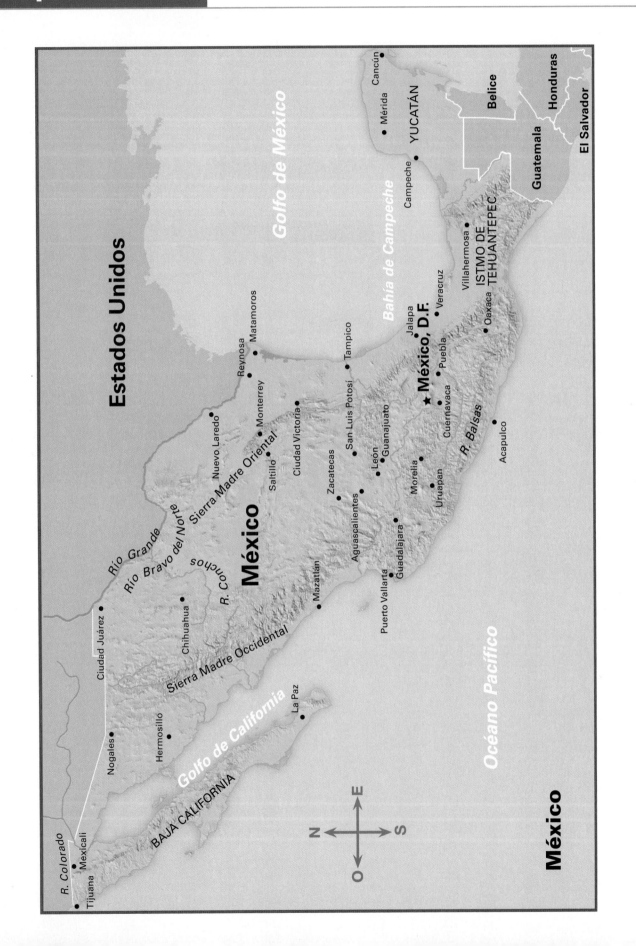

Estados Unidos

Golfo de México

R. Colorado
Mexicali
Tijuana
Nogales
Hermosillo
Ciudad Juárez
Chihuahua
R. Conchos
Río Grande
Río Bravo del Norte
Sierra Madre Occidental
Sierra Madre Oriental
Nuevo Laredo
Monterrey
Reynosa
Matamoros
Saltillo
Ciudad Victoria
Zacatecas
Mazatlán
Aguascalientes
San Luis Potosí
Tampico
León
Guanajuato
Guadalajara
Puerto Vallarta
Morelia
Uruapan
Cuernavaca
Puebla
México, D.F.
Jalapa
Veracruz
Villahermosa
Oaxaca
Acapulco
R. Balsas
ISTMO DE TEHUANTEPEC
Bahía de Campeche
Campeche
YUCATÁN
Mérida
Cancún
Belice
Guatemala
Honduras
El Salvador

México

BAJA CALIFORNIA
Golfo de California
La Paz
Océano Pacífico

N
E
S
O

México

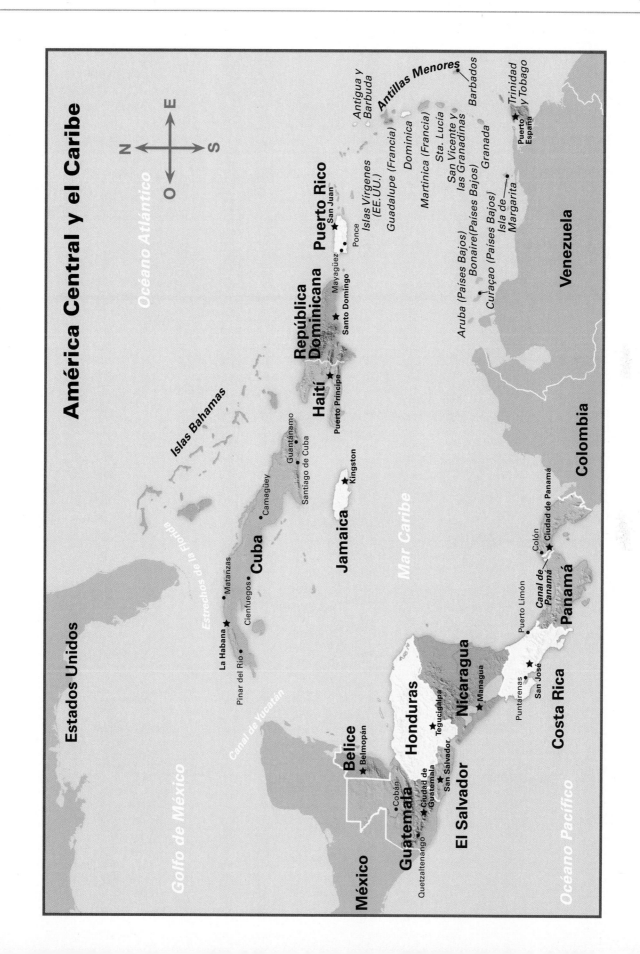

América Central y el Caribe

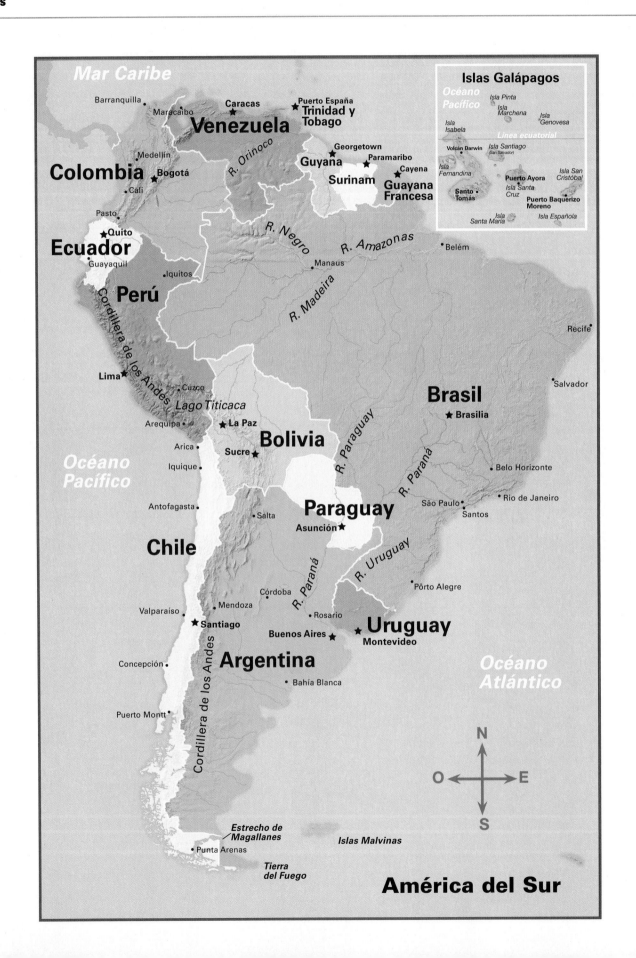

Mar Caribe

Barranquilla
Maracaibo
★ Caracas
Venezuela
Puerto España
★ Trinidad y Tobago

Medellín
Colombia
★ Bogotá
Cali

Georgetown
Guyana ★ Paramaribo
Surinam ● Cayena
Guayana Francesa

R. Orinoco

Pasto
Quito ★
Ecuador
Guayaquil
Iquitos

R. Negro
R. Amazonas
● Belém
Manaus

Perú

R. Madeira

Cordillera de los Andes

Recife

Lima ★
Cuzco
Lago Titicaca

Brasil
● Salvador
★ Brasilia

Arequipa
★ La Paz
Bolivia

Océano Pacífico

Arica
Sucre ★
Iquique

R. Paraguay
R. Paraná

Belo Horizonte

Antofagasta

Paraguay
São Paulo ● Rio de Janeiro
Santos

● Salta
Asunción ★

Chile

R. Paraná
R. Uruguay

Pôrto Alegre

Córdoba
Mendoza
Valparaíso
★ Santiago

R. Paraná
● Rosario
Buenos Aires ★
Uruguay
Montevideo

Océano Atlántico

Concepción

Argentina
● Bahía Blanca

Cordillera de los Andes

Puerto Montt

N
O ← → E
S

Estrecho de Magallanes
Islas Malvinas
● Punta Arenas
Tierra del Fuego

América del Sur

Islas Galápagos

Océano Pacífico
Isla Pinta
Isla Marchena
Isla Genovesa
Isla Isabela
Línea ecuatorial
Volcán Darwin
Isla Santiago (San Salvador)
Isla Fernandina
Puerto Ayora
Isla San Cristóbal
Santo Tomás
Isla Santa Cruz
Puerto Baquerizo Moreno
Isla Santa María
Isla Española

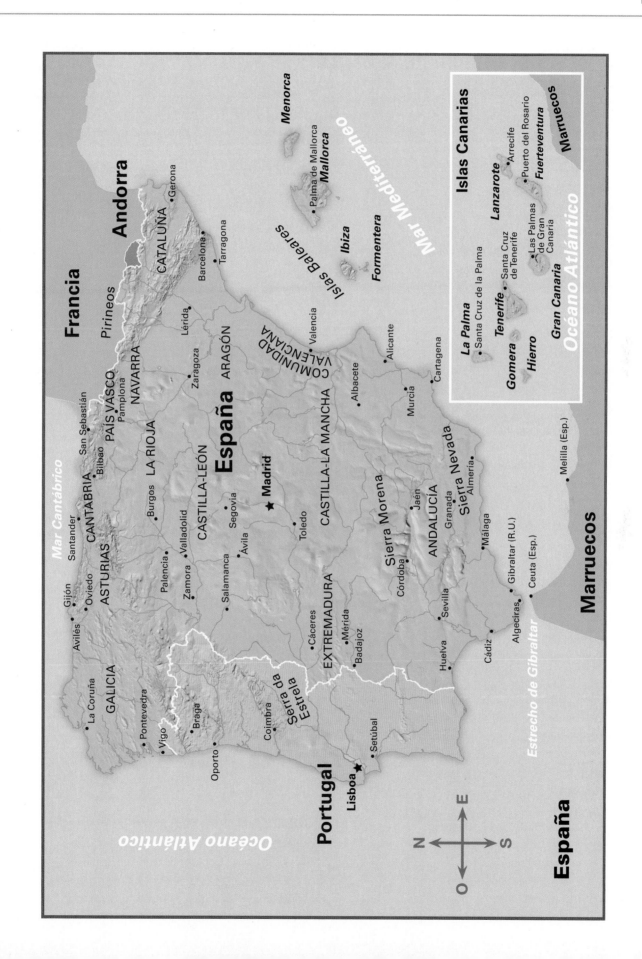

Glossary of Grammatical Terms

ADJECTIVE A word that modifies or describes a noun or pronoun.

muchos libros
many books

un hombre **rico**
*a **rich** man*

las mujeres **altas**
*the **tall** women*

Demonstrative adjective An adjective that points out a specific noun.

esta fiesta
***this** party*

ese chico
***that** boy*

aquellas flores
***those** flowers*

Possessive adjective An adjective that indicates ownership or possession.

mi mejor vestido
***my** best dress*

Éste es **mi** hermano.
*This is **my** brother.*

Stressed possessive adjective A possessive adjective that emphasizes the owner or possessor.

Es un libro **mío**.
*It's **my book**./It's a book **of mine**.*

Es amiga **tuya**; yo no la conozco.
*She's a friend **of yours**; I don't know her.*

ADVERB A word that modifies or describes a verb, adjective, or another adverb.

Pancho escribe **rápidamente**.
*Pancho writes **quickly**.*

Este cuadro es **muy** bonito.
*This picture is **very** pretty.*

ARTICLE A word that points out either a specific (definite) noun or a non-specific (indefinite) noun.

Definite article An article that points out a specific noun.

el libro
***the** book*

la maleta
***the** suitcase*

los diccionarios
***the** dictionaries*

las palabras
***the** words*

Indefinite article An article that points out a noun in a general, non-specific way.

un lápiz
***a** pencil*

una computadora
***a** computer*

unos pájaros
***some** birds*

unas escuelas
***some** schools*

CLAUSE A group of words that contains both a conjugated verb and a subject, either expressed or implied.

Main (or Independent) clause A clause that can stand alone as a complete sentence.

Pienso ir a cenar pronto.
I plan to go to dinner soon.

Subordinate (or Dependent) clause A clause that does not express a complete thought and therefore cannot stand alone as a sentence.

Trabajo en la cafetería **porque necesito dinero para la escuela**.
*I work in the cafeteria **because I need money for school**.*

COMPARATIVE A word or construction used with an adjective, adverb, or noun to express a comparison between two people, places, or things.

Este programa es **más interesante que** el otro.
*This program is **more interesting than** the other one.*

Tomás no es **tan alto como** Alberto.
*Tomás is not **as tall as** Alberto.*

CONJUGATION A set of the forms of a verb for a specific tense or mood, or the process by which these verb forms are presented.

Preterite conjugation of **cantar**:

cant**é**	cant**amos**
cant**aste**	cant**asteis**
cant**ó**	cant**aron**

CONJUNCTION A word or phrase used to connect words, clauses, or phrases.

Susana es de Cuba **y** Pedro es de España.
*Susana is from Cuba **and** Pedro is from Spain.*

No quiero estudiar, **pero** tengo que hacerlo.
*I don't want to study, **but** I have to do it.*

CONTRACTION The joining of two words into one. The only contractions in Spanish are **al** and **del**.

Mi hermano fue **al** concierto ayer.
*My brother went **to the** concert yesterday.*

Saqué dinero **del** banco.
*I took money **from the** bank.*

DIRECT OBJECT A noun or pronoun that directly receives the action of the verb.

Tomás lee **el libro**.   **La** pagó ayer.
*Tomás reads **the book**.*   *She paid **it** yesterday.*

GENDER The grammatical categorizing of certain kinds of words, such as nouns and pronouns, as masculine, feminine, or neuter.

Masculine
articles **el**, un
pronouns **él**, **lo**, **mío**, **éste**, **ése**, aquél
adjective simpátic**o**

Feminine
articles **la**, un**a**
pronouns **ella**, **la**, **mía**, **ésta**, **ésa**, aquéll**a**
adjective simpátic**a**

IMPERSONAL EXPRESSION A third-person expression with no expressed or specific subject.

Es muy importante.   **Llueve** mucho.
It's very important.   *It's raining hard.*

Aquí **se habla** español.
*Spanish **is spoken** here.*

INDIRECT OBJECT A noun or pronoun that receives the action of the verb indirectly; the object, often a living being, to or for whom an action is performed.

Eduardo **le** dio un libro **a Linda**.
*Eduardo gave a book **to Linda**.*

Carlos **me** prestó cincuenta pesos.
*Carlos loaned **me** fifty pesos.*

INFINITIVE The basic form of a verb. Infinitives in Spanish end in -**ar**, -**er**, or -**ir**.

hablar   correr   abrir
to speak   *to run*   *to open*

INTERROGATIVE An adjective, adverb, or pronoun used to ask a question.

¿**Quién** habla?   ¿**Cuántos** compraste?
Who *is speaking?*   **How many** *did you buy?*

¿**Qué** piensas hacer hoy?
What *do you plan to do today?*

INVERSION Changing the word order of a sentence, often to form a question.

Statement: Elena pagó la cuenta del restaurante.

Inversion: ¿Pagó Elena la cuenta del restaurante?

MOOD A grammatical distinction of verbs that indicates whether the verb is intended to make a statement or command, or to express doubt, emotion, or a condition contrary to fact.

Imperative mood Verb forms used to make commands.

Di la verdad.   **Caminen** ustedes conmigo.
Tell *the truth.*   **Walk** *with me.*

¡**Comamos** ahora!
Let's eat *now!*

Indicative mood Verb forms used to state facts, actions, and states considered to be real.

Sé que **tienes** el dinero.
I know *that **you have** the money.*

Subjunctive mood Verb forms used principally in subordinate (or dependent) clauses to express wishes, desires, emotions, doubts, and certain conditions, such as contrary-to-fact situations.

Prefieren que **hables** en español.
*They prefer that **you speak** in Spanish.*

Dudo que Luis **tenga** el dinero necesario.
*I doubt that Luis **has** the necessary money.*

NOUN A word that identifies people, animals, places, things, and ideas.

hombre   gato
man   *cat*

México   casa
Mexico   *house*

libertad   libro
freedom   *book*

NUMBER A grammatical term that refers to singular or plural. Nouns in Spanish and English have number. Other parts of a sentence, such as adjectives, articles, and verbs, can also have number.

Singular	Plural
una cosa	**unas** cosas
a thing	*some things*
el profesor	**los** profesor**es**
the professor	*the professors*

NUMBERS Words that represent amounts.

Cardinal numbers Words that show specific amounts.

cinco minutos
five minutes

el año **dos mil diecinueve**
the year 2019

Ordinal numbers Words that indicate the order of a noun in a series.

el **cuarto** jugador	la **décima** hora
the fourth player	*the tenth hour*

PAST PARTICIPLE A past form of the verb used in compound tenses. The past participle may also be used as an adjective, but it must then agree in number and gender with the word it modifies.

Han **buscado** por todas partes.
They have searched everywhere.

Yo no había **estudiado** para el examen.
I hadn't studied for the exam.

Hay una **ventana rota** en la sala.
There is a broken window in the living room.

PERSON The form of the verb or pronoun that indicates the speaker, the one spoken to, or the one spoken about. In Spanish, as in English, there are three persons: first, second, and third.

Person	Singular		Plural	
1st	**yo**	*I*	**nosotros/as**	*we*
2nd	**tú, Ud.**	*you*	**vosotros/as, Uds.**	*you*
3rd	**él, ella**	*he/she*	**ellos, ellas**	*they*

PREPOSITION A word that describes the relationship, most often in time or space, between two other words.

Anita es **de** California.
Anita is from California.

La chaqueta está **en** el carro.
The jacket is in the car.

¿Quieres hablar **con** ella?
Do you want to talk to her?

PRESENT PARTICIPLE In English, a verb form that ends in *-ing*. In Spanish, the present participle ends in **–ndo**, and is often used with **estar** to form a progressive tense.

Mi hermana está **hablando** por teléfono ahora mismo.
My sister is talking on the phone right now.

PRONOUN A word that takes the place of a noun or nouns.

Demonstrative pronoun A pronoun that takes the place of a specific noun.

Quiero **ésta**.
I want this one.

¿Vas a comprar **ése**?
Are you going to buy that one?

Juan prefirió **aquéllos**.
Juan preferred those (over there).

Object pronoun A pronoun that functions as a direct or indirect object of the verb.

Te digo la verdad.
I'm telling you the truth.

Me lo trajo Juan.
Juan brought it to me.

Reflexive pronoun A pronoun that indicates that the action of a verb is performed by the subject on itself. These pronouns are often expressed in English with *-self: myself, yourself,* etc.

Yo **me bañé** antes de salir.
I bathed (myself) before going out.

Elena **se acostó** a las once y media.
Elena went to bed at eleven-thirty.

Relative pronoun A pronoun that connects a subordinate clause to a main clause.

El chico **que** nos escribió viene a visitarnos mañana.
*The boy **who** wrote us is coming to visit us tomorrow.*

Ya sé **lo que** tenemos que hacer.
*I already know **what** we have to do.*

Subject pronoun A pronoun that replaces the name or title of a person or thing and acts as the subject of a verb.

Tú debes estudiar más.
***You** should study more.*

Él llegó primero.
***He** arrived first.*

SUBJECT A noun or pronoun that performs the action of a verb and is often implied by the verb.

María va al supermercado.
***María** goes to the supermarket.*

(Ellos) Trabajan mucho.
***They** work hard.*

Esos **libros** son muy caros.
*Those **books** are very expensive.*

SUPERLATIVE A word or construction used with an adjective or adverb to express the highest or lowest degree of a specific quality among three or more people, places, or things.

Entre todas mis clases, ésta es **la más interesante**.
*Among all my classes, this is **the most interesting**.*

Raúl es **el menos simpático** de los chicos.
*Raúl is **the least pleasant** of the boys.*

TENSE A set of verb forms that indicates the time of an action or state: past, present, or future.

Compound tense A two-word tense made up of an auxiliary verb and a present or past participle. In Spanish, **estar** and **haber** are often auxiliary verbs.

En este momento, **estoy estudiando**.
*At this time, **I am studying**.*

El paquete no **ha llegado** todavía.
*The package **has not arrived** yet.*

Simple tense A tense expressed by a single verb form.

María **estaba** mal anoche.
*María **was** sick last night.*

Juana **hablará** con su mamá mañana.
*Juana **will speak** with her mom tomorrow.*

VERB A word that expresses actions or states of being.

Auxiliary verb A verb used with a present or past participle to form a compound tense. **Haber** is the most commonly used auxiliary verb in Spanish.

Los chicos **han** visto los elefantes.
*The children **have** seen the elephants.*

Espero que **hayas** comido.
*I hope you **have** eaten.*

Reflexive verb A verb that describes an action performed by the subject on itself and is always used with a reflexive pronoun.

Me compré un carro nuevo.
***I bought myself** a new car.*

Pedro y Adela **se levantan** muy temprano.
*Pedro and Adela **get (themselves) up** very early.*

Spelling change verb A verb that undergoes a predictable change in spelling in order to reflect its actual pronunciation in the various conjugations.

practicar	c → qu	practi**c**o	practi**qué**
dirigir	g → j	diri**j**o	diri**gí**
almorzar	z → c	almor**z**ó	almor**cé**

Stem-changing verb A verb whose stem vowel undergoes one or more predictable changes in the various conjugations.

ent**e**nder (e:ie)	ent**ie**ndo
p**e**dir (e:i)	p**i**den
d**o**rmir (o:ue, u)	d**ue**rmo, d**u**rmieron

Verb Conjugation Tables

The verb lists

The list of verbs below and the model-verb tables that start on page 446 show you how to conjugate the verbs taught in **Aventuras**. Each verb in the list is followed by a model verb conjugated according to the same pattern. The number in parentheses indicates where in the tables you can find the conjugated forms of the model verb. If you want to find out how to conjugate **divertirse**, for example, look up number 33, **sentir**, the model for verbs that follow the **e:ie** stem-change pattern.

How to use the verb tables

In the tables you will find the infinitive, present and past participles, and all the simple forms of each model verb. The formation of the compound tenses of any verb can be inferred from the table of compound tenses, pages 446–453, either by combining the past participle of the verb with a conjugated form of **haber** or combining the present participle with a conjugated form of **estar**.

---

abrir like vivir (3) *except* past participle is **abierto**

aburrir(se) like vivir (3)

acabar like hablar (1)

acampar like hablar (1)

aconsejar like hablar (1)

acordar(se) (o:ue) like contar (24)

acostar(se) (o:ue) like contar (24)

adelgazar (z:c) like cruzar (37)

afeitar(se) like hablar (1)

ahorrar like hablar (1)

alegrar(se) like hablar (1)

aliviar like hablar (1)

almorzar (o:ue) like contar (24) *except* (z:c)

alquilar like hablar (1)

apagar (g:gu) like llegar (41)

aprender like comer (2)

apurar(se) like hablar (1)

arrancar (c:qu) like tocar (44)

arreglar like hablar (1)

asistir like vivir (3)

aumentar like hablar (1)

bailar like hablar (1)

bajar(se) like hablar (1)

bañar(se) like hablar (1)

barrer like comer (2)

beber like comer (2)

brindar like hablar (1)

bucear like hablar (1)

buscar (c:qu) like tocar (44)

caer(se) (5)

calentarse (e:ie) like pensar (30)

cambiar like hablar (1)

caminar like hablar (1)

cantar like hablar (1)

cargar like llegar (41)

casarse like hablar (1)

celebrar like hablar (1)

cenar like hablar (1)

cepillar(se) like hablar (1)

cerrar (e:ie) like pensar (30)

chatear like hablar (1)

chocar (c:qu) like tocar (44)

cobrar like hablar (1)

cocinar like hablar (1)

comenzar (e:ie) (z:c) like empezar (26)

comer (2)

compartir like vivir (3)

comprar like hablar (1)

comprender like comer (2)

comprometerse like comer (2)

conducir (c:zc) (6)

conectar(se) like hablar (1)

confirmar like hablar (1)

conocer (c:zc) (35)

conseguir (e:i) (g:gu) like seguir (32)

conservar like hablar (1)

consumir like vivir (3)

contaminar like hablar (1)

contar (o:ue) (24)

contestar like hablar (1)

contratar like hablar (1)

controlar like hablar (1)

conversar like hablar (1)

correr like comer (2)

costar (o:ue) like contar (24)

creer (y) (36)

cruzar (z:c) (37)

cuidar like hablar (1)

cumplir like vivir (3)

dañar like hablar (1)

dar(se) (7)

deber like comer (2)

decidir like vivir (3)

decir (e:i) (8)

dejar like hablar (1)

depositar like hablar (1)

desarrollar like hablar (1)

desayunar like hablar (1)

descansar like hablar (1)

descargar like llegar (41)

describir like vivir (3) *except* past participle is **descrito**

descubrir like vivir (3) *except* past participle is **descubierto**

desear like hablar (1)

despedir (e:i) like pedir (29)

despertar(se) (e:ie) like pensar (30)

destruir (y) (38)

dibujar like hablar (1)

disfrutar like hablar (1)

divertirse (e:ie) like sentir (33)

divorciarse like hablar (1)

doblar like hablar (1)

doler (o:ue) like volver (34) *except* past participle is regular

dormir(se) (o:ue, u) (25)

duchar(se) like hablar (1)

dudar like hablar (1)

echar like hablar (1)

empezar (e:ie) (z:c) (26)

enamorarse like hablar (1)

encantar like hablar (1)

encontrar (o:ue) like contar (24)

enfermarse like hablar (1)

engordar like hablar (1)

enojar(se) like hablar (1)

enseñar like hablar (1)

ensuciar like hablar (1)

entender (e:ie) (27)

entrenar(se) like hablar (1)

entrevistar like hablar (1)

enviar (envío) (39)

escalar like hablar (1)

escanear like hablar (1)

escribir like vivir (3) *except* past participle is **escrito**

escuchar like hablar (1)

esperar like hablar (1)

esquiar (esquío) like enviar (39)
estacionar like hablar (1)
estar (9)
estornudar like hablar (1)
estudiar like hablar (1)
evitar like hablar (1)
explicar (c:qu) like tocar (44)
faltar like hablar (1)
fascinar like hablar (1)
firmar like hablar (1)
fumar like hablar (1)
funcionar like hablar (1)
ganar like hablar (1)
gastar like hablar (1)
grabar like hablar (1)
graduarse (gradúo) (40)
guardar like hablar (1)
gustar like hablar (1)
haber (hay) (10)
hablar (1)
hacer (11)
importar like hablar (1)
imprimir like vivir (3)
indicar (c:qu) like tocar (44)
insistir like vivir (3)
interesar like hablar (1)
invertir (e:ie) like sentir (33)
invitar like hablar (1)
ir(se) (12)
jubilarse like hablar (1)
jugar (u:ue) (g:gu) (28)
lastimar(se) like hablar (1)
lavar(se) like hablar (1)
leer (y) like creer (36)
levantar(se) like hablar (1)
limpiar like hablar (1)
llamar(se) like hablar (1)
llegar (g:gu) (41)
llenar like hablar (1)
llevar(se) like hablar (1)
llover (o:ue) like volver (34) *except*
past participle is regular
mandar like hablar (1)
manejar like hablar (1)
mantenerse (e:ie) like tener (20)

maquillar(se) like hablar (1)
mejorar like hablar (1)
merendar (e:ie) like pensar (30)
mirar like hablar (1)
molestar like hablar (1)
montar like hablar (1)
morir (o:ue) like dormir (25)
except past participle is **muerto**
mostrar (o:ue) like contar (24)
mudarse like hablar (1)
nacer (c:zc) like conocer (35)
nadar like hablar (1)
necesitar like hablar (1)
negar (e:ie) like pensar (30)
except (g:gu)
nevar (e:ie) like pensar (30)
obtener (e:ie) like tener (20)
odiar like hablar (1)
ofrecer (c:zc) like conocer (35)
oír (13)
olvidar like hablar (1)
pagar (g:gu) like llegar (41)
parar like hablar (1)
parecer (c:zc) like conocer (35)
pasar like hablar (1)
pasear like hablar (1)
patinar like hablar (1)
pedir (e:i) (29)
peinar(se) like hablar (1)
pensar (e:ie) (30)
perder (e:ie) like entender (27)
pescar (c:qu) like tocar (44)
planchar like hablar (1)
poder (o:ue) (14)
poner(se) (15)
practicar (c:qu) like tocar (44)
preferir (e:ie) like sentir (33)
preguntar like hablar (1)
prender like comer (2)
preocupar(se) like hablar (1)
preparar like hablar (1)
prestar like hablar (1)
probar(se) (o:ue) like contar (24)
prohibir (42)
proteger (g:j) (43)

quedar(se) like hablar (1)
querer (e:ie) (16)
quitar(se) like hablar (1)
recetar like hablar (1)
recibir like vivir (3)
reciclar like hablar (1)
recoger (g:j) like proteger (43)
recomendar (e:ie) like pensar (30)
recordar (o:ue) like contar (24)
reducir (c:zc) like conducir (6)
regalar like hablar (1)
regatear like hablar (1)
regresar like hablar (1)
reír(se) (e:i) (31)
relajarse like hablar (1)
renunciar like hablar (1)
repetir (e:i) like pedir (29)
resolver (o:ue) like volver (34)
respirar like hablar (1)
revisar like hablar (1)
rogar (o:ue) like contar (24)
except (g:gu)
romper(se) like comer (2) *except*
past participle is **roto**
saber (17)
sacar(se) (c:qu) like tocar (44)
sacudir like vivir (3)
salir (18)
seguir (e:i) (32)
sentarse (e:ie) like pensar (30)
sentir(se) (e:ie) (33)
separarse like hablar (1)
ser (19)
servir (e:i) like pedir (29)
solicitar like hablar (1)
sonar (o:ue) like contar (24)
sonreír (e:i) like reír(se) (31)
sorprender like comer (2)
subir like vivir (3)
sudar like hablar (1)
sufrir like vivir (3)
sugerir (e:ie) like sentir (33)
suponer like poner (15)
temer like comer (2)
tener (e:ie) (20)

terminar like hablar (1)
textear like hablar (1)
tomar like hablar (1)
torcerse (o:ue)
like volver (34) *except* (c:z)
and past participle is regular;
e.g., **yo tuerzo**
toser like comer (2)
trabajar like hablar (1)
traducir (c:zc) like conducir (6)
traer (21)
tratar like hablar (1)
usar like hablar (1)
vender like comer (2)
venir (e:ie) (22)
ver (23)
vestir(se) (e:i) like pedir (29)
viajar like hablar (1)
visitar like hablar (1)
vivir (3)
volver (o:ue) (34)

Regular verbs: simple tenses

Infinitive	INDICATIVE					SUBJUNCTIVE		IMPERATIVE
	Present	Imperfect	Preterite	Future	Conditional	Present	Past	
1 hablar	hablo	hablaba	hablé	hablaré	hablaría	hable	hablara	
	hablas	hablabas	hablaste	hablarás	hablarías	hables	hablaras	habla tú (no hables)
Participles:	habla	hablaba	habló	hablará	hablaría	hable	hablara	hable Ud.
hablando	hablamos	hablábamos	hablamos	hablaremos	hablaríamos	hablemos	habláramos	hablemos
hablado	habláis	hablabais	hablasteis	hablaréis	hablaríais	habléis	hablarais	hablad (no habléis)
	hablan	hablaban	hablaron	hablarán	hablarían	hablen	hablaran	hablen Uds.
2 comer	como	comía	comí	comeré	comería	coma	comiera	
	comes	comías	comiste	comerás	comerías	comas	comieras	come tú (no comas)
Participles:	come	comía	comió	comerá	comerían	coma	comiera	coma Ud.
comiendo	comemos	comíamos	comimos	comeremos	comeríamos	comamos	comiéramos	comamos
comido	coméis	comíais	comisteis	comeréis	comeríais	comáis	comierais	comed (no comáis)
	comen	comían	comieron	comerán	comerían	coman	comieran	coman Uds.
3 vivir	vivo	vivía	viví	viviré	viviría	viva	viviera	
	vives	vivías	viviste	vivirás	vivirías	vivas	vivieran	vive tú (no vivas)
Participles:	vive	vivía	vivió	vivirá	viviría	viva	viviera	viva Ud.
viviendo	vivimos	vivíamos	vivimos	viviremos	viviríamos	vivamos	viviéramos	vivamos
vivido	vivís	vivíais	vivisteis	viviréis	viviríais	viváis	vivierais	vivid (no viváis)
	viven	vivían	vivieron	vivirán	vivirían	vivan	vivieran	vivan Uds.

All verbs: compound tenses

PERFECT TENSES					
INDICATIVE				SUBJUNCTIVE	
Present Perfect	Past Perfect	Future Perfect	Conditional Perfect	Present Perfect	Past Perfect
he	había	habré	habría	haya	hubiera
has	habías	habrás	habrías	hayas	hubieras
ha hablado	había hablado	habrá hablado	habría hablado	haya hablado	hubiera hablado
hemos comido	habíamos comido	habremos comido	habríamos comido	hayamos comido	hubiéramos comido
habéis vivido	habíais vivido	habréis vivido	habríais vivido	hayáis vivido	hubierais vivido
han	habían	habrán	habrían	hayan	hubieran

PROGRESSIVE TENSES

INDICATIVE				SUBJUNCTIVE	
Present Progressive	Past Progressive	Future Progressive	Conditional Progressive	Present Progressive	Past Progressive
estoy	estaba	estaré	estaría	esté	estuviera
estás	estabas	estarás	estarías	estés	estuvieras
está	estaba	estará	estaría	esté	estuviera
estamos hablando comiendo viviendo	estábamos hablando comiendo viviendo	estaremos hablando comiendo viviendo	estaríamos hablando comiendo viviendo	estemos hablando comiendo viviendo	estuviéramos hablando comiendo viviendo
estáis	estabais	estaréis	estaríais	estéis	estuvierais
están	estaban	estarán	estarían	estén	estuvieran

Irregular verbs

Infinitive	INDICATIVE					SUBJUNCTIVE		IMPERATIVE
	Present	Imperfect	Preterite	Future	Conditional	Present	Past	
4 caber	**quepo**	cabía	**cupe**	**cabré**	**cabría**	**quepa**	**cupiera**	
	cabes	cabías	**cupiste**	**cabrás**	**cabrías**	**quepas**	**cupieras**	cabe tú (no **quepas**)
Participles:	cabe	cabía	**cupo**	**cabrá**	**cabría**	**quepa**	**cupiera**	**quepa** Ud.
cabiendo	cabemos	cabíamos	**cupimos**	**cabremos**	**cabríamos**	**quepamos**	**cupiéramos**	**quepamos**
cabido	cabéis	cabíais	**cupisteis**	**cabréis**	**cabríais**	**quepáis**	**cupierais**	cabed (no **quepáis**)
	caben	cabían	**cupieron**	**cabrán**	**cabrían**	**quepan**	**cupieran**	**quepan** Uds.
5 caer(se)	**caigo**	caía	caí	caeré	caería	**caiga**	**cayera**	
	caes	caías	**caíste**	caerás	caerías	**caigas**	**cayeras**	cae tú (no **caigas**)
Participles:	cae	caía	**cayó**	caerá	caería	**caiga**	**cayera**	**caiga** Ud.
cayendo	caemos	caíamos	**caímos**	caeremos	caeríamos	**caigamos**	**cayéramos**	**caigamos**
caído	caéis	caíais	**caísteis**	caeréis	caeríais	**caigáis**	**cayerais**	caed (no **caigáis**)
	caen	caían	**cayeron**	caerán	caerían	**caigan**	**cayeran**	**caigan** Uds.
6 conducir (c:zc)	**conduzco**	conducía	**conduje**	conduciré	conduciría	**conduzca**	**condujera**	
	conduces	conducías	**condujiste**	conducirás	conducirías	**conduzcas**	**condujeras**	conduce tú (no **conduzcas**)
	conduce	conducía	**condujo**	conducirá	conduciría	**conduzca**	**condujera**	**conduzca** Ud.
Participles:	conducimos	conducíamos	**condujimos**	conduciremos	conduciríamos	**conduzcamos**	**condujéramos**	**conduzcamos**
conduciendo	conducís	conducíais	**condujisteis**	conduciréis	conduciríais	**conduzcáis**	**condujerais**	conducid (no **conduzcáis**)
conducido	conducen	conducían	**condujeron**	conducirán	conducirían	**conduzcan**	**condujeran**	**conduzcan** Uds.

		INDICATIVE				SUBJUNCTIVE		IMPERATIVE
Infinitive	**Present**	**Imperfect**	**Preterite**	**Future**	**Conditional**	**Present**	**Past**	
7 dar	**doy**	daba	**di**	daré	daría	**dé**	diera	
	das	dabas	**diste**	darás	darías	**des**	dieras	da tú (no des)
Participles:	da	daba	**dio**	dará	daría	**dé**	diera	**dé** Ud.
dando	damos	dábamos	**dimos**	daremos	daríamos	**demos**	diéramos	**demos**
dado	dais	dabais	**disteis**	daréis	daríais	**deis**	dierais	dad (no **deis**)
	dan	daban	**dieron**	darán	darían	**den**	dieran	**den** Uds.
8 decir (e:i)	**digo**	decía	**dije**	**diré**	**diría**	diga	dijera	
	dices	decías	**dijiste**	**dirás**	**dirías**	digas	dijeras	**di** tú (no **digas**)
Participles:	**dice**	decía	**dijo**	**dirá**	**diría**	diga	dijera	**diga** Ud.
diciendo	decimos	decíamos	**dijimos**	**diremos**	**diríamos**	digamos	dijéramos	**digamos**
dicho	decís	decíais	**dijisteis**	**diréis**	**diríais**	digáis	dijerais	decid (no **digáis**)
	dicen	decían	**dijeron**	**dirán**	**dirían**	digan	dijeran	**digan** Uds.
9 estar	**estoy**	estaba	**estuve**	estaré	estaría	**esté**	estuviera	
	estás	estabas	**estuviste**	estarás	estarías	**estés**	estuvieras	**está** tú (no **estés**)
Participles:	**está**	estaba	**estuvo**	estará	estaría	**esté**	estuviera	**esté** Ud.
estando	estamos	estábamos	**estuvimos**	estaremos	estaríamos	estemos	**estuviéramos**	estemos
estado	estáis	estabais	**estuvisteis**	estaréis	estaríais	estéis	**estuvierais**	estad (no estéis)
	están	estaban	**estuvieron**	estarán	estarían	**estén**	estuvieran	**estén** Uds.
10 haber	**he**	había	**hube**	**habré**	**habría**	haya	hubiera	
	has	habías	**hubiste**	**habrás**	**habrías**	hayas	hubieras	
Participles:	**ha**	había	**hubo**	**habrá**	**habría**	haya	hubiera	
habiendo	**hemos**	habíamos	**hubimos**	**habremos**	**habríamos**	hayamos	hubiéramos	
habido	**habéis**	habíais	**hubisteis**	**habréis**	**habríais**	hayáis	hubierais	
	han	habían	**hubieron**	**habrán**	**habrían**	hayan	hubieran	
11 hacer	**hago**	hacía	**hice**	**haré**	**haría**	haga	hiciera	
	haces	hacías	**hiciste**	**harás**	**harías**	hagas	hicieras	**haz** tú (no **hagas**)
Participles:	hace	hacía	**hizo**	**hará**	**haría**	haga	hiciera	**haga** Ud.
haciendo	hacemos	hacíamos	**hicimos**	**haremos**	**haríamos**	hagamos	hiciéramos	**hagamos**
hecho	hacéis	hacíais	**hicisteis**	**haréis**	**haríais**	hagáis	hicierais	haced (no **hagáis**)
	hacen	hacían	**hicieron**	**harán**	**harían**	hagan	hicieran	**hagan** Uds.
12 ir	**voy**	iba	**fui**	iré	iría	vaya	fuera	
	vas	ibas	**fuiste**	irás	irías	vayas	fueras	**ve** tú (no **vayas**)
Participles:	va	iba	**fue**	irá	iría	vaya	fuera	**vaya** Ud.
yendo	vamos	íbamos	**fuimos**	iremos	iríamos	vayamos	fuéramos	**vamos** (no **vayamos**)
ido	vais	ibais	**fuisteis**	iréis	iríais	vayáis	fuerais	id (no **vayáis**)
	van	iban	**fueron**	irán	irían	vayan	fueran	**vayan** Uds.
13 oír (y)	**oigo**	oía	**oí**	oiré	oiría	oiga	oyera	
	oyes	oías	**oíste**	oirás	oirías	oigas	oyeras	**oye** tú (no **oigas**)
Participles:	**oye**	oía	**oyó**	oirá	oiría	oiga	oyera	**oiga** Ud.
oyendo	**oímos**	oíamos	**oímos**	oiremos	oiríamos	oigamos	oyéramos	**oigamos**
oído	**oís**	oíais	**oísteis**	oiréis	oiríais	oigáis	oyerais	oíd (no **oigáis**)
	oyen	oían	**oyeron**	oirán	oirían	oigan	oyeran	**oigan** Uds.

		INDICATIVE				SUBJUNCTIVE		IMPERATIVE
Infinitive	Present	Imperfect	Preterite	Future	Conditional	Present	Past	
14 poder (o:ue)	**puedo**	podía	**pude**	podré	podría	**pueda**	**pudiera**	
	puedes	podías	**pudiste**	podrás	podrías	**puedas**	**pudieras**	**puede** tú (no **puedas**)
Participles:	**puede**	podía	**pudo**	podrá	podría	**pueda**	**pudiera**	**pueda** Ud.
pudiendo	podemos	podíamos	**pudimos**	podremos	podríamos	podamos	**pudiéramos**	podamos
podido	podéis	podíais	**pudisteis**	podréis	podríais	podáis	**pudierais**	poded (no podáis)
	pueden	podían	**pudieron**	podrán	podrían	**puedan**	pudieran	**puedan** Uds.
15 poner	**pongo**	ponía	**puse**	pondré	pondría	**ponga**	**pusiera**	
	pones	ponías	**pusiste**	pondrás	pondrías	**pongas**	**pusieras**	**pon** tú (no **pongas**)
Participles:	pone	ponía	**puso**	pondrá	pondría	**ponga**	**pusiera**	**ponga** Ud.
poniendo	ponemos	poníamos	**pusimos**	pondremos	pondríamos	**pongamos**	**pusiéramos**	**pongamos**
puesto	ponéis	poníais	**pusisteis**	pondréis	pondríais	**pongáis**	**pusierais**	poned (no **pongáis**)
	ponen	ponían	**pusieron**	pondrán	pondrían	**pongan**	**pusieran**	**pongan** Uds.
16 querer (e:ie)	**quiero**	quería	**quise**	**querré**	**querría**	**quiera**	**quisiera**	
	quieres	querías	**quisiste**	**querrás**	**querrías**	**quieras**	**quisieras**	**quiere** tú (no **quieras**)
Participles:	**quiere**	quería	**quiso**	**querrá**	**querría**	**quiera**	**quisiera**	**quiera** Ud.
queriendo	queremos	queríamos	**quisimos**	**querremos**	**querríamos**	queramos	**quisiéramos**	queramos
querido	queréis	queríais	**quisisteis**	**querréis**	**querríais**	queráis	**quisierais**	quered (no queráis)
	quieren	querían	**quisieron**	**querrán**	**querrían**	**quieran**	**quisieran**	**quieran** Uds.
17 saber	**sé**	sabía	**supe**	**sabré**	**sabría**	**sepa**	**supiera**	
	sabes	sabías	**supiste**	**sabrás**	**sabrías**	**sepas**	**supieras**	sabe tú (no **sepas**)
Participles:	sabe	sabía	**supo**	**sabrá**	**sabría**	**sepa**	**supiera**	**sepa** Ud.
sabiendo	sabemos	sabíamos	**supimos**	**sabremos**	**sabríamos**	**sepamos**	**supiéramos**	**sepamos**
sabido	sabéis	sabíais	**supisteis**	**sabréis**	**sabríais**	**sepáis**	**supierais**	sabed (no **sepáis**)
	saben	sabían	**supieron**	**sabrán**	**sabrían**	**sepan**	**supieran**	**sepan** Uds.
18 salir	**salgo**	salía	salí	**saldré**	**saldría**	**salga**	saliera	
	sales	salías	saliste	**saldrás**	**saldrías**	**salgas**	salieras	**sal** tú (no **salgas**)
Participles:	sale	salía	salió	**saldrá**	**saldría**	**salga**	saliera	**salga** Ud.
saliendo	salimos	salíamos	salimos	**saldremos**	**saldríamos**	**salgamos**	saliéramos	**salgamos**
salido	salís	salíais	salisteis	**saldréis**	**saldríais**	**salgáis**	salierais	salid (no **salgáis**)
	salen	salían	salieron	**saldrán**	**saldrían**	**salgan**	salieran	**salgan** Uds.
19 ser	**soy**	era	**fui**	seré	sería	**sea**	**fuera**	
	eres	eras	**fuiste**	serás	serías	**seas**	**fueras**	**sé** tú (no **seas**)
Participles:	es	era	**fue**	será	sería	**sea**	**fuera**	sea Ud.
siendo	**somos**	**éramos**	**fuimos**	seremos	seríamos	**seamos**	**fuéramos**	**seamos**
sido	**sois**	erais	**fuisteis**	seréis	seríais	**seáis**	fuerais	sed (no **seáis**)
	son	eran	**fueron**	serán	serían	sean	fueran	sean Uds.
20 tener	**tengo**	tenía	**tuve**	**tendré**	**tendría**	**tenga**	**tuviera**	
	tienes	tenías	**tuviste**	**tendrás**	**tendrías**	**tengas**	**tuvieras**	**ten** tú (no **tengas**)
Participles:	**tiene**	tenía	**tuvo**	**tendrá**	**tendría**	**tenga**	**tuviera**	tenga Ud.
teniendo	tenemos	teníamos	**tuvimos**	**tendremos**	**tendríamos**	**tengamos**	**tuviéramos**	**tengamos**
tenido	tenéis	teníais	**tuvisteis**	**tendréis**	**tendríais**	**tengáis**	**tuvierais**	tened (no **tengáis**)
	tienen	tenían	**tuvieron**	**tendrán**	**tendrían**	**tengan**	**tuvieran**	**tengan** Uds.

	Infinitive	INDICATIVE					SUBJUNCTIVE		IMPERATIVE
		Present	Imperfect	Preterite	Future	Conditional	Present	Past	
21	traer	**traigo**	traía	**traje**	traeré	traería	**traiga**	**trajera**	
		traes	traías	**trajiste**	traerás	traerías	**traigas**	**trajeras**	trae tú (no **traigas**)
	Participles:	trae	traía	**trajo**	traerá	traería	**traiga**	**trajera**	**traiga** Ud.
	trayendo	traemos	traíamos	**trajimos**	traeremos	traeríamos	**traigamos**	**trajéramos**	**traigamos**
	traído	traéis	traíais	**trajisteis**	traeréis	traeríais	**traigáis**	**trajerais**	traed (no **traigáis**)
		traen	traían	**trajeron**	traerán	traerían	**traigan**	**trajeran**	**traigan** Uds.
22	venir	**vengo**	venía	**vine**	**vendré**	**vendría**	**venga**	**viniera**	
		vienes	venías	**viniste**	**vendrás**	**vendrías**	**vengas**	**vinieras**	**ven** tú (no **vengas**)
	Participles:	**viene**	venía	**vino**	**vendrá**	**vendría**	**venga**	**viniera**	**venga** Ud.
	viniendo	venimos	veníamos	**vinimos**	**vendremos**	**vendríamos**	**vengamos**	**viniéramos**	**vengamos**
	venido	venís	veníais	**vinisteis**	**vendréis**	**vendríais**	**vengáis**	**vinierais**	venid (no **vengáis**)
		vienen	venían	**vinieron**	**vendrán**	**vendrían**	**vengan**	**vinieran**	**vengan** Uds.
23	ver	**veo**	**veía**	**vi**	veré	vería	**vea**	**viera**	
		ves	**veías**	**viste**	verás	verías	**veas**	**vieras**	**ve** tú (no **veas**)
	Participles:	ve	**veía**	**vio**	verá	vería	**vea**	**viera**	**vea** Ud.
	viendo	vemos	**veíamos**	**vimos**	veremos	veríamos	**veamos**	**viéramos**	**veamos**
	visto	veis	**veíais**	**visteis**	veréis	veríais	**veáis**	**vierais**	ved (no **veáis**)
		ven	**veían**	**vieron**	verán	verían	**vean**	**vieran**	**vean** Uds.

Stem-changing verbs

	Infinitive	INDICATIVE					SUBJUNCTIVE		IMPERATIVE
		Present	Imperfect	Preterite	Future	Conditional	Present	Past	
24	contar	**cuento**	contaba	conté	contaré	contaría	**cuente**	contara	
	(o:ue)	**cuentas**	contabas	contaste	contarás	contarías	**cuentes**	contaras	**cuenta** tú (no **cuentes**)
		cuenta	contaba	contó	contará	contaría	**cuente**	contara	**cuente** Ud.
	Participles:	contamos	contábamos	contamos	contaremos	contaríamos	contemos	contáramos	contemos
	contando	contáis	contabais	contasteis	contaréis	contaríais	contéis	contarais	contad (no contéis)
	contado	**cuentan**	contaban	contaron	contarán	contarían	**cuenten**	contaran	**cuenten** Uds.
25	dormir	**duermo**	dormía	dormí	dormiré	dormiría	**duerma**	**durmiera**	
	(o:ue)	**duermes**	dormías	dormiste	dormirás	dormirías	**duermas**	**durmieras**	**duerme** tú (no **duermas**)
		duerme	dormía	**durmió**	dormirá	dormiría	**duerma**	**durmiera**	**duerma** Ud.
	Participles:	dormimos	dormíamos	dormimos	dormiremos	dormiríamos	**durmamos**	**durmiéramos**	**durmamos**
	durmiendo	dormís	dormíais	dormisteis	dormiréis	dormiríais	**durmáis**	**durmierais**	dormid (no **durmáis**)
	dormido	**duermen**	dormían	**durmieron**	dormirán	dormirían	**duerman**	**durmieran**	**duerman** Uds.
26	empezar	**empiezo**	empezaba	**empecé**	empezaré	empezaría	**empiece**	empezara	
	(e:ie) (z:c)	**empiezas**	empezabas	empezaste	empezarás	empezarías	**empieces**	empezaras	**empieza** tú (no **empieces**)
		empieza	empezaba	empezó	empezará	empezaría	**empiece**	empezara	**empiece** Ud.
	Participles:	empezamos	empezábamos	empezamos	empezaremos	empezaríamos	**empecemos**	empezáramos	**empecemos**
	empezando	empezáis	empezabais	empezasteis	empezaréis	empezaríais	**empecéis**	empezarais	empezad (no **empecéis**)
	empezado	**empiezan**	empezaban	empezarán	empezarán	empezarían	**empiecen**	empezaran	**empiecen** Uds.

Infinitive	INDICATIVE					SUBJUNCTIVE		IMPERATIVE
	Present	**Imperfect**	**Preterite**	**Future**	**Conditional**	**Present**	**Past**	
27 entender (e:ie)	**entiendo**	entendía	entendí	entenderé	entendería	**entienda**	entendiera	
	entiendes	entendías	entendiste	entenderás	entenderías	**entiendas**	entendieras	**entiende** tú (no **entiendas**)
	entiende	entendía	entendió	entenderá	entendería	**entienda**	entendiera	**entienda** Ud.
Participles:	entendemos	entendíamos	entendimos	entenderemos	entenderíamos	entendamos	entendiéramos	entendamos
entendiendo	entendéis	entendíais	entendisteis	entenderéis	entenderíais	entendáis	entendierais	entended (no entendáis)
entendido	**entienden**	entendían	entendieron	entenderán	entenderían	**entiendan**	entendieran	**entiendan** Uds.
28 jugar (u:ue) (g:gu)	**juego**	jugaba	**jugué**	jugaré	jugaría	**juegue**	jugara	
	juegas	jugabas	jugaste	jugarás	jugarías	**juegues**	jugaras	**juega** tú (no **juegues**)
	juega	jugaba	jugó	jugará	jugaría	**juegue**	jugara	**juegue** Ud
Participles:	jugamos	jugábamos	jugamos	jugaremos	jugaríamos	juguemos	jugáramos	juguemos
jugando	jugáis	jugabais	jugasteis	jugaréis	jugaríais	juguéis	jugarais	jugad (no juguéis)
jugado	**juegan**	jugaban	jugaron	jugarán	jugarían	**jueguen**	jugaran	**jueguen** Uds.
29 pedir (e:i)	**pido**	pedía	pedí	pediré	pediría	**pida**	**pidiera**	
	pides	pedías	pediste	pedirás	pedirías	**pidas**	**pidieras**	**pide** tú (no **pidas**)
Participles:	**pide**	pedía	**pidió**	pedirá	pediría	**pida**	**pidiera**	**pida** Ud.
pidiendo	pedimos	pedíamos	pedimos	pediremos	pediríamos	**pidamos**	**pidiéramos**	**pidamos**
pedido	pedís	pedíais	pedisteis	pediréis	pediríais	**pidáis**	**pidierais**	pedid (no **pidáis**)
	piden	pedían	**pidieron**	pedirán	pedirían	**pidan**	**pidieran**	**pidan** Uds.
30 pensar (e:ie)	**pienso**	pensaba	pensé	pensaré	pensaría	**piense**	pensara	
	piensas	pensabas	pensaste	pensarás	pensarías	**pienses**	pensaras	**piensa** tú (no **pienses**)
	piensa	pensaba	pensó	pensará	pensaría	**piense**	pensara	**piense** Ud.
Participles:	pensamos	pensábamos	pensamos	pensaremos	pensaríamos	pensemos	pensáramos	pensemos
pensando	pensáis	pensabais	pensasteis	pensaréis	pensaríais	penséis	pensarais	pensad (no penséis)
pensado	**piensan**	pensaban	pensaron	pensarán	pensarían	**piensen**	pensaran	**piensen** Uds.
31 reír (e:i)	**río**	reía	**reí**	reiré	reiría	**ría**	riera	
	ríes	reías	**reíste**	reirás	reirías	**rías**	rieras	**ríe** tú (no **rías**)
Participles:	**ríe**	reía	**rio**	reirá	reiría	**ría**	riera	ría Ud.
riendo	**reímos**	reíamos	**reímos**	reiremos	reiríamos	**riamos**	riéramos	**riamos**
reído	**reís**	reíais	**reísteis**	reiréis	reiríais	**riáis**	rierais	reíd (no **riáis**)
	ríen	reían	**rieron**	reirán	reirían	**rían**	rieran	**rían** Uds.
32 seguir (e:i) (gu:g)	**sigo**	seguía	seguí	seguiré	seguiría	**siga**	**siguiera**	
	sigues	seguías	seguiste	seguirás	seguirías	**sigas**	**siguieras**	**sigue** tú (no **sigas**)
	sigue	seguía	**siguió**	seguirá	seguiría	**siga**	**siguiera**	**siga** Ud.
Participles:	seguimos	seguíamos	seguimos	seguiremos	seguiríamos	**sigamos**	**siguiéramos**	**sigamos**
siguiendo	seguís	seguíais	seguisteis	seguiréis	seguiríais	**sigáis**	**siguierais**	seguid (no **sigáis**)
seguido	**siguen**	seguían	**siguieron**	seguirán	seguirían	**sigan**	**siguieran**	**sigan** Uds.
33 sentir (e:ie)	**siento**	sentía	sentí	sentiré	sentiría	**sienta**	sintiera	
	sientes	sentías	sentiste	sentirás	sentirías	**sientas**	sintieras	**siente** tú (no **sientas**)
Participles:	**siente**	sentía	**sintió**	sentirá	sentiría	**sienta**	sintiera	**sienta** Ud.
sintiendo	sentimos	sentíamos	sentimos	sentiremos	sentiríamos	**sintamos**	**sintiéramos**	**sintamos**
sentido	sentís	sentíais	sentisteis	sentiréis	sentiríais	**sintáis**	sintierais	sentid (no **sintáis**)
	sienten	sentían	**sintieron**	sentirán	sentirían	**sientan**	sintieran	**sientan** Uds.

	Infinitive	INDICATIVE					SUBJUNCTIVE		IMPERATIVE
		Present	Imperfect	Preterite	Future	Conditional	Present	Past	
34	volver	**vuelvo**	volvía	volví	volveré	volvería	**vuelva**	volviera	
	(o:ue)	**vuelves**	volvías	volviste	volverás	volverías	**vuelvas**	volvieras	**vuelve** tú (no **vuelvas**)
		vuelve	volvía	volvió	volverá	volvería	**vuelva**	volviera	**vuelva** Ud.
	Participles:	volvemos	volvíamos	volvimos	volveremos	volveríamos	volvamos	volviéramos	volvamos
	volviendo	volvéis	volvíais	volvisteis	volveréis	volveríais	volváis	volvierais	volved (no volváis)
	vuelto	**vuelven**	volvían	volvieron	volverán	volverían	**vuelvan**	volvieran	**vuelvan** Uds.

Verbs with spelling changes only

	Infinitive	INDICATIVE					SUBJUNCTIVE		IMPERATIVE
		Present	Imperfect	Preterite	Future	Conditional	Present	Past	
35	conocer	**conozco**	conocía	conocí	conoceré	conocería	**conozca**	conociera	
	(c:zc)	conoces	conocías	conociste	conocerás	conocerías	**conozcas**	conocieras	conoce tú (no **conozcas**)
		conoce	conocía	conoció	conocerá	conocería	**conozca**	conociera	**conozca** Ud.
	Participles:	conocemos	conocíamos	conocimos	conoceremos	conoceríamos	**conozcamos**	conociéramos	**conozcamos**
	conociendo	conocéis	conocíais	conocisteis	conoceréis	conoceríais	**conozcáis**	conocierais	conoced (no **conozcáis**)
	conocido	conocen	conocían	conocieron	conocerán	conocerían	**conozcan**	conocieran	**conozcan** Uds.
36	creer (y)	creo	creía	**creí**	creeré	creería	crea	**creyera**	
		crees	creías	**creíste**	creerás	creerías	creas	**creyeras**	cree tú (no creas)
	Participles:	cree	creía	**creyó**	creerá	creería	crea	**creyera**	crea Ud.
	creyendo	creemos	creíamos	**creímos**	creeremos	creeríamos	creamos	**creyéramos**	creamos
	creído	creéis	creíais	**creísteis**	creeréis	creeríais	creáis	**creyerais**	creed (no creáis)
		creen	creían	**creyeron**	creerán	creerían	crean	**creyeran**	crean Uds.
37	cruzar (z:c)	cruzo	cruzaba	**crucé**	cruzaré	cruzaría	**cruce**	cruzara	
		cruzas	cruzabas	cruzaste	cruzarás	cruzarías	**cruces**	cruzaras	cruza tú (no **cruces**)
	Participles:	cruza	cruzaba	cruzó	cruzará	cruzaría	**cruce**	cruzara	**cruce** Ud.
	cruzando	cruzamos	cruzábamos	cruzamos	cruzaremos	cruzaríamos	**crucemos**	cruzáramos	**crucemos**
	cruzado	cruzáis	cruzabais	cruzasteis	cruzaréis	cruzaríais	**crucéis**	cruzarais	cruzad (no **crucéis**)
		cruzan	cruzaban	cruzaron	cruzarán	cruzarían	**crucen**	cruzaran	**crucen** Uds.
38	destruir (y)	**destruyo**	destruía	destruí	destruiré	destruiría	**destruya**	**destruyera**	
		destruyes	destruías	destruiste	destruirás	destruirías	**destruyas**	**destruyeras**	**destruye** tú (no **destruyas**)
	Participles:	**destruye**	destruía	**destruyó**	destruirá	destruiría	**destruya**	**destruyera**	**destruya** Ud.
	destruyendo	destruimos	destruíamos	destruimos	destruiremos	destruiríamos	**destruyamos**	**destruyéramos**	**destruyamos**
	destruido	destruís	destruíais	destruisteis	destruiréis	destruiríais	**destruyáis**	**destruyerais**	destruid (no **destruyáis**)
		destruyen	destruían	**destruyeron**	destruirán	destruirían	**destruyan**	**destruyeran**	**destruyan** Uds.
39	enviar	**envío**	enviaba	envié	enviaré	enviaría	**envíe**	enviara	
	(envío)	**envías**	enviabas	enviaste	enviarás	enviarías	**envíes**	enviaras	**envía** tú (no **envíes**)
		envía	enviaba	envió	enviará	enviaría	**envíe**	enviara	**envíe** Ud.
	Participles:	enviamos	enviábamos	enviamos	enviaremos	enviaríamos	**enviemos**	enviáramos	enviemos
	enviando	enviáis	enviabais	enviasteis	enviaréis	enviaríais	**enviéis**	enviarais	enviad (no **enviéis**)
	enviado	**envían**	enviaban	enviaron	enviarán	enviarían	**envíen**	enviaran	**envíen** Uds.

		INDICATIVE					SUBJUNCTIVE		IMPERATIVE
Infinitive	Present	Imperfect	Preterite	Future	Conditional	Present	Past	
40 graduarse (gradúo)	**gradúo**	graduaba	gradué	graduaré	graduaría	**gradúe**	graduara	
	gradúas	graduabas	graduaste	graduarás	graduarías	**gradúes**	graduaras	**gradúa** tú (no **gradúes**)
	gradúa	graduaba	graduó	graduará	graduaría	**gradúe**	graduara	**gradúe** Ud.
Participles:	graduamos	graduábamos	graduamos	graduaremos	graduaríamos	graduemos	graduáramos	graduemos
graduando	graduáis	graduabais	graduasteis	graduaréis	graduaríais	graduéis	graduarais	graduad (no **graduéis**)
graduado	**gradúan**	graduaban	graduaron	graduarán	graduarían	**gradúen**	graduaran	**gradúen** Uds.
41 llegar (g:gu)	llego	llegaba	**llegué**	llegaré	llegaría	**llegue**	llegara	
	llegas	llegabas	llegaste	llegarás	llegarías	**llegues**	llegaras	llega tú (no **llegues**)
Participles:	llega	llegaba	llegó	llegará	llegaría	**llegue**	llegara	**llegue** Ud.
llegando	llegamos	llegábamos	llegamos	llegaremos	llegaríamos	**lleguemos**	llegáramos	**lleguemos**
llegado	llegáis	llegabais	llegasteis	llegaréis	llegaríais	**lleguéis**	llegarais	llegad (no **lleguéis**)
	llegan	llegaban	llegaron	llegarán	llegarían	**lleguen**	llegaran	**lleguen** Uds.
42 prohibir (prohíbo)	**prohíbo**	prohibía	prohibí	prohibiré	prohibiría	**prohíba**	prohibiera	**prohíbe** tú (no **prohíbas**)
	prohíbes	prohibías	prohibiste	prohibirás	prohibirías	**prohíbas**	prohibieras	**prohíba** Ud.
	prohíbe	prohibía	prohibió	prohibirá	prohibiría	**prohíba**	prohibiera	prohibamos
Participles:	prohibimos	prohibíamos	prohibimos	prohibiremos	prohibiríamos	prohibamos	prohibiéramos	prohibid (no prohibáis)
prohibiendo	prohibís	prohibíais	prohibisteis	prohibiréis	prohibiríais	prohibáis	prohibierais	**prohíban** Uds.
prohibido	**prohíben**	prohibían	prohibieron	prohibirán	prohibirían	**prohíban**	prohibieran	
43 proteger (g:j)	**protejo**	protegía	protegí	protegeré	protegería	**proteja**	protegiera	
	proteges	protegías	protegiste	protegerás	protegerías	**protejas**	protegieras	protege tú (no **protejas**)
	protege	protegía	protegió	protegerá	protegería	**proteja**	protegiera	**proteja** Ud.
Participles:	protegemos	protegíamos	protegimos	protegeremos	protegeríamos	**protejamos**	protegiéramos	**protejamos**
protegiendo	protegéis	protegíais	protegisteis	protegeréis	protegeríais	**protejáis**	protegierais	proteged (no **protejáis**)
protegido	protegen	protegían	protegieron	protegerán	protegerían	protejan	protegieran	**protejan** Uds.
44 tocar (c:qu)	toco	tocaba	**toqué**	tocaré	tocaría	**toque**	tocara	
	tocas	tocabas	tocaste	tocarás	tocarías	**toques**	tocaras	toca tú (no **toques**)
Participles:	toca	tocaba	tocó	tocará	tocaría	**toque**	tocara	**toque** Ud.
tocando	tocamos	tocábamos	tocamos	tocaremos	tocaríamos	**toquemos**	tocáramos	**toquemos**
tocado	tocáis	tocabais	tocasteis	tocaréis	tocaríais	**toquéis**	tocarais	tocad (no **toquéis**)
	tocan	tocaban	tocaron	tocarán	tocarían	**toquen**	tocaran	**toquen** Uds.
45 vencer (c:z)	**venzo**	vencía	vencí	venceré	vencería	**venza**	venciera	
	vences	vencías	venciste	vencerás	vencerías	**venzas**	vencieras	vence tú (no **venzas**)
Participles:	vence	vencía	venció	vencerá	vencería	**venza**	venciera	**venza** Ud.
venciendo	vencemos	vencíamos	vencimos	venceremos	venceríamos	**venzamos**	venciéramos	**venzamos**
vencido	vencéis	vencíais	vencisteis	venceréis	venceríais	**venzáis**	vencierais	venced (no **venzáis**)
	vencen	vencían	vencieron	vencerán	vencerían	**venzan**	vencieran	**venzan** Uds.

Guide to Vocabulary

Note on alphabetization

For purposes of alphabetization, **ch** and **ll** are not treated as separate letters, but **ñ** still follows **n**. Therefore, in this glossary you will find that **año**, for example, appears after **anuncio**.

Abbreviations used in this glossary

adj.	adjective	*form.*	formal	*poss.*	possessive
adv.	adverb	*indef.*	indefinite	*prep.*	preposition
art.	article	*interj.*	interjection	*pron.*	pronoun
conj.	conjunction	*i.o.*	indirect object	*ref.*	reflexive
def.	definite	*m.*	masculine	*sing.*	singular
d.o.	direct object	*obj.*	object	*sub.*	subject
f.	feminine	*p.p.*	past participle	*v.*	verb
fam.	familiar	*pl.*	plural		

Spanish-English

A

a *prep.* at; to **1**
  ¿A qué hora...? At what time...? **1, 9**
  a dieta on a diet **15**
  a la derecha de to the right of **2**
  a la izquierda de to the left of **2**
  a la plancha grilled
  a la(s) + *time* at + *time* **1**
  a menos que *conj.* unless **13**
  a menudo often **10**
  a mi nombre in my name
  a nombre de in the name of
  a plazos in installments **14**
  A sus órdenes. At your service.
  a tiempo on time **10**
  a veces sometimes **10**
  a ver let's see
abierto/a *adj.* open **5**; *p.p.* opened **15**
abogado/a *m., f.* lawyer **16**
abrazar(se) *v.* to hug; to embrace (each other)
abrazo *m.* hug
abrigo *m.* coat **6**
abril *m.* April **5**
abrir *v.* to open **3**
abuelo/a *m., f.* grandfather; grandmother **3**
abuelos *pl.* grandparents **3**
aburrido/a *adj.* bored; boring **5**
aburrir *v.* to bore **7**
aburrirse *v.* to get bored
acabar de (+ *inf.*) *v.* to have just (*done something*) **6**
acampar *v.* to camp **5**
accidente *m.* accident **10**
acción *f.* action
aceite *m.* oil **8**

acompañar *v.* to go with; to accompany
aconsejar *v.* to advise **12**
acontecimiento *m.* event
acordarse (de) (o:ue) *v.* to remember **7**
acostarse (o:ue) *v.* to lie down; to go to bed **7**
activo/a *adj.* active **15**
actor *m.* actor **16**
actriz *f.* actress **16**
actualidades *f., pl.* news; current events
adelgazar *v.* to lose weight; to slim down **15**
además (de) *adv.* furthermore; besides **10**; in addition (to)
adicional *adj.* additional
adiós *m.* goodbye **1**
adjetivo *m.* adjective
administración de empresas *f.* business administration **2**
adolescencia *f.* adolescence **9**
¿adónde? *adv.* where (to)? (*destination*) **2, 9**
aduana *f.* customs **5**
aeróbico/a *adj.* aerobic **15**
aeropuerto *m.* airport **5**
afectado/a *adj.* affected **13**
afeitarse *v.* to shave **7**
aficionado/a *adj.* fan **4**
afirmativo/a *adj.* affirmative
afueras *f., pl.* suburbs; outskirts **12**
agencia de bienes raíces *f.* real estate agency **12**
agosto *m.* August **5**
agradable *adj.* pleasant
agrio/a *adj.* sour **8**
agua *f.* water **8**
  agua mineral mineral water **8**
ahora *adv.* now
  ahora mismo right now **5**
ahorrar *v.* to save money **14**

ahorros *m., pl.* savings **14**
aire *m.* air **13**
ajo *m.* garlic **8**
al (*contraction of* a + el) **4**
  al aire libre open-air **6**
  al contado in cash **14**
  (al) este (to the) east **14**
  al fondo (de) at the end (of)
  al lado de next to **2**
  (al) norte (to the) north **14**
  (al) oeste (to the) west **14**
  (al) sur (to the) south **14**
alcoba *f.* bedroom **12**
alcohol *m.* alcohol **15**
alcohólico/a *adj.* alcoholic **15**
alegrarse (de) *v.* to be happy **13**
alegre *adj.* happy **5**
alegría *f.* happiness **9**
alemán, alemana *adj.* German **3**
alérgico/a *adj.* allergic **10**
alfombra *f.* carpet; rug **12**
algo *pron.* something; anything **7**
alguien *pron.* someone; anyone **7**
algún, alguno/a(s) *adj.* any; some **7**
aliviar *v.* to relieve **15**
  aliviar el estrés/la tensión to relieve stress/tension **15**
allí *adv.* there
almacén *m.* department store **6**
almohada *f.* pillow **12**
almorzar (o:ue) *v.* to have lunch **8**
almuerzo *m.* lunch **8**
¿Aló? *interj.* Hello? (*on the telephone*)
alojamiento *m.* lodging **5**
alquilar *v.* to rent **12**
alquiler *m.* rent **12**
altillo *m.* attic **12**
alto/a *adj.* tall **3**
aluminio *m.* aluminum **13**
amable *adj.* friendly
amargo/a *adj.* bitter **8**
amarillo/a *adj.* yellow **6**
amigo/a *m., f.* friend **3**

amistad *f.* friendship **9**
amo/a *m., f.* **de casa** homemaker **12**
amor *m.* love **9**
anaranjado/a *adj.* orange **6**
animal *m.* animal **13**
aniversario (de bodas) *m.* (wedding) anniversary **9**
anoche *adv.* last night **6**
anteayer *adv.* the day before yesterday **6**
antes *adv.* before **7**
  antes de *prep.* before **7**
  antes (de) que *conj.* before **13**
antibiótico *m.* antibiotic **10**
antipático/a *adj.* unpleasant **3**
anunciar *v.* to announce; to advertise
anuncio *m.* advertisement **16**
año *m.* year **5**
  el año pasado last year **6**
apagar *v.* to turn off **11**
apartamento *m.* apartment **12**
apellido *m.* last name **9**
apenas *adv.* hardly; scarcely **10**
aplaudir *v.* to applaud
aplicación *f.* app **11**
apreciar *v.* to appreciate
aprender *v.* to learn **3**
apurarse *v.* to hurry; to rush **15**
aquel, aquella *adj.* that (over there) **6**
aquél, aquélla *pron.* that (one) (over there) **6**
aquello *neuter, pron.* that; that thing; that fact **6**
aquellos/as *pl. adj.* those (over there) **6**
aquéllos/as *pl. pron.* those (ones) (over there) **6**
aquí *adv.* here
árbol *m.* tree **13**
archivo *m.* file **11**
argentino/a *adj.* Argentine **3**
armario *m.* closet **12**
arqueólogo/a *m., f.* archeologist **16**
arquitecto/a *m., f.* architect **16**
arrancar *v.* to start (*a car*) **11**
arreglar *v.* to fix; to arrange **11**; to straighten up **12**
arriba *adv.* up
arroz *m.* rice **8**
arte *m.* art **2**
artes *f., pl.* arts
artesanía *f.* craftsmanship; crafts
artículo *m.* article
artista *m., f.* artist **3**
artístico/a *adj.* artistic
arveja *m.* pea **8**
asado/a *adj.* roasted **8**
ascenso *m.* promotion **16**
ascensor *m.* elevator **5**
así *adj.* like this; so (*in such a way*) **10**
  así así so-so
asistir (a) *v.* to attend **3**

aspiradora *f.* vacuum cleaner **12**
aspirante *m., f.* candidate; applicant **16**
aspirina *f.* aspirin **10**
atún *m.* tuna **8**
aumentar *v.* **de peso** to gain weight **15**
aumento *m.* increase
  aumento de sueldo pay raise **16**
aunque *conj.* although
autobús *m.* bus **1**
auto(móvil) *m.* car **5**
autopista *f.* highway
ave *f.* bird
avenida *f.* avenue
aventura *f.* adventure
avergonzado/a *adj.* embarrassed **5**
avión *m.* airplane **5**
¡Ay! *interj.* Oh!
ayer *adv.* yesterday **6**
ayudar *v.* to help
ayudarse *v.* to help each other
azúcar *m.* sugar **8**
azul *adj.* blue **6**

B

bailar *v.* to dance **2**
bailarín/bailarina *m., f.* dancer **16**
baile *m.* dance
bajar *v.* to go down **11**
bajar(se) de *v.* to get out of (a vehicle) **11**
bajo/a *adj.* short (*in height*) **3**
balcón *m.* balcony **12**
ballena *f.* whale **13**
ballet *m.* ballet
baloncesto *m.* basketball **4**
banana *f.* banana **8**
banco *m.* bank **14**
banda *f.* band
bandera *f.* flag
bañarse *v.* to take a bath **7**
baño *m.* bathroom **7**
barato/a *adj.* cheap **6**
barco *m.* boat **5**
barrer *v.* to sweep **12**
  barrer el suelo to sweep the floor **12**
barrio *m.* neighborhood **12**
bastante *adv.* enough; quite **10**
basura *f.* trash **12**
baúl *m.* trunk **11**
beber *v.* to drink **3**
bebida *f.* drink; beverage **8**
  bebida alcohólica alcoholic beverage **15**
béisbol *m.* baseball **4**
bellas artes *f., pl.* fine arts
belleza *f.* beauty **14**
beneficio *m.* benefit; profit **16**
besar(se) *v.* to kiss (each other)
beso *m.* kiss **6**
biblioteca *f.* library **2**
bicicleta *f.* bicycle **4**

bien *adv.* well **1**
bienestar *m.* well-being **15**
¡Bienvenido(s)/a(s)! *adj.* Welcome!
billete *m.* paper money
billón trillion **6**
biología *f.* biology **2**
bistec *m.* steak **8**
blanco/a *adj.* white **6**
bluejeans *m., pl.* jeans **6**
blusa *f.* blouse **6**
boca *f.* mouth **10**
boda *f.* wedding **9**
boleto *m.* ticket
bolsa *f.* bag; purse **6**
bombero/a *m., f.* firefighter **16**
bonito/a *adj.* pretty **3**
borrador *m.* eraser **2**
bosque *m.* forest **13**
  bosque tropical tropical forest; rain forest **13**
bota *f.* boot **6**
botella *f.* bottle **9**
  botella de vino bottle of wine **9**
brazo *m.* arm **10**
brindar *v.* to toast (*drink*) **9**
bucear *v.* to scuba dive **4**
buen, bueno/a *adj.* good **3, 6**
  ¡Buen viaje! Have a good trip!
  buena forma good shape (*physical*) **15**
  Buenas noches. Good evening; Good night. **1**
  Buenas tardes. Good afternoon. **1**
  ¿Bueno? Hello? (*on telephone*)
  Buenos días. Good morning. **1**
bulevar *m.* boulevard
buscar *v.* to look for **2**
buzón *m.* mailbox **14**
  buzón de voz voicemail **11**

C

caballo *m.* horse **5**
cabaña *f.* cabin **5**
cabe: no cabe duda de there's no doubt **13**
cabeza *f.* head **10**
cada *adj.* each **6**
caerse *v.* to fall **10**
café *m.* café **4**; *adj.* brown **6**; coffee **8**
cafetera *f.* coffee maker
cafetería *f.* cafeteria **2**
caído/a *p.p.* fallen **15**
caja *f.* cash register **6**
cajero/a *m., f.* cashier
  cajero automático ATM **14**
calcetín *m.* sock **6**
calculadora *f.* calculator **11**
calentamiento global *m.* global warming **13**
calentarse (e:ie) *v.* to warm up **15**
calidad *f.* quality
calle *f.* street **11**

calor *m.* heat
caloría *f.* calorie 15
calzar *v.* to take size ... shoes
cama *f.* bed 5
cámara digital digital camera 11
camarero/a *m., f.* waiter 8
camarón *m.* shrimp 8
cambiar (de) *v.* to change 9
cambio *m.* **de moneda** currency
    exchange
caminar *v.* to walk 2
camino *m.* route 11
camión *m.* truck; bus
camisa *f.* shirt 6
camiseta *f.* t-shirt 6
campo *m.* countryside 5
canadiense *adj.* Canadian 3
canal *m.* channel (TV)
canción *f.* song
candidato/a *m., f.* candidate
cansado/a *adj.* tired 5
cantante *m., f.* singer 16
cantar *v.* to sing 2
capital *f.* capital city
capó *m.* (car) hood 11
cara *f.* face 7
caramelo *m.* caramel
cargador *m.* charger 11
cargar *v.* to charge; to upload 11
carne *f.* meat 8
    carne de res beef 8
carnicería *f.* butcher shop 14
caro/a *adj.* expensive 6
carpintero/a *m., f.* carpenter 16
carrera *f.* career 16
carretera *f.* highway; (main) road
carro *m.* car 11
carta *f.* letter 4; (playing) card
cartel *m.* poster
cartera *f.* wallet 6
cartero/a *m., f.* mail carrier 14
casa *f.* house 4; home
casado/a *adj.* married 9
casarse (con) *v.* to get married (to) 9
casi *adv.* almost 10
catorce fourteen 1
caza *f.* hunting 13
cebolla *f.* onion 8
celebrar *v.* to celebrate 9
cena *f.* dinner 8
cenar *v.* to have dinner 8
centro *m.* downtown 4
    centro comercial shopping mall 6
cepillarse los dientes/el pelo *v.* to
    brush one's teeth/one's hair 7
cerámica *f.* pottery
cerca de *prep.* near 2
cerdo *m.* pork 8
cereales *m., pl.* cereal; grains 8
cero zero 1
cerrado/a *adj.* closed 5
cerrar (e:ie) *v.* to close 4
cerveza *f.* beer 8
césped *m.* grass 13

chaleco *m.* vest
champán *m.* champagne 9
champiñón *m.* mushroom 8
champú *m.* shampoo 7
chaqueta *f.* jacket 6
chatear *v.* to chat 11
chau *fam., interj.* bye 1
cheque *m.* (bank) check 14
chévere *adj., fam.* terrific
chico/a *m., f.* boy/girl 1
chino/a *adj.* Chinese 3
chocar (con) *v.* to run into; to crash 11
chocolate *m.* chocolate
choque *m.* collision
chuleta *f.* chop (*food*) 8
    chuleta de cerdo pork chop 8
ciclismo *m.* cycling 4
cielo *m.* sky 13
cien(to) one hundred 2, 6
    por ciento percent
ciencia *f.* science
    ciencia ficción science fiction
científico/a *m., f.* scientist 16
cierto *m.* certain; true 13
    es cierto it's true/certain 13
    no es cierto it's not true/certain 13
cifra *f.* figure
cinco five 1
cincuenta fifty 2
cine *m.* movie theater 4
cinturón *m.* belt 6
circulación *f.* traffic
cita *f.* date; appointment 9
ciudad *f.* city 4
ciudadano/a *adj.* citizen
claro que sí *fam.* of course
clase *f.* class 2
    clase de ejercicios aeróbicos
        aerobics class 15
clásico/a *adj.* classical
cliente/a *m., f.* client 6
clínica *f.* clinic 10
cobrar *v.* to cash a check 14; to
    charge for a product or service 14
coche *m.* car 11
cocina *f.* kitchen 12
cocinar *v.* to cook 12
cocinero/a *m., f.* cook, chef 16
cola *f.* line 14
colesterol *m.* cholesterol 15
color *m.* color 6
comedia *f.* comedy; play
comedor *m.* dining room 12
comenzar (e:ie) *v.* to begin 4
comer *v.* to eat 3
comercial *adj.* commercial;
    business-related 16
comida *f.* food; meal 8
como *prep.* like, as 8
¿cómo? what?; how? 1, 2
    ¿Cómo es...? What's... like?
    ¿Cómo está usted? How are you?
        form. 1

¿Cómo estás? How are you?
    fam. 1
¿Cómo se llama usted?
    What's your name? *form.* 1
¿Cómo te llamas (tú)?
    What's your name? *fam.* 1
cómoda *f.* chest of drawers 12
cómodo/a *adj.* comfortable 5
compañero/a de clase *m., f.*
    classmate 2
compañero/a de cuarto *m., f.*
    roommate 2
compañía *f.* company; firm 16
compartir *v.* to share 3
compositor(a) *m., f.* composer
comprar *v.* to buy 2
    comprar en línea to buy online 6
compras *f., pl.* purchases
    ir de compras go shopping 6
comprender *v.* to understand 3
comprobar *v.* to check
comprometerse (con) *v.* to get
    engaged (to) 9
computación *f.* computer science 2
computadora *f.* computer 1, 11
computadora portátil *f.* laptop 11
comunicación *f.* communication
comunicarse (con) *v.* to communicate
    (with)
comunidad *f.* community 1
con *prep.* with
    Con él/ella habla. This is
        he/she. (*on telephone*)
    con frecuencia *adv.* frequently 10
    Con permiso. Pardon me.,
        Excuse me.
    con tal (de) que *conj.* provided
        that 13
concierto *m.* concert
concordar *v.* to agree
concurso *m.* contest; game show
conducir *v.* to drive 8, 11
conductor(a) *m., f.* driver 1
conectarse *v.* **a Internet** to get
    connected to the Internet 11
conexión *f.* **inalámbrica** wireless
    connection 11
confirmar *v.* to confirm 5
    confirmar una reservación to
        confirm a reservation 5
congelador *m.* freezer
congestionado/a *adj.* congested 10
conmigo *pron.* with me
conocer *v.* to know; to be acquainted
    with 8
conocido/a *adj.* known
conseguir (e:i) *v.* to get; to obtain 4
consejero/a *m., f.* counselor; advisor 16
consejo *m.* advice 9
conservación *f.* conservation 13
conservar *v.* to conserve 13
construir *v.* to build
consultorio *m.* doctor's office 10
consumir *v.* to consume 15

contabilidad *f.* accounting 2
contador(a) *m., f.* accountant 16
contaminación *f.* pollution 13; contamination
   contaminación del aire/del agua air/water pollution 13
contaminado/a *adj.* polluted 13
contaminar *v.* to pollute 13
contento/a *adj.* content 5
contestar *v.* to answer 2
contigo *pron.* with you
contratar *v.* to hire 16
control *m.* control
   control remoto remote control 11
controlar *v.* to control 13
conversación *f.* conversation 1
conversar *v.* to talk; to chat 2
copa *f.* wineglass 12
corazón *m.* heart 10
corbata *f.* tie 6
corredor(a) *m., f.* **de bolsa** stockbroker 16
correo *m.* post office; mail 14
   correo electrónico e-mail 4
correr *v.* to run 3
cortesía *f.* courtesy
cortinas *f., pl.* curtains 12
corto/a *adj.* short (*in length*) 6
cosa *f.* thing 1
costar (o:ue) *v.* to cost 6
costarricense *adj.* Costa Rican 3
cráter *m.* crater 13
creer *v.* to believe 13
   creer (en) *v.* to believe (in) 3
creído/a *p.p.* believed 15
crema de afeitar *f.* shaving cream 7
crimen *m.* crime; murder
cruzar *v.* to cross 14
cuaderno *m.* notebook 1
cuadra *f.* city block 14
cuadro *m.* picture 12
cuadros *m., pl.* plaid
¿cuál(es)? which?; which one(s)? 2; what? 9
   ¿Cuál es la fecha de hoy? What is today's date? 5
cuando *conj.* when 13
¿cuándo? *adv.* when? 2, 9
¿cuánto(s)/a(s)? *adv.* how much?, how many? 1, 2
   ¿Cuánto cuesta...? How much does... cost?
   ¿Cuántos años tienes/tiene? How old are you?
cuarenta forty 2
cuarto *m.* room
cuarto/a *adj.* quarter 1; fourth 5
   menos cuarto quarter to (time) 1
   y cuarto quarter after (time) 1
cuarto de baño *m.* bathroom
cuatro four 1
cuatrocientos/as four hundred 6
cubano/a *adj.* Cuban 3

cubiertos *m., pl.* silverware
cubierto/a *p.p.* covered
cubrir *v.* to cover
cuchara *f.* spoon 12
cuchillo *m.* knife 12
cuello *m.* neck 10
cuenta *f.* bill 9; account 14
   cuenta corriente checking account 14
   cuenta de ahorros savings account 14
cuento *m.* story
cuerpo *m.* body 10
cuidado *m.* care
cuidar *v.* to take care of 13
cultura *f.* culture
cumpleaños *m., sing.* birthday 9
cumplir años *v.* to have a birthday 9
cuñado/a *m., f.* brother-in-law; sister-in-law 3
currículum *m.* résumé 16
curso *m.* course 2

D

danza *f.* dance
dañar *v.* to damage; to break down 10
dar *v.* to give 6
   dar un consejo to give advice
   darse con *v.* to bump into; to run into
   darse prisa to hurry; to rush 15
de *prep.* of; from 1
   ¿de dónde? from where? 2
   ¿De dónde eres? *fam.* Where are you from? 1
   ¿De dónde es usted? *form.* Where are you from? 1
   ¿De parte de quién? Who is calling? (*on telephone*)
   ¿de quién...? whose...? (*sing.*) 1
   ¿de quiénes...? whose...? (*pl.*) 1
   de aluminio (made of) aluminum 13
   de compras shopping
   de cuadros plaid
   de excursión hiking 4
   de ida y vuelta round-trip 5
   de la mañana in the morning; A.M. 1
   de la noche in the evening; at night; P.M. 1
   de la tarde in the afternoon; in the early evening; P.M. 1
   de lunares polka-dotted
   de moda in fashion
   De nada. You're welcome. 1
   de niño/a as a child 10
   de parte de on behalf of
   de plástico (made of) plastic 13
   de rayas striped
   de repente suddenly 6
   de vez en cuando from time to time 10

   de vidrio (made of) glass 13
debajo de *prep.* below; under 2
deber (+ inf.) *v.* should (*do something*) 3
deber *m.* responsibility; obligation
debido a due to; the fact that
débil *adj.* weak 15
decidir *v.* to decide 3
décimo/a *adj.* tenth 5
decir *v.* to say; to tell 6
declarar *v.* to declare; to say
dedo *m.* finger 10
deforestación *f.* deforestation 13
dejar *v.* to let; to quit; to leave behind 16
   dejar de (+ inf.) to stop (*doing something*) 13
   dejar una propina to leave a tip 9
del (*contraction of* **de + el**) of the; from the
delante de *prep.* in front of 2
delgado/a *adj.* thin 3
delicioso/a *adj.* delicious 8
demás *pron.* the rest
demasiado *adv.* too much
dentista *m., f.* dentist 10
dentro de *adv.* within
dependiente/a *m., f.* clerk 6
deporte *m.* sport 4
deportista *m.* sports person
deportivo/a *adj.* sports-related 4
depositar *v.* to deposit 14
derecha *f.* right 2
   a la derecha de to the right of 2
derecho *adv.* straight (ahead) 14
derechos *m., pl.* rights
desarrollar *v.* to develop 13
desastre natural *m.* natural disaster
desayunar *v.* to have breakfast 8
desayuno *m.* breakfast 8
descafeinado/a *adj.* decaffeinated 15
descansar *v.* to rest 2
descargar *v.* to download 11
descompuesto/a *adj.* not working; out of order 11
describir *v.* to describe 3
descrito/a *p.p.* described 15
descubierto/a *p.p.* discovered 15
descubrir *v.* to discover 13
desde *prep.* from 6
desear *v.* to want; to wish 2; to desire 12
desempleo *m.* unemployment
desierto *m.* desert 13
desigualdad *f.* inequality
desordenado/a *adj.* disorderly 5
despacio *adj.* slowly
despedida *f.* farewell; goodbye
despedir (e:i) *v.* to fire 16
despejado/a *adj.* clear (*weather*) 5
despertador *m.* alarm clock 7
despertarse (e:ie) *v.* to wake up 7
después *adv.* afterward; then 7

después de *prep.* after 7
después (de) que *conj.* after 13
destruir *v.* to destroy 13
detrás de *prep.* behind 2
día *m.* day 1
día de fiesta holiday 9
diario *m.* diary 1; newspaper
diario/a *adj.* daily 7
dibujar *v.* to draw 2
dibujo *m.* drawing
dibujos animados *m., pl.* cartoons
diccionario *m.* dictionary 1
dicho/a *p.p.* said 15
diciembre *m.* December 5
dictadura *f.* dictatorship
diecinueve nineteen 1
dieciocho eighteen 1
dieciséis sixteen 1
diecisiete seventeen 1
diente *m.* tooth 7
dieta *f.* diet 15
dieta equilibrada balanced
diet 15
diez ten 1
difícil *adj.* difficult 3
¿Diga? Hello? (*on telephone*)
diligencia *f.* errand 14
dinero *m.* money 6
dirección *f.* address 14
director(a) *m., f.* director; (*musical*)
conductor
disco *m.* disk
discriminación *f.* discrimination
discurso *m.* speech
diseñador(a) *m., f.* designer 16
diseño *m.* design
disfrutar (de) *v.* to enjoy; to reap the
benefits (of) 15
diversión *f.* entertainment; fun
activity 4
divertido/a *adj.* fun
divertirse (e:ie) *v.* to have fun 9
divorciado/a *adj.* divorced 9
divorciarse (de) *v.* to get divorced
(from) 9
divorcio *m.* divorce 9
doblar *v.* to turn 14
doble *adj.* double
doce twelve 1
doctor(a) *m., f.* doctor 3, 10
documental *m.* documentary
documentos de viaje *m., pl.* travel
documents
doler (o:ue) *v.* to hurt 10
dolor *m.* ache; pain 10
dolor de cabeza *m.* headache 10
domingo *m.* Sunday 2
dominicano/a *adj.* Dominican 3
don/doña title of respect used with a
person's first name
donde *prep.* where
¿dónde? where? 1, 2
¿Dónde está...? Where is...?
dormir (o:ue) *v.* to sleep 4

dormirse (o:ue) *v.* to go to sleep; to
fall asleep 7
dos two 1
dos veces twice 6
doscientos/as two hundred 6
drama *m.* drama; play
dramático/a *adj.* dramatic
dramaturgo/a *m., f.* playwright
droga *f.* drug 15
drogadicto/a *m., f.* drug addict 15
ducha *f.* shower
ducharse *v.* to shower 7
duda *f.* doubt 13
dudar *v.* to doubt 13
dueño/a *m., f.* owner 8
dulce *adj.* sweet 8
dulces *m., pl.* sweets; candy 9
durante *prep.* during 7
durar *v.* to last

E

e *conj. (used instead of y before words
beginning with i and hi)* and
echar *v.* to throw
echar una carta al buzón to put a
letter in the mailbox; to mail a
letter 14
ecología *f.* ecology 13
ecológico/a *adj.* ecological 13
ecologista *m., f.* ecologist 13
economía *f.* economics
ecoturismo *m.* ecotourism 13
ecuatoriano/a *adj.* Ecuadorian 3
edad *f.* age
edificio *m.* building 12
edificio de apartamentos
apartment building 12
efectivo *m.* cash
ejercicio *m.* exercise 15
ejercicios aeróbicos aerobic
exercises 15
ejercicios de estiramiento
stretching exercises 15
ejército *m.* army
el *m., sing., def. art.* the 1
él *sub. pron.* he 1; *obj. pron.* him
elección *f.* election
electricista *m., f.* electrician 16
electrodoméstico *m.* electrical
appliance 12
elegante *adj. m., f.* elegant 6
elegir *v.* to elect
ella *sub. pron.* she 1; *obj. pron.* her
ellos/as *sub. pron.* they 1; them
embarazada *adj.* pregnant 10
emergencia *f.* emergency 10
emitir *v.* to broadcast
emocionante *adj.* exciting
empezar (e:ie) *v.* to begin 4
empleado/a *m., f.* employee 5
empleo *m.* job; employment 16
empresa *f.* company; firm 16

en *prep.* in; on; at 2
en casa at home
en caso (de) que *conj.* in case
(that) 13
en cuanto *conj.* as soon as 13
en efectivo in cash
en exceso in excess; too much 15
en línea online 6
en punto on the dot; sharp
(*time*) 1
¿En qué puedo servirles?
How can I help you?
enamorado/a *adj.* **(de)** in love
(with) 5
enamorarse (de) *v.* to fall in love
(with) 9
encantado/a *adj.* pleased to meet you 1
encantar *v.* to like very much; to love
(*objects*) 7
encima de *prep.* on top of 2
encontrar (o:ue) *v.* to find 4
encuesta *f.* poll; survey
energía *f.* energy 13
energía nuclear nuclear energy 13
energía solar solar energy 13
enero *m.* January 5
enfermarse *v.* to get sick 10
enfermedad *f.* illness 10
enfermero/a *m., f.* nurse 10
enfermo/a *adj.* sick 10
enfrente de *prep.* opposite; facing 14
engordar *v.* to gain weight 15
enojado/a *adj.* angry 5
enojarse *v.* **(con)** to get angry
(with) 7
ensalada *f.* salad 8
enseguida *adv.* right away
enseñar *v.* to teach 2
ensuciar *v.* to get (something) dirty 12
entender (e:ie) *v.* to understand 4
entonces *adv.* then 7
entrada *f.* entrance 12; ticket
entre *prep.* between; among 2
entremeses *m., pl.* appetizers 8
entrenarse *v.* to train 15
entrevista *f.* interview 16
entrevistador(a) *m., f.* interviewer 16
entrevistar *v.* to interview 16
envase *m.* container 13
enviar *v.* to send 14; to mail
equilibrado/a *adj.* balanced 15
equipaje *m.* luggage 5
equipo *m.* team 4
equivocado/a *adj.* wrong 5
eres you are *fam. sing.* 1
es you are *form. sing.*; he/she/it is 1
Es una lástima... It's a shame... 13
Es bueno que... It's good that... 12
Es extraño... It's strange... 13
Es importante que... It's
important that . . . 12
Es imposible... It's impossible... 13
Es improbable... It's improbable...13
Es la una. It's one o'clock. 1

Es malo que... It's bad that... **12**
Es mejor que... It's better that... **12**
Es necesario que... It's
necessary that... **12**
Es obvio... It's obvious... **13**
Es ridículo... It's ridiculous... **13**
Es seguro... It's certain... **13**
Es terrible... It's terrible... **13**
Es triste... It's sad... **13**
Es urgente que... It's urgent
that... **12**
Es verdad... It's certain... **13**
esa(s) *f., adj.* that; those **6**
ésa(s) *f., pron.* those (ones) **6**
escalar *v.* to climb **4**
  escalar montañas *f., pl.* to go
    mountain climbing **4**
escalera *f.* stairs **12**
escanear *v.* to scan **11**
escoger *v.* choose
escribir *v.* to write **3**
  escribir una carta to write a letter **4**
  escribir un mensaje electrónico
    to write an e-mail **4**
  escribir una (tarjeta) postal
    to write a postcard **4**
escrito/a *p.p.* written **15**
escritor(a) *m., f.* writer **16**
escritorio *m.* desk **2**
escuchar *v.* to listen (to) **2**
  escuchar la radio to listen to
    the radio
  escuchar música to listen to music
escuela *f.* school **1**
esculpir *v.* to sculpt
escultor(a) *m., f.* sculptor **16**
escultura *f.* sculpture
ese *m., sing., adj.* that **6**
ése *m., sing., pron.* that (one) **6**
eso *neuter, pron.* that; that thing **6**
esos *m., pl., adj.* those **6**
ésos *m., pl., pron.* those (ones) **6**
español *m.* Spanish (*language*) **2**
español(a) *adj.* Spanish **3**
espárragos *m., pl.* asparagus
especialización *f.* field of study **16**;
  specialization
espectacular *adj.* spectacular
espectáculo *m.* show
espejo *m.* mirror **7**
esperar *v.* to wait (for); to hope **2**;
  to wish **13**
esposo/a *m., f.* husband/wife;
  spouse **3**
esquí (acuático) *m.* (water) skiing **4**
esquiar *v.* to ski **4**
esquina *m.* corner **14**
está he/she/it is, you are *form.* **1**
  Está despejado. It's clear.
    (*weather*) **5**
  Está (muy) nublado. It's
    (very) cloudy. (*weather*) **5**
esta(s) *f., adj.* this; these **6**
  esta noche tonight

ésta(s) *f., pron.* this (one); these
  (ones) **6**
  Ésta es... *f.* This is...
    (*introducing someone*) **1**
establecer *v.* to establish
estación *f.* station **5**; season **5**
  estación de autobuses bus
    station **5**
  estación del metro subway
    station **5**
  estación del tren train station **5**
estacionar *v.* to park **11**
estadio *m.* stadium **2**
estado civil *m.* marital status **9**
estadounidense *adj.* from the
  United States **3**
estampilla *f.* stamp **14**
estante *m.* bookcase; bookshelf **12**
estar *v.* to be **2**
  estar a dieta to be on a diet **15**
  estar aburrido/a to be bored **5**
  estar afectado/a (por) to be
    affected (by) **13**
  estar contaminado/a to be
    polluted **13**
  estar de acuerdo to agree
  estar de moda to be in fashion
  estar de vacaciones to be on
    vacation **5**
  estar en buena forma to be in
    good shape **15**
  estar enfermo/a to be sick **10**
  estar listo/a to be ready **5**
  estar perdido/a to be lost **14**
  estar roto/a to be broken
  estar seguro/a (de) to be sure
    (of) **5, 13**
estatua *f.* statue
este *m.* east **14**
este *m., sing., adj.* this **6**
éste *m., sing., pron.* this (one) **6**
  Éste es... *m.* This is...
    (*introducing someone*) **1**
estilo *m.* style
estiramiento *m.* stretching **15**
esto *neuter pron.* this; this thing **6**
estómago *m.* stomach **10**
estornudar *v.* to sneeze **10**
estos *m., pl., adj.* these **6**
éstos *m., pl., pron.* these (ones) **6**
estrella *f.* star **13**
  estrella de cine movie star
estrés *m.* stress **15**
estudiante *m., f.* student **1**
estudiantil *adj. m., f.* student
estudiar *v.* to study **2**
estufa *f.* stove **12**
estupendo/a *adj.* stupendous
etapa *f.* stage **9**; step
evitar *v.* to avoid **13**
examen *m.* test; exam **2**
  examen médico physical exam **10**
excelente *adj.* excellent
exceso *m.* excess; too much **15**

excursión *f.* hike; tour;
  excursion **4**
excursionista *m., f.* hiker **4**
éxito *m.* success
experiencia *f.* experience
explicar *v.* to explain **2**
explorar *v.* to explore
expresión *f.* expression
extinción *f.* extinction **13**
extranjero/a *adj.* foreign
extraño/a *adj.* strange **13**

F

fábrica *f.* factory **13**
fabuloso/a *adj* fabulous
fácil *adj.* easy **3**
falda *f.* skirt **6**
faltar *v.* to lack; to need **7**
familia *f.* family **3**
famoso/a *adj.* famous
farmacia *f.* pharmacy **10**
fascinar *v.* to fascinate; to like very
  much **7**
favorito/a *adj.* favorite **4**
febrero *m.* February **5**
fecha *f.* date **5**
feliz *adj.* happy **5**
  ¡Felicidades! Congratulations!
    (*for an event such as a birthday
    or anniversary*)
  ¡Felicitaciones! Congratulations!
    (*for an event such as an engagement
    or a good grade on a test*)
  ¡Feliz cumpleaños! Happy
    birthday!
fenomenal *adj.* great; phenomenal
feo/a *adj.* ugly **3**
festival *m.* festival
fiebre *f.* fever **10**
fiesta *f.* party **9**
fijo/a *adj.* set, fixed **6**
fin *m.* end **4**
  fin de semana weekend **4**
finalmente *adv.* finally
firmar *v.* to sign (*a document*) **14**
física *f.* physics **2**
flan *m.* baked custard **9**
flexible *adj.* flexible **15**
flor *f.* flower **13**
folclórico/a *adj.* folk; folkloric
folleto *m.* brochure
forma *f.* shape **15**
formulario *m.* form **14**
foto(grafía) *f.* photograph **1**
francés, francesa *adj.* French **3**
frenos *m., pl.* brakes **11**
fresco/a *adj.* cool
frijoles *m., pl.* beans **8**
frío *m.* cold **3**
frito/a *adj.* fried
fruta *f.* fruit **8**
frutería *f.* fruit shop **14**
fuera *adv.* outside

fuerte *adj.* strong **15**
fumar *v.* to smoke **15**
   no fumar not to smoke **15**
funcionar *v.* to work **11**; to function
fútbol *m.* soccer **4**
fútbol americano football **4**
futuro/a *adj.* future
   en el futuro in the future

G

gafas (de sol) *f., pl.* (sun)glasses **6**
galleta *f.* cookie **9**
ganar *v.* to win **4**; to earn (money) **16**
ganga *f.* bargain
garaje *m.* garage; (mechanic's) repair
   shop **11**; garage **12**
garganta *f.* throat **10**
gasolina *f.* gasoline **11**
gasolinera *f.* gas station **11**
gastar *v.* to spend (*money*) **6**
gato/a *m., f.* cat **3**
gente *f.* people **3**
geografía *f.* geography **2**
gerente *m., f.* manager **16**
gimnasio *m.* gym, gymnasium **4**
gobierno *m.* government **13**
golf *m.* golf **4**
gordo/a *adj.* fat **3**
grabar *v.* to record **11**
gracias *f., pl.* thank you; thanks **1**
graduarse (de) *v.* to graduate (from) **9**
gran *adj.* great **3**
grande *adj.* big **3**
grasa *f.* fat **15**
gratis *adj.* free of charge **14**
grave *adj.* grave; serious **10**
gripe *f.* flu **10**
gris *adj.* gray **6**
gritar *v.* to scream
guantes *m., pl.* gloves **6**
guapo/a *adj.* good-looking **3**
guardar *v.* to save (on a computer) **11**
guerra *f.* war
guía *m., f.* guide
gustar *v.* to be pleasing to; to like **2, 7**
   Me gustaría(n)... I would like **7**
gusto *m.* pleasure **1**
   El gusto es mío. The pleasure
      is mine. **1**
   Mucho gusto. Pleased to meet you. **1**

H

haber (*aux.*) *v.* to have (*done
   something*) **15**
habitación *f.* room **5**
   habitación doble double room **5**
   habitación individual single
      room **5**
habitantes *m., pl.* inhabitants
hablar *v.* to talk; to speak **2**
hacer *v.* to do; to make **4**

Hace buen tiempo. The weather is
   nice. **5**
Hace (mucho) calor. It's (very) hot.
   (*weather*) **5**
Hace fresco. It's cool. (*weather*) **5**
Hace (mucho) frío. It's (very) cold.
   (*weather*) **5**
Hace mal tiempo. The weather is
   bad **5**
Hace (mucho) sol. It's (very) sunny.
   (*weather*) **5**
Hace (mucho) viento. It's (very)
   windy. (*weather*) **5**
hacer cola to stand in line **14**
hacer diligencias to run
   errands **14**
hacer ejercicio to exercise **15**
hacer ejercicios aeróbicos to do
   aerobics **15**
hacer ejercicios de estiramiento
   to do stretching exercises **15**
hacer el papel to play a role
hacer gimnasia to work out **15**
hacer juego (con) to match **6**
hacer la cama to make the bed **12**
hacer las maletas to pack (one's
   suitcases) **5**
hacer los quehaceres domésticos
   to do household chores **12**
hacer turismo to go sightseeing **5**
hacer un viaje to take a trip **5**
hacer una excursión to go on a
   hike; to go on a tour **5**
hacia *prep.* toward **14**
hambre *f.* hunger
hamburguesa *f.* hamburger **8**
   hamburguesa vegetariana *f.*
      veggie burger **8**
hasta *prep.* until **6**; toward
   Hasta la vista. See you later. **1**
   Hasta luego. See you later. **1**
   Hasta mañana. See you tomorrow. **1**
   hasta que *conj.* until **13**
   Hasta pronto. See you soon. **1**
hay there is; there are **1**
   Hay (mucha) niebla. It's (very)
      foggy. **5**
   No hay de qué. You're welcome. **1**
   no hay duda de there's no
      doubt **13**
hecho/a *p.p.* done **15**
heladería *f.* ice cream shop **14**
helado *m.* ice cream **9**
helado/a *adj.* iced **8**
hermanastro/a *m., f.* stepbrother/
   stepsister **3**
hermano/a *m., f.* brother/sister **3**
hermano/a mayor/menor *m., f.* older/
   younger brother/sister
hermanos *m., pl.* siblings (brothers
   and sisters) **3**
hermoso/a *adj.* beautiful **6**
hierba *f.* grass **13**
hijastro/a *m., f.* stepson/stepdaughter **3**

hijo/a *m., f.* son/daughter **3**
   hijo/a único/a only child
   hijos *m., pl.* children; sons **3**
historia *f.* history **2**; story
hockey *m.* hockey **4**
hogar *m.* home **12**
hola *interj.* hello **1**
hombre *m.* man **1**
   hombre de negocios businessman
      16
hora *f.* hour
horario *m.* schedule **2**
horno *m.* oven **12**
hospital *m.* hospital **10**
hotel *m.* hotel **5**
hoy *adv.* today **2**
   hoy día nowadays
   Hoy es... Today is... **2**
huelga *f.* strike (labor)
hueso *m.* bone **10**
huésped *m., f.* guest **5**
huevo *m.* egg **8**
humanidades *f., pl.* humanities
huracán *m.* hurricane

I

ida *f.* one way (*travel*)
idea *f.* idea
iglesia *f.* church **4**
igualdad *f.* equality
igualmente *adv.* likewise **1**
impermeable *m.* raincoat **6**
importante *adj.* important **3**
importar *v.* to be important (to);
   to matter **7, 12**
imposible *adj.* impossible **13**
impresora *f.* printer **11**
imprimir *v.* to print **11**
improbable *adj.* improbable **13**
impuesto *m.* tax
incendio *m.* fire
increíble *adj.* incredible
indicar cómo llegar *v.* to give
   directions **14**
infección *f.* infection **10**
informar *v.* to inform
informe *m.* report; paper (*written
   work*)
ingeniero/a *m., f.* engineer **3**
inglés *m.* English (*language*) **2**
inglés, inglesa *adj.* English **3**
insistir (en) *v.* to insist (on) **12**
inspector(a) de aduanas *m., f.*
   customs inspector **5**
inteligente *adj.* intelligent **3**
intercambiar *v.* exchange
interesante *adj.* interesting **3**
interesar *v.* to be interesting to;
   to interest **7**
internacional *adj.* international
Internet Internet **11**
inundación *f.* flood
invertir (e:ie) *v.* to invest **16**

invierno *m.* winter 5
invitado/a *m., f.* guest (*at a function*) 9
invitar *v.* to invite; to treat 9
inyección *f.* injection 10
ir *v.* to go 4
  ir a (+ *inf.*) to be going to do something 4
  ir a la playa to go to the beach 5
  ir de compras to go shopping 6
  ir de excursión (a las montañas) to go for a hike (in the mountains) 4
  ir de pesca to go fishing 5
  ir de vacaciones to go on vacation 5
  ir en autobús to go by bus 5
  ir en auto(móvil) to go by car 5
  ir en avión to go by plane 5
  ir en barco to go by boat 5
  ir en metro to go by subway 5
  ir en motocicleta to go by motorcycle 5
  ir en taxi to go by taxi 5
  ir en tren to go by train
irse *v.* to go away; to leave 7
italiano/a *adj.* Italian
izquierda *f.* left 2
  a la izquierda de to the left of 2

J

jabón *m.* soap 7
jamás *adv.* never; not ever 7
jamón *m.* ham 8
japonés, japonesa *adj.* Japanese 3
jardín *m.* garden; yard 12
jefe, jefa *m., f.* boss 16
joven *adj.* young 3
joven *m., f.* young person 1
joyería *f.* jewelry store 14
jubilarse *v.* to retire (*from work*) 9
juego *m.* game
jueves *m., sing.* Thursday 2
jugador(a) *m., f.* player 4
jugar (u:ue) *v.* to play 4
  jugar a las cartas to play cards
jugo *m.* juice 8
  jugo de fruta fruit juice 8
julio *m.* July 5
jungla *f.* jungle
junio *m.* June 5
juntos/as *adj.* together 9
juventud *f.* youth 9

K

kilómetro *m.* kilometer 11

l

la *f., sing., def. art.* the 1
la *f., sing., d.o. pron.* her, it, *form.* you 5

laboratorio *m.* laboratory 2
lago *m.* lake 13
lámpara *f.* lamp 12
langosta *f.* lobster 8
lápiz *m.* pencil 1
largo/a *m.* long (*in length*) 6
las *f., pl., def. art.* the 1
las *f., pl., d.o. pron.* them; you 5
lástima *f.* shame 13
lastimarse *v.* to injure oneself 10
  lastimarse el pie to injure one's foot 10
lata *f.* (*tin*) can 13
lavabo *m.* sink
lavadora *f.* washing machine 12
lavandería *f.* laundromat 14
lavaplatos *m., sing.* dishwasher 12
lavar *v.* to wash 12
lavarse *v.* to wash oneself 7
  lavarse la cara to wash one's face 7
  lavarse las manos to wash one's hands 7
le *sing., i.o. pron.* to/for him, her, you *form.* 6
Le presento a... I would like to introduce... to you. *form.* 1
lección *f.* lesson 1
leche *f.* milk 8
lechuga *f.* lettuce 8
leer *v.* to read 3
  leer el correo electrónico to read e-mail 4
  leer el periódico to read the newspaper 4
  leer una revista to read a magazine 4
leído/a *p.p.* read 15
lejos de *prep.* far from 2
lengua *f.* language 2
  lenguas extranjeras *f., pl.* foreign languages 2
lentes de contacto *m., pl.* contact lenses
lento/a *adj.* slow 11
les *pl., i.o. pron.* to/for them, you *pl.* 6
letrero *m.* sign 14
levantar *v.* to lift 15
  levantar pesas to lift weights 15
levantarse *v.* to get up 7
ley *f.* law 13
libertad *f.* liberty; freedom
libre *adj.* free 4
librería *f.* bookstore 2
libro *m.* book 2
licencia de conducir *f.* driver's license 11
limón *m.* lemon 8
limpiar *v.* to clean 12
  limpiar la casa to clean the house 12
limpio/a *adj.* clean 5
listo/a *adj.* smart; ready 5

literatura *f.* literature
llamar *v.* to call 11
  llamar por teléfono to call on the phone
llamarse to be named 7
llanta *f.* tire 11
llave *f.* key 5
llegada *f.* arrival 5
llegar *v.* to arrive 2
llenar *v.* to fill
  llenar el tanque to fill the tank 11
  llenar un formulario to fill out a form 14
lleno/a *adj.* full 11
llevar *v.* to carry 2; to take; to wear 6
  llevar una vida sana to lead a healthy lifestyle 15
  llevarse bien/mal (con) to get along well/badly (with) 9
llover (o:ue) *v.* to rain 5
  Llueve. It's raining. 5
lluvia *f.* rain
lo *m., sing. d.o. pronoun.* him, it, you *form.* 5
  lo mejor the best (thing)
  lo peor the worst (thing)
  lo que what; that which 9
  Lo siento. I'm sorry. 1
loco/a *adj.* crazy 6
locutor(a) *m., f.* TV or radio announcer
los *m., pl., def. art.* the 1
los *m., pl., do. pron.* them, you *pl.* 5
luchar (contra), (por) *v.* to fight; to struggle (against), (for)
luego *adv.* afterward, then 7; *adv.* later 1
lugar *m.* place 4
luna *f.* moon 13
lunar *m.* polka dot
lunes *m., sing.* Monday 2
luz *f.* light; electricity 12

M

madrastra *f.* stepmother 3
madre *f.* mother 3
madurez *f.* maturity; middle age 9
maestro/a *m., f.* teacher 16
magnífico/a *adj.* magnificent
maíz *m.* corn 8
mal, malo/a *adj.* bad 3; sick 5
maleta *f.* suitcase 1
mamá *f.* mom
mandar *v.* to order 12; to send 14; to mail
manejar *v.* to drive 11
manera *f.* way
mano *f.* hand 1
manta *f.* blanket 12
mantener *v.* to maintain
  mantenerse en forma to stay in shape 15
mantequilla *f.* butter 8

manzana *f.* apple **8**
mañana *f.* morning **1**; tomorrow **1**
mapa *m.* map **1**
maquillaje *m.* makeup **7**
maquillarse *v.* to put on makeup **7**
mar *m.* sea **5**
maravilloso/a *adj.* marvelous
marcador *m.* dry-erase marker **2**
mareado/a *adj.* dizzy; nauseated **10**
margarina *f.* margarine **8**
mariscos *m., pl.* seafood **8**
marrón *adj. m., f.* brown
martes *m., sing.* Tuesday **2**
marzo *m.* March **5**
más *adj., adv.* more **8**
  el/la/los/las más the most **8**
  más de (+ *number*) more
    than (+ *number*) **8**
  más tarde later (on) **7**
  más... que more... than **8**
masaje *m.* massage **15**
matemáticas *f., pl.* mathematics **2**
materia *f.* course
matrimonio *m.* marriage; married
  couple **9**
mayo *m.* May **5**
mayonesa *f.* mayonnaise **8**
mayor *adj.* older **8**
  el/la mayor *adj.* the oldest **8**
me *pron.* me **5, 6**
  Me gusta(n)... I like... **2**
  No me gusta(n)... I don't like... **2**
  Me gustaría(n)... I would like... **7**
  Me llamo... My name is... **1**
mecánico/a *m., f.* mechanic **11**
mediano/a *adj.* medium
medianoche *f.* midnight **1**
medias *f., pl.* pantyhose, stockings **6**
medicamento *m.* medication **10**
medicina *f.* medicine **10**
médico/a *m., f.* doctor **3**;
  adj. medical **10**
medio/a *m. adj.* half **3**
  medio ambiente environment **13**
  medio/a hermano/a
    half-brother/half-sister **3**
  medios de comunicación *m., pl.*
    means of communication; media
  y media thirty minutes past the
    hour (*time*) **1**
mediodía *m.* noon **1**
mejor *adj.* better **8**
  el/la mejor *m., f.* the best **8**
mejorar *v.* to improve **13**
melocotón *m.* peach
menor *adj.* younger **3, 8**
  el/la menor *m., f.* the youngest **8**
menos *adj., adv.* less **10**
  el/la/los/las menos the least **8**
  menos cuarto/menos quince
    quarter to (*time*) **1**
  menos de (+ *number*) less
    than (+ *number*) **8**
  menos... que less... than **8**

mensaje de texto text message **11**
mensaje electrónico *m.* e-mail
  message **4**
mentira *f.* lie **6**
menú *m.* menu **8**
mercado *m.* market **6**
  mercado al aire libre open-air
    market **6**
merendar (e:ie) *v.* to have a(n)
  (afternoon) snack **15**
merienda *f.* (afternoon) snack **15**
mes *m.* month **5**
mesa *f.* table **2**
mesita *f.* end table **12**
  mesita de noche nightstand **12**
metro *m.* subway **5**
mexicano/a *adj.* Mexican **3**
mí *pron. obj. of prep.* me
mi(s) *poss. adj.* my **3**
microondas *m., sing.* microwave **12**
miedo *m.* fear
mientras *conj.* while **10**
miércoles *m., sing.* Wednesday **2**
mil one thousand **6**
  mil millones billion **6**
milla *f.* mile **11**
millón million **6**
millones (de) millions (of) **6**
mineral *m.* mineral **15**
minuto *m.* minute
mío(s)/a(s) *poss.* my; (of) mine **11**
mirar *v.* to look (at); to watch **2**
  mirar (la) televisión to watch
    television
mismo/a *adj.* same
mochila *f.* backpack **1**
moda *f.* fashion
moderno/a *adj.* modern
molestar *v.* to bother; to annoy **7**
mono *m.* monkey **13**
montaña *f.* mountain **4**
montar *v.* **a caballo** to ride a horse **5**
monumento *m.* monument **4**
morado/a *adj.* purple **6**
moreno/a *adj.* dark-haired **3**
morir (o:ue) *v.* to die **8**
mostrar (o:ue) *v.* to show **4**
moto(cicleta) *f.* motorcycle **5**
motor *m.* motor **11**
muchacho/a *m., f.* boy; girl **3**
mucho/a *adj., adv.* many; a lot;
  much **2, 3**
  (Muchas) gracias. Thank you
    (very much). **1**
  muchas veces a lot; many
    times **10**
  Mucho gusto. Pleased to meet
    you. **1**
mudarse *v.* to move (from one house
  to another) **12**
muebles *m., pl.* furniture **12**
muela *f.* tooth **10**
muerte *f.* death **9**
muerto/a *p.p.* died **15**

mujer *f.* woman **1**
  mujer de negocios
    businesswoman **16**
  mujer policía female police
    officer **11**
multa *f.* fine; ticket **11**
mundial *adj.* worldwide
mundo *m.* world **13**
municipal *adj.* municipal
músculo *m.* muscle **15**
museo *m.* museum **4**
música *f.* music
musical *adj.* musical
músico/a *m., f.* musician
muy *adv.* very **1**
  (Muy) bien, gracias. (Very) well,
    thanks. **1**

N

nacer *v.* to be born **9**
nacimiento *m.* birth **9**
nacional *adj.* national
nacionalidad *f.* nationality **1**
nada *pron., adv.* nothing **1**; not
  anything **7**
nadar *v.* to swim **4**
  nadar en la piscina to swim in
    the pool **4**
nadie *pron.* no one, not anyone **7**
naranja *m.* orange **8**
nariz *f.* nose **10**
natación *f.* swimming **4**
natural *adj.* natural **13**
naturaleza *f.* nature **13**
navegador GPS GPS **11**
Navidad *f.* Christmas **9**
necesario/a *adj.* necessary **12**
necesitar *v.* to need **2, 12**
negar (e:ie) *v.* to deny **13**
negativo/a *m.* negative
negocios *m., pl.* business;
  commerce **16**
negro/a *adj.* black **6**
nervioso/a *adj.* nervous **5**
nevar (e:ie) *v.* to snow **5**
  Nieva. It's snowing. **5**
ni... ni *conj.* neither... nor **7**
niebla *f.* fog
nieto/a *m., f.* grandson/
  granddaughter **3**
nieve *f.* snow
ningún, ninguno/a(s) *adj.* no; none;
  not any **7**
niñez *f.* childhood **9**
niño/a *m., f.* child; boy/girl **3**
no *adv.* no; not **1**
  no cabe duda de there is no
    doubt **13**
  No es seguro... It's not certain...
    13
  No es verdad... It's not true... **13**
  no estar de acuerdo to disagree

no estar seguro/a (de) not to be sure (of) **13**

No estoy seguro. I'm not sure.

no hay there is not; there are not **1**

No hay de qué. You're welcome. **1**

no hay duda de there is no doubt **13**

no muy bien not very well **1**

¿no? right? **2**

no sé I don't know

no tener razón to be wrong **3**

noche *f.* night **1**

nombre *m.* name

norte *m.* north **14**

norteamericano/a *adj.* (North) American **3**

nos *pron.* us **5, 6**

Nos vemos. See you. **1**

nosotros/as *sub. pron.* we **1**

noticias *f., pl.* news

noticiero *m.* newscast

novecientos/as nine hundred **6**

noveno/a *adj.* ninth **5**

noventa ninety **2**

noviembre *m.* November **5**

novio/a *m., f.* boyfriend/girlfriend **3**

nube *f.* cloud **13**

nublado/a *adj.* cloudy **5**

Está (muy) nublado. It's (very) cloudy. **5**

nuclear *adj.* nuclear **13**

nuera *f.* daughter-in-law **3**

nuestro(s)/a(s) *poss. adj.* our **3;** of ours **11**

nueve nine **1**

nuevo/a *adj.* new **6**

número *m.* number **1;** (shoe) size

nunca *adj.* never; not ever **7**

nutrición *f.* nutrition **15**

O

o *conj.* or **7**

o... o *conj.* either . . . or **7**

obedecer *v.* to obey

obra *f.* work (*of art, literature, music, etc.*)

obra maestra masterpiece

obtener *v.* to obtain; to get **16**

obvio/a *adj.* obvious **13**

océano *m.* ocean **13**

ochenta eighty **2**

ocho eight **1**

ochocientos/as eight hundred **6**

octavo/a *adj.* eighth **5**

octubre *m.* October **5**

ocupación *f.* occupation **16**

ocupado/a *adj.* busy **5**

ocurrir *v.* to occur; to happen

odiar *v.* to hate **9**

oeste *m.* west **14**

oferta *f.* offer

oficina *f.* office **12**

oficio *m.* trade **16**

ofrecer *v.* to offer **8**

oído *m.* sense of hearing; inner ear

oído/a *p.p.* heard **15**

oír *v.* to hear **4**

ojalá (que) *interj.* I hope (that); I wish (that) **13**

ojo *m.* eye **10**

olvidar *v.* to forget **10**

once eleven **1**

ópera *f.* opera

operación *f.* operation **10**

ordenado/a *adj.* orderly **5;** well organized

ordinal *adj.* ordinal (*number*)

oreja *f.* (outer) ear **10**

orquesta *f.* orchestra

ortográfico/a *adj.* spellling

os *fam., pl. pron.* you **5, 6**

otoño *m.* autumn **5**

otro/a *adj.* other; another **6**

otra vez again

P

paciente *m., f.* patient **10**

padrastro *m.* stepfather **3**

padre *m.* father **3**

padres *m., pl.* parents **3**

pagar *v.* to pay **6**

pagar a plazos to pay in installments **14**

pagar al contado to pay in cash **14**

pagar con to pay with **6**

pagar en efectivo to pay in cash

pagar la cuenta to pay the bill **9**

página *f.* page **11**

página principal home page **11**

país *m.* country **1**

paisaje *m.* landscape **13;** countryside

pájaro *m.* bird **13**

palabra *f.* word **1**

pan *m.* bread **8**

pan tostado toasted bread **8;** toast

panadería *f.* bakery **14**

pantalla *f.* screen **11**

pantalones *m., pl.* pants **6**

pantalones cortos shorts **6**

papa *f.* potato **8**

papas fritas *f., pl.* French fries **8**

papá *m.* dad

papás *m., pl.* parents

papel *m.* paper **2;** role

paquete *m.* package **14**

par *m.* pair **6**

par de zapatos pair of shoes **6**

para *prep.* for; in order to; toward; in the direction of; by; used for; considering **11**

para que *conj.* so that **13**

parabrisas *m., sing.* windshield **11**

parar *v.* to stop **11**

parecer *v.* to seem **8**

pared *f.* wall **12**

pareja *f.* couple; partner **9**

parientes *m., pl.* relatives **3**

parque *m.* park **4**

párrafo *m.* paragraph

partido *m.* game **4;** match (*sports*)

pasado/a *adj.* last; past **6**

pasaje *m.* ticket **5**

pasaje de ida y vuelta *m.* round-trip ticket **5**

pasajero/a *m., f.* passenger **1**

pasaporte *m.* passport **5**

pasar *v.* to pass

pasar la aspiradora to vacuum **12**

pasar por la aduana to go through customs **5**

pasar el tiempo to spend time **4**

pasarlo bien/mal to have a good/bad time **9**

pasatiempo *m.* pastime, hobby **4**

pasear *v.* to take a walk; to stroll

pasear en bicicleta to ride a bicycle **4**

pasear por la ciudad/el pueblo to walk around the city/town **4**

pasillo *m.* hallway **12**

pastel *m.* cake **9**

pastel de chocolate chocolate cake

pastel de cumpleaños birthday cake **9**

pastelería *f.* pastry shop **14**

pastilla *f.* pill **10**

patata *f.* potato **8**

patatas fritas *f., pl.* French fries **8**

patinar *v.* to skate **4**

patio *m.* patio; yard **12**

pavo *m.* turkey **8**

paz *f.* peace

pedir (e:i) *v.* to ask for; to request **4, 12;** to order (*food*) **8**

pedir prestado/a to borrow **14**

pedir un préstamo to apply for a loan **14**

peinarse *v.* to comb one's hair **7**

película *f.* movie **4**

peligro *m.* danger **13**

peligroso/a *adj.* dangerous

pelirrojo/a *adj.* red-haired **3**

pelo *m.* hair **7**

pelota *f.* ball **4**

peluquería *f.* hair salon **14**

peluquero/a *m., f.* hairdresser **16**

penicilina *f.* penicillin

pensar (e:ie) *v.* to think **4**

pensar (+ inf.) to intend; to plan (*to do something*) **4**

pensar en to think about **4**

pensión *f.* boarding house **5**

peor *adj.* worse **8**

el/la peor the worst **8**

pequeño/a *adj.* small **3**

pera *f.* pear

perder (e:ie) *v.* to lose; to miss **4**

perdido/a *adj.* lost **14**

Perdón. Pardon me.; Excuse me.
perezoso/a *adj.* lazy
perfecto/a *adj.* perfect
periódico *m.* newspaper 4
periodismo *m.* journalism 2
periodista *m., f.* journalist 3
permiso *m.* permission
pero *conj.* but 2
perro/a *m., f.* dog 3
persona *f.* person 3
personaje *m.* character
   personaje principal main character
pesas *f., pl.* weights 15
pesca *f.* fishing 5
pescadería *f.* fish market 14
pescado *m.* fish (*cooked*) 8
pescador(a) *m., f.* fisherman/
   fisherwoman
pescar *v.* to fish 5
peso *m.* weight 15
pez *m.* fish (*live*) 13
picante *adj.* spicy 8
pie *m.* foot 10
piedra *f.* stone 13
pierna *f.* leg 10
pimienta *f.* pepper 8
piña *f.* pineapple
pintar *v.* to paint
pintor(a) *m., f.* painter 16
pintura *f.* painting 12
piscina *f.* swimming pool 4
piso *m.* floor (*of a building*) 5
pizarra *f.* whiteboard 2
placer *m.* pleasure
planchar la ropa *v.* to iron clothes 12
planta *f.* plant 13
   planta baja ground floor 5
plástico *m.* plastic 13
plato *m.* dish (*in a meal*) 8;
   plate 12
   plato principal main dish 8
playa *f.* beach 5
pluma *f.* pen 2
población *f.* population 13
pobre *m., f., adj.* poor 6
pobreza *f.* poverty
poco *adv.* little 10
poder (o:ue) *v.* to be able to; can 4
poema *m.* poem
poesía *f.* poetry
poeta *m., f.* poet 16
policía *f.* police (force) 11; *m.* (male)
   police officer 11
política *f.* politics
político/a *m., f.* politician 16
pollo *m.* chicken 8
   pollo asado roast chicken 8
poner *v.* to put; to place 4; to turn on
   (*electrical appliances*) 11
   poner la mesa to set the table 12
   poner una inyección to give an
     injection 10

ponerse (+ adj.) to become (+ *adj.*) 7;
   to put on 7
por *prep.* in exchange for; for; by;
   in; through; by means of; along;
   during; around; in search of; by way
   of; per 11
   por aquí around here 11
   por avión by plane
   por ciento percent
   por ejemplo for example 11
   por eso that's why; therefore 11
   Por favor. Please. 1
   por fin finally 11
   por la mañana in the morning 7
   por la noche at night 7
   por la tarde in the afternoon; in
     the (early) evening 7
   por lo menos at least 10
   ¿por qué? why? 2, 9
   por supuesto of course
   por teléfono by phone; on the phone
   por último finally 7
posesivo/a *adj.* possessive
posible *adj.* possible 13
   es posible it's possible 13
   no es posible it's not possible 13
postal *f.* postcard 4
postre *m.* dessert 9
practicar *v.* to practice 2
   practicar deportes *m., pl.* to play
     sports 4
precio (fijo) *m.* (fixed) price 6
preferir (e:ie) *v.* to prefer 4, 12
pregunta *f.* question
preguntar *v.* to ask (*a question*) 2
premio *m.* prize; award
prender *v.* to turn on 11
prensa *f.* press
preocupado/a (por) *adj.* worried
   (about) 5
preocuparse (por) *v.* to worry
   (about) 7
preparar *v.* to prepare 2
preposición *f.* preposition
presentación *f.* introduction
presentar *v.* to introduce; to put on
   (*a performance*)
presiones *f., pl.* pressure 15
prestado/a *adj.* borrowed
préstamo *m.* loan 14
prestar *v.* to loan 6
primavera *f.* spring 5
primer, primero/a *adj.* first 5
primo/a *m., f.* cousin 3
principal *adj.* main 8
probable *adj. m., f.* probable 13
   es probable it's probable 13
   no es probable it's not probable 13
probar (o:ue) *v.* to taste; to try 8
probarse (o:ue) *v.* to try on 7
problema *m.* problem 1
profesión *f.* profession 16
profesor(a) *m., f.* teacher; professor 1

programa *m.* program 1
   programa de computación
     software 11
   programa de entrevistas talk show
programador(a) *m., f.* programmer 3
prohibir *v.* to prohibit 10, 12; to forbid
pronombre *m.* pronoun
pronto *adj.* soon 10
propina *f.* tip 9
propio/a *adj.* own
proteger *v.* to protect 13
proteína *f.* protein 15
próximo/a *adj.* next
prueba *f.* test; quiz 2
psicología *f.* psychology 2
psicólogo/a *m., f.* psychologist 16
publicar *v.* to publish
público *m.* audience
pueblo *m.* town 4
puerta *f.* door 2
puerto *m.* **USB** USB port 11
puertorriqueño/a *adj.* Puerto
   Rican 3
pues *conj.* well; then
puesto *m.* position; job 16
puesto/a *p.p.* put 15
puro/a *adj.* pure 13

Q

que *pron.* that; who; which 9
¡Qué...! How...!
   ¡Qué sorpresa! What a surprise!
¿qué? what?; which? 1, 2, 9
   ¿Qué día es hoy? What day is it?
   ¿Qué es? What is it? 1
   ¿Qué hay de nuevo? What's
     new? 1
   ¿Qué hicieron ellos/ellas? What
     did they do? 6
   ¿Qué hicieron ustedes? What did
     you (*pl.*) do? 6
   ¿Qué hiciste? What did you
     (*fam., sing.*) do? 6
   ¿Qué hizo él/ella? What did
     he/she do? 6
   ¿Qué hizo usted? What did you
     (*form., sing.*) do? 6
   ¿Qué hora es? What time is it? 1
   ¿Qué pasa? What's going on? 1
   ¿Qué pasó? What happened?;
     What's wrong?
   ¿Qué precio tiene? What is the
     price?
   ¿Qué tal? How is it going? 1
   ¿Qué tiempo hace? How's the
     weather? 5
quedar *v.* to be left over; to fit
   (*clothing*) 7; to be left behind 10; to
   be located 14
quedarse *v.* to stay 7
quehaceres domésticos *m., pl.*
   household chores 12

querer (e:ie) *v.* to want **4, 12**; to love **4**

queso *m.* cheese **8**

quien(es) *pron.* who **1**; whom; that **9**

  ¿Quién es? Who is it? **1**

  ¿Quién habla? Who is speaking? (*telephone*)

  ¿quién(es)? who?; whom? **1, 2**

química *f.* chemistry **2**

quince fifteen **1**

  menos quince quarter to (time) **1**

  y quince quarter after (time) **1**

quinceañera *f.* young woman celebrating her fifteenth birthday **9**

quinientos/as five hundred **6**

quinto/a *adj.* fifth **5**

quisiera *v.* I would like

quitar la mesa *v.* to clear the table **12**

quitarse *v.* to take off **7**

quizás *adv.* maybe **13**

R

racismo *m.* racism

radio *f.* radio (*medium*)

radio *m.* radio (set) **11**

radiografía *f.* X-ray **10**

rápido/a *adj.* fast

ratón *m.* mouse **11**

ratos libres *m., pl.* spare time **4**

raya *f.* stripe

razón *f.* reason

rebaja *f.* sale **6**

recado *m.* (telephone) message

receta *f.* prescription **10**

recetar *v.* to prescribe **10**

recibir *v.* to receive **3**

reciclaje *m.* recycling **13**

reciclar *v.* to recycle **13**

recién casado/a *m., f.* newlywed **9**

recoger *v.* to pick up **13**

recomendar (e:ie) *v.* to recommend **8, 12**

recordar (o:ue) *v.* to remember **4**

recurso *m.* resource **13**

  recurso natural natural resource **13**

red *f.* network; Web **11**

reducir *v.* to reduce **13**

refresco *m.* soft drink **8**

refrigerador *m.* refrigerator **12**

regalar *v.* to give (*as a gift*) **9**

regalo *m.* gift **6**

regatear *v.* to bargain **6**

región *f.* region; area **13**

regresar *v.* to return **2**

regular *adj. m., f.* so-so **1**

reído/a *p.p.* laughed **15**

reírse (e:i) *v.* to laugh **9**

relaciones *f., pl.* relationships

relajarse *v.* to relax **9**

reloj *m.* clock; watch **2**

renovable *adj.* renewable **13**

renunciar (a) *v.* to resign (from) **16**

repetir (e:i) *v.* to repeat **4**

---

reportaje *m.* report

reportero/a *m., f.* reporter **16**; journalist

representante *m., f.* representative

resfriado *m.* cold (*illness*) **10**

residencia estudiantil *f.* dormitory **2**

resolver (o:ue) *v.* to resolve; to solve **13**

respirar *v.* to breathe **13**

respuesta *f.* answer **9**

restaurante *m.* restaurant **4**

resuelto/a *p.p.* resolved **15**

reunión *f.* meeting **16**

revisar *v.* to check **11**

  revisar el aceite to check the oil **11**

revista *f.* magazine **4**

rico/a *adj.* rich **6**; *adj.* tasty **8**

ridículo *adj.* ridiculous **13**

río *m.* river **13**

rodilla *f.* knee **10**

rogar (o:ue) *v.* to beg **12**

rojo/a *adj.* red **6**

romántico/a *adj.* romantic

romper (con) *v.* to break up (with) **9**

romper(se) *v.* to break **10**

  romperse la pierna to break one's leg **10**

ropa *f.* clothing **6**

  ropa interior underwear **6**

rosado/a *adj.* pink **6**

roto/a *p.p.* broken **15**

rubio/a *adj.* blond **3**

ruso/a *adj.* Russian

rutina *f.* routine **7**

  rutina diaria daily routine **7**

S

sábado *m.* Saturday **2**

saber *v.* to know; to know how **8**

sabroso/a *adj.* delicious **8**

sacar *v.* to take out **12**

  sacar fotos to take pictures **5**

  sacar la basura to take out the trash **12**

  sacar(se) una muela to have a tooth pulled **10**

sacudir *v.* to dust **12**

  sacudir los muebles to dust the furniture **12**

sal *f.* salt **8**

sala *f.* living room **12**; room

  sala de emergencia(s) emergency room **10**

salado/a *adj.* salty **8**

salario *m.* salary **16**

salchicha *f.* sausage **8**

salida *f.* departure; exit **5**

salir *v.* to leave **4**; to go out

  salir con to leave with; to go out with **4, 9**; to date (*someone*) **9**

  salir de to leave from **4**

  salir para to leave for (*a place*) **4**

salmón *m.* salmon **8**

salón de belleza *m.* beauty salon **14**

---

salón de clases *m.* classroom **2**

salud *f.* health **10**

saludable *adj.* healthy **10**

saludar(se) *v.* to greet (each other)

saludo *m.* greeting

  saludos a... say hello to... **1**

sandalia *f.* sandal **6**

sándwich *m.* sandwich **8**

sano/a *adj.* healthy **10**

se *ref.pron.* himself, herself, itself, *form.* yourself, themselves, yourselves **7**

secadora *f.* clothes dryer **12**

secretario/a *m., f.* secretary **16**

secuencia *f.* sequence

sed *f.* thirst

sedentario/a *adj.* sedentary **15**

seguir (e:i) *v.* to follow; to continue; to keep (doing something) **4**

  seguir una dieta equilibrada to eat a balanced diet **15**

según *prep.* according to

segundo/a *adj.* second **5**

seguro/a *adj.* sure; safe; confident **5**

seis six **1**

seiscientos/as six hundred **6**

sello *m.* stamp **14**

selva *f.* jungle **13**

semáforo *m.* traffic light **11**

semana *f.* week **2**

  fin *m.* **de semana** weekend **4**

  la semana pasada last week **6**

semestre *m.* semester **2**

sendero *m.* trail **13**

sentarse (e:ie) *v.* to sit down **7**

sentir (e:ie) *v.* to be sorry; to regret **13**

sentirse (e:ie) *v.* to feel **7**

señor (Sr.) *m.* Mr.; sir **1**

señora (Sra.) *f.* Mrs.; ma'am **1**

señorita (Srta.) *f.* Miss **1**; young woman

separado/a *adj.* separated **9**

separarse (de) *v.* to separate (from) **9**

septiembre *m.* September **5**

séptimo/a *adj.* seventh **5**

ser *v.* to be **1**

  ser aficionado/a (a) to be a fan (of) **4**

  ser alérgico/a (a) to be allergic (to) **10**

  ser gratis to be free of charge **14**

serio/a *adj.* serious

servilleta *f.* napkin **12**

servir (e:i) *v.* to serve **8**

sesenta sixty **2**

setecientos/as seven hundred **6**

setenta seventy **2**

sexismo *m.* sexism

sexto/a *adj.* sixth **5**

sí *adv.* yes

si *conj.* if

siempre *adv.* always **7**

siete seven 1
silla *f.* chair 2
sillón *m.* armchair 12
similar *adj. m., f.* similar
simpático/a *adj.* nice 3
sin *prep.* without 13, 15
   sin duda without a doubt
   sin embargo *adv.* however
   sin que *conj.* without 13
sino *conj.* but 7
síntoma *m.* symptom 10
sitio *m.* **web** website 11
situado/a *p.p.* located
sobre *m.* envelope 14; *prep.* on;
   over 2
sobrino/a *m., f.* nephew/niece 3
sociología *f.* sociology 2
sofá *m.* sofa 12
sois *fam. pl.* you are 1
sol *m.* sun 13
solar *adj.* solar 13
solicitar *v.* to apply (*for a job*) 16
solicitud (de trabajo) *f.* (job)
   application 16
sólo *adv.* only
soltero/a *adj.* single 9; unmarried
solución *f.* solution 13
sombrero *m.* hat 6
somos we are 1
son you *pl.*/they are 1
   Son las... It's... o'clock. 1
sonar (o:ue) *v.* to ring 11
sonreído/a *p.p.* smiled 15
sonreír (e:i) *v.* to smile 9
sopa *f.* soup 8
sorprender *v.* to surprise 9
sorpresa *f.* surprise 9
sótano *m.* basement 12
soy I am 1
   soy de... I'm from... 1
su(s) *poss. adj.* his; her; its; *form.*
   your; their 3
subir *v.* to go up 11
subir(se) a to get into
   (a vehicle) 11
sucio/a *adj.* dirty 5
sudar *v.* to sweat 15
suegro/a *m., f.* father-in-law;
   mother-in-law 3
sueldo *m.* salary 16
suelo *m.* floor 12
sueño *m.* sleep
suerte *f.* luck
suéter *m.* sweater 6
sufrir *v.* to suffer 15
   sufrir muchas presiones to
     be under a lot of pressure 15
sugerir (e:ie) *v.* to suggest 12
supermercado *m.* supermarket 14
suponer *v.* to suppose 4
sur *m.* south 14
sustantivo *m.* noun

suyo(s)/a(s) *poss.* (of) his/her; (of)
   hers; (of) its; (of) *form.* your, (of)
   yours, (of) theirs; their 11

T

tableta *f.* tablet (computer) 11
tal vez *adv.* maybe 5
talentoso/a *adj.* talented
talla *f.* size
taller *m.* **(mecánico)** (mechanic's)
   repair shop 11
también *adv.* also; too 7
tampoco *adv.* neither; not either 7
tan *adv.* as 8
   tan pronto como *conj.* as soon
     as 13
   tan... como as... as 8
tanque *m.* tank 11
tanto *adv.* so much
   tanto... como as much... as 8
   tantos/as... como as
     many... as 8
tarde *adv.* late 7
tarde *f.* afternoon; early evening 1
tarea *f.* homework 2
tarjeta *f.* (post) card 4
   tarjeta de crédito credit card 6
   tarjeta de débito debit card 6
   tarjeta postal postcard 4
taxi *m.* taxi(cab) 5
taza *f.* cup; mug 12
te *fam. sing. pron.* you 5, 6
   Te presento a... I would like to
     introduce... to you. *fam.* 1
   ¿Te gustaría? Would you like to?
   ¿Te gusta(n)... ? Do you like...? 2
té *m.* tea 8
   té helado iced tea 8
teatro *m.* theater
teclado *m.* keyboard 11
técnico/a *m., f.* technician 16
tejido *m.* weaving
teleadicto/a *m., f.* couch potato 15
teléfono celular *m.* cell phone 11
telenovela *f.* soap opera
teletrabajo *m.* telecommuting 16
televisión *f.* television
televisor *m.* television set 11
temer *v.* to be afraid 13
temperatura *f.* temperature 10
temprano *adv.* early 7
tenedor *m.* fork 12
tener *v.* to have 3
   tener... años to be... years old 3
   tener (mucho) calor to be (very)
     hot 3
   tener (mucho) cuidado to be
     (very) careful 3
   tener éxito to be successful 16
   tener fiebre to have a fever 10
   tener (mucho) frío to be (very)
     cold 3

   tener ganas de (+ *inf.*) to feel
     like (*doing something*) 3
   tener (mucha) hambre *f.* to be
     (very) hungry 3
   tener (mucho) miedo to be (very)
     afraid/scared 3
   tener miedo (de) que to be afraid
     that 13
   tener (mucha) prisa to be in a
     (big) hurry 3
   tener que (+ *inf.*) *v.* to have to
     (*do something*) 3
   tener razón to be right 3
   tener (mucha) sed to be (very)
     thirsty 3
   tener (mucho) sueño to be (very)
     sleepy 3
   tener (mucha) suerte to be (very)
     lucky 3
   tener tiempo to have time
   tener una cita to have a date,
     an appointment 9
tenis *m.* tennis 4
tensión *f.* tension 15
tercer, tercero/a *adj.* third 5
terminar *v.* to end; to finish 2
terremoto *m.* earthquake
terrible *adj.* terrible 13
textear *v.* to text 11
ti *obj. of prep., fam. sing.* you
tiempo *m.* time 4; weather
   tiempo libre free time 4
tienda *f.* store 6
   tienda de campaña *f.* tent 5
tierra *f.* land; soil 13
tinto/a *adj.* red (wine) 8
tío/a *m., f.* uncle/aunt 3
tíos *m.* aunts and uncles 3
título *m.* title
tiza *f.* chalk
toalla *f.* towel 7
tobillo *m.* ankle 10
tocar *v.* to play (*a musical
   instrument*); to touch
todavía *adv.* yet; still 5
todo *m.* everything
todo(s)/a(s) *adj.* all; whole
   todos los días every day 10
todos *m., pl.* all of us; *m., pl.*
   everybody; everyone
tomar *v.* to take; to drink 2
   tomar clases to take classes
   tomar el sol to sunbathe 4
   tomar fotos to take pictures
   **tomar(le) la temperatura (a
     alguien)** to take (someone's)
     temperature 10
tomate *m.* tomato 8
tonto/a *adj.* foolish 3
torcerse (o:ue) (el tobillo) *v.* to sprain
   (one's ankle) 10
torcido/a *adj.* twisted; sprained
tormenta *f.* storm

tornado *m.* tornado
tortuga marina *f.* sea turtle 13
tos *f., sing.* cough 10
toser *v.* to cough 10
tostado/a *adj.* toasted 8
tostadora *f.* toaster
trabajador(a) *adj.* hard-working 3
trabajar *v.* to work 2
trabajo *m.* job; work 16; written
    work
traducir *v.* to translate 8
traer *v.* to bring 4
tráfico *m.* traffic 11
tragedia *f.* tragedy
traído/a *p.p.* brought 15
traje *m.* suit 6
    traje de baño bathing suit 6
tranquilo/a *adj.* calm; quiet 15
    ¡Tranquilo! Stay calm!
transmitir to broadcast
tratar de (+ *inf.*) *v.* to try (*to do
    something*) 15
trece thirteen 1
treinta thirty 1
    y treinta thirty minutes past the
        hour (*time*) 1
tren *m.* train 5
tres three 1
trescientos/as three hundred 6
trimestre *m.* trimester; quarter 2
triste *adj.* sad 5
tú *fam. sing. sub. pron.* you 1
tu(s) *fam. poss. adj.* your 3
turismo *m.* tourism
turista *m., f.* tourist 1
turístico/a *adj.* touristic
tuyo(s)/a(s) *fam. poss. pron.* your;
    (of) yours 11

U

Ud. *form., sing. sub. pron.* you 1
Uds. *pl. sub. pron.* you 1
último/a *adj.* last
un, uno/a *indef. art.* a; one 1
    una vez once 6
único/a *adj.* only
universidad *f.* university 2; college
unos/as *pron.* some 1
urgente *adj.* urgent 12
usar *v.* to wear; to use 6
usted *form., sing. sub. pron.* you 1
ustedes *pl. sub. pron.* you 1
útil *adj.* useful
uva *f.* grape 8

V

vacaciones *f., pl.* vacation 5
valle *m.* valley 13
vamos let's go 4
varios/as *adj., pl.* several
vaso *m.* glass 12

vecino/a *m., f.* neighbor 12
veinte twenty 1
veinticinco twenty-five 1
veinticuatro twenty-four 1
veintidós twenty-two 1
veintinueve twenty-nine 1
veintiocho twenty-eight 1
veintiséis twenty-six 1
veintisiete twenty-seven 1
veintitrés twenty-three 1
veintiún, veintiuno/a twenty-one 1
vejez *f.* old age 9
velocidad *f.* speed 11
    velocidad máxima speed limit 11
vendedor(a) *m., f.* salesperson 6
vender *v.* to sell 6
venezolano/a *adj.* Venezuelan 3
venir *v.* to come 3
ventana *f.* window 2
ver *v.* to see; to watch 4
    ver películas *f., pl.* to watch movies 4
    a ver let's see
verano *m.* summer 5
verbo *m.* verb
verdad *f.* truth 6
    ¿verdad? right? 2
verde *adj.,* green; not ripe 5
verduras *pl., f.* vegetables 8
vestido *m.* dress 6
vestirse (e:i) *v.* to get dressed 7
vez *f.* time
viajar *v.* to travel 2
viaje *m.* trip 5
viajero/a *m., f.* traveler 5
vida *f.* life 9
video *m.* video 1
videoconferencia *f.*
    videoconference 16
vidrio *m.* glass 13
viejo/a *adj.* old 3
viento *m.* wind
viernes *m., sing.* Friday 5
vinagre *m.* vinegar 8
vino *m.* wine 8
    vino blanco white wine 8
    vino tinto red wine 8
violencia *f.* violence
visitar *v.* to visit 4
    visitar un monumento to visit a
        monument 4
visto/a *p.p.* seen 15
vitamina *f.* vitamin 15
viudo/a *adj.* widowed 9
vivienda *f.* housing 12
vivir *v.* to live 3
vivo/a *adj.* clever; alive 5; bright
volante *m.* steering wheel 11
volcán *m.* volcano 13
vóleibol *m.* volleyball 4
volver (o:ue) *v.* to return 4
vos *pron.* you
vosotros/as *fam., pl. sub. pron.*
    you 1

votar *v.* to vote
vuelta *f.* return trip
vuelto/a *p.p.* returned 15
vuestro(s)/a(s) *fam., pl. poss. adj.*
    your 3; (of) yours 11

Y

y *conj.* and 1
    y cuarto quarter after (time) 1
    y media half past (time) 1
    y quince quarter after (time) 1
    y treinta thirty (minutes past
        the hour) 1
    ¿Y tú? *fam.* And you? 1
    ¿Y usted? *form.* And you? 1
ya *adv.* already 6
yerno *m.* son-in-law 3
yo *sub. pron.* I 1
yogur *m.* yogurt

Z

zanahoria *f.* carrot 8
zapatería *f.* shoe store 14
zapato *m.* shoe 6
    par de zapatos pair of shoes 6
    zapatos de tenis sneakers 6

English-Spanish

A

able: be able to **poder (o:ue)** *v.* 4
accident **accidente** *m.* 10
accompany **acompañar** *v.*
account **cuenta** *f.* 14
accountant **contador(a)** *m., f.* 16
accounting **contabilidad** *f.* 2
ache **dolor** *m.* 10
acquainted: be acquainted with
  conocer *v.* 8
action **acción** *f.*
active **activo/a** *adj.* 15
actor **actor** *m.* 16
actress **actriz** *f.* 16
addict (*drug*) **drogadicto/a** *m., f.* 15
additional **adicional** *adj.*
address **dirección** *f.* 14
adjective **adjetivo** *m.*
adolescence **adolescencia** *f.* 9
adventure **aventura** *f.*
advertise **anunciar** *v.*
advertisement **anuncio** *m.* 16
advice **consejo** *m.* 9
  give advice **dar** *v.* **un consejo**
advise **aconsejar** *v.* 12
advisor **consejero/a** *m., f.* 16
aerobic **aeróbico/a** *adj.* 15
  aerobic exercises **ejercicios**
    aeróbicos 15
  aerobics class **clase de**
    ejercicios aeróbicos 15
affected **afectado/a** *adj.* 13
  be affected (by) **estar** *v.*
    afectado/a (por) 13
affirmative **afirmativo/a** *adj.*
afraid: be (very) afraid **tener (mucho)**
    miedo 3
  be afraid **temer** *v.* 13
after **después de** *prep.* 7; **después**
    (de) que *conj.* 13
afternoon **tarde** *f.* 1
afterward **después** *adv.* 7; **luego** *adv.*7
again **otra vez** *adv.*
age **edad** *f.*
agree **concordar** *v.* agree; **estar** *v.* **de**
    acuerdo
agreement **acuerdo** *m.*
air **aire** *m.* 13
  air pollution **contaminación del**
    aire 13
airplane **avión** *m.* 5
airport **aeropuerto** *m.* 5
alarm clock **despertador** *m.* 7
alcohol **alcohol** *m.* 15
alcoholic **alcohólico/a** *adj.* 15
  alcoholic beverage **bebida**
    alcohólica 15
alive **vivo/a** *adj.* 5

all **todo(s)/toda(s)** *adj.*
allergic **alérgico/a** *adj.* 10
  be allergic (to) **ser alérgico/a (a)** 10
alleviate **aliviar** *v.* 15
almost **casi** *adv.* 10
alone **solo/a** *adj.*
along **por** *prep.* 11
already **ya** *adv.* 6
also **también** *adv.* 7
although **aunque** *conj.*
aluminum **aluminio** *m.* 13
  (made of) aluminum **de aluminio** 13
always **siempre** *adv.* 7
American (*North*)
    norteamericano/a *adj.* 3
among **entre** *prep.* 2
and **y** 1; **e** (*before words beginning*
    with **i** *or* **hi**)
    And you? **¿Y tú?** *fam.* 1;
      ¿Y usted? *form.* 1
angry **enojado/a** *adj.* 5
  get angry (with) **enojarse (con)** *v.* 7
animal **animal** *m.* 13
ankle **tobillo** *m.* 10
anniversary **aniversario** *m.* 9
  wedding anniversary **aniversario**
    de bodas 9
announce **anunciar** *v.*
announcer (*TV/radio*) **locutor(a)** *m., f.*
annoy **molestar** *v.* 7
another **otro/a** *adj.* 6
answer **contestar** *v.* 2; **respuesta** *f.* 9
antibiotic **antibiótico** *m.* 10
any **algún, alguno/a(s)** *adj.* 7
anyone **alguien** *pron.* 7
anything **algo** *pron.* 7
apartment **apartamento** *m.*12
apartment building **edificio** *m.* **de**
    apartamentos 12
app **aplicación** *f.* 11
appetizers **entremeses** *m., pl.* 8
applaud **aplaudir** *v.*
apple **manzana** *f.* 8
appliance (electrical) **electrodoméstico**
    m. 12
applicant **aspirante** *m., f.* 16
application **solicitud** *f.* 16
  job application **solicitud de**
    trabajo 16
apply (*for a job*) **solicitar** *v.* 16
  apply for a loan **pedir** *v.* **un**
    préstamo 14
appointment **cita** *f.* 9
  have an appointment **tener** *v.*
    una cita 9
appreciate **apreciar** *v.*
April **abril** *m.* 5
archeologist **arqueólogo/a** *m., f.* 16
architect **arquitecto/a** *m., f.* 16
area **región** *f.* 13
Argentine **argentino/a** *adj.* 3
arm **brazo** *m.* 10
armchair **sillón** *m.* 12

army **ejército** *m.*
around **por** *prep.* 11
around here **por aquí** 11
arrange **arreglar** *v.* 11
arrival **llegada** *f.* 5
arrive **llegar** *v.* 2
art **arte** *m.* 2
  fine arts **bellas artes** *f., pl.*
article *m.* **artículo**
artist **artista** *m., f.* 3
artistic **artístico/a** *adj.*
arts **artes** *f., pl.*
as **como** *conj.* 8
  as… as **tan… como** 8
  as a child **de niño/a** 10
  as many… as **tantos/as… como** 8
  as much… as **tanto… como** 8
  as soon as **en cuanto** *conj.* 13;
    tan pronto como *conj.* 13
ask (*a question*) **preguntar** *v.* 2
  ask for **pedir (e:i)** *v.* 4, 12
asparagus **espárragos** *m., pl.*
aspirin **aspirina** *f.* 10
at **a** *prep.* 1; **en** *prep.* 2
  at + *time* **a la(s)** + *time* 1
  at home **en casa**
  at least **por lo menos** 10
  at night **de la noche** 1; **por la**
    noche 7
  at the end (of) **al fondo (de)**
  At what time…? **¿A qué hora…?**
    1, 9
  At your service. **A sus órdenes.**
ATM **cajero** *m.* **automático** 14
attend **asistir (a)** *v.* 3
attic **altillo** *m.* 12
attract **atraer** *v.*
audience **público** *m.*
August **agosto** *m.* 5
aunt **tía** *f.* 3
  aunts and uncles **tíos** *m., pl.* 3
autumn **otoño** *m.* 5
avenue **avenida** *f.*
avoid **evitar** *v.* 13
award **premio** *m.*

B

backpack **mochila** *f.* 1
bad **mal, malo/a** *adj.* 3, 5
  It's bad that… **Es malo que…** 12
bag **bolsa** *f.* 6
bakery **panadería** *f.* 14
balanced **equilibrado/a** *adj.* 15
  balanced diet **dieta equilibrada** 15
balcony **balcón** *m.* 12
ball **pelota** *f.* 4
ballet **ballet** *m.*
banana **banana** *f.* 8
band **banda** *f.*
bank **banco** *m.* 14
bargain **ganga** *f.*; **regatear** *v.* 6

baseball (*game*) **béisbol** *m.* 4
basement **sótano** *m.* 12
basketball (*game*) **baloncesto** *m.* 4
bath **baño** *m.*
   take a bath **bañarse** *v.* 7
bathing suit **traje** *m.* **de baño** 6
bathroom **baño** *m.* 7; **cuarto de**
   baño *m.*
be **ser** *v.* 1; **estar** *v.* 2
be… years old **tener… años** 3
beach **playa** *f.* 5
   go to the beach **ir a la playa** 5
beans **frijoles** *m., pl.* 8
beautiful **hermoso/a** *adj.* 6
beauty **belleza** *f.* 14
   beauty salon **peluquería** *f.*;
      salón *m.* **de belleza** 14
because of **por** *prep.*
become (+ *adj.*) **ponerse (+ *adj.*)** 7;
   convertirse *v.*
bed **cama** *f.* 5
   go to bed **acostarse (o:ue)** *v.* 7
bedroom **alcoba** *f.* 12; **cuarto** *m.*;
   recámara *f.*
beef **carne** *f.* **de res** 8
beer **cerveza** *f.*.8
before **antes** *adv.* 7; **antes de** *prep.* 7;
   antes (de) que *conj.* 13
beg **rogar (o:ue)** *v.* 12
begin **comenzar (e:ie)** *v.* 4; **empezar**
   (e:ie) *v.* 4
behind **detrás de** *prep.* 2
believe **creer** *v.* 13
   believe (in) **creer** *v.* **(en)** 3
believed **creído/a** *p.p.* 15
beloved **enamorado/a** *adj.*
below **debajo de** *prep.* 2
belt **cinturón** *m.* 6
benefit **beneficio** *m.* 16
besides **además (de)** *adv.* 10
best **mejor** *adj.* 8
   the best **el/la mejor** *m., f.* 8;
      lo mejor *neuter*
better **mejor** *adj.* 8
   It's better that… **Es mejor que…** 12
between **entre** *prep.* 2
bicycle **bicicleta** *f.* 4
big **grande** *adj.* 3
bill **cuenta** *f.* 9
billion **mil millones** 6
biology **biología** *f.* 2
bird **pájaro** *m.* 13; **ave** *f.*
birth **nacimiento** *m.* 9
birthday **cumpleaños** *m., sing.* 9
   birthday cake **pastel de**
      cumpleaños 9
   have a birthday **cumplir** *v.* **años** 9
bitter **amargo/a** *adj.* 8
black **negro/a** *adj.* 6
blanket **manta** *f.* 12
block (city) **cuadra** *f.* 14
blond **rubio/a** *adj.* 3

blouse **blusa** *f.* 6
blue **azul** *adj.* 6
boarding house **pensión** *f.* 5
boat **barco** *m.* 5
body **cuerpo** *m.* 10
bone **hueso** *m.* 10
book **libro** *m.* 2
bookcase **estante** *m.* 12
bookshelves **estante** *m.* 12
bookstore **librería** *f.* 2
boot **bota** *f.* 6
bore **aburrir** *v.* 7
bored **aburrido/a** *adj.* 5
   be bored **estar** *v.* **aburrido/a** 5
   get bored **aburrirse** *v.*
boring **aburrido/a** *adj.* 5
born: be born **nacer** *v.* 9
borrow **pedir prestado/a** 14
borrowed **prestado/a** *adj.*
boss **jefe** *m.*, **jefa** *f.* 16
bottle **botella** *f.* 9
   bottle of wine **botella de**
      vino 9
bother **molestar** *v.* 7
bottom **fondo** *m.*
boulevard **bulevar** *m.*
boy **chico** *m.* 1; **muchacho** *m.* 3; **niño**
   m. 3
boyfriend **novio** *m.* 3
brakes **frenos** *m., pl.* 11
bread **pan** *m.* 8
break **romper(se)** *v.* 10
   break (one's leg) **romperse (la**
      pierna) 10
break down **dañar** *v.* 10
break up (with) **romper** *v.* **(con)** 9
breakfast **desayuno** *m.* 8
   have breakfast **desayunar** *v.* 8
breathe **respirar** *v.* 13
bring **traer** *v.* 4
broadcast **transmitir** *v.*; **emitir** *v.*
brochure **folleto** *m.*
broken **roto/a** *p.p.* 15
brother **hermano** *m.* 3
   brother-in-law **cuñado** *m.* 3
   brothers and sisters **hermanos** *m.,*
      pl. 3
brought **traído/a** *p.p.* 15
brown **café** *adj.* 6; **marrón** *adj.*
brunet(te) **moreno/a** *adj.*
brush **cepillarse** *v.* 7
   brush one's hair **cepillarse el pelo** 7
   brush one's teeth **cepillarse los**
      dientes 7
build **construir** *v.*
building **edificio** *m.* 12
bump into (*meet accidentally*) **darse**
   con
bus **autobús** *m.* 1
   bus station **estación** *f.* **de**
      autobuses 5

business **negocios** *m., pl.* 16
   business administration
      administración *f.* **de**
      empresas 2
   business-related **comercial** *adj.* 16
businessman **hombre** *m.* **de negocios**
   16
businesswoman **mujer** *f.* **de negocios**
   16
busy **ocupado/a** *adj.* 5
but **pero** *conj.* 2; **sino** *conj.* 7
   (*in negative sentences*)
butcher shop **carnicería** *f.* 14
butter **mantequilla** *f.* 8
buy **comprar** *v.* 2
   buy online **comprar en línea** 6
by **por** *conj.* 11; **para** *prep.* 11
   by means of **por** *prep.* 11
   by phone **por teléfono**
   by plane **en avión** 5
   by way of **por** *prep.* 11
Bye. **Chau.** *interj. fam.* 1

C

---

cabin **cabaña** *f.* 5
café **café** *m.* 4
cafeteria **cafetería** *f.* 2
cake **pastel** *m.* 9
calculator **calculadora** *f.* 11
call **llamar** *v.* 11
   call on the phone **llamar por**
      teléfono
calm **tranquilo/a** *adj.* 15
   Stay calm! **¡Tranquilo/a!**
calorie **caloría** *f.* 15
camera **cámara** *f.* 11
   digital camera **cámara digital** 11
camp **acampar** *v.* 5
can **lata** *f.* 13
can **poder (o:ue)** *v.* 4
Canadian **canadiense** *adj.* 3
candidate **aspirante** *m. f.* 16;
   candidato/a *m., f.*
candy **dulces** *m., pl.* 9
capital city **capital** *f.*
car **coche** *m.* 11; **carro** *m.* 11;
   auto(móvil) *m.* 5
caramel **caramelo** *m.*
card **tarjeta** *f.* 4; (*playing*) **carta** *f.*
care **cuidado** *m.*
   take care of **cuidar** *v.* 13
career **carrera** *f.* 16
careful: be (very) careful **tener** *v.*
   (mucho) cuidado 3
carpenter **carpintero/a** *m., f.* 16
carpet **alfombra** *f.* 12
carrot **zanahoria** *f.* 8
carry **llevar** *v.* 2
cartoons **dibujos** *m., pl.* **animados**
case: in case (that) **en caso (de)**
   que *conj.* 13

cash (a check) **cobrar** *v.* 14; **efectivo** *m.*
   cash register **caja** *f.* 6
   pay in cash **pagar** *v.* **al contado** 14; **pagar en efectivo**
cashier **cajero/a** *m., f.*
cat **gato/a** *m., f.* 3
celebrate **celebrar** *v.* 9
cell phone **teléfono** *m.* **celular** 11
cereal **cereales** *m., pl.* 8
certain **cierto** *m.* 13; **seguro** *m.* 13
   it's (not) certain **(no) es seguro/cierto** 13
chair **silla** *f.* 2
chalk **tiza** *f.*
champagne **champán** *m.* 9
change **cambiar** *v.* **(de)** 9
channel (*TV*) **canal** *m.*
character (*fictional*) **personaje** *m.*
   main character **personaje principal**
charge (a device) **cargar** *v.* 11; (for a product or service) **cobrar** *v.* 14
charger **cargador** *m.* 11
chat **conversar** *v.* 2; **chatear** *v.* 11
cheap **barato/a** *adj.* 6
check **comprobar** *v.;* **revisar** *v.* 11; (*bank*) **cheque** *m.* 14
   check the oil **revisar el aceite** 11
checking account **cuenta** *f.* **corriente** 14
cheese **queso** *m.* 8
chef **cocinero/a** *m., f.* 16
chemistry **química** *f.* 2
chest of drawers **cómoda** *f.* 12
chicken **pollo** *m.* 8
child **niño/a** *m., f.* 3
childhood **niñez** *f.* 9
children **hijos** *m., pl.* 3
Chinese **chino/a** *adj.* 3
chocolate **chocolate** *m.*
   chocolate cake **pastel** *m.* **de chocolate**
cholesterol **colesterol** *m.* 15
choose **escoger** *v.*
chop (*food*) **chuleta** *f.* 8
Christmas **Navidad** *f.* 9
church **iglesia** *f.* 4
citizen **ciudadano/a** *m., f.*
city **ciudad** *f.* 4
class **clase** *f.* 2
   take classes **tomar** *v.* **clases**
classical **clásico/a** *adj.*
classmate **compañero/a** *m., f.* **de clase** 2
classroom **salón** *m.* **de clases** 2
clean **limpio/a** *adj.* 5; **limpiar** *v.* 12
   clean the house **limpiar** *v.* **la casa** 12
clear (*weather*) **despejado/a** *adj.* 5
   clear the table **quitar** *v.* **la mesa** 12
   It's clear. (*weather*) **Está despejado.** 5
clerk **dependiente/a** *m., f.* 6
clever **vivo/a** *adj.* 5

client **cliente/a** *m., f.* 6
clinic **clínica** *f.* 10
clock **reloj** *m.* 2
close **cerrar (e:ie)** *v.* 4
closed **cerrado/a** *adj.* 5
closet **armario** *m.* 12
clothes dryer **secadora** *f.* 12
clothing **ropa** *f.* 6
cloud **nube** *f.* 13
cloudy **nublado/a** *adj.* 5
   It's (very) cloudy. **Está (muy) nublado.** 5
coat **abrigo** *m.* 6
coffee **café** *m.* 8
   coffee maker **cafetera** *f.*
cold **frío** *m.* 3; (*illness*) **resfriado** *m.* 10
   be (very) cold (*feel*) **tener (mucho) frío** 3
   It's (very) cold. (*weather*) **Hace (mucho) frío.** 5
college **universidad** *f.*
collision **choque** *m.*
color **color** *m.* 6
comb one's hair **peinarse** *v.* 7
come **venir** *v.* 3
comedy **comedia** *f.*
comfortable **cómodo/a** *adj.* 5
commerce **negocios** *m., pl.* 16
commercial **comercial** *adj.* 16
communicate (with) **comunicarse** *v.* **(con)**
communication **comunicación** *f.*
   means of communication **medios** *m., pl.* **de comunicación**
community **comunidad** *f.* 1
company **compañía** *f.* 16; **empresa** *f.* 16
comparison **comparación** *f.*
composer **compositor(a)** *m., f.*
computer **computadora** *f.* 1, 11
   computer disc **disco** *m.*
   computer programmer **programador(a)** *m., f.* 3
   computer science **computación** *f.* 2
concert **concierto** *m.*
conductor (*musical*) **director(a)** *m., f.*
confident **seguro/a** *adj.* 5
confirm **confirmar** *v.* 5
   confirm a reservation **confirmar una reservación** 5
congested **congestionado/a** *adj.* 10
Congratulations! (*for an event such as a birthday or anniversary*) **¡Felicidades!;** (*for an event such as an engagement or a good grade on a test*) *f., pl.* **¡Felicitaciones!**
conservation **conservación** *f.* 13
conserve **conservar** *v.* 13
considering **para** *prep.* 11
consume **consumir** *v.* 15
contact lenses **lentes** *m. pl.* **de contacto**
container **envase** *m.* 13
contamination **contaminación** *f.*

content **contento/a** *adj.* 5
contest **concurso** *m.*
continue **seguir (e:i)** *v.* 4
control **control** *m.;* **controlar** *v.* 13
conversation **conversación** *f.* 1
cook **cocinar** *v.* 12; **cocinero/a** *m., f.* 16
cookie **galleta** *f.* 9
cool **fresco/a** *adj.*
   It's cool. (*weather*) **Hace fresco.** 5
corn **maíz** *m.* 8
corner **esquina** *m.* 14
cost **costar (o:ue)** *v.* 6
Costa Rican **costarricense** *adj.* 3
couch potato **teleadicto/a** *m., f.* 15
cough **tos** *f.* 10; **toser** *v.* 10
counselor **consejero/a** *m., f.* 16
country (*nation*) **país** *m.* 1
countryside **campo** *m.* 5; **paisaje** *m.*
couple **pareja** *f.* 9
   couple (married) **matrimonio** *m.* 9
course **curso** *m.* 2; **materia** *f.*
courtesy **cortesía** *f.*
cousin **primo/a** *m., f.* 3
cover **cubrir** *v.*
covered **cubierto** *p.p.*
crafts **artesanía** *f.*
craftsmanship **artesanía** *f.*
crash **chocar** *v.* **(con)** 11
crater **cráter** *m.* 13
crazy **loco/a** *adj.* 6
create **crear** *v.*
credit **crédito** *m.* 6
   credit card **tarjeta** *f.* **de crédito** 6
crime **crimen** *m.*
cross **cruzar** *v.* 14
Cuban **cubano/a** *adj.* 3
culture **cultura** *f.*
cup **taza** *f.* 12
currency exchange **cambio** *m.* **de moneda**
current events **actualidades** *f., pl.*
curtains **cortinas** *f., pl.* 12
custard (*baked*) **flan** *m.* 9
custom **costumbre** *f.*
customer **cliente/a** *m., f.* 6
customs **aduana** *f.* 5
   customs inspector **inspector(a)** *m., f.* **de aduanas** 5
cycling **ciclismo** *m.* 4

D

dad **papá** *m.*
daily **diario/a** *adj.* 7
   daily routine **rutina** *f.* **diaria** 7
damage **dañar** *v.* 10
dance **bailar** *v.* 2; **danza** *f.* **baile** *m.*
dancer **bailarín/bailarina** *m., f.* 16
danger **peligro** *m.* 13
dangerous **peligroso/a** *adj.*
dark-haired **moreno/a** *adj.* 3
date (*appointment*) **cita** *f.* 9; (*calendar*)

fecha *f.* 5; (*someone*) **salir** *v.* **con (alguien)** 9
   date: have a date **tener** *v.* **una cita** 9
daughter **hija** *f.* 3
daughter-in-law **nuera** *f.* 3
day **día** *m.* 1
   day before yesterday **anteayer** *adv.* 6
death **muerte** *f.* 9
debit card **tarjeta** *f.* **de débito** 6
decaffeinated **descafeinado/a** *adj.* 15
December **diciembre** *m.* 5
decide **decidir** *v.* 3
declare **declarar** *v.*
deforestation **deforestación** *f.* 13
delicious **delicioso/a** *adj.* 8; **rico/a** *adj.* 8; **sabroso/a** *adj.* 8
dentist **dentista** *m., f.* 10
deny **negar (e: ie)** *v.* 13
department store **almacén** *m.* 6
departure **salida** *f.* 5
deposit **depositar** *v.* 14
describe **describir** *v.* 3
described **descrito/a** *p.p.* 15
desert **desierto** *m.* 13
design **diseño** *m.*
designer **diseñador(a)** *m., f.* 16
desire **desear** *v.* 12
desk **escritorio** *m.* 2
dessert **postre** *m.* 9
destroy **destruir** *v.* 13
develop **desarrollar** *v.* 13
diary **diario** *m.* 1
dictatorship **dictadura** *f.*
dictionary **diccionario** *m.* 1
die **morir (o:ue)** *v.* 8
died **muerto/a** *p.p.* 15
diet **dieta** *f.* 15
   balanced diet **dieta equilibrada** 15
   be on a diet **estar** *v.* **a dieta** 15
   eat a balanced diet **seguir una dieta equilibrada** 15
difficult **difícil** *adj.* 3
dining room **comedor** *m.* 12
dinner **cena** *f.* 8
   have dinner **cenar** *v.* 8
direction: in the direction of **para** *prep.* 11
directions: give directions **indicar cómo llegar** *v.* 14
director **director(a)** *m., f.*
dirty **sucio/a** *adj.* 5
   get (something) dirty **ensuciar** *v.* 12
disagree **no estar de acuerdo**
disaster **desastre** *m.*
discover **descubrir** *v.* 13
discovered **descubierto** *p.p.* 15
discrimination **discriminación** *f.*
dish **plato** *m.* 8
   main dish **plato principal** 8
dishwasher **lavaplatos** *m., sing.* 12
disk **disco** *m.*
disorderly **desordenado/a** *adj.* 5

dive **bucear** *v.* 4
divorce **divorcio** *m.* 9
divorced **divorciado/a** *adj.* 9
   get divorced (from) **divorciarse** *v.* **(de)** 9
dizzy **mareado/a** *adj.* 10
do **hacer** *v.* 4
   do aerobics **hacer ejercicios aeróbicos** 15
   do household chores **hacer quehaceres domésticos** 12
   do stretching exercises **hacer ejercicios de estiramiento** 15
doctor **médico/a** *m., f.* 3; **doctor(a)** *m., f.* 3, 10
documentary (*film*) **documental** *m.*
dog **perro/a** *m., f.* 3
Dominican **dominicano/a** *adj.* 3
done **hecho/a** *p.p.* 15
door **puerta** *f.* 2
dormitory **residencia** *f.* **estudiantil** 2
double **doble** *adj.* 5
   double room **habitación** *f.* **doble** 5
doubt **duda** *f.* 13; **dudar** *v.* 13
   There is no doubt… **No cabe duda de…** 13; **No hay duda de…** 13
download **descargar** *v.* 11
downtown **centro** *m.* 4
drama **drama** *m.*
dramatic **dramático/a** *adj.*
draw **dibujar** *v.* 2
drawing **dibujo** *m.*
dress **vestido** *m.* 6
   get dressed **vestirse (e:i)** *v.* 7
drink **beber** *v.* 3; **bebida** *f.* 8; **tomar** *v.* 2
drive **conducir** *v.* 8, 11; **manejar** *v.* 11
driver **conductor(a)** *m., f.* 1
drug *f.* **droga** 15
   drug addict **drogadicto/a** *m., f.* 15
dry-erase marker **marcador** *m.* 2
due to **por** *prep.*
   due to the fact that **debido a**
during **durante** *prep.* 7; **por** *prep.* 11
dust **sacudir** *v.* 12
   dust the furniture **sacudir los muebles** 12

E

each **cada** *adj.* 6
ear (outer) **oreja** *f.* 10
early **temprano** *adv.* 7
earn **ganar** *v.* 16
earthquake **terremoto** *m.*
ease **aliviar** *v.* 15
east **este** *m.* 14
   to the east **al este** 14
easy **fácil** *adj.* 3
eat **comer** *v.* 3
ecological **ecológico/a** *adj.* 13
ecologist **ecologista** *m., f.* 13
ecology **ecología** *f.* 13

economics **economía** *f.*
ecotourism **ecoturismo** *m.* 13
Ecuadorian **ecuatoriano/a** *adj.* 3
effective **eficaz** *adj. m., f.*
egg **huevo** *m.* 8
eight **ocho** 1
eight hundred **ochocientos/as** 6
eighteen **dieciocho** 1
eighth **octavo/a** *adj.* 5
eighty **ochenta** 2
either… or **o… o** *conj.* 7
elect **elegir** *v.*
election **elecciones** *f., pl.*
electrician **electricista** *m., f.* 16
electricity **luz** *f.* 12
elegant **elegante** *adj.* 6
elevator **ascensor** *m.* 5
eleven **once** 1
e-mail **correo** *m.* **electrónico** 4
   e-mail message **mensaje** *m.* **electrónico** 4
   read e-mail **leer** *v.* **el correo electrónico** 4
   write an e-mail **escribir** *v.* **un mensaje electrónico** 4
embarrassed **avergonzado/a** *adj.* 5
embrace (each other) **abrazar(se)** *v.*
emergency **emergencia** *f.* 10
   emergency room **sala** *f.* **de emergencia(s)** 10
employee **empleado/a** *m., f.* 5
employment **empleo** *m.* 16
end **fin** *m.* 4; **terminar** *v.* 2
   end table **mesita** *f.* 12
energy **energía** *f.* 13
engaged: get engaged (to) **comprometerse** *v.* **(con)** 9
engineer **ingeniero/a** *m., f.* 3
English (*language*) **inglés** *m.* 2; **inglés, inglesa** *adj.* 3
enjoy **disfrutar** *v.* **(de)** 15
enough **bastante** *adv.* 10
entertainment **diversión** *f.* 4
entrance **entrada** *f.* 12
envelope **sobre** *m.* 14
environment **medio ambiente** *m.* 13
equality **igualdad** *f.*
eraser **borrador** *m.* 2
errand *f.* **diligencia** 14
establish **establecer** *v.*
event **acontecimiento** *m.*
every day **todos los días** 10
everybody **todos** *m., pl.*
everything **todo** *m.*
exam **examen** *m.* 2
excellent **excelente** *adj.*
excess **exceso** *m.* 15
   in excess **en exceso** 15
exchange **intercambiar** *v.*
   in exchange for **por** 11
exciting **emocionante** *adj. m., f.*
excuse **disculpar** *v.*
Excuse me. (*May I?*) **Con permiso.**; (*I beg your pardon.*) **Perdón.**

exercise **ejercicio** *m.* 15
  hacer *v.* **ejercicio** 15
exit **salida** *f.* 5
expensive **caro/a** *adj.* 6
experience **experiencia** *f.*
explain **explicar** *v.* 2
explore **explorar** *v.*
expression **expresión** *f.*
extinction **extinción** *f.* 13
eye **ojo** *m.* 10

F

fabulous **fabuloso/a** *adj.*
face **cara** *f.* 7
facing **enfrente de** *prep.* 14
factory **fábrica** *f.* 13
fall **caerse** *v.* 10
  fall asleep **dormirse (o:ue)** *v.* 7
  fall in love (with) **enamorarse** *v.*
  (de) 9
fallen **caído/a** *p.p.* 15
family **familia** *f.* 3
famous **famoso/a** *adj.*
fan **aficionado/a** *adj.* 4
  be a fan (of) **ser aficionado/a (a)** 4
far from **lejos de** *prep.* 2
farewell **despedida** *f.*
fascinate **fascinar** *v.* 7
fashion **moda** *f.*
  be in fashion **estar** *v.* **de moda**
fast **rápido/a** *adj.*
fat **gordo/a** *adj.* 3; **grasa** *f.* 15
father **padre** *m.* 3
father-in-law **suegro** *m.* 3
favorite **favorito/a** *adj.* 4
fear **miedo** *m.*
February **febrero** *m.* 5
feel *v.* **sentir(se) (e:ie)** 7
  feel like (*doing something*) **tener
  ganas de (+ *inf.*)** 3
festival **festival** *m.*
fever **fiebre** *f.* 10
  have a fever **tener** *v.* **fiebre** 10
few **pocos/as** *adj. pl.*
field: field of study **especialización**
  f. 16
fifteen **quince** 1
fifth **quinto/a** *adj.* 5
fifty **cincuenta** 2
fight **luchar** *v.* **(por)**
figure (*number*) **cifra** *f.*
file **archivo** *m.* 11
fill **llenar** *v.*
  fill out a form **llenar un formulario**
  14
  fill the tank **llenar el tanque** 11
finally **finalmente** *adv*; **por último** 7;
  por fin 11
find **encontrar (o:ue)** *v.* 4
fine **multa** *f.* 11
fine arts **bellas artes** *f., pl.*
finger **dedo** *m.* 10

finish **terminar** *v.* 2
fire **incendio** *m.*; **despedir (e:i)** *v.* 16
firefighter **bombero/a** *m., f.* 16
firm **compañía** *f.* 16; **empresa** *f.* 16
first **primer, primero/a** *adj.* 5
fish (*food*) **pescado** *m.* 8; **pescar** *v.* 5;
  (*live*) **pez** *m.* 13
  fish market **pescadería** *f.* 14
fisherman **pescador** *m.*
fisherwoman **pescadora** *f.*
fishing **pesca** *f.* 5
fit (*clothing*) **quedar** *v.* 7
five **cinco** 1
five hundred **quinientos/as** 6
fix (*put in working order*) **arreglar** *v.* 11
fixed **fijo/a** *adj.* 6
flag **bandera** *f.*
flexible **flexible** *adj.* 15
flood **inundación** *f.*
floor (*story in a building*) **piso** *m.* 5;
  suelo *m.*12
  ground floor **planta** *f.* **baja** 5
flower **flor** *f.* 13
flu **gripe** *f.* 10
fog **niebla** *f.*
foggy: It's (very) foggy. **Hay (mucha)
  niebla.** 5
folk **folclórico/a** *adj.*
follow **seguir (e:i)** *v.* 4
food **comida** *f.* 8
foolish **tonto/a** *adj.* 3
foot **pie** *m.* 10
football **fútbol** *m.* **americano** 4
for **para** *prep.* 11; **por** *prep.* 11
  for example **por ejemplo** 11
forbid **prohibir** *v.* 12
foreign **extranjero/a** *adj.*
  foreign languages **lenguas**
  f., pl. **extranjeras** 2
forest **bosque** *m.* 13
forget **olvidar** *v.* 10
fork **tenedor** *m.* 12
form **formulario** *m.* 14
forty **cuarenta** 2
four **cuatro** 1
four hundred **cuatrocientos/as** 6
fourteen **catorce** 1
fourth **cuarto/a** *adj.* 5
free **libre** *adj.* 4
  be free of charge **ser gratis** 14
  free time **tiempo** *m.* **libre** 4;
  ratos *m., pl.* **libres** 4
freedom **libertad** *f.*
freezer **congelador** *m.*
French **francés, francesa** *adj.* 3
  French fries **papas** *f., pl* **fritas** 8;
  patatas *f., pl* **fritas** 8
frequently **frecuentemente** *adv.*; **con
  frecuencia** 10
Friday **viernes** *m., sing.* 2
fried **frito/a** *adj.*
friend **amigo/a** *m., f.* 3
friendly **amable** *adj.*
friendship **amistad** *f.* 9

from **de** *prep.* 1; **desde** *prep.* 6
  from where? **¿de donde?** 2, 9
  from the United States
  estadounidense *adj.* 3
  from time to time **de vez en
  cuando** 10
  I'm from… **Soy de…** 1
fruit **fruta** *f.* 8
  fruit juice **jugo** *m.* **de fruta** 8
  fruit shop **frutería** *f.* 14
full **lleno/a** *adj.* 11
fun **divertido/a** *adj.*
  fun activity **diversión** *f.* 4
  have fun **divertirse (e:ie)** *v.* 9
function **funcionar** *v.*
furniture **muebles** *m., pl.* 12
furthermore **además (de)** *adv.* 10
future **futuro** *m.*
  in the future **en el futuro**

G

gain weight **aumentar** *v.* **de peso** 15;
  engordar *v.* 15
game (*match*) **partido** *m.* 4; **juego** *m.*
  game show **concurso** *m.*
garage **garaje** *m.* 11, 12
garden **jardín** *m.* 12
garlic **ajo** *m.* 8
gas station **gasolinera** *f.* 11
gasoline **gasolina** *f.* 11
geography **geografía** *f.* 2
German **alemán, alemana** *adj.* 3
get **conseguir (e:i)** *v.* 4; **obtener** *v.* 16
  get along well/badly (with)
  llevarse bien/mal (con) 9
  get bored **aburrirse** *v.*
  get connected to the Internet
  conectarse *v.* **a Internet** 11
  get out of (a vehicle)
  bajar(se) *v.* **de** 11
  get into (a vehicle) **subir(se)** *v.* **a** 11
  get up **levantarse** *v.* 7
gift **regalo** *m.* 6
girl **chica** *f.* 1; **muchacha** *f.* 3; **niña**
  f. 3
girlfriend **novia** *f.* 3
give **dar** *v.* 6; (*as a gift*) **regalar** 9
  give directions **indicar cómo llegar**
  v. 14
glass (*drinking*) **vaso** *m.* 12; **vidrio**
  m. 13
  (made of) glass **de vidrio** 13
glasses **gafas** *f., pl.* 6
  sunglasses **gafas de sol** 6
global warming **calentamiento global**
  m. 13
gloves **guantes** *m., pl.* 6
go **ir** *v.* 4
  go away **irse** 7
  go by boat **ir en barco** 5
  go by bus **ir en autobús** 5
  go by car **ir en auto(móvil)** 5

go by motorcycle **ir en motocicleta** 5
go by plane **ir en avión** 5
go by subway **ir en metro**
go by taxi **ir en taxi** 5
go by train **ir en tren**
go down **bajar** *v.* 11
go fishing **ir de pesca** 5
go for a hike (in the mountains) **ir de excursión (a las montañas)** 4
go mountain climbing **escalar montañas** 4
go out **salir** *v.* 9
go out with **salir con** 4, 9
go through customs **pasar por la aduana** 5
go up **subir** *v.* 11
go with **acompañar** *v.*
Let's go. **Vamos.** 4
going to: be going to (*do something*) **ir a (+ inf.)** 4
golf **golf** *m.* 4
good **buen, bueno/a** *adj.* 1, 3
   Good afternoon. **Buenas tardes.** 1
   Good evening. **Buenas noches.** 1
   Good morning. **Buenos días.** 1
   Good night. **Buenas noches.** 1
   It's good that… **Es bueno que…** 12
goodbye **adiós** *m.* 1
good-looking **guapo/a** *adj.* 3
government **gobierno** *m.* 13
GPS **navegador GPS** *m.* 11
graduate (from) **graduarse** *v.* (de) 9
grains **cereales** *m., pl.* 8
granddaughter **nieta** *f.* 3
grandfather **abuelo** *m.* 3
grandmother **abuela** *f.* 3
grandparents **abuelos** *m., pl.* 3
grandson **nieto** *m.* 3
grape **uva** *f.* 8
grass **hierba** *f.* 13; **césped** *m.* 13
grave **grave** *adj.* 10
gray **gris** *adj. m., f.* 6
great **gran** *adj.* 3; **fenomenal** *adj.*
green **verde** *adj. m., f.* 5, 6
greet (each other) **saludar(se)** *v.*
greeting **saludo** *m.*
grilled (*food*) **a la plancha**
ground floor **planta** *f.* **baja** 5
guest (*at a house/hotel*) **huésped** *m., f.* 5; (*invited to a function*) **invitado/a** *m., f.* 9
guide **guía** *m., f.*
gym **gimnasio** *m.* 4
gymnasium **gimnasio** *m.* 4

H

hair **pelo** *m.* 7
hair salon **peluquería** *f.* 14
hairdresser **peluquero/a** *m., f.* 16

half **medio/a** *adj.* 3
   half-brother **medio hermano** *m.* 3
   half-sister **media hermana** *f.* 3
   half-past (*time*) **y media** 1
hallway **pasillo** *m.* 12
ham **jamón** *m.* 8
hamburger **hamburguesa** *f.* 8
   veggie burger **hamburguesa vegetariana** *f.* 8
hand **mano** *f.* 1
happen **ocurrir** *v.*
happiness **alegría** *f.* 9
happy **alegre** *adj.* 5; **feliz** *adj.* 5
   be happy **alegrarse** *v.* (de) 13
Happy birthday! **¡Feliz cumpleaños!**
hard-working **trabajador(a)** *adj.* 3
hardly **apenas** *adv.* 10
hat **sombrero** *m.* 6
hate **odiar** *v.* 9
have **tener** *v.* 3
   Have a good trip! **¡Buen viaje!**
   have a tooth pulled **sacar(se) una muela** 10
he **él** *sub. pron.* 1
head **cabeza** *f.* 10
headache **dolor** *m.* **de cabeza** 10
health **salud** *f.* 10
healthy **sano/a, saludable** *adj.* 10
   lead a healthy lifestyle **llevar** *v.* **una vida sana** 15
hear **oír** *v.* 4
heard **oído/a** *p.p.* 15
hearing: sense of hearing **oído** *m.*
heart **corazón** *m.* 10
heat **calor** *m.*
Hello. **Hola.** *interj.* 1; (*on the telephone*) **Aló.; ¿Bueno?; Diga.**
help **ayudar** *v.*
   help each other **ayudarse** *v.*
her **su(s)** *poss. adj.* 3; **la** *pron.* 5; **le** *pron.* 6
here **aquí** *adv.*
hers **suyo(s)/a(s)** *poss. pron.* 11
highway **autopista** *f.*; **carretera** *f.*
hike **excursión** *f.* 4
   go on a hike **hacer una excursión** 5; **ir de excursión** 4
hiker **excursionista** *m., f.* 4
hiking **de excursión** 4
him **lo** *pron.* 5; **le** *pron.* 6
hire **contratar** *v.* 16
his **su(s)** *poss. adj.* 3; **suyo(s)/a(s)** *poss. pron.* 11
history **historia** *f.* 2
hobby **pasatiempo** *m.* 4
hockey **hockey** *m.* 4
holiday **día** *m.* **de fiesta** 9
home **hogar** *m.* 12
   home page **página** *f.* **principal** 11
homemaker **amo/a** *m., f.* **de casa** 12
homework **tarea** *f.* 2
hood (*car*) **capó** *m.* 11
hope **esperar** *v.* 2, 13
   I hope (that) **ojalá (que)** *interj.* 13

horror **terror** *m.*
horse **caballo** *m.* 5
hospital **hospital** *m.* 10
hot: be (very) hot (*feel*) **tener (mucho) calor** 3; (*weather*) **hacer (mucho) calor** 5
hotel **hotel** *m.* 5
hour **hora** *f.*
house **casa** *f.* 4
household chores **quehaceres** *m., pl.* **domésticos** 12
housing **vivienda** *f.* 12
How…! **¡Qué…!**
   how **¿cómo?** *adv.* 1, 2
   How are you? **¿Cómo estás?** *fam.* 1
   How are you? **¿Cómo está usted?** *form.* 1
   How can I help you? **¿En qué puedo servirles?**
   How is it going? **¿Qué tal?** 1
   How much/many? **¿Cuánto(s)/a(s)?** 1, 2
   How much does… cost? **¿Cuánto cuesta…?** 6
   How old are you? **¿Cuántos años tienes?** *fam.*
   How's the weather? **¿Qué tiempo hace?** 5
however **sin embargo** *adv.*
hug (each other) **abrazar(se)** *v.*
humanities **humanidades** *f., pl.*
hunger **hambre** *f.*
hundred **cien** 2; **ciento** 6
hungry: be (very) hungry **tener** *v.* **(mucha) hambre** 3
hunting **caza** *f.* 13
hurricane **huracán** *m.*
hurry **apurarse** *v.* 15; **darse** *v.* **prisa** 15
   be in a (big) hurry *v.* **tener (mucha) prisa** 3
hurt **doler (o:ue)** *v.* 10
husband **esposo** *m.* 3

I

I **yo** *sub. pron.* 1
   I hope (that) **Ojalá (que)** *interj.* 13
   I wish (that) **Ojalá (que)** *interj.* 13
   I would like… **me gustaría(n)…** 7
   I would like to introduce… to you. **Le presento a…** *form.* 1; **Te presento a…** *fam.* 1
ice cream **helado** *m.* 9
   ice cream shop **heladería** *f.* 14
iced tea **té helado** *m.* 8
idea **idea** *f.*
if **si** *conj.*
illness **enfermedad** *f.* 10
important **importante** *adj.* 3
   be important to **importar** *v.* 7, 12
   It's important that… **Es importante que…** 12

impossible **imposible** *adj.* 13
  It's impossible… **Es imposible…** 13
improbable **improbable** *adj.* 13
  It's improbable… **Es improbable…** 13
improve **mejorar** *v.* 13
in **en** *prep.* 2; **por** *prep.* 11
  in the afternoon **de la tarde** 1; **por la tarde** 7
  in the morning **de la mañana** 1; **por la mañana** 7
  in love (with) **enamorado/a (de)** 5
  in front of **delante de** *prep.* 2
increase **aumento** *m.*
incredible **increíble** *adj.*
inequality **desigualdad** *f.*
infection **infección** *f.* 10
inform **informar** *v.*
inhabitants **habitantes** *m., pl.*
injection **inyección** *f.* 10
  give an injection **poner** *v.* **una inyección** 10
injure (oneself) **lastimarse** *v.* 10
  injure (one's foot) **lastimarse (el pie)** 10
inner ear **oído** *m.*
insist (on) **insistir** *v.* **(en)** 12
installments: pay in installments **pagar** *v.* **a plazos** 14
intelligent **inteligente** *adj.* 3
intend **pensar** *v.* **(+ inf.)** 4
interest **interesar** *v.* 7
interesting **interesante** *adj.* 3
  be interesting to **interesar** *v.* 7
international **internacional** *adj. m., f.*
Internet **red** *f.*; **Internet** 11
  get connected to the Internet **conectarse** *v.* **a Internet** 11
interview **entrevista** *f.* 16; **entrevistar** *v.* 16
interviewer **entrevistador(a)** *m., f.* 16
introduction **presentación** *f.*
invest **invertir (e:ie)** *v.* 16
invite **invitar** *v.* 9
iron clothes **planchar** *v.* **la ropa** 12
it **lo/la** *pron.* 5
Italian **italiano/a** *adj.*
its **su(s)** *poss. adj.* 3; **suyo(s)/a(s)** *poss. pron.* 11

J

jacket **chaqueta** *f.* 6
January **enero** *m.* 5
Japanese **japonés, japonesa** *adj.* 3
jeans **bluejeans** *m., pl.* 6
jewelry store **joyería** *f.* 14
job **empleo** *m.* 16; **puesto** *m.* 16; **trabajo** *m.* 16
  job application **solicitud** *f.* **de trabajo** 16
journalism **periodismo** *m.* 2
journalist **periodista** *m., f.* 3

juice **jugo** *m.* 8
July **julio** *m.* 5
June **junio** *m.* 5
jungle **selva** *f.* 13, **jungla** *f.*
just: have just done something **acabar de (+ inf.)** 6

K

keep (doing something) **seguir (e:ie)** *v.* 4
key **llave** *f.* 5
keyboard **teclado** *m.* 11
kilometer **kilómetro** *m.* 11
kiss (each other) **besar(se)** *v.*; **beso** *m.* 6
kitchen **cocina** *f.* 12
knee **rodilla** *f.* 10
knife **cuchillo** *m.* 12
know **saber** *v.* 8; **conocer** *v.* 8
know how **saber** *v.* 8

L

laboratory **laboratorio** *m.* 2
lack **faltar** *v.* 7
lake **lago** *m.* 13
lamp **lámpara** *f.* 12
land **tierra** *f.* 13
landscape **paisaje** *m.* 13
language **lengua** *f.* 2
laptop (computer) **computadora** *f.* **portátil** 11
last **durar** *v.*; **pasado/a** *adj.* 6; **último/a** *adj.*
  last name **apellido** *m.* 9
  last night **anoche** *adv.* 6
  last week **la semana pasada** 6
  last year **el año pasado** 6
late **tarde** *adv.* 7
later (on) **más tarde** *adv.* 7
  See you later. **Hasta la vista.** 1; **Hasta luego.** 1
laugh **reírse (e:i)** *v.* 9
laughed **reído/a** *p.p.* 15
laundromat **lavandería** *f.* 14
law **ley** *f.* 13
lawyer **abogado/a** *m., f.* 16
lazy **perezoso/a** *adj.*
learn **aprender** *v.* 3
least, (the) **el/la/los/las menos** 8
leave **salir** *v.* 4; **irse** *v.* 7
  leave a tip **dejar una propina** 9
  leave for (*a place*) **salir para** 4
  leave from **salir de** 4
  leave behind **dejar** *v.* 16
left **izquierda** *f.* 2
  be left behind **quedar** *v.* 10
  be left over **quedar** *v.* 7
  to the left of **a la izquierda de** 2
leg **pierna** *f.* 10
lemon **limón** *m.* 8
lend **prestar** *v.* 6

less **menos** *adj., adv.* 10
  less… than **menos… que** 8
  less than (+ *number*) **menos de (+ *number*)** 8
lesson **lección** *f.* 1
letter **carta** *f.* 4
lettuce **lechuga** *f.* 8
liberty **libertad** *f.*
library **biblioteca** *f.* 2
license (*driver's*) **licencia** *f.* **de conducir** 11
lie **mentira** *f.* 6
lie down **acostarse (o:ue)** *v.* 7
life **vida** *f.* 9
lifestyle: lead a healthy lifestyle **llevar una vida sana** 15
lift **levantar** *v.* 15
  lift weights **levantar pesas** 15
light **luz** *f.* 12
like **como** *prep.*; **gustar** *v.* 2, 7
  like this **así** *adv.* 10
  like very much **encantar** *v.* 7; **fascinar** *v.* 7
  I like… **me gusta(n)…** 2
  Do you like… ? **¿Te gusta(n)…?** 2
likewise **igualmente** *adv.* 1
line **cola** (*queue*) *f.* 14
listen (to) **escuchar** *v.* 2
  listen to music **escuchar música**
  listen to the radio **escuchar la radio**
literature **literatura** *f.*
little (*quantity*) **poco** *adv.* 10
live **vivir** *v.* 3
living room **sala** *f.* 12
loan **préstamo** *m.* 14; **prestar** *v.* 6
lobster **langosta** *f.* 8
located **situado/a** *adj.*
  be located **quedar** *v.* 14
lodging **alojamiento** *m.* 5
long **largo/a** *adj.* 6
look (at) **mirar** *v.* 2
look for **buscar** *v.* 2
lose **perder (e:ie)** *v.* 4
  lose weight **adelgazar** *v.* 15
lost **perdido/a** *adj.* 14
  be lost **estar perdido/a** 14
lot, a **muchas veces** 10
love (*another person*) **querer (e:ie)** *v.* 4; (*things*) **encantar** *v.* 7; **amor** *m.* 9; in love (with) **enamorado/a (de)** *adj.* 5
luck **suerte** *f.*
lucky: be (very) lucky **tener (mucha) suerte** 3
luggage **equipaje** *m.* 5
lunch **almuerzo** *m.* 8
  have lunch **almorzar (o:ue)** *v.* 8

M

ma'am **señora (Sra.)** *f.* 1
magazine **revista** *f.* 4
  read a magazine **leer una revista** 4

magnificent **magnífico/a** *adj.*
mail **correo** *m.* 14; **enviar** *v.*, **mandar** *v.*
  mail a letter **echar una carta al buzón** 14
  mail carrier **cartero/a** *m., f.* 14
mailbox **buzón** *m.* 14
main **principal** *adj. m., f.* 8
maintain **mantener** *v.*
make **hacer** *v.* 4
  make the bed **hacer la cama** 12
makeup **maquillaje** *m.* 7
man **hombre** *m.* 1
manager **gerente** *m., f.* 16
many **mucho/a** *adj.* 3
  many times **muchas veces** 10
map **mapa** *m.* 1
March **marzo** *m.* 5
margarine **margarina** *f.* 8
marital status **estado** *m.* **civil** 9
marker **marcador** *m.* 2
market **mercado** *m.* 6
  open-air market **mercado al aire libre** 6
marriage **matrimonio** *m.* 9
married **casado/a** *adj.* 9
  get married (to) **casarse** *v.* **(con)** 9
marvelous **maravilloso/a** *adj.*
massage **masaje** *m.* 15
masterpiece **obra** *f.* **maestra**
match (*sports*) **partido** *m.* 4
  match **hacer** *v.* **juego (con)** 6
mathematics **matemáticas** *f., pl.* 2
matter **importar** *v.* 7, 12
maturity **madurez** *f.* 9
May **mayo** *m.* 5
maybe **tal vez** *adv.* 13; **quizás** *adv.* 13
mayonnaise **mayonesa** *f.* 8
me **me** *pron.* 5, 6
meal **comida** *f.* 8
means of communication **medios** *m., pl.* **de comunicación**
meat **carne** *f.* 8
mechanic **mecánico/a** *m., f.* 11
  (mechanic's) repair shop **taller** *m.* **mecánico** 11; **garaje** *m.* 11
media **medios** *m., pl.* **de comunicación**
medical **médico/a** *adj.* 10
medication **medicamento** *m.* 10
medicine **medicina** *f.* 10
medium **mediano/a** *adj.*
meeting **reunión** *f.* 16
menu **menú** *m.* 8
message (*telephone*) **recado** *m.*
Mexican **mexicano/a** *adj.* 3
microwave **microondas** *m., sing.* 12
middle age **madurez** *f.* 9
midnight **medianoche** *f.* 1
mile **milla** *f.* 11
milk **leche** *f.* 8

million **millón** *m.* 6
  million of **millón de** 6
mine **mío/a(s)** *poss. pron.* 11
mineral **mineral** *m.* 15
  mineral water **agua** *f.* **mineral** 8
minute **minuto** *m.*
mirror **espejo** *m.* 7
Miss **señorita (Srta.)** *f.* 1
miss **perder (e:ie)** *v.* 4
modern **moderno/a** *adj.*
mom **mamá** *f.*
Monday **lunes** *m., sing.* 2
money **dinero** *m.* 6
monkey **mono** *m.* 13
month **mes** *m.* 5
monument **monumento** *m.* 4
moon **luna** *f.* 13
more **más** *adj., adv.* 8
  more… than **más… que** 8
  more than (+ *number*) **más de (+ *number*)** 8
morning **mañana** *f.* 1
most, (the) **el/la/los/las más** 8
mother **madre** *f.* 3
mother-in-law **suegra** *f.* 3
motor **motor** *m.* 11
motorcycle **moto(cicleta)** *f.* 5
mountain **montaña** *f.* 4
mouse **ratón** *m.* 11
mouth **boca** *f.* 10
move (*to another house/city/country*) **mudarse** *v.* 12
movie **película** *f.* 4
  movie star **estrella** *f.* **de cine**
  movie theater **cine** *m.* 4
Mr. **señor (Sr.)** *m.* 1
Mrs. **señora (Sra.)** *f.* 1
much **mucho/a** *adj.* 3
mug **taza** *f.* 12
municipal **municipal** *adj.*
murder **crimen** *m.*
muscle **músculo** *m.* 15
museum **museo** *m.* 4
mushroom **champiñón** *m.* 8
music **música** *f.*
musical **musical** *adj.*
musician **músico/a** *m., f.*
my **mi(s)** *poss. adj.* 3; **mío(s)/a(s)** *poss. pron.* 11

N

name **nombre** *m.*
  in my name **a mi nombre**
  in the name of **a nombre de**
  last name **apellido** *m.* 9
  My name is… **Me llamo…** 1
  be named **llamarse** *v.* 7
napkin **servilleta** *f.* 12
national **nacional** *adj., m., f.*

nationality **nacionalidad** *f.* 1
natural **natural** *adj., m., f.* 13
  natural disaster **desastre** *m.* **natural**
  natural resource **recurso** *m.* **natural** 13
nature **naturaleza** *f.* 13
nauseated **mareado/a** *adj.* 10
near **cerca de** *prep.* 2
necessary **necesario/a** *adj.* 12
  It's necessary that… **Es necesario que…** 12
neck **cuello** *m.* 10
need **faltar** *v.* 7; **necesitar** *v.* 2, 12
negative **negativo/a** *adj.*
neighbor **vecino/a** *m., f.* 12
neighborhood **barrio** *m.* 12
neither… nor **ni… ni** *conj.* 7; neither **tampoco** *adv.* 7
nephew **sobrino** *m.* 3
nervous **nervioso/a** *adj.* 5
network **red** *f.* 11
never **nunca** *adv.* 7; **jamás** *adv.* 7
new **nuevo/a** *adj.* 6
newlywed **recién casado/a** *m., f.* 9
news **noticias** *f., pl.*; **actualidades** *f., pl.*
newscast **noticiero** *m.*
newspaper **periódico** *m.* 4; **diario** *m.*
  read the newspaper **leer el periódico** 4
next **próximo/a** *adj.*
next to **al lado de** 2
nice **simpático/a** *adj.* 3; **amable** *adj.*
niece **sobrina** *f.* 3
night **noche** *f.* 1
nightstand **mesita** *f.* **de noche** 12
nine **nueve** 1
nine hundred **novecientos/as** 6
nineteen **diecinueve** 1
ninety **noventa** 2
ninth **noveno/a** *adj.* 5
no **no** 1; **ningún, ninguno/a(s)** *adj.* 7
  no one **nadie** *pron.* 7
none **ningún, ninguno/a(s)** *adj.* 7
noon **mediodía** *m.* 1
nor **ni** *conj.* 7
north **norte** *m.* 14
  to the north **al norte** 14
nose **nariz** *f.* 10
not **no** 1
  not any **ningún, ninguno/a(s)** *adj.* 7
  not anyone **nadie** *pron.* 7
  not anything **nada** *pron.* 7
  not either **tampoco** *adv.* 7
  not ever **nunca** *adv.* 7; **jamás** *adv.* 7
  Not very well. **No muy bien.** 1
  not working **descompuesto/a** *adj.* 11
notebook **cuaderno** *m.* 1
nothing **nada** *pron.* 1; 7
noun **sustantivo** *m.*

November **noviembre** *m.* 5
now **ahora** *adv.*
nowadays **hoy día** *adv.*
nuclear energy **energía** *f.* **nuclear** 13
number **número** *m.* 1
nurse **enfermero/a** *m., f.* 10
nutrition **nutrición** *f.* 15

O

o'clock: It's… o'clock. **Son las…** 1
    It's one o'clock. **Es la una.** 1
obey **obedecer** *v.*
obligation **deber** *m.*
obtain **conseguir (e:i)** *v.* 4; **obtener** *v.* 16
obvious **obvio** *adj.* 13
    it's obvious **es obvio** 13
occupation **ocupación** *f.* 16
occur **ocurrir** *v.*
ocean **océano** *m.* 13
October **octubre** *m.* 5
of **de** *prep.* 1
    of course **claro que sí; por supuesto**
offer **oferta** *f.*; **ofrecer** *v.* 8
office **oficina** *f.* 12
    doctor's office **consultorio** *m.* 10
often **a menudo** *adv.* 10
Oh! **¡Ay!**
oil **aceite** *m.* 8
old **viejo/a** *adj.* 3
old age **vejez** *f.* 9
older **mayor** *adj., m., f.* 8
    older brother, sister **hermano/a mayor** *m., f.*
oldest **el/la mayor** 8
on **en** *prep.* 2; **sobre** *prep.* 2
    on the dot **en punto** *adv.* 1
    on time **a tiempo** *adv.* 10
    on top of **encima de** *prep.* 2
once **una vez** 6
one **un, uno/a** 1
    one hundred **cien** 2; **ciento** 6
    one million **un millón** 6
    one thousand **mil** 6
    one way (*travel*) **ida** *f.*
onion **cebolla** *f.* 8
online: buy online **comprar** *v.* **en línea** 6
only **sólo** *adv.*; **único/a** *adj.*
    only child **hijo/a único/a** *m., f.*
open **abrir** *v.* 3; **abierto/a** *adj.* 5
open-air **al aire libre** 6
opened **abierto/a** *p.p.* 15
opera **ópera** *f.*
operation **operación** *f.* 10
opposite **en frente de** *prep.* 14
or **o** *conj.* 7
orange **anaranjado/a** *adj.* 6; **naranja** *f.* 8
orchestra **orquesta** *f.*

order **mandar** 12; (*food*) **pedir (e:i)** *v.* 8
    in order to **para** *prep.* 11
orderly **ordenado/a** *adj.* 5
ordinal (*numbers*) **ordinal** *adj.*
other **otro/a** *adj.* 6
our **nuestro(s)/a(s)** *poss. adj.* 3; *poss. pron.* 11
out of order **descompuesto/a** *adj.* 11
outside **fuera** *adv.*
outskirts **afueras** *f., pl.* 12
oven **horno** *m.* 12
over **sobre** *prep.* 2
own **propio/a** *adj.*
owner **dueño/a** *m., f.* 8

P

pack (one's suitcases) **hacer** *v.* **las maletas** 5
package **paquete** *m.* 14
page **página** *f.* 11
pain **dolor** *m.* 10
paint **pintar** *v.*
painter **pintor(a)** *m., f.* 16
painting **pintura** *f.* 12
pair **par** *m.* 6
    pair of shoes **par de zapatos** 6
pants **pantalones** *m., pl.* 6
pantyhose **medias** *f., pl.* 6
paper **papel** *m.* 2; (*report*) **informe** *m.*
    paper money **billete** *m.*
paragraph **párrafo** *m.*
Pardon me. (*May I?*) **Con permiso.** (*Excuse me.*) **Perdón.**
parents **padres** *m., pl.* 3; **papás** *m., pl.*
park **parque** *m.* 4; **estacionar** *v.* 11
partner (*one of a couple*) **pareja** *f.* 9
party **fiesta** *f.* 9
pass **pasar** *v.*
passenger **pasajero/a** *m., f.* 1
passport **pasaporte** *m.* 5
past **pasado/a** *adj.* 6
pastime **pasatiempo** *m.* 4
pastry shop **pastelería** *f.* 14
patient **paciente** *m., f.* 10
patio **patio** *m.* 12
pay **pagar** *v.* 6
    pay in cash **pagar** *v.* **al contado** 14; **pagar en efectivo**
    pay in installments **pagar** *v.* **a plazos** 14
    pay the bill **pagar** *v.* **la cuenta** 9
    pay with **pagar con** 6
pea **arveja** *f.* 8
peace **paz** *f.*
peach **melocotón** *m.*
pear **pera** *f.*
pen **pluma** *f.* 2
pencil **lápiz** *m.* 1
penicillin **penicilina** *f.*
people **gente** *f.* 3

pepper **pimienta** *f.* 8
per **por** *prep.* 11
percent **por ciento**
perfect **perfecto/a** *adj.*
perhaps **quizás** *adv.*; **tal vez** *adv.*
permission **permiso** *m.*
person **persona** *f.* 3
pharmacy **farmacia** *f.* 10
phenomenal **fenomenal** *adj.*
photograph **foto(grafía)** *f.* 1
physical (*exam*) **examen** *m.* **médico** 10
physics **física** *f., sing.* 2
pick up **recoger** *v.* 13
picture **foto** *f.* 5; **cuadro** *m.* 12
pie **pastel** *m.*
pill (tablet) **pastilla** *f.* 10
pillow **almohada** *f.* 12
pineapple **piña** *f.*
pink **rosado/a** *adj.* 6
place **lugar** *m.* 4; **poner** *v.* 4
plaid **de cuadros** *adj.*
plan (*to do something*) **pensar** *v.* (+ *inf.*) 4
plane **avión** *m.* 5
plant **planta** *f.* 13
plastic **plástico** *m.* 13
    (made of) plastic **de plástico** 13
plate **plato** *m.* 12
play **drama** *m.*; **comedia** *f.*; **jugar (u:ue)** *v.* 4; (*a musical instrument*) **tocar** *v.*; (*a role*) **hacer** *v.* **el papel**; (*cards*) **jugar** *v.* **a (las cartas)**; (*sports*) **practicar** *v.* **deportes** 4
player **jugador(a)** *m., f.* 4
playwright **dramaturgo/a** *m., f.*
pleasant **agradable** *adj.*
Please. **Por favor.** 1
Pleased to meet you. **Mucho gusto.** 1; **Encantado/a.** *adj.* 1
pleasing: be pleasing to **gustar** *v.* 7
pleasure **gusto** *m.* 1; **placer** *m.*
    The pleasure is mine. **El gusto es mío.** 1
poem **poema** *m.*
poet **poeta** *m., f.* 16
poetry **poesía** *f.*
police (force) **policía** *f.* 11
    police officer **policía** *m.*, **mujer** *f.* **policía** 11
political **político/a** *adj.*
politician **político/a** *m., f.* 16
politics **política** *f.*
polka-dotted **de lunares** *adj.*
poll **encuesta** *f.*
pollute **contaminar** *v.* 13
polluted **contaminado/a** *adj.* 13
    be polluted **estar contaminado/a** 13
pollution **contaminación** *f.* 13
pool **piscina** *f.* 4
poor **pobre** *adj.* 6

population **población** *f.* 13
pork **cerdo** *m.* 8
  pork chop **chuleta** *f.* **de cerdo** 8
position **puesto** *m.* 16
possessive **posesivo/a** *adj.*
possible **posible** *adj.* 13
  it's (not) possible **(no) es posible** 13
post office **correo** *m.* 14
postcard **postal** *f.* 4; **tarjeta** *f.* **postal** 4
poster **cartel** *m.*
potato **papa** *f.* 8; **patata** *f.* 8
pottery **cerámica** *f.*
practice **practicar** *v.* 2
prefer **preferir (e:ie)** *v.* 4, 12
pregnant **embarazada** *adj. f.* 10
prepare **preparar** *v.* 2
preposition **preposición** *f.*
prescribe *(medicine)* **recetar** *v.* 10
prescription **receta** *f.* 10
present **regalo** *m.* 6; **presentar** *v.*
press **prensa** *f.*
pressure: be under a lot of pressure
  sufrir *v.* **muchas presiones** 15
pretty **bonito/a** *adj.* 3
price **precio** *m.* 6
  fixed price **precio** *m.* **fijo** 6
print **imprimir** *v.* 11
printer **impresora** *f.* 11
prize **premio** *m.*
probable **probable** *adj.* 13
  it's (not) probable **(no) es probable** 13
problem **problema** *m.* 1
profession **profesión** *f.* 16
professor **profesor(a)** *m., f.* 1
profit **beneficios** *m., pl.* 16
program **programa** *m.* 1
programmer **programador(a)** *m., f.* 3
prohibit **prohibir** *v.* 10, 12
promotion *(career)* **ascenso** *m.* 16
pronoun **pronombre** *m.*
protect **proteger** *v.* 13
protein **proteína** *f.* 15
provided that **con tal (de) que** *conj.* 13
psychologist **psicólogo/a** *m., f.* 16
psychology **psicología** *f.* 2
publish **publicar** *v.*
Puerto Rican **puertorriqueño/a** *adj.* 3
pull a tooth **sacar** *v.* **una muela**
purchases **compras** *f., pl.*
pure **puro/a** *adj.* 13
purple **morado/a** *adj.* 6
purse **bolsa** *f.* 6
put **poner** *v.* 4; **puesto/a** *p.p.* 15
  put a letter in the mailbox **echar** *v.*
  una carta al buzón 14
  put on *(a performance)* **presentar** *v.*
  put on *(clothing)* **ponerse** *v.* 7
  put on makeup **maquillarse** *v.* 7

Q

quality **calidad** *f.*
quarter **trimestre** *m.* 2
  quarter after *(time)* **y cuarto** 1;
  y quince 1
  quarter to *(time)* **menos cuarto** 1;
  menos quince 1
question **pregunta** *f.*
quickly **rápido** *adv.*
quiet **tranquilo/a** *adj.* 15
quit **dejar** *v.* 16
quite **bastante** *adv.* 10
quiz **prueba** *f.* 2

R

racism **racismo** *m.*
radio *(medium)* **radio** *f.*;
  radio *(set)* **radio** *m.* 11
rain **llover (o:ue)** *v.* 5
  It's raining. **Llueve.** 5
rain forest **bosque** *m.* **tropical** 13
raincoat **impermeable** *m.* 6
raise *(salary)* **aumento** *m.* **de sueldo**
  16
read **leer** *v.* 3; **leído/a** *p.p.* 15
ready **listo/a** *adj.* 5
real estate agency **agencia** *f.* **de**
  bienes raíces 12
reap the benefits (of) **disfrutar** *v.* **(de)**
  15
reason **razón** *f.*
receive **recibir** *v.* 3
recommend **recomendar (e:ie)** *v.*
  8, 12
record **grabar** *v.* 11
recycle **reciclar** *v.* 13
recycling **reciclaje** *m.* 13
red **rojo/a** *adj.* 6
red-haired **pelirrojo/a** *adj.* 3
reduce **reducir** *v.* 13
  reduce stress/tension **aliviar** *v.* **el**
  estrés/la tensión 15
refrigerator **refrigerador** *m.* 12
region **región** *f.* 13
regret **sentir (e:ie)** *v.* 13
relationships **relaciones** *f., pl.*
relatives **parientes** *m., pl.* 3
relax **relajarse** *v.* 9
relieve stress/tension **aliviar el**
  estrés/la tensión 15
remember **recordar (o:ue)** *v.* 4;
  acordarse (o:ue) *v.* **(de)** 7
remote control **control** *m.* **remoto** 11
renewable **renovable** *adj.* 13
rent **alquilar** *v.* 12; **alquiler** *m.* 12
repeat **repetir (e:i)** *v.* 4
report **informe** *m.*; **reportaje** *m.*
reporter **reportero/a** *m., f.* 16
representative **representante** *m., f.*
request **pedir (e:i)** *v.* 4

reservation **reservación** *f.* 5
resign (from) **renunciar (a)** *v.* 16
resolve **resolver (o:ue)** *v.* 13
resolved **resuelto/a** *p.p.* 15
resource **recurso** *m.* 13
responsibility **deber** *m.*
rest **descansar** *v.* 2
  the rest **lo/los/las demás** *pron.*
restaurant **restaurante** *m.* 4
résumé **currículum** *m.* 16
retire (from work) **jubilarse** *v.* 9
return **regresar** *v.* 2; **volver (o:ue)** *v.* 4
  return trip **vuelta** *f.*
returned **vuelto/a** *p.p.* 15
rice **arroz** *m.* 8
rich **rico/a** *adj.* 6
ride **pasear** *v.* 4
  ride a bicycle **pasear en bicicleta** 4
  ride a horse **montar a caballo** 5
ridiculous **ridículo/a** *adj.* 13
  it's ridiculous **es ridículo** 13
right **derecha** *f.* 2
  right away **enseguida** *adv.*
  right now **ahora mismo** 5
  be right **tener** *v.* **razón** 3
  to the right of **a la derecha de** 2
  right? *(question tag)* **¿no?**;
  ¿verdad? 2
rights **derechos** *m., pl.*
ring **sonar (o:ue)** *v.* 11
river **río** *m.* 13
road **camino** *m.*
roast chicken **pollo** *m.* **asado** 8
roasted **asado/a** *adj.* 8
role **papel** *m.*
romantic **romántico/a** *adj.*
room **habitación** *f.* 5; **cuarto** *m.*;
  (large, living) **sala** *f.*
roommate **compañero/a** *m., f.*
  de cuarto 2
round-trip **de ida y vuelta** 5
  round-trip ticket **pasaje** *m.* **de**
  ida y vuelta 5
route **camino** *m.* 11
routine **rutina** *f.* 7
rug **alfombra** *f.* 12
run **correr** *v.* 3
  run errands **hacer diligencias** 14
  run into *(have an accident)*
  chocar *v.* **(con)** 11; *(meet*
  accidentally) **darse** *v.* **con**
rush **apurarse** *v.* 15; **darse** *v.* **prisa** 15
Russian **ruso/a** *adj.*

S

sad **triste** *adj.* 5
  it's sad **es triste** 13
safe **seguro/a** *adj.* 5
said **dicho/a** *p.p.* 15
salad **ensalada** *f.* 8
salary **salario** *m.* 16; **sueldo** *m.* 16

sale **rebaja** *f.* 6

salesperson **vendedor(a)** *m., f.* 6

salmon **salmón** *m.* 8

salt **sal** *f.* 8

salty **salado/a** *adj.* 8

same **mismo/a** *adj.*

sandal **sandalia** *f.* 6

sandwich **sándwich** *m.* 8

Saturday **sábado** *m.* 2

sausage **salchicha** *f.* 8

save (*on a computer*) **guardar** *v.* 11;
    save (*money*) **ahorrar** *v.* 14

savings **ahorros** *m., pl.* 14
    savings account **cuenta** *f.* **de**
        ahorros 14

say **decir** *v.* 6
    say hello to... **saludos** *m., pl.* **a...** 1

scan **escanear** *v.* 11

scarcely **apenas** *adv.* 10

scared: be (very) scared **tener** *v.*
    (mucho) miedo 3

schedule **horario** *m.* 2

school **escuela** *f.* 1

science **ciencia** *f.*
    science fiction **ciencia ficción** *f.*

scientist **científico/a** *m., f.* 16

scream **gritar** *v.*

screen **pantalla** *f.* 11

scuba dive **bucear** *v.* 4

sculpt **esculpir** *v.*

sculptor **escultor(a)** *m., f.* 16

sculpture **escultura** *f.*

sea **mar** *m.* 5

sea turtle **tortuga** *f.* **marina** 13

seafood **mariscos** *m., pl.* 8

search: in search of **por** *prep.* 11

season **estación** *f.* 5

second **segundo/a** *adj.* 5

secretary **secretario/a** *m., f.* 16

sedentary **sedentario/a** *adj.* 15

see **ver** *v.* 4
    See you. **Nos vemos.** 1
    See you later. **Hasta la vista.** 1;
        Hasta luego. 1
    See you soon. **Hasta pronto.** 1
    See you tomorrow. **Hasta**
        mañana. 1

seem **parecer** *v.* 8

seen **visto/a** *p.p.* 15

sell **vender** *v.* 6

semester **semestre** *m.* 2

send **enviar** *v.* 14; **mandar** *v.* 14

separate (from) **separarse** *v.* **(de)** 9

separated **separado/a** *adj.* 9

September **septiembre** *m.* 5

sequence **secuencia** *f.*

serious **grave** *adj.* 10

serve **servir (e:i)** *v.* 8

set (*fixed*) **fijo** *adj.* 6
    set the table **poner** *v.* **la mesa** 12

seven **siete** 1

seven hundred **setecientos/as** 6

seventeen **diecisiete** 1

seventh **séptimo/a** *adj.* 5

seventy **setenta** 2

several **varios/as** *adj., pl.*

sexism **sexismo** *m.*

shame **lástima** *f.* 13
    It's a shame. **Es una lástima.** 13

shampoo **champú** *m.* 7

shape **forma** *f.* 15
    be in good shape **estar en**
        buena forma 15

share **compartir** *v.* 3

sharp (*time*) **en punto** 1

shave **afeitarse** *v.* 7

shaving cream **crema** *f.* **de afeitar** 7

she **ella** *sub. pron.* 1

shellfish **mariscos** *m., pl.*

ship **barco** *m.*

shirt **camisa** *f.* 6

shoe **zapato** *m.* 6
    pair of shoes **par de zapatos** 6
    shoe size **número** *m.* **de zapato**
    shoe store **zapatería** *f.* 14

shopping, to go **ir** *v.* **de compras** 6
    shopping mall **centro** *m.* **comercial**
        6

short (*in height*) **bajo/a** *adj.* 3; (*in*
    length) **corto/a** *adj.* 6

short story **cuento** *m.*

shorts **pantalones cortos** *m., pl.* 6

should (*do something*) **deber** *v.*
    (+ inf.) 3

show **mostrar (o:ue)** *v.* 4; **espectáculo**
    m.

shower **ducha** *f.*; **ducharse** *v.* 7

shrimp **camarón** *m.* 8

siblings **hermanos** *m., pl.* 3

sick **mal, malo/a** 5; **enfermo/a** *adj.*
    10
    be sick **estar enfermo/a** 10
    get sick **enfermarse** *v.* 10

sightseeing: go sightseeing **hacer** *v.*
    turismo 5

sign **firmar** *v.* 14; **letrero** *m.* 14

silverware **cubierto** *m.*

similar **similar** *adj. m., f.*

since **desde** *prep.*

sing **cantar** *v.* 2

singer **cantante** *m., f.* 16

single **soltero/a** *adj.* 9
    single room **habitación** *f.*
        individual 5

sink **lavabo** *m.*

sir **señor (Sr.)** *m.* 1

sister **hermana** *f.* 3

sister-in-law **cuñada** *f.* 3

sit down **sentarse (e:ie)** *v.* 7

six **seis** 1

six hundred **seiscientos/as** 6

sixteen **dieciséis** 1

sixth **sexto/a** *adj.* 5

sixty **sesenta** 2

size **talla** *f.*
    shoe size **número** *m.* **de zapato**

skate **patinar** *v.* 4

ski **esquiar** *v.* 4

skiing **esquí** *m.* 4
    water-skiing **esquí acuático** 4

skirt **falda** *f.* 6

sky **cielo** *m.* 13

sleep **dormir (o:ue)** *v.* 4; **sueño** *m.*
    go to sleep **dormirse (o:ue)** *v.* 7

sleepy: be (very) sleepy **tener** *v.*
    (mucho) sueño 3

slim down **adelgazar** *v.* 15

slow **lento/a** *adj.* 11

slowly **despacio** *adv.*

small **pequeño/a** *adj.* 3

smart **listo/a** *adj.* 5

smile **sonreír (e:i)** *v.* 9

smiled **sonreído/a** *p.p.* 15

smoke **fumar** *v.* 15
    not to smoke **no fumar** *v.* 15

snack (in the afternoon) **merendar**
    (e:ie) *v.* 15; (afternoon snack)
    merienda *f.* 15
    have a snack **merendar (e:ie)** *v.* 15

sneakers **zapatos** *m., pl.* **de tenis** 6

sneeze **estornudar** *v.* 10

snow **nevar (e:ie)** *v.* 5; **nieve** *f.*
    snowing: It's snowing. **Nieva.** 5

so (*in such a way*) **así** *adv.* 10
    so much **tanto** *adv.*
    so-so **regular** 1; **así así**
    so that **para que** *conj.* 13

soap **jabón** *m.* 7
    soap opera **telenovela** *f.*

soccer **fútbol** *m.* 4

sociology **sociología** *f.* 2

sock **calcetín** *m.* 6

sofa **sofá** *m.* 12

soft drink **refresco** *m.* 8

software **programa** *m.* **de**
    computación 11

soil **tierra** *f.* 13

solar energy **energía** *f.* **solar** 13

solution **solución** *f.* 13

solve **resolver (o:ue)** *v.* 13

some **algún, alguno/a(s)** *adj.* 7;
    unos/as *m., f., pl. indef. art.* 1

somebody **alguien** *pron.* 7

someone **alguien** *pron.* 7

something **algo** *pron.* 7

sometimes **a veces** *adv.* 10

son **hijo** *m.* 3

song **canción** *f.*

son-in-law **yerno** *m.* 3

soon **pronto** *adj.* 10
    See you soon. **Hasta pronto.** 1

sorry: be sorry **sentir (e:ie)** *v.* 13
    I'm sorry. **Lo siento.** 1

soup **sopa** *f.* 8

sour **agrio/a** *adj.* 8

south **sur** *m.* 14
    to the south **al sur** 14

Spanish (*language*) **español** *m.* 2;
    español(a) *adj.; m., f.* 3

spare time **ratos** *m., pl.* **libres** 4
speak **hablar** *v.* 2
specialization **especialización** *f.*
spectacular **espectacular** *adj.*
speech **discurso** *m.*
speed **velocidad** *f.* 11
  speed limit **velocidad máxima** 11
spelling **ortográfico/a** *adj.*
spend (*money*) **gastar** *v.* 6
  spend time **pasar** *v.* **el tiempo** 4
spicy **picante** *adj.* 8
spoon (*table or large*) **cuchara** *f.* 12
sport **deporte** *m.* 4
  sports-related **deportivo/a** *adj.* 4
spouse **esposo/a** *m., f.* 3
sprain (one's ankle) **torcerse** *v.*
  (el tobillo) 10
sprained **torcido/a** *adj.*
spring **primavera** *f.* 5
stadium **estadio** *m.* 2
stage **etapa** *f.* 9
stairs **escalera** *f.* 12
stamp **estampilla** *f.* 14; **sello** *m.* 14
stand in line **hacer** *v.* **cola** 14
star **estrella** *f.* 13
start (*a vehicle*) **arrancar** *v.* 11
state **estado** *m.*
station **estación** *f.* 5
statue **estatua** *f.*
status: marital status **estado** *m.* **civil** 9
stay **quedarse** *v.* 7
  Stay calm! **¡Tranquilo/a!**
  stay in shape **mantenerse** *v.* **en**
    forma 15
steak **bistec** *m.* 8
steering wheel **volante** *m.* 11
step **etapa** *f.*
stepbrother **hermanastro** *m.* 3
stepdaughter **hijastra** *f.* 3
stepfather **padrastro** *m.* 3
stepmother **madrastra** *f.* 3
stepsister **hermanastra** *f.* 3
stepson **hijastro** *m.* 3
still **todavía** *adv.* 5
stockbroker **corredor(a)** *m., f.* **de**
  bolsa 16
stockings **medias** *f., pl.* 6
stomach **estómago** *m.* 10
stone **piedra** *f.* 13
stop **parar** *v.* 11
  stop (*doing something*) **dejar** *v.* **de**
    (+ *inf.*) 13
store **tienda** *f.* 6
storm **tormenta** *f.*
story **cuento** *m.*; **historia** *f.*
stove **estufa** *f.* 12
straight (ahead) **derecho** *adv.* 14
straighten up **arreglar** *v.* 12
strange **extraño/a** *adj.* 13
  It's strange... **Es extraño...** 13
street **calle** *f.* 11
stress **estrés** *m.* 15

stretching **estiramiento** *m.* 15
  stretching exercises **ejercicios**
    m., pl. **de estiramiento** 15
strike (*labor*) **huelga** *f.*
stripe **raya** *f.*
  striped **de rayas** *adj.*
stroll **pasear** *v.* 4
strong **fuerte** *adj.* 15
struggle (for) **luchar** *v.* **(por)**
student **estudiante** *m., f.* 1;
  estudiantil *adj.*
study **estudiar** *v.* 2
stupendous **estupendo/a** *adj.*
style **estilo** *m.*
suburbs **afueras** *f., pl.* 12
subway **metro** *m.* 5
  subway station **estación** *f.* **del**
    metro 5
success **éxito** *m.*
successful: be successful **tener** *v.* **éxito** 16
suddenly **de repente** *adv.* 6
suffer **sufrir** *v.* 15
sugar **azúcar** *m.* 8
suggest **sugerir (e:ie)** *v.* 12
suit **traje** *m.* 6
suitcase **maleta** *f.* 1
summer **verano** *m.* 5
sun **sol** *m.* 13
sunbathe **tomar** *v.* **el sol** 4
Sunday **domingo** *m.* 2
sunglasses **gafas** *f., pl.* **de sol** 6
sunny: It's (very) sunny. **Hace (mucho)**
  sol. 5
supermarket **supermercado** *m.* 14
suppose **suponer** *v.* 4
sure **seguro/a** *adj.* 5
  be sure (of) **estar** *v.* **seguro/a (de)**
    5, 13
surprise **sorprender** *v.* 9; **sorpresa** *f.* 9
survey **encuesta** *f.*
sweat **sudar** *v.* 15
sweater **suéter** *m.* 6
sweep the floor **barrer** *v.* **el suelo** 12
sweet **dulce** *adj.* 8
sweets **dulces** *m., pl.* 9
swim **nadar** *v.*
  swim in the pool **nadar en la**
    piscina 4
swimming **natación** *f.* 4
  swimming pool **piscina** *f.* 4
symptom **síntoma** *m.* 10

T

table **mesa** *f.* 2
tablespoon **cuchara** *f.* 12
tablet (computer) **tableta** *f.* 11
take **tomar** *v.* 2, 8; **llevar** *v.* 6
  take care of **cuidar** *v.* 13
  take (someone's) temperature
    tomar(le) *v.* **la temperatura**
    (a alguien) 10
  take (*wear*) a shoe size **calzar** *v.*

take a bath **bañarse** *v.* 7
take off **quitarse** *v.* 7
take out the trash **sacar** *v.* **la**
  basura 12
take pictures **sacar** *v.* **fotos** 5;
  tomar fotos
talented **talentoso/a** *adj.*
talk **hablar** *v.* 2; **conversar** *v.* 2
  talk show **programa** *m.* **de**
    entrevistas
tall **alto/a** *adj.* 3
tank **tanque** *m.* 11
taste **probar (o:ue)** *v.* 8
tasty **rico/a** *adj.* 8; **sabroso/a** *adj.* 8
tax **impuesto** *m.*
taxi(cab) **taxi** *m.* 5
tea **té** *m.* 8
teach **enseñar** *v.* 2
teacher **profesor(a)** *m., f.*;
  maestro/a *m., f.* 16
team **equipo** *m.* 4
technician **técnico/a** *m., f.* 16
telecommuting **teletrabajo** *m.* 16
telephone **teléfono** *m.* 11
  cell phone **teléfono celular** 11
television **televisión** *f.*
  television set **televisor** *m.* 11
tell **decir** *v.* 6
temperature **temperatura** *f.* 10
ten **diez** 1
tennis **tenis** *m.* 4
  tennis shoes **zapatos** *m., pl.* **de**
    tenis 6
tension **tensión** *f.* 15
tent **tienda** *f.* **de campaña** 5
tenth **décimo/a** *adj.* 5
terrible **terrible** *adj. m., f.* 13
  it's terrible **es terrible** 13
terrific **chévere** *adj.*
test **prueba** *f.* 2; **examen** *m.* 2
text **textear** *v.* 11
text message **mensaje** *m.* **de texto** 11
Thank you. **Gracias.** *f., pl.* 1
  Thank you (very much).
    (Muchas) gracias. 1
that **que; quien(es); lo que** *rel. pron.* 9
  that (one) **ése, ésa, eso** *pron.* 6;
    ese, esa *adj.* 6
  that (*over there*) **aquél, aquélla,**
    aquello *pron.* 6;
    aquel, aquella *adj.* 6
  that which **lo que** *rel. pron.* 9
  that's why **por eso** 11
the **el** *m.*, **la** *f. sing., def. art.*; **los** *m.*,
  las *f. pl., def. art.* 1
theater **teatro** *m.*
their **su(s)** *poss., adj.* 3; **suyo(s)/a(s)**
  poss., pron. 11
them **los/las** *pron.* 5; **les** *pron.* 6
then **después** (*afterward*) *adv.* 7;
  entonces (*as a result*) *adv.* 7;
  luego (*next*) *adv.* 7

there **allí** *adv.*
> There is/are… **Hay…** 1
> There is/are not… **No hay…** 1

therefore **por eso** *adv.* 11

these **éstos, éstas** *pron.* 6;
> **estos, estas** *adj.* 6

they **ellos/as** *sub. pron.* 1

thin **delgado/a** *adj.* 3

thing **cosa** *f.* 1

think **pensar (e:ie)** *v.* 4; (believe)
> **creer** *v.*
> think about **pensar en** 4

third **tercer, tercero/a** *adj.* 5

thirst **sed** *f.*

thirsty: be (very) thirsty **tener** *v.*
> **(mucha) sed** 3

thirteen **trece** 1

thirty **treinta** 1; thirty (*minutes past the hour*) **y treinta** 1; **y media** 1

this **este, esta** *adj.; *éste, ésta, esto**
> *pron.* 6
> This is… (*introduction*) **Éste/a es…** 1
> This is he/she. (*on telephone*)
> **Con él/ella habla.**

those **ésos, ésas** *pron.* 6; **esos, esas**
> *adj.* 6

those (over there) **aquéllos, aquéllas**
> *pron.* 6; **aquellos, aquellas** *adj.* 6

thousand **mil** *m.* 6

three **tres** 1

three hundred **trescientos/as** 6

throat **garganta** *f.* 10

through **por** *prep.* 11

throw **echar** *v.*

Thursday **jueves** *m., sing.* 2

ticket **boleto** *m.;* **entrada** *f.;* **pasaje** *m.*
> 5; (traffic) **multa** *f.* 11

tie **corbata** *f.* 6

time **vez** *f.;* **tiempo** *m.* 4
> have a good/bad time
> **pasarlo** *v.* **bien/mal** 9

times **veces** *f., pl.*
> many times **muchas veces** 10

tip **propina** *f.* 9

tire **llanta** *f.* 11

tired **cansado/a** *adj.* 5

title **título** *m.*

to **a** *prep.* 1

toast (*drink*) **brindar** *v.* 9
> toast **pan** *m.* **tostado** 8

toasted **tostado/a** *adj.* 8

toaster **tostadora** *f.*

today **hoy** *adv.* 2
> Today is . . . **Hoy es…** 2, 5

together **juntos/as** *adj.* 9

tomato **tomate** *m.* 8

tomorrow **mañana** *adv.* 1
> See you tomorrow. **Hasta mañana.** 1

tonight **esta noche** *adv.*

too **también** *adv.* 7
> too much **demasiado** *adv.;*
> **en exceso** 15

tooth **diente** *m.* 7; tooth **muela** *f.* 10

tornado **tornado** *m.*

touch **tocar** *v.*

tour **excursión** *f.*
> go on a tour **hacer** *v.* **una excursión** 5

tourism **turismo** *m.*

tourist **turista** *m., f.* 1; **turístico/a** *adj.*

toward **para** *prep.* 11; **hacia** *prep.* 14

towel **toalla** *f.* 7

town **pueblo** *m.* 4

trade **oficio** *m.* 16

traffic **circulación** *f.;* **tráfico** *m.* 11
> traffic light **semáforo** *m.* 11

tragedy **tragedia** *f.*

trail **sendero** *m.* 13

train **entrenarse** *v.* 15; **tren** *m.* 5
> train station **estación** *f.* **del tren** *m.* 5

translate **traducir** *v.* 8

trash **basura** *f.* 12

travel **viajar** *v.* 2
> travel documents **documentos** *m., pl.* **de viaje**

traveler **viajero/a** *m., f.* 5

treat (*entertain*) **invitar** *v.* 9

tree **árbol** *m.* 13

trillion **billón** 6

trimester **trimestre** *m.* 2

trip **viaje** *m.* 5
> take a trip **hacer** *v.* **un viaje** 5

tropical forest **bosque** *m.* **tropical** 13

truck **camión** *m.*

true **cierto/a** *adj.* 13
> it's (not) true **(no) es cierto/verdad** 13

trunk **baúl** *m.* 11

truth **verdad** *f.* 6

try **intentar** *v.;* **probar (o:ue)** *v.* 8
> try (*to do something*) **tratar** *v.* **de (+ *inf.*)** 15
> try on **probarse (o:ue)** *v.* 7

t-shirt **camiseta** *f.* 6

Tuesday **martes** *m., sing.* 2

tuna **atún** *m.* 8

turkey **pavo** *m.* 8

turn **doblar** *v.* 14
> turn off (*electricity/appliance*)
> **apagar** *v.* 11
> turn on (*electricity/appliance*)
> **poner** *v.* 11; **prender** *v.* 11

turtle **tortuga** *f.* 13
> sea turtle **tortuga marina** 13

twelve **doce** 1

twenty **veinte** 1

twenty-eight **veintiocho** 1

twenty-five **veinticinco** 1

twenty-four **veinticuatro** 1

twenty-nine **veintinueve** 1

twenty-one **veintiún, veintiuno/a** 1

twenty-seven **veintisiete** 1

twenty-six **veintiséis** 1

twenty-three **veintitrés** 1

twenty-two **veintidós** 1

twice **dos veces** 6

twisted **torcido/a** *adj.*

two **dos** 1

two hundred **doscientos/as** 6

U

ugly **feo/a** *adj.* 3

uncle **tío** *m.* 3

under **debajo de** *prep.* 2; **bajo** *prep.*

understand **comprender** *v.* 3;
> **entender (e:ie)** *v.* 4

underwear **ropa** *f.* **interior** 6

unemployment **desempleo** *m.*

university **universidad** *f.* 2

unless **a menos que** *conj.* 13

unmarried **soltero/a** *adj.* 9

unpleasant **antipático/a** *adj.* 3

until **hasta** *prep.* 6; **hasta que** *conj.* 13

up **arriba** *adv.*

upload **cargar** *v.* 11

urgent **urgente** *adj.* 12
> It's urgent that… **Es urgente que…** 12

us **nos** *pron.* 5, 6

USB port **puerto** *m.* **USB** 11

use **usar** *v.* 6

used for **para** *prep.* 11

useful **útil** *adj.*

V

vacation **vacaciones** *f., pl.* 5
> be on vacation **estar** *v.* **de vacaciones** 5
> go on vacation **ir** *v.* **de vacaciones** 5

vacuum **pasar** *v.* **la aspiradora** 12
> vacuum cleaner **aspiradora** *f.* 12

valley **valle** *m.* 13

various **varios/as** *adj., pl.*

vegetables **verduras** *f., pl.* 8

Venezuelan **venezolano/a** *adj.* 3

verb **verbo** *m.*

very **muy** *adv.* 1
> (Very) well, thanks. **(Muy) bien, gracias.** 1

vest **chaleco** *m.*

video **video** *m.* 1

videoconference
> **videoconferencia** *f.* 16

vinegar **vinagre** *m.* 8

violence **violencia** *f.*

visit **visitar** *v.* 4
> visit a monument **visitar un monumento** 4

vitamin **vitamina** *f.* 15

voicemail **buzón** *m.* **de voz** 11

volcano **volcán** *m.* 13

volleyball **vóleibol** *m.* 4

vote **votar** *v.*

W

wait (for) **esperar** *v.* 2
waiter **camarero/a** *m., f.* 8
wake up **despertarse (e:ie)** *v.* 7
walk **caminar** *v.* 2
  take a walk **pasear** *v.* 4
  walk around the city/town **pasear por la ciudad/el pueblo** 4
wall **pared** *f.* 12
wallet **cartera** *f.* 6
want **desear** *v.* 2; **querer (e:ie)** *v.* 4, 12
war **guerra** *f.*
warm up **calentarse (e:ie)** *v.* 15
wash **lavar** *v.* 12
  wash one's face/hands **lavarse** *v.* **la cara/las manos** 7
  wash oneself **lavarse** 7
washing machine **lavadora** *f.* 12
watch **mirar** *v.* 2; **reloj** *m.* 2; **ver** *v.* 4
  watch television **mirar (la) televisión**
  watch movies **ver películas** 4
water **agua** *f.* 8
  water pollution **contaminación del agua** 13
  water-skiing **esquí** *m.* **acuático** 4
way **manera** *f.*
we **nosotros/as** *sub. pron.* 1
weak **débil** *adj.* 15
wear **llevar** *v.* 6; **usar** *v.* 6; **calzar** *v.* (shoes)
weather **tiempo** *m.* 5
  It's bad weather. **Hace mal tiempo.** 5
  It's nice weather. **Hace buen tiempo.** 5
weaving **tejido** *m.*
Web **red** *f.* 11
website **sitio** *m.* **web** 11
wedding **boda** *f.* 9
Wednesday **miércoles** *m., sing.* 2
week **semana** *f.* 2
weekend **fin** *m.* **de semana** 4
weight **peso** *m.* 15
  lift weights **levantar** *v.* **pesas** *f., pl.* 15
Welcome! **¡Bienvenido(s)/a(s)!** *adj.*
well **pues** *adv.*
well-being **bienestar** *m.* 15
well organized **ordenado/a** *adj.* 5
west **oeste** *m.* 14
  to the west **al oeste** 14
whale **ballena** *f.* 13
what **lo que** *rel. pron.* 9
  what? **¿qué?** *adj., pron.* 1, 2, 9; **¿cuál(es)?** 9
  At what time…? **¿A qué hora…?** 1
  What a… ! **¡Qué…!**
  What a surprise! **¡Qué sorpresa!**
  What day is it? **¿Qué día es hoy?**

What did he/she do? **¿Qué hizo él/ella?** 6
What did they do? **¿Qué hicieron ellos/ellas?** 6
What did you do? **¿Qué hiciste?** *fam., sing.;* **¿Qué hizo usted?** *form., sing.;* **¿Qué hicieron ustedes?** *pl.* 6
What did you say? **¿Cómo?**
What happened? **¿Qué pasó?**
What is it? **¿Qué es?** 1
What is the price? **¿Qué precio tiene?**
What is today's date? **¿Cuál es la fecha de hoy?** 5
What time is it? **¿Qué hora es?** 1
What's going on? **¿Qué pasa?** 1
What's… like? **¿Cómo es…?**
What's new? **¿Qué hay de nuevo?** 1
What's wrong? **¿Qué pasó?**
What's your name? **¿Cómo se llama usted?** *form.* 1
What's your name? **¿Cómo te llamas (tú)?** *fam.* 1
when **cuando** *conj.* 13
  When? **¿Cuándo?** 2
where **donde** *adj., conj.*
  where? (*destination*) **¿adónde?** 2; (*location*)**¿dónde?** 1, 2
  Where are you from? **¿De dónde eres?** *fam.* 1; **¿De dónde es usted?** *form.* 1
  Where is…? **¿Dónde está…?**
  (to) where? **¿adónde?** 2
which **que** *rel. pron.* 9
which? **¿cuál(es)?** *pron.* 2, 9; **¿qué?** 2, 9
  which one(s)? **¿cuál(es)?** 2
while **mientras** *conj.* 10
white **blanco/a** *adj.* 6
  white wine **vino** *m.* **blanco** 8
whiteboard **pizarra** *f.* 2
who **que; quien(es)** *rel. pron.* 9
  who? **¿quién(es)?** 1, 2, 9
  Who is it? **¿Quién es?** 1
  Who is calling? (*on telephone*) **¿De parte de quién?**
  Who is speaking? (*on telephone*) **¿Quién habla?**
whole **todo/a** *adj.*
whom **quien(es)** *rel. pron.* 9
whose…? **¿de quién(es)…?** 1
why? **¿por qué?** *adv.* 2, 9
widowed **viudo/a** *adj.* 9
wife **esposa** *f.* 3
win **ganar** *v.* 4
wind **viento** *m.*
window **ventana** *f.* 2
windshield **parabrisas** *m., sing.* 11

windy: It's (very) windy. **Hace (mucho) viento.** 5
wine **vino** *m.* 8
  red wine **vino tinto** 8
  white wine **vino blanco** 8
wineglass **copa** *f.* 12
winter **invierno** *m.* 5
wireless connection **conexión** *f.* **inalámbrica** 11
wish **desear** *v.* 2; **esperar** *v.* 13
  I wish (that) **Ojalá que** 13
with **con** *prep.*
  with me **conmigo**
  with you **contigo** *fam.*
within **dentro de** *prep.*
without **sin** *prep.* 13, 15; **sin que** *conj.* 13
  without a doubt **sin duda**
woman **mujer** *f.* 1
word **palabra** *f.* 1
work **trabajar** *v.* 2; **funcionar** *v.* 11; **trabajo** *m.* 16
  work (of art, literature, music, etc.) **obra** *f.*
  work out **hacer** *v.* **gimnasia** 15
world **mundo** *m.* 13
worldwide **mundial** *adj. m., f.*
worried (about) **preocupado/a (por)** *adj.* 5
worry (about) **preocuparse** *v.* (**por**) 7
worse **peor** *adj. m., f.* 8
worst **el/la peor** 8; **lo peor**
Would you like to? **¿Te gustaría?**
write **escribir** *v.* 3
  write a letter/post card/e-mail **escribir una carta/(tarjeta) postal/mensaje** *m.* **electrónico** 4
writer **escritor(a)** *m., f.* 16
written **escrito/a** *p.p.* 15
wrong **equivocado/a** *adj.* 5
  be wrong **no tener** *v.* **razón** 3

X

X-ray **radiografía** *f.* 10

Y

yard **jardín** *m.* 12; **patio** *m.* 12
year **año** *m.* 5
  be… years old **tener** *v.* **… años** 3
yellow **amarillo/a** *adj.* 6
yes **sí** *interj.*
yesterday **ayer** *adv.* 6
yet **todavía** *adv.* 5
yogurt **yogur** *m.*
you **tú** *sub. pron. fam. sing.* 1; **usted** *sub. pron. form. sing.* 1; **vosotros/as** *sub. pron. fam. pl.* 1; **ustedes** *sub. pron. pl.* 1; **te** *d.o. pron.*

fam. sing. 5; **lo** *d.o. pron. m. form.*
sing. 5; **la** *d.o. pron. f. form. sing.*
5; **os** *d.o. pron. fam. pl.* 5; **los** *d.o.*
pron. m. pl. 5; **las** *d.o. pron.*
f. pl. 5; **le(s)** *i.o. pron.*
form. 6
You're welcome. **De nada.** 1; **No**
hay de qué. 1
young **joven** *adj.* 3
young person **joven** *m., f.* 1
young woman **señorita** *f.*
younger **menor** *adj. m., f.* 8
younger brother, sister **hermano/a**
menor *m., f.*
youngest **el/la menor** *m., f.* 8
your **su(s)** *poss., adj., form.* 3
your **tu(s)** *poss., adj., fam. sing.* 3
your **vuestro(s)/a(s)** *poss., adj.*
fam., pl. 3
your(s) **suyo(s)/a(s)**
poss. pron., form. 11
your(s) **tuyo(s)/a(s)** *poss.,*
fam., sing. 11
youth **juventud** *f.* 9

Z

zero **cero** *m.* 1

A

abbreviations (14) **361**
absolute superlative (8) **213**
acabar de + *infinitive* (6) **153**
academic courses (2) **28, 52**
accents (4) **89**, (10) **257**
    on homonyms (11) **285**
accidental occurrences with **se** (10) **264**
adjectives
    demonstrative (6) **156**
    descriptive (3) **68**
    nationality (3) **69**
    past participles used as (15) **394**
    position (3) **69**
    possessive (3) **70**
    stressed possessive (11) **294**
adverbs (10) **266**
al (contraction) (4) **94**
animals (3), (13) **59, 82, 332, 354**
appliances, household (12) **304, 326**
articles, definite and indefinite (1) **12**
Aventuras en los países hispanos
    Argentina (10) **275**
    Bolivia (10) **275**
    Canadá (2) **53**
    Chile (10) **275**
    Colombia (8) **221**
    Costa Rica (14) **379**
    Cuba (6) **165**
    Ecuador (8) **221**
    El Salvador (12) **327**
    España (16) **431**
    Estados Unidos, los (2) **53**
    Guatemala (12) **327**
    Honduras (12) **327**
    México (4) **109**
    Nicaragua (14) **379**
    Panamá (14) **379**
    Paraguay (10) **275**
    Perú (8) **221**
    Puerto Rico (6) **165**
    República Dominicana (6) **165**
    Uruguay (10) **275**
    Venezuela (8) **221**

B

b and **v** (5), (15) **119, 389**
bank terms (14) **357, 378**
bathroom objects (7) **170, 194**
birthdays (9) **226, 250**
body parts (7), (10) **170, 194, 252, 274**
buildings
    campus (2) **28, 52**
    general (4) **85, 108**

C

c (8) **201**
campus buildings (2) **28, 52**
capitalization (12) **309**
car terms (11) **280, 302**
celebrations (9) **226, 250**
chores, household (12) **304, 326**
classroom objects and people (2) **28, 52**
clothing (6) **140, 164**
colors (6) **141**
commands
    familiar (**tú**) (14) **368**
    with **nosotros** (14) **370**
    with **Ud.** and **Uds.** (12) **314**
comparatives and superlatives (8) **212**
computer terms (11) **281, 302**
conditional tense (16) **420**
conducir
    present tense (8) **210**
    preterite tense (9) **236**
conjunctions
    requiring subjunctive (13) **346, 354**
    requiring subjunctive or indicative (13) **347, 354**
conocer and **saber** (8) **210**
courses (academic) (2) **28, 52**
courtesy expressions (1) **3, 26**
Cultura *Readings*
    Año Nuevo (9) **234**
    Balcones que enamoran (12) **312**
    Las bicicletas en la ciudad (14) **364**
    El Camino Inca (5) **122**
    ¿Cómo te llamas? (3) **66**
    Desayunos exquisitos (8) **204**
    La elección de una carrera universitaria (2) **36**
    La entrevista de trabajo (16) **416**
    Espacios públicos saludables (15) **392**
    Jóvenes por el medio ambiente (13) **340**
    Los mercados al aire libre (6) **148**
    Real Madrid y Barça: rivalidad total (4) **92**
    Las redes sociales (11) **288**
    Los saludos y el espacio personal (1) **10**
    Servicios de salud (10) **260**
    La siesta (7) **178**

D

d and **t** (6) **145**
daily routine (7) **170, 194**
dar
    present tense (6) **155**
    preterite tense (9) **237**
dates (5) **115, 138**
days of the week (2) **29, 52**
decir
    present tense (6) **155**
    preterite tense (9) **236**
definite articles (1) **12**
del (contraction) (1) **17**
demonstrative adjectives and pronouns (6) **156**

describing clothes (6) **141, 147, 164**
describing routines (7) **170**, **194**
descriptive adjectives (3) **68**
diphthongs and linking (3) **63**
direct objects: nouns and pronouns (5) **130**
directions, getting and giving (14) **357, 378**
double object pronouns (8) **208**
downtown shops (14) **356, 378**

E

ecology terms (13) **332, 354**
emergencies, health-related (10) **252, 274**
environmental terms (13) **332, 354**
estar
    present tense (2) **42**
    preterite tense (9) **236**
    comparing **ser** and **estar** (5) **128**
    with health conditions (2) **42**
    with location (2) **42**
    with conditions (5) **124**
    with emotions (5) **124**
exercise terms (15) **384, 406**

F

familiar (**tú**) commands (14) **368**
family members and relatives (3) **58, 82**
farewells (1) **2, 26**
fitness terms (15) **384, 406**
Flash cultura
    La casa de Frida (12) **313**
    La comida latina (8) **205**
    Comprar en los mercados (6) **149**
    Encuentros en la plaza (1) **11**
    ¿Estrés? ¿Qué estrés? (15) **393**
    Los estudios (2) **37**
    La familia (3) **67**
    Las fiestas (9) **235**
    ¡Fútbol en España! (4) **93**
    Maravillas de la tecnología (11) **289**
    El metro del D.F. (14) **365**
    El mundo del trabajo (16) **417**
    Naturaleza en Costa Rica (13) **341**
    La salud (10) **261**
    Tapas para todos los días (7) **179**
    ¡Vacaciones en Perú! (5) **123**
food and drink (8) **196, 220**
    parties, related foods (9) **226, 250**
forming questions (2) **40**
furniture (12) **305, 326**
future tense (16) **418**

G

g (9) **231**
greetings and introductions (1) **2, 26**
grooming, personal (7) **170, 194**
gusta(n), me/te (2) **39**

gustar (2), (7) **39, 186**
    verbs like **gustar** (7) **186**

H

h (9), (16) **231, 413**
h, j, and **g** (9) **231**
hacer
    present tense (4) **100**
    preterite tense (9) **236**
hay (1) **14**
health
    conditions with **estar** (5) **128**
    emergencies (10) **252, 274**
    fitness terms (15) **384, 406**
    questions (1), **2, 26**
    stress terms (15) **385, 406**
hotels (5) **114, 138**
housing
    appliances (12) **304, 326**
    chores (12) **305, 326**
    furniture (12) **305, 326**
    general terms (12) **304, 326**
    rooms (12) **304, 326**

I

imperfect and preterite contrasted (11) **290**
imperfect (*past*) subjunctive (16) **422**
imperfect tense, regular and irregular verbs (10) **262**
impersonal constructions with **se** (10) **264**
indefinite articles (1) **12**
indefinite words (7) **182**
indirect object pronouns (6) **154**
information questions (2) **40**
Internet terms (11) **281, 302**
interrogative words (2) **41**
intonation, question (2) **40**
introductions (1) **3, 26**
ir
    imperfect tense (10) **262**
    present tense (4) **94**
    preterite tense (7) **184**
    ir a + *infinitive* (4) **94**
irregular verbs
    imperfect tense (10) **262**
    preterite tense (9) **236**

J

j (9) **231**
job terms (16) **408, 430**

L

life stages (9) **227, 250**
linking (3) **63**
ll (8), (16) **201, 413**
location with **estar** (2) **42**

M

mail terms (14) **356, 378**
meals (8) **196, 220**
months of the year (5) **115**

N

nationalities (3) **69**
nature terms (13) **332, 354**
negation with **no** (2) **39**
negative words (7) **182**
nosotros/as commands (14) **370**
nouns (1) **12, 26**
numbers
    0-30 (1) **14**
    31-100 (2) **44**
    101 and higher (6) **150**

Ñ

ñ (8) **201**

O

object pronouns
    direct (5) **130**
    double (8) **208**
    indirect (6) **154**
    reflexive (7) **180**
occupations (16) **408, 430**
ofrecer, present tense (8) **210**
oír, present tense (4) **101**
ordinal numbers (5) **115**

P

parecer, present tense (8) **210**
participles
    past used as adjectives (15) **394**
    present with progressive tenses (5) **126**
parties, related people, items, foods (9) **226, 250**
parts of the body (7), (10) **170, 194, 252, 274**
past participles as adjectives (15) **394**
past perfect tense (15) **398**
past (*imperfect*) subjunctive (16) **422**
perfect tenses
    past perfect (15) **398**
    present perfect (15), **396**
pero vs. **sino** (7) **183**
personal **a** (5) **130**
place settings (12) **304, 326**
plural of nouns (1) **13**
poder, preterite tense (9) **236**
poner
    present tense (4) **100**
    preterite tense (9) **236**
por and **para,** uses (11) **292**
position of adjectives (3) **69**

possessive adjectives (3) **70**
possessive pronouns (11) **295**
post office terms (14) **356, 378**
present perfect tense (5) **396**
present progressive tense (5) **126**
prepositions of location (2) **43**
present subjunctive (12) **316**
preterite vs. imperfect (11) **290**
preterite tense
    regular verbs (6) **152**
    irregular verbs (9) **236**
    stem-changing verbs (8) **206**
    verbs that change meaning in (9) **238**
professions (3), (16) **59, 82, 408, 430**
pronouns
    demonstratives (6) **156**
    direct object (5) **130**
    double object (8) **208**
    indirect object (6) **154**
    possessive (11) **295**
    reflexive (7) **180**
    relative (9) **240**
    subject (1) **16**
    use and omission of subject (2) **39**
punctuation (13) **337**

Q

querer, preterite tense (9) **236**
questions, forming (2) **40**
    information questions (2) **40**
    intonation for questions (2) **40**
    ¿Qué? and **¿cuál?** (9) **242**

R

r (7) **175**
reflexive verbs (7) **170, 171, 180, 181, 194**
regular verbs
    present tense
        -**ar** verbs (2) **38**
        -**er** and -**ir** verbs (3) **72**
    preterite (6) **152**
relative pronouns (9) **240**
restaurants (8) **196, 220**
routines (7) **170, 194**

S

saber
    and **conocer** (8) **210**
    preterite tense (9) **236**
salir, present tense (4) **100**
seasons of the year (5) **115**
sequencing actions, words for (7) **171, 194**
se constructions
    accidental occurrences (10) **264**
    impersonal expressions (10) **264**
    reflexive verbs (7) **180**
    unplanned occurrences (10) **264**

ser
 imperfect tense (10) **262**
 present tense (1) **16**
 preterite tense (7) **184**
 comparing **ser** and **estar** (5) **128**
 to show identity (1) **17**
 to show origin (1) **17**
 to show possession (1) **17**
 with professions (1) **17**
shape, staying in (15) **384**, **406**
shopping (6) **140**, **164**
shops downtown (14) **356**, **378**
sickness vocabulary (10) **252**, **274**
Spanish alphabet (1) **7**
sports and leisure activities (4) **84**, **108**
stages of life (9) **227**, **250**
stem-changing verbs
 present tense (4) **96**, **98**
 preterite tense (8) **206**
stress and accent marks (4) **89**
stressed possessive adjectives (11) **294**
subject pronouns (1) **16**
 use and omission (2) **39**
subjunctive
 past (*imperfect*) (16) **422**
 present (12) **316**
 following certain conjunctions (13) **346**
 to express indefiniteness and nonexistence (14) **366**
 with expressions of will and influence (12) **318**
 with expressions of emotion (13) **342**
 with expressions of doubt, disbelief, and denial (13) **344**
superlatives (8) **213**
 absolute superlatives (8) **213**
suponer, present tense (4) **100**

T

t (6) **145**
table settings (12) **304**, **326**
technology terms (11) **281**, **302**
tener
 present tense (3) **74**
 preterite tense (9) **236**
 expressions with (3) **75**
telling time (1) **18**
town places (14) **356**, **378**
traducir
 present tense (8) **210**
 preterite tense (9) **236**
traer
 present tense (4) **100**
 preterite tense (9) **236**
travel terms (5) **114**, **138**

U

Ud. and **Uds.** commands (12) **314**
unplanned occurrences with **se** (10) **264**

V

v (5), (15) **119**, **389**
venir
 present tense (3) **74**
 preterite tense (9) **236**
ver
 imperfect tense (10) **262**
 present tense (4) **101**
verbs describing routines and personal grooming (7) **170**, **194**
verbs with irregular **yo** forms (**hacer, oír, poner, salir, suponer, traer,** and **ver**) (4) **100**

W

weather expressions (5) **114**, **138**
work-related terms (16) **408**, **430**
written accents (4), (10), (11) **89**, **257**, **285**

Y

y (16) **413**
years (e.g., 2015) (6) **151**
yes-no questions (2) **40**

Z

z (8) **201**

Every effort has been made to trace the copyright holders of the works published herein. If proper copyright acknowledgment has not been made, please contact the publisher and we will correct the information in future printings.

Photography and Art Credits

All images © by Vista Higher Learning unless otherwise noted.

Cover: Kelly Cheng Travel Photography/Moment/Getty Images.

Front Matter (SE): iii: Carlos Muñoz; **xxvi:** (The Cast, all) Carlos Muñoz; (Aventuras, all) Carlos Muñoz; (Panorama cultural, l) Eucagallery/Getty Images; (Panorama cultural, r) Rick Ray/Shutterstock.

Front Matter (IAE): IAE-5: Carlos Muñoz; **IAE-28:** (The Cast, all) Carlos Muñoz; (Aventuras, all) Carlos Muñoz; (Panorama cultural, l) Eucagallery/Getty Images; (Panorama cultural, r) Rick Ray/Shutterstock; **IAE-44:** (all) Carlos Muñoz; **IAE-45:** (quetzal) Mallardg500/Moment Open/Getty Images.

Lesson 1: 1: Carlos Muñoz; **2:** (l) Paula Díez; (r) Sam Edwards/Media Bakery; **3:** (l) Hero/Media Bakery; (r) Laurence Mouton/Media Bakery; **5:** Martín Bernetti; **6:** (l, m) Martín Bernetti; (r) Frank and Helena/Media Bakery; **8:** (all) Carlos Muñoz; **9:** (all) Carlos Muñoz; **10:** (all) Paula Díez; **12:** (left col: r, l) Carlos Muñoz; (right col: t, bl, br) Annie Pickert Fuller; (right col: ml) Zentilia/Fotolia; (right col: mr) Martín Bernetti; **13:** (t) Darío Eusse Tobón; (mt) Tiero/Fotolia; (mmt) Invictus99/123RF; (mmb, mb) Martín Bernetti; (b) Gchutka/iStockphoto; **14:** Blend Images/Alamy; **15:** Carlos Muñoz; **16:** (left col: tl) Paula Díez; (left col: tm) Andresr/Shutterstock; (left col: tr) Elenathewise/123RF; (left col: b) Spaxiax/Fotolia; (right col: t) Helga Esteb/Shutterstock; (right col: mtl) Andrea Raffin/Shutterstock; (right col: mtr) Cooper Neill/MLB Photos/Getty Images; (right col: mbl) Everett Collection/Newscom; (right col: mbr) WireImage/Getty Images; (right col: bl) Rafiquar Rahman/Reuters; (right col: br) Kathy Hutchins/Shutterstock; **17:** (l) Kathy Hutchins/Shutterstock; (m, r) Carlos Muñoz; **19:** Prathan Chorruangsak/Shutterstock; **20:** (all) Carlos Muñoz; **22:** (t) Hanibaram/iStockphoto; (b) Gary Conner/Getty Images; **23:** Philip Lange/123RF.

Lesson 2: 27: Carlos Muñoz; **28:** (tl) Radu Razvan Gheorghe/123RF; (tr) WavebreakmediaMicro/Fotolia; (bl) West Coast Surfer/Media Bakery; (br) Alexander Raths/Fotolia; **29:** (t) Annie Pickert Fuller; (bl) Mmarcius/Fotolia; (bm, br) Martín Bernetti; **30:** Paula Díez; **31:** (t) Bettmann/Getty Images; (b) Johnny Lye/iStockphoto; **34:** (all) Carlos Muñoz; **35:** (left col: all) Carlos Muñoz; (r) Angel Gracia; **36:** (l) Lorena Natalia Fernández/123RF; (r) Pablo Corral V/Corbis/VCG/Getty Images; **38:** (all) Carlos Muñoz; **39:** (t) Zero Creatives/Media Bakery; (ml, br) Martín Bernetti; (mr) Paula Díez; (bl) Ken Hurst/Shutterstock; **40:** (all) Carlos Muñoz; **41:** Paula Díez; **42:** (all) Carlos Muñoz; **43:** (all) Carlos Muñoz; **44:** Carlos Muñoz; **45:** (t) Martín Bernetti; (b) Adalberto Roque/AFP/Getty Images; **46:** Oneinchpunch/Fotolia; **48:** (tl) Paula Díez; (tr) Darío Eusse Tobón; (b) Annie Pickert Fuller; **49:** (t) Michaeljung/Fotolia; (b) David R. Frazier Photolibrary, Inc/Alamy; **50:** José Blanco; **51:** (t) Pascal Pernix; (b) Hongqi Zhang/123RF; **53:** Bryan Smith/ZUMA Press/Newscom; **54:** (tl) Ian Dagnall/Alamy; (tr) Sylvain Grandadam/AGE Fotostock; (bl) Lou Rocco/Disney ABC Television Group/Getty Images; (bml) Alliance Images/Alamy; (bmr) DFree/Shutterstock; (br) Spacephotos/AGE Fotostock; **55:** (tl) Wilber Vazquez/NortePhoto/Alamy; (tr) Richard Cummins/Corbis Documentary/Getty Images; (tm) Danny Lehman/Corbis/VCG/Getty Images; (b) Roberto Machado Noa/LightRocket/Getty Images.

Lesson 3: 57: Carlos Muñoz; **58:** Martín Bernetti; **59:** (t) Rob Marmion/Shutterstock; (bl) Media Bakery; (br) Monkey Business/Fotolia; **61:** (t) Martín Bernetti; (ml) Tyler Olson/Fotolia; (mm) Paula Díez; (mr) Dann Tardif/The Image Bank Unreleased/Getty Images; (bl) Golubovy/Fotolia; (bm) Cristovao/Deposit Photos; (br) Ariel Skelley/Media Bakery; **62:** Jack Hollingsworth/Media Bakery; **64:** (all) Carlos Muñoz; **65:** (left col: all) Carlos Muñoz; (r) Raquel Rodríguez/123RF; **66:** (tl) David Cantor/AP Images; (tr) Rafael Perez/Reuters; (b) Martial Trezzini/EPA/Shutterstock; **68:** (tl) Chris Fertnig/iStockphoto; (tm) Grigorita Ko/Fotolia; (tr) Daniel Ernst/Fotolia; (bl) Olena

Lesson 7: 169: Carlos Muñoz; **170:** (l) Paula Díez; (m, r) Martín Bernetti; **171:** (t) Martín Bernetti; (b) Lightwavemedia/Shutterstock; **174:** (t, ml, br) Paula Díez; (mm) Radnatt/Fotolia; (mr) Kemter/iStockphoto; (bl) Zeljkosantrac/iStockphoto; (bm) Easy Production/Media Bakery; **176:** (all) Carlos Muñoz; **177:** (left col: all) Carlos Muñoz; (r) Lucas Vallecillos/AGE Fotostock; **178:** Stewart Cohen/Getty Images; **180:** (left col: all) Carlos Muñoz; (right col: tl, tr, ml, mr, bl) Martín Bernetti; (right col: br) Stockbyte/Getty Images; **181:** (all) Martín Bernetti; **182:** (all) Carlos Muñoz; **183:** (t) Photographee EU/Fotolia; (b) JGI/Tom Grill/Media Bakery; **184:** (left col: all) Carlos Muñoz; (r) Anyaberkut/Fotolia; **185:** Masterfile; **186:** (all) Carlos Muñoz; **187:** AntonioDiaz/Fotolia; **190:** Anne Loubet; **191:** Bartosz Hadyniak/Media Bakery.

Lesson 8: 195: Carlos Muñoz; **196:** (l) Paula Díez; (r) Jack Puccio/iStockphoto; **197:** (tl) Barry Gregg/Corbis; (tr) Martín Bernetti; (m) Annie Pickert Fuller; (bl) Paula Díez; (br) Marcel Kriegl/Shutterstock; **202:** (all) Carlos Muñoz; **203:** (all) Carlos Muñoz; **204:** (tl) Antonio Gravante/123RF; (tr) Ana Maria Mejia/Alamy; (m) Sheridan Stancliff/SuperStock; (b) Luna Marina/Deposit Photos; **206:** (all) Carlos Muñoz; **207:** (left col: t) Darío Eusse Tobón; (left col: b) Thomas Northcut/Media Bakery; (right col: l) Rodolfo Benitez/StockFood/AGE Fotostock; (right col: ml) Janet Dracksdorf; (right col: mr) Andrade Gustavo/StockFood/AGE Fotostock; (right col: r) José Blanco; **208:** (all) Carlos Muñoz; **209:** (all) Carlos Muñoz; **211:** (left col: t) Ben Blankenburg/Corbis; (left col: ml) Corbis; (left col: mm, bm, br) Martín Bernetti; (left col: mr, bl) Darío Eusse Tobón; (r) Jack Hollingsworth/Corbis; **212:** (all) Carlos Muñoz; **216:** Commercial Eye/The Image Bank/Getty Images; **221:** Galen Rowell/Mountain Light/Media Bakery; **222:** (tl) John Beatty/Getty Images; (tr) David Barnes/Danita Delimont; (b) Jeff Luckett/iStockphoto; **223:** (t) Piero Pomponi/Getty Images; (bl) Tommy Lindholm/Alamy; (br) Jeremy Horner/The Image Bank Unreleased/Getty Images.

Lesson 9: 225: Carlos Muñoz; **226:** (tl) Susana/Fotocolombia; (tr, b) Martín Bernetti; **232:** (all) Carlos Muñoz; **233:** (all) Carlos Muñoz; **234:** (l) Martin-dm/E+/Getty Images; (r) Mauricio Duenas/EPA/Shutterstock; **237:** (all) Carlos Muñoz; **239:** (left col: l) Darío Eusse Tobón; (left col: m) Martín Bernetti; (left col: r) Monkey Business/Fotolia; (right col: t) Nikolai Sorokin/Fotolia; (right col: b) Ecliff6/iStockphoto; **240:** (l, m) Carlos Muñoz; (r) Martín Bernetti; **241:** (all) Carlos Muñoz; **243:** (left col: t) Monkey Business/Fotolia; (left col: ml) Africa Studio/Fotolia; (left col: mr) Martín Bernetti; (left col: bl) Tyler Olson/Shutterstock; (left col: br) SelectStock/iStockphoto; (right col: t) Tim Pannell/Media Bakery; (right col: b) Padnpen/iStockphoto; **244:** Kzenon/Shutterstock; **245:** Jupiterimages/Brand X/Alamy; **248:** (l) Katrina Brown/123RF; (r) Digital Vision/Media Bakery; **249:** Carlos Hernandez/Media Bakery.

Lesson 10: 251: Carlos Muñoz; **252:** (t) Martín Bernetti; (b) José Blanco; **253:** (t) Karel Miragaya/Deposit Photos; (b) James Steidl/Shutterstock; **254:** Martín Bernetti; **258:** (all) Carlos Muñoz; **259:** (left col: all) Carlos Muñoz; (r) Imanol Urquizu/123RF; **260:** (l) Ricardo Figueroa/AP Images; (r) José Blanco; **262:** (all) Carlos Muñoz; **265:** (all) Carlos Muñoz; **267:** (all) Martín Bernetti; **268:** JupiterImages/Photos.com/Alamy; **270:** Paula Díez; **271:** Stephanie Maze/The Image Bank Unreleased/Getty Images; **272-273:** Martín Bernetti; **275:** Tips RF/Media Bakery; **276:** (t) Ali Burafi; (b) Annie Pickert Fuller; **277:** (t, m, br) Ali Burafi; (bl) Ricardo Za/Shutterstock.

Lesson 11: 279: Carlos Muñoz; **280:** (t) Martín Bernetti; (b) Paula Díez; **281:** (l) Dmitry Kutlayev/iStockphoto; (r) Aleksandr Kurganov/Shutterstock; **282:** Martín Bernetti; **283:** WavebreakMediaMicro/Fotolia; **286:** (all) Carlos Muñoz; **287:** (left col: all)Carlos Muñoz; (r) Sean Pavone/123RF; **288:** (l) Quka/Shutterstock; (r) GM Visuals/AGE Fotostock; **290:** (all) Carlos Muñoz; **291:** JPL-Caltech/NASA; **292:** (all) Carlos Muñoz; **294:** (t) LdF/iStockphoto; (tml) AHBE/Fotolia; (tmr) Aleksandr Kurganov/Shutterstock; (bml) Oleksiy Mark/Shutterstock; (bmr) Bet Noire/Getty Images; (bl) Martín Bernetti; (br) Nebojsa Markovic/Shutterstock; **295:** (left col: t) LdF/iStockphoto; (left col: b) Greg Nicholas/iStockphoto; (right col: all) Carlos Muñoz.

Lesson 12: 303: Carlos Muñoz; **304:** (t) Martín Bernetti; (b) Darío Eusse Tobón; **305:** (t) Comstock Images/Jupiterimages; (bl, br) Martín Bernetti; **306:** (all) Martín Bernetti; **308:** (l) Terry J Alcorn/iStockphoto; (r) Harry Neave/Fotolia; **310:** (all) Carlos Muñoz; **311:** (left col: all) Carlos Muñoz; (r) Juan Jimenez Fernandez/123RF; **312:** (tl) Jess Kraft/Shutterstock; (tr) Scharfsinn/Shutterstock; (b) Daniel Ferreira-Leites Ciccarino/123RF; **314:** (all)

Carlos Muñoz; **318:** Nelia Sapronova/Shutterstock; **319:** (all) Carlos Muñoz; **323:** Tony Arruza/The Image Bank Unreleased/Getty Images; **324:** Chile DesConocido/Alamy; **327:** Owen Franken/The Image Bank Unreleased/Getty Images; **328:** (t) Kato Inowe/Shutterstock; (bl) Dave G. Houser/Corbis Documentary/Getty Images; (br) Craig Lovell/The Image Bank/Getty Images; **329:** (tl) Kevin Schafer/The Image Bank/Getty Images; (tr) Tony Arruza/ Corbis Documentary/Getty Images; (m) Johan Ordonez/AFP/Getty Images; (b) Jim Engelbrecht/Danita Delimont/Alamy.

Lesson 13: 331: Carlos Muñoz; **332:** (t) Simone van den Berg/iStockphoto; (m) Rachel Distler; (b) Soleg/123RF; **333:** (l) Martín Bernetti; (m) Ron Masessa/iStockphoto; (r) Darren Greenwood/Design Pics/Corbis; **334:** (tl) Fotos 593/ Fotolia; (tr) Daniel Stein/iStockphoto; (bl) Martín Bernetti; (br) Dean Pennala/iStockphoto; **336:** Dmitry Pichugin/ Fotolia; **338:** (all) Carlos Muñoz; **339:** (left col: all) Carlos Muñoz; (r) Raul Ortega Marinas/123RF; **340:** (l) Roberto Almeida Aveledo/ZUMA Press/Alamy; (r) Erik McGregor/Sipa USA/Newscom; **342:** (all) Carlos Muñoz; **343:** Martín Bernetti; **344:** (all) Carlos Muñoz; **345:** Carsten Koall/Getty Images; **346:** (left col: all) Carlos Muñoz; (r) Rick Rusing/Getty Images; **347:** (all) Carlos Muñoz; **350:** Deron Rodehaver/123RF; **351:** Brian Lasenby/ Fotolia; **352:** (sunflower) Richard Griffin/Fotolia; (picture frame) Vlntn/Fotolia; (woman) Drobot Dean/Fotolia **352–353:** Morokey/123RF.

Lesson 14: 355: Carlos Muñoz; **356:** (l) Martín Bernetti; (m) Media Bakery; (r, carriage) Lefteris Papaulakis/Fotolia; (r, soccer player) Grafissimo/iStockphoto; (r, woman) Freedom Studio/Shutterstock; (r, birds) DBI Studio/Alamy; **357:** (t) Martín Bernetti; (bl) Skynesher/iStockphoto; (br) Bilge/iStockphoto; **358:** Wavebreakmedia Ltd UC8/Alamy; **362:** (all) Carlos Muñoz; **363:** (left col; all) Carlos Muñoz; (r) Bibi57/iStockphoto/Getty Images; **364:** (l) Hugh Mitton/Alamy; (r) Carol Smiljan/NurPhoto/Getty Images; **366:** (all) Carlos Muñoz; **367:** Tarras79/iStockphoto; **368:** (all) Carlos Muñoz; **370:** (left col: tl, tr) Carlos Muñoz; (left col: b) Monkey Business/Fotolia; (r) Darío Eusse Tobón; **374:** Martín Bernetti; **375:** David Parsons/iStockphoto; **376–377:** (open book) Rangizzz/123RF **379:** Bettmann/Getty Images; **380:** (t) Richard Cummins/AGE Fotostock/Media Bakery; (bl) John Nakata/Corbis; (br) Bettmann/Getty Images; **381:** (tl) Courtesy of excelenciaspanama.com; (tr) William Gentile/Corbis Historical/Getty Images; (b) Agencia el Universal GDA Photo Service/Newscom.

Lesson 15: 383: Carlos Muñoz; **384:** (t) Manley099/iStockphoto; (bl) Neyya/Getty Images; (br) Martín Bernetti; **385:** Annie Pickert Fuller; **386:** Diego Cervo/iStockphoto; **390:** (all) Carlos Muñoz; **391:** (left col: all) Carlos Muñoz; (r) Photooiasson/Deposit Photos; **392:** (l) Milton Rodriguez/Shutterstock; (r) Jason Sheil/SOPA Images/ LightRocket;Getty Images; **394:** (l) Darío Eusse Tobón; (r) Martín Bernetti; **395:** (all) Martín Bernetti; **396:** (all) Carlos Muñoz; **397:** (all) Carlos Muñoz; **398:** (all) Carlos Muñoz; **399:** Martín Bernetti; **402:** Stasique/Fotolia; **403:** Meunierd/Shutterstock; **404:** Martín Bernetti.

Lesson 16: 407: Carlos Muñoz; **408:** (tl) Peathegee Inc/Media Bakery; (tr) Glyn Jones/Corbis; (bl) Andersen Ross/ Media Bakery; (br) Pressmaste/Fotolia; **409:** (tl, b) Martín Bernetti; (tr) Jeff Cleveland/Shutterstock; **410:** Paula Díez; **414:** (all) Carlos Muñoz; **415:** (left col: all) Carlos Muñoz; (r) Sean Pavone/123RF; **416:** (l) Martín Bernetti; (r) Tempura/E+/Getty Images; **423:** (all) Carlos Muñoz; **424:** (l) Track5/iStockphoto; (r) Forgiss/Fotolia; **427:** Paula Díez; **428:** Kostic Dusan/123RF; **431:** Greg Gerla/AGE Fotostock; **432:** (t) Graficart.net/Alamy; (b) Reuters; **433:** (tl) *Las Meninas* or the *Family of Philip IV* (1656), Diego Rodríguez Velázquez. Oil on canvas, 276 x 318 cm. Museo del Prado, Madrid, Spain. Ali Burafi; (tr) José Blanco; (bl) Pete Goding/SIME/eStockphoto; (br) Paul Almasy/Corbis Historical/Getty Images.

Back Cover: Demaerre/iStockphoto.

Text Credits

300: Juan Matias Loiseau/TUTE; **352:** © Anderson Imbert, Enrique, "La foto", *Dos mujeres y un Julián*. Buenos Aires, Corregidor, 1999; **376:** © Fundación Mario Benedetti. c/o Schavelzon Graham Agencia Literaria. www. schavelzongraham.com; **404:** Cristina Peri Rossi; **428:** © 1978, Augusto Monterroso. Reimpreso por permiso de International Editors' Co.

Video Credits

21: Mastercard; **47:** EFE News Service, Inc.; **77:** Banco Galicia/Mercado McCann; **103:** Feel Sales/ContentLine; **133:** ANA INES CIBILS MARIO VASQUEZ/AFPTV/AFP; **159:** Juguettos; **189:** MARINA DE RUSSÉ IVAN COURONNE ELODIE MARTINEZ/AFPTV/AFP; **215:** PABLO ALBUERNE "GIPSY CHEF" / LA VANGUARDIA / GIPSYCHEF@GMAIL.COM; **245:** Watch the full video on the YouTube Channel: Sin Portal; **269:** Getting Better Creative Studio; **297:** Banco Galicia/Mercado McCann; **321:** Conforama España; **349:** Entropic Films; **373:** Ogilvy & Mathers Honduras; **401:** Cámara\\TBWA Agencia Publicitaria; **425:** EFE News Service, Inc.

About the Authors

José A. Blanco founded Vista Higher Learning in 1998. A native of Barranquilla, Colombia, Mr. Blanco holds a B.A. in Literature from the University of California, Santa Cruz, and an M.A. in Hispanic Studies from Brown University. He has worked as a writer, editor, and translator for Houghton Mifflin and D.C. Heath and Company, and has taught Spanish at the secondary and university levels. Mr. Blanco is also the co-author of several other Vista Higher Learning programs: **Vistas**, **Panorama**, **¡Adelante!** and **¡Viva!** at the introductory level; **Perspectivas**, **Enlaces**, **Facetas**, **Enfoques**, **Imagina**, and **Sueña** at the intermediate level; and **Revista** at the advanced conversation level.

Philip Redwine Donley received his M.A. in Hispanic Literature from the University of Texas at Austin in 1986 and his Ph.D. in Foreign Language Education from the University of Texas at Austin in 1997. Dr. Donley taught Spanish at Austin Community College, Southwestern University, and the University of Texas at Austin. He published articles and conducted workshops about language anxiety, language anxiety management, and the development of critical thinking skills, and was involved in research about teaching languages to the visually impaired. Dr. Donley was also the co-author of three other introductory college Spanish textbook programs published by Vista Higher Learning: **Vistas**, **Panorama**, and **¡Viva!**.